Introduction to TCP/IP

Understanding Data Communications Across the Internet

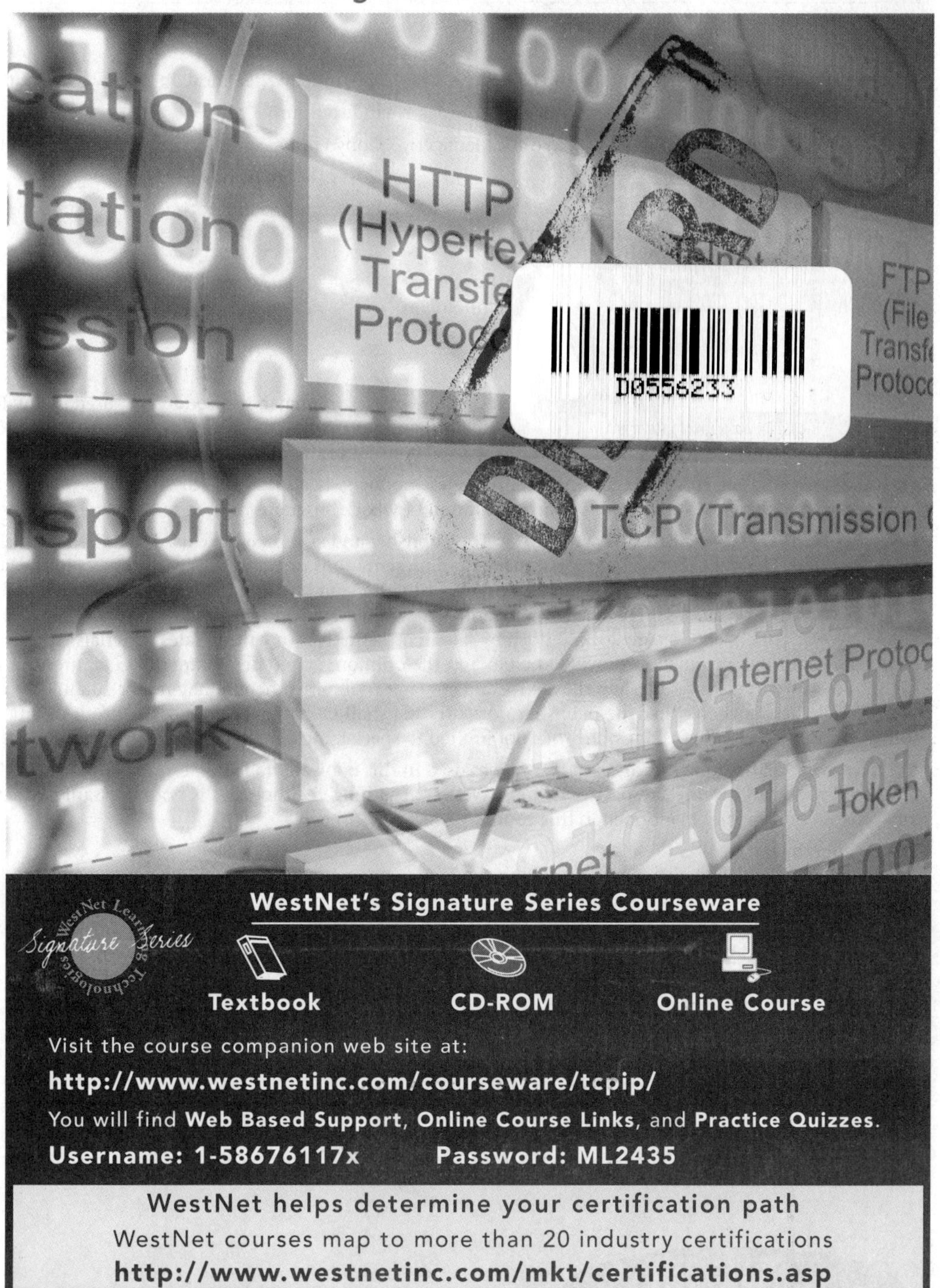

CREDITS

Author and Development Editor: Kenneth D. Reed
Editorial and Production Manager: Marilee E. Aust
Book Design and Composition, and Copy Editor Manager: D. Kari Luraas, Clairvoyance Design
Illustrator: Lynn Siefken
Proofreaders: Judy Leszczynski, Kim Pearman, Larry Beckett

Technical Writer and Editor: David M. Watts
Indexer: Amy Casey
Copy Editor: Sheryl Shapiro, Clairvoyance Design
Cover Design: David Jones
Printer: Johnson Printing

ISBN: 1-58676-117-X (softcover)

Printed in the United States of America

Reed, Kenneth D.
Introduction to TCP/IP
800 pp., includes illustrations and index

1. TCP/IP Structure and Addressing 2. Overview of TCP/IP Applications 3. TCP/IP Addressing and Subnets
4. TCP/IP Protocols 5. TCP/IP Services 6. Routing TCP/IP 7. How TCP/IP Applications Work
8. Troubleshooting a TCP/IP Network

WB47.0

For instructor-led training, self-paced courses,
turn-key curricula solutions, or more information contact:

WestNet Learning Technologies (dba: WestNet Inc.)
5420 Ward Road, Suite 150, Arvada, CO 80002 USA
E-mail: Info@westnetinc.com

To access the WestNet student resource site, go to http://www.westnetinc.com/student

Preface

The world's largest network, the Internet, is also one of the world's most powerful communication tools. Learn the underlying applications, components and protocols of Transmission Control Protocol/Internet Protocol (TCP/IP) and its necessary link to the Internet. The Introduction to TCP/IP course will help participants learn how to identify TCP/IP layers, components, and functions. Navigation tools, TCP/IP services, and troubleshooting methodologies are also covered in this course.

Prerequisites

The *Introduction to Networking* course is a prerequisite for this course.

Key Topics

- Using TCP/IP applications such as TCP, browsers, e-mail, and network management
- TCP/IP and IP routing structures
- TCP/IP addressing and subnetting
- How TCP/IP addresses are discovered and used in computer networks
- IP routing and router usage
- Moving information from source to destination across a TCP/IP network
- How TCP/IP applications work
- Troubleshooting a TCP/IP network

Course Objectives

- Recognize TCP/IP layers, components, and functions, and map these to the Open Systems Interconnection (OSI) model
- Describe and implement TCP/IP application services that support e-mail, remote terminal access, network management, Web access, and file transport across routed networks
- Explain TCP/IP protocols used to transport data over intranets, extranets, and the Internet
- Identify and utilize Internet navigation and searching tools such as Web browsers (Hypertext Transfer Protocol [HTTP]) and file transfer services (File Transfer Protocol [FTP], Trivial File Transfer Protocol [TFTP])
- Design and implement subnetworks
- Design and implement Classless Interdomain Routing (CIDR)
- Choose a routing protocol based on network size and service requirements, including quality of service/type of service (QoS/ToS) routing, variable-length subnet mask (VLSM), and link redundancy
- Describe TCP/IP support services, including Domain Name Service (DNS) and Dynamic Host Configuration Protocol (DHCP)
- Use TCP/IP tools to troubleshoot and isolate internetwork communications failures
- Explain how TCP/IP supports converged voice and data networks

Pedagogical Features

Several pedagogical features are included in this text to enhance the presentation of the materials so you can easily understand the concepts and apply them. Throughout the book, emphasis is placed on applying concepts to real-world scenarios through end-of-lesson Activities, Extended Activities, and other exercises and examples.

Learning Objectives, Unit Summaries, Discussion Questions, and Activities/Exercises

Learning objectives, unit summaries, discussion questions, and activities/exercises are designed to function as integrated study tools. Learning objectives reflect what you should be able to accomplish after completing each unit or chapter. Chapter summaries highlight the key concepts you should master. The discussion questions help guide critical thinking about those key concepts, and the Activities/Exercises provide you with opportunities to practice important techniques.

Key Terms

The information technology field includes many unique terms that are critical to creating a workable language when it is combined with the world of business. Definitions of key terms are provided in alphabetical order at the beginning of each unit and in a glossary at the end of the textbook.

Supplements

When this course is used in an academic or instructor-led setting, it is accompanied by an Instructor's Resource Tool Kit. The online-based kit includes an Instructor's Guide with the answers to Activities/Exercises, Lesson and Unit Quizzes, and the End-of-Course Exam. It also includes PowerPoint presentations organized by lesson, unit, and course. The Instructor's Resource site may also include sample syllabi, discussion topics, puzzles, cryptograms, and up-to-the-minute updates to the textbooks and supplemental course materials.

WestNet Learning Technologies' cutting edge Administrative Tools offer a unique online Windows-based exam software. The Online Course Exam engine includes lesson-, unit-, and course-level questions. These exams can be accessed by individual students and is presented in random order, ensuring that no student ever gets the same question with the same sequence of answers. This feature allows you to create printed and online pretests, practice tests, and actual examinations.

Advancing Your Level of Technical Expertise

WestNet Learning Technologies envisions a new communications paradigm for the 21st century—a paradigm based on increased bandwidth and digital exchange. Moving forward, WestNet is integrating these capacities with data/telephony/IP educational solutions that will give its students a complete range of communications skills and knowledge.

Why Choose WestNet?

WestNet Learning Technologies offers comprehensive information technologies (IT) educational and certification programs and curricula to secondary schools, colleges and universities, as well as corporations, resellers, and individual participants around the globe. These programs provide participants with the tools necessary to further their technical knowledge and skills, and to obtain hands-on experience. This unique program, which is vendor neutral, helps prepare participants to pursue IT careers, earn secondary and post-secondary educational degrees, and/or obtain industry certification.

Contents

INTRODUCTION

The term "architecture" refers to the design and construction of an object. If a building is referred to as having Gothic or Victorian architecture, a certain style comes to mind with regard to how the building was constructed, as well as specific features of the building's exterior. A similar concept holds true in networking. There are several networking architectures in existence today; some are constructed for small networks, and others are designed for large networks.

This course looks at the Transmission Control Protocol/Internet Protocol (TCP/IP) system architecture, which is designed from top to bottom for a specific purpose. That purpose is to route data across networks, between endpoints, reliably and efficiently.

OVERVIEW OF ARCHITECTURES

There are four types of system architectures:

- IBM Systems Network Architecture (SNA)
- DECnet
- AppleTalk
- TCP/IP

Except for TCP/IP, these architectures are all considered proprietary. Therefore, TCP/IP has become the most significant architecture in today's networking environments. Although TCP/IP has been around for a long time (Vinton G. Cerf and Robert E. Kahn proposed TCP/IP in 1974), it has gained a tremendous amount of popularity as the architecture of choice in most computer networks. There are a number of reasons for this, including:

- TCP/IP's nonproprietary nature
- Growing public and private Internet, intranet, and extranet usage
- Vendors' inclusion of TCP/IP in operating system (OS) software

Unlike other architectures, TCP/IP is "open," that is, the specifications describing TCP/IP and related protocols are open to the general public, free of charge. You can simply go to the Internet and download each protocol's specifications. These specifications exist as Request for Comments (RFCs), posted by the programs' developers, and as TCP/IP-provided protocols.

Another reason for the widespread acceptance of TCP/IP, and its adoption by most organizations, is the growth of the Internet and the number of organizations and users that attach to it. Because the Internet is TCP/IP-based, users who access the Internet use TCP/IP at each desktop.

And finally, network OSs such as UNIX and NetWare include TCP/IP as an integral part of their overall structure. Desktop OSs such as Macintosh OS and Microsoft Windows 2000 also include TCP/IP.

Unit 1
TCP/IP Structure and Addressing

This unit introduces the Transmission Control Protocol/Internet Protocol (TCP/IP) protocol suite. We begin with a review of the Open Systems Interconnection (OSI) model. We then introduce the TCP/IP Network, Transport, and Application Layer protocols. Then we explore the different address types necessary to move information from one user's application to another's across a TCP/IP network. We review IP address structures and how they are divided into logical and physical groups called subnets.

To end the unit, we review some of the most common network devices responsible for moving data across networks.

Lessons

1. OSI Model Review
2. Internet Protocol Suite
3. Internet Addressing
4. Internetworking Devices

Terms

100BaseFX—100BaseFX is a 100BaseT variant that runs over fiber optic cabling. 100BaseFX is generally used for high-speed LAN backbones.

100BaseT—100BaseT is based on 802.3 Ethernet and uses twisted pair cabling, as does 10BaseT Ethernet. However, 100BaseT runs 10 times faster than 10Base2 and 10Base5, at 100 Mbps.

10Base2—10Base2 is one of several physical cabling standards for 802.3 Ethernet networks. 10Base2 uses thin RG-58A/U coaxial cabling for connecting nodes on a bus topology, as does 10Base5. 10Base2 is also known as Thinnet.

10Base5—Also known as Thicknet, 10Base5 was the original Ethernet cabling standard. It is called Thicknet because it used a coaxial cable approximately 0.5 inches thick.

10BaseT—10BaseT is one of several physical cabling standards for 802.3 Ethernet LANs. 10BaseT networks use twisted pair cabling for connecting nodes in a star topology.

Address Resolution Protocol (ARP)—ARP is the protocol used by IP (as in TCP/IP) for address resolution. Address resolution refers to the ability of a station to resolve another station's MAC (hardware) address given its IP address.

AppleTalk—AppleTalk is Apple's proprietary protocol suite for Macintosh networks. It provides a multilayer, peer-to-peer architecture that uses built-in OS services. AppleTalk corresponds to the OSI seven-layer model.

Asynchronous Transfer Mode (ATM)—ATM is a cell-switching network that consists of multiple ATM switches that forward each individual cell to its final destination. ATM can provide transport services for audio, data, and video.

Bootstrap Protocol (BOOTP)—BOOTP is an Internet protocol for enabling a diskless workstation to boot and determine its configuration information, such as its IP address, from information available on a BOOTP server.

bridge—A bridge is a hardware device that connects LANs. It can be used to connect LANs of the same type, such as two Token Ring segments, or LANs with different types of media, such as Ethernet and Token Ring. A bridge operates at the Data Link Layer of the OSI reference model.

bridge router (Brouter)—A Brouter is an internetworking device that combines the functions of both a bridge and a router. See router.

broadcast—The term broadcast is used in several different ways in communications and networking. With respect to LANs, the term refers to information (that is, frames) sent to all devices on the physical segment. For example, a bus topology, in which a common cable is used to connect devices, is considered a broadcast technology. Another common use of the term broadcast relates to frames. Broadcast frames contain a special destination address that instructs all devices on the network to receive the frame.

checksum—A checksum is a simple error detection strategy that computes a running total based on a packet's transmitted byte values and then applies a simple operation to compute the checksum value. The receiver compares the checksums computed by the sender and the receiver, and, if they match, assumes error-free transmission.

collision—A collision occurs in an Ethernet network when two frames are put onto the physical medium at the same time and overlap fully or partially. When a collision occurs, the data on the physical segment is no longer valid.

datagram—A datagram is a unit of information processed by the Network Layer of the OSI reference model. The packet header contains the logical (network) address of the destination node. Intermediate nodes forward a packet until it reaches its destination. A packet can contain an entire message generated by higher OSI layers or a segment of a much larger message.

DECnet—DECnet is a proprietary network architecture created by DEC (now Compaq). The most recent DECnet model, DECnet Phase V, specifies seven layers that correspond to the OSI reference model. The DECnet architecture specifies 20-byte addresses and allows for the creation of separate routing and administration domains.

Domain Name System or Service (DNS)—In a TCP/IP network, a user can communicate with another user by specifying a name, such as johnd@engr.company.com. TCP and IP require Internet addresses for messages, thus one must be translated to the other. This is the job of the DNS; given a name, it returns an Internet address.

Dynamic Host Configuration Protocol (DHCP)—DHCP is used on a TCP/IP network to allow hosts to obtain configuration information from a DHCP server. DHCP provides for address leases, which release an address after a set lease period. DHCP can pass to a DHCP client computer such information as its DNS server and default gateway addresses and subnet mask.

Ethernet—Ethernet technology, originally developed in the 1970s by Xerox Corporation in conjunction with Intel and DEC, is now the primary medium for LANs. The original Ethernet has 10-Mbps throughput and uses the CSMA/CD method to access the physical media. Fast Ethernet (100-Mbps Ethernet) and Gigabit Ethernet (1,000-Mbps Ethernet) are also used.

expansion card—An expansion card is a printed circuit board that can be inserted into a PC to add capabilities. Expansion card examples are NICs, video cards, and modems.

extranet—An extranet is an external intranet offering select Internet users controlled access to an internal network segment. External users can view and update data stored on the internal network without actually traversing the network.

Fiber Distributed Data Interface (FDDI)—FDDI is a LAN standard specifying a 100-Mbps token-passing network using fiber optic cable.

File Transfer Protocol (FTP)—FTP is a TCP/IP Application Layer protocol used to transfer files between two computers.

hub—Also referred to as a wiring concentrator, a simple hub is a repeater with multiple ports. A signal coming into one port is repeated out the other ports.

Hypertext Transfer Protocol (HTTP)—HTTP is the Application Layer protocol used to request and transmit documents by means of the Web.

Institute of Electrical and Electronic Engineers (IEEE)—IEEE is a professional organization composed of engineers, scientists, and students. Founded in 1884, IEEE publishes computer and electronics standards, including the 802 series that defines shared-media networks such as Ethernet and Token Ring.

Internet—The Internet is the worldwide internetwork of various research, defense, and commercial networks, all tied together for sharing information with one another and public and private users of all sizes and concerns. The Internet consists of millions of interconnected hosts.

Internet Control Message Protocol (ICMP)—ICMP is an integral part of IP that handles error and control messages. Gateways and hosts use ICMP to report problems about datagrams back to the original source that sent the datagram. ICMP also includes an echo request/reply used to test whether a destination is reachable and responding.

Internet Corporation of Assigned Names and Numbers (ICANN)—ICANN is a private, nonprofit organization responsible for overseeing the domain name registration process, assigning IP addresses, assigning protocol parameters, and managing the DNS root servers. Learn more about ICANN at **http://www.icann.org**.

Internet Engineering Task Force (IETF)—IETF is a large, open, international community of network designers, operators, vendors, and researchers concerned with the evolution of the Internet architecture and smooth operation of the Internet.

Internet Group Management Protocol (IGMP)—IGMP is the Internet standard by which hosts can communicate their multicast group membership status to multicast routers. IGMP is used to keep up-to-date information on which host is in which multicast group.

Internet Packet Exchange/Sequenced Packet Exchange (IPX/SPX)—IPX is NetWare's proprietary Network Layer protocol. SPX is the connection-oriented transport protocol concerned with connection-oriented services such as sequencing packets and guaranteeing their delivery, which provides reliability for IPX communications.

Internet Protocol (IP)—IP is the TCP/IP standard protocol that defines the IP datagram as the unit of information passed across an internet. IP provides the basis for connectionless, best-effort packet delivery service, and includes ICMP. The entire protocol suite is often referred to as TCP/IP because TCP and IP are the two most fundamental protocols.

internetwork—Internetwork is a term used to describe a set of connected networks communicating across routers using routable protocols such as TCP/IP or IPX/SPX. The Internet is a very large internetwork; smaller internetworks are corporate networks spanning several floors, buildings, or sites.

intranet—An intranet is an internal network. An intranet is generally only accessible by corporate network users, but it runs all the same protocols and services as does an Internet site.

loopback—The TCP/IP loopback function allows a network administrator to test IP software without concern for the hardware or drivers. The loopback address 127.0.0.1 is the designated software loopback interface for the machine.

Medium Access Control (MAC)—MAC is one of the media-specific IEEE 802 standards (802.3, 802.4, and 802.5) that defines the protocol and frame formats for Ethernet, Token Bus, and Token Ring. It is the lower sublayer of the Data Link Layer of the OSI model used to transmit frames between NICs.

network interface card (NIC)—A NIC is an expansion board inserted into a computer to enable the computer to be connected to a network.

Network News Transfer Protocol (NNTP)—NNTP is the TCP/IP protocol used to distribute news article collections, or news feeds, over the Internet.

Open Systems Interconnection (OSI)—OSI began as a reference model, that is, an abstract model for data communications. However, now the OSI model has been implemented and is used in some data communications applications. The seven-layer OSI model falls logically into two parts. Layers 1 through 4, the "lower" layers, are concerned with the communication of raw data. Layers 5 through 7, the "higher" layers, are concerned with the networking of applications.

PC card—Previously known as a PCMCIA card, a PC card is a small, rectangular expansion card for portable devices, such as laptop and palm computers. PC cards can be NICs, modems, and hard drives, to name a few.

Post Office Protocol (POP)—POP is used to transfer information from a mail server to a user's computer so the information can be read by a mail program at the user's desk. POP3 is the latest iteration of the protocol.

protocol data unit (PDU)—A PDU is a datagram created by a particular layer of an open system reference model. A PDU is used to provide peer-to-peer communications between local and remote processes.

repeater—A repeater connects one cable segment of a LAN to other segments, including connecting differing media. For example, a repeater connects thin Ethernet cables to thick Ethernet cables. It regenerates electrical signals from one segment of cable onto all other segments. Because a repeater reproduces exactly what it receives, bit by bit, it also reproduces errors.

Request for Comment (RFC)—RFCs are the working documents of the Internet research and development community. A document in this series may be on essentially any topic related to computer communication and may be anything from a meeting report to the specification of a standard.

router—A router is a Layer 3 device with several ports that can each connect to a network or another router. The router examines the logical network address of each packet, then uses its internal routing table to forward the packet to the routing port associated with the best path to the packet's destination. If the packet is addressed to a network that is not connected to the router, the router forwards the packet to another router that is closer to the final destination. Each router, in turn, evaluates each packet and then either delivers the packet or forwards it to another router.

Simple Network Management Protocol (SNMP)—SNMP is a TCP/IP Application Layer protocol used to send and receive information about the status of network resources on a TCP/IP network.

switch—A switch is a device that operates at the Data Link Layer of the OSI reference model. It can connect LANs or segments of the same media access type and dedicates its entire bandwidth to each frame it switches.

Systems Network Architecture (SNA)—SNA is IBM's architecture for computer networking, which was designed for transaction processing in mission-critical applications. SNA networks usually involve a large number of terminals communicating with a mainframe.

Telnet—Telnet is a TCP/IP Application Layer protocol that provides a remote login capability to another computer on a network.

Token Ring—Token Ring is a network architecture that uses a ring topology and a token passing strategy to control network access. The IEEE 802.5 standard defines the token ring architecture and how it operates at the OSI model Physical and Data Link Layers.

Transmission Control Protocol (TCP)—TCP is the TCP/IP Transport Layer protocol that provides reliable, full-duplex, stream service. TCP allows a process on one computer to send data to a process on another computer. TCP software implementations normally reside in the OS and use IP to transmit information across the underlying internet.

Trivial File Transfer Protocol (TFTP)—TFTP is a simple file transfer protocol designed for use on top of connectionless UDP. TFTP requires an acknowledgement for each packet before it sends another.

unicast—A unicast is a transmission sent to a single network address. This is in contrast to a broadcast, which is sent to all network addresses simultaneously, and a multicast, which is sent to several addresses at once.

UNIX to UNIX Copy Program (UUCP)—UUCP is an Application Layer protocol used for transferring files between UNIX systems.

USB adapter—A USB adapter is a PC expansion device that conforms to the USB standard. USB devices support data transfer rates of up to 12 Mbps and up to 127 devices on the same bus. USB device examples include NICs, modems, scanners, and CD-ROM drives.

User Datagram Protocol (UDP)—UDP is the TCP/IP protocol that allows an application program on one computer to send a datagram to an application program on another computer. UDP uses IP to deliver datagrams. The difference between UDP datagrams and IP datagrams is that UDP includes a protocol port number, allowing the sender to distinguish among multiple destinations (application programs) on the remote computer. UDP also includes a checksum for the data being sent.

Lesson 1—OSI Model Review

This lesson reviews some of the OSI model's key principles. The OSI model is used as a frame of reference in almost all computer networking texts and courses, and in this course, as well. The information reviewed in this lesson is critical to understanding computer networking.

Objectives

At the end of this lesson you will be able to:

- Describe each OSI model layer's primary function
- List the two main address types found in most computer networks
- Explain why three address types are used to move information from source to destination

Key Point

There are two main types of computer addresses: physical and logical.

Primary Functions of the OSI Model Layers

The OSI Model Layers Table provides an overview of each OSI model layer's primary functions. It also presents the layer's unit of information and address type where appropriate.

OSI Model Layers

OSI Model Layer	Layer Function	Unit of Information	Address Type
Application	User functionality	Program	
Presentation	Character representation Compression Security	Characters and words	
Session	Establishing, conducting, and ending sessions		

OSI Model Layers (Continued)

OSI Model Layer	Layer Function	Unit of Information	Address Type
Transport	Transmitting messages from sending computer process to receiving computer process	Message	Process to process between applications
Network	Transmitting individual packets across a network	Packet	Packet address identifying receiver's network and host location
Data Link	Transmitting frames containing a packet across a link en route to final destination	Frame	NIC (next node in network)
Physical	Transmitting bits in the form of signals across physical media	Bit	

Physical Addresses

A physical address is also referred to as a:

- Hardware address
- Adapter address
- Network interface card (NIC) address
- Medium Access Control (MAC) address

A physical address is required for network devices to ultimately deliver information to a given network node. The word "ultimately" is used because information often starts out (at the higher layers) addressed to some symbolic name, such as the host name in the command "ftp serverhost." The name "serverhost" refers to the name of the target host computer the user is attempting to contact using the ftp (TCP/IP) application and protocol. For the user to connect to this host, a physical address must somehow be derived from the symbolic name, and then used in an agreed-upon addressing scheme to reach the target. In this case, a name service such as the Domain Name Service (DNS) derives a logical software address from the symbolic name. The TCP/IP protocol suite calls this logical address an IP address.

The Physical Layer

You may want to associate a physical address with the OSI model Physical Layer; indeed, this seems natural. However, the OSI model Data Link Layer actually processes the physical address. The Physical Layer only transmits bits to, and receives bits from, the physical medium, and does not "see" the bits as organized into meaningful patterns, such as an address. The Physical Layer operates depending on the chosen network topology. For example, Ethernet networks format, frame, and time bits in a different manner than do Token Ring networks.

The Data Link Layer

We can categorize physical addresses, for the purposes of networking, into two general types: local area network (LAN) addresses and wide area network (WAN) addresses. A LAN address is commonly found in an Ethernet or Token Ring LAN environment, while we use WAN addresses in High-Level Data Link Control (HDLC) or frame relay network protocol addressing.

Physical addresses support a flat network model. This means that physical addresses are not routable; they only designate a host, not both a network and host. To be routable, as in TCP/IP, a protocol must designate both a host and network address. Devices communicating with a Layer 2 only addressing scheme cannot communicate across network (Layer 3) boundaries.

Logical Addresses

A logical address differs from a physical address in that it is generally implemented as a software entity rather than a hardware entity. There are two primary types of logical addresses, as follows:

- Network addresses, processed at the Network Layer
- Port or process addresses, processed at the Transport Layer

The Network Layer

One example of a logical address is an IP address (network), such as 144.25.54.8. The network administrator assigns each host on an IP network a unique IP address. The IP address is a 32-bit address that designates both a host portion and a network portion.

Because layer protocols designate both a host and a network, they allow us to build hierarchical networks. The Three-Layer Network Hierarchy Diagram illustrates this concept.

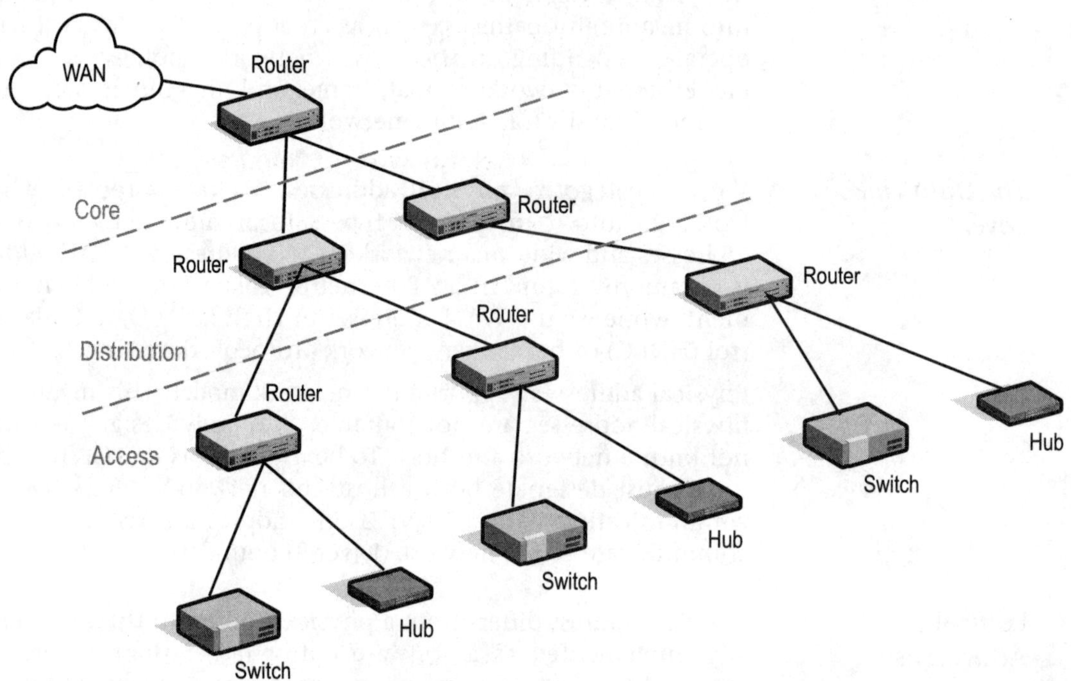

Three-Layer Network Hierarchy

Layer 3 addresses allow us to create multiple routed networks. We can use the three-layer hierarchical model to isolate traffic to local network segments, only passing traffic between layers when hosts on one segment must communicate with hosts on other segments. Ideally, we would isolate traffic to the bottom two layers, the access and distribution layer, and only pass WAN traffic to the core layer. Routing and Layer 3 addresses make this possible.

The Transport Layer

Another logical address example is a port number (process address), such as "23." Devices use port addresses to pass information to the higher layers. Devices use port numbers to keep track of multiple simultaneous conversations.

Software developers use well-known port numbers to initiate conversations. The Well-Known Port Numbers Table lists some of the more commonly used TCP and User Datagram Protocol (UDP) addresses.

Well-Known Port Numbers

Decimal	Protocol-Description
20	TCP-FTP Data
21	TCP-FTP
23	TCP-Telnet
25	TCP-SMTP
53	TCP/UDP-DNS
67	UDP-BOOTP/DHCP
69	UDP-TFTP
161	UDP-SNMP

The Transport Layer is responsible not only for application addressing, but also for providing reliable communications over the best effort Layer 3 protocols. The Transport Layer provides flow control, windowing, data sequencing, and recovery.

Layers 5 through 7

The remaining OSI model layers work with the data itself. These layers leave the end-to-end data transport issues to the lower four layers.

The Session Layer

The Session Layer establishes, manages, and terminates sessions between applications. Sessions consist of dialogs between two or more Presentation Layer entities.

The Session Layer provides its services to the Presentation Layer. The Session Layer synchronizes dialog between Presentation Layer entities and manages their data exchange. In addition to regulating conversations (sessions), the Session Layer can provide for dialog unit synchronization, class of service (CoS), and Layer 5, 6, and 7 session exception reporting.

The Presentation Layer

The Presentation Layer ensures that information sent by the Application Layer of one system is formatted in a manner in which the destination system's Application Layer can read it. The Presentation Layer can translate between multiple data representation formats, if necessary.

The Application Layer

The Application Layer is the layer closest to the user. It provides user application services to application processes outside the OSI model's scope and does not support the other layers.

The Application Layer identifies and establishes the intended communication partners availability, synchronizes cooperating applications, and establishes agreed procedures for application error recovery and data integrity control. It also determines whether sufficient resources exist for the intended communications.

Addressing Summary

The most important fact to remember concerning logical addresses is that a logical address will not transmit information "into the box." Only the physical address, whether it is a broadcast, multicast (group), or single destination (unicast) address, can accomplish this.

Activities

1. The OSI model Physical Layer serves which primary purpose?
   a. It provides physical addresses for moving information into the box.
   b. It builds frames that carry higher layer PDU across network segments.
   c. It uses network and host addresses to route packets across networks.
   d. It transmits data in the form of bits across the physical medium.
2. Which is the primary purpose of the OSI model Session Layer?
   a. It builds frames that carry higher layer PDU across network segments.
   b. It builds a flat network model with unroutable physical addresses.
   c. It establishes, manages, and terminates dialogs between Presentation Layer entities.
   d. It defines the format in which Application Layer information is sent across the network.
3. Which is the primary purpose of the OSI model Presentation Layer?
   a. It establishes, manages, and terminates sessions between applications.
   b. It uses logical addresses to identify higher layer applications.
   c. It builds a flat network model with unroutable physical addresses.
   d. It defines the format in which Application Layer information is sent across the network.
4. The OSI model Data Link Layer serves which primary purpose?
   a. It builds a flat network model with unroutable physical addresses.
   b. It transmits data in the form of bits across the physical medium.
   c. It creates multiple routed networks with logical addresses.
   d. It establishes, manages, and terminates sessions between applications.

5. The OSI model Application Layer serves which primary purpose?
   a. It defines well-known logical port addresses for communications between applications.
   b. It controls dialogs between two or more Presentation Layer entities.
   c. It establishes user application procedures for error recovery and data integrity.
   d. It creates a hierarchical addressing model for moving information across networks.

Extended Activities

1. On a windows PC, select Start, Find, Files, or Folders. In the named box, type **services**. Select the drive on which the operating systems is installed (typically C:) in the Look In box.

   In the results window, double-click the Services file (there is no extension). When prompted for a program with which to open the file, choose Notepad. Notepad will open the file; this file contains all the TCP and UDP well-known service ports as defined by RFC 1060.
2. Locate in the Services file the following services and list their port numbers.
   a. BOOTP
   b. Chargen
   c. POP3
   d. NNTP
   e. Nbname (NetBIOS name)

Lesson 2—Internet Protocol Suite

The Internet protocol suite is the combination of protocols that make up TCP/IP software. This lesson covers important aspects and protocols of a TCP/IP system.

Objectives

At the end of this lesson you will be able to:

- Describe the Internet protocol suite
- List the Application Layer protocols
- List the Transport Layer protocols
- List the Network Layer protocols

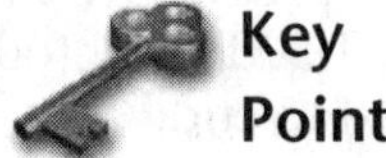

Key Point

Each TCP/IP architecture layer has a specific purpose.

Overview of the TCP/IP Protocol Suite

The TCP/IP Protocols Diagram shows a detailed picture of the TCP/IP layers; the corresponding OSI layers are also presented. This lesson describes, in the context of a network, the services and protocols these layers provide.

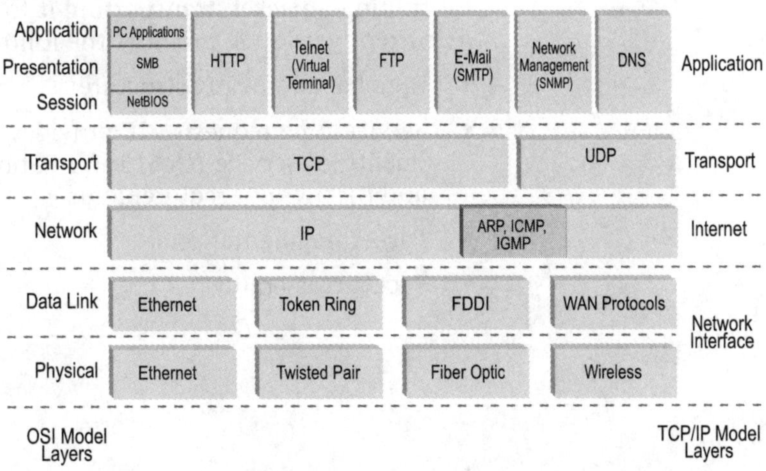

TCP/IP Protocols

As shown, the TCP/IP protocols map to specific OSI model layers; TCP/IP also provides its own layered model. The TCP/IP Protocols Diagram also shows the TCP/IP model layers.

The TCP/IP model layers function as follows:

- Network Interface Layer—Encompasses the functions of the OSI model Physical and Data Link Layers, providing bit and frame transmission services, depending on the network type.
- Internetwork Layer—Delivers packets to their destination across multiple networks, as does the OSI model Network Layer.
- Transport Layer—Provides reliability and flow control similar to the OSI model Transport Layer.
- Application Layer—Provides the high-level protocols users and application programs use for communicating over the network.

Network Interface Layer Protocols

Although messaging services are primarily provided by Application Layer protocols, the lower layer TCP/IP protocols are required for carrying the messages from end to end.

The Network Interface Layer protocols define rules that determine how a host accesses a LAN. These low-level protocols define how a host connects to the network. The physical network's operation is left up to the physical network topology's specific Layer 1 and 2 protocols.

Internetwork Layer Protocols

The Internetwork Layer protocols define the basic unit of transfer across a network and provide support for a global addressing scheme and routing. IP is the Network Layer protocol responsible for routing a packet, transporting it to its final destination. IP, in its current version 4, provides the following functions:

- A global addressing structure
- Service type requests—IP provides, within the packet header, quality of service (QoS) information, such as packet priority and throughput requirements
- Packet fragmentation
- Packet reassembly

Other protocols at the Internetwork Layer include:

- Address Resolution Protocol (ARP)/ Reverse ARP (RARP)—Maps an IP host address to a physical address (ARP) or a physical address to an IP address (RARP). RARP is often used in master/slave network environments where a terminal must download an IP address before it can communicate with the host server.
- Internet Control Message Protocol (ICMP)—Provides troubleshooting utilities, such as ping and traceroute, for testing and verifying network connectivity between devices through error and status messages intended for use by the TCP/IP software rather than for users.
- Internet Group Management Protocol (IGMP)—Used to allow hosts to participate in IP multicast (group) addressing schemes.

A new version of the IP protocol, version 6, is now in development. It expands the IP Address fields from 32 to 128 bits.

Transport Layer Protocols

The Transport Layer's primary function is to provide communication from one application program to another.

A Network Layer protocol only provides a packet delivery service, allowing a host to inject packets into the Internet with some degree of confidence that they will be delivered to the correct destination. User applications, however, typically require a specific service level. This may involve specific levels of reliability, error rate, delay, or some combination of these characteristics. A Transport Layer protocol provides the Application Layer's required level of service.

TCP/IP provides applications two different levels of service:

- TCP—Provides an end-to-end data stream service containing mechanisms to ensure reliable data transmission. These mechanisms include checksums, sequence numbers, timers, acknowledgements, and retransmission procedures. TCP, a connection-oriented protocol, provides reliable, sequenced data delivery for the Application Layer.
- UDP—Provides an end-to-end, transaction-oriented, best-effort, connectionless service for those applications that do not require a reliable data delivery service. An application uses UDP when it depends more on speed than reliability, or when the application itself provides reliability.

Application Layer Protocols

An application passes data to the Transport Layer protocols, which sequence the data into messages, or byte streams, for transport across the network. The TCP/IP protocol suite includes the following Application Layer protocols:

- Telnet—Telnet is a remote terminal access protocol that uses TCP's connection-oriented services. Telnet allows a local host terminal to communicate with a remote host program as if the local terminal were directly connected to the remote.
- File Transfer Protocol (FTP)—FTP enables a facility to send files from one host to another. Like Telnet, FTP uses the reliable service provided by TCP to ensure the file segments are not lost.
- Simple Mail Transfer Protocol (SMTP)—SMTP contains the electronic mail (e-mail) mechanisms. SMTP also uses TCP for reliable mail message transfers. Though not commonly used explicitly (most frequently implemented by a server or client service), SMTP provides a simple protocol for sending e-mail between a client or a server and another server.
- Simple Network Management Protocol (SNMP)—SNMP provides a standardized network management protocol that allows management of TCP/IP hosts and routers. At the Transport Layer, SNMP uses UDP.
- DNS—DNS provides a name-to-address look-up service. DNS allows us to enter a Uniform Resource Locator (URL) instead of an IP address and still access the remote server. DNS may use either UDP or TCP, first attempting a TCP connection.
- Post Office Protocol 3 (POP3)—POP3 is the protocol that allows us to retrieve our e-mail from the mail server on which it is stored. POP3 uses TCP at the Transport Layer.
- Hypertext Transfer Protocol (HTTP)—HTTP allows web clients and servers to negotiate and interact with each other. HTTP is a stateless protocol; that means that when the transaction is completed, the logical connection is dropped. HTTP uses TCP at the Transport Layer.
- Network News Transfer Protocol (NNTP)—NNTP is the TCP/IP protocol used to distribute news article collections, or news feeds, over the Internet. NNTP allows companies to publicly post information that users may readily download to a news reader client. NNTP uses TCP at the Transport Layer. Many e-mail systems provide NNTP services.

- UNIX-to-UNIX Copy Program (UUCP) protocol—UUCP allows us to transfer files between UNIX systems. It is commonly used as an Internet low-end access protocol.

Communication Using TCP/IP

Consider an example in which you wish to send an e-mail message to another host on the network. The following sections describe this process.

Application Layer

There is an Application Layer protocol for e-mail; in TCP/IP it is SMTP. This protocol defines a set of commands that one computer sends to another. These commands are used to specify both the sender and recipient of the message, as well as the message text.

The data stream shown on the Your Mail E-Mail Message 1 Diagram makes up the e-mail message:

Your Mail E-Mail Message 1

This stream of data is sent to the TCP module that is responsible for ensuring that the e-mail message gets through to the other end. Think of TCP as a library of routines that applications use for reliable network communication with other computers.

Transport Layer

TCP breaks a large e-mail message into manageable pieces, as shown on the Your Mail E-Mail Message 2 Diagram. Each piece (or segment) will eventually be placed in its own packet. It is the responsibility of the destination station to reassemble the individual segments into the complete e-mail message.

Your Mail E-Mail Message 2

After it breaks up the message into segments, TCP keeps track of the pieces by placing a header on the front of each, as shown on the Your Mail E-Mail Message 3 Diagram. The TCP header includes a source port, destination port, and sequence number. If we, for the sake of illustration, abbreviate the TCP header as "T," the entire e-mail file now looks like this:

Your Mail E-Mail Message 3

The packet (or datagram) is now passed down to the Network Layer for processing and eventual transmission by IP. TCP tracks what it sends, and retransmits anything that does not get through.

Network Layer

The interface between TCP and IP is relatively simple. TCP simply hands a datagram with a destination to IP. IP has no knowledge of how this datagram relates to any other datagram before or after it; IP merely exists to deliver the packet to the end node.

IP's job is to find a route for the datagram and get it to its final destination. IP places a header on each segment to send the encapsulating datagram on to its final destination, as shown on the Your Mail E-Mail Message 4 Diagram. The IP header includes the source and destination IP addresses, a protocol number indicating the Transport Layer protocol (in this example, TCP), and a checksum. If we abbreviate the IP header as "I," the e-mail message now looks like this:

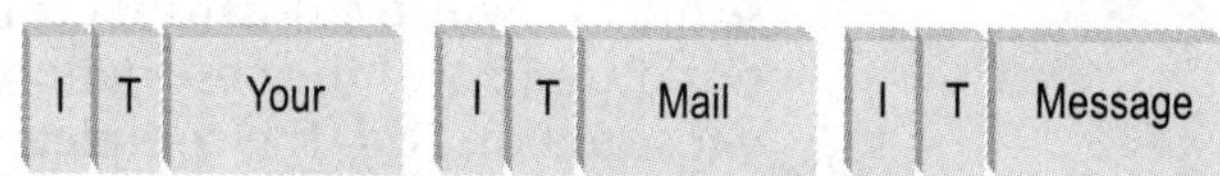

Your Mail E-Mail Message 4

Each datagram is now passed down to the Network Interface Layer for injection into the physical network as a sequence of bits.

Network Interface Layer

The physical network places its own header on each datagram. Assume we are trying to access an Ethernet network. If we represent the Ethernet header by an "E," and the Ethernet checksum with a "C," the e-mail message is now composed of the following three datagrams, as shown on the Your Mail E-Mail Message 5 Diagram.

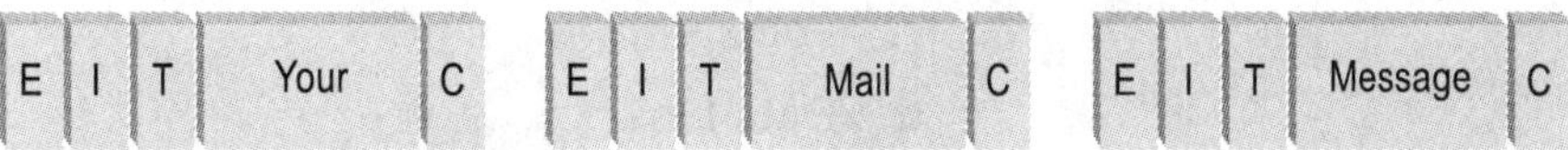

Your Mail E-Mail Message 5

Destination Station

When the destination station receives the packets, the datagrams are processed, in reverse, by the various protocol stack layers. The Ethernet interface looks at the Ethernet Type field and passes the datagram up to IP.

IP looks at the Protocol field and passes the datagram up to TCP. TCP looks at the sequence numbers and other information to recombine the segments into the original e-mail message. The Transport Layer then passes the message up to the e-mail application on the destination computer.

Activities

1. The TCP/IP model Network Interface Layer maps to which OSI model layer(s)? (Choose all that apply.)
   a. Physical
   b. Network
   c. Transport
   d. Data Link
2. Which three of the following are functions of the TCP/IP Internetwork Layer protocols? (Choose three.)
   a. A global addressing structure
   b. Packet fragmentation
   c. End-to-end data stream service
   d. Service type requests
3. Which three of the following are TCP/IP Internetwork Layer protocols? (Choose three.)
   a. IGMP
   b. IP
   c. UDP
   d. ARP
4. Which TCP/IP Application Layer protocol allows companies to publicly post information over the Internet?
   a. FTP
   b. SMTP
   c. UUCP
   d. NNTP
5. Which TCP/IP Transport Layer protocol provides an end-to-end, transaction-oriented, best-effort, connectionless service?
   a. TCP
   b. UDP
   c. RTP
   d. RSVP

6. Given the TCP/IP Communications Diagram, label each layer in the e-mail process with the appropriate TCP/IP model layer name.

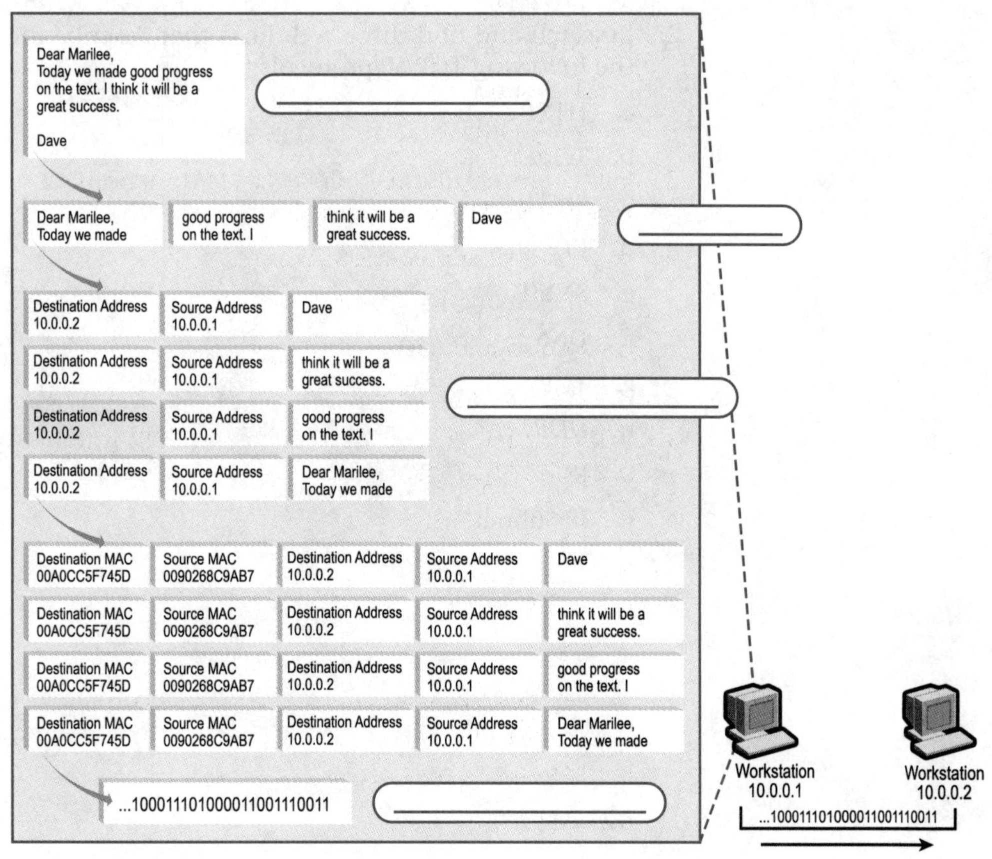

TCP/IP Communications

Extended Activities

1. Download and review the following RFCs at **http://www.ietf.org/rfc. 814** "Name, Addresses, Ports, and Routes," D. D. Clark, July 1982.
2. Research and find three Web links that describe the details of the following TCP/IP protocols:
   a. HTTP
   b. Telnet
   c. SMTP
   d. FTP
   e. SNMP
   f. DNS
   g. TCP
   h. UDP
   i. IP
   j. IP Subnet

Lesson 3—Internet Addressing

Any global communications system requires a universally accepted method to identify individual computers. Computing devices, or hosts (also called nodes), on a TCP/IP-based network, are assigned unique addresses called IP addresses. These hosts may be personal computers (PCs), terminal servers, ports on a terminal server, routers, network management stations, UNIX hosts, and so forth. This lesson presents the structure of IP addresses.

Objectives

At the end of this lesson you will be able to:

- Describe IP addressing fundamentals
- Explain IP address routing and bridging

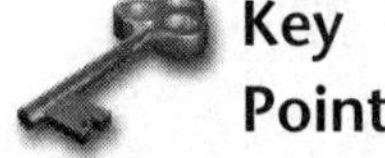

Key Point

Unique addressing is critical in networking.

IP Addresses

There is one thing that all computers running the TCP/IP suite have in common: each is assigned its own IP address. The Internet Corporation of Assigned Names and Numbers (ICANN), a private, nongovernment organization, issues all IP addresses. Some devices, such as routers, which have physical connections to more than one network, must be assigned a unique IP address for each network connection, or port.

IP addressing uses a 32-bit Address field; the bits in the Address field are numbered 0 to 31. This field is then divided into two parts: the right part identifies the host (the host portion), and the left part identifies the network on which the host resides (the network portion). Hosts attached to the same network must share a common prefix designating their network number.

Note: The IP software residing on network hosts uses a unique bit pattern to identify the address class. After the IP software has identified the address class, it can determine which bits represent the network number and which bits identify the host portion of the address.

IP addresses take the form of four numeric fields, consisting of 3 characters each, separated by periods.

field1.field2.field3.field4

There are five IP address classes; Classes A-E. We can easily determine the address class from its leading (highest-order) bits.

Class A Address

A Class A network address has the leading bit set to 0, a 7-bit network number, and a 24-bit local host address. The first octet ranges from 0–127, although 0 and 127 are reserved and cannot be assigned to networks and hosts, as shown on the Class A Network Address Diagram. We can define a total of 126 Class A networks, with up to 16,777,214 hosts per network.

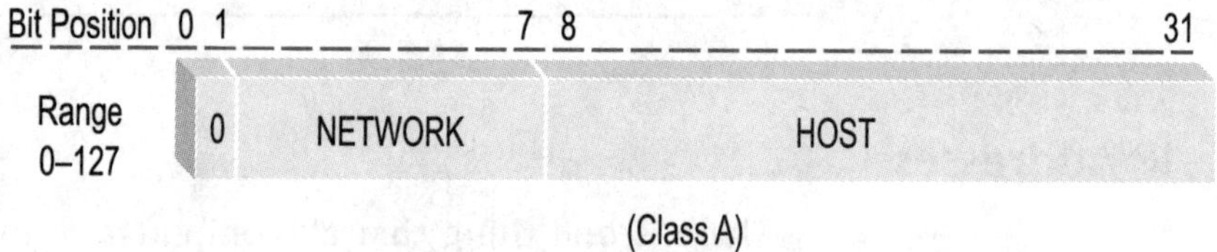

Class A Network Address

Note: Internet Engineering Task Force (IETF) Request For Comments (RFCs) specify that in a range of IP addresses, certain addresses are reserved. The first address, with the host portion set to all 0s, specifies *this* network, and cannot be assigned to a host. The last address, with the host portion set to all 1s specifies *all hosts*, and also cannot be assigned to a specific host.

Additionally, network addresses 0.x.y.z and 127.x.y.z are reserved for special functions, that we will learn about later. Therefore, we can only assign the Class A ranges 1.x.y.z through 126.x.y.z to network hosts.

Although 2^{24} equates to 16,777,216, we can only assign 16,777,214 host addresses per Class A network. Recall that we cannot assign a host address of all 0s nor all 1s. Consequently, we then have to subtract these two unassignable addresses from the total number of available host addresses. We will revisit this addressing restriction again when we discuss subnetting in a later unit.

Class B Address

A Class B network address has the two highest-order bits set to 1-0, a 14-bit network number, and a 16-bit local host address. The first octet ranges from 128–191, as shown on the Class B Network Address Diagram. A total of 16,382 Class B networks can be defined with up to 65,534 usable hosts per network.

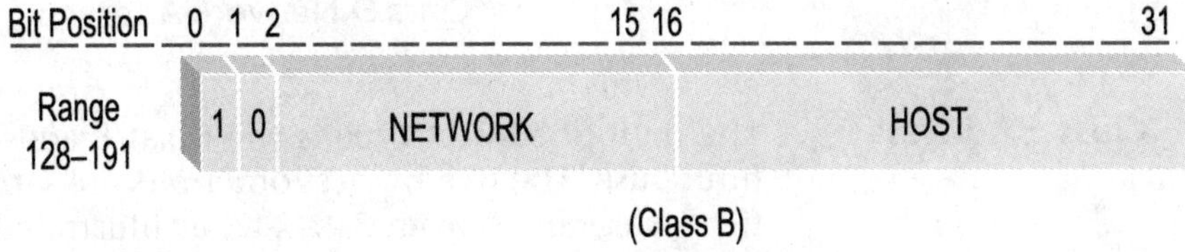

Class B Network Address

Class C Address

A Class C network address has the three leading bits set to 1-1-0, a 21-bit network number, and an 8-bit local host address. The first octet ranges from 192–223, as shown on the Class C Network Address Diagram. A total of 2,097,152 Class C networks may be defined with up to 254 usable hosts per network.

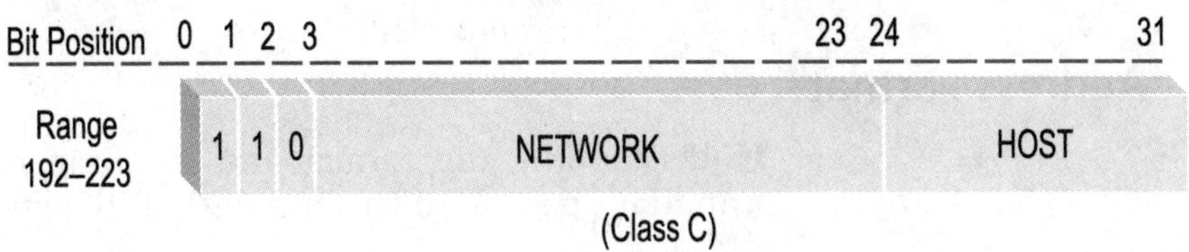

Class C Network Address

Class D Address

The fourth address type, Class D, is used as a multicast address. The four highest order bits are set to 1-1-1-0, and the remaining 28 bits specify a multicast group ID. The first octet ranges from 224–239. This concept is illustrated on the Class D Network Address Diagram. We discuss the use of Class D addresses later in this course.

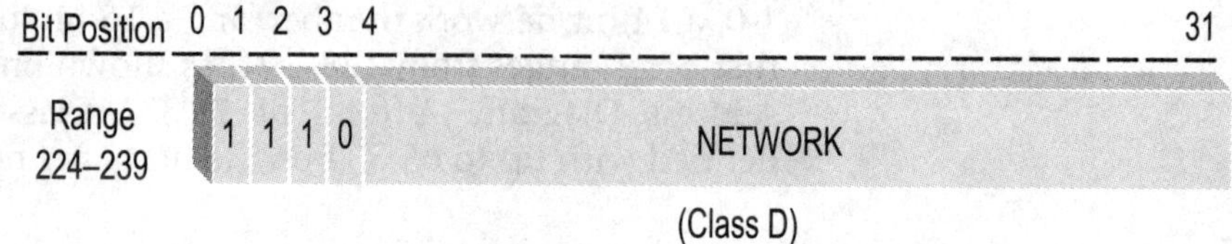

Class D Network Address

Class E Address

The final IP address type is the Class E address; it is reserved for future use. The five highest order bits are set to 1-1-1-1-0, and the first octet ranges from 240–247, as illustrated on the Class E Network Address Diagram.

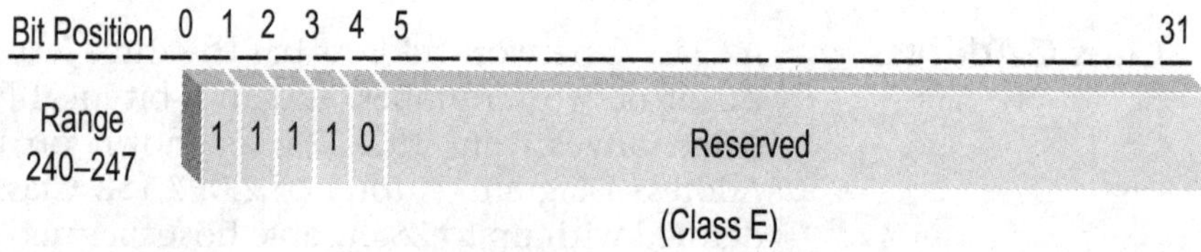

Class E Network Address

Address Format

Understanding the format and meaning of IP addresses is an important part of understanding TCP/IP networks and subnets.

Dotted Decimal Notation

To make it easier for people to read and understand IP addresses, the addresses are often written as four decimal numbers, each separated by a dot. This format is called dotted decimal notation.

This notation divides the 32-bit address into four 8-bit (byte) fields, or octets, and independently specifies the value of each field as a decimal number. For example, if given the Class B IP address specified by the bit pattern:

10000001 00001111 00010001 00000011

The value of each byte, specified in a string of four decimal numbers, is:

129 15 17 3

The complete IP address, shown in dotted decimal notation, is:

129.15.17.3

The valid network numbers for each address class are provided below. The "hhh" represents the host portion of the address assigned by the network administrator.

Class A: 001.hhh.hhh.hhh through 127.hhh.hhh.hhh

Class B: 128.001.hhh.hhh through 191.254.hhh.hhh

Class C: 192.000.001.hhh through 223.255.254.hhh

Class D: 224.000.000.000 through 239.255.255.255

Class E: 240.xxx.yyy.zzz through 247.xxx.yyy.zzz

Addressing Rules

The following rules pertain to assigning IP addresses:

- The bits that define the host portion of an IP address should not be all 1 bits. According to the RFCs, any IP address with the host portion consisting of all 1s is interpreted as meaning "all," as in "all hosts." For example, the address 128.1.255.255 is interpreted as meaning all hosts on Network 128.1.0.0.
- The bits used to define the network portion of an IP address should not be all 0 bits. According to the RFCs, a host portion address of all 0s is interpreted as meaning "this," as in "this network." For example, the address 0.0.0.63 is interpreted as meaning Host 63 on this network.
- The Class A network number 127 is assigned the loopback function. This means that a datagram sent by a higher level protocol to a Network 127 address should loop back inside the host.

In some cases, (UNIX) network sockets are used not only for communication with other computers, but also used for inter-process communication. In a UNIX environment, if Program A wishes to communicate with Program B running on the same computer, they would do so using IP network number 127. No datagram should ever appear on any network with a source or destination network address of 127.

- The ICANN has designated certain address ranges as private or reserved addresses. These ranges are:
  - 10.0.0.0 through 10.255.255.255
  - 172.16.0.0 through 172.31.255.255
  - 192.168.0.0 through 192.168.255.255

  Internet routers do not route these address ranges. The ICANN suggests organizations use these address ranges when:
  - The network hosts do not require access to other enterprises or the Internet.
  - Mediating gateways, such as Application Layer gateways, routers, or firewalls, can act on the network hosts' behalf. Hosts may only require limited Internet services, or the mediating gateway can translate private addresses to Internet routable public addresses.

  Organizations benefit from using these private addresses by:
  - Conserving globally unique IP addresses when this uniqueness is not required
  - Gain more network design flexibility, because a large address range is available
  - Preventing address clashes when obtaining Internet access without obtaining a full range of ICANN assigned addresses

  Private IP addressing has its drawbacks, as well:
  - To provide hosts future Internet access, you will have to renumber some hosts, or perform address translation at the Internet access point. Address translation is discussed later in this course.
  - In the case of a corporate merger, if all hosts on both networks use private IP addresses, you will likely have to reassign at least some of the host addresses.

Sample Network Using Class A Address Format

Segments connected by switches share the same network fields, while having different host fields. Segments interconnected by routers must have different network fields, as illustrated on the Sample Class A Network Diagram.

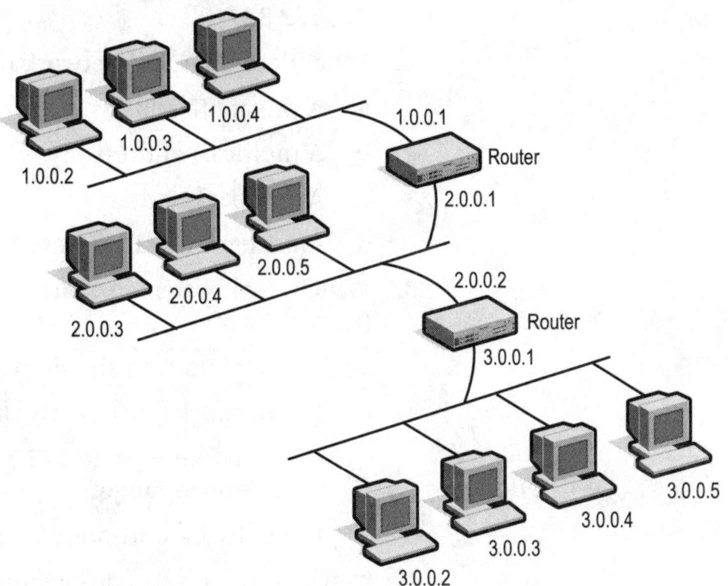

Sample Class A Network

In this example, we have 3 separate Class A networks, each using a different first octet number. We must connect these separate networks through routers for them to communicate. Routers, which are Layer 3 devices, route IP packets across networks based on source and destination addresses, such as IP logical addresses.

Whenever a host on the 2.0.0.0 network wishes to communicate with a host on the 1.0.0.0 network, it must first send its message to its local router port. The local router then determines the appropriate path to use to forward the packet along to the destination network.

The destination network router receives the packet sent from the originating router, and determines if the destination host is on its local network. If so, the destination router forwards the packet out its local network port to the destination host. If not, the router forwards the packet on to the next hop router in the packet's path.

Activities

1. Which are considered private IP addresses?
   a. 10.0.0.0
   b. 172.31.255.255
   c. 192.168.0.0
   d. 172.32.0.0
2. What does the Class network number 127.x.y.z designate?
   a. A private IP address
   b. A multicast address
   c. A loopback address
   d. An experimental address
3. Which two statements are true concerning IP addressing? (Choose two.)
   a. The host portion should not be all 1s.
   b. The network portion bits should usually be all 0s.
   c. The IP address range 172.16.0.0–172.31.255.255 is a public IP address range.
   d. The network portion bits should not be all 0s.
4. In which three ways do organizations benefit from using private IP addresses? (Choose three.)
   a. They conserve private IP addresses when uniqueness is required.
   b. They gain more network design flexibility with a large address range.
   c. They prevent Internet address clashes when obtaining only a small range of ICANN assigned addresses.
   d. They conserve public IP addresses when uniqueness is not required.
5. Which two of the following are considered reserved IP addresses? (Choose two.)
   a. 0.x.y.z
   b. 172.16.y.z
   c. 127.x.y.z
   d. 126.x.y.z

6. Fill in the blanks to the right of each address range with its IP Class.
   a. 240.xxx.yyy.zzz through 247.xxx.yyy.zzz _______
   b. 128.001.hhh.hhh through 191.254.hhh.hhh _______
   c. 001.hhh.hhh.hhh through 127.hhh.hhh.hhh _______
   d. 224.000.000.000 through 239.255.255.255 _______
   e. 192.000.001.hhh through 223.255.254.hhh _______

   Class A
   Class B
   Class C
   Class D
   Class E

Extended Activities

1. On your PC, open a command prompt or MS-DOS prompt window. Type the command **ping 127.0.0.1**. Note the response.
2. In the same command prompt windows, type **ping localhost**. Note the response. How does this compare to the first response?
3. Ping the hostname that appeared next to the loopback IP address 127.0.0.1 in the first line of Step 2's response. What is the response?

Lesson 4—Internetworking Devices

In IP networks, the primary network connectivity device is the router. However, other devices, such as NICs, hubs, repeaters, and switches, play crucial roles in network operations.

This lesson reviews the most common, frequently used networking devices.

Objectives

At the end of this lesson you will be able to:

- Describe the most commonly used networking devices
- Explain how routers control broadcast traffic
- Explain how routers make packet forwarding decisions

Key Point

Many network device types comprise a network

Common Network Components

Computer networks require a great deal of equipment to function properly. LANs and WANs typically include NICs, repeaters, hubs, switches, and routers. A typical network might appear as shown in the Networking Devices Diagram.

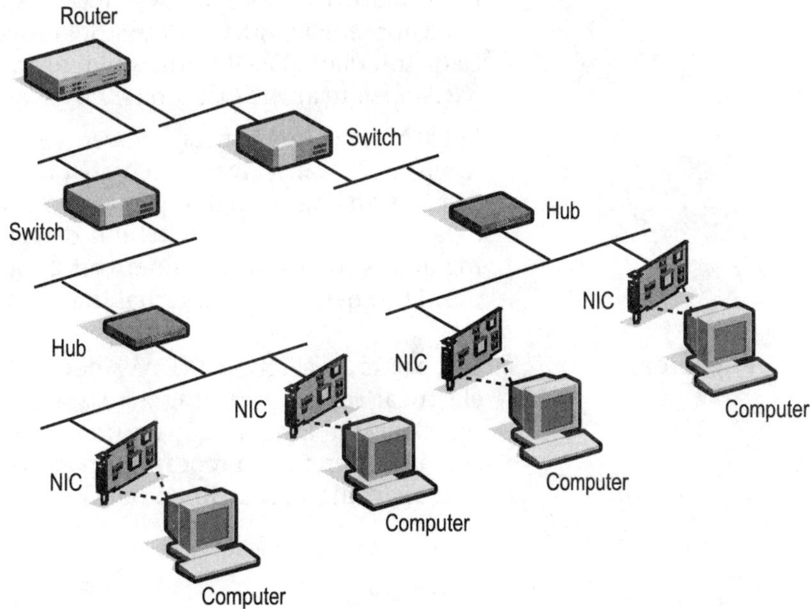

Networking Devices

NIC

Each network node uses a NIC, also called a network adapter card. The NIC is the interface between the computer and the network, and can take the form of an internal expansion card, a PC card, or a Universal Serial Bus (USB) adapter. The Network Adapters Diagram illustrates these devices.

Network Adapters

No matter where it resides, the NIC communicates with the computer through a NIC device driver. Network cables connect NICs to the network. NICs are available to support many different network topologies, such as Ethernet, Token Ring, Fiber Distributed Data Interface (FDDI), and Asynchronous Transfer Mode (ATM). NICs operate at the OSI model Physical and Data Link Layers.

Most NICs contain a transceiver, which is short for transmitter-receiver. A transceiver is a network device that transmits and receives analog or digital signals. In LANs, the transceiver places data onto the network wire and detects and receives data traveling across the wire. Some network types, such as 10Base5 (Thicknet) Ethernet, require external transceivers.

Repeaters

A repeater is a Physical Layer device that amplifies and repeats electrical signals traveling across a cable segment, as shown on the Repeater Diagram. It ensures that electronic signals do not degrade; therefore, a repeater can connect computers that are farther apart than the defined network standard allows.

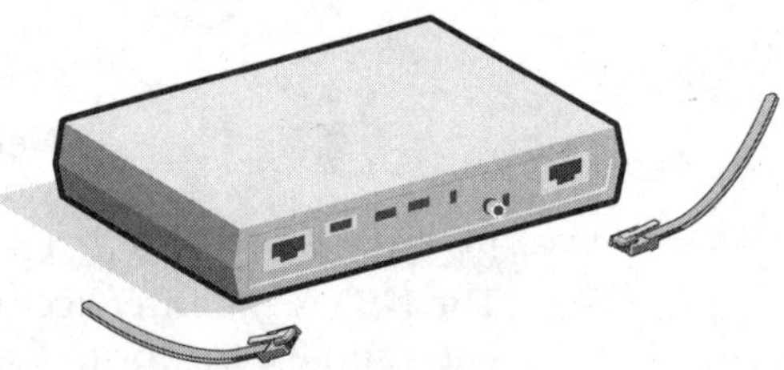

Repeater

Repeaters only transmit binary representations of the transmitted data. As a cable segment approaches its maximum allowed length, the data signal weakens and eventually breaks down. The Maximum Segment Length Table lists various topologies and their maximum cable lengths.

Maximum Segment Length

Topology	Maximum Unrepeated Cable Length	Maximum Repeated Cable Length
10Base2	185 m	925 m
10Base5	500 m	2,500 m

Maximum Segment Length (Continued)

Topology	Maximum Unrepeated Cable Length	Maximum Repeated Cable Length
10BaseT	100 m	N/A (star topology)
100BaseT	100 m	N/A (star topology)
100BaseFX	2 to 10 Km	N/A

Hubs

Hubs are OSI model Layer 1 devices that connect computers in a star-configured network so they can exchange information. Hubs function as multiple-port repeaters, repeating and regenerating bits. Rather than have all devices connected to a common physical segment, as on a bus, a star network collapses the bus backbone into the hub. The hub provides port connections into which we can plug individual network cables. This collapsed network backbone serves to concentrate network connections at a single, central device.

Most hubs are active hubs; in other words, they regenerate and repeat the network's electronic signals. The Network Hub Diagram illustrates a small, active hub.

Network Hub

Hubs can be daisy chained together, and connected to switches, bridges, and routers to increase the number of network nodes.

Bridges

Bridges are OSI model Layer 2 devices. Bridges filter traffic by MAC addresses, helping to control network collisions by dividing a single network into two segments.

Bridges maintain in memory MAC address to port mappings. These mappings allow bridges to store information regarding devices connected to their ports. By referencing these MAC address tables before they forward frames, bridges can determine whether a frame is destined for a device on the source segment, or whether it needs to forward the frame to another segment. This ensures that frames only travel on network segments on which their source and destination devices are located, reducing network traffic and increasing available bandwidth.

Bridges may also connect different network topologies, such as connecting an Ethernet network to a Token Ring network. The Network Bridge Diagram illustrates a network bridge device.

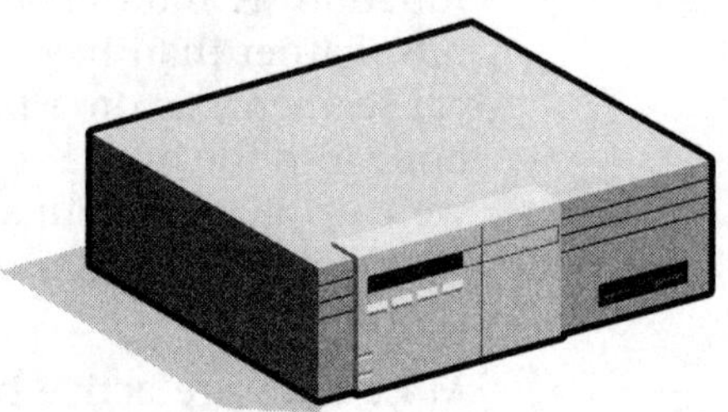

Network Bridge

Bridges operate independently of all upper layer protocols, allowing them to forward frames containing many different upper layer protocol data units (PDUs).

Switches

Switches work as multiple-port bridges. As do bridges, switches filter Layer 2 frames by MAC addresses, by learning and maintaining port to address mappings. Switches create multiple network segments, with each segment offering its full bandwidth to its connected devices. The Network Switch Diagram illustrates this device.

Network Switch

Switches break up collisions, as do bridges. For example, on a 10-port hub, each connected device shares the network's bandwidth with the other devices. Each has to wait for the other attached devices' network traffic to clear before they can transmit their frames. However, on a 10-port switch, each device has its own entire network segment. Each only competes for the network bandwidth with the switch port itself, dramatically reducing delays caused by network bandwidth contention. The Shared vs. Switched Network Diagram illustrates this concept.

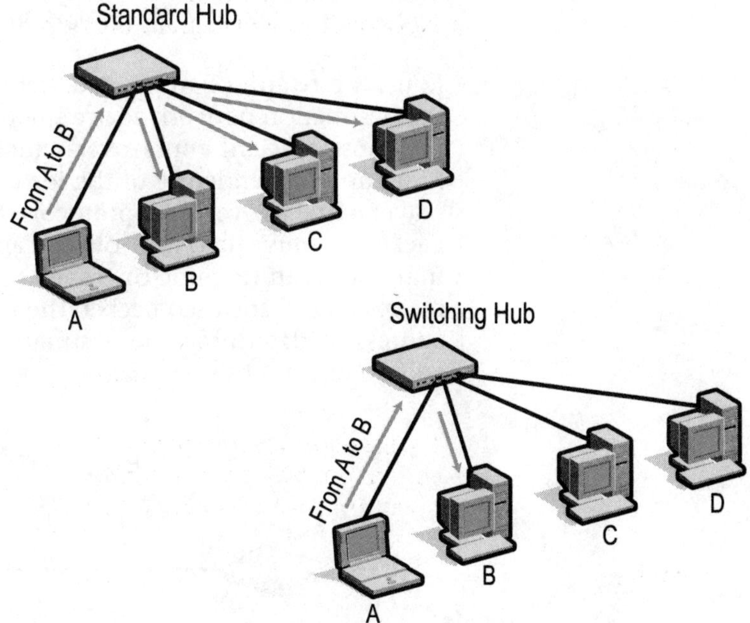

Shared vs. Switched Network

By using a switch, network performance is increased when traffic is sent between different nodes attached to the switch. For example, if client A sends information to client C at the same time client B sends information to client D, the performance of the network is doubled. In other words, the full port bandwidth is available to every device attached to a switch port, instead of its being shared among multiple stations. If the network is 10-megabytes-per-second (Mbps) Ethernet, each port has 10-Mbps bandwidth available. Similarly, if the network is 100-Mbps Ethernet, each port has 100-Mbps bandwidth available.

Routers

Routers are OSI model Layer 3 devices that implement the network service. Routers function essentially as do bridges, making forwarding decisions based on addresses. However, because routers operate at Layer 3, they make their forwarding decisions based on logical addresses instead of physical addresses. The Network Router Diagram illustrates this device.

Network Router

Routers forward, or route, data between networks. They identify the destination network device's network address, then determine the most efficient route over which to send the data. Routers function independently of the lower (Layers 1 and 2) and higher (Layer 4 and above) layer protocols. For a router to forward a data packet, it must first strip off (decapsulate) the Data Link Layer frame so it can examine the Layer 3 packet the frame carries. After it exposes the enclosed packet, the router reads the destination IP address to determine the destination network. The Packet Diagram illustrates this process.

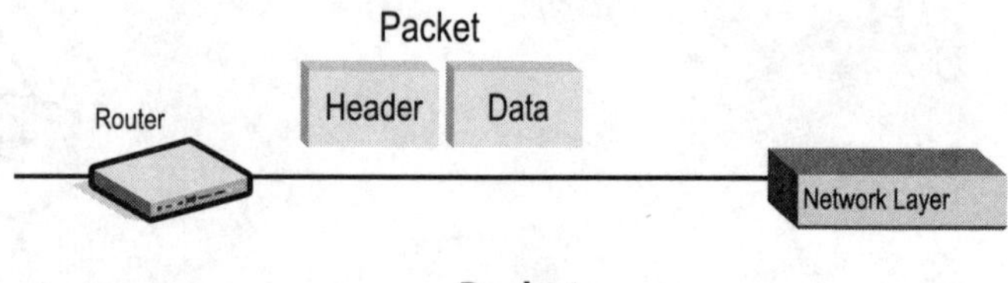

Packet

Routers are Layer 3 protocol-dependent. For a network architecture to be routable, it must have a Network Layer; TCP/IP and Internetwork Packet Exchange/Sequenced Packet Exchange (IPX/SPX) are routable protocols. A router operates based on the Layer 3 protocol's addressing structure. Addresses must have the form network:node; the network portion determines the "wire" on which the host resides, and the node portion addresses the specific host on the wire.

IP uses a 32-bit address, with the network and host portions varying in size, depending on the address class. IPX uses a 10-byte (80-bit) logical address, of which one part (4 bytes) is the administrator assigned network address, and the other part is the 6-byte MAC address. A router must support a specific Layer 3 protocol, otherwise it will drop these unrecognizable packets.

Broadcast Isolation

Routers break up collisions, just as do bridges and switches, but bridges and switches cannot isolate broadcast traffic. A broadcast frame results from a number of different Layer 2 protocols and services. The sending device sets the broadcast frame's physical destination address to a MAC address of all "Fs." Switches and bridges can only handle this global address in one manner, and that is to forward the frame out all ports; no one network device can have the physical address FF:FF:FF:FF:FF:FF.

Because they make decisions at the Network Layer, routers control broadcast traffic. If a frame does not carry routable Layer 3 data, the router will drop the frame. This isolates broadcast traffic to the local network, preserving bandwidth on any remote networks attached to the router's ports. The Broadcast Isolation Diagram illustrates this concept.

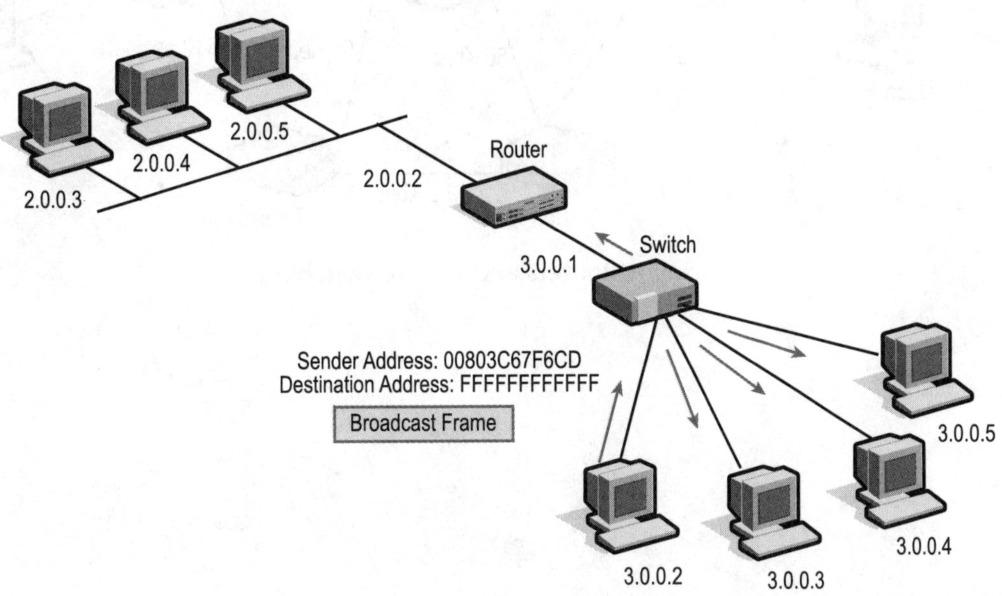

Broadcast Isolation

Making Forwarding Decisions

A router has several ports through which it can route packets to a network or other routers. To make forwarding decisions, the router examines the network address portion (and the subnet portion within internetworks) to determine the logical network on which the destination host resides. It looks up this address in its routing table (similar to the bridge or switch's MAC address table) and locates the router port to which it needs to forward the packet. If the packet is addressed to a network not connected to the router, the router forwards the packet to another router that is closer to the destination network, as shown in the Routers and Packet Switching Diagram. Each router, in turn, evaluates each packet and either delivers the packet or forwards it to the next router.

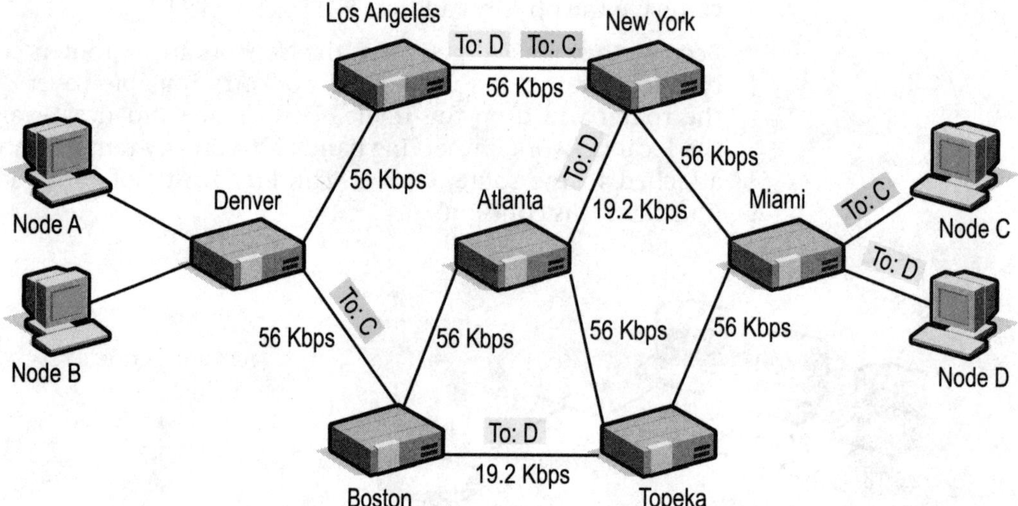

Routers and Packet Switching

Activities

1. Which three of the following networking devices break up collisions? (Choose three.)
   a. Hub
   b. Bridge
   c. Switch
   d. Router
2. IPX uses which address size?
   a. 32-bit
   b. 48-bit
   c. 64-bit
   d. 80-bit
3. Which three of the following OSI model layers do routers support? (Choose three.)
   a. 1
   b. 2
   c. 3
   d. 4
4. Hubs connect network hosts in which configuration?
   a. Bus
   b. Ring
   c. Mesh
   d. Star
5. Which two devices transmit the binary representations of the network data? (Choose two.)
   a. Hub
   b. Bridge
   c. Repeater
   d. Router

6. Which device provides the connection point between a workstation or PC and the network?
   a. NIC
   b. Hub
   c. Repeater
   d. Modem
7. At what segment length would we require a repeater to extend an existing 10Base2 Ethernet segment?
   a. 100 m
   b. 185 m
   c. 200 m
   d. 250 m

Extended Activities

1. Given the Example Network Diagram, label each network device as the type best suited for the application. The network segments run the network topologies indicated. Explain why you placed a certain device in a particular position.

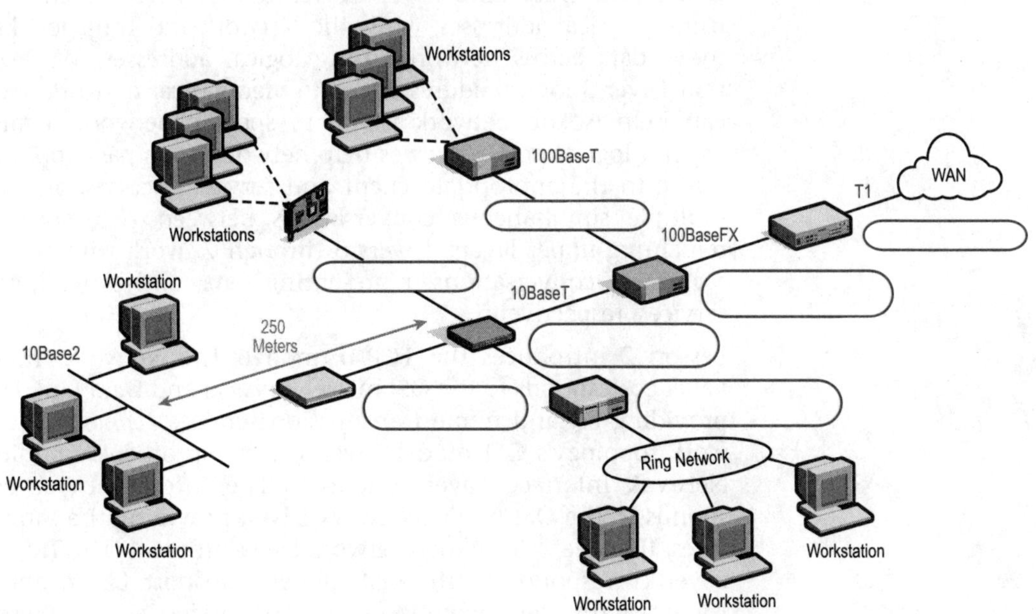

Example Network

a. Hub
b. Repeater
c. Switch
d. NIC
e. Router
f. Bridge

Summary

This Unit reviewed terminology covered in previous courses, and added some new information, as well. In Lesson 1, we revisited the OSI model. We reviewed each layer's function, unit of information, and address type. We learned that networks use physical and logical addresses to move information between networks and nodes. The Data Link Layer moves frames between end nodes using physical addresses, while the Network and Transport Layers move data across networks using logical addresses. We learned that Layer 3 logical addresses create hierarchical networks, which can help isolate network traffic to specific network segments. Layer 4 logical port addresses help network hosts pass application traffic to the appropriate client and server processes, and allow multiple simultaneous conversations between two hosts. The remaining upper layers, Layers 5 through 7, work with the data, regulating conversations, representing data, and providing user services, respectively.

Lesson 2 introduces the TCP/IP model. The Network Interface Layer corresponds to the OSI model Physical and Data Link layers, providing bit and frame transmission services. The specific network topology's OSI model Layer 1 and 2 protocols handle the Network Interface Layer functions. The Internet Layer corresponds to the OSI model Network Layer, providing the same services; IP is the TCP/IP Internetwork Layer protocol. The Transport Layer corresponds to the OSI model Transport Layer, and the Application Layer encompasses the OSI model Session, Presentation, and Application Layers. At the Transport Layer, TCP and UDP provide connection-oriented and connectionless services, respectively. TCP/IP provides numerous applications, such as those used for sharing e-mail (POP3, SMTP), name resolution (DNS), sharing data and information (FTP, HTTP), and remote access (Telnet).

Lesson 3 introduces IP addresses, 32-bit logical addresses used to designate unique hosts on an IP network. IP addresses feature two parts: a network portion and a host portion. In order to communicate, IP hosts on the same network segment must share the same network portion. Five IP address classes are defined: Class A, B, C, D, and E. Class A addresses use the first octet address range of 1–126 (0 and 127 are reserved). Class B addresses range from 128–191, and Class C addresses range from 192–223. Class D addresses are special purpose, multicast addresses, and Class E addresses are reserved for future use. We represent IP addresses in dotted decimal format.

Lesson 4 reviewed internetworking devices. End nodes use NICs to connect to the physical network; NICs are both OSI model Layer 1 and 2 devices. NICs come in different forms, as expansion boards, PC cards, and USB devices, and in order to operate, require device drivers loaded on the host. Repeaters are OSI model Layer 1 devices, merely repeating what they receive out all attached ports. Hubs also are Layer 1 devices, operating as multi-port repeaters. Bridges and switches operate at Layer 2, and filter traffic based on MAC addresses. Bridges can connect dissimilar topologies, and both bridges and switches isolate collisions, though switches provide multiple interfaces used to create multiple collision domains. Each switch interface provides the network topology's full bandwidth to each attached device.

In Lesson 4 we also learned that routers are OSI model Layer 3 devices used to contain broadcasts and route Layer 3 protocols. Routers determine the best path to the destination network by looking up an IP packet's destination network address in their routing tables. Routers do not forward broadcast traffic, and so create separate broadcast domains on each port.

Unit 1 Quiz

1. Which of the following is the primary purpose of the OSI model Transport Layer?
   a. It defines well-known logical port addresses for communications between applications.
   b. It establishes, manages, and terminates sessions between applications.
   c. It establishes user application procedures for error recovery and data integrity.
   d. It controls dialogs between two or more Presentation Layer entities.
2. The OSI model Network Layer serves which primary purpose?
   a. It establishes, manages, and terminates sessions between applications.
   b. It uses Layer 3 addresses to create multiple routed networks.
   c. It uses logical addresses to identify higher layer applications.
   d. It builds frames that carry higher layer PDU across network segments.
3. Telnet is an example of which TCP/IP layer protocol?
   a. Network Interface
   b. Internetwork
   c. Transport
   d. Application
4. Which TCP/IP Internetwork Layer protocol provides troubleshooting utilities, such as ping and traceroute?
   a. ICMP
   b. IGMP
   c. ARP
   d. IARP

5. The TCP/IP model Application Layer maps to which three OSI model layers? (Choose three.)
   a. Application
   b. Session
   c. Presentation
   d. Transport
6. Which is the valid Class A IP address range?
   a. 1.hhh.hhh.hhh–191.hhh.hhh.hhh
   b. 0.hhh.hhh.hhh –91.hhh.hhh.hhh
   c. 128.hhh.hhh.hhh–191.hhh.hhh.hhh
   d. 1.hhh.hhh.hhh–127.hhh.hhh.hhh
7. Which network device allows us to connect dissimilar network topologies?
   a. Hub
   b. NIC
   c. Bridge
   d. Switch
8. Which is the valid Class C IP address range?
   a. 192.000.001.hhh–223.255.254.hhh
   b. 192.hhh.hhh.hhh–239.255.255.255
   c. 224.000.000.000–239.255.255.255
   d. 128.001.hhh.hhh–191.254.hhh.hhh
9. A Class C network address provides for how many network and host bits?
   a. 16 network, 16 hosts
   b. 8 network, 24 hosts
   c. 24 network, 8 hosts
   d. 30 network, 2 hosts

10. A Class D address is also known as which type of address?
    a. Unicast
    b. Broadcast
    c. Private
    d. Multicast
11. Which is a valid Class B network address?
    a. 15.129.89.76
    b. 151.129.89.76
    c. 193.129.89.76
    d. 223.129.89.76
12. Which network device allows communication between separate IP networks?
    a. Hub
    b. Bridge
    c. Layer 2 switch
    d. Router
13. Which three devices forward broadcast traffic? (Choose three.)
    a. Switch
    b. Bridge
    c. Repeater
    d. Router
14. Which is the valid Class B IP address range?
    a. 1.hhh.hhh.hhh–191.254.hhh.hhh
    b. 128.001.hhh.hhh–191.254.hhh.hhh
    c. 128.hhh.hhh.hhh–223.254.hhh.hhh
    d. 192.254.hhh.hhh–223.255.254.hhh
15. Which Layer 2 device creates multiple network segments, each offering the full network bandwidth?
    a. Router
    b. Switch
    c. Hub
    d. Repeater

16. TCP includes which three types of information in its PDU message headers? (Choose three.)
    a. Source port
    b. Destination port
    c. Checksum
    d. Sequence number
17. Which network device requires a device driver in order to connect hosts to the network segment?
    a. Bridge
    b. NIC
    c. Hub
    d. Switch
18. A Class C address provides for a maximum of how many hosts?
    a. 16
    b. 256
    c. 65,536
    d. 16,777,216
19. The Network Layer must do what to a received frame first in order to determine the route over which it will forward the datagram to the next network?
    a. Encapsulate the packet
    b. Change the IP address
    c. Change the MAC address
    d. Decapsulate the packet
20. A hub that repeats and regenerates signals is called which type of hub?
    a. Passive
    b. Bridging
    c. Active
    d. Layer 2

Unit 2
Overview of TCP/IP Applications

The acronym for Transmission Control Protocol/Internet Protocol (TCP/IP) represents the names of two protocols developed for the original Advanced Research Projects Agency Network (ARPANET). However, TCP/IP is often used to denote much more than just the protocols themselves. The TCP/IP "world" includes three major components:

- Networks, when taken collectively, are referred to as the Internet.
- Entire suites of protocols, software, and applications that are standard parts of many operating systems (OSs), such as File Transfer Protocol (FTP) and Telnet.
- Actual networking protocols such as TCP and IP.

This course uses the term "TCP/IP" to include all three of these components. This unit introduces the protocols and applications built upon these components, which logically form the Open Systems Interconnection (OSI) model Application Layer.

Lessons

1. Summary of TCP/IP Applications
2. Web Browsers and Servers
3. Telnet
4. FTP
5. E-Mail
6. Network Management
7. Other Applications

Terms

Advanced Research Projects Agency Network (ARPANET)—ARPANET is a long-haul network funded by the ARPA (later DARPA) and built by Bolt, Beranek, and Newman, Inc. From 1969 through 1990, ARPANET served as the basis for early networking research, as well as a central backbone during development of the Internet.

American Standard Code for Information Interchange (ASCII)—ASCII is one of the most widely used codes for representing text in computers. ASCII codes represent letters, numerals, punctuation, and keyboard characters as numbers. For example, when the character "A" is pressed on the keyboard, the ASCII binary representation of that character is 100 0001 (hexadecimal 41). The basic ASCII character set uses 7 bits to represent the 128 text and keyboard elements.

attribute—When related to HTML, an attribute is used to distinguish elements of the same type by their details. An example of an HTML attribute is the SIZE attribute, which specifies an element's height. Another HTML attribute is HREF, which specifies a referenced file's URL.

Base64—Base64 is a standard algorithm for encoding and decoding non-ASCII data for attachment to an e-mail message; it is the foundation for MIME. Base64 uses a 65-character subset of ASCII to represent non-ASCII data in e-mail attachments.

cc:Mail—cc:Mail is a Lotus Development Corporation proprietary mail system. cc:Mail does not provide Internet mail access, and thus must use an e-mail gateway to send and receive SMTP mail.

country code top level domain (ccTLD)—Each country in the world is assigned an Internet country code, a two-character code designating the country in which a domain resides. This country code is appended to the end of the FQDN.

daemon—A daemon is a UNIX process that runs in the background and performs an operation at a specified time or in response to a certain event. A Microsoft Windows equivalent to a daemon is a service or system agent.

digital signature—A digital signature is a digital code that can be embedded into a document to prove its authenticity. Digital signatures are an application of public-key encryption technology; the sender of a document uses a private encryption key to encrypt a text string or the digest of the message. Document recipients use the sender's public-encryption key to decrypt the signature and authenticate the sender.

disk operating system (DOS)—DOS is the low-level software that resides on many PCs and controls the operation of a computer and its peripheral devices. MS-DOS is the operating system that preceded Microsoft Windows and still exists as an extension of the Windows OS.

fully qualified domain name (FQDN)—The FQDN is the complete Internet system name. The FQDN includes the hostname and the domain name. An example of a FQDN is ken.westnetinc.com.

graphical user interface (GUI)—A GUI provides easy access to computer programs and often hides details of a program from the user.

graphics interchange format (GIF)—GIF is one of two graphic image formats used in HTML (JPEG is the other type). GIF files, the more popular format for small or simple images, are limited to 256 colors, have a lower resolution than JPEG files, offer lossless compression, and can be made transparent for a popular type of borderless effect.

Hypertext Markup Language (HTML)—HTML is the authoring language used to create documents for use on the Web.

Internet Message Access Protocol (IMAP)—IMAP is a protocol used for retrieving e-mail messages from a mail server. IMAP4 is a version of IMAP similar to POP3, but it supports additional features such as allowing keyword searches in e-mail messages while the messages remain on the mail server.

Joint Photographic Experts Group (JPEG)—JPEG is an open standard that defines a method of compressing still images. See JPEG File Interchange Format.

JPEG File Interchange Format (JFIF)—JFIF is a public domain graphic compression format that conforms to the JPEG standard for image compression. It is one of two popular graphic image formats used in HTML pages (GIF is the other). JPEG/JFIF files offer higher resolution, with up to 16.7 million colors, and are generally used in continuous-tone images such as photographs. However, JPEG/JFIF compression is lossy (some image information is lost), even at the highest quality setting.

management information base (MIB)—A MIB is an SNMP database that lists information objects relevant to each managed object. A managed element's MIB includes its own information objects. The management application's MIB is a compilation of all the individual managed element's MIBs.

Motion Picture Experts Group (MPEG)—MPEG is a standard for compressing video to fewer bits for storage and transmission.

Multipurpose Internet Mail Extension (MIME)—MIME is an extension of SMTP that supports the exchange of a wide variety of document files by means of an e-mail system.

Network Basic Input/Output System (NetBIOS)—IBM and Sytek developed NetBIOS to link a NOS to specific hardware, augmenting DOS to provide LAN functions to the operating system. NetBIOS uses SMBs as the message format for sharing Windows files, directories, and devices.

public-key encryption—Public-key encryption is a cryptographic system that uses two mathematically related keys; one key is used to encrypt a message and the other is used to decrypt it. People who need to receive encrypted messages distribute their public keys but keep their private keys secret.

Remote Monitoring (RMON)—The Remote Monitoring protocol gathers network information at a central workstation. RMON defines additional SNMP MIBs that provide more detailed information about network usage and status.

Reverse Address Resolution Protocol (RARP)—RARP is the protocol a diskless computer uses at startup to find its IP address. The computer broadcasts a request that contains its physical hardware address, and a server responds by sending the computer its IP address. RARP takes its name and message format from the IP ARP.

RMON probe—An RMON probe is a firmware or hardware device installed in a network component, or attached to a network segment, designed to monitor the network and its devices. The probe sends information it has gathered to the network monitoring station.

RMON2—RMON2 improves upon RMON by providing traffic data at the Network Layer in addition to the Physical Layer. This allows administrators to analyze traffic by protocol.

Secure/MIME (S/MIME)—S/MIME is a MIME version that supports message encryption using public-key encryption technology. This ensures that e-mail is sent and received in a manner that is secure from interception or tampering.

Sendmail—Sendmail is a UNIX application that handles electronic mail. Sendmail supports backend message routing and handling for SMTP-based e-mail systems.

shell—A shell is another term for a user interface. OSs sometimes provide an alternative shell to make program interaction easier. For example, the shell may provide a menu-driven system that translates user menu choices to OS commands.

store-and-forward—In a messaging system, a store-and-forward application accepts messages on their way to their final destination and stores them until the destination host requests them. When the destination host requests the messages, the store-and-forward system forwards them on to the requesting host. POP3 is a store-and-forward application protocol.

tag—A tag is an HTML command inserted in a document that specifies how a Web browser should format the document or a portion of the document.

terminal emulation—A terminal emulation program allows a local computer to connect to a remote computer and appear to be logged on to the remote computer locally. Terminal emulation programs are often used to access mainframe computers.

top level domain (TLD)—TLDs are the groupings of lower level domain types. A TCP/IP network can be segmented into a hierarchy of domains or groupings; the Internet is an example of this segmentation type. For example, the .com TLD groups commercial domains, while the .edu TLD groups educational institutions.

Usenet—Usenet is a global news distribution service that relies on the Internet for much of its news traffic. News servers agree to share and distribute newsfeeds, which are collections of related news articles. Users post news messages in newsfeeds using a news reader client.

Uuencode—Uuencode is a set of algorithms for converting e-mail attachments into a series of 7-bit ASCII characters for transmission over the Internet. Uuencode originally stood for UNIX-to-UNIX encode, but is now considered a universal protocol used to transfer file attachments between different operating system platforms. Nearly all e-mail applications support uuencoding.

Waveform Audio File (WAV)—WAV is one of several formats for storing sound in files developed jointly by Microsoft and IBM. Support for WAV files is built-in to Windows 95 making it the de facto standard for sound on PCs. WAV sound files end with a .WAV extension and can be played by nearly all Windows applications that support sound.

Windows Internet Naming Service (WINS)—WINS is a Microsoft client/server application that resolves network computer host names to IP addresses. WINS works in conjunction with DHCP, where the WINS server maintains a dynamic database of hostname-to-address mappings. Because DHCP clients may not maintain the same address over time, WINS works well for this application. Standard DNS supports only hosts with statically assigned IP addresses.

Windows service—A Windows service is the equivalent of a UNIX daemon. Windows services provide specific functions, such as enabling file sharing or automatic virus protection, and can start automatically on system startup, manually as directed by the user, or when scheduled to run at a particular time of the day.

WINS node type—A WINS node type designates the type of NetBIOS name resolution the client uses; WINS supports several different node types. For example, a client might broadcast for name resolution (B-node) or first broadcast, then directly request name resolution (M-node).

Lesson 1—Summary of TCP/IP Applications

This lesson introduces you to the most common TCP/IP applications used today. It also provides a brief overview of the two primary methods used to run TCP/IP applications.

Objectives

At the end of this lesson you will be able to:

- Describe the two methods used to access TCP/IP applications
- Name common TCP/IP applications and how they are used

Key Point

TCP/IP architecture includes many Application Layer protocols.

Accessing TCP/IP Applications

There are two methods for accessing TCP/IP applications. The first and oldest method is by means of a command line. Using a command line means typing in text-based commands. For example, if we want to run an FTP application, we can type **ftp** at a UNIX or disk operating system (DOS) command line, as the Command Line FTP Screen Diagram shows.

```
C:\WINNT\System32\cmd.exe - ftp

C:\>ftp
ftp> open ftp.microsoft.com
Connected to ftp.microsoft.com.
220 CPMSFTFTPA04 Microsoft FTP Service (Version 5.0).
User (ftp.microsoft.com:(none)):
```

Command Line FTP Screen

The second method is by means of a graphical user interface (GUI), most commonly a World Wide Web (Web) browser. Instead of having to type commands such as **get file**, we simply use a mouse to point and click on the file we want to download. The Browser FTP Screen Diagram shows this method.

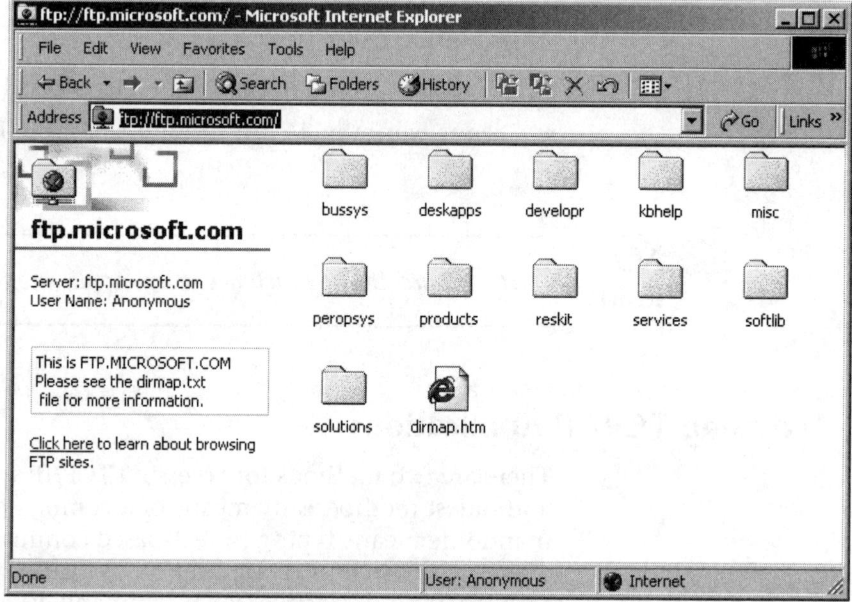

Browser FTP Screen

Common TCP/IP Applications

TCP/IP software is packaged with many applications. The predominant applications that ship with TCP/IP software are discussed in more detail in the following sections.

Browsers (HTTP)

A Web browser is a TCP/IP client application that allows a user to retrieve hypertext documents from a remote host computer called a Hypertext Transfer Protocol (HTTP) server. Request for Comments (RFCs) 1945 and 2616 define HTTP as the Application Layer protocol browsers use to request and transmit documents between themselves and an HTTP server. Web browsers are the front end to access HTTP servers by means of the Internet. HTTP servers are commonly referred to as Web servers.

Telnet

Telnet is a terminal emulation program that provides remote login capability on a TCP/IP network. The look and operation is similar to working from an OS's command prompt. For example, the user types **telnet delta** on the command line and receives a login prompt from the computer called "delta." After logging in, the user can type commands to manipulate the remote device and services.

Telnet is an old application, but has widespread use. Telnet implementations usually work between different OSs. For example, we can initiate a Telnet session between a Microsoft Windows client and a UNIX server. RFC 854 defines Telnet.

FTP

FTP, which is as old as Telnet, also uses TCP and has widespread use. The operation and appearance is as if we used Telnet to connect to a remote computer. Instead of typing the usual commands, we have to make do with a short list of commands for directory listings and the like. FTP commands allow us to copy files between computers.

Quite often, browser-initiated Internet downloads call on FTP processes to handle the actual file transfer. The Web browser and server hide the FTP process details from us, issuing Connect, File Transfer, and Disconnect commands on our behalf. RFC 959 defines FTP.

TFTP

Diskless workstations use Trivial File Transfer Protocol (TFTP) to initialize; TFTP works with Bootstrap Protocol (BOOTP), discussed later. Where FTP uses TCP, TFTP uses User Datagram Protocol (UDP). Because TFTP is simple and small, it can be imbedded in a device's read-only memory (ROM). Network devices, such as routers and switches, use TFTP for software and firmware upgrades and can download configuration information from a central TFTP server. RFC 1350 defines TFTP.

NNTP

Network News Transfer Protocol (NNTP) allows Internet sites to exchange USENET news articles, which are organized into topic areas such as programming in C++ or Quake user groups. To access a newsgroup, one opens a news browser client, which connects to a news server. One must be authorized to access the news server to read and post information. RFC 977 defines NNTP.

E-Mail

Simple Mail Transfer Protocol (SMTP) is the Internet standard protocol for transferring e-mail messages from one computer to another. Unlike other communication protocols that use binary codes in structured fields, SMTP uses plain English headers. SMTP defines a protocol and set of protocol processes to transfer e-mail messages between mail systems; it does not define the programs used to store and retrieve mail messages. In fact, although a basic mail "reader" program is included with TCP/IP on virtually every OS, many different mail readers have been developed. RFC 821 defines SMTP.

Post Office Protocol (POP3) often works with SMTP, to provide servers a means to store e-mail and provide clients a means to download their messages from the POP3 server. POP3 stores the incoming e-mail until the server authorizes a client mail application and downloads the messages. RFC 1939 defines POP3.

Network Management

Simple Network Management Protocol (SNMP) is a standardized network management scheme designed for TCP/IP network management. A central network management station (NMS) uses SNMP to collect data from other network computers. SNMP defines the collected data's format; it is up to the central station or network manager to interpret it. SNMP features low network resource requirements, portability, and widespread acceptance. RFC 1157 defines SNMP.

Remote Monitoring (RMON) supplements SNMP. Whereas SNMP gathers network information from a single management information base (MIB) and presents to the monitoring station a view of a collection of separate entities, RMON defines additional MIBs that allow monitoring stations to view the network as a whole. RMON uses RMON probes, sometimes called RMON agents, which are either firmware built into a network device or a special hardware device, designed to monitor a network segment and its devices. An RMON probe tracks and analyzes network traffic and gathers statistics, reporting this information to the monitoring station. RFC 1757 defines RMON, while RFC 2021 defines the more advanced, Layer 3 RMON2.

DNS

Domain Name Server (DNS) is a mechanism, primarily used on the Internet, which TCP/IP devices use to translate host computer names into IP addresses. DNS provides a centralized name resolution database running on a DNS server. Client applications, such as Telnet or browsers, contact DNS servers when using fully qualified domain names (FQDNs) to resolve these names to IP addresses.

Remember that TCP/IP uses numerical logical addresses to find hosts across a routed network; thus, in order to find a server on the Internet, the application needs to know the server's IP address. DNS looks up the FQDN, for example **http://www.microsoft.com**, in its database and returns to the client the corresponding IP address (207.46.230.229). RFCs 1034 and 1035 define DNS.

BOOTP

BOOTP is a method by which diskless TCP/IP hosts can automatically discover their IP address, a BOOTP server's address, and download a file from which they can boot. A single BOOTP message specifies many items a workstation might need at startup, including its gateway to the Internet (a router port address) and a DNS server's address. RFC 951 specifies BOOTP.

DHCP

Dynamic Host Configuration Protocol (DHCP) is a protocol TCP/IP clients use to locate and download IP addressing and configuration information. It is based on BOOTP, but improves upon it dramatically. While a BOOTP administrator must manually identify requesting hosts and their corresponding information, DHCP blindly passes information to any host that requests it. DHCP servers can pass vendor-specific device configuration information using option codes, and provide a mechanism for automatic address renewal, based on a lease period. Many Internet service providers (ISPs) (and local area networks [LANs], as well) use this leasing mechanism to oversubscribe their address ranges, signing more clients than they have addresses to support.

Like BOOTP, DHCP reduces network administration workload because clients need not be configured manually. Indeed, Microsoft clients, such as Windows 98 and Windows 2000, configure themselves "out of the box" to use DHCP when the TCP/IP protocol stack is installed. Other OSs that run TCP/IP, such as Linux and Mac OS, support DHCP as well. RFC 2131 specifies DHCP.

Different Applications Use Different Protocols

The TCP/IP Network Diagram illustrates that different types of applications attached to a TCP/IP network use different Application Layer protocols. For example, when sending mail from a mail client to a mail server, SMTP is used to transfer information across the TCP/IP network to and from the client and server.

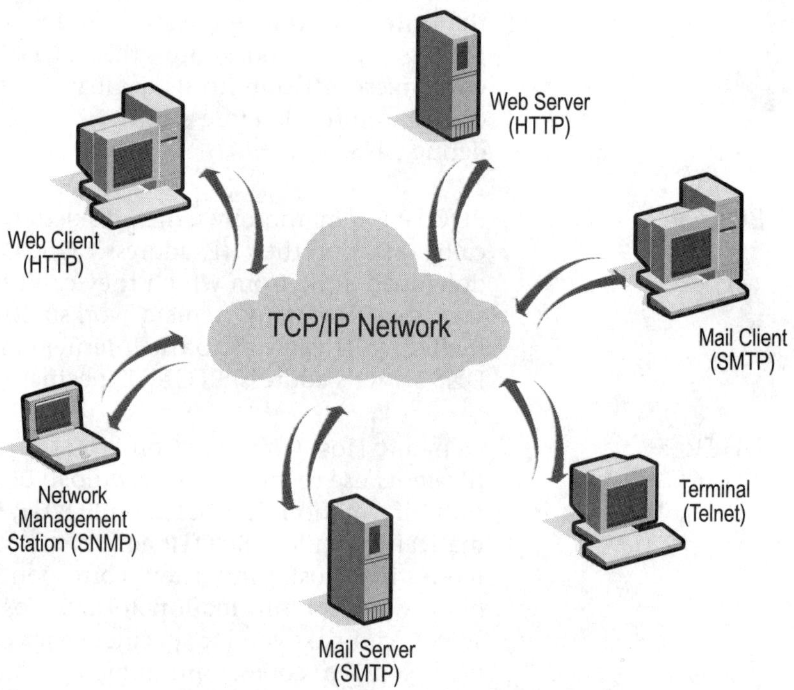

TCP/IP Network

In the TCP/IP Network Diagram, we can see that there are many different types of servers that can be attached to a TCP/IP network. Primary requirements for attachment to a TCP/IP network are a unique address and use of the TCP/IP protocols. If a client wanted to access files from a file server, for example, the client would need to know the address of the file server and have permission to access files from that file server. The client would also need to run the correct protocols to communicate across the TCP/IP network.

If a client wants to access files from a file server attached to a TCP/IP network, the client must have a program, such as FTP, as well as permission to access an FTP server. This is shown in the Client File Access Diagram.

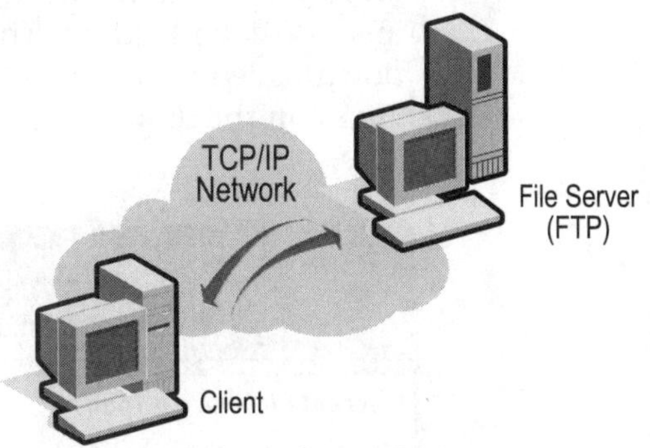

Client File Access

As mentioned in the beginning of this lesson, there are two ways the client can access this server. One is by using a program such as FTP directly, usually through a command line interface. The user types in **ftp** and the FTP program starts. The user then types FTP commands to access the appropriate files. An example screen shot showing the DOS FTP program is shown on the DOS FTP Screen Diagram.

DOS FTP Screen

The user would have to understand how to use FTP and the commands necessary to access directories, download files, and close the session when using the command line interface.

Another method used to send and retrieve files using a TCP/IP network is by means of a browser. A browser hides details of FTP and the application from the user. The user still has to know the appropriate file server address and have server file access rights, but the user does not have to know individual commands. The FTP Using a Browser Diagram shows a Web browser with a list of files available for downloading. The diagram shows three files that can be downloaded from the FTP site at westnetinc.com. The user simply clicks on the desired file, and the download process begins.

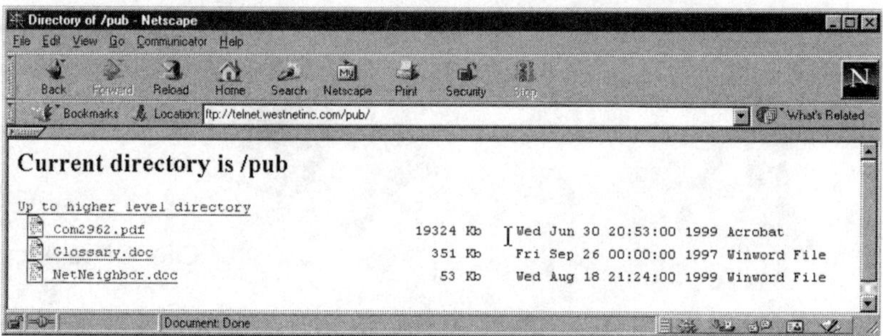

FTP Using a Browser

Activities

1. Which TCP/IP application allows a network user to remotely log on and manipulate a network device?
   a. Browser
   b. Telnet
   c. FTP
   d. Rlogin
2. Which TCP/IP application allows us to transfer files either within a browser or at the command line?
   a. FTP
   b. Telnet
   c. Xwindows
   d. TFTP
3. Internet e-mail uses which two protocols? (Choose two.)
   a. SNMP
   b. SMTP
   c. LDAP
   d. POP3
4. How does DNS resolve FQDNs to IP addresses?
   a. By looking up the names in a centralized MIB database
   b. By looking up names in a centralized name database
   c. By referring inquiries to SNMP servers
   d. By looking up names in a local hosts file
5. Which two choices are examples of TFTP use? (Choose two.)
   a. Download news articles
   b. Download router upgrades
   c. Initialize diskless workstations
   d. Remote terminal emulation

Extended Activity

Fill in the missing layers of the following protocol stacks.

Web Services	Network Management	File Services	Virtual Terminal
TCP	UDP	TCP	TCP
IP	IP	IP	IP
LAN/WAN Protocols	LAN/WAN Protocols	LAN/WAN Protocols	LAN/WAN Protocols
Physical Layer Protocols	Physical Layer Protocols	Physical Layer Protocols	Physical Layer Protocols

Lesson 2—Web Browsers and Servers

A Web browser is a TCP/IP client application that allows a user to retrieve hypertext documents from a remote host computer called an HTTP server. HTTP is the Application Layer protocol used to request and transmit documents by means of the Internet, or Web.

Objectives

At the end of this lesson you will be able to:

- Explain the relationship between HTTP, Web browsers, and Web servers
- Describe the basics of Web browsers and Web servers

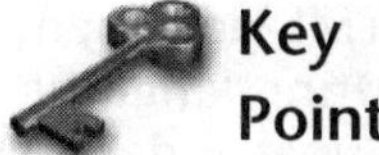

Key Point

HTTP is the Application Layer protocol of Web browsers and servers.

Browsers and Servers Overview

Web browsers are the front-end software used to access HTTP servers over an intranet, extranet, or the Internet. HTTP servers are commonly referred to as Web servers. A typical Web server can handle thousands of client requests in a short time period. In a typical session, the following actions take place:

1. The Web browser sends a connection request to the HTTP server.
2. The HTTP server accepts the request and notifies the browser of the successful connection.
3. The browser then transmits the document request to the server.
4. The server retrieves the document and transmits its contents to the browser.
5. The browser receives the incoming document data and displays it for the user.
6. After the server has transmitted the entire document, the server breaks the connection with the browser.

One reason HTTP servers can handle thousands, and perhaps millions, of requests per hour is because Web connections are stateless. That is, after the browser downloads the requested document, picture, or media file, it and the server disconnect that session. A browser opens multiple simultaneous sessions, one for every file it downloads. Every time a client browser wants to retrieve a document, a separate request is sent to the server. Because the browser/server connection drops after the browser retrieves the file, if a user spends several hours reading a particular Web page, the server has no knowledge of it. The browser maintains the file(s) open in local memory until the user moves on to another page, or closes the browser.

The Web browser's job is to display documents retrieved from HTTP servers; these documents are HyperText Markup Language (HTML) documents. HTML is text-based formatting language used to generically format text using a variety of tags and attributes. The Web browser reads the HTML document and displays it as indicated by the HTML formatting language. Because the browser provides the intelligence to format and display HTML documents, these documents are generally fairly small. The Home Page Screen Diagram shows a typical Web browser's display of a Web page.

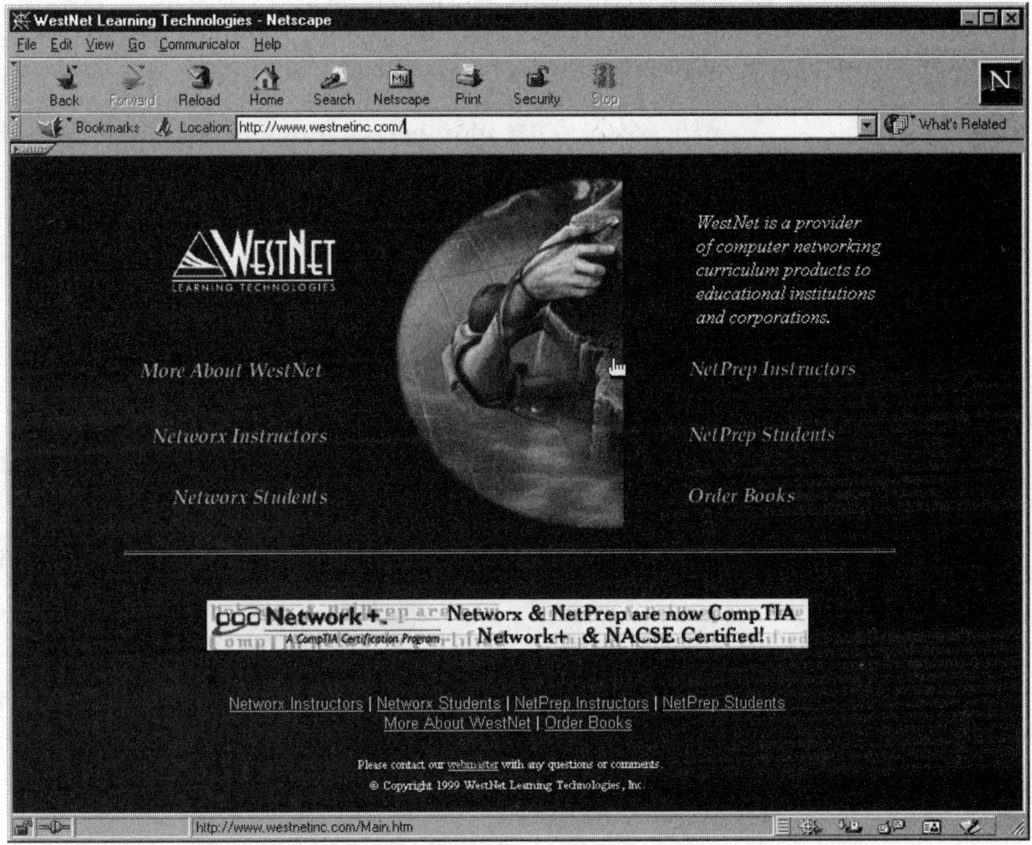

Home Page Screen

A Web site is a collection of documents and applications that create documents or pages. The site is organized around the Web server process, which runs either as a daemon process on UNIX, or as a Windows NT/2000 service. The Web server service listens for connection requests on TCP Port 80, and provides security, database connectivity, and Web site management tools.

Web Browsers

The mid-1990s marked the dawn of a new era for the Internet, the World Wide Web. What once was the domain of command line tools and UNIX servers became the world of the Web browser. The Web Browser and Server Diagram illustrates the two key components used in retrieving information from the Web. Due in large part to the GUI of modern-day computers, the Internet has become a key information sharing technology.

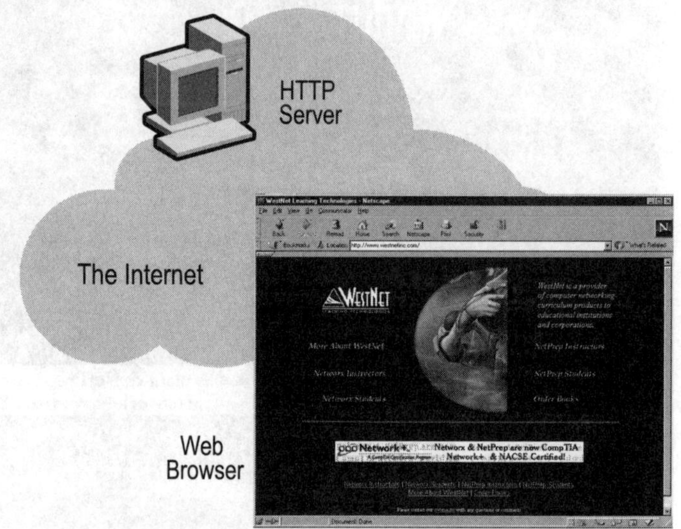

Web Browser and Server

Each time we run our browser, it can load a document we designate as our home page. A home page is the starting place for exploring the Internet. Home pages generally have links to various topics of interest to the user.

Browser Basics

We must understand at least the basics of using a Web browser; thus, we can obtain the most benefit out of the Internet. Fortunately, learning to use a browser is relatively easy. The Web Browser Toolbar Diagram details a toolbar from one version of Microsoft's Internet Explorer. The diagram highlights various navigation tools available on the toolbar.

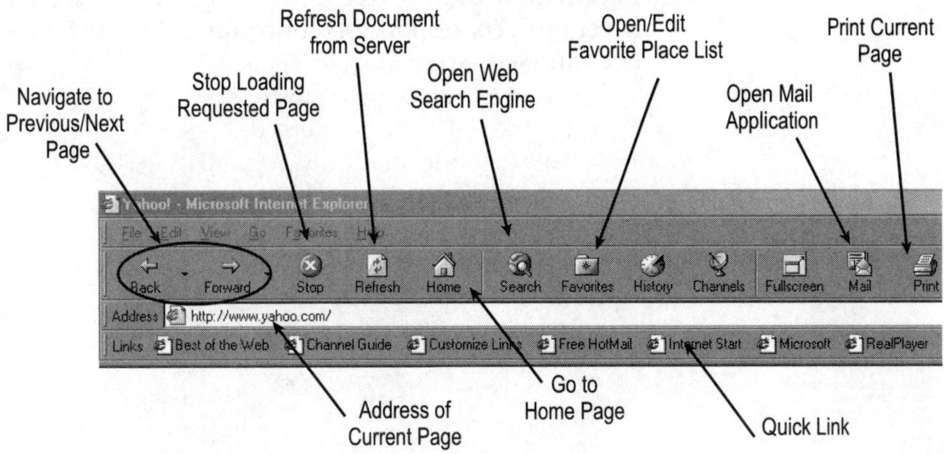

Web Browser Toolbar

The toolbar contains most of the tools we use to navigate the Web. The Toolbar Descriptions Table briefly explains each tool.

Toolbar Descriptions

Toolbar Button	Purpose
Back	Retraces back through pages already viewed in this session
Forward	Traces forward through pages already viewed (after Back is used)
Stop	Interrupts loading of current page
Refresh	Reloads current page from the source Web server
Home	Returns to home page
Search	Opens the search engine configured in the browser
Favorites	Displays editable list of links for quickly returning to pages
Print	Prints current page
Font	Increases or decreases font size of the current page
Mail	Opens e-mail application

In summary, a Web browser is a client application that accesses information from a Web server. HTTP is the TCP/IP Application Layer protocol responsible for communication between a Web client and Web server.

Activities

1. The HTTP server process can run as which two of the following? (Choose two.)
   a. Terminate and stay resident program
   b. Device driver
   c. Daemon
   d. Windows service
2. On which well-known TCP port does the HTTP server service listen for connection requests?
   a. 23
   b. 25
   c. 69
   d. 80
3. What happens when the browser application finishes downloading the files necessary to display a Web page?
   a. The browser maintains the connection while it displays the page's contents.
   b. The server maintains the connection so the browser can quickly reload the page elements.
   c. The browser and server drop all but the last connection, so the browser can quickly reload the page if needed.
   d. The browser and server drop the connections, and the browser maintains the page and its elements in memory.

Extended Activities

For each subject below, go the Web site listed to research additional information on each topic. Write a brief description of your findings.

1. HTTP—**http://www.w3.org/Protocols/Specs.html**

   ____

   ____

   ____

2. HTTP servers—**http://www.yahoo.com/Computers_and_Internet/Software/Internet/World_Wide_Web/Servers/**

3. Netcraft Web Server Survey—**http://www.netcraft.co.uk/Survey/**

4. Macintosh—**http://www.starnine.com/**

5. UNIX—**http://hoohoo.ncsa.uiuc.edu/**

6. Windows—**http://www.iplanet.com/downloads/download/0104.htmll**

7. Microsoft Internet Information Server—**http://www.microsoft.com/iis/**

8. Lotus Domino Server—**http://domino.lotus.com/**

   ____

   ____

   ____

9. Using a browser, create a favorite links file that includes the following folders:

   a. Networking vendors

   b. TCP/IP applications

   c. TCP/IP protocols

   Using the Web, find at least five links per subject, and add these to the folders.

Lesson 3—Telnet

Telnet is another Internet protocol that uses TCP/IP. The Telnet application facilitates remote login, that is, users log on to a remote computer system from a local computer. Telnet is one of the first services to take advantage of Internet connectivity. Many years ago, before the widespread distribution of microcomputers, terminals were used to communicate with large mainframes and minicomputers. Telnet is simply a way to offer this same kind of interaction over a TCP/IP network. In today's world of fancy and flashy graphical interfaces, Telnet may seem archaic.

Objectives

At the end of this lesson you will be able to:

- Describe common Telnet uses
- Demonstrate use of Telnet with a browser
- Demonstrate use of Telnet with a command line

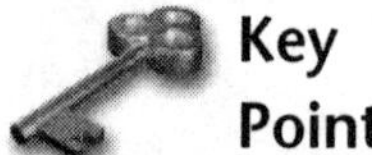

Key Point

Telnet is commonly used to run a program on a remote computer.

Common Telnet Uses

Telnet is a way to remotely connect to another system, with privileges to run specific programs on that system. Common Telnet uses include:

- Connecting to a system to use specific programs, such as e-mail and statistics programs
- Connecting to a networking device for information or configuration purposes

- Connecting to an online database of information
- Connecting to an online forum to interact and communicate with other users

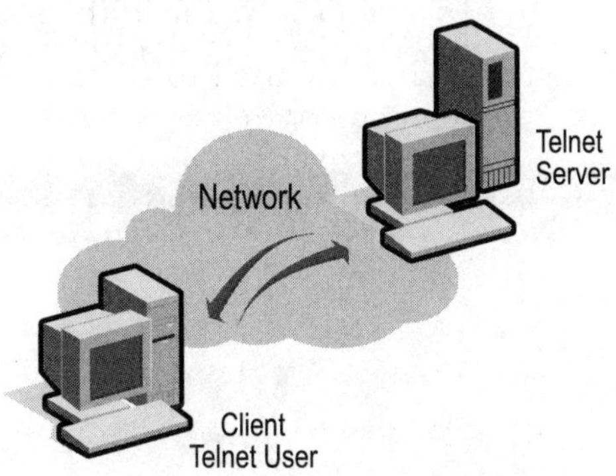

Telnet Session

How to Use Telnet by Means of a Command Line

To use Telnet on your Windows client, type **telnet** at the command prompt, and press ENTER. After the Telnet client opens, you can connect to the Telnet host with which you wish to communicate. You can also connect to a port or service other than the standard Telnet port. This particular Telnet feature is useful when a Telnet client is used to access something other than a Telnet process. After your host connects to the remote system, the Telnet window title bar shows the remote system's name. Depending on the OS, there are several ways to run Telnet. A sample session follows.

Using Telnet with Windows

The following steps illustrate how to use Windows Telnet client to initiate a remote login to an Internet host.

1. Start Telnet. This step will be different for different OSs. Telnet can normally be started from the PC DOS prompt or from within a browser. The Telnet From Command Prompt Screen Diagram shows the initial screen that appears when **telnet** is typed into the Run dialog box using Windows 95 or 98.

Telnet From Command Prompt Screen

2. Under the Connect menu, select Remote System. A dialog box like the one shown in the Telnet Connect Screen Diagram will appear.

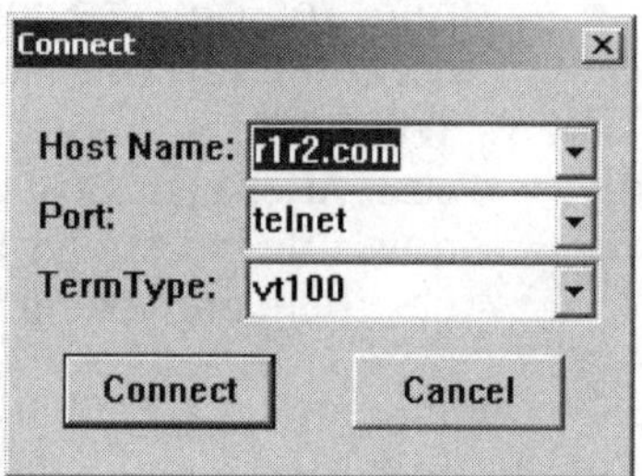

Telnet Connect Screen

3. In the box marked Host Name, enter the Telnet address for your desired location (you can use r1r2.com).

4. Click Connect, or press ENTER, to initiate the connection. The Telnet Connectivity Screen Diagram is displayed.

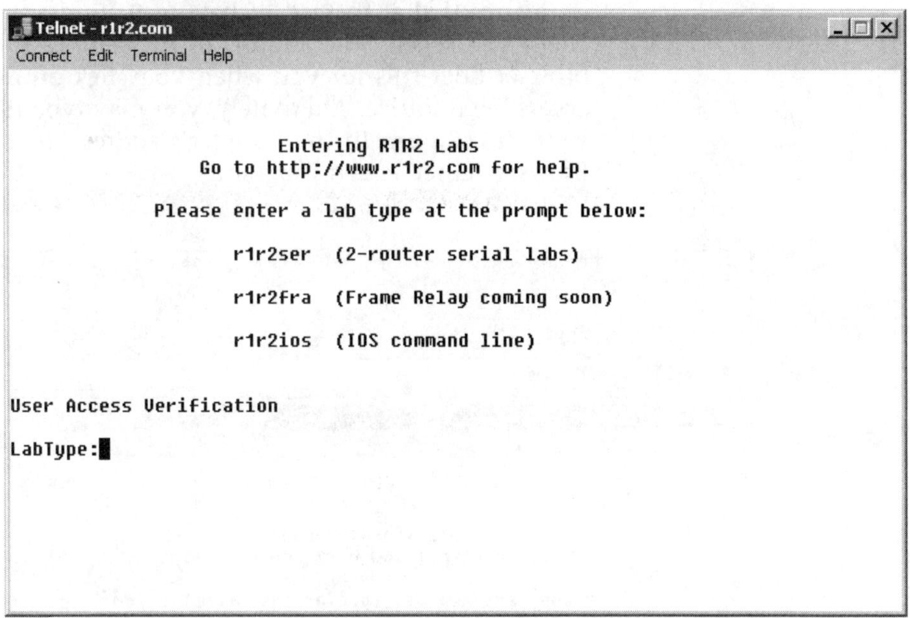
Telnet - r1r2.com
Connect Edit Terminal Help
Entering R1R2 Labs
Go to http://www.r1r2.com for help.
Please enter a lab type at the prompt below:
r1r2ser (2-router serial labs)
r1r2fra (Frame Relay coming soon)
r1r2ios (IOS command line)
User Access Verification
LabType:

Telnet Connectivity Screen

Note: After you log on to the remote site, pay attention to the instructions that appear on the screen to help you navigate on that particular system. Menu options are usually easy to understand; however, commands vary from system to system. You can usually get help by typing **help** or **?** as you navigate.

Basic Telnet commands include:

- Open—Establishes a connection to the specified host.
- Close—Closes an open connection and leaves you in the Telnet software.
- Quit—Closes any open Telnet sessions and exits the Telnet software.

5. To end your session, type **exit** or **logout** at the command line. You may also go to the Connect menu and choose Disconnect.

Using Telnet by Means of a Web Browser

Using Telnet to access a remote computer by means of a Web browser is basically the same as using Telnet directly. The primary difference is that instead of having to find and open the Telnet client and specify the address of the remote computer, the Web browser does this for you when you click on a link to a Telnet-accessible resource. Alternately, you may type the command **telnet://r1r2.com** in the browser's address line, as shown in the Browser Telnet Screen Diagram.

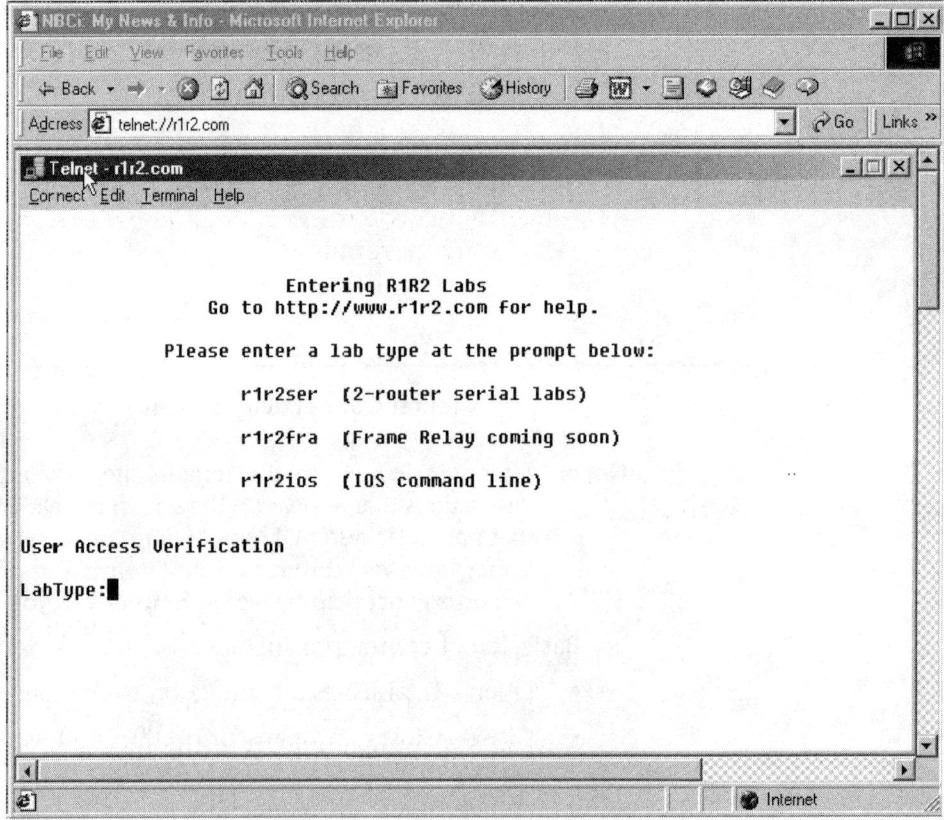

Browser Telnet Screen

Activities

1. Which three of the following are common Telnet application uses? (Choose three.)
   a. Connect to an online database
   b. Run a program on the local computer
   c. Connect remotely to run a specific application
   d. Connect to a router for network information
2. Which basic Telnet command opens a session to a specified host?
   a. Open
   b. Close
   c. Hello
   d. Quit
3. Which Telnet command closes a Telnet session but leaves the Telnet software running?
   a. Quit
   b. Close
   c. Exit
   d. Logout

Extended Activities

This activity has you Telnet into a publicly available site that provides free access to Cisco routers. You will examine the router configuration and list the commands you might issue from the router privileged EXEC mode.

1. On your PC, start a Telnet session:
   a. Open a Command prompt window
   b. Type **telnet**
2. At the Telnet> prompt, type **open r1r2.com**
3. At the LabType: prompt, type **r1r2ser**
4. At the Username: prompt, type **cisco**
5. At the Password: prompt, type **ccna**. A welcome screen appears.
6. Press the Enter key on your keyboard. A Router prompt, similar to Router>, appears.

7. If the prompt reads Router>, type **en**. The prompt changes to Router#. The "#" indicates that you are in the router privileged EXEC mode.

Note: The router may prompt for another password. If it does, disconnect and try later. These are publicly used routers, and others can set passwords at their discretion. The site managers reset the router configurations from time to time, thus you will be able to access the routers at a later time.

8. At the Router# prompt, type **show running**. This displays the router's current configuration.
9. Press the space bar to scroll the screen pages.
10. At the Router# prompt, type **?**. This lists all the commands that you can issue from the Router# prompt. Scroll the pages with the space bar.
11. At the Router# prompt, type **exit**. This logs you out of the router.
12. Close your Telnet session.

Lesson 4—FTP

FTP is designed to allow computers to communicate with each other across the Internet and arrange for file transfers from one computer's storage area to another's.

Objectives

At the end of this lesson you will be able to:

- Explain basic FTP use
- Demonstrate the difference between using command line FTP and browser-based FTP

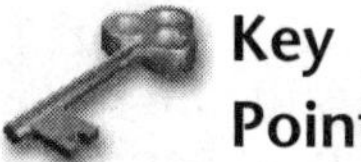

Key Point

FTP is used to move files between two computers.

Why Use FTP?

FTP is used to transfer files between hosts on a TCP/IP network. Although other avenues exist for passing files, FTP is the best choice when we must work with large files. For example, many of us are used to sending and receiving files as e-mail attachments. This works fine for smaller files; however, who has not waited for several minutes for their e-mail to download over a dial-up connection because a well-meaning friend or colleague sent a 1 or 2 megabyte (MB) file attachment? Additionally, many ISPs conserve mail server resources by limiting e-mail attachment sizes to 2 MB or less.

FTP is ideal for downloading large file attachments. FTP offloads the burden these large files place on the e-mail server and the network and allows us to better control file downloads. If the e-mail server experiences file-transfer problems, you may not receive it at all. Additionally, the mail server may hold the file in queue for delivery until an administrator deletes it. With FTP, if you experience an error, you simply initiate the transfer again.

Purpose of Browser and Server Software

Not all computers on the Internet allow for or are capable of FTP. First, to allow connections, the computer must run an FTP server. This server service or daemon manages connections from clients requesting file retrieval or transmission. In effect, an FTP server is like a window into the remote computer's hard drive. The user who sets up an FTP server controls what areas of the hard drive are visible, what files can be read or written, and who can access them. If no one configured an FTP server on a computer, an FTP client cannot read that computer's file.

FTP servers are set up for private use, and usernames and passwords control access. This means that an administrator must give a user explicit access to the FTP server, and that user must have been assigned a unique username and password so they may access the server's facilities.

An FTP server logs all traffic. You can consult the server logs to determine the amounts of traffic the server handles, what is accessed, and who is accessing it.

Where Can We Use FTP?

In addition to using FTP for an organization's internal use, there are many public-access documents and software archives, including shareware and public domain archives, that use FTP services. Users access these archives by what is known as anonymous FTP, where the FTP server requires a username, but the username is "anonymous." The associated password is normally an e-mail address.

To protect sensitive resources on the FTP server, administrators first verify that no sensitive information is accessible by anonymous FTP. One reason for using anonymous FTP is security; FTP passes credentials as plain text data. Hackers can intercept these unencrypted usernames and passwords and use them to steal or destroy sensitive data. If an administrator allows anonymous FTP, then users will pass no sensitive credentials across the network.

Is Anonymous FTP Really Anonymous?

When using anonymous FTP, most FTP servers will require that the user supply his or her e-mail address as a password. This means the archive maintainers will have a record of the user's e-mail address, cross-referenced with the files the user transferred. However, most archive maintainers stipulate that the e-mail address will be used only for their own purposes, such as demographic studies and pursuing any abuse of the archive services. A user is unlikely to receive unsolicited e-mail in connection with using an anonymous FTP archive.

Note: Few FTP servers verify that the e-mail address you supply is valid, thus you do not have to use your own. Indeed, you can make one up, if you wish.

How Can We Use FTP?

There are a large number of programs available that can be used for FTP, with varying user interfaces. The most basic is a program called "ftp." This program offers a command line interface, similar in some ways to a DOS or UNIX shell, which can be used to explore a remote computer's directory tree transfer files. The program has one main advantage; it is standard and has been written for most computer platforms.

There are also numerous programs available that provide a user a more graphical, point-and-click interface to FTP. Space does not permit a discussion of the various programs available for different platforms, but you may visit a number of Web sites that provide downloadable software archives for examples. It is worth noting that most Web browsers can also be used to obtain files by means of FTP; we will demonstrate this in a later lesson.

Using Command Line FTP

The following is a demonstration of a command line FTP session and illustrates how some of the basic commands work:

1. Issue FTP command.
2. At the command prompt, type **ftp** followed by an FTP site, for example:

   ftp telnet.westnetinc.com

You may also type **ftp** at the command line. You must then use the OPEN command to open the appropriate FTP site. This is illustrated in the Command Line FTP Screen Diagram.

```
C:\WINNT\System32\cmd.exe - ftp

C:\>ftp
ftp> open telnet.westnetinc.com
Connected to telnet.westnetinc.com.
220 telnet Microsoft FTP Service (Version 5.0).
User (telnet.westnetinc.com:(none)): _
```

Command Line FTP Screen

Recognize that the FTP site address could have easily been **ftp.westnetinc.com**, but in this case we use the same computer as both a Telnet and an ftp server.

The computer responds with the following message:

User <telnet.westnetinc.com:<none>>:

3. At the prompt, type **anonymous**.

   The server responds with:

   331 Anonymous access allowed, send identity (e-mail name) as password

4. At the prompt, type in your complete e-mail address.

   If the server accepts your login information, it responds with:

   ftp>

5. At the prompt, type the **dir** or **ls** command to see what files are located in this directory. A screen similar to the one in the FTP DIR Command Screen Diagram will appear.

```
Command Prompt - ftp telnet.westnetinc.com
Microsoft Windows 2000 [Version 5.00.2195]
(C) Copyright 1985-2000 Microsoft Corp.

C:\>ftp telnet.westnetinc.com
Connected to telnet.westnetinc.com.
220 telnet Microsoft FTP Service (Version 5.0).
User (telnet.westnetinc.com:(none)): anonymous
331 Anonymous access allowed, send identity (e-mail name) as password.
Password:
230-Welcome to the WestNet Learning Technologies FTP site. All documents herein
are copyright WestNet Learning Technologies. All rights reserved.
230 Anonymous user logged in.
ftp> dir
200 PORT command successful.
150 Opening ASCII mode data connection for /bin/ls.
drwxrwxrwx   1 owner    group                  0 Aug 13 12:30 ~tmp
-rwxrwxrwx   1 owner    group                  0 Aug 12 11:53 file_id.diz
-rwxrwxrwx   1 owner    group                  0 Jun 23  8:37 mT200kbOham
drwxrwxrwx   1 owner    group                  0 Aug 17  9:20 pub
226 Transfer complete.
ftp: 273 bytes received in 0.01Seconds 27.30Kbytes/sec.
ftp>
```

FTP DIR Command Screen

After issuing the DIR command, the first part of the file listing has a series of letters and dashes. If the first series is a "-" it means the item is a file. If it is a "d" it indicates a directory. The FTP DIR Command Screen shows all directories.

You can change directories with the CD command. Use CD PUB to change to the pub directory. You can then type **dir**, and the screen illustrated in the Listing of Pub Directory Screen Diagram will appear.

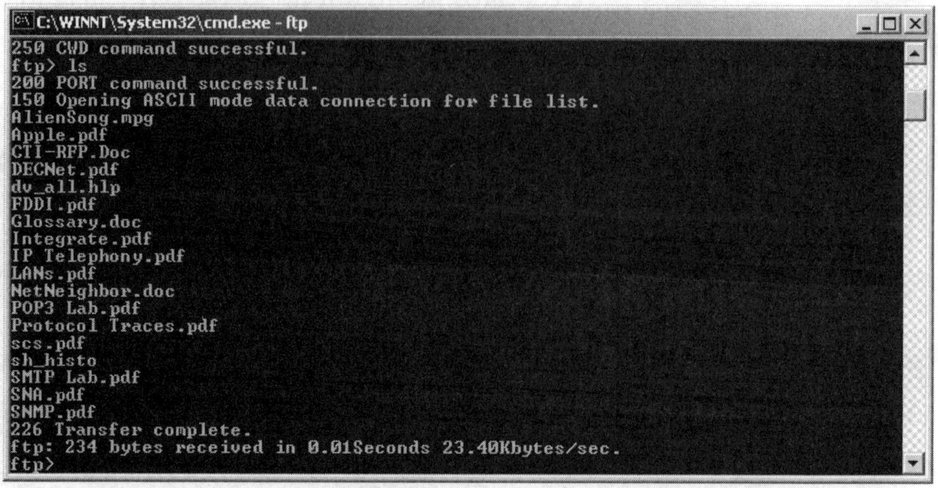

```
C:\WINNT\System32\cmd.exe - ftp
250 CWD command successful.
ftp> ls
200 PORT command successful.
150 Opening ASCII mode data connection for file list.
AlienSong.mpg
Apple.pdf
CTI-RFP.Doc
DECNet.pdf
dv_all.hlp
FDDI.pdf
Glossary.doc
Integrate.pdf
IP Telephony.pdf
LANs.pdf
NetNeighbor.doc
POP3 Lab.pdf
Protocol Traces.pdf
scs.pdf
sh_histo
SMTP Lab.pdf
SNA.pdf
SNMP.pdf
226 Transfer complete.
ftp: 234 bytes received in 0.01Seconds 23.40Kbytes/sec.
ftp>
```

Listing of Pub Directory Screen

The directory listing shows the files available for manipulation in the designated directory. For example, if we choose to download the file GLOSSARY.DOC, we can type the command get Glossary.doc at the ftp> prompt and retrieve the designated file.

Using FTP with a Browser

You can also connect to an FTP site using a Web browser:

1. Open a browser.
2. Type the FTP site address in the space where Uniform Resource Locators (URLs) are entered. For example, to access the westnetinc.com FTP site, you must type the following in your browser:

   ftp://telnet.westnetinc.com/pub

This will allow you to download files using FTP from the telnet.westnetinc.com/pub address. Recognize that we have gone directly to the pub directory in this example, as illustrated on the FTP Using a Browser Screen Diagram.

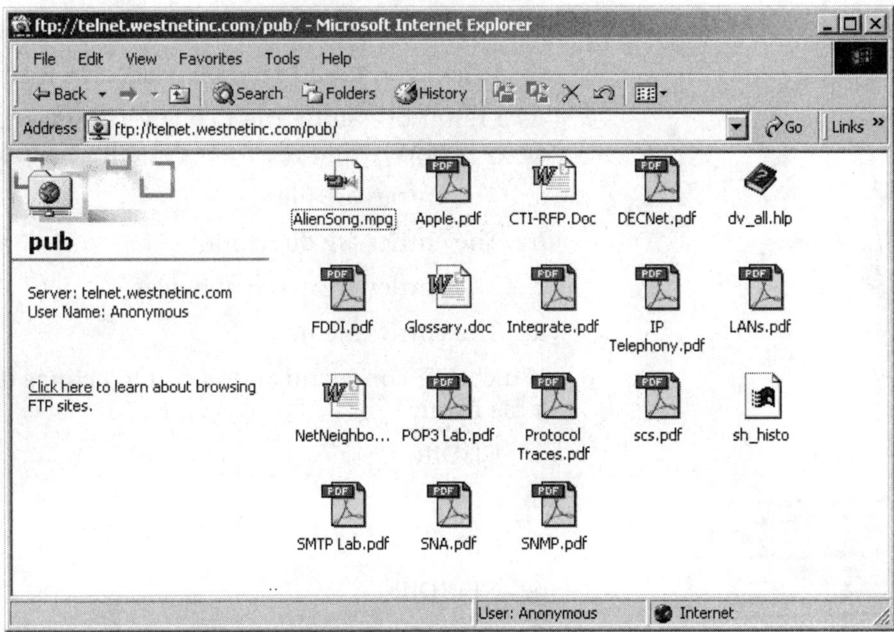

FTP Using a Browser Screen

3. You can then download information by clicking the file of choice.

FTP is used in both examples; only the user interface is different.

Activities

1. Which is the best reason to use the FTP application?
   a. When you need to configure a router or switch
   b. When you need to access a Web site
   c. When you need to pass large files over a slow connection
   d. When you need to remotely access a mainframe computer
2. As a result of issuing the FTP DIR command, each file listing entry begins with a "-"; what does the "-" indicate?
   a. The entries are files
   b. The entries are directories
   c. The entries are executable files
   d. The entries are invalid
3. Which FTP command allows you to change directories within a file listing?
   a. CHDIR
   b. CDIR
   c. CD
   d. NEWDIR
4. An FTP server administrator can control server access in which three ways? (Choose three.)
   a. Allow only remote access
   b. Make only portions of the drive visible
   c. Control read and write privileges
   d. Limit file access

Extended Activities

1. Go to the Website **http://www.downloads.com**, and download the latest version of the Ipswitch, Inc. FTP application WS_FTP LE. Scan the download for viruses and install the application.
2. FTP to the telnet.westnetinc.com site using both command line FTP and the WS_FTP application. Change to the Pub directory, and locate and download the file GLOSSARY.DOC. Which is easier to use, the command line utility or the WS_FTP application?

Lesson 5—E-Mail

E-mail is the most popular and widely used Internet application. E-mail is a fast and efficient way to communicate with anyone connected to the Internet. We can use e-mail to communicate with one or thousands of persons at a time. We can receive and send files and other information with our e-mail messages (see Lesson 4). We can even subscribe to electronic journals and newsletters. Literally, billions of e-mail messages are sent every day across the Internet.

Objectives

At the end of this lesson you will be able to:

- Explain basic e-mail operations
- Describe the parts of an e-mail address
- Identify the key protocols used to send and receive e-mail

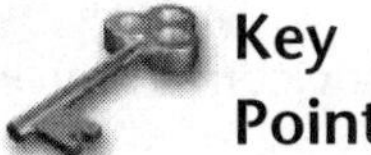

Key Point

E-mail is the most widely used Internet application.

How Does E-Mail Work?

E-mail is an asynchronous communication form, that is, the person whom you want to read your message does not have to be available at the precise moment you send it. This is a great convenience for both you and the recipient. In contrast, the telephone, which is a synchronous communication medium, requires that to communicate both you and your listener must be on the line at the same time (unless you leave a voice message).

It will be impossible to discuss all the details of the many e-mail packages available to Internet users. Fortunately, most of these programs share basic functionality that allow you to:

- Send and receive e-mail messages
- Save e-mail messages in a file
- Print e-mail messages
- Reply to e-mail messages
- Attach a file to an e-mail message

There are many e-mail packages, both server and client, available for use in a TCP/IP network. Some examples include the Microsoft Outlook Express and Netscape Messenger clients, and UNIX's sendmail client/server e-mail system.

Reading an IP Address

To use Internet e-mail successfully, we must understand how names and addresses for both computers and people are formatted on the Internet. Mastering this technique is just as important as knowing how to use telephone numbers or postal addresses correctly. Fortunately, IP addresses are usually no more complex than phone numbers and postal addresses. And, like using telephone numbers or street addresses to identify a person, organization, or geographic location, IP addresses have rules and conventions for their use.

An example of an IP address is kdr@westnetinc.com. IP addresses have three parts, as follows:

- Username (kdr in the example)
- "@" (at sign)
- The user's mail server address (westnetinc.com in the example)

The mail server's address, for example, westnetinc.com, is called the domain name and is related to the server's IP address. Every Internet connected server has a numeric IP address.

Because it is easier for humans to remember names rather than numbers, each server can also have a corresponding domain name. This name associates the server's numeric IP address with a name that is easier to remember. Both the IP address and domain name should work the same, that is, their use establishes a connection to the correct Internet server.

It is sometimes useful to read an Internet address or domain name from right to left, because this helps us determine information about the addresses source. An address like 1234@westnetinc.com does not tell us much about the person sending us a message. Nonetheless, the suffix ".com" at the address's end allows us to conclude that the sender has some affiliation with a commercial institution. Domain name suffixes, called top level domains (TLDs), usually adhere to the following naming conventions:

- .edu—Educational sites in the United States
- .com—Commercial sites in the United States

- .gov—Government sites in the United States
- .net—Network administrative organizations
- .mil—Military sites in the United States
- .org—Organizations in the United States not covered by the categories above (for example, nonprofit organizations)

Additionally, TLD name suffixes exist for each country, called country code top level domains (ccTLDs). Though space does not allow us to list them all, here are some examples:

- .au—Australia
- .ca—Canada
- .cn—China
- .de—Germany
- .it—Italy
- .jp—Japan
- .ke—Kenya
- .pr—Puerto Rico
- .uk—United Kingdom
- .us—United States

Although there are variations, when describing an Internet address, the @ symbol is typically pronounced "at," and the "." (period) is pronounced "dot."

E-Mail Protocols

TCP/IP networks combine several protocols for implementing an e-mail network, including:

- SMTP
- UNIX-to-UNIX encoding (Uuencode)
- Multipurpose Internet Mail Extensions (MIME)
- POP
- Internet Message Access Protocol (IMAP) 4

SMTP

SMTP is an Application Layer protocol used to transfer mail across a TCP/IP network. When e-mail is being sent across a TCP/IP network such as the Internet, it is encapsulated in a SMTP header before traversing the network.

One of SMTP's limitations is that it limits e-mail messages to 1,000 or less 7-bit ASCII characters. Before sending a message, users are forced to convert any nontextual data (file attachments) into 7-bit bytes represented as printable ASCII characters. One of the first of these encoding methods is Uuencode; another is MIME.

Uuencode

Uuencode takes a binary file such as a word document and converts it to ASCII for transmission; Uuencode originated on UNIX systems. Though the encoded file is visible in any text editor, it makes no sense until decoded. Some mail systems do not support MIME, thus file attachments must be encoded with Uuencode.

MIME

MIME is used in conjunction with SMTP for supporting more than just standard ASCII text files. Using MIME, many different types of data can be sent through e-mail. Examples of MIME-supported data types are:

- Binary information—Word processed documents or spreadsheets
- Graphic images—Graphic Interchange Format (GIF) or Joint Photographic Experts Group (JPEG) files
- Video—Moving Pictures Expert Group (MPEG) files
- Audio—Waveform Audio File (WAV) files

MIME is actually an SMTP extension. It enables encoding and transporting within a single message multiple objects that represent body text and character sets, and allows extensions to the original MIME standard. Exceptions include ASCII, images, and audio fragments. RFC 1341 initially described MIME; this has been superseded by RFCs 1521 and 2045.

MIME creates an "envelope" around the attachment consisting of several header fields, indicating the MIME version, the message's content, the type of encoding used, and other extended fields. The MIME-Encoded Message Diagram illustrates these header fields.

```
From: User <yyyyy@usa.net>
To: xxxxx@pcisys.net
Subject: Mime test
X-Mailer: USANET web-mailer (34FM.0700.4.03)
Mime-Version: 1.0
Content-Type: multipart/mixed;
        boundary="----NetAddressPart-00--=_guWG6352S78799040cb"
X-UIDL: c20989a861a45681c8e9c5c112a5fda7
Status: RO

This is a multi-part message in MIME format.

------NetAddressPart-00--=_guWG6352S78799040cb
Content-Type: text/plain; charset=US-ASCII
Content-Transfer-Encoding: quoted-printable

User, MCP, MCP+I, MCSE, MCT, NCNI
Instructor/Consultant
yyyyy@usa.net

------NetAddressPart-00--=_guWG6352S78799040cb
Content-Type: application/java; name="Marquee.class"
Content-Transfer-Encoding: base64
Content-Disposition: inline; filename="Marquee.class"

yv66vgADAC0BSQgA1ggBSAgBDggAtwgAyAgAyggBNAgBLQgBKggBMwgBPQgA/QgA4wgBBQgB
CgAvAJAKAC4AeAoAMQCBCQAoAHMKAC0AoAoAIwB0CQAoAJoKACMAfgkAKACjCQAoAKYKACgA
AAIAAQAAAAoqtwBwKgS1AEuxAAAAAQCyAAAADgADAAAAEwAEABgACQATAAEA4AAAAAIBPw==

------NetAddressPart-00--=_guWG6352S78799040cb--

.
```

MIME-Encoded Message

- The Mime-Version line indicates that this is a MIME version 1.0 message. The verbatim text entry "Mime-Version: 1.0" indicates this message is an RFC 2045-formatted message.
- The Content-Type entry may take several forms. In this message, the first Content-Type entry indicates that this message is a multipart message of mixed media types, as indicated by the entry "Content-Type: multipart/mixed;..."

The first part of the message is encoded as plain text, as indicated by the entry "Content-Type: text/plain: charset=US-ASCII." The entry "Content-Type: application/java; name="Marquee.class"" indicates that the second message part is a Java application attachment named Marquee.class.

- The "Content-Transfer-Encoding:" entry specifies how the body text was initially encoded, indicating to the receiver how it should be decoded. Printable characters of the ASCII character set represent the text portion of this message, therefore the term "Quoted-Printable."

  The message's second part uses the Base64 Content-Transfer-Encoding type. Base64 uses a 65-character subset of ASCII to represent non-ASCII data in e-mail message attachments. Each printed character represents 6 bits of the original binary attachment, and the encoding algorithm creates an overhead of approximately 33 percent beyond the original file size.

S/MIME

Secure/MIME (S/MIME) is a specification for secure electronic messaging. In 1995, software vendors created S/MIME to solve a very real problem: interception and forgery of e-mail. Protecting sensitive data is a real concern, especially in a world becoming increasingly more connected. The S/MIME specification was designed to be easily integrated into e-mail and messaging products.

MIME represents e-mail attachment data with a simple Base64 coding technique. Though the attachment is encoded, any device capable of decoding Base64 can intercept and decode the message. To resolve the inherent security risks MIME presents, RSA Data Security developed S/MIME. S/MIME uses digital signatures and public-key encryption to ensure hackers do not tamper with messages in transit. S/MIME encrypts the message and encloses it in a digital envelope, which may only be opened by someone holding the sender's public key.

POP

POP is used to transfer information from a mail server to a user's computer so users can read, delete, or otherwise manage their e-mail; POP3 is the latest version. A POP mail server stores e-mail until the client requests it. The user uses a desktop e-mail program, such as Lotus Notes, Eudora, or Outlook, to access the mail server and download messages. The POP3 server is responsible for authorizing access in the form of a username and password.

IMAP4

IMAP is another protocol for e-mail message retrieval. The latest version, IMAP4, is similar to POP, but it supports some additional features. POP requires that we first download our messages before we can work with them. With IMAP4, we can search for keywords in our e-mail messages while the messages remain on the mail server. As a result, we can download only those messages we choose. Like POP, IMAP uses SMTP for communication between the e-mail client and server. Refer to **http://www.imap.org/** for more information. RFC 1730 specifies IMAP4.

Mail Server Configuration

The E-Mail Communication Diagram illustrates a typical e-mail configuration. The components in this diagram are local mail clients, remote mail clients, and a mail server.

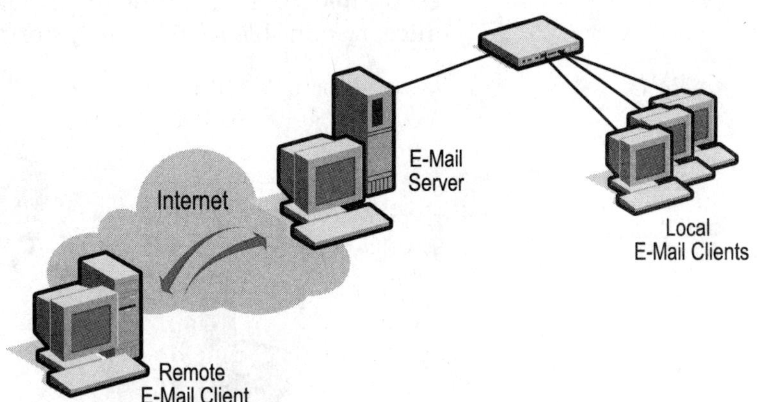

E-Mail Communication

The mail server is the computer that stores and forwards e-mail for all clients that use this particular mail server. Each client must be configured to access the mail server; the clients must know either the server's FQDN or IP address, and present to the server the correct authorization information. Most mail servers today support POP, thus each network client can retrieve information as needed. It is also important that the mail server use MIME for transferring binary information.

Mail gateway software is also used on the mail server to send e-mail messages between different types of e-mail programs. Some e-mail programs use SMTP, while others use proprietary e-mail protocols such as cc:mail. Mail gateways are only needed in systems that do not use SMTP.

Store-and-Forward Mail Systems

SMTP provides delivery of mail from source to destination, that is, end-to-end delivery or direct delivery. Other protocols are referred to as "store-and-forward," meaning the information is sent to a mail server and then to the final destination. The problem with direct delivery of mail is that when the receiving device is turned off, mail cannot be delivered, and the delivery fails. The Direct vs. Store-and-Forward E-Mail Diagram demonstrates the difference between the two types of systems. SMTP is like a mail carrier, responsible for transporting mail. POP and IMAP4 are like the post office, responsible for receiving, storing, and forwarding mail.

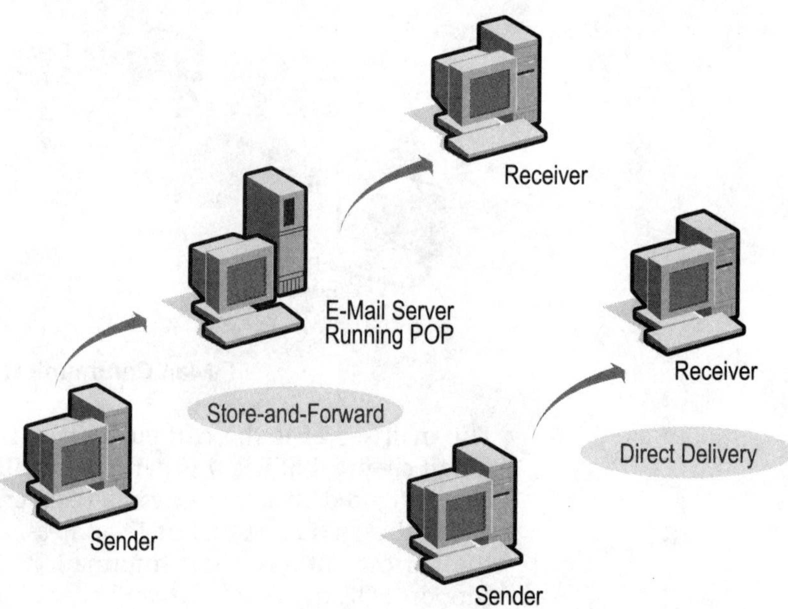

Direct vs. Store-and-Forward E-Mail

Most systems send e-mail to a server first. The information is stored on the server until the host requests the information. The most common method for doing this is to send mail to a server that uses a protocol to move information to the final destination. POP or IMAP4 are used for this purpose.

Activities

1. Which two of the following are examples of e-mail clients? (Choose two.)
   a. Microsoft Outlook
   b. Microsoft Word
   c. UNIX sendmail
   d. UNIX samba
2. Which is a valid e-mail address?
   a. westnetinc.com@kdr
   b. kdr.westnetinc.com
   c. com westnetinc@.kdr
   d. kdr@westnetinc.com
3. Which two choices are TCP/IP e-mail protocols? (Choose two.)
   a. SMTP
   b. SNMP
   c. LDAP
   d. IMAP
4. Which two protocols deliver e-mail directly to the e-mail client? (Choose two.)
   a. POP3
   b. IMAP4
   c. SMTP
   d. MIME
5. How does S/MIME protect e-mail from forgery and interception?
   a. It only sends messages to the designated recipient.
   b. It encrypts the messages using Base64 encoding.
   c. It hides the sender address from all but the designated recipient.
   d. It uses digital signatures and public-key encryption techniques.

6. Your network Help desk calls and asks you to help troubleshoot an e-mail problem. Several users have complained that when they send e-mail messages with attachments, the recipients reply that the attachments are unreadable. The message body is legible, however. You know that your users encode all attachments using MIME. Which is the best solution to this problem?
   a. Install new e-mail clients for the complaining users, and set the encoding method to MIME.
   b. Tell the users to fax the attachments instead.
   c. Have the users only send text attachments.
   d. Contact the recipients, and have them use MIME to decode attachments.
7. You are a networking consultant for a major telecommunications firm. They ask you to help them resolve a hacked e-mail problem. It seems that someone is intercepting e-mails between district offices and inserting pornographic pictures in place of legitimate e-mail attachments. How might you resolve this problem for them?
   a. Have the users send attachments as Base64 encoded text.
   b. Implement S/MIME encoding on all outbound e-mail attachments.
   c. Implement Uuencoding on all outbound external e-mail attachments.
   d. Switch users from a POP e-mail client to an IMAP client.

Extended Activities

This activity has you Telnet into your POP mail server and list the messages waiting for retrieval. You should close your e-mail client before performing this activity. Some e-mail services, such as MSN or AOL, may not allow this.

1. In your e-mail client, look up your ISP's POP e-mail server's FQDN. It will take the form mail.<isp>.net or pop.<isp>.net. Note the FQDN.
2. Open a Telnet session.

3. At the Telnet> prompt, type the FQDN you noted in Step 1. Enter the port number 110.

Note: In the Windows Telnet utility, enter the port number in the Port: line. At the Command prompt, type the FQDN followed by the port number, as in **mail.yahoo.com 110**.

4. After the "+OK POP3..." line, type **user** followed by your username.
5. After the "+OK Password required for <user> line," type **pass** followed by your password.
6. After the "+OK <user> has x messages line," type **list**. This lists the messages waiting for retrieval from the server.
7. Close the Telnet session.

Lesson 6—Network Management

The 1970s were the decade of the centralized network. In a period dominated by mainframe processing, data communications consisted primarily of a system of terminals connected to a mainframe. Typically low-speed, asynchronous transmission was used for the communications link. These mainframe/terminal systems had very little direct interaction with other computer systems or the outside world. Furthermore, support and management of the systems were typically supplied by the mainframe manufacturer (IBM) and communications company (AT&T).

The 1980s brought changes in computer technology that altered the face of traditional data communications. First, microprocessors burst onto the scene. They offered significant price and performance advantages over mainframes, and ignited the fuse of the personal computer (PC) explosion. Second, as the number of microcomputers increased, so did the user's desire to share applications and data. This desire led to a dramatic increase in the number of LANs. The increase in LANs caused high-speed, wide-area transmission facilities, such as T-carrier circuits, to emerge and provide connectivity between microcomputer-based LANs.

When the 1990s rolled around, network managers were left with a big problem. Not only was there a connectivity problem between the many products, but there was a bigger problem of how to manage this internetwork of technologies. This led to the development of network management products. These products were developed around network protocols to help network managers deal with the complexity of everyday computing. SNMP is a popular management protocol defined by the Internet community for TCP/IP networks. RMON builds upon SNMP to define more advanced management and monitoring functionality.

Objectives

At the end of this lesson you will be able to:

- Describe basic SNMP concepts
- Explain how SNMP is used to manage network components
- Describe how RMON improves upon simple SNMP network management

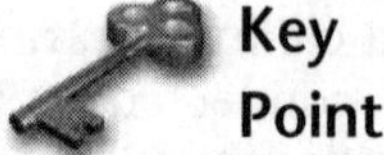
Key Point

SNMP is the de facto standard in network management.

Network Management Concepts

Introducing some basic network management concepts is worthwhile so we have a better idea of what we wish to manage. A generic managed device classification leads to the term "devices" as a catchall name for the information network managers want to view (from the statistical standpoint) and/or control (from the system configuration standpoint).

In addition to the classic management model, the network management community is shifting from instrumentation to problem solving. Instrumentation describes placing monitoring tools on various network devices in order to monitor their performance. Problem solving describes proactively monitoring network activity and performance so we can act before an issue becomes a problem.

Finally, there are two network management axioms that have been widely accepted as industry doctrine:

- The increased traffic the management information creates should not significantly burden the managed network.
- The managed device agent should not significantly increase the device's processing overhead such that its primary function is negatively affected.

Types of Managed Nodes/Devices

Vendors have built increased functionality into their various products' management elements through either software or firmware. The Types of Managed Nodes/Devices Diagram illustrates a representative sampling of the different kinds of managed entities that typically exist in today's networks.

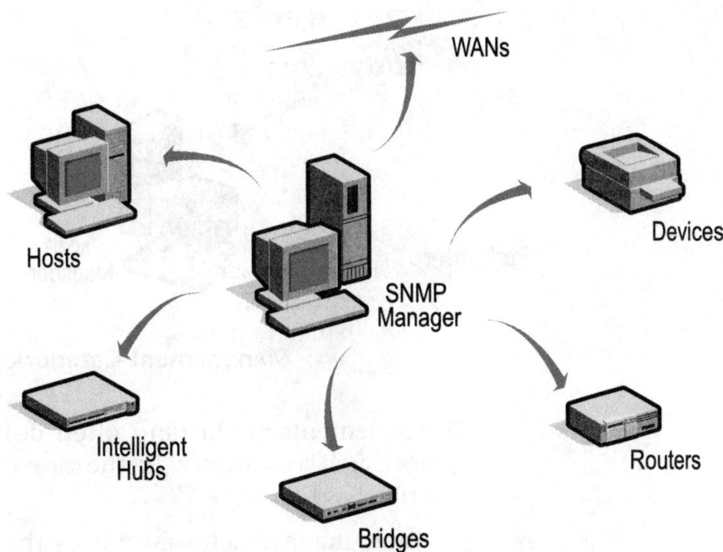

Types of Managed Nodes/Devices

Items other than managed devices are not depicted in the diagram. The management domain does include other items, such as applications and databases. An example of a managed item is a piece of intelligence, such as an application. Here, we could monitor the number of current application users and the highest number of simultaneous users to date.

Functional categories provide another perspective on what the network manager is attempting to manage. The Management Categories Diagram presents a breakdown of the various functional elements.

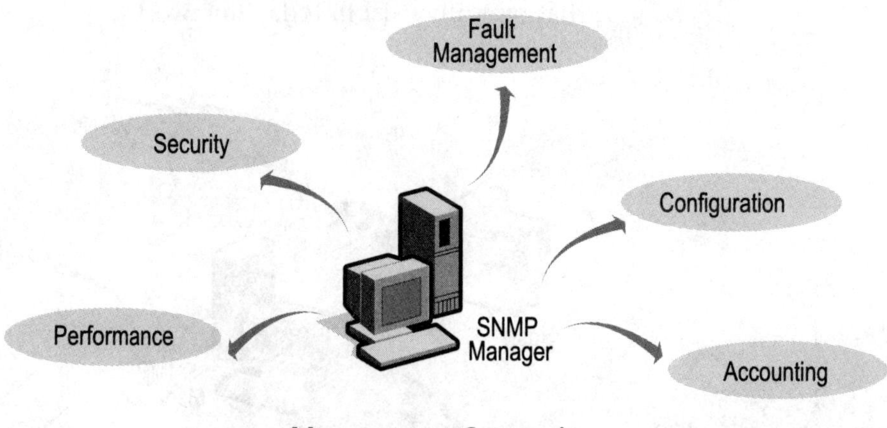

Management Categories

These elements could (and often do) exist in a single network device, such as a router. In the case of a router, each element is described as follows:

- Fault management—Monitors the state of the router's LAN and wide area network (WAN) links.
- Configuration—Reads and changes the router's routing tables and route costs.
- Accounting—Gathers statistics on path use for billing purposes.
- Performance—Discovers how many datagrams were forwarded and how many were discarded.
- Security—Changes the valid authentication codes for routing protocols, such as Open Shortest Path First (OSPF).

Network Management Model

We have briefly discussed two parts of the network management model; the types of managed devices/elements and the managed functional elements. To round out the network management framework, refer to the Management Model Diagram.

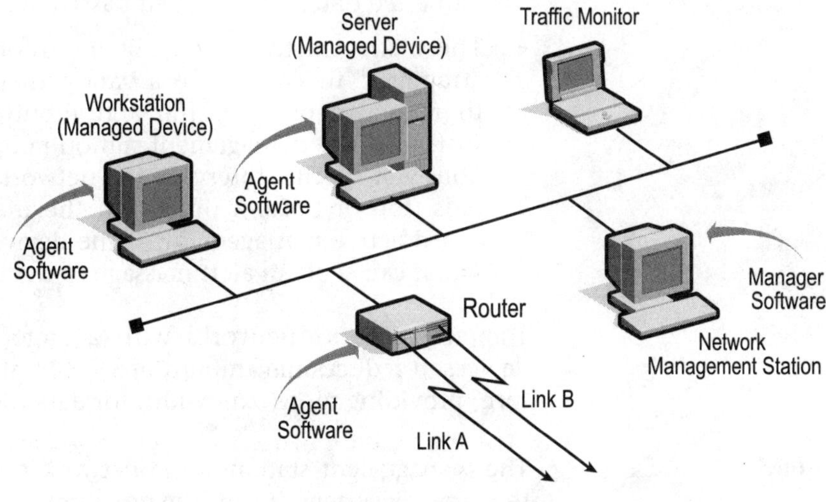

Management Model

The model consists of essentially four parts, namely:

- Managed nodes/devices
- Software (or firmware) that runs in the managed nodes, called agents
- The NMS, which runs the management application
- The Network Management Protocol, used to exchange management information between NMS and the agent (SNMP)

Managed Nodes/ Devices

The managed nodes are the network devices we wish to monitor. On these devices reside the MIBs, which have a database structure. The database contains a series of objects, which are resource data gathered on the managed device. Some of the MIB categories include port interface, TCP, and ICMP data.

SNMP Agents

The SNMP management agent is the software component the managed devices contain. Bridges, routers, hubs, switches, and servers may contain SNMP agents, thus the management station can control them. The management agent responds to the management station in two ways:

- The management station polls the managed device, requesting data from the agent. The agent, in turn, responds with the requested data. This is called passive management.
- The management station obtains information by the agent "trapping" it. Trapping is a data gathering method designed to reduce network traffic and monitor device processing. Instead of the management station polling the agents continuously at specific intervals, the network manager sets thresholds (top or bottom limits) on the managed device; this is called active management. If the device exceeds this threshold, it can send an alert message to the management station.

Trapping benefits networks with a large number of managed devices. It reduces the amount of SNMP traffic on the network, in turn, providing more bandwidth for data transfer.

NMS

The management station is the network manager's interface into the network system. It runs the programs that manipulate data and control the network. The management station also maintains a database of MIB extracted from the devices under its management.

Network Management Protocol

SNMP is the network management protocol used. It has three key capabilities:

- GET—The management console retrieves data from the agent.
- PUT—The management console sets object values on the agent.
- TRAP—The agent notifies the management console of significant events.

Recognize that the Management Model Diagram also shows a device called a Traffic Monitor. SNMP defines a type of device/element that allows a network manager to query the Traffic Monitor for such things as network traffic statistics and other events that may affect network performance. This tool is designed to monitor network media, rather than devices. We can include network media in the types of devices managed by a network manager.

The Network Management Protocol Diagram depicts another network management framework view. It illustrates not only where SNMP fits into the overall management picture, but also reintroduces the MIB.

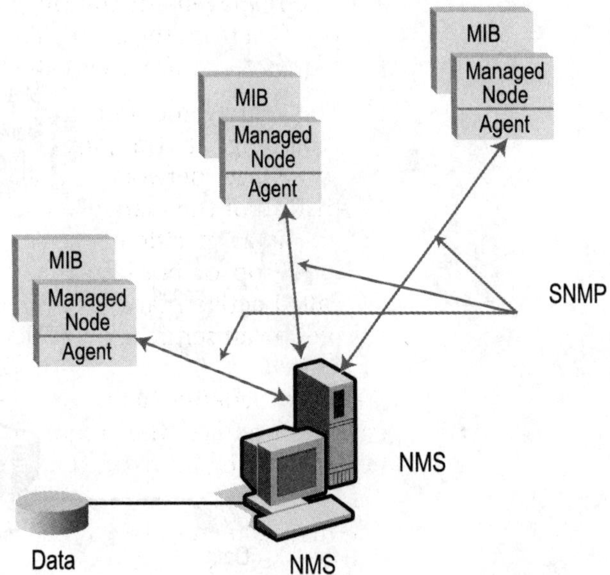

Network Management Protocol

Network Management Modes

We are all likely familiar with the terms "micromanager" and "hands-off manager," as they apply to a person's management style. Similarly, network management can be categorized into general operation modes, including:

- Passive management—Simply gathering statistics/information
- Active management—Changing a device's characteristics and operating parameters
- Exception management—Being notified only of conditions worthy of some action

Passive Management

The Passive Management Diagram illustrates an NMS polling a device's agent process to collect information about specific data variables. The device's MIB has previously defined these data variables, thus they are available upon an authorized manager's request.

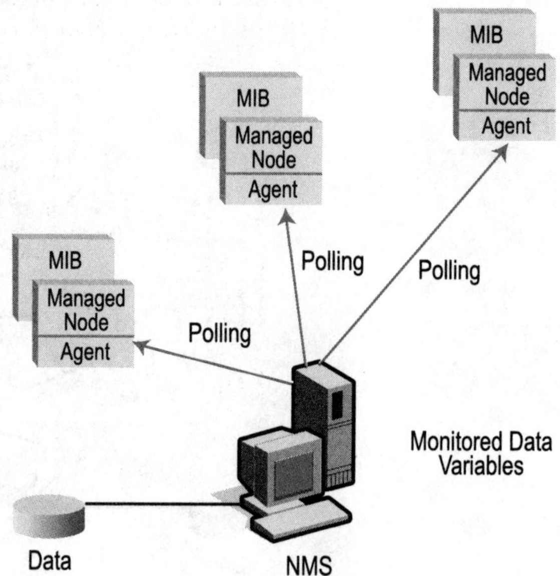

Passive Management

The Polling and Traffic Statistics Diagram depicts a management station polling the Traffic Monitor for the network's current utilization status (in this case an Ethernet network). The network operator might have received a Help desk call stating that the network appeared to be running slow. As a starting point in making a determination of what could be causing the bottleneck, a snapshot of the current network traffic utilization might be helpful.

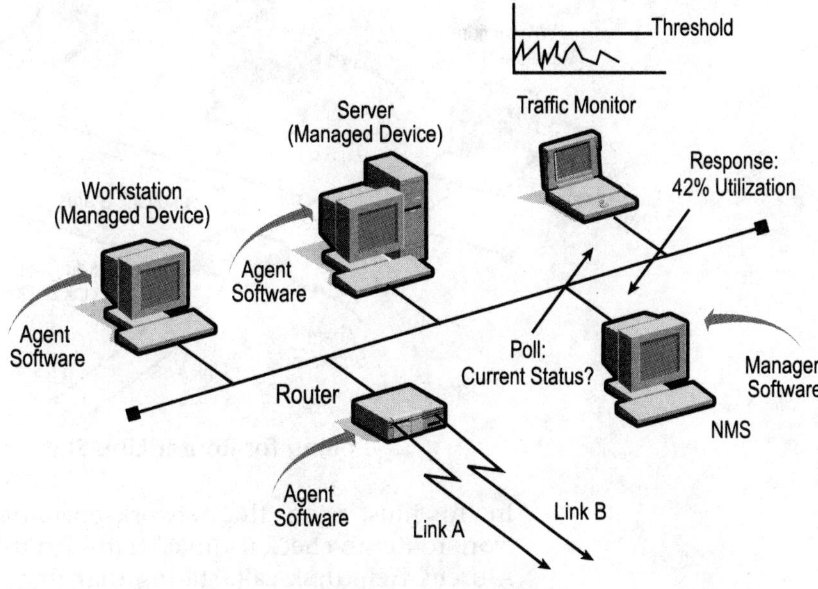

Polling and Traffic Statistics

Another example of passive management (information gathering) is shown on the Polling for Router Link Status Diagram.

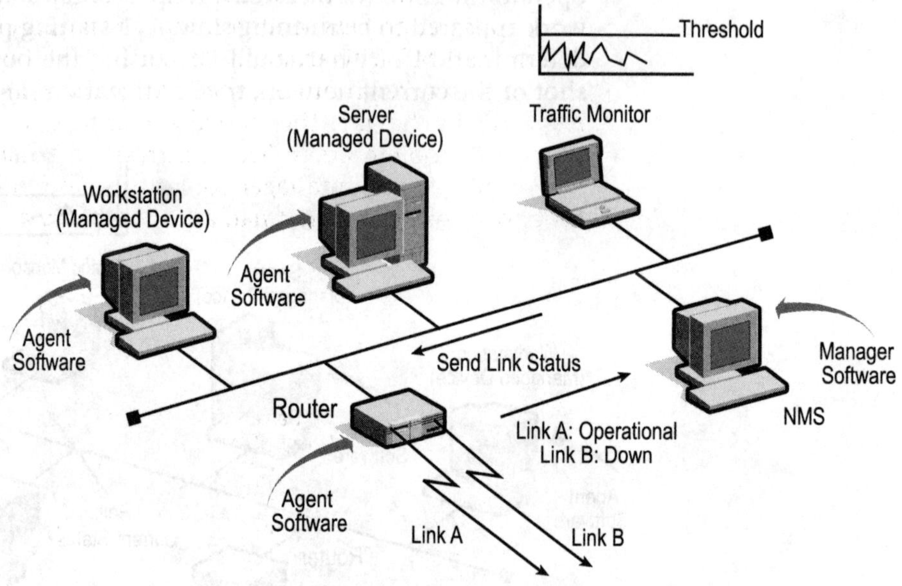

Polling for Router Link Status

In this illustration, the network operator polls a particular network router to check its links' status (in this case, the WAN links). A user's Help desk call, stating that they were no longer able to reach a certain destination on the company's intranet, may have triggered the manager's examination of the router's WAN links. Another reason the manager may have chosen to examine the links may be that network access times have seriously degraded, for instance, the network lost a high-speed T1 link. On this diagram, Link A is operational and Link B is down, causing all network traffic to flow over the single WAN Link A.

Active Management

Active management is the second network management operation mode. In this mode, the network manager changes a specific network device's operational parameters. For example, if the managed device is a bridge, the network manager may add to the bridge configuration additional filtering parameters that prevent it from forwarding certain frames to another network segment.

Exception Management

The last network management mode is the exception mode, as illustrated on the Exception Management Diagram. In this example, the network has exceeded a previously configured parameter (in this case, a traffic utilization threshold). In response, the device's agent process sends a notification of the exceeded threshold to the NMS. This example demonstrates how a network manager could take a more proactive posture in controlling the network, by having the network component inform them of potential problem areas. This contrasts to passive management, where the network manager could only respond to network performance conditions that had already occurred.

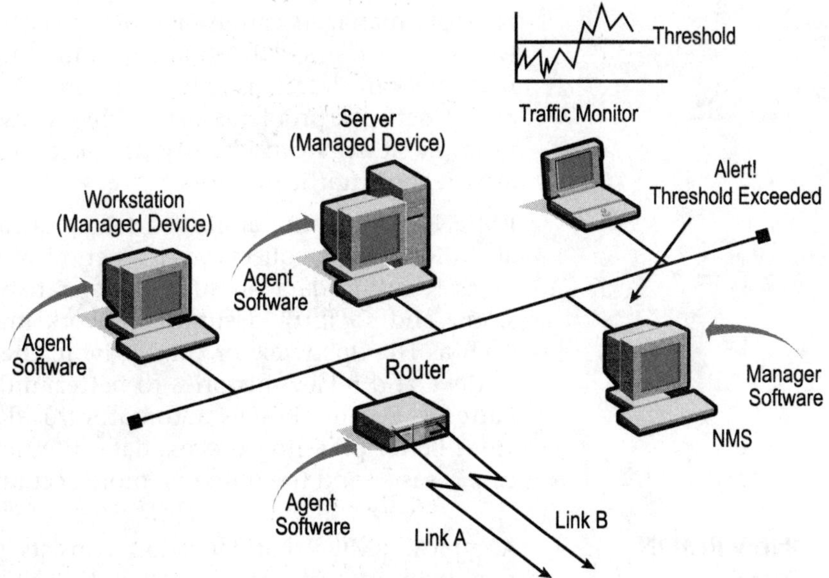

Exception Management

The exception mode of network management goes by several other names; a trap, alert, and event are three descriptions that appear in documentation. For example, SNMP calls these notifications traps. The device software directs these notifications to a certain NMS software destination, where they can trigger certain actions. One such action would be to automatically page the person who can address the particular situation.

RMON

RMON is a standard MIB that defines current and historical Medium Access Control (MAC)-Layer statistics and control objects, allowing the NMS to capture real-time information across the entire network. The RMON standard is an Ethernet SNMP MIB definition described in RFC 1757.

The RMON MIB provides a standard method to monitor an Ethernet network's basic operations, providing inoperability between SNMP management stations and monitoring agents. RMON also provides a powerful alarm and event mechanism for setting network thresholds and for notifying network managers of changes in network behavior.

Network managers can use RMON to centrally analyze and monitor network traffic data obtained from remote LAN segments. The manager can detect, isolate, diagnose, and report potential and actual network problems before they cause network outages. For example, RMON can identify the hosts on a network that generate the most traffic or errors.

RMON provides the ability to set up automatic histories, which an RMON agent collects over a period of time. This history provides trending data on such basic statistics as utilization, collisions, and so forth. Using a network management application such as HP Openview or IBM's Tivoli, the network manager can retrieve and review histories to better understand network usage patterns. Because RMON automates this data collection, and provides better planning process data, the network monitoring process is easier and the outcome more accurate.

How RMON Works

A typical RMON configuration consists of a central NMS and remote monitoring devices called RMON agents. The NMS can be a Windows- or UNIX-based workstation, or a PC running a network management application. From the management station, the network manager can issue SNMP commands requesting information from the RMON agent. The RMON agent sends the requested information to the management station, which then processes and displays this information on its console.

The RMON agent, also known as an RMON probe, is either firmware built into a network device, such as a server or router, or a specifically designed network device inserted into a network segment. A probe provides the same functionality as an SNMP agent. The probe tracks and analyzes network traffic and gathers statistics, which it sends to the monitoring station. As packets travel across the network, the RMON probe continuously collects and analyzes remote LAN segment data, in real-time, and stores the data locally. Multiple RMON agents can run on different network segments, usually one per subnet, as shown on the RMON Agents Diagram.

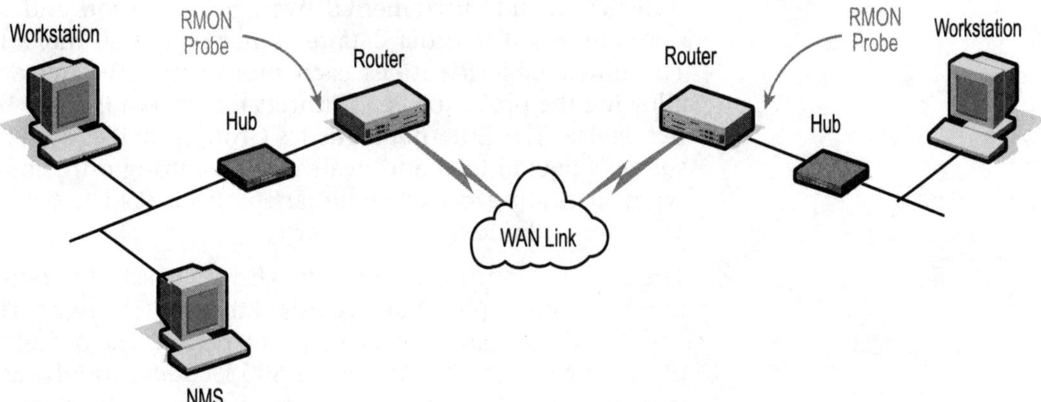

RMON Agents

Probes can be inserted at various points in the network; where we choose to insert the probes determines the information we gather. For example, if we wish to measure overall network congestion, we would choose to insert an external probe into a passive tap on the network backbone. In a hierarchical network design, our backbone carries traffic between network segments; therefore, we will see the majority of the network traffic on the backbone. This probe can capture performance statistics by IP address, port, protocol, or application, and generate threshold alerts and alarms and log traffic errors.

RMON provides for redundant management consoles. These redundant management consoles provide two major benefits to network management processes:

- The ability to have more than one network administrator located in different physical locations to monitor and manage the same network; for example one in Denver and one in Dallas.
- Having two or more management consoles provides management redundancy. This means if one of the consoles fails, the other console can still be used to monitor and control the network until the first console is repaired.

RMON Extensions to SNMP

The RMON extension to the SNMP protocol creates new data monitoring categories. These categories add more branches to the MIB database. The major categories are as follows:

- The Ethernet Statistics Group—The Ethernet Statistics Group contains statistics gathered for each monitored subnet. These statistics include incremental byte, packet, error, and frame size counters. The other data reference type is an index table. The index table identifies each monitored Ethernet device, allowing the probe to keep counters for each individual Ethernet device. The Ethernet Statistics Group provides a view of a subnet's overall load and health by measuring different error types, including cyclic redundancy check (CRC), collisions, and over and under-sized packets.
- The History Control Group—The History Control Group contains a data table that records Ethernet Statistics Group counter samples over a specified time period. The default sampling time is every 30 minutes (1,800 seconds) and the default table size is 50 entries, providing a total of 25 continuous hours of monitoring. As a specified counter's history is created, the probe creates a new entry at each sample interval until the table meets its maximum entry limit. When the table reaches its limit, the device deletes the oldest entry as it creates each new entry. These samples provide a network baseline we can compare against the original baseline to identify and resolve problems, or we can use it to update the baseline as the network changes.
- The Alarm Group—The Alarm Group uses limits specified by network managers, called thresholds. If the monitored data counters cross the thresholds, the NMS sends a message or alarm to the specified people. This process, known as an error trap, can automate many network monitoring functions. This is the RMON exception management function.
- The Host Group—The Host Group contains counters maintained about each host the MIB discovers on a subnet or segment. Packets, octets, errors, and broadcasts are some of the counter categories maintained. Examples of these types of counters are total packets, packets received, and packets sent.

- The Host TOPN Group—The Host TOPN Group is used to prepare reports about a group of hosts that top a statistical list, based on a measured parameter. For example, the MIB could generate a report for the day's top ten broadcasting hosts. Another report might be generated for the most packets transmitted during the day. This category provides a simple tool for determining who and what type of data traffic most occupies the selected subnetwork.
- The Matrix Group—The Matrix Group records the data communication between two hosts on a subnetwork; a matrix (a multidimensional table) stores this data. One of the reports the MIB can generate from this category is which hosts utilize a server. By reorganizing the matrix order, we can create other reports. For example, one report might show all the users of a particular server, while another report shows all the servers used by a particular host.
- The Filter Group—The Filter Group provides a way that a management console can instruct an RMON probe to gather selected packets from a specific interface on a particular subnetwork. This selection is based on two filters: the data filter and the status filter. The data filter is designed to either match (or not) particular data patterns, allowing the NMS to select that particular data. The status filter is based on the type of packet examined, for instance, a CRC or a valid packet. We can combine these filters using the logical "and" and "or" functions to create very complicated conditions. The filter group allows the network administrator to selectively look at different packet types, in order to provide better network analysis and troubleshooting.
- The Packet Capture Group—The Packet Capture Group allows the administrator to specify a method to capture packets the Filter Group selects. By capturing specified packets, the network administrator can look at the exact details of packets that match the basic filter. The packet group also specifies the individual captured packet quantities and the total number of packets captured.

- The Event Group—The Event Group contains events generated by other groups in the MIB database. For example, a counter could exceed its threshold specified in the Alarm Group; consequently, this action would generate an Event Group event. Based upon this event, the NMS could generate an action such as issuing a warning e-mail message to all the recipients listed in the Alarm Group's parameters, or it could create a logged entry in the event table. An event is generated for all comparison operations in the RMON MIB extensions.
- The Token Ring Group—The Token Ring Group creates counters necessary to use RMON to monitor and manage Token Ring networks.

RMON2

The newest RMON version, RMON2, provides data about higher layer network traffic. This capability allows administrators to analyze traffic by protocol, including checking network performance all the way to the individual port level on RMON2-compatible routers or switches. It also allows a single RMON probe to monitor multiple protocol types on a single segment, and allows much more flexibility in the way probes are configured for reporting and network response time measurements.

RMON has its problems. High costs and lots of vendor implementation incompatibilities plagued RMON1; RMON2 suffers these same difficulties. As with other management standards, RMON tool vendors have added to their products' proprietary RMON extensions, making them more attractive to managers hungry for more functionality. However, although these proprietary extensions look good on the surface, there is a risk of an organization becoming dependent on a single vendor management solution. Therefore, network managers wishing to implement RMON2 might choose to make this move cautiously.

Activities

1. Which three of the following are devices manageable with SNMP? (Choose three.)
   a. PBXs
   b. Applications
   c. Bridges
   d. Routers
2. Which three of the following are examples of SNMP router management categories? (Choose three.)
   a. Performance
   b. Storage
   c. Configuration
   d. Security
3. What results from trapping data with an SNMP agent?
   a. Increased network bandwidth usage
   b. Decreased network bandwidth usage
   c. The management station alerts the managed device of a threshold violation
   d. Increased management station polling intervals
4. Which SNMP capability sets object values on an agent?
   a. SET
   b. TRAP
   c. GET
   d. PUT
5. Which SNMP management mode allows us to change a device's characteristics and operating parameters?
   a. Passive management
   b. Active management
   c. Reactive management
   d. Exception management

6. RMON uses which devices, placed on remote network segments, to gather network information?
   a. Probes
   b. Traps
   c. Taps
   d. Trap agents
7. An RMON probe can capture a network segment's performance statistics based on which three of the following? (Choose three.)
   a. IP address
   b. Port number
   c. MAC address
   d. Application
8. How does RMON2 differ from RMON?
   a. RMON2 uses probes, where RMON uses agents.
   b. RMON allows a single probe to monitor multiple protocols on a single segment.
   c. RMON2 only monitors Layer 3 traffic, while RMON looks at Layer 4 and beyond.
   d. RMON2 looks at Layer 3 traffic, while RMON only looks at Layers 1 and 2.

Extended Activities

1. Go to the following Web sites that contain SNMP-related information, and summarize your findings.
   a. **http://www.hio.hen.nl/rfc/snmp/**
   b. **http://www.linas.org/linux/NMS.html**
   c. **http://www.ee.umanitoba.ca/~blight/snmp.html**
2. Using your favorite search engine, find at least four other sites containing information about SNMP.

Lesson 7—Other Applications

Thus far, we have covered some of the more predominant TCP/IP applications. This lesson covers other applications normally included in TCP/IP software.

Objectives

At the end of this lesson you will be able to:

- Name other applications bundled with TCP/IP software
- Describe these applications' functions

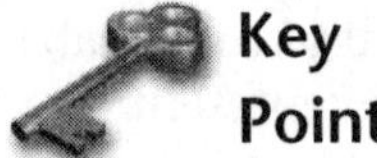

Key Point

TCP/IP software ships with many useful applications.

NFS

NFS, originally developed by Sun Microsystems, uses UDP for accessing UNIX file systems on multiple computers. A diskless workstation, for example, can access a server's hard disk as if the disk were local to the workstation.

NFS is included in many TCP/IP software packages for PC applications. It is a client/server application, where the server gives clients access to its file system. The NFS File Server Diagram illustrates the application. The client uses the remote file system as if it were part of the local file system. Attaching a remote directory to the local file system (done by the client) is called mounting in accordance with NFS terminology. Mounting is similar to mapping drives with a PC.

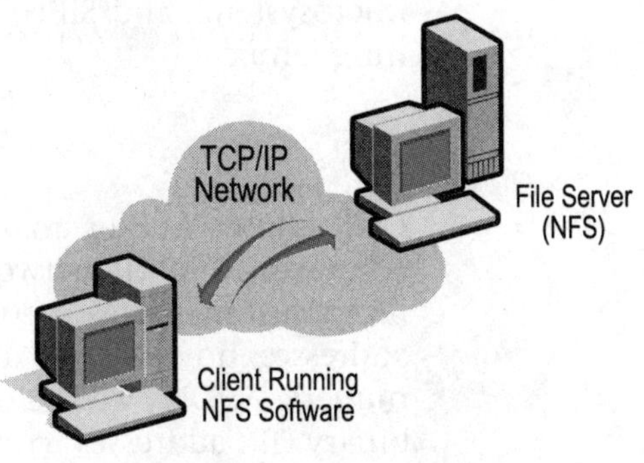

NFS File Server

Rlogin

The application name Rlogin stands for remote login. Rlogin is a UNIX-to-UNIX remote access facility. Suppose you are logged in on your own workstation but need to run a complicated inquiry on a database that resides on another workstation. You could FTP the file to your system, but a very large file transfer could take hours. You could choose to mount the file using NFS, but because your database software would access the data records across the network, response time could be very slow.

Assuming you have a login ID established on the other system, you can use the Rlogin utility to connect to the other system and execute commands as if you were physically sitting at that workstation. The database activity would be local to the database's host file system, and only the characters that represent input statements and displayed or printed results would have to be transmitted across the network. Because Rlogin only supports UNIX-to-UNIX connectivity, the remote system understands the environment in which you are running. This means, for example, that you could direct the output of an inquiry command to be stored in a file on your own system rather than on the remote system.

X-Window

The X-Window application uses the TCP X-Window protocol to draw windows on a UNIX or Linux workstation's display screen. X-Windows is much more than a utility for drawing windows; it is an entire philosophy for designing a user interface.

X-Window, also known simply as "X," is a portable, network-transparent window system that runs on many different computers. It is frequently used in conjunction with the UNIX OS. Popular platforms include workstations from companies such as Sun Microsystems and Silicon Graphics, Inc., and standard PCs running Linux.

DNS

DNS allows a user to communicate with another user using addresses. TCP/IP networks require addresses for sending and receiving messages between hosts. Ultimately, these are IP addresses; however, we need a mechanism to translate the alphanumeric FQDNs we use in Internet URLs to the machine-unique, binary IP addresses computers understand. The name server resolves these alphanumeric Internet addresses to binary IP addresses. When given a domain name, the server will return an Internet address in binary format.

The DNS Server Diagram presents the interaction between client and server. Given the domain name **http://www.westnetinc.com**, a DNS server will resolve the name from right to left. DNS will first locate a specified server on the Internet that knows the locations for commercial sites (.coms). That DNS server will then locate the company WestNet and ask for the address of the **http://www.westnetinc.com**. When found, the server will return the binary number (01101101...) that relates to the requested host name **http://www.westnetinc.com**.

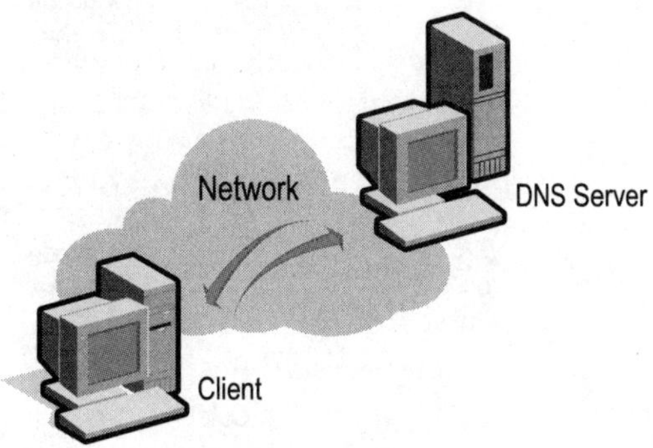

DNS Server

We discuss DNS in much more detail in a future lesson.

TFTP

TFTP is a very simple FTP created for use on TCP/IP networks. TFTP is a connectionless protocol (it uses UDP at the Transport Layer), and uses a "lock-step" packet delivery approach. In other words, TFTP requires an acknowledgement for each transmitted packet before it sends the next. TFTP supports only a few packet types:

- Read Request (RRQ)—Sent when the client wishes to download a file. The packet's opcode = 1.
- Write Request (WRQ)—Sent when the client wishes to upload a file or when the packet begins "mail" mode. The packet's opcode = 2.
- Data (DATA)—Contains up to 512 bytes of data. Though Data fields are typically 512 bytes long, the last packet may have a shortened Data field. The packet's opcode = 3.

- Acknowledgement (ACK)—Sent by a device in response to a correctly received packet. The packet's opcode = 4.
- Error (ERROR)—Sent if an error occurs, for example, if a packet is lost or a device experiences an input/output (I/O) error. Error packets may be sent in reply, instead of ACK packets. The packet's opcode = 5.

The TFTP Packets Diagram shows the five packet types.

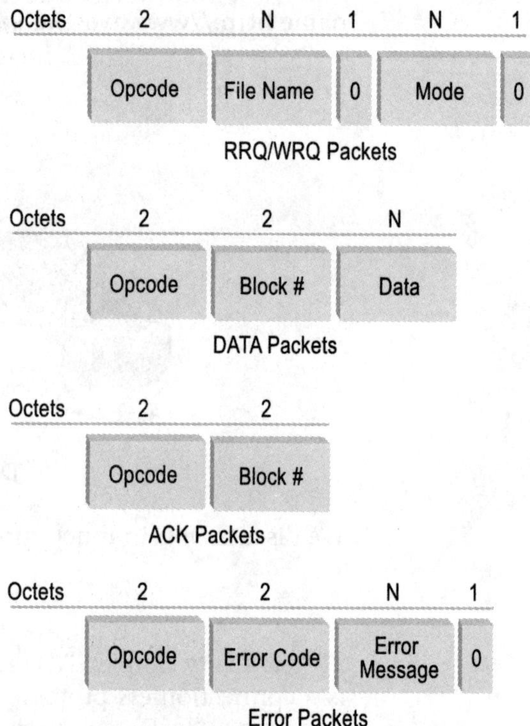

TFTP Packets

The only field the five packet types have in common is the Opcode field. ACK packets are the only ones that are of a fixed size. The other packet fields include:

- Filename—Contains the file name to be written or read. This is an ASCII text string.

- Mode—The Mode field specifies one of three data format values: netascii, octet, or mail. Netascii data uses the 8-bit ASCII format. Octet mode is used to transfer a file using the source machine's native 8-bit file format. Mail is similar to netascii, except that a username is placed in the Filename field and the transmission begins with a WRQ packet.
- Block #—Block # provides a way to identify successive packets. The protocol assigns block numbers consecutively, beginning with 1. The only time the protocol assigns a block # of 0 is when the devices are initially establishing communications. The receiving device sends an ACK with a block number of 0 in response to the sender's WRQ packet.
- Data—The Data field provides the variable size field for actually carrying the data between devices. This field can vary from 0 to 512 bytes. TFTP considers any packet containing a Data field less than 512 bytes long as the transmission's end.
- Error Code—This 16-bit field contains an integer representation of an error type. TFTP error codes are:
  - 0—Not defined, see error message
  - 1—File not found
  - 2—Access violation
  - 3—Disk full or allocation exceeded
  - 4—Illegal TFTP operation
  - 5—Unknown transfer ID
  - 6—File already exists
  - 7—No such user
- ErrMsg—ErrMsg is a string associated with a particular error code.

TFTP transfers files. It does not provide a directory listing and is not particularly reliable. However, it is very easy to implement, uses few network and host resources, and provides built-in rate and error-control in the form of the required ACK packets.

NNTP

As mentioned earlier, NNTP is the TCP/IP protocol used to distribute news articles, or newsfeeds, on TCP/IP networks. Commonly, we find newsfeeds on the Internet; however, we can also place NNTP servers on local internets, intranets, and on extranets. The NNTP server stores, maintains, and distributes a central database of news articles and newsgroups. NNTP allows a news reader client to post articles to and retrieve articles from a newsgroup, and allows news servers to interact by exchanging newsfeeds.

NNTP is reliable in that it uses TCP as a transport protocol. Because of its interactive capabilities, it provides advantages over other server-to-server or client-to-server copy programs. Rather than transferring an entire database file between communicating nodes, NNTP only transfers the database contents a client or server request. Clients can pick from a list which news articles they wish to read, leaving the remainder on the server.

The NNTP News Reader Screen Diagram shows Microsoft Outlook Express used as a news client.

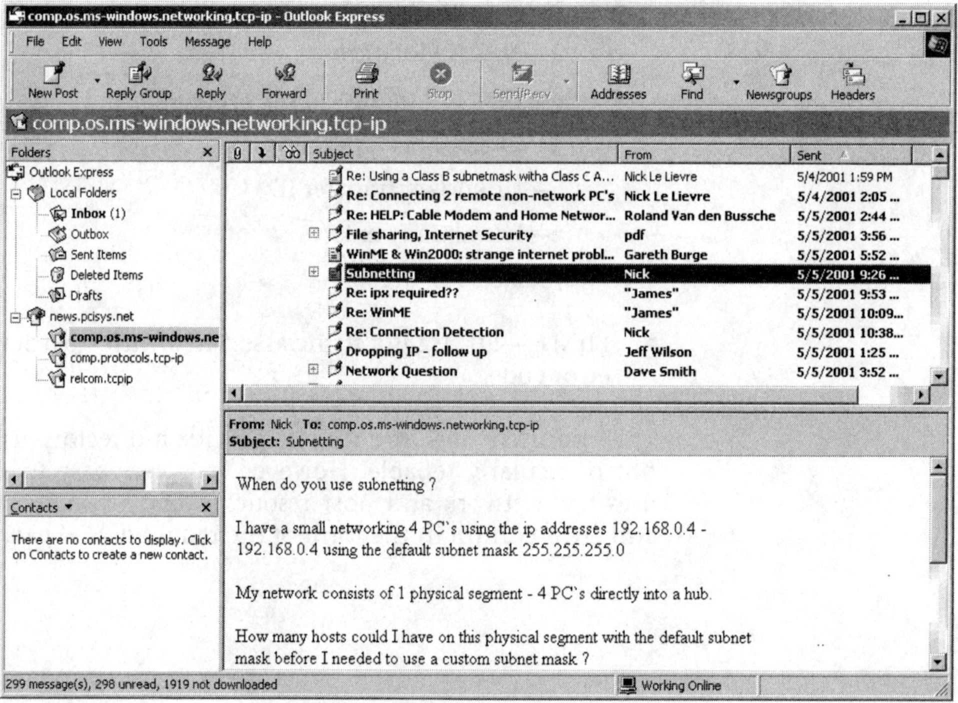

NNTP News Reader Screen

The user can download from the news server a list of available newsgroups, and then pick those that pertain to their needs. The user then downloads the news messages into the reader, and sorts them as they do their e-mail messages. Newsfeeds can be great information sources on a variety of subjects, including TCP/IP.

DHCP/BOOTP

On an IP network, a DHCP server provides host configuration information to the network's clients. This can significantly reduce client configuration and support times on TCP/IP networks large and small.

ISPs dynamically assign most clients IP addresses when they connect to the ISP's network. This simplifies remote client support by automatically passing such information as the ISP's DNS server and default gateway router addresses, and the client's network address and subnet mask.

DHCP is similar to BOOTP, as we have already learned. DHCP is also similar to another TCP/IP protocol, Reverse Address Resolution Protocol (RARP), which provides a client an IP address given a MAC layer address. However, DHCP far exceeds the capabilities of either of these two protocols.

In addition to being a protocol for exchanging client configuration information, DHCP provides three mechanisms for allocating network addresses:

- Automatic address allocation—Assigns a host a permanent IP address.
- Dynamic address allocation—Assigns a host a temporary IP address. This is the mechanism that distinguishes DHCP from the others (BOOTP and RARP).
- Manual allocation—The network administrator assigns an IP address to a particular node, and the DHCP server merely transfers the assigned address to the host.

A client may request a configuration from any available DHCP server by broadcasting a server discovery message on its subnet. This message contains the requesting device's MAC address and computer name. Servers receiving the request respond with a broadcast message stating that they have an address to offer. In the mean time, the offering server(s) reserves the offered address so they cannot offer the same address to another client.

If an immediate response is not received, the client may find it necessary to repeat their request several times, over set time periods. When the client receives a server's offer, it responds, again with a broadcast message, to the server that it has accepted the offer. If other servers offered addresses, they withdraw their offers and return the offered address to their address pools.

The winning server then broadcasts to the client its acknowledgement of the client's offer acceptance, and the client then binds to itself the address and any other information provided. After this binding, the client is able to use TCP/IP on the network.

Servers lease addresses to clients for an administrator-definable time period. Some administrators like to set this to a short time period; for example, an ISP might set the lease renewal period to 600 seconds. This ensures that unused addresses are quickly returned to the pool. Others may choose to set the time period to several days, to keep to a minimum network broadcast traffic.

The client attempts lease renewal when 50 percent of the lease time has expired. This occurs using a simplified version of the initial lease procedure, only requiring a client request and a server acknowledgement. If the first renewal attempt fails, the client next attempts renewal after 87.5 percent of the original lease time has expired.

The DHCP Server Screen Diagram illustrates a configured Microsoft Windows NT 4.0 DHCP server.

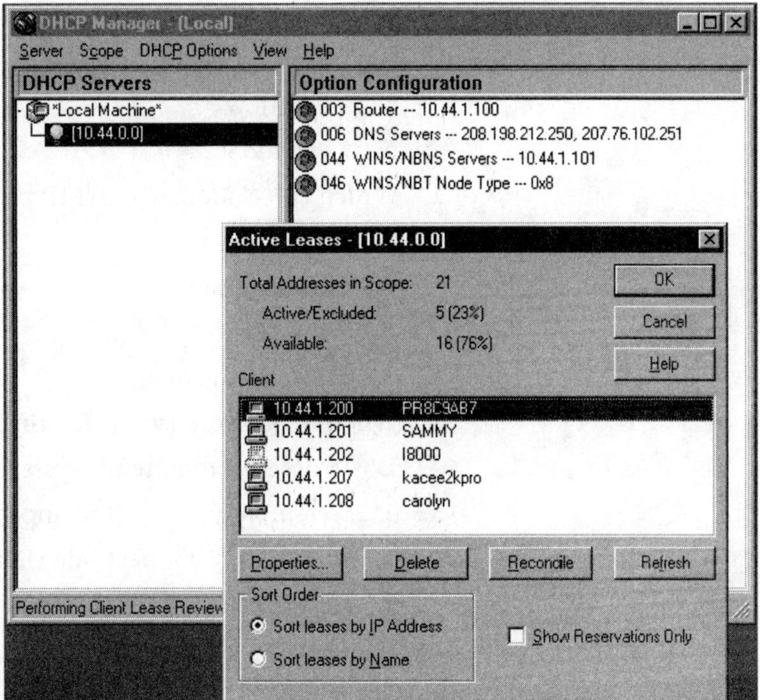

DHCP Server Screen

Here, we see the server's active client leases. Of the total of 21 addresses defined in the DHCP scope, 5, or 23 percent, are active. In the DHCP Manager window, we see several DHCP options configured. These include the gateway router address, the DNS server addresses, the Windows Internet Naming Service (WINS) server address, and the WINS node type.

We will discuss DHCP in more detail later in this text. For more information on WINS, visit **http://www.webopedia.com/term/w/wins.html**.

Activities

1. Which TCP/IP application allows users to display locally a remote UNIX host's screen?
   a. Telnet
   b. Rlogin
   c. R-Window
   d. X-Window
2. Which three choices are TFTP packet types? (Choose three.)
   a. Read request
   b. Data request
   c. Write request
   d. Acknowledgement
3. When might you use the Rlogin TCP/IP application?
   a. To access a remote file system as if it were local
   b. To remotely connect to another Windows PC
   c. To remotely connect one UNIX workstation to another
   d. To bring up a remote window from another workstation
4. Which TCP/IP application distributes news articles read from a central database?
   a. DNS
   b. NNTP
   c. SMTP
   d. IMAP
5. Which three of the following are DHCP address allocation mechanisms? (Choose three.)
   a. Automatic
   b. Dynamic
   c. Static
   d. Manual

Extended Activities

1. Examples of news reader clients are Microsoft Outlook and Outlook Express, and Netscape Messenger. Using one of these news readers, connect to your ISP's news server. Download the list of available newsgroups.
2. Search for the following terms in the newsgroup list. Review some of the postings found. Answer someone else's posting, if you can.
   a. Rlogin
   b. X-Windows
   c. DNS
   d. NNTP
   e. NFS
   f. DHCP

Summary

This unit provided an overview of some of the more important application programs shipped with TCP/IP software. We began the unit by looking at ways to access TCP/IP applications, either through the command line or a browser. When accessed, the applications use TCP, IP, and other protocols to move information between sending and receiving application programs.

HTTP is used to move information between browsers and Web servers in TCP/IP networks. HTTP is widely used in today's networking environments because of the continued Internet, intranet, and extranet connectivity growth.

Telnet is used to connect to remote computers. A user calls a Telnet program, either from the command line or through an Internet browser, such as Netscape. Telnet allows a local computer to run applications on the remote computer. One common Telnet use is to connect to a device, such as a switch or router, in order to configure it.

FTP is another common TCP/IP application program. As with Telnet, FTP can be run from a command line or a browser. This program sends and retrieves files across a network. Many different clients can access an FTP server, as long as they are also running the FTP program. Transferring files is the most common use for FTP.

E-mail is the most frequently used application in computer networking. SMTP is the TCP/IP Application Layer protocol used to send and receive mail in a TCP/IP environment. Other important applications related to SMTP are POP, MIME, and IMAP. POP is used to transfer information from a client to a mail server. MIME is used to attach various file types to an e-mail message. IMAP allows clients to manipulate messages directly on the server, allowing them to download only those files they choose.

SNMP is used to manage networking resources. Software is located throughout the network to gather information about networking devices. This information can be displayed at a central point in the network, called an NMS, for management purposes. SNMP is the protocol used to move information between devices in the network and the central management station. RMON and RMON2 extend SNMP to allow the NMS and RMON probes to gather and manipulate more information than can SNMP alone.

Other application protocols are also used in TCP/IP networks; however, the emphasized protocols are the most widely used. These applications all use underlying TCP/IP protocols to move information across LANs, campus networks, metropolitan area networks (MANs), and WANs, between source and destination computers.

Unit 2 Quiz

1. Which two TCP/IP protocols are used for network management? (Choose two.)
   a. SMTP
   b. MONR
   c. RMON
   d. SNMP
2. SNMP gathers network information from what type of database?
   a. RMON
   b. MIB
   c. DNS
   d. FQDN
3. NNTP allows TCP/IP users to perform which of the following?
   a. Terminal emulation
   b. Download e-mail
   c. Collect network information
   d. Download news articles
4. A daemon is the equivalent to which Windows component?
   a. Device driver
   b. Kernel
   c. Service
   d. Control
5. Which best describes why an HTTP server can handle multiple simultaneous connections?
   a. It maintains state information about each connection so that it can quickly reconnect if the browser experiences an error.
   b. HTTP is stateless, which means the server has no knowledge of previous connections after they are dropped.
   c. The server maintains each file in its memory, so that the application need not read files from the hard disk.
   d. HTTP is stateful, which means that the server maintains information about each connection.

6. For what purpose would you choose to run the Telnet application?
   a. To access a Web site
   b. To configure a router
   c. To download a file
   d. To manage the network
7. FTP is used for what purpose?
   a. To manage remote devices
   b. To download e-mail files
   c. To download HTML files
   d. To download large files
8. Why does SMTP need additional protocols to carry nontext data as attachments?
   a. An SMTP packet is limited to 1,000 bits in size.
   b. SMTP only carries ASCII text characters.
   c. SMTP is incompatible with MIME attachments.
   d. SMTP is too slow on its own to carry large attachments.
9. Which SNMP RMON extension maintains a data table recording Ethernet Statistics Group counter samples collected over a period of time?
   a. The Alarm Group
   b. The History Control Group
   c. The Event Group
   d. The Data History Group
10. SMTP is which type of message delivery system?
    a. Store-and-forward
    b. Direct delivery
    c. Unreliable
    d. Best-effort

11. Which three of the following are SNMP network management model components? (Choose three.)

    a. Managed devices

    b. NMS

    c. Network management protocol

    d. Management probes

12. Which SNMP capability notifies the management station of the occurrence of a significant event?

    a. GET

    b. PUT

    c. TRAP

    d. NOTE

13. When a management station polls a device agent process to collect information, the network management system is operating in which SNMP network management mode?

    a. Passive

    b. Active

    c. Proactive

    d. Exception

14. Which SNMP RMON extension prepares reports about a group of devices that head a measured parameter's statistical list?

    a. The Host TOPN Group

    b. The Host Group

    c. The Alarm Group

    d. The Filter Group

15. Which two of the following are MIME supported data types? (Choose two.)

    a. Uuencode

    b. MPEG

    c. GIF

    d. POP

16. Which TCP/IP application uses a lock-step packet delivery approach for file transfers?
    a. TFTP
    b. FTP
    c. SMB
    d. HTTP
17. To resolve FQDNs to binary IP addresses, resolvers contact which type of TCP/IP application server?
    a. WINS
    b. NetBIOS
    c. DHCP
    d. DNS
18. Which TCP/IP protocol has us attach a remote device to the local file system by mounting it?
    a. NFS
    b. NNTP
    c. UUCP
    d. FTP
19. Which TCP/IP UNIX specific application would allow us to connect to a remote database over the network, but restrict database activity to the remote host?
    a. Xwindows
    b. Telnet
    c. Rlogin
    d. NNTP
20. Which DHCP network address allocation mechanism assigns a host a temporary IP address?
    a. Automatic
    b. Dynamic
    c. Manual
    d. Static

Unit 3
TCP/IP Addressing and Subnets

Subnetting is one of the most complex of Internet Protocol (IP) network management tasks. Many a network administrator has maintained a Transmission Control Protocol (TCP)/IP network with little understanding of how to build subnetworks, instead depending on their Internet service provider (ISP) or carrier for these solutions.

Subnetting allows us to build smaller networks from a large IP address group. Why do we need smaller networks? Subnetting conserves our host addresses, controls broadcast traffic, and provides network scalability.

This unit introduces subnetting concepts, beginning with Class C networks, and building to subnetted Class A networks. We also discuss Classless Interdomain Routing (CIDR) and supernetting, an addressing scheme designed to conserve addresses and reduce routing table entries.

Lessons

1. Number Conversion
2. Subnetting Fundamentals
3. Subnetting Class C Networks
4. Subnetting Class B Networks
5. Subnetting Class A Networks
6. CIDR

Terms

address mask—An address mask is a bit mask used to select bits from an IP address for subnet addressing. The mask is 32 bits long and selects the network portion of the IP address and one or more bits of the local portion.

AND function—The AND function is a Boolean operator that only returns a true (1) value when both operands are true. Otherwise, the result is false (0).

base 10—See decimal.

base 2—See binary.

binary—The binary number system is one that uses just two unique digits, 1 and 0. Computers and other networking devices are based on the binary numbering system. All operations that are possible in the decimal system (addition, subtraction, multiplication, division) are equally possible in the binary system. For network devices, because of their electrical nature (on versus off), the binary system is more natural than the decimal system.

classful protocol—A classful protocol is a routing protocol that does not send along subnet mask information along with routing updates. A classful routing protocol cannot differentiate between a default network's network address and the all 0s subnet, making that subnet unusable.

Classless Interdomain Routing (CIDR)—CIDR replaces the older network addressing system based on classes A, B, and C. With CIDR, a single IP address can be used to designate many unique IP addresses. A CIDR IP address looks like a normal IP address except that it ends with a slash followed by a number, called the IP prefix. The IP prefix specifies how many addresses are covered by the CIDR address, with lower prefix values covering more addresses. For example, an IP prefix of /16, can be used to address 256 former Class C addresses.

classless protocol—A classless protocol is a routing protocol that passes subnet mask information with its routing updates; this makes subnetting more efficient. CIDR uses classless protocols.

convergence—Convergence is the speed and ability of a group of internetworking devices running a specific routing protocol to agree on the topology of an internetwork after a change in that topology.

decimal—Decimal refers to numbers in base 10 (the numbers we use in everyday life), represented by the digits 0–9. Decimal numbers are more natural for us to work with, thus most network devices perform binary-to-decimal and decimal-to-binary conversion for us.

dotted decimal notation—Dotted decimal notation is the syntactic representation for a 32-bit integer that consists of four 8-bit numbers with periods (dots) separating them. Many TCP/IP application programs accept dotted decimal notation in place of destination computer names (205.169.85.200).

least significant bit (LSB)—In a binary number, the LSB is the bit position with the lowest place value (2^0).

most significant bit (MSB)—In a binary number, the MSB is the bit position with the highest place value. In an 8-bit number, the MSB in the bit position with the place value of 2^7.

multicast—Multicast is a technique that allows copies of a single packet to be passed to a select subset of all possible destinations. Some hardware (such as Ethernet) supports multicast by allowing a network interface to belong to one or more multicast groups. IP supports an internet multicast facility.

Network Address Translation (NAT)—NAT is an Internet standard that enables a LAN to use one set of IP addresses for internal traffic and a second set of addresses for external traffic. A network device, such as a router or a firewall, located where the LAN meets the external network, translates the internal addresses to external addresses, and external to internal. NAT serves two main purposes: it provides a type of firewall by hiding internal IP addresses and enables a company to use more internal IP addresses than ICANN has assigned them. Since these addresses are used internally only, there is no possibility of conflict with IP addresses used by other companies and organizations.

network mask—The network mask is the number of mask bits in an IP address class used to determine the network on which a host resides. The mask octets set to all 1s determines the network, while the mask octets set to all 0s determines the host.

OR function—The OR function is a Boolean operator that returns a true (1) when the operands are both true, or when either is true and the other is false (0). The only time the OR function results in a false condition is when both operands are false.

routed protocol—A routed protocol is one that is routed across an internetwork. Routed protocols contain source and destination network and host addresses, in the form of logical addresses, to enable network devices to move data from its source host and network to the destination network and host.

routing protocol—A routing protocol is a protocol that implements the movement of Layer 3 protocol traffic across an internetwork. Routing protocols gather network path information from neighboring network devices and use this information to determine the best path over which to forward traffic towards its destination.

subnet address— Subnet address is an extension of the IP addressing scheme that allows a site to use a single IP network address for multiple physical networks. Gateways and hosts using subnet addressing interpret the local portion of the address by dividing it into a physical network portion and host portion.

subnetwork—A subnetwork is a smaller network created by borrowing host bits (subnetting), from a larger Class A, B, or C network.

supernet—A supernet is an aggregate of smaller, classful networks presented to a border router as a single, routing table entry. Supernetting is the basis for CIDR.

Lesson 1—Number Conversion

Although we write IP addresses as dotted decimal numbers (192.168.0.0), network devices work with these addresses in their binary form (11000000101010000000000000000000). For us to understand how routers work with subnets, we must be able to work with IP addresses in both decimal and binary forms. This lesson reviews essential concepts related to binary-to-decimal and decimal-to-binary number conversion.

Objectives

At the end of this lesson you will be able to:

- Convert decimal numbers to binary
- Convert binary numbers to decimal

Key Point

To work with subnets, we must understand the router's binary number system.

Decimal to Binary Conversion

In the base 10 (decimal) numbering system, each character position has a placeholder value represented by a power of 10. For example, the decimal number 1,679 is represented in the base 10 numbering system as:

Power of 10	1×10^3	6×10^2	7×10^1	9×10^0
Value	1,000	600	70	9

Note: The 10^0 power is always equal to 1.

Summing the resultant values gives us the original decimal number, 1,679:

1,000 + 600 + 70 + 9 = 1,679

In binary, each position has a value represented by a power of 2 rather than a power of 10, as in the base 10 system. For example, the above number represented in binary appears as follows:

Power of 2	2^{10}	2^9	2^8	2^7	2^6	2^5	2^4	2^3	2^2	2^1	2^0
Binary Number	1	1	0	1	0	0	0	1	1	1	1
Decimal Value	1,024	512	0	128	0	0	0	8	4	2	1

Note: The 2^0 power is always equal to 1.

Summing the resultant place values gives us in the original decimal number, 1,679:

1,024 + 512 + 0 + 128 + 0 + 0 + 0 + 8 + 4 + 2 + 1 = 1,679

How did we make the conversion from the original decimal number to binary? One method we can use for performing this conversion is the divide by two process.

Divide by Two

In the divide by two process, we lay out our conversion problem as follows.

- Decimal number/base = quotient, remainder
- Quotient/base = quotient, remainder, etc.

Using the above example, we start the decimal to binary conversion process.

1. Divide the decimal number 1,679 by the base, 2.

   1,679 divided by 2 = 839, remainder 1

   The result, 839, is an odd number, and the remainder is 1.
2. Next, divide the quotient, 839 by the base, 2, again.

   839 divided by 2 = 419, remainder 1

   The result again is an odd number with a remainder of 1.
3. Continue on, dividing the results by the base. Note the remainders, whether a 1 or a 0, on the right.

   1,679 divided by 2 = 839, remainder 1

   839 divided by 2 = 419, remainder 1

419 divided by 2 = 209, remainder 1

209 divided by 2 = 104, remainder 1

104 divided by 2 = 52, remainder 0

52 divided by 2 = 26, remainder 0

26 divided by 2 = 13, remainder 0

13 divided by 2 = 6, remainder 1

6 divided by 2 = 3, remainder 0

3 divided by 2 = 1, remainder 1

1 divided by 2 = 0.5 (effectively 0), remainder 1

4. Stop the division process when the quotient equals a fraction, in other words, the quotient divided by the base is no longer a whole number. List the final remainder as a whole number.
5. To finish the exercise, carry down the remainders, starting from top to bottom, arranging them from right to left. The right most remainder character becomes the binary number's least significant bit (LSB) and the left most character becomes the most significant bit (MSB). The resulting binary number looks as follows:

   11010001111

This is the binary representation of the decimal number 1,679.

Binary to Decimal Conversion

To convert binary to decimal, the simplest method is to sum the decimal representation of each binary place value. Working with our example, we express each binary bit position as its decimal equivalent value:

Powers of 2	2^{10}	2^9	2^8	2^7	2^6	2^5	2^4	2^3	2^2	2^1	2^0
Binary Number	1	1	0	1	0	0	0	1	1	1	1
Decimal Value	1,024	512	0	128	0	0	0	8	4	2	1

Summing the resultant place values results in the original decimal number, 1,679:

1,024 + 512 + 0 + 128 + 0 + 0 + 0 + 8 + 4 + 2 + 1 = 1,679

Decimal to Binary Conversion Related to IP Addressing

In working with IP addresses, particularly when building subnets, we frequently have to convert decimal IP address values to binary, or binary representations to decimal. The following are examples of each.

Example 1: Convert the address 64.16.8.32 to binary.

Represent each octet as its binary equivalent:

1. First octet

   64 divided by 2 = 32, remainder 0

   32 divided by 2 = 16, remainder 0

   16 divided by 2 = 8, remainder 0

   8 divided by 2 = 4, remainder 0

   4 divided by 2 = 2, remainder 0

   2 divided by 2 = 1, remainder 0

   1 divided by 2 = 0, remainder 1

   Result: 01000000

Note: Remember to include leading 0s as placeholders, so the binary result is always 8 characters.

2. Second octet

   16 divided by 2 = 8, remainder 0

   8 divided by 2 = 4, remainder 0

   4 divided by 2 = 2, remainder 0

   2 divided by 2 = 1, remainder 0

   1 divided by 2 = 0, remainder 1

   Result: 00010000

3. Third octet

   8 divided by 2 = 4, remainder 0

   4 divided by 2 = 2, remainder 0

   2 divided by 2 = 1, remainder 0

   1 divided by 2 = 0, remainder 1

   Result: 00001000

4. Fourth octet

    32 divided by 2 = 16, remainder 0

    16 divided by 2 = 8, remainder 0

    8 divided by 2 = 4, remainder 0

    4 divided by 2 = 2, remainder 0

    2 divided by 2 = 1, remainder 0

    1 divided by 2 = 0, remainder 1

    Result: 00100000

The resulting binary IP address is:

01000000.00010000.00001000.00100000

Example 2: Convert the binary IP address 10001000.00100000.01000000.00000111 to its decimal representation.

Convert each octet to its decimal equivalent:

1. First octet

Powers of 2	2^7	2^6	2^5	2^4	2^3	2^2	2^1	2^0
Binary Number	1	0	0	0	1	0	0	0
Decimal Value	128	0	0	0	8	0	0	0

10001000 = 128 + 0 + 0 + 0 + 8+ 0 + 0 + 0 = 136

2. Second octet

Powers of 2	2^7	2^6	2^5	2^4	2^3	2^2	2^1	2^0
Binary Number	0	0	1	0	0	0	0	0
Decimal Value	0	0	32	0	0	0	0	0

00100000 = 0 + 0 + 32 + 0 + 0+ 0 + 0 + 0 = 32

3. Third octet

Powers of 2	2^7	2^6	2^5	2^4	2^3	2^2	2^1	2^0
Binary Number	0	1	0	0	0	0	0	0
Decimal Value	0	64	0	0	0	0	0	0

01000000 = 0 + 64 + 0 + 0 + 0+ 0 + 0 + 0 = 64

4. Fourth octet

Powers of 2	2^7	2^6	2^5	2^4	2^3	2^2	2^1	2^0
Binary Number	0	0	0	0	0	1	1	1
Decimal Value	0	0	0	0	0	4	2	1

00000111 = 0 + 0 + 0 + 0 + 0+ 4 + 2 + 1 = 7

The result is the original decimal IP address, 136.32.64.7.

Activities

1. Which is another name for the decimal number system?
   a. Base 2
   b. Base 8
   c. Base 10
   d. Base 16
2. Which is another name for the binary number system?
   a. Base 2
   b. Base 8
   c. Base 10
   d. Base 16
3. What is the decimal value of the binary number 1000?
   a. 64
   b. 16
   c. 8
   d. 4
4. What is the decimal equivalent of the binary number 1010?
   a. 12
   b. 10
   c. 6
   d. 5
5. What is the binary equivalent of the decimal number 129?
   a. 10001000
   b. 10010000
   c. 11001000
   d. 10000001
6. What is the binary equivalent of the decimal number 254?
   a. 11111110
   b. 01111111
   c. 10111111
   d. 00111111

7. Match the decimal place value with the binary placeholder value.

   2 ____

   128 ____

   1 ____

   4 ____

   32 ____

   16 ____

   64 ____

   8 ____

   2^7

   2^6

   2^5

   2^4

   2^3

   2^2

   2^1

   2^0

Extended Activities

1. Convert the following IP addresses from decimal to binary.

   a. 172.68.10.2

   ____

   b. 10.0.12.3

   ____

   c. 127.0.0.1

   ____

d. 192.168.200.0

____

e. 13.45.36.128

____

2. Convert the following binary addresses to decimal.

a. 10000000.01010101.10100000.00001111

____

b. 00011100.00010001.01000010.11001110

____

c. 01110011.11001000. 00101100.00000010

____

d. 00101110.10110000.11111100.11111111

____

e. 11011110.00111111.10111100.00011100

____

Lesson 2—Subnetting Fundamentals

Subnets are logical subdivisions of a single Internet network number. For technical or administrative reasons, many organizations divide their TCP/IP networks into several smaller network segments. We use networking devices, such as routers, to connect these smaller networks. The main advantage of subnetting is to provide IP addressing flexibility.

Objectives

At the end of this lesson you will be able to:

- Define subnet addressing
- Explain basic subnetting principles
- Recognize when a network requires subnetting
- Describe IP broadcast addresses

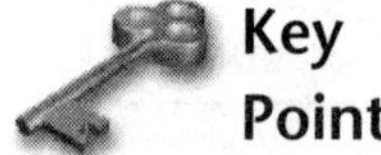

Key Point

A subnet is a network subdivision.

The Value of Subnetting

The Open Systems Interconnection (OSI) model Network Layer is responsible for moving data through internetworks. Remember that for devices to communicate over a routed network, their network protocols must supply them a Layer 3 address. Through the Layer 3 protocols, organizations build a hierarchical addressing scheme. This hierarchical addressing allows networks to easily scale from few to many hosts, and across geographical locations. Network Layer protocols provide a means of routing data between networks, and work with Layer 3 devices to control broadcast traffic.

When an organization does not need Internet access, they can build their TCP/IP network with the three private IP address ranges. However, when an organization wishes to connect to the Internet, they must lease or purchase a routable Class A, B, or C network number from their ISP, carrier, or the Internet Corporation for Assigned Names and Numbers (ICANN).

The IP Address Crisis

Many of you have likely heard the world is running short of available IP addresses. In fact, if each organization needing Internet access used an entire Class A, B, or C network address, less than 17 million network segments could be uniquely addressed before all the IP network addresses were depleted. Additionally, many host addresses would be wasted in the process. For example, if a small organization of 256 hosts owned an entire Class B address, they would leave over 65,000 host addresses unused. Subnetting, along with CIDR and Network Address Translation (NAT) (discussed in more detail in later lessons), has helped mitigate this problem by allowing organizations to segment their TCP/IP networks and more efficiently utilize their available host addresses.

Why Multiple Network Segments?

There are good reasons why an organization would need multiple network segments. If they grow significantly, their local network segment traffic can increase to the point where it becomes unmanageable. Many businesses run networks consisting of several hundred segments, all assigned their own network addresses. These addresses usually come from a larger single network address, such as a Class A or B address. Global enterprises need some method of communicating between remote sites. If they wish to communicate over the public Internet, they must somehow break up their assigned network addresses. Subnetting allows network administrators to break up a single network address into smaller network addresses, creating router-connected network segments, all with their own unique network address space.

Interconnection of TCP/IP Networks

To interconnect multiple TCP/IP networks across routers, we must assign each network a different network address. We may create subnets from any of the Class A, B, or C network addresses.

For example, in the Subnet Addressing Diagram, the network's administrator has created two subnetworks from a single Class B network address, 135.15.0.0, using the network address's third byte (135.15.x.0). The router receives all inbound traffic for Network 135.15.0.0 and selects the correct outbound interface based on this subnetted third byte (the subnet identifier, or subnet portion, of the network address).

If the network had not been broken into subnets, it would have required each network segment to have a separate Class B network address. Depending on the number of hosts on each segment, many host addresses could have remained unused.

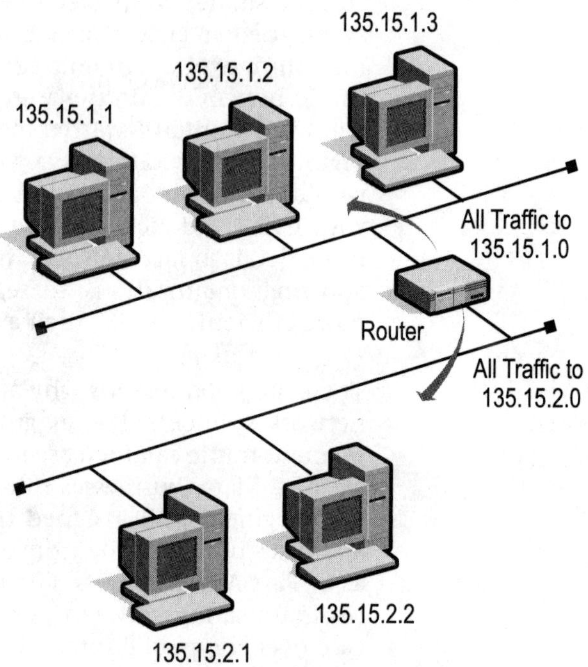

Subnet Addressing

When we subnet, we divide an IP network address's host portion into two parts, as shown on the Subnetted Address Diagram.

- One left part is used to identify the subnet address portion.
- One right part is used to identify the host address portion.

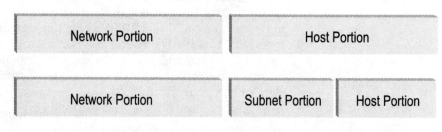

Original Network Address

Network Portion	Host Portion	
Network Portion	Subnet Portion	Host Portion

Subnetted Address

We subnet by borrowing bits from the host address portion to create the subnet address portion. Recall that a router uses the network portion to determine the network on which a host resides:

- Class A network portion—the first octet
- Class B network portion—the first and second octets
- Class C network portion—the first, second, and third octets

The remaining octet(s) are the host portion, which identifies the destination node. Network devices determine these portions using the network mask.

The Network Mask

A network mask (net mask) is a 32-bit binary number network device used to isolate an IP address's network portion from its host portion.

Each IP address class is assigned a default net mask, as shown in the Default Net Mask Table.

Default Net Mask

Class	Decimal	Binary
A	255.0.0.0	11111111.00000000.00000000.00000000
B	255.255.0.0	11111111.11111111.00000000.00000000
C	255.255.255.0	11111111.11111111.11111111.00000000

Note the octets in each class where the net mask reads 255 (all binary 1s) and where it reads 0 (all binary 0s). In Class A addresses, the first octet reads "255" while the last three octets read "0.0.0." The binary 1s in the mask designate the network portion, and the binary 0s designate the host portion.

Network devices make the distinction between the network and host portions by performing a logical AND function on the binary network address and the net mask. Let us return to the Subnet Addressing Diagram as an example:

1. Here we start with a Class B address (the first octet falls in the Class B address range). Let us represent the host IP address 135.15.2.1 in binary:

   135.15.2.1 = 10000111.00001111.00000010.00000001

2. Next, let us represent in binary the default Class B net mask, 255.255.0.0:

   255.255.0.0 = 11111111.11111111.00000000.00000000

We want to isolate the IP address's network portion. To perform this isolation, a network device "ANDs" the IP address with the net mask. When "ANDing" binary digits, devices use the following Binary AND Truth Table:

Binary AND Truth
(A AND B = Result)

A	B	Result
0	0	0
1	0	0
0	1	0
1	1	1

The only time the AND function provides a 1 result is when both "ANDed" bits are 1s; otherwise, the function's result is 0.

3. Let us find the network portion by "ANDing" the host address with the net mask:

   10000111.00001111.00000010.00000001 = 135.15.2.1

   <u>11111111.11111111.00000000.00000000</u> = 255.255.0.0

   10000111.00001111.00000000.00000000 = 135.15.0.0

4. Finally, we convert the binary AND result to decimal and find that the network address portion is 135.15.0.0; this is the default network address for this Class B IP address. Notice that the AND process sets the host bits to 0, while the network portion bits "fall through" in their original states (1 or 0).

Creating Subnets

A subnet mask is a modified net mask that extends into a network address's host portion. Just as we use the default net mask to determine the network address portion of an IP address, we can use extended net masks to create subnet masks. We use the subnet mask to determine which bits from an address's host portion define the subnet portion. This subnet portion then becomes part of the subnetted network address's network portion.

What does all that mean? Let us return to the Subnet Addressing Diagram. We have broken up the 135.15.0.0 Class B network into two separate subnetworks. We do this by borrowing bits from the default host portion and assigning them to the network portion.

The default network address is 135.15.0.0. We wish to create 2^8, or 256, subnetworks. We do this by borrowing 8 bits from the third octet and assigning them to the 135.15.0.0 network address's network portion. The resultant subnet mask looks as follows:

11111111.11111111.*11111111*.00000000 or 255.255.*255*.0

When we borrow the 8 bits from the host portion, we set them to all 1s. We must always borrow host bits in descending order, starting from the left most bit position (MSB) and working to the right (LSB), as shown in the Borrowed Bits Diagram.

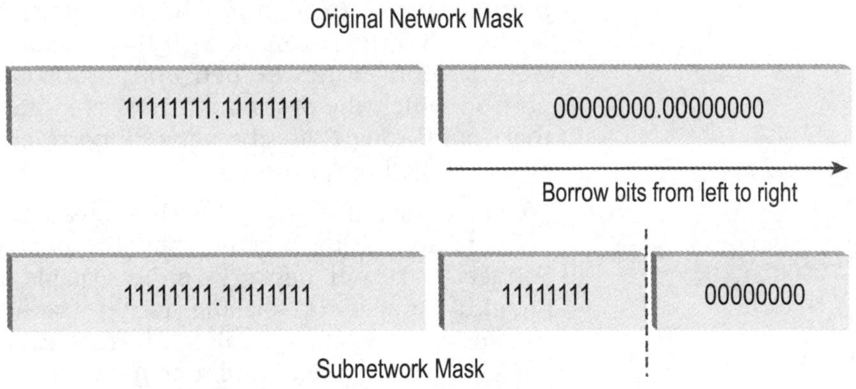

Borrowed Bits

The subnet mask's decimal representation now shows the third octet as 255 instead of 0. When we AND our IP address with the subnet mask, the first three octets "fall through":

10000111.00001111.00000010.00000001

11111111.11111111.11111111.00000000

10000111.00001111.00000010.00000000 = 135.15.2.0

The result of subnetting the 135.15.0.0 network is that host 135.15.2.1 is now located on subnet 135.15.2.0. The router in the diagram connects it to the other network we created, 135.15.1.0, when we set our subnet mask.

Recapping What We Have Learned Thus Far

Now is a good time to review what we have covered thus far.

Each IP address Class has a default net mask, as shown in the Default Net Masks Table.

Default Net Masks

Class	Decimal	Binary
A	255.0.0.0	11111111.00000000.00000000.00000000
B	255.255.0.0	11111111.11111111.00000000.00000000
C	255.255.255.0	11111111.11111111.11111111.00000000

The net mask bits are set to 1 to identify the IP address's network portion, and 0 to identify the host portion. Layer 3 network devices AND the net mask with the IP address to isolate the network portion, using the network portion to identify the router port on which the destination host is located. The resulting bits that "fall through" are the network portion, while the bits set to all 0s are the host portion.

We create subnets when we wish to create more flexibility in our network addressing scheme than the default net mask allows. Subnets make our networks more scalable and help us control broadcast traffic by placing routers between our local data streams. This isolates local traffic to local segments, and only passes traffic destined for remote networks.

A subnet is a subset of a major Class A, B, or C network. We create subnets by borrowing bits from the network address's host portion, working in descending bit order from left to right. Network devices AND the IP address with the subnet mask to determine an IP address's network and subnet portions. The bits that fall through are the newly created network portion, encompassing both the original network portion and the new subnet portion, while the remaining 0 bits define the host portion.

Maximum Usable Subnets and Hosts

The beauty of subnetting also makes it somewhat of a beast. Subnetting does not limit us to a certain subnet size, indeed it provides us a great deal of flexibility in determining the number of subnetworks we can create and the number of hosts we can support on each subnetwork. These numbers vary by the network address Class, as the Subnet and Hosts Table lists.

Subnets and Hosts

Address Class	Maximum Number of Hosts	Maximum Number of Subnetworks
A	16,777,214	4,194,304
B	65,534	16,384
C	254	64

Why the discrepancy between the maximum number of hosts and the maximum number of subnetworks? When we borrow from the host portion, we must leave at least two host bits. Recall that our maximum number of hosts on a default network is 2 to the power of the number of host bits, minus 2 ($2^{\text{host bits}}-2$). This means when we borrow bits, we have to leave behind at least 4 (2^2) host addresses per subnetwork. If we leave behind fewer than 4 host addresses, then when we subtract the subnet's network and broadcast addresses, we are left with zero hosts. For example, if we were to leave only 1 host bit, when we subtract the network and broadcast addresses, the number of addresses available for host use is 0 ($2^1 - 2 = 0$).

The maximum number of hosts per subnet depends on the number of subnets we create. Because Class C subnets are the easiest to work with, we will use Class C addresses as an example. The Class C Hosts vs. Subnets Table illustrates the relationship between the available hosts and number of subnets.

Class C Hosts vs. Subnets

Borrowed Bits	Maximum Number of Subnets Created/ Usable*	Maximum Number of Hosts per Subnet/ Usable
0	0 (default address)	2^8 = 256/ 254 usable
1	2^1 = 2/ 0 usable	2^7 = 128/0 usable
2	2^2 = 4/ 2 usable	2^6 = 64/ 62 usable
3	2^3 = 8/ 6 usable	2^5 = 32/ 30 usable

Class C Hosts vs. Subnets (Continued)

Borrowed Bits	Maximum Number of Subnets Created/ Usable*	Maximum Number of Hosts per Subnet/ Usable
4	2^4 = 16/ 14 usable	2^4 = 16/ 14 usable
5	2^5 = 32/ 30 usable	2^3 = 8/ 6 usable
6	2^6 = 64/ 62 usable	2^2 = 4/ 2 usable
7	2^7 = 128/ 0 usable	2^1 = 2/ 0 usable
8	2^8 = 256/ 0 usable	2^0 = 1/ 0 usable
*The first and last subnets are unusable. See below.		

Several things in this table are important for us to notice:

- We show nine possible bit borrowing conditions. The first is where we use the default Class C subnet mask, and have 8 bits available for hosts (254 usable hosts). The remaining entries show the results of borrowing the number of host bits the first column lists. The last condition is impossible, because borrowing 8 bits leaves us with 0 host bits left.
- The usable subnets are 2 subnets less than the maximum number of subnets. Some routing protocols, called Classful protocols, cannot differentiate between an all 0 subnet (the subnet portion is all 0s) and a default network address. For example, a Classful router would think the address 135.15.0.0 with the net mask 255.255.0.0 is the same address as 135.15.0.0 with a subnet mask of 255.255.255.0. Additionally, Classful routers cannot tell the difference between an all 1s subnet portion and the default broadcast address. Therefore, we show that when we borrow 1 bit, the subnetworks are unusable (2 – 2 = 0).
- Remember that we have to leave at least 2 host bits, so when we subtract the network and broadcast addresses, we still have at least 2 usable hosts left. Therefore, we cannot borrow 7 bits, as this leaves only 1 host bit ($2^1 - 2 = 0$).

This leaves us with five usable Class C subnet entries, as shown in the Usable Class C Subnets and Hosts Table.

Usable Class C Subnets and Hosts

Borrowed Bits	Number of Usable Subnets Created	Number of Usable Hosts/Subnet	Usable Networks * Usable Hosts	Resulting Subnet Mask
2	2^2 = 4, 2 usable	2^6 = 64, 62 usable	124	255.255.255.192
3	2^3 = 8, 6 usable	2^5 = 32, 30 usable	180	255.255.255.224
4	2^4 = 16, 14 usable	2^4 = 16, 14 usable	196	255.255.255.240
5	2^5 = 32, 30 usable	2^3 = 8, 6 usable	180	255.255.255.248
6	2^6 = 64, 62 usable	2^2 = 4, 2 usable	124	255.255.255.252

Here we have added a column to show the total usable hosts corresponding to the bits borrowed (Usable Networks * Usable Hosts). We gain or lose usable hosts depending on the number of bits we borrow. The usable subnet masks for a Class C network address are as follows:

255.255.255.192, borrow 2 bits

255.255.255.224, borrow 3 bits

255.255.255.240, borrow 4 bits

255.255.255.248, borrow 5 bits

255.255.255.252, borrow 6 bits

IP Prefixes

We can represent the subnet mask in another manner, as a prefix rather than a mask. Rather than writing out the subnet mask, for instance, 255.255.255.240, we can represent the same mask as "/28." This is a shorthand notation for the combined network and subnet mask.

The number 28 in our example represents the total number of the subnet mask bits set to 1. Let us represent the subnet mask 255.255.255.240 in binary:

11111111.11111111.11111111.1111|0000 = 255.255.255.240

We place a separator between the mask's last binary 1 and its first binary 0. We count the number of 1s in the binary subnet mask, and determine they equal 28. Rather than writing out the subnet mask in four decimal octets, we can write it as "/28." Therefore, to represent address 192.14.16.8 on subnet 255.255.255.240, we can write it as 192.14.16.8/28.

The Complete Class C Subnets Table ties this Class C subnetting information together, while the Complete Class B and A Subnets Tables show the Class B and A subnetting information.

Complete Class C Subnets

Borrowed Bits	Subnet Mask	Prefix	Usable Subnets Created	Usable Hosts/Subnet	Usable Networks * Usable Hosts
2	255.255.255.192	/26	2 usable	62 usable	124
3	255.255.255.224	/27	6 usable	30 usable	180
4	255.255.255.240	/28	14 usable	14 usable	196
5	255.255.255.248	/29	30 usable	6 usable	180
6	255.255.255.252	/30	62 usable	2 usable	124

Complete Class B Subnets

Borrowed Bits	Subnet Mask	Prefix	Usable Subnets Created	Usable Hosts/Subnet	Usable Networks * Usable Hosts
2	255.255.192.0	/18	2 usable	16,382 usable	32,764
3	255.255.224.0	/19	6 usable	8,190 usable	49,140
4	255.255.240.0	/20	14 usable	4,094 usable	57,316
5	255.255.248.0	/21	30 usable	2,046 usable	61,380
6	255.255.252.0	/22	62 usable	1,022 usable	63,364
7	255.255.254.0	/23	126 usable	510 usable	64,260
8	255.255.255.0	/24	254 usable	254 usable	64,516

Complete Class B Subnets (Continued)

Borrowed Bits	Subnet Mask	Prefix	Usable Subnets Created	Usable Hosts/Subnet	Usable Networks * Usable Hosts
9	255.255.255.128	/25	510 usable	126 usable	64,260
10	255.255.255.192	/26	1,022 usable	62 usable	63,364
11	255.255.255.224	/27	2,046 usable	30 usable	61,380
12	255.255.255.240	/28	4,094 usable	14 usable	57,316
13	255.255.255.248	/29	8,190 usable	6 usable	49,140
14	255.255.255.252	/30	16,382 usable	2 usable	32,764

Complete Class A Subnets

Borrowed Bits	Subnet Mask	Prefix	Usable Subnets Created	Usable Hosts/Subnet	Usable Networks *Usable Hosts
2	255.192.0.0	/10	2 usable	4,194,302 usable	8,388,604
3	255.224.0.0	/11	6 usable	2,097,150 usable	15,282,900
4	255.240.0.0	/12	14 usable	1,048,574 usable	14,680,036
5	255.248.0.0	/13	30 usable	524,286 usable	15,728,580
6	255.252.0.0	/14	62 usable	262,142 usable	16,252,804
7	255.254.0.0	/15	126 usable	131,070 usable	16,514,820
8	255.255.0.0	/16	254 usable	65,534 usable	16,645,636
9	255.255.128.0	/17	510 usable	32,766 usable	16,710,660
10	255.255.192.0	/18	1,022 usable	16,382 usable	16,742,404
11	255.255.224.0	/19	2,046 usable	8,190 usable	16,756,740
12	255.255.240.0	/20	4,094 usable	4,094 usable	16,760,836
13	255.255.248.0	/21	8,190 usable	2,046 usable	16,756,740

Complete Class A Subnets (Continued)

Borrowed Bits	Subnet Mask	Prefix	Usable Subnets Created	Usable Hosts/Subnet	Usable Networks *Usable Hosts
14	255.255.252.0	/22	16,382 usable	1,022 usable	16,742,404
15	255.255.254.0	/23	32,766 usable	510 usable	16,710,660
16	255.255.255.0	/24	65,534 usable	254 usable	16,645,636
17	255.255.255.128	/25	131,070 usable	126 usable	16,514,820
18	255.255.255.192	/26	262,142 usable	62 usable	16,252,804
19	255.255.255.224	/27	524,286 usable	30 usable	15,728,580
20	255.255.255.240	/28	1,048,574 usable	14 usable	14,680,036
21	255.255.255.248	/29	2,097,150 usable	6 usable	12,582,900
22	255.255.255.252	/30	4,194,302 usable	2 usable	8,388,604

Determining Subnet Requirements

We now have something of an idea of how subnetting works, but how do we know how many subnets we need? Because we have the three Complete Class A, B, and C Subnet Tables above, we simply determine the number of hosts or networks we need to support, and look these figures up in the tables.

Suppose you work for a company that owns a Class B address. The Chief Information Officer (CIO), your boss, tells you the company is planning to expand from their current single site to a dozen (12) sites located across the county. He and the managing partners want you to break up their existing Class B address into enough subnets to support these new sites and provide for 100-percent growth over the next two years. They plan only 300 hosts per subnet initially, but again want you to allow for 100-percent growth. How do you meet their requirements while most efficiently utilizing the Class B addresses to avoid unused hosts?

Looking in the Complete Class B Subnet Table, we find two potential row entries, shown in the Complete Class B Subnet Table Excerpt.

Complete Class B Subnet Table Excerpt

Borrowed Bits	Subnet Mask	Prefix	Usable Subnets Created	Usable Hosts/Subnet	Usable Networks * Usable Hosts
5	255.255.248.0	/21	30 usable	2,046 usable	61,380
6	255.255.252.0	/22	62 usable	1,022 usable	63,364

The first entry, where we borrow 5 bits, provides for 30 subnets. This allows you to meet all of your boss's existing and future subnetting requirements. However, it also provides 2,046 hosts per subnet, well above the projected 600 hosts per subnet. This leaves over 1,400 hosts per subnet unused.

The second entry provides 62 subnets, well above the required 24. However, it only allows for 1,022 hosts per subnet, thus we leave only 422 hosts per subnet unused. Not only does this choice more efficiently use each subnet's available host addresses, but it also leaves much more room for network growth. The second choice is the best choice, for both reasons.

IP Broadcast Addresses

As we learned earlier, the network and/or host IP address portions cannot be set to all 1s. When this is the case, we create broadcast addresses, which are special purpose addresses networks use to pass data to multiple destinations simultaneously.

There are four IP broadcast address types:

- Limited broadcast—The address is set to 255.255.255.255. This address is used for configuring hosts at startup, such as when a host obtains an IP address from a Dynamic Host Configuration Protocol (DHCP) or Bootstrap Protocol (BOOTP) server.
- Nondirected broadcast—This address takes the form *netid*.255.255.255; for example, *126*.255.255.255. Networks use this address to send packets to all hosts on a specific network segment.

- Subnet-directed broadcast—In a subnetted network, a subnet-directed broadcast is limited to only those hosts on the specified subnet.
- All-subnets-directed broadcasts—On a subnetted internetwork, network devices can send broadcasts to all hosts on all subnets. This is now considered obsolete, and has been replaced by Class D multicast addresses.

Limited Broadcast

A packet sent to IP address 255.255.255.255 is classified as a "limited broadcast" packet. In a broadcast packet destined for the local network, the destination address network and host portions are all 1s (255.255.255.255). Limited broadcasts should never pass through a router, only through repeaters and Medium Access Control (MAC) Layer bridges.

Directed Broadcast

A packet sent to a destination IP address where only the host portion of the IP address is all 1s, such as 180.100.255.255, is classified as a "directed broadcast" packet. Directed broadcasts may pass through a router and will be broadcast to all hosts on the target network. Directed broadcast can be a network-directed or subnetwork-directed broadcast.

- A network-directed broadcast IP address has the host portion of the IP address as all 1s and a valid network portion. The broadcast reaches all hosts on the network.
- A subnetwork-directed broadcast IP address has the host portion of the IP address as all 1s, a valid network portion, and a valid subnet portion. The broadcast reaches all hosts on the subnet.

Activities

1. If we borrow 3 bits from a Class C network address, how many usable subnets have we created?
   a. 3
   b. 6
   c. 8
   d. 12
2. If we borrow 12 bits from a Class B address, how many usable subnets have we created?
   a. 2,046
   b. 2,048
   c. 4,094
   d. 4,096
3. AND the following network addresses and their corresponding network or subnet masks. Show the resulting network address in both binary and decimal.
   a. 193.100.56.3

      ____

      255.255.255.0

      ____

      Network address

      ____

   b. 214.69.15.6

      ____

      255.255.255.252

      ____

      Network address

      ____

c. 129.89.125.17

____

255.255.224.0

____

Network address

____

d. 101.56.110.41

____

255.255.0.0

____

Network address

____

e. 96.78.120.28

____

255.255.240.0

____

Network address

____

f. 52.91.130.6

____

255.0.0.0

____

Network address

____

4. Represent the following borrowed host bits as powers of 2 and their decimal equivalent. (Example, 6 $2^6 = 32$.)

   a. 2

   ____

   b. 4

   ____

   c. 10

   ____

   d. 8

   ____

   e. 20

   ____

   f. 12

   ____

5. Represent the following subnet masks with the appropriate IP prefixes.

   a. 255.224.0.0

   ____

   b. 255.254.0.0

   ____

   c. 255.255.128.0

   ____

   d. 255.255.248.0

   ____

   e. 255.255.254.0

   ____

   f. 255.255.255.192

   ____

6. List and explain reasons why an organization would subnet their TCP/IP network.

____

____

____

____

7. Explain the difference between a default net mask and a subnet mask.

____

____

____

____

8. Explain the difference between a limited and a directed broadcast address.

____

____

____

____

____

____

____

____

Extended Activity

1. Your customer is building a network to support 115 remote offices located around the world. They own the Class B address 190.17.0.0/16. They will initially support 200 hosts per subnet, but expect this to increase to 500 hosts per subnet in the next three years. Additionally, they want to reserve 10 networks for future offices.

   They ask you to plan their addressing scheme. You need to determine the subnet mask that will allow them to most efficiently utilize their available host addresses, while at the same time meeting their present and future network requirements.

   Which subnet mask will you choose? How many total and usable subnets and host will that create? How many hosts per subnet are left unused if your customer meets their growth projections? How many subnets are left over?

   ____

   ____

   ____

   ____

2. You are a major corporation's CIO. Your parent company recently merged with a competitor.

   You support a network consisting of 700 routed segments, created by subnetting a Class A network address. You will need to create 450 more segments from the same Class A address.

   You choose to rebuild your subnets. Your current subnet mask is 255.255.192.0. Which subnet mask will allow you to meet your subnetting requirements, while supporting no more than 4,094 hosts per subnet?

   ____

   ____

3. A major manufacturing company hires you to help them evaluate and resolve network performance issues on their home office campus. The Home Office Campus Network Diagram illustrates the network.

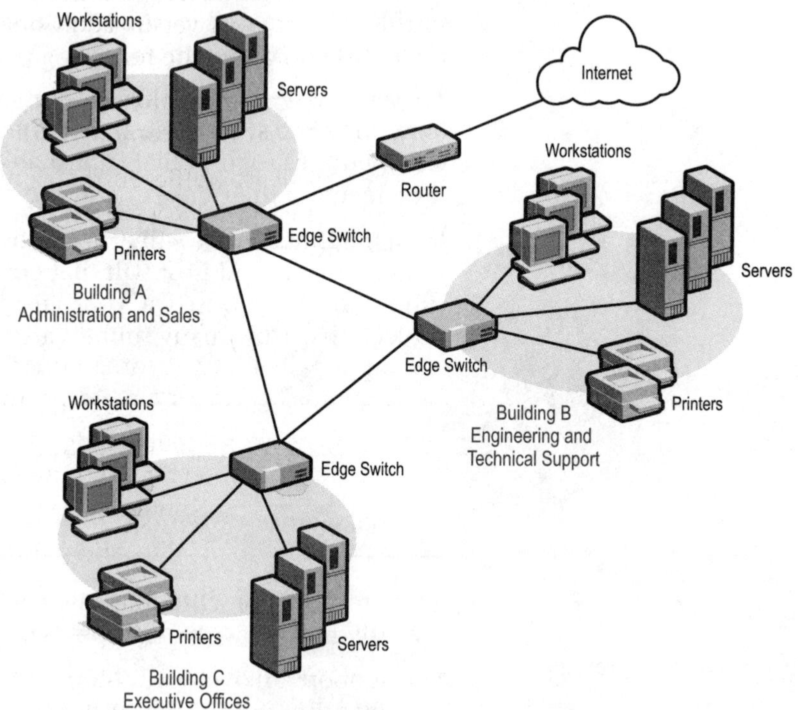

Home Office Campus Network

In your initial evaluation, you find the following:

- The campus network consists of 1,000 nodes (servers, workstations, and printers) scattered among three buildings.
- The network is flat, that is, the only network router is the one that connects the network to the Internet. Switches provide all other network connectivity.
- The network backbone is 100-megabits-per-second (Mbps) switched Ethernet, with fiber optic cabling connecting the buildings.
- Each building isolates collisions using a single, multiport, Layer 2 Ethernet switch.

- They own Class B address 131.28.0.0/16.
- They have users and services roughly arranged by workgroups, with each workgroup isolated to a specific area within a single building.

You decide to isolate network traffic by workgroup using subnetting and routers versus additional Layer 2 switches. You make this choice for the following reasons:

- The company plans 50-percent growth in all departments over the next five years.
- The broadcast traffic on the network measures over one-half the total network traffic during the busiest hours of the day.

You survey the network users and determine the workgroup locations and specific workgroup hosts are as follows:

- The administrative workgroup—Bldg. A. 77 workstations, 2 administrative servers, 15 printers
- The sales workgroup—Bldg. A. 40 workstations, 1 file server, 1 e-mail server, 10 printers
- The engineering workgroup—Bldg. B. 422 workstations, 4 file servers, 30 printers and plotters
- The technical support workgroup—Bldg. B. 300 workstations, 5 file servers, 2 communications servers, 20 printers
- The executive workgroup—Bldg. C. 45 workstations, 2 files servers, 2 communications servers, 22 printers

You recommend that they break up their network by workgroups, using routers to isolate broadcast traffic and creating subnets for each workgroup out of their existing Class B address. You must determine how many subnets to create and how many hosts each subnet must support. You will use a classful routing protocol and must allow for your customer's projected growth.

How many subnets will you create and how many hosts per subnet will they support?

____

____

____

____

Lesson 3—Subnetting Class C Networks

Now that we are familiar with subnetting terms and concepts, let us dig a little deeper. We start by subnetting Class C addresses. We introduce subnetting's intricacies, including determining each subnet's address ranges and identifying the network number on which an address resides.

Objectives

At the end of this lesson you will be able to:

- Determine a Class C subnet's valid IP address ranges
- Identify the subnet on which an address resides
- List each subnet's network and broadcast addresses

Key Point

Class C networks are the easiest to subnet but provide less addressing flexibility than either Class A or B subnets.

Determining Address Ranges

The Complete Class C Subnets Table shows the available Class C subnets.

Complete Class C Subnets

Borrowed Bits	Subnet Mask	Prefix	Usable Subnets Created	Usable Hosts/Subnet	Usable Networks * Usable Hosts
2	255.255.255.192	/26	2 usable	62 usable	124
3	255.255.255.224	/27	6 usable	30 usable	180
4	255.255.255.240	/28	14 usable	14 usable	196
5	255.255.255.248	/29	30 usable	6 usable	180
6	255.255.255.252	/30	62 usable	2 usable	124

Each subnet provides a certain number of usable hosts, and each host can (and must) have a unique IP address within the subnet. Recall that a host's IP address network portion must match its segment's network address; otherwise, it cannot communicate on that segment.

Network Address Ranges

For example, on a default Class C network with the network address 198.124.200.0, all hosts must have a network portion matching the network address's first three octets, *198.124.200*. If we assign a host on this segment an address of 199.124.200.3, this host cannot communicate with other hosts on this, or any other network segment. When we AND the default Class C net mask (255.255.255.0) with the host address 199.124.200.3, all bits fall through but the host portion. The decimal result is the network address 199.124.200.0:

11000111.01111100.11001000.00000011 = 199.124.200.3

<u>11111111.11111111.11111111.00000000</u> = 255.255.255.0

11000111.01111100.11001000.00000000 = 199.124.200.0

This network address, 199.124.200.0, does not match the original network address 198.124.200.0. The first network, 198.124.200.0, has a valid address range from 198.124.200.0 to 198.124.200.255. Any other address using the Class C network mask is on another network.

Subnetwork Address Ranges

Similarly, hosts on subnetworks must include in their IP address's network and subnet portions the same bit pattern as that of their subnet's network address.

Assume we have a host on a subnetted Class C network using the subnet mask 255.255.255.192. The subnet's network address is 204.56.178.64; we will talk about why this is the network address shortly. The host address is 204.56.178.126. How do we know if this host can communicate on the subnet?

1. Let us start from basics. Convert the subnet's network address to binary:

   204.56.178.64 = 11001100.00111000.10110010.01000000

2. Write the subnet mask in binary:

   255.255.255.192 = 11111111.11111111.11111111.11000000

3. AND them together:

   204.56.178.64 = 11001100.00111000.10110010.01000000

   255.255.255.192 = 11111111.11111111.11111111.11000000

   204.56.178.64 = 11001100.00111000.10110010.01000000

   The result is the network address 204.56.178.64.

4. To determine whether the host is on the same subnet, write the host address in binary:

   204.56.178.126 = 11001100.00111000.10110010.01111110

5. AND it with the subnet mask:

   11001100.00111000.10110010.01111110 = 204.56.178.126

   11111111.11111111.11111111.11000000 = 255.255.255.192

   11001100.00111000.10110010.01000000 = 204.56.178.64

   The bits that fall through match the network address bits shown in Step 3. Therefore, this address is on the same subnet, and the host can communicate across it. Address 204.56.178.126 falls within the 204.56.178.64 subnetwork's valid address range (204.56.178.64–204.56.178.127). We will build the range in the next section.

   Because we used the subnet mask 255.255.255.192 in the preceding example, to finish up the example let us explore all the usable subnets we can create with this mask. The Class C with 2 Borrowed Bits Table lists all the possible subnet address portion patterns available with the 255.255.255.192 subnet mask.

Class C with 2 Borrowed Bits

Network Address Portion			Subnetwork Portion	Host Portion	Decimal Address
11001100	00111000	10110010	00	0000000	204.56.178.0
11001100	00111000	10110010	01	0000000	204.56.178.64
11001100	00111000	10110010	10	0000000	204.56.178.128
11001100	00111000	10110010	11	0000000	204.56.178.192

Each of these individual subnetworks provides a range of addresses. These ranges begin with each subnet's network address and end with the subnet's broadcast address. Recall that the first and last default network addresses are unusable, because the host portion is set to all 0s or all 1s. Classful routers cannot differentiate between the default network address and the first subnet's network address; thus, the subnet portion cannot be all 0s. Similarly, because classful routers cannot tell the difference between the default network's broadcast address and the last subnet's broadcast address, the subnet portion cannot be all 1s. Therefore, the first and last subnetworks are unusable.

With the subnet mask 255.255.255.192, we have borrowed 2 bits from the default host portion. This leaves 6 bits for the hosts. We determine the number of hosts per subnet by expressing 2 to the power of the number of left over host bits, or $2^{(\text{host bits} - \text{bits borrowed})}$. The subnet mask 255.255.255.192 leaves us a maximum of 2^6 hosts, or 64 hosts maximum per subnet. We subtract 2 host addresses (the network and the broadcast addresses) to arrive at the total usable hosts per subnet, 62.

Building the Range

Let us build a Subnetting Exercise Table, and fill it out as we build our address ranges:

Subnetting Exercise

Target IP Address:		Subnet Mask:	
Subnet ID	**Network (Wire) Address**	**Subnet Usable Address Range**	**Broadcast Address**

- The Subnet ID column helps us identify the numeric network on which an address resides. This is mostly for identification purposes, providing an index for us to easily locate a subnetwork in the table.
- The Network Address column is where we place the first address in a subnet's address range. This is the address where the host portion is all 0s. Another term for network address is wire address. The wire address is the network segment's identifier.

- The Subnet Address Range column is where we identify our subnet's usable host addresses. These are the addresses where the host portion does not equal all 0s nor all 1s.
- The Broadcast Address column is where we identify the last address in the range, the broadcast address. The broadcast address is the address in the range where the host portion is all 1s.

Using the subnet mask 255.255.255.192, let us build the complete subnet table for our address 204.56.178.126.

Note: In practice, we rarely ever borrow just 2 bits. This creates just 2 usable subnets, leaving only 124 of the 256 total Class C host addresses usable. We use this subnet mask as an example and work up to more complex problems later in this and subsequent lessons.

1. Start by numbering the Network ID column, starting at 1, and ending with the maximum number of subnets our mask allows.

Subnetting Exercise

Target IP Address: 204.56.178.126		Subnet Mask: 255.255.255.192	
Network ID	**Network (Wire) Address**	**Subnet Usable Address Range**	**Broadcast Address**
1			
2			
3			
4			

The subnet mask 255.255.255.192 creates a maximum of 4 subnets ($2^2 = 4$), thus we number the column's cells from 1 to 4.

2. Next, we determine the first wire address and fill in the appropriate cell.

Subnetting Exercise

Target IP Address: 204.56.178.126		Subnet Mask: 255.255.255.192	
Network ID	**Network (Wire) Address**	**Subnet Usable Address Range**	**Broadcast Address**
1	204.56.178.0		
2			
3			
4			

Our example host address is 204.56.178.126. When we "ANDed" this address with our subnet mask, the resulting subnetwork address was 204.56.178.64; this was the first usable wire address. However, when building subnet tables, we always start with the first subnet address the subnet mask creates; this is the address where both the subnet portion and the host portion are all 0s. This address, when we look at the Class C with 2 Borrowed Bits Table, is 204.56.178.0.

Note: Though it may seem pointless to include unusable subnets and addresses in the table, their inclusion provides an addressing starting and ending point that will help us determine and fill in each subnet's valid address ranges.

3. Next we fill in the last broadcast address. This is the last address on the last subnet, where the host and subnetwork portions are all 1s.

Subnetting Exercise

Target IP Address: 204.56.178.126		**Subnet Mask: 255.255.255.192**	
Network ID	**Network (Wire) Address**	**Subnet Usable Address Range**	**Broadcast Address**
1	204.56.178.0		
2			
3			
4			204.56.178.255

Note that the first wire address and the last broadcast address are always the first and last addresses under the default network mask, regardless of the subnet mask. We can always fill in these cells using this rule. Reverting back to our default networks for a moment, a Class C default network starts at x.y.z.0 and ends at x.y.z.255. These will always be the first wire address and the last broadcast address in a set of subnets.

4. Now that we have the first wire and the last broadcast addresses, we need to determine the first subnet's broadcast address. We know that with this subnet mask, 255.255.255.192, we have 6 host bits left over; $2^6 = 64$, thus each subnet contains a maximum of 64 hosts (62 usable). We start at 0 when we count hosts in the first subnet, thus to cover all 64 of the first subnet's host addresses, we end our first range at 63.

Subnetting Exercise

Target IP Address: 204.56.178.126		**Subnet Mask: 255.255.255.192**	
Network ID	**Network (Wire) Address**	**Subnet Usable Address Range**	**Broadcast Address**
1	204.56.178.0		204.56.178.63
2			
3			
4			204.56.178.255

If you were to count on your fingers (and your neighbor's fingers, etc.) from 0 to 63, you would need 64 fingers to represent each symbol. This results in the last address in the first range, 204.56.178.63. If you were to go back and AND the address 204.56.178.63 with the subnet mask, you would find that the first wire address and this address's fall through bits are identical. Additionally, this address's host portion is set to all 1s, designating a broadcast address.

If you were to represent the subnet's address range in binary, it would appear as follows:

00000000 = 0 (network, hosts bits all 0s, unusable)

00000001 = 1

00000010 = 2

...

00111110 = 62

00111111 = 63 (broadcast, hosts bits all 1s, unusable)

5. Notice that we now have both the first (wire) address and the last (broadcast) address in the first subnet. All we need do now is fill in the remaining addresses. Because our range spans the addresses 204.56.178.0–204.57.178.63, the remaining usable addresses, excluding .0 and .63, range from 204.56.178.1–204.57.178.62.

Subnetting Exercise

Target IP Address: 204.56.178.126		Subnet Mask: 255.255.255.192	
Network ID	**Network (Wire) Address**	**Subnet Usable Address Range**	**Broadcast Address**
1	204.56.178.0	204.56.178.1–204.56.178.62	204.56.178.63
2			
3			
4			204.56.178.255

6. We know the last address in the first subnet, thus we can drop down one row, beneath the first wire address, and fill in the the second subnet's wire address. The IP address 204.56.178.64 follows 204.56.178.63. The host portion in address 204.56.178.64 are all 0s.

Subnetting Exercise

Target IP Address: 204.56.178.126		Subnet Mask: 255.255.255.192	
Network ID	**Network (Wire) Address**	**Subnet Usable Address Range**	**Broadcast Address**
1	204.56.178.0	204.56.178.1–204.56.178.62	204.56.178.63
2	204.56.178.64		
3			
4			204.56.178.255

Have you noticed a pattern? Do you see how the wire addresses increment by 64, the maximum number of hosts per subnet? If not, you will soon. Patterns are important when performing subnetting, especially when we move on to Class A and B subnets. We will point them out as we go along.

7. Next, fill in the second subnet's broadcast address. This is the last address that will cover all 64 of the subnet's hosts. Just as before, we count hosts starting with the wire address, thus if we had 64 fingers, we would count from 64 to 127. We fill in the second subnet's broadcast address with the address 204.56.178.127.

Note: 63 + 64 = 127. There's the pattern again.

Subnetting Exercise

Target IP Address: 204.56.178.126		**Subnet Mask: 255.255.255.192**	
Network ID	**Network (Wire) Address**	**Subnet Usable Address Range**	**Broadcast Address**
1	204.56.178.0	204.56.178.1–204.56.178.62	204.56.178.63
2	204.56.178.64		204.56.178.127
3			
4			204.56.178.255

8. We now have the second subnet's first and last addresses. We now fill in the remaining usable addresses.

Subnetting Exercise

Target IP Address: 204.56.178.126		**Subnet Mask: 255.255.255.192**	
Network ID	**Network (Wire) Address**	**Subnet Usable Address Range**	**Broadcast Address**
1	204.56.178.0	204.56.178.1–204.56.178.62	204.56.178.63
2	204.56.178.64	204.56.178.65–204.56.178.126	204.56.178.127
3			

Subnetting Exercise (Continued)

Target IP Address: 204.56.178.126		Subnet Mask: 255.255.255.192	
4			204.56.178.255

9. To fill in the next subnet's wire address, we increment the second subnet's broadcast address by 1.

Subnetting Exercise

Target IP Address: 204.56.178.126		Subnet Mask: 255.255.255.192	
Network ID	**Network (Wire) Address**	**Subnet Usable Address Range**	**Broadcast Address**
1	204.56.178.0	204.56.178.1–204.56.178.62	204.56.178.63
2	204.56.178.64	204.56.178.65–204.56.178.126	204.56.178.127
3	204.56.178.128		
4			204.56.178.255

10. The last address on the third subnet is 205.56.178.191.

Subnetting Exercise

Target IP Address: 204.56.178.126		Subnet Mask: 255.255.255.192	
Network ID	**Network (Wire) Address**	**Subnet Usable Address Range**	**Broadcast Address**
1	204.56.178.0	204.56.178.1–204.56.178.62	204.56.178.63
2	204.56.178.64	204.56.178.65–204.56.178.126	204.56.178.127
3	204.56.178.128		204.56.178.191
4			204.56.178.255

11. We then fill in the third subnet's usable address range.

Subnetting Exercise

Target IP Address: 204.56.178.126		Subnet Mask: 255.255.255.192	
Network ID	**Network (Wire) Address**	**Subnet Usable Address Range**	**Broadcast Address**
1	204.56.178.0	204.56.178.1—204.56.178.62	204.56.178.63
2	204.56.178.64	204.56.178.65–204.56.178.126	204.56.178.127
3	204.56.178.128	204.56.178.129–204.56.178.190	204.56.178.191
4			204.56.178.255

12. Fill in the last subnet's wire address. The address following 204.56.178.191 is 204.56.178.192.

Subnetting Exercise

Target IP Address: 204.56.178.126		Subnet Mask: 255.255.255.192	
Network ID	**Network (Wire) Address**	**Subnet Usable Address Range**	**Broadcast Address**
1	204.56.178.0	204.56.178.1–204.56.178.62	204.56.178.63
2	204.56.178.64	204.56.178.65–204.56.178.126	204.56.178.127
3	204.56.178.128	204.56.178.129–204.56.178.190	204.56.178.191
4	204.56.178.192		204.56.178.255

13. The final entry is the last subnet's usable address range. This fills the gap between the last wire and the last broadcast address.

Subnetting Exercise

Target IP Address: 204.56.178.126		**Subnet Mask: 255.255.255.192**	
Network ID	**Network (Wire) Address**	**Subnet Usable Address's Range**	**Broadcast Address**
1	204.56.178.0	204.56.178.1–204.56.178.62	204.56.178.63
2	204.56.178.64	204.56.178.65–204.56.178.126	204.56.178.127
3	204.56.178.128	204.56.178.129–204.56.178.190	204.56.178.191
4	204.56.178.192	204.56.178.193–204.56.178.254	204.56.178.255

Finished! Let us talk about some things that you have probably noticed:

- The wire addresses always end the last octet in an even number; this is true for all address Classes. This is a quick check you can use to ensure that you are on track.
- The broadcast addresses always end the last octet in an odd number, again true for all Classes. Another quick check.
- Both the wire and broadcast addresses increment by an amount equal to the maximum number of hosts per subnet. With the subnet mask 255.255.255.192, we create a maximum of 64 hosts per subnet. Add 204.56.178.0 + .64 and the result is 204.56.178.64, the second subnet's wire address. Similarly, add 64 to the second subnet's wire address to obtain the third, and so on.
- Add 64 to the first subnet's broadcast address, 204.56.178.63, and we obtain the second subnet's broadcast address. Add to this address 64, and we obtain the third, and so on.

- If you multiply the maximum number of subnets and the maximum number of hosts per subnet (and you subnetted correctly) your result will be the maximum number of hosts available with the default net mask. In our example, 4 subnets x 64 hosts equals 256, the maximum number of hosts we can have on a default Class C network. One more check.

The following is a form you can use to work the subnet exercises that follow in this lesson and subsequent lessons' extended activities. This form is available for download in Word 97 format at:

ftp://telnet.westnetinc.com/pub/subnet.doc

IP address: ______________________ Borrow __________ bits.

1. What class is the IP address?

   ____

2. What is the maximum number of bits that can be borrowed in this class?

   ____

3. How many octets in this class are dedicated to the network?

   ____

4. How many octets in this class are dedicated to the host?

   ____

5. What is the maximum number of hosts in this class?

   ____

6. What is the subnet mask?

   ____

7. What is the subnet prefix?

   ____

8. With this subnet mask, what is the maximum number of subnets possible?

   ____

9. With this subnet mask, what is the maximum number of hosts/subnets possible?

____

10. What is this subnet's usable number of subnets?

____

11. What is the usable number of hosts per subnet?

____

12. What is the total number of usable hosts across all subnets?

____

13. What is this subnet's network number?

____

14. What is this subnet's broadcast number?

____

15. Show the first two address ranges.

____

16. Show the last two address ranges.

____

17. Show the IP address in binary.

____

18. Show the subnet mask in binary.

____

19. AND them together.

____

20. Convert the ANDed binary number to dotted decimal.

____

Sample Problem #1

Fill out the subnetting activity form using the address 202.125.39.129 borrowing 4 bits.

1. **What class is the IP address?**

   Class C

   The first octet in a Class C address ranges from 192 to 223.

2. **What is the maximum number of bits that can be borrowed in this class?**

   6

   Of the eight default Class C host portion bits, we can borrow 6 leaving 2 behind for hosts.

3. **How many octets in this class are dedicated to the network?**

   3

4. **How many octets in this class are dedicated to the host?**

   1

5. **How many maximum hosts in this class?**

   256

   $2^8 = 256$

6. **What is the subnet mask?**

   255.255.255.240

   Represent the subnet mask in binary, 11111111.11111111.11111111.11110000, and you can recognize the four borrowed bits. Convert the last octet back to decimal, 128 + 64 + 32 + 16 = 240.

7. **What is the subnet prefix?**

   /28

   Count the number of subnet bits that comprise the network and host portions.

8. **With this subnet mask, what is the maximum number of subnets possible?**

   16

   $2^4 = 16$

9. With this subnet mask, what is the maximum number of hosts/subnets possible?

   16

   $2^4 = 16$

10. What is this subnet's usable number of subnets?

    14

    $2^4 - 2 = 14$

11. What is the usable number of hosts per subnet?

    14

    $2^4 - 2 = 14$

12. What is the total number of usable hosts across all subnets?

    196

    14 x 14 = 196. Look back at the Complete Class C Subnets Table in Lesson 2.

13. What is this subnet's network number (wire address)?

    202.125.39.128

    Build the Subnet Exercise table.

Sample Problem 1, Step 13

Target IP Address: 202.125.39.129		**Subnet Mask: 255.255.255.240**	
Network ID	**Network (Wire) Address**	**Subnet Usable Address Range**	**Broadcast Address**
1 Unusable	202.125.39.0	202.125.39.1–202.125.39.14	202.125.39.15
2	202.125.39.16	202.125.39.17–202.125.39.30	202.125.39.31
3	202.125.39.32	202.125.39.33–202.125.39.46	202.125.39.47
4	202.125.39.48	202.125.39.49–202.125.39.62	202.125.39.63
5	202.125.39.64	202.125.39.65–202.125.39.78	202.125.39.79

Sample Problem 1, Step 13 (Continued)

Target IP Address: 202.125.39.129		**Subnet Mask: 255.255.255.240**	
6	202.125.39.80	202.125.39.81–202.125.39.94	202.125.39.95
7	202.125.39.96	202.125.39.97–202.125.39.126	202.125.39.127
8	202.125.39.128	202.125.39.129–202.125.39.142	202.125.39.143
9	202.125.39.144	202.125.39.145–202.125.39.158	202.125.39.159
10	202.125.39.160	202.125.39.161-202.125.39.174	202.125.39.175
11	202.125.39.176	202.125.39.177–202.125.39.190	202.125.39.191
12	202.125.39.192	202.125.39.193–202.125.39.206	202.125.39.207
13	202.125.39.208	202.125.39.209–202.125.39.222	202.125.39.223
14	202.125.39.224	202.125.39.225–202.125.39.238	202.125.39.239
15	202.125.39.240	202.125.39.241–202.125.39.246	202.125.39.247
16 Unusable	202.125.39.248	202.125.39.249–202.125.39.254	202.125.39.255

14. What is this subnet's broadcast number?

    202.125.39.143

15. Show the first two address ranges

    202.125.39.0–202.125.39.15 Unusable

    202.125.39.16–202.125.39.31

16. Show the last two address ranges.

    202.125.39.240–202.125.39.247

    202.125.39.248–202.125.39.255 Unusable

17. Show the IP address in binary.

    11001010.01111101.00100111.10000001

18. Show the subnet mask in binary.

    11111111.11111111.11111111.11110000

19. AND them together.

    11001010.01111101.00100111.10000000

20. Convert the ANDed binary number to dotted decimal.

    202.125.39.128

    This is the original address's subnet wire address.

Sample Problem # 2

Fill out the subnetting activity form, using the address 194.120.36.35 borrowing 3 bits.

1. What class is the IP address?

   Class C

2. What is the maximum number of bits that can be borrowed in this class?

   6

3. How many octets in this class are dedicated to the network?

   3

4. How many octets in this class are dedicated to the host?

   1

5. How many maximum hosts in this class?

   256

6. What is the subnet mask?

   255.255.255.224

7. What is the subnet prefix?

   /27

   Count the number of subnet bits that comprise the network and host portions.

8. **With this subnet mask, what is the maximum number of subnets possible?**

   8

9. **With this subnet mask, what is the maximum number of hosts/subnets possible?**

   32

10. **What is this subnet's usable number of subnets?**

    6

11. **What is the usable number of hosts per subnet?**

    30

12. **What is the total number of usable hosts across all subnets?**

    180

13. **What is this subnet's network number (wire address)?**

    194.120.36.32

14. **What is this subnet's broadcast number?**

    194.120.36.63

15. **Show the first two address ranges.**

    194.120.36.0–194.120.36.31 Unusable

    194.120.36.32–194.120.36.63

16. **Show the last two address ranges.**

    194.120.36.192–194.120.36.223

    194.120.36.224–194.120.36.255 Unusable

17. **Show the IP address in binary.**

    11000010.01111000.00100100.00100011

18. **Show the subnet mask in binary.**

    11111111.11111111.11111111.11100000

19. **AND them together.**

    11000010.01111000. 00100100.00100000

20. **Convert the ANDed binary number to dotted decimal.**

    194.120.36.32

Activities

1. In order for a host to communicate on a subnetted network segment, which two portions of its IP address must match those of the subnet address? (Choose two.)
   a. The host portion
   b. The subnet portion
   c. The router portion
   d. The network portion
2. Using the default Class C subnet mask, 255.255.255.0, which two addresses will be able to communicate on the same network segment? (Choose two.)
   a. 192.128.200.3
   b. 192.200.129.18
   c. 192.127.250.223
   d. 192.200.129.179
3. Using the subnet mask 255.255.255.248, which two addresses are on the same subnet? (Choose two.)
   a. 194.212.56.18
   b. 194.212.56.25
   c. 194.212.56.13
   d. 194.212.56.20
4. Using the subnet mask 255.255.255.240, which two addresses are on the same subnet? (Choose two.)
   a. 200.193.15.18
   b. 200.193.15.42
   c. 200.193.15.49
   d. 200.193.15.61
5. A subnet's broadcast address has which portion's bits set to all ones?
   a. The subnet portion
   b. The network portion
   c. The mask portion
   d. The host portion

6. In a set of subnet address ranges, which is the first wire address in the first subnet?
   a. The IP address where all bits are set to 0
   b. The first address on the first usable subnet
   c. The same as the first host address
   d. The default network's wire address
7. Fill out the Subnetting Exercise Table with the address ranges created with the following information: IP address 203.16.97.43, subnet mask 255.255.255.248.

Target IP Address:		**Subnet Mask:**	
Network ID	**Network (Wire) Address**	**Subnet Address Range**	**Broadcast Address**
1 Unusable			

Target IP Address:		Subnet Mask:	
Unusable			

Extended Activities

1. For the following exercises, complete the subnetting activity form available for download at: **ftp://telnet.westnetinc.com/pub/subnet.doc.**
   a. IP address: 199.16.156.34, Borrow 3 bits

   b. IP address: 220.178.220.89, Borrow 4 bits

c. IP address: 208.36.3.156, Borrow 2 bits

d. IP address: 195.195.200.50, Borrow 5 bits

Lesson 4—Subnetting Class B Networks

Class C networks only give us 6 host bits with which to work, allowing us to create a maximum of 62 subnets, each with only 2 hosts per subnet. These numbers are rarely acceptable for larger companies with many networks and hosts to support. Therefore, larger organizations lease or purchase Class A or B network addresses and subnet them. In this lesson we learn how to subnet Class B networks.

Objectives

At the end of this lesson you will be able to:

- Determine a Class B subnet's valid IP address ranges
- Identify the subnet on which an address resides
- List each subnet's network and broadcast addresses

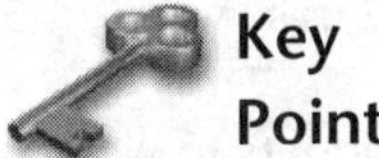

Key Point

Class B subnets are better suited to large network use than are Class C subnets.

Building the Address Range

The Complete Class B Subnets Table shows the available Class B subnets.

Complete Class B Subnets

Borrowed Bits	Subnet Mask	Prefix	Usable Subnets Created	Usable Hosts/Subnet	Usable Networks * Usable Hosts
2	255.255.192.0	/18	2 usable	16,382 usable	32,764
3	255.255.224.0	/19	6 usable	8,190 usable	49,140
4	255.255.240.0	/20	14 usable	4,094 usable	57,316
5	255.255.248.0	/21	30 usable	2,046 usable	61,380

Complete Class B Subnets (Continued)

Borrowed Bits	Subnet Mask	Prefix	Usable Subnets Created	Usable Hosts/Subnet	Usable Networks * Usable Hosts
6	255.255.252.0	/22	62 usable	1,022 usable	63,364
7	255.255.254.0	/23	126 usable	510 usable	64,260
8	255.255.255.0	/24	254 usable	254 usable	64,516
9	255.255.255.128	/25	510 usable	126 usable	64,260
10	255.255.255.192	/26	1,022 usable	62 usable	63,364
11	255.255.255.224	/27	2,046 usable	30 usable	61,380
12	255.255.255.240	/28	4,094 usable	14 usable	57,316
13	255.255.255.248	/29	8,190 usable	6 usable	49,140
14	255.255.255.252	/30	16,382 usable	2 usable	32,764

Obviously, Class B addresses give us more subnets to work with than do Class C addresses. Thus, how do we subnet Class B networks?

Let us start with a problem. Given a Class B IP address, 131.20.3.125, and the subnet mask 255.255.224.0, let us build the Subnetting Exercise Table.

1. Let us start by numbering the Network IDs:

Subnetting Exercise

Target IP Address: 131.20.3.125		Subnet Mask: 255.255.224.0	
Network ID	**Network (Wire) Address**	**Subnet Usable Address Range**	**Broadcast Address**
1			
2			
3			
4			
5			

Subnetting Exercise (Continued)

Target IP Address: 131.20.3.125		Subnet Mask: 255.255.224.0	
6			
7			
8			

We borrow 3 bits from the host portion. Remember, a default Class B network portion is 2 octets long, leaving the remaining 2 octets for the hosts. Thus, the subnet mask 255.255.224.0 takes us 3 bits into the host portion (128 + 64 + 32 = 224). We have created 2^3 (8) maximum subnets.

2. Next, let us fill in the first wire address.

Subnetting Exercise

Target IP Address: 131.20.3.125		Subnet Mask: 255.255.224.0	
Network ID	**Network (Wire) Address**	**Subnet Usable Address Range**	**Broadcast Address**
1	131.20.0.0		
2			
3			
4			
5			
6			
7			
8			

Just as with Class C subnets, the first wire address is always the default Class B network address. All the host bits (and the subnet portion bits) are set to 0.

3. Fill in the last broadcast address.

Subnetting Exercise

Target IP Address: 131.20.3.125		Subnet Mask: 255.255.224.0	
Network ID	**Network (Wire) Address**	**Subnet Usable Address Range**	**Broadcast Address**
1	131.20.0.0		
2			
3			
4			
5			
6			
7			
8			131.20.255.255

As in Class C subnetting (and Class A, as we will soon find), the last broadcast address is the default Class B network broadcast address. All the host and subnet bits are set to 1.

4. Next, fill in the first subnet's broadcast address.

Subnetting Exercise

Target IP Address: 131.20.3.125		Subnet Mask: 255.255.224.0	
Network ID	**Network (Wire) Address**	**Subnet Usable Address Range**	**Broadcast Address**
1	131.20.0.0		131.20.31.255
2			
3			
4			
5			
6			

Subnetting Exercise (Continued)

Target IP Address: 131.20.3.125		Subnet Mask: 255.255.224.0	
7			
8			131.20.255.255

Where did this address come from? Remember, we are working with many more host bits, thus we have to cover more hosts per subnet. Go back and look at the Complete Class B Subnets Table.

With 3 borrowed bits in a Class B network, we leave 13 bits for hosts, creating a maximum of 2^{13} (8,192) hosts per subnet (the maximum number of hosts per subnet is 2 to the number of hosts bits left). Therefore, we have to cover 8,192 hosts in our first address range.

Covering hosts was fairly easy in Class C networks when we only had to work with one octet; now we have to work with two. Let us look at this from the binary point of view. Following is our subnet mask in binary:

11111111.11111111.11100000.00000000 = 255.255.224.0

The first two octets are the default Class B network portion, the remaining two are the host portion. We move 3 bits right into the host portion to create the subnet portion. This leaves 16 – 3 = 13 bits for hosts, and 2^{13} = 8,192 maximum hosts per subnet (8,190 usable). Check it: 8,192 x 2^3 (8) = 65,536, the maximum number of hosts created with the default Class B subnet mask.

To cover 8,192 hosts on the first subnet, we have to account for all the 13 host bits. The first subnet, in binary, ranges from:

10000011.00010100.*00000000.00000000* = 131.20.0.0

To:

10000011.00010100.*00011111.11111111* = 131.20.31.255

Notice that in the broadcast address, the 13 host bits are all 1s.

The next wire address looks as follows:

10000011.00010100.*001*00000.00000000 = 131.20.32.0

Notice that the subnet portion (shown in italics) incremented by one. Look at the Class B with 3 Borrowed Bits Table.

Class B with 3 Borrowed Bits

Network Address Portion		Subnetwork Portion	Host Portion	Decimal Address
10000011	00010100	000	00000.00000000	131.20.0.0
		001		131.20.32.0
		010		131.20.64.0
		011		131.20.96.0
		100		131.20.128.0
		101		131.20.160.0
		110		131.20.192.0
		111		131.20.224.0

Also, notice that on each consecutive subnet the binary subnetwork portion counts up one decimal value (0,1,2, etc.) and the wire address' third octet increments by 32. We observed a similar occurrence in our Class C subnetting problems, but only on the last octet.

Before we return to our exercise, here is a trick that might help:

Divide any hosts per subnet that exceed 255 (the maximum decimal value for any one octet) by 256. In our example, we have 8,192 hosts per subnet. Thus:

8,192 / 256 = 32

The result is the first address of the next subnet, 131.20.32.0. From this division exercise, we also see that our subnetted octet increments by decimal 32.

Back to our problem.

5. Now that we have the first subnet's broadcast address, we can fill in the first subnet's address range.

Subnetting Exercise

Target IP Address: 131.20.3.125		**Subnet Mask: 255.255.224.0**	
Network ID	**Network (Wire) Address**	**Subnet Usable Address Range**	**Broadcast Address**
1	131.20.0.0	131.20.0.1–131.20.31.254	131.20.31.255
2			
3			
4			
5			
6			
7			
8			131.20.255.255

Make this easy on yourself. Start with the first address following the subnet's wire address (132.20.0.1) and end with the last address preceding the first subnet's broadcast address (131.20.31.254).

6. Next, we need the second subnet's wire address.

Subnetting Exercise

Target IP Address: 131.20.3.125		**Subnet Mask: 255.255.224.0**	
Network ID	**Network (Wire) Address**	**Subnet Usable Address Range**	**Broadcast Address**
1	131.20.0.0	131.20.0.1–131.20.31.254	131.20.31.255
2	131.20.32.0		
3			

Subnetting Exercise (Continued)

Target IP Address: 131.20.3.125		Subnet Mask: 255.255.224.0	
4			
5			
6			
7			
8			131.20.255.255

Remember that we subnetted on the third octet, so this is where our subnets increment. The wire address' host bits are all 0s, while the subnet portion incremented by one. Review the Class B with 3 Borrowed Bits Table.

7. Fill in the second subnet's broadcast address.

Subnetting Exercise

Target IP Address: 131.20.3.125		Subnet Mask: 255.255.224.0	
Network ID	**Network (Wire) Address**	**Subnet Usable Address Range**	**Broadcast Address**
1	131.20.0.0	131.20.0.1–131.20.31.254	131.20.31.255
2	131.20.32.0		131.20.63.255
3			
4			
5			
6			
7			
8			131.20.255.255

This is the address on the second subnet where the host bits are all 1s. The subnet portion does not change bit patterns until the start of the next subnet.

Do you see the pattern? The third octet increments by 32 on each consecutive subnet.

8. Recognizing the pattern, we can fill in the remaining wire and broadcast addresses.

Subnetting Exercise

Target IP Address: 131.20.3.125		**Subnet Mask: 255.255.224.0**	
Network ID	**Network (Wire) Address**	**Subnet Usable Address Range**	**Broadcast Address**
1	131.20.0.0	131.20.0.1–131.20.31.254	131.20.31.255
2	131.20.32.0		131.20.63.255
3	131.20.64.0		131.20.95.255
4	131.20.96.0		131.20.127.255
5	131.20.128.0		131.20.159.255
6	131.20.160.0		131.20.191.255
7	131.20.192.0		131.20.223.255
8	131.20.224.0		131.20.255.255

9. All we have left to fill in are the ranges.

Subnetting Exercise

Target IP Address: 131.20.3.125		Subnet Mask: 255.255.224.0	
Network ID	**Network (Wire) Address**	**Subnet Usable Address Range**	**Broadcast Address**
1	131.20.0.0	131.20.0.1–131.20.31.254	131.20.31.255
2	131.20.32.0	131.20.32.1–131.20.63.254	131.20.63.255
3	131.20.64.0	131.20.64.1–131.20.95.254	131.20.95.255
4	131.20.96.0	131.20.96.1–131.20.127.254	131.20.127.255
5	131.20.128.0	131.20.128.1–131.20.159.254	131.20.159.255
6	131.20.160.0	131.20.160.1–131.20.191.254	131.20.191.255
7	131.20.192.0	131.20.192.1–131.20.223.254	131.20.223.255
8	131.20.224.0	131.20.224.1–131.20.255.254	131.20.255.255

Each range entry must account for each subnet's remaining hosts, and we can easily do this by showing the range's first usable address as the address following the subnet's wire address, and the range's last usable address as the address preceding the subnet's broadcast address.

Sample Problem #1

Fill out the subnetting activity form using the address 175.25.250.62 borrowing 6 bits.

1. **What class is the IP address?**

   Class B

   The first octet in a Class B address ranges from 128 to 191.

2. **What is the maximum number of bits that can be borrowed in this class?**

   14

   Of the 16 default Class B host portion bits, we can borrow 14, leaving 2 behind for hosts.

3. **How many octets in this class are dedicated to the network?**

   2

4. **How many octets in this class are dedicated to the host?**

   2

5. **How many maximum hosts in this class?**

   65,536

   2^{16} = 65,536

6. **What is the subnet mask?**

   255.255.252.0

   Represent the subnet mask in binary, 11111111.11111111.11111100.00000000, and you can recognize the 6 borrowed bits. Convert the third octet, the one from which we borrowed the host bits, back to decimal, 128 + 64 + 32 + 16 + 8 + 4 = 252.

7. **What is the subnet prefix?**

   /22

   Count the number of subnet bits that comprise the network and host portions.

8. **With this subnet mask, what is the maximum number of subnets possible?**

   64

   2^6 = 64

9. With this subnet mask, what is the maximum number of hosts/subnets?

   1,024

   2^{10} = 1,024. Check it: 64 x 1,024 = 65,536, the maximum Class B default hosts.

10. What is this subnet's usable number of subnets?

    62

    $2^6 - 2 = 62$

11. What is the usable number of hosts per subnet?

    1,022

    $2^{10} - 2 = 1,022$

12. What is the total number of usable hosts across all subnets?

    63,364

    62 x 1,022 = 63,364. Look back at the Complete Class B Subnets Table.

13. What is this subnet's network number (wire address)?

    175.25.248.0

Build the Subnet Exercise Table.

Subnet Exercise

Target IP Address: 175.25.250.62		**Subnet Mask: 255.255.252.0**	
Network ID	**Network (Wire) Address**	**Subnet Usable Address Range**	**Broadcast Address**
1	175.25.0.0	175.25.0.1–175.25.3.254	175.25.3.255
2	175.25.4.0	175.25.4.1–175.25.7.254	175.25.7.255
3	175.25.8.0	175.25.8.1–175.25.11.254	175.25.11.255
4	175.25.12.0	175.25.12.1–175.25.15.254	175.25.15.255

Subnet Exercise (Continued)

Target IP Address: 175.25.250.62		Subnet Mask: 255.255.252.0	
5	175.25.16.0	175.25.16.1–175.25.19.254	175.25.19.255
6	175.25.20.0	175.25.20.1–175.25.23.254	175.25.23.255
7	175.25.24.0	175.25.24.1–175.25.27.254	175.25.27.255
8	175.25.28.0	175.25.28.1–175.25.31.254	175.25.31.255
9	175.25.32.0	175.25.32.1–175.25.35.254	175.25.35.255
10	175.25.36.0	175.25.36.1–175.25.39.254	175.25.39.255
11	175.25.40.0	175.25.40.1–175.25.43.254	175.25.43.255
12	175.25.44.0	175.25.44.1–175.25.47.254	175.25.47.255
13	175.25.48.0	175.25.48.1–175.25.51.254	175.25.51.255
14	175.25.52.0	175.25.52.1–175.25.55.254	175.25.55.255
15	175.25.56.0	175.25.56.1–175.25.59.254	175.25.59.255
16	175.25.60.0	175.25.60.1–175.25.63.254	175.25.63.255
17	175.25.64.0	175.25.64.1–175.25.67.254	175.25.67.255
18	175.25.68.0	175.25.68.1–175.25.71.254	175.25.71.255
19	175.25.72.0	175.25.72.1–175.25.75.254	175.25.75.255

Subnet Exercise (Continued)

Target IP Address: 175.25.250.62		**Subnet Mask: 255.255.252.0**	
20	175.25.76.0	175.25.76.1–175.25.79.254	175.25.79.255
21	175.25.80.0	175.25.80.1–175.25.83.254	175.25.83.255
22	175.25.84.0	175.25.84.1–175.25.87.254	175.25.87.255
23	175.25.88.0	175.25.88.1–175.25.91.254	175.25.91.255
24	175.25.92.0	175.25.92.1–175.25.95.254	175.25.95.255
25	175.25.96.0	175.25.96.1–175.25.99.254	175.25.99.255
26	175.25.100.0	175.25.101.1–175.25.103.254	175.25.103.255
27	175.25.104.0	175.25.104.1–175.25.107.254	175.25.107.255
28	175.25.108.0	175.25.108.1–175.25.111.254	175.25.111.255
29	175.25.112.0	175.25.112.1–175.25.115.254	175.25.115.255
30	175.25.116.0	175.25.116.1–175.25.119.254	175.25.119.255
31	175.25.120.0	175.25.120.1–175.25.123.254	175.25.123.255
32	175.25.124.0	175.25.124.1–175.25.127.254	175.25.127.255
33	175.25.128.0	175.25.128.1–175.25.131.254	175.25.131.255
34	175.25.132.0	175.25.132.1–175.25.135.254	175.25.135.255

Subnet Exercise (Continued)

Target IP Address: 175.25.250.62		Subnet Mask: 255.255.252.0	
35	175.25.136.0	175.25.136.1–175.25.139.254	175.25.139.255
36	175.25.140.0	175.25.140.1–175.25.143.254	175.25.143.255
37	175.25.144.0	175.25.144.1–175.25.147.254	175.25.147.255
38	175.25.148.0	175.25.148.1–175.25.151.254	175.25.151.255
39	175.25.152.0	175.25.152.1–175.25.155.254	175.25.155.255
40	175.25.156.0	175.25.156.1–175.25.159.254	175.25.159.255
41	175.25.160.0	175.25.160.1–175.25.163.254	175.25.163.255
42	175.25.164.0	175.25.164.1–175.25.167.254	175.25.167.255
43	175.25.168.0	175.25.168.1–175.25.171.254	175.25.171.255
44	175.25.172.0	175.25.172.1–175.25.175.254	175.25.175.255
45	175.25.176.0	175.25.176.1–175.25.179.254	175.25.179.255
46	175.25.180.0	175.25.180.1–175.25.183.254	175.25.183.255
47	175.25.184.0	175.25.184.1–175.25.187.254	175.25.187.255
48	175.25.188.0	175.25.188.1–175.25.191.254	175.25.191.255
49	175.25.192.0	175.25.192.1–175.25.195.254	175.25.195.255

Subnet Exercise (Continued)

Target IP Address: 175.25.250.62		Subnet Mask: 255.255.252.0	
50	175.25.196.0	175.25.196.1–175.25.199.254	175.25.199.255
51	175.25.200.0	175.25.200.1–175.25.203.254	175.25.203.255
52	175.25.204.0	175.25.204.1–175.25.207.254	175.25.207.255
53	175.25.208.0	175.25.208.1–175.25.211.254	175.25.211.255
54	175.25.212.0	175.25.212.1–175.25.215.254	175.25.215.255
55	175.25.216.0	175.25.216.1–175.25.219.254	175.25.219.255
56	175.25.220.0	175.25.220.1–175.25.223.254	175.25.223.255
57	175.25.224.0	175.25.224.1–175.25.227.254	175.25.227.255
58	175.25.228.0	175.25.228.1–175.25.231.254	175.25.231.255
59	175.25.232.0	175.25.232.1–175.25.235.254	175.25.235.255
60	175.25.236.0	175.25.236.1–175.25.239.254	175.25.239.255
61	175.25.240.0	175.25.240.1–175.25.243.254	175.25.243.255
62	175.25.244.0	175.25.244.1–175.25.247.254	175.25.247.255
63	175.25.248.0	175.25.248.1–175.25.251.254	175.25.251.255
64	175.25.252.0	175.25.252.1–175.25.255.254	175.25.255.255

14. What is this subnet's broadcast number?

    175.25.251.255

15. Show the first two address ranges using Steps 2 through 16.

    175.25.0.0–175.25.3.255 Unusable

    175.25.4.0–175.25.7.255

16. Show the last two address ranges.

    175.25.248.0–175.25.251.255

    175.25.252.0–175.25.255.255 Unusable

17. Show the IP address in binary.

    10101111.00011001.11111010.00111110

18. Show the subnet mask in binary.

    11111111.11111111.11111100.00000000

19. AND them together.

    10101111.00011001.11111000.00000000

20. Convert the ANDed binary number to dotted decimal.

    175.25.248.0

    This is the original address's subnet wire address.

Sample Problem # 2

Fill out the subnetting activity form using the address 146.32.72.210 borrowing 12 bits.

1. What class is the IP address?

   Class B

2. What is the maximum number of bits that can be borrowed in this class?

   14

3. How many octets in this class are dedicated to the network?

   2

4. How many octets in this class are dedicated to the host?

   2

5. How many maximum hosts in this class?

   65,536

6. What is the subnet mask?

   255.255.255.240

   The subnet portion carries into the fourth octet.

   11111111.11111111.11111111.11110000 = 255.255.255.240

7. What is the subnet prefix?

   /28

8. With this subnet mask, what is the maximum number of subnets possible?

   4,096

   2^{12} = 4,096

9. With this subnet mask, what is the maximum number of hosts/subnets possible?

   16

   2^{4} = 16. Check it: 4,096 x 16 = 65,536

10. What is this subnet's usable number of subnets?

    4,094

11. What is the usable number of hosts per subnet?

    14

12. What is the total number of usable hosts across all subnets?

    57,316

13. What is this subnet's network number (wire address)?

    146.32.72.208

Target IP Address: 146.32.72.210		**Subnet Mask: 255.255.255.240**	
Network ID	**Network (Wire) Address**	**Subnet Usable Address Range**	**Broadcast Address**
1	146.32.0.0	146.32.0.1–146.32.0.14	146.32.0.15
2	146.32.0.16	146.32.0.17–146.32.0.30	146.32.0.31

Target IP Address: 146.32.72.210		**Subnet Mask: 255.255.255.240**	
3	146.32.0.32	146.32.0.33–146.32.0.46	146.32.0.47
4	146.32.0.48	146.32.0.49–146.32.0.62	146.32.0.63
...			
1,166	146.32.72.208	146.32.72.209–146.32.72.222	146.32.72.223
...			
4,093	146.32.255.192	146.32.255.193–146.32.255.196	146.32.255.207
4,094	146.32.255.208	146.32.255.209–146.32.255.222	146.32.255.223
4,095	146.32.255.224	146.32.255.225–146.32.255.238	146.32.255.239
4,096	146.32.255.240	146.32.255.241–146.32.255.254	146.32.255.255

Write out the entire table, until you become comfortable with the patterns. We show only a portion to conserve space.

14. What is this subnet's broadcast number?

    146.32.72.223

15. Show the first two address ranges.

    146.32.0.0–146.32.0.15 Unusable

    146.32.0.16–146.32.0.31

16. Show the last two address ranges.

    146.32.255.224–146.32.255.239

    146.32.255.240–146.32.255.255 Unusable

17. Show the IP address in binary.

    10010010.00100000.01001000.11010010

18. Show the subnet mask in binary.

    11111111.11111111.11111111.11110000

19. AND them together.

    10010010.00100000.01001000.11010000

20. Convert the ANDed binary number to dotted decimal.

    146.32.72.208

Activities

1. How many total bits does a Class B subnet allow us to borrow from the host portion?
   a. 16
   b. 14
   c. 8
   d. 6
2. If a Class B address's subnet mask is 255.255.254.0, in which octet does our subnet portion increment?
   a. First
   b. Second
   c. Third
   d. Fourth
3. When subnetting Class B addresses, what is the first subnet's wire address equal to?
   a. The default subnet's wire address
   b. The first subnet's first usable host
   c. A Class C default wire address
   d. The default network wire address
4. When written in binary, the first part of a subnetted Class B network's wire address will show which bit pattern?
   a. The network portion set to all 1s, the subnet portion to all 0s, and the host portion to all 1s.
   b. The network portion set as the default Class B network portion, the subnet portion to all 0s, and the host portion to all 0s.
   c. The network portion set as the default Class B network portion, the subnet portion to all 1s, and the host portion to all 0s.
   d. The network portion set to all 0s, the subnet portion to all 0s, and the host portion to all 0s.

5. With the subnet mask 255.255.255.128, how frequently will the Class B subnets increment, and in which octet?
   a. Every 128 hosts; fourth octet only
   b. Every 128 hosts; third and fourth octets
   c. Every 128 hosts; third octet only
   d. Every 256 hosts; third and fourth octets
6. In a subnetted Class B network, in what state will the host bits be on each subnet's broadcast address?
   a. Each subnet's host bits are set to all 1s
   b. Each subnet's host bits are set to all 0s
   c. They will match the first wire address
   d. They will match the following subnet's wire address
7. If a Class B address's subnet mask is 255.255.255.192, in which octet does the subnet portion increment?
   a. First and second
   b. Second and third
   c. Third and fourth
   d. Fourth only
8. If the number of hosts per subnet exceeds 255, how might you solve for the subnet incremental range?
   a. Divide the number of subnets by 256
   b. Divide the number of networks by 65,536
   c. Divide the number of hosts by 256
   d. Divide the number of networks by the number of subnets

Extended Activities

1. Use the subnetting activity form for the following exercises.
   a. IP address: 130.73.68.1, Borrow 2 bits.

   b. IP address: 129.89.125.17, Borrow 5 bits

c. IP address: 188.92.61.25, Borrow 10 bits

d. IP address: 140.195.200.50, Borrow 14 bits

Lesson 5—Subnetting Class A Networks

Our final Class to subnet is Class A networks. The numbers we work with are quite large, thus you must be able to recognize the patterns that form as the subnets increment. Do not attempt Class A subnets until you feel comfortable with subnetting Class B and C networks.

Objectives

At the end of this lesson you will be able to:

- Determine a Class A subnet's valid IP address ranges
- Identify the subnet on which an address resides
- List each subnet's network and broadcast addresses

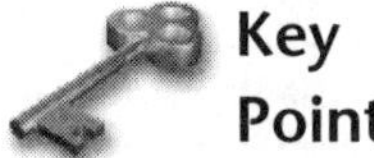

Key Point

Subnetting Class A networks is easiest when you learn to recognize the number patterns.

Building the Address Range

The Complete Class A Subnets Table shows the available Class A subnets.

Complete Class A Subnets

Borrowed Bits	Subnet Mask	Prefix	Usable Subnets Created	Usable Hosts/ Subnet	Usable Networks * Usable Hosts
2	255.192.0.0	/10	2 usable	4,194,302 usable	8,388,604
3	255.224.0.0	/11	6 usable	2,097,150 usable	12,582,900
4	255.240.0.0	/12	14 usable	1,048,574 usable	14,680,036
5	255.248.0.0	/13	30 usable	524,286 usable	15,728,580
6	255.252.0.0	/14	62 usable	262,142 usable	16,252,804

Complete Class A Subnets (Continued)

Borrowed Bits	Subnet Mask	Prefix	Usable Subnets Created	Usable Hosts/ Subnet	Usable Networks * Usable Hosts
7	255.254.0.0	/15	126 usable	131,070 usable	16,514,820
8	255.255.0.0	/16	254 usable	65,534 usable	16,645,636
9	255.255.128.0	/17	510 usable	32,766 usable	16,710,660
10	255.255.192.0	/18	1,022 usable	16,382 usable	16,742,404
11	255.255.224.0	/19	2,046 usable	8,190 usable	16,756,740
12	255.255.240.0	/20	4,094 usable	4,094 usable	16,760,836
13	255.255.248.0	/21	8,190 usable	2,046 usable	16,756,740
14	255.255.252.0	/22	16,382 usable	1,022 usable	16,742,404
15	255.255.254.0	/23	32,766 usable	510 usable	16,710,660
16	255.255.255.0	/24	65,534 usable	254 usable	16,645,636
17	255.255.255.128	/25	131,070 usable	126 usable	16,514,820
18	255.255.255.192	/26	262,142 usable	62 usable	16,252,804
19	255.255.255.224	/27	524,286 usable	30 usable	15,728,580
20	255.255.255.240	/28	1,048,574 usable	14 usable	14,680,036
21	255.255.255.248	/29	2,097,150 usable	6 usable	12,582,900
22	255.255.255.252	/30	4,194,302 usable	2 usable	8,388,604

Notice that the network and hosts counts become quite large. In reality, you will likely not have to work with millions of networks, or hosts for that matter. Nonetheless, you may have to break up a portion of a Class A network, and thus you need to understand how to subnet Class A networks.

Let us start on an example. We want to subnet the Class A address 90.64.32.16 using the subnet mask 255.240.0.0.

1. Start with the Subnet Exercise Table and fill in the Network IDs.

Subnetting Exercise

Target IP Address: 90.64.32.16		**Subnet Mask: 255.240.0.0**	
Network ID	**Network (Wire) Address**	**Subnet Usable Address Range**	**Broadcast Address**
1			
2			
3			
4			
5			
6			
7			
8			
9			
10			
11			
12			
13			
14			
15			
16			

We borrow 4 bits from the host portion, and thus create a maximum of 16 subnets.

2. Fill in the first wire address.

Subnetting Exercise

Target IP Address: 90.64.32.16		**Subnet Mask: 255.240.0.0**	
Network ID	**Network (Wire) Address**	**Subnet Usable Address Range**	**Broadcast Address**
1	90.0.0.0		
2			
3			
4			
5			
6			
7			
8			
9			
10			
11			
12			
13			
14			
15			
16			

Just as with Class B and C, the first wire address is the default Class A wire address. All 20 remaining host bits are set to 0, as are the subnet portion bits.

3. Fill in the last broadcast address.

Subnetting Exercise

Target IP Address: 90.64.32.16		**Subnet Mask: 255.240.0.0**	
Network ID	**Network (Wire) Address**	**Subnet Usable Address Range**	**Broadcast Address**
1	90.0.0.0		
2			
3			
4			
5			
6			
7			
8			
9			
10			
11			
12			
13			
14			
15			
16			90.255.255.255

This is the address where all the host bits and subnet bits are set to 1.

4. Fill in the first subnet's broadcast address.

Subnetting Exercise

Target IP Address: 90.64.32.16		**Subnet Mask: 255.240.0.0**	
Network ID	**Network (Wire) Address**	**Subnet Usable Address Range**	**Broadcast Address**
1	90.0.0.0		90.15.255.255
2			
3			
4			
5			
6			
7			
8			
9			
10			
11			
12			
13			
14			
15			
16			90.255.255.255

This is the address in the first subnet where the host portion bits are all set to 1.

Before we move on to the next wire address, I offer you another trick. Write the subnet mask out in binary:

11111111.11110000.00000000.00000000 = 255.240.0.0

Now, circle the last 1 bit in the subnet portion (the last 1 bit on the right).

11111111.111(1)0000.00000000.00000000 = 255.240.0.0

Note the octet in which this bit is set. This is the octet where the subnets will increment. Also note this bit's decimal value; this is the decimal amount this octet increments on each subnet.

Thus, we see that we increment our subnets in the second octet. The bit's decimal value is 16, thus we start with address 90.*0*.0.0, the next subnet starts with address 90.*16*.0.0, and so on.

5. Fill in the next wire address.

Subnetting Exercise

Target IP Address: 90.64.32.16		**Subnet Mask: 255.240.0.0**	
Network ID	**Network (Wire) Address**	**Subnet Usable Address Range**	**Broadcast Address**
1	90.0.0.0		90.15.255.255
2	90.16.0.0		
3	90.32.0.0		
4	90.48.0.0		
5	90.64.0.0		
6	90.80.0.0		
7	90.96.0.0		
8	90.112.0.0		
9	90.128.0.0		
10	90.144.0.0		
11	90.160.0.0		
12	90.176.0.0		
13	90.192.0.0		

Subnetting Exercise (Continued)

Target IP Address: 90.64.32.16		Subnet Mask: 255.240.0.0	
14	90.208.0.0		
15	90.224.0.0		
16	90.240.0.0		90.255.255.255

Using our trick, we can fill in the rest of the wire addresses, as well.

6. Fill in the broadcast addresses.

Subnetting Exercise

Target IP Address: 90.64.32.16		Subnet Mask: 255.240.0.0	
Network ID	**Network (Wire) Address**	**Subnet Usable Address Range**	**Broadcast Address**
1	90.0.0.0		90.15.255.255
2	90.16.0.0		90.31.255.255
3	90.32.0.0		90.47.255.255
4	90.48.0.0		90.63.255.255
5	90.64.0.0		90.79.255.255
6	90.80.0.0		90.95.255.255
7	90.96.0.0		90.111.255.255
8	90.112.0.0		90.127.255.255
9	90.128.0.0		90.143.255.255
10	90.144.0.0		90.159.255.255
11	90.160.0.0		90.175.255.255
12	90.176.0.0		90.191.255.255
13	90.192.0.0		90.207.255.255
14	90.208.0.0		90.223.255.255

Subnetting Exercise (Continued)

Target IP Address: 90.64.32.16		Subnet Mask: 255.240.0.0	
15	90.224.0.0		90.239.255.255
16	90.240.0.0		90.255.255.255

7. Fill in the ranges on each subnet.

Subnetting Exercise

Target IP Address: 90.64.32.16		Subnet Mask: 255.240.0.0	
Network ID	**Network (Wire) Address**	**Subnet Usable Address Range**	**Broadcast Address**
1	90.0.0.0	90.0.0.1–90.15.255.254	90.15.255.255
2	90.16.0.0	90.16.0.1–90.31.255.254	90.31.255.255
3	90.32.0.0	90.32.0.1–90.47.255.254	90.47.255.255
4	90.48.0.0	90.48.0.1–90.63.255.254	90.63.255.255
5	90.64.0.0	90.64.0.1–90.79.255.254	90.79.255.255
6	90.80.0.0	90.80.0.1–90.95.255.254	90.95.255.255
7	90.96.0.0	90.96.0.1–90.111.255.254	90.111.255.255
8	90.112.0.0	90.112.0.1–90.127.255.254	90.127.255.255
9	90.128.0.0	90.128.0.1–90.143.255.254	90.143.255.255
10	90.144.0.0	90.144.0.1–90.159.255.254	90.159.255.255

Subnetting Exercise (Continued)

Target IP Address: 90.64.32.16		Subnet Mask: 255.240.0.0	
11	90.160.0.0	90.160.0.1–90.175.255.254	90.175.255.255
12	90.176.0.0	90.176.0.1–90.191.255.254	90.191.255.255
13	90.192.0.0	90.192.0.1–90.207.255.254	90.207.255.255
14	90.208.0.0	90.208.0.1–90.223.255.254	90.223.255.255
15	90.224.0.0	90.224.0.1–90.239.255.254	90.239.255.255
16	90.240.0.0	90.240.0.1–90.255.255.254	90.255.255.255

That is all there is to it. Do not let Class A subnets intimidate you, they work just as Class B and C, but just with larger numbers.

Let us try some sample problems.

Sample Problem #1

Fill out the subnetting activity form using the address 10.129.212.17 and borrowing 12 bits.

Note: Although this is a private IP address, we can still subnet it.

1. What class is the IP address?

   Class A

   The first octet in a Class A address ranges from 1 to 126 (127 is reserved for loopback, local host, etc.).

2. What is the maximum number of bits that can be borrowed in this class?

   22

   Of the 24 default class C host portion bits, we can borrow 22 leaving 2 behind for hosts.

3. How many octets in this class are dedicated to the network?

   1

4. **How many octets in this class are dedicated to the host?**

   3

5. **How many maximum hosts in this class?**

   16,777,216

   2^{24} = 16,777,216

6. **What is the subnet mask?**

   255.255.240.0

   Represent the subnet mask in binary, 11111111.11111111. 11110000.00000000, and you can recognize the four borrowed bits. Convert the third octet back to decimal, 128 + 64 + 32 + 16 = 240.

7. **What is the subnet prefix?**

   /20

8. **With this subnet mask, what is the maximum number of subnets possible?**

   4,096

   2^{12} = 4,096

9. **With this subnet mask, what is the maximum number of hosts/subnets possible?**

   4,096

   2^{12} = 4,096. Check it: 4096 x 4096 = 16,777,216

10. **What is this subnet's usable number of subnets?**

    4,094

    $2^{12} - 2$ = 4,094

11. **What is the usable number of hosts per subnet?**

    4,094

    $2^{12} - 2$ = 4,094

12. **What is the total number of usable hosts across all subnets?**

    16,760,836

    4,094 x 4,094 = 16,760,836. Look back at the Complete Class A Subnets Table.

13. **What is this subnet's network number (wire address)?**

    10.129.208.0

    Note: Building the table is somewhat ungainly. However, you can build the first few rows to get the pattern down, then mathematically calculate the IP address's wire address.

    We know that the third octet is the incrementing octet. We find using our trick that it increments by decimal 16:

    11111111.11111111.11110000.00000000 = 255.255.240.0

    Our subject IP address, 10.129.212.17, has a third octet decimal value of 212. Divide 212 by 16, and the result is 13.25. Drop the fraction and multiply 13 by 16; the result is 208. This is the third octet of subject IP address' subnet wire address, 10.129.*208*.0.

14. **What is this subnet's broadcast number?**

    10.129.223.255

    Use the pattern. The next wire address is 10.129.224.0 (add 16 to 208). Subtract one host address from the next wire address to obtain the subject IP address' subnet broadcast address 10.129.223.255.

15. **Show the first two address ranges.**

    10.0.0.0–10.0.15.255 Unusable

    10.0.16.0–10.0.31.255

16. **Show the last two address ranges.**

    10.255.224.0–10.255.239.255

    10.255.240.0–10.255.255.255 Unusable

    Use the pattern.

    Subtract 16 from the final broadcast address' third octet (255 – 16) = 239, which gives you the previous broadcast address' third octet, 10.255.*239*.255.

    Fill in the last wire address, 10.255.240.0, then subtract 16 from this wire address' third octet (240 – 16 = 224) to obtain the previous wire address' third octet, 10.255.*224*.0.

    Each wire address' host portions are all 0s, and each broadcast address' host portion is all 1s.

17. Show the IP address in binary.

    00001010.10000001.11010100.00010001

18. Show the subnet mask in binary.

    11111111.11111111.11110000.00000000

19. AND them together.

    00001010.10000001.11010000.00000000

20. Convert the ANDed binary number to dotted decimal.

    10.129.208.0

    This is the original address's subnet wire address.

Sample Problem # 2

Fill out the subnetting activity form using the address 125.225.198.93 borrowing 21 bits.

1. What class is the IP address?

   Class A

2. What is the maximum number of bits that can be borrowed in this class?

   22

3. How many octets in this class are dedicated to the network?

   1

4. How many octets in this class are dedicated to the host?

   3

5. How many maximum hosts in this class?

   16,777,216

6. What is the subnet mask?

   255.255.255.252

7. What is the subnet prefix?

   /29

   Count the number of subnet bits that comprise the network and host protions.

8. With this subnet mask, what is the maximum number of subnets possible?

   2^{21} = 2,097,152

9. With this subnet mask, what is the maximum number of hosts/subnets possible?

   8

10. What is this subnet's usable number of subnets?

    2,097,150

11. What is the usable number of hosts per subnet?

    6

12. What is the total number of usable hosts across all subnets?

    12,582,900

13. What is this subnet's network number (wire address)?

    125.225.198.88

    We subnetted on the fourth octet, so this is where our subnets increment. The subnet changes every 8 hosts. Divide 93 by 8, and the result is 11.625. Drop the fraction, and multiply 11 by 8. The result is the wire address, 125.225.198.88.

    The broadcast address is 8 addresses higher.

    (88 + 8 – 1 = 95)

14. What is this subnet's broadcast number?

    125.225.198.95

15. Show the first two address ranges.

    125.0.0.0–125.0.0.7 Unusable

    125.0.0.8–125.0.0.15

16. Show the last two address ranges.

    125.255.255.240–125.255.255.247

    125.255.255.248–125.255.255.255 Unusable

17. Show the IP address in binary.

    01111101.11100001.11000110.01011101

18. Show the subnet mask in binary.

    11111111.11111111.11111111.11111000

19. AND them together.

    01111101.11100001.11000110.01011000

20. Convert the ANDed binary number to dotted decimal.

    125.225.198.88

Activities

1. Given the subnet mask 255.255.254.0, and considering the trick you learned in Lesson 5 for identifying patterns, in which octet will the subnet wire addresses increment?
   a. First
   b. Second
   c. Third
   d. Fourth
2. When subnetting Class A addresses, which two of the following is the first subnet's wire address equal to? (Choose two.)
   a. The default wire address
   b. The default broadcast address
   c. Netid.255.255.255
   d. Netid.0.0.0
3. Show how you might easily determine the incrementing subnet octet and the increment's decimal magnitude.
   a. 255.192.0.0

      ____

      ____

      ____

      ____

   b. 255.252.0.0

      ____

      ____

   c. 255.255.128.0

      ____

      ____

   d. 255.255.240.0

      ____

      ____

e. 255.255.255.224

f. 255.255.255.252

Extended Activities

1. Use the subnetting activity form for the following exercises.

   a. IP address: 103.224.17.129, Borrow 7 bits

   b. IP address: 129.89.125.17, Borrow 5 bits

c. IP address: 52.98.150.85, Borrow 13 bits

d. IP address: 11.100.165.9, Borrow 18 bits

2. Go to **http://www.wildpackets.com/products/demos** and download their subnet calculator application. Use this to check your work.

   Alternately, use the online subnet calculator at **http://www.docutech.com/calc/subcalc.htm**.

Lesson 6—CIDR

Someone connects a new network to the Internet every 30 seconds, according to Pacific Bell Internet. Even though subnetting techniques conserve IP addresses, they still leave as many as 97 percent of the available addresses unused. Had the Internet Engineering Task Force (IETF) not designed CIDR, Internet growth would have screeched to a halt years ago.

Request for Comments (RFCs) 1518 and 1519 specified supernetting, or CIDR, as an addressing scheme that would conserve Internet addresses and reduce Internet router routing table entries. This lesson discusses CIDR.

Objectives

At the end of this lesson you will be able to:

- Explain why we need CIDR
- Describe how CIDR aggregates IP network addresses
- Explain how CIDR reduces Internet router routing table sizes
- Build supernets

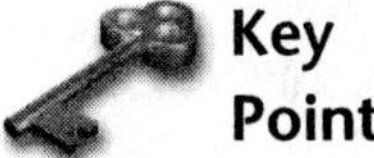

CIDR conserves IP addresses and reduces routing table sizes.

Why Do We Need CIDR?

The Internet continues to nearly double in size every year. The Internet Growth Diagram illustrates Internet growth between the years 1996 and early 2001.

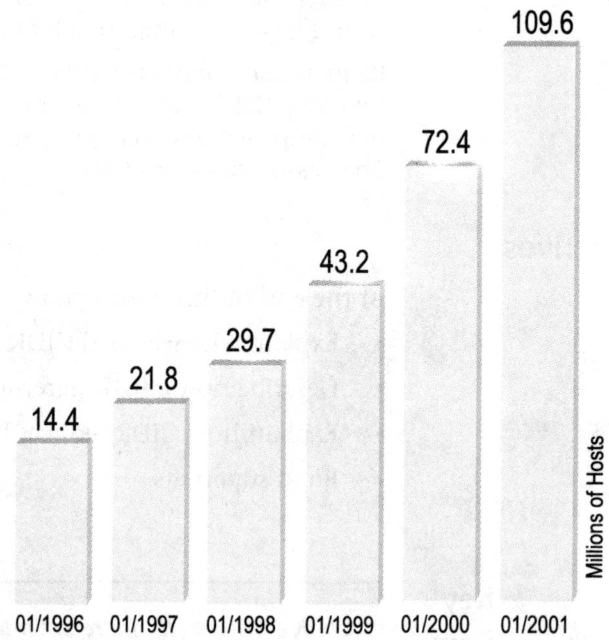

Internet Growth

The global Internet is a loose coalition of semiautonomous networks (ISPs and carriers), each operating with its own policies, services, and customers. Each network makes independent decisions about where and how to secure the various components needed to create the Internet service. Routers provide the Internet packet–switching backbone, making these independent packet-handling decisions based on the service provider's policies.

A common address space (IP) is the glue that ties these separate networks into a cohesive whole. Routing protocols, such as the Interior Gateway Routing Protocol (IGRP) used within autonomous systems, and the Exterior Gateway Protocol (EGP) used between autonomous systems, ensure routers know how to move packets from one network segment to another. We discuss BGP and EGP more in Unit 6.

Routers use routing tables to locate the best path over which to route packets between networks; routing protocols build routing tables. A routing table entry could look as shown in the Sample Routing Table:

Sample Routing

Destination Address	Subnet Mask	Gateway Address
220.80.88.0	255.255.255.0	220.80.89.1
220.80.89.0	255.255.255.0	220.80.89.1
220.80.90.0	255.255.255.0	220.80.89.1
220.80.91.0	255.255.255.0	220.80.89.1
220.80.92.0	255.255.255.0	220.80.89.1
220.80.93.0	255.255.255.0	220.80.89.1
220.80.94.0	255.255.255.0	220.80.89.1
220.80.95.0	255.255.255.0	220.80.89.1

A router needs to know where to send packets destined for remote networks, and it makes these decisions by looking in its routing table. The Routed Network Diagram illustrates a small, routed internetwork.

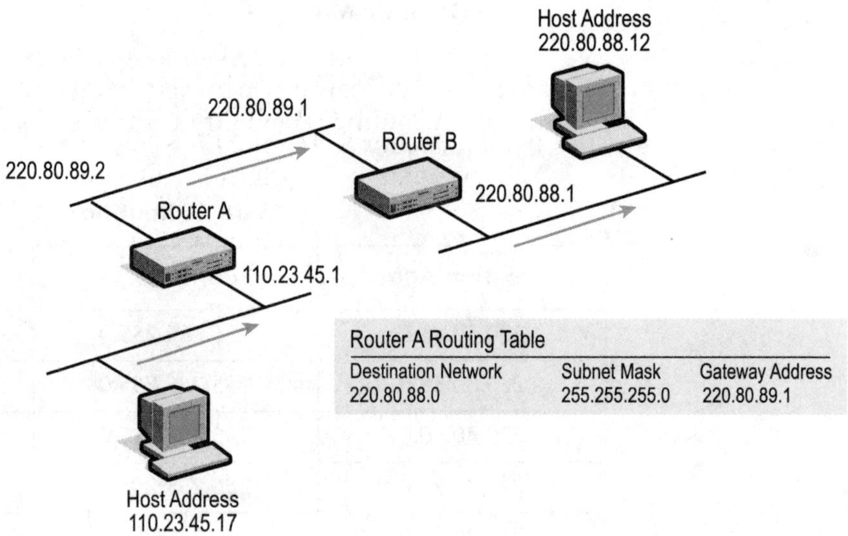

Routed Network

To find how to send packets to the host 220.80.88.12, the source network Router A looks in its routing table for an entry for network 220.80.88.0. Router A sends the packets to the gateway address 220.80.89.1, which is a port on the directly connected remote Router B.

Studies performed in the early 1990s indicated that by mid-1994, Internet router routing tables would have reached their maximum theoretical size of 60,000 entries, effectively shutting down Internet growth. Additionally, too many addresses went unused. The default Class B address ranges supplied more address than most single organizations could use, and Class C address ranges supplied too few. Therefore, organizations had no choice but to obtain a Class B range, and hold many unused addresses in reserve.

CIDR is designed to resolve these two issues. CIDR supports address summarization, or aggregation. Address aggregation assigns a network provider a contiguous Class C address block. The provider then suballocates these blocks to their customers. The provider only advertises routes to the aggregate block's network address, not the individual customer addresses.

Additionally, CIDR provides more flexible address assignments, allowing organizations to more efficiently cover their host addressing requirements by obtaining consecutive Class C addresses, rather than a single Class B. CIDR treats these consecutive addresses as a single, aggregate supernetwork.

How CIDR Works

CIDR restructures the old, classful routing process of assigning Class A, B, and C addresses. Instead of limiting addresses to network portions 8, 16, or 24 bits long, CIDR provides prefixes from 13 to 27 bits in length. Administrators can assign address blocks to as few as 32 hosts, or to over 500,000. These address block assignments can much more closely fit an organization's specific addressing needs.

A CIDR address includes the standard 32-bit-long IP address and information on how many bits compose the network prefix. For example, the CIDR address 207.14.3.48/25 represents the first 25 address bits as the address's network portion, leaving the remaining bits as host bits. The CIDR Prefixes Table lists the CIDR prefixes, the number of Class C addresses each creates, and the number of hosts per network.

CIDR Prefixes

CIDR Prefix	Number of Equivalent Class C Networks	Number of Host Addresses per Network
/27	1/8 of a Class C	32
/26	1/4 of a Class C	64
/25	1/2 of a Class C	128
/24	1	256
/23	2	512
/22	4	1,024
/21	8	2,048
/20	16	4,096
/19	32	8,192
/18	64	16,384

CIDR Prefixes (Continued)

CIDR Prefix	Number of Equivalent Class C Networks	Number of Host Addresses per Network
/17	128	32,768
/16	256 (1 Class B)	65,536
/15	512	131,072
/14	1,024	262,144
/13	2,048	524,288

CIDR is based on supernetting, a derivative of subnetting; think of supernetting as subnetting in reverse. Recall that subnetting incorporates bits borrowed from the host portion into an address's network portion. On the other hand, supernetting allows us to move the network portion to the left, giving more bits to the host portion. This classless supernetting technique reduces the number of routing table entries carriers present to the Internet routing domain, aggregating a group of smaller, classful networks into one larger, single routing table entry.

Large ISPs obtain address blocks prefixed with 15 or more bits (512 Class Cs, 131,072 hosts). They then suballocate these blocks to their customers with /27 to /19 prefixes; this suballocation process is called nesting. In turn, these customers may suballocate, or nest, their blocks even further. An important concept concerning CIDR is that the ISP's routers only advertise the ISP's single address block; any Internet traffic destined for the nested customer address blocks routes first to the ISP's router interfaces. The ISP's internal routers route the customer traffic to their individual networks. The Nested IP Network Diagram illustrates this concept.

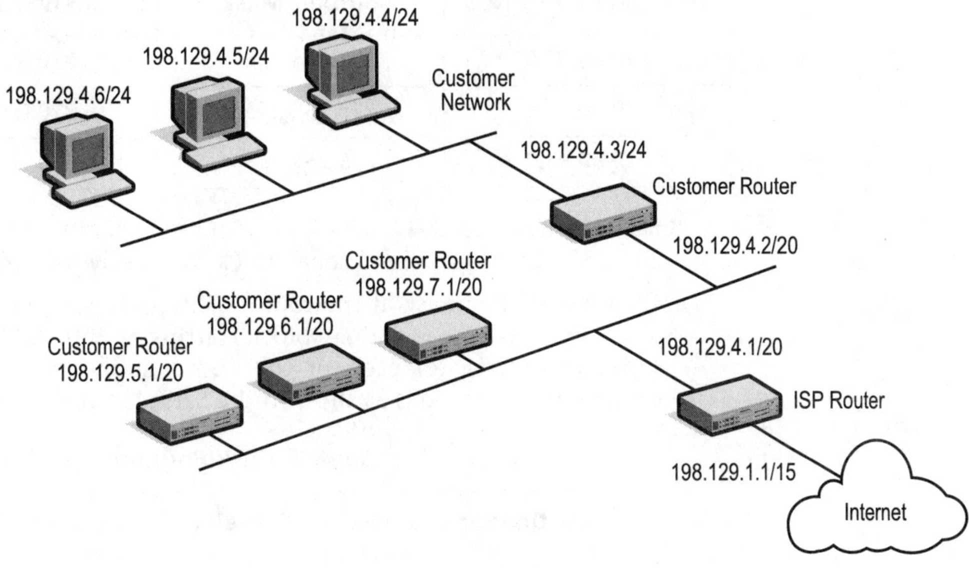

Nested IP Network

Creating a Supernet

Looking at the Sample Routing Table, we see that in order to route traffic to separate Class C networks using subnetting techniques, we need to build a routing table entry for each network.

Sample Routing

Destination Address	Subnet Mask	Gateway Address
220.80.88.0	255.255.255.0	220.80.88.1
220.80.89.0	255.255.255.0	220.80.88.1
220.80.90.0	255.255.255.0	220.80.88.1
220.80.91.0	255.255.255.0	220.80.88.1
220.80.92.0	255.255.255.0	220.80.88.1

Sample Routing (Continued)

Destination Address	Subnet Mask	Gateway Address
220.80.93.0	255.255.255.0	220.80.88.1
220.80.94.0	255.255.255.0	220.80.88.1
220.80.95.0	255.255.255.0	220.80.88.1

Each address 220.80.x.0 entry, with the default network mask 255.255.255.0, specifies a separate Class C network wire address.

CIDR alters this mask at the router's internetwork (outside) interface. Given a Class C address block starting at 220.80.88.0, we can supernet (aggregate) each of the above addresses and create a router entry that looks as show in the Sample CIDR Routing Table.

Sample CIDR Routing

Destination Address	IP Prefix	Gateway Address
220.80.88.0	/21	220.80.88.1

This entry represents the eight separate Class C networks as one aggregated router table entry assigned the new 21-bit prefix.

The supernet member addresses should form a complete, contiguous set of the Class C addresses. Let us look at this from a binary standpoint:

11111111.11111111.11111000.00000000 = /21 (prefix bits)

11011100.01010000.01011000.00000000 = 220.80.88.0/24

11011100.01010000.01011001.00000000 = 220.80.89.0/24

11011100.01010000.01011010.00000000 = 220.80.90.0/24

11011100.01010000.01011011.00000000 = 220.80.91.0/24

11011100.01010000.01011100.00000000 = 220.80.92.0/24

11011100.01010000.01011101.00000000 = 220.80.93.0/24

11011100.01010000.01011110.00000000 = 220.80.94.0/24

11011100.01010000.01011111.00000000 = 220.80.95.0/24

*11011100.01010000.01011*000.00000000 = 220.80.88.0/21

CIDR prefixed address: *11011100.01010000.01011*000.00000000 = 220.80.88.0/21

The aggregate address' 21-bit mask retains the same bit pattern across all eight of the Class C network addresses. The remaining bits 22–24, known as the difference bits, designate the eight separate networks within the aggregate, covering all eight possible binary bit patterns from 000 to 111. These 3 different bits extend the individual network prefixes to 24 bits, representing the eight separate nested networks.

CIDR benefits include reduced network bandwidth used by routing table updates, and fewer router central processing unit (CPU) and memory resources tied up in the router convergence process. CIDR has worked to maintain current global routing tables at approximately 35,000 entries, significantly below the theoretical maximum.

Let us work some problems and build some supernets.

Sample Problem #1

Given the address block 192.168.16.0/20, create a supernet consisting of 16 Class C networks.

1. Start by showing the prefix in binary:

   11111111.11111111.11110000.00000000 = /20

2. Create 16 separate Class C networks. Determine how many third octet bits we will need to form a contiguous network set, from 0000–1111 (0–15).

   11111111.11111111.1111*xxxx*.00000000

   The italicized bits cover the bit patterns 0000–1111.

3. Determine all the set's subnet wire addresses. We know the first 20 bits retain their current pattern, thus we need to determine which third octet decimal number ranges complete the set.

   Write the addresses in binary, and convert to decimal, including the individual network prefixes:

   11000000.10101000.0001*0000*.00000000 = 192.168.16.0/24

   11000000.10101000.0001*0001*.00000000 = 192.168.17.0/24

   11000000.10101000.0001*0010*.00000000 = 192.168.18.0/24

   11000000.10101000.0001*0011*.00000000 = 192.168.19.0/24

   11000000.10101000.0001*0100*.00000000 = 192.168.20.0/24

   11000000.10101000.0001*0101*.00000000 = 192.168.21.0/24

   11000000.10101000.0001*0110*.00000000 = 192.168.22.0/24

   11000000.10101000.0001*0111*.00000000 = 192.168.23.0/24

11000000.10101000.0001*1000*.00000000 = 192.168.24.0/24

11000000.10101000.0001*1001*.00000000 = 192.168.25.0/24

11000000.10101000.0001*1010*.00000000 = 192.168.26.0/24

11000000.10101000.0001*1011*.00000000 = 192.168.27.0/24

11000000.10101000.0001*1100*.00000000 = 192.168.28.0/24

11000000.10101000.0001*1101*.00000000 = 192.168.29.0/24

11000000.10101000.0001*1110*.00000000 = 192.168.30.0/24

11000000.10101000.0001*1111*.00000000 = 192.168.31.0/24

Note that the highlighted bits, the difference bits, increment from 0000–1111. This covers the entire bit pattern range.

4. Write the aggregate address the provider's router advertises to outside networks:

   192.168.16.0/20

   Our supernet bits cover the first 20 bits, leaving the rest for networks and host.

Sample Problem #2

Let us take one of the Class C networks we created above, 192.168.24.0/24, and suballocate it, creating four nested subnetworks. This leaves 64 hosts per subnetwork, meaning we need to leave 6 (2^6) host bits.

1. Start by showing the subnetwork's binary prefix bits:

   11111111.11111111.11111111.00000000 = /24

2. Determine how many fourth octet bits provide for four separate subnetworks. These must form a contiguous set, from 00–11 (0–4). As in subnetting, we assign bits from left to right.

   11111111.11111111.11111111.*xx*000000

   The highlighted bits cover the bit patterns 00–11.

3. Determine the subnet wire addresses included in the nested set. We know from the original prefix bits (/24) that the first 24 bits remain in their current pattern, thus we need to determine what fourth octet decimal ranges complete the set.

Write the address range in binary, and convert to decimal:

11000000.10101000.00011000.*00*000000 = 192.168.24.0/26

11000000.10101000.00011000.*01*000000 = 192.168.24.64/26

11000000.10101000.00011000.*10*000000 = 192.168.24.128/26

11000000.10101000.00011000.*11*000000 = 192.168.24.192/26

Note that the highlighted difference bits increment from 00–11. This covers the entire bit pattern range.

4. Write the CIDR address the provider's router advertises to the outside network.

   192.168.24.0/24

   Our supernet bits cover the first 24 bits, leaving the rest for networks and host.

Sample Problem #3

This problem is an example of how an organization might use supernetting to solve a network integration problem:

Your company has just acquired several other firms, each with its own network. You need to integrate these networks with your own existing IP network. You also want to ensure that all locations can access internal and external network resources while maintaining the service levels and performance they experienced prior to the merger. You will use CIDR to advertise these networks to the Internet.

The individual network addresses are:

Your company: 172.16.0.0/28

Firm A: 172.16.1.48/28

Firm B: 172.16.1.176/28

Firm C: 172.16.1.160/28

Firm D: 172.16.1.128/28

Firm E: 172.16.1.144/28

We need to determine how we will advertise these networks. First, let us look at these addresses in binary.

10101100.00010000.00000000.*0000*0000 = 172.16.0.0/28

10101100.00010000.00000001.*0011*0000 = 172.16.1.48/28

10101100.00010000.00000001.*1011*0000 = 172.16.1.176/28

10101100.00010000.00000001.*1010*0000 = 172.16.1.160/28

10101100.00010000.00000001.*1000*0000 = 172.16.1.128/28

10101100.00010000.00000001.*1001*0000 = 172.16.1.144/28

Looking at the different bit patterns, we can see that 172.16.0.0/28 and 172.16.1.48 can not be summarized together, as their bit patterns are too different. However, the rest of the addresses can be summarized, as the twenty-fifth and twenty-sixth bits are the same. This gives us a CIDR address of 172.16.1.128/26. As a result, the routing table entries for the individual networks would contain the following network addresses:

172.16.1.128/26

172.16.1.48/28

172.16.0.0/28

Without CIDR, the routing table would need to store all six network addresses.

Note: The organization aggregating networks must own the entire block from which the supernet is derived. Otherwise, addressing conflicts will occur.

Activities

1. Why did IETF design CIDR?
   a. To eliminate the need for subnet masks
   b. To expand routing table sizes
   c. To reduce routing table entries
   d. To add additional Class B networks
2. How does a router determine where to send packets addressed to hosts on remote networks?
   a. It pings the remote network for its gateway address and subnet mask.
   b. It adds a routing table entry for each unknown host address.
   c. It modifies the destination address to a local address.
   d. It looks in its routing table for an entry for the destination network.
3. Which two of the following result from implementing CIDR? (Choose two.)
   a. Increased router resource usage
   b. Reduced network bandwidth utilization
   c. Conservation of available addresses
   d. Reduced number of Class C networks
4. If we assign a customer a CIDR address block 199.16.64.0/27, how many subnetworks do we create?
   a. 1/8
   b. 1/4
   c. 4
   d. 8

5. Given the following CIDR prefixes and the CIDR Prefixes Table, write the number of hosts and Class C networks each creates.

CIDR Prefixes

CIDR Prefix	Number of Equivalent Class C Networks	Number of Host Addresses per Network
/27	1/8 of a Class C	32
/26	1/4 of a Class C	64
/25	1/2 of a Class C	128
/24	1	256
/23	2	512
/22	4	1,024
/21	8	2,048
/20	16	4,096
/19	32	8,192
/18	64	16,384
/17	128	32,768
/16	256 (1 Class B)	65,536
/15	512	131,072
/14	1,024	262,144
/13	2,048	524,288

a. /14

____

b. /19

____

c. /22

____

d. /24

____

6. Explain how CIDR resolves the problems associated with Internet addressing and expanding routing table sizes.

____

____

____

____

____

____

Extended Activities

1. Create a supernet of 64 aggregated Class C networks from the address block 222.156.64.0/18. Show the individual network wire addresses and prefixes.
2. Create from the address block 198.14.0.0/16 a supernet of 256 aggregated Class C networks. Show the nested network addresses and prefixes.
3. Visit the following URLs to read more on CIDR:
   a. **http://public.pacbell.net/dedicated/cidr.html**
   b. **http://www.freesoft.org/CIE/Course/Subnet/index.htm**

Summary

Unit 3 covered IP addressing in great detail. First, we looked at how network devices look at IP addresses as a set of 32 binary digits, although we work best with decimal numbers. To properly configure routers on a TCP/IP network, we need to know how to convert from binary numbers to decimal, and back. We used the divide by two method to convert from decimal to binary, and to convert from binary to decimal, we added the individual place values to obtain their decimal equivalent.

Lesson 2 introduced subnetting fundamentals. We learned the difference between a default Class A, B, or C network mask and a subnet mask. We learned why organizations would want to define separate subnetworks; to allow for more scalable networks, to contain broadcast traffic, and to conserve host addresses. To create the address's subnet portion, we borrow bits from the host address portion. These bits, in conjunction with the subnet mask, create the subnetwork address on which a host resides. A subnet's first two network and host addresses are unusable (in classful routing), and thus to create the usable host and address ranges we must reduce our maximum hosts and subnets by 2. We learned that IP prefixes provide us a shorthand for representing the number of bits that compose the subnet's network and subnet portions. We learned how to determine the appropriate subnet to suit a particular network addressing need, allowing for the required present and future hosts and subnets, while most efficiently utilizing our allocated host and network addressing space. Finally, we learned of the different broadcast addresses: limited, nondirected, subnet directed, and all-subnet-directed.

Lesson 3 provided instructions on Class C network subnetting, including tricks and techniques applicable to all IP network classes. We learned that in Class C networks we can borrow from 2 to 6 host bits, creating 2 to 62 usable subnets; the subnet mask determines the subnets and their address ranges. To communicate on the same network segment, hosts must share the same network and subnet address portions. We learned that the subnet portion determines the subnet's incremental range, and that we determine the number of hosts per subnet by subtracting 2 from the remaining host bits ($2^{(\text{host bits} - \text{borrowed bits})} - 2$). We found that building a subnetting table helps us to lay out our subnets and host address ranges. We learned that when determining address ranges, we must begin the count from 0. Finally, we learned some quick methods for checking our work, and some patterns to look for when building subnets.

Lesson 4 covered the more complex Class B subnetting procedures. Although the concepts are the same as we used in Class C subnetting, the numbers are larger. Again, we build the subnetting tables to help us organize our subnet ranges. In Class B subnets, we may subnet on either the third or fourth octet. We must recognize the octet in which the subnets increment, and the address' incremental ranges. We found that by dividing a host count greater than 255 by 256, we can determine the incremental subnet range, and the first usable subnet address.

Lesson 5 demonstrated subnetting Class A networks. In Class A networks, we can subnet in the second, third, or fourth octets. We learned a technique that will allow us to quickly determine the subnet increments, and the first usable subnet wire address.

Lesson 6 introduced CIDR, an addressing method designed to reduce routing table size and conserve host addresses. We learned that CIDR supports address aggregation, or summarization, thus Internet routers only need advertise the aggregate address, rather than many smaller subnet addresses. CIDR provides a means of better designing network addressing to better suit a customer's needs, reducing the number of unused addresses. CIDR creates supernets, consisting of a set of subordinate Class C addresses. Network service providers can suballocate these supernets, creating nested networks or subnetworks, which customers can suballocate even further.

Unit 3 Quiz

1. Which broadcast address type broadcasts to the local segment only?
   a. Limited broadcast
   b. Nondirected broadcast
   c. Subnet-directed broadcast
   d. All-subnet-directed broadcast
2. Using the Subnet Exercise Form, subnet the following addresses:
   a. 10.5.43.205, Borrow 7 bits

   b. 130.228.67.13, Borrow 5 bits

c. 123.223.89.203, Borrow 20 bits

d. 20. 221.12.93.129, Borrow 3 bits

e. 180.36.65.202, Borrow 14 bits

f. 132.198.224.17, Borrow 5 bits

3. Your customer is planning to franchise their network services division, initially selling 14 franchises, but planning as much as 300-percent growth in five years. Each franchise includes 30 TCP/IP network nodes, plus two router ports. The home office currently leases from their ISP a Class B network address, 131.17.0.0. Part of the franchise agreement is that the franchiser provides the franchisees high-speed Internet access through the home office network. Your customer (the franchiser) plans to provide this connectivity with dedicated T1 lines run from the home office router to the franchise locations.

   They want you to set up an IP addressing scheme that will provide for their five-year growth plans, and yet most efficiently allocate their host addresses. How will you subnet this network, and why?

   ___

   ___

   ___

   ___

   ___

   ___

   ___

   ___

4. You work for an ISP that uses Qwest Communications as their carrier. Qwest assigns your employer the CIDR address block 218.2.0.0/16. They want you to suballocate this address block to provide 254 host addresses to each of your corporate customers.

   How many nested networks must you create? List each nested network's wire address and prefix.

6. Convert the following binary numbers to decimal:
   a. 11001110
   b. 00111010
   c. 10001101
   d. 00001011
   e. 11110011

7. Convert the following decimal numbers to binary:
   a. 193
   b. 253
   c. 98
   d. 131
   e. 47

8. Represent the following subnet masks with prefix bits.

   a. 255.255.0.0

   ____

   b. 255.224.0.0

   ____

   c. 255.255.254.0

   ____

   d. 255.255.255.240

   ____

   e. 255.255.248.0

   ____

Unit 4
TCP/IP Protocols

This unit takes a detailed look at how the underlying Transmission Control Protocol/Internet Protocol (TCP/IP) works. When information must be sent between two applications on a TCP/IP network, the applications must use the services of TCP, User Datagram Protocol (UDP), IP, plus local area network (LAN) and wide area network (WAN) protocols for the particular network.

We begin by looking at IP and how IP packets, or datagrams, are routed through a TCP/IP network. We look at the various IP packet header components, and how IP processes divide packets into fragments before sending them down to the Data Link Layer.

We investigate two IP-related protocols, Address Resolution Protocol (ARP) and Reverse Address Resolution Protocol (RARP), and their uses for resolving logical addresses to physical addresses, and physical addresses to logical.

We also look at the operation of the two transport protocols, UDP and TCP. UDP, used in connectionless networks, is normally coupled with applications such as Simple Network Management Protocol (SNMP) and Domain Name System (DNS). TCP, the connection-oriented counterpart to UDP, is coupled with applications such as File Transfer Protocol (FTP) and Hypertext Transfer Protocol (HTTP).

We conclude the unit by looking at how all the protocols work together to move information between communicating applications.

Lessons

1. IP
2. Address Resolution
3. UDP
4. TCP and Connection Establishment
5. TCP and Data Transmission
6. Moving Information Across a TCP/IP Network

Terms

fragmentation—Fragmentation is the IP process of dividing a datagram into smaller pieces that will better suit the transporting network's MTU.

IP Version 6—IPv6, also known as IP next generation, is a new version of the IP currently being reviewed in the IETF standards committees. IPv6 adds features over the current IPv4, including longer addresses (128 bits) and better QoS support.

mailbox—When referring to IP sockets, this is a software-specified storage area where the local IP process forwards inbound segments to the TCP process. TCP, in turn, forwards the data to the destination application.

Maximum Transmission Unit (MTU)—MTU is the maximum amount of information that can be carried by a datagram or frame. For example, the MTU of Ethernet is 1,500 bytes of information.

Proxy ARP—Proxy ARP is a variation of the ARP protocol, where an intermediate device, such as a router, sends an ARP response to the requesting host on behalf of the end node.

socket—A socket is a software object that connects an application to a network protocol. In UNIX, for example, a program can send and receive TCP/IP messages by opening a socket and reading and writing data to and from the socket. A TCP process creates a socket from the host's IP address combined with a port number, and each TCP connection includes two sockets, one for each connected host.

Time to Live (TTL)—TTL is a technique used in best-effort delivery systems to avoid packet loops. Each IP datagram is assigned an integer TTL when it is created. IP gateways decrement the TTL field when they process a datagram and discard it if the TTL value reaches zero.

Lesson 1—IP

IP is responsible for transmitting blocks of data (datagrams) through an interconnected set of networks. IP receives these blocks from higher level protocols such as TCP or UDP, and transmits them through the Internet.

Objectives

At the end of this lesson you will be able to:

- Describe the basic functions provided by IP
- Discuss IP frame encapsulation
- Describe internet datagram fragmentation and reassembly
- Define an internet datagram's lifetime
- List the network monitoring features provided by IP options
- Describe the IP header format and field description

Key Point

IP provides connectionless delivery of datagrams across a TCP/IP network.

Overview of IP

IP provides a connectionless (datagram) delivery service between end-stations. Each datagram carries a full destination IP address, and is routed through the system independent of all other datagrams. No connections or logical circuits are established.

Individual network segments can set varying maximum packet sizes, called the Maximum Transmission Unit (MTU). IP provides a mechanism for fragmenting and reassembling datagrams to match a network's MTU.

An IP software module resides in all hosts and routers running the TCP/IP protocol stack. These modules share common rules for internet datagram address field interpretation and fragmenting and reassembling. Additionally, these modules provide procedures for making routing decisions and other help functions, such as ARP and Internet Control Message Protocol (ICMP) messages.

IP provides internetwork communication by passing a datagram from one host's IP module to the IP module on another host, until the datagram reaches its final destination. The datagram can traverse several hosts on its way to its destination; each host through which the datagram passes is called a hop. The network routes the datagram from host to host, based on the destination IP address carried in the IP header. The datagram may travel through several networks before reaching its final destination, as shown in the Routed Network Diagram.

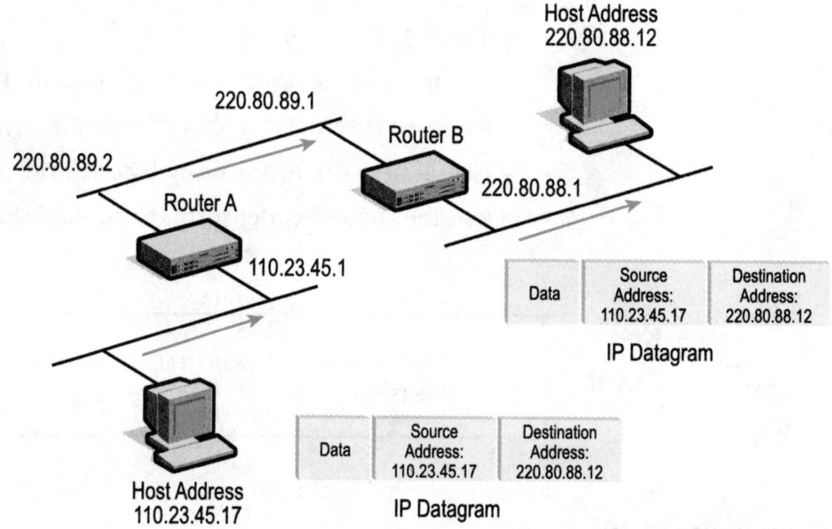

Routed Network

Specific IP characteristics include:

- There is little data error control. IP provides a 16-bit header checksum, calculated from the header's length, that receiving stations use to validate a packet. The receiving station discards packets with invalid checksums.
- There are no end-to-end or hop-by-hop receipt acknowledgements.
- There are no provisions for the retransmission of lost or corrupted data.
- There are no packet sequencing or flow control mechanisms.

The IP and OSI Model Diagram illustrates the role of IP relative to the Open Systems Interconnection (OSI) reference model.

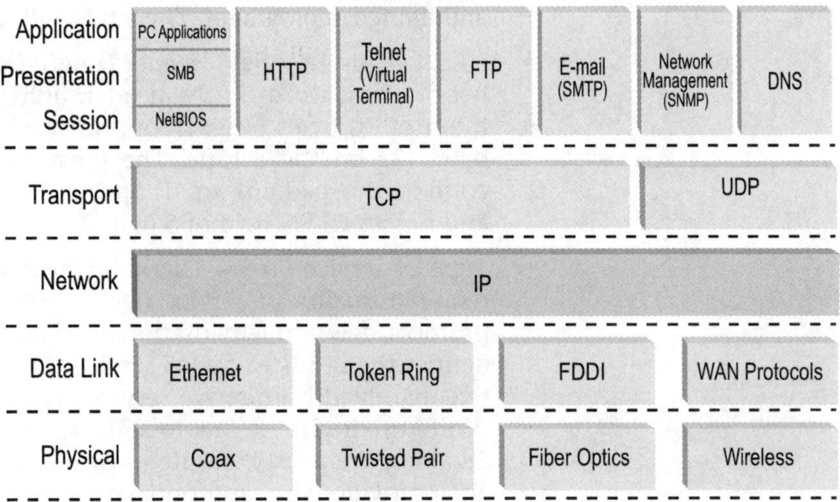

IP and OSI Model

IP Header Format and Field Descriptions

The IP Header Format Diagram illustrates the various fields incorporated into an IP datagram. These fields are described below.

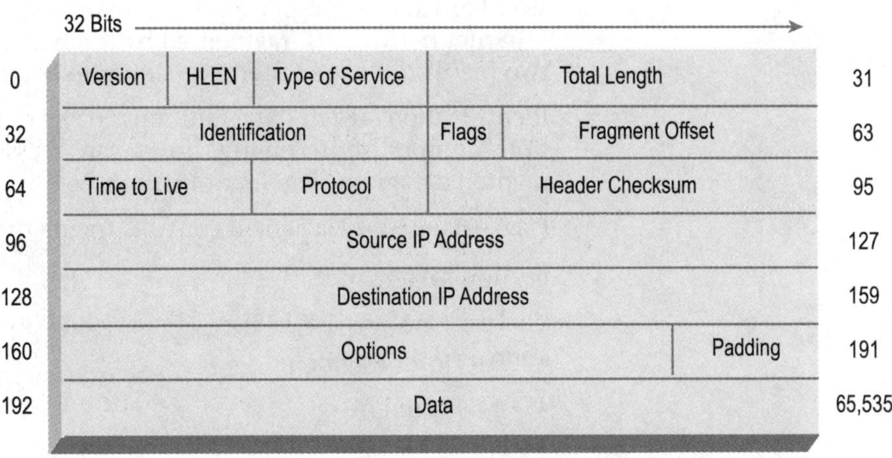

IP Header Format

- Version—This 4-bit field contains the IP version used to create the datagram. This field ensures that the sender, receiver, and intervening gateways agree on the correct datagram format. The most widely used IP version is version 4; IPv6 is now in testing and limited deployment. These bits will read 0100 for IPv4.
- HLEN—This 4-bit field Header Length field provides the number of 32-bit words in the header. IP headers must be a minimum of 20 bytes long. IP options can extend the field by 4 bytes (32 bits) at a time. The most common header, which contains no padding or IP options, measures 20 bytes long and has an HLEN field of 5 (0101).
- Type of service (ToS)—This 8-bit field specifies a datagram's required quality of service (QoS). Because IP is a best effort protocol, few implementations use the ToS fields as RFC791 defines them. Instead, QoS services used for such delay-sensitive, bandwidth-intensive services as video and Voice over IP (VoIP) modify these bits to suit their needs. Network devices all along the packet's route must recognize these bit settings, and provide the appropriate network services. RFC1349 refines the original ToS designations.
- Total Length—This 16-bit field provides an IP datagram's length in bytes, including the header and data (Data Length = Total Length – HLEN). The maximum size is 65,535 bytes, and all hosts must be able to handle a packet of at least 576 bytes.

  Identification, Flags, and Fragment Offset control datagram's fragmentation and reassembly. Most datagrams are fragmented and encapsulated into multiple frames of a smaller size. For example, a packet 2,500 bytes long, carried over an Ethernet network, is fragmented by the transmitting host into two pieces to fit the Ethernet maximum MTU of 1,500 bytes.
- Identification—Each datagram must have a unique identification number so receiving hosts can reassemble the fragmented datagram. The Identification field is 16 bits long.
- Flags—The 3-bit Flags field controls fragmentation

  Bit 0—Reserved

  Bit 1—Don't fragment bit:

  - 0—Don't fragment
  - 1—Fragment

Bit 2—More fragments bit:

- 0—Last fragment
- 1—More fragments follow

If a network device is preparing to send a datagram longer than the network MTU and sees the don't fragment bit set, it returns an ICMP error message to the sender and discards the packet. All fragments but the last have the more fragments bit set to 1.

- Fragment Offset—The 13-bit Fragment Offset field specifies the fragment's location in the original datagram. The first fragment has offset 0, and the remaining fragments are measured as eight 8-byte units, representing the fragment's beginning in relation to the start of the original payload.
- Time to Live (TTL)—This 8-bit field specifies the time (in seconds) the datagram is allowed to remain on the internetwork. Each gateway and host the packet traverses decrements this field by one; after the packet's TTL expires, network devices remove it from the network. Because network devices almost always forward a packet in less than 1 second, the TTL is used as the packet's hop count.
- Protocol—The 8-bit Protocol field specifies which high-level protocol was used to create the message carried in the Data area of a datagram. For example, TCP is assigned protocol number 6, and UDP is assigned protocol number 17.
- Header Checksum—This 16-bit field is used as an IP header checksum only. Because some Header fields change as the packet traverses the network (for example, the TTL or the ToS bits), each hop where the header is processed recomputes the checksum.
- Source and Destination IP Addresses—These 32-bit fields specify the sender and expected recipient IP addresses. They do not change as the packets traverse the network.
- Options—This variable-length field is used for various options, such as recording the route taken, specifying the route to be taken, and time stamping. The option field can be zero or more bits in length. Padding is used to ensure that the option field fills at least 32 bits.
- Padding—This field consists of a specific number of 0 bits added to guarantee the IP header ends on a 32-bit boundary.

ToS

The ToS field is used to indicate the QoS desired by the original source of a datagram. Unfortunately, there is no guarantee the other devices on the Internet will honor the source station's request for a particular ToS. The ToS Field Diagram illustrates the bit layout for this field.

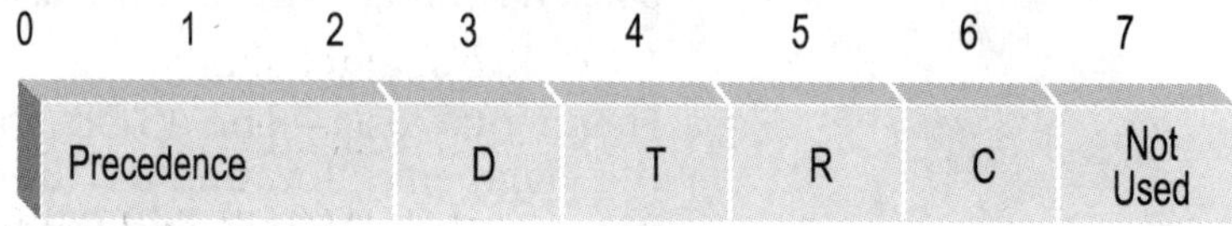

ToS Field

Precedence Bits

The ToS field Precedence bits (bits 0–2) are used by a source host to convey to other devices on the internetwork a datagram's relative importance (precedence). These bits were designed to provide a mechanism that would allow a router to treat certain datagrams as more important than other types of traffic; for example, a network can only accept datagrams above a certain precedence at times of high network load. This field's values range from 0 (low) to 7 (high). The bits can be set as follows, from highest to lowest:

111—Network Control

110—Internetwork Control

101—Critical

100—Flash override

011—Flash

010—Immediate

001—Priority

000—Routine

D-T-R-C Bits

Until recently, most network devices ignored the ToS field D-T-R-C bits (bits 3–7). With the advent of the Open Shortest Path First (OSPF) routing protocol, IP routers began to support ToS routing. The D-T-R-C bits are described below.

Bit 3: D-(Delay) bit—Used by a source host to request either low delay or normal delay. The defined bit states are:

- 0—Normal delay
- 1—Low delay

Bit 4: T-(Throughput) bit—Used by a source host to request either high or normal throughput. The defined bit states are:

- 0—Normal throughput
- 1—High throughput

Bit 5: R-(Reliability) bit—Used by a source host to request either high reliability or normal reliability. The defined bit states are:

- 0—Normal reliability
- 1—High reliability

Bits 6–7—Reserved for future use. The defined bit states are:

- 00—Reserved

Typically, Routing Information Protocol (RIP) ignores ToS bits, but OSPF can route according to ToS requests.

Fragmentation

Fragmentation is the process of dividing a large IP datagram into several smaller pieces. This is necessary when the IP module is forced to transmit a large packet through a "small packet" network (one with a smaller MTU).

MTU

A network's MTU is the maximum packet or frame size, in bytes, that a network interface can handle. At the time an end-to-end connection is established, the receiving host announces to the sender the maximum Transport Layer segment size it can handle. The sender then encapsulates these segments into IP packets of a size suitable to the network interface's MTU.

However, in a routed network, packets may traverse multiple network devices, each likely with a different MTU. The sending and receiving hosts have no knowledge of these MTU variances. As a result, although the source station's Transport Layer protocols efficiently divided the data stream into segments, and the IP module built packets for efficient delivery across its directly connected network, the resulting packets may eventually be fragmented to match another network segment's MTU.

The datagram fragments traverse the Internet as individual, smaller datagrams, until they reach their final destination. The destination host is responsible for reassembling the fragments into the original message. The concept of fragmentation is illustrated on the Fragmentation Diagram.

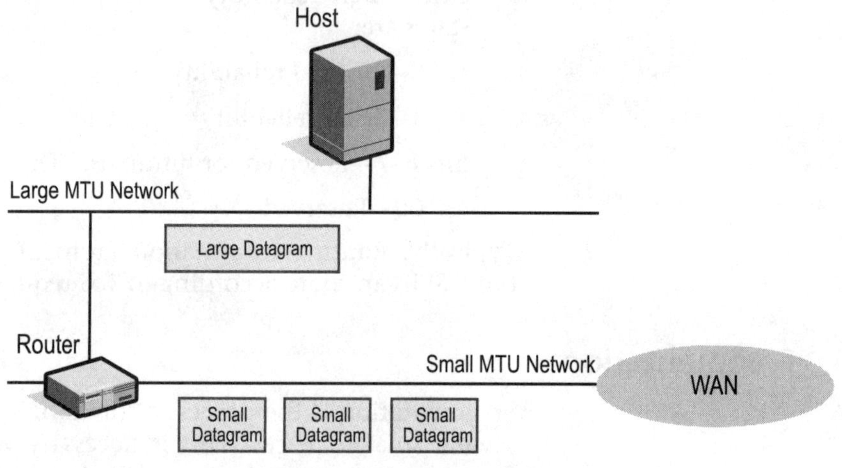

Fragmentation

An Internet datagram may be marked as "don't fragment." If it becomes necessary to transmit a "don't fragment" datagram through a network with a smaller MTU, the datagram will be discarded, and the discarding device will send an ICMP error message to the originator informing it of this action.

Fragmentation can allow different parts of an internetwork to maximize performance without requiring that each host know each intervening network's specific MTU. Routers can correct mismatched MTUs using a built-in automatic translation service.

Fields Controlling Fragmentation

Four fields in the IP header are used to control datagram fragmentation and reassembly:

- Identification—Provides a unique integer that identifies a datagram's fragments. The datagram's source assigns this value to the original, unfragmented datagram. If a device fragments the datagram, it copies this value into the Identification field of all resulting fragments. As the fragments arrive at the final destination, this value, along with the source address, identifies the original datagram to which the fragment belongs.

- Total Length—Provides the total length of the datagram (measured in bytes), including the IP header and data. All hosts must be prepared to accept datagrams of up to 576 bytes. Hosts should only send datagrams larger than 576 bytes when the network administrator is certain the destination is prepared to accept larger datagrams.
- Fragment Offset—Indicates where in the original datagram the fragment belongs. The value is a measure in units of 8 bytes from the start of the original datagram. The first fragment has offset zero.
- Flags—Controls fragmentation. These bits' settings determine whether a datagram may be fragmented. If a datagram is fragmented, the Flags field is used to indicate whether there are more fragments, or whether this is the last fragment "n" in a series.

Fragmentation Example

In the following example, a datagram arrives at a router and must be fragmented so it can be transmitted across a "small packet" (or one with a smaller MTU) network. This example is illustrated in the Packet Fragment Diagram.

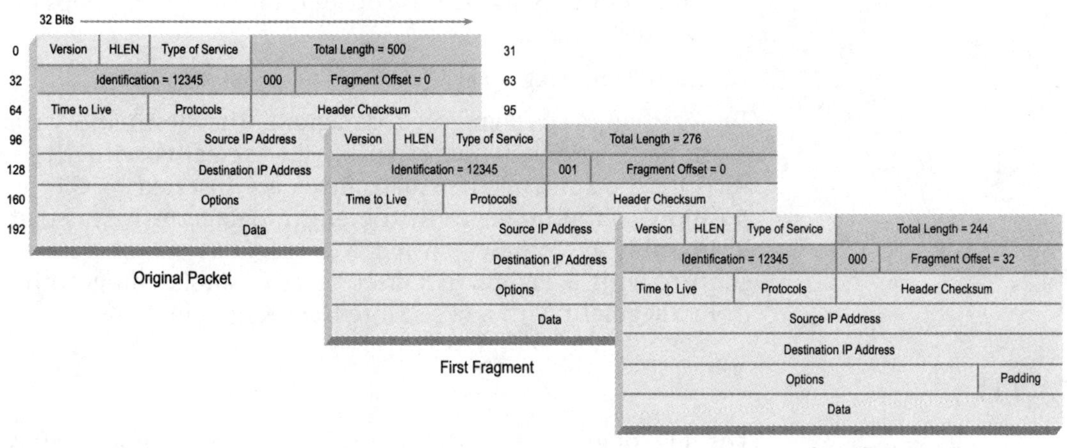

Packet Fragment

Assume the MTU is 280 bytes, and the IP header is 20 bytes in length.

- Original Datagram:

  Identification = 12345

  Total Length = 500 (20 IP header bytes + 480 data bytes)

  Fragment Offset = 0

  More Data Flag = False

The router divides the datagram into two fragments:

- First Fragment:

  Identification = 12345

  Total Length = 276 (20 IP header bytes + 256 data bytes)

  Fragment Offset = 0

  More Data Flag = True

- Second Fragment:

  Identification = 12345

  Total Length = 244 (20 IP header bytes + 224 data bytes)

  Fragment Offset = 32 (The offset is measured in groups of 8 bytes)

  More Data Flag = False

To reassemble a fragmented datagram, the destination station must have sufficient buffer space. As segments with the same Identification arrive, their data fields are inserted in the proper position in the buffer until the entire datagram is reassembled. Reassembly is complete when a contiguous set of data exists, starting with a Fragment Offset of zero, and ending with data from a segment with a false More Data Flag field.

TTL

The TTL field is set by the original source host and specifies the time a datagram is allowed to circulate in the internetwork. If dynamic or static routing is used, a datagram can potentially loop through the network indefinitely. The looping is caused by inaccurate or misconfigured routing tables. An endlessly circulating datagram consumes valuable network resources and may interfere with the Transport Layer protocol's efforts to keep track of the missing datagram.

Each datagram is marked with a TTL value to help avoid these problems. Each host or router decrements the TTL field by one each time they process the datagram. When the TTL field is reduced to zero, the datagram is discarded. If a router or host discards a datagram because of an expired TTL, the router or host sends an ICMP message to the source host indicating the datagram has been discarded.

Protocol

The Protocol field provides a way for IP datagrams to carry more than one Transport Layer protocol in a given data stream. For example, two communicating hosts might be sharing HTTP and DNS information simultaneously. As we already know, HTTP uses TCP as its Transport Layer protocol, and DNS can use UDP. The Protocol field allows the sending device to multiplex segments from these two different Transport Layer protocols into one packet stream destined for the same end node.

Multiplexing is a process that places multiple types of communication signals over a single communication channel. Demultiplexing, on the other hand, refers to the practice of separating a single input into several outputs, as illustrated on the Demultiplexing Transport Protocols Diagram.

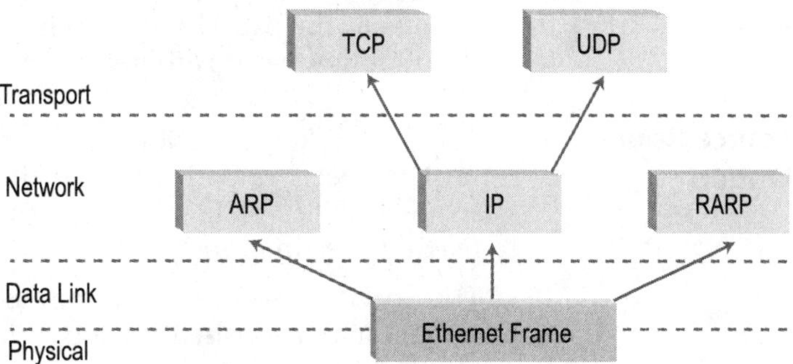

Demultiplexing Transport Protocols

Incoming datagrams are demultiplexed and sent to the appropriate Transport Layer protocol based on the Protocol field. If the receiving device sees a Protocol field set to 6, it knows to send the datagram's data to the TCP protocol. If it sees 17 in the Protocol field, it knows to send the data to the UDP protocol.

The original source of an IP datagram places a value in the Protocol field to indicate whether the source Transport Layer protocol was TCP or UDP. The receiving computer uses this information to forward the incoming datagram to the correct Transport Layer process. RFC790 specifies the assigned protocol numbers.

Addressing

The fundamental purpose of IP is to move datagrams through an interconnected set of networks. Devices route the datagrams from one Internet module to another, through individual networks, based on the interpretation of the IP address. One important feature of IP is the implementation and recognition of IP addressing.

Options

Although the Options fields are just that, optional, nonetheless all network device IP modules must support these fields. The Options field's main purpose is to provide network administrators with a tool to test and debug the network. Options used in any particular datagram is at the network administrator's discretion.

Record Route Option

The Record Route Option feature allows a source host to reserve space in the datagram header for an empty list of IP addresses. Each router that processes the datagram is required to add its IP address to the list. This option is useful to monitor the path a datagram follows as it is routed through the Internet.

Source Route Option

The Source Route Option feature provides a method for a source host to specify a path through the Internet. The sender places a sequenced list of IP addresses that a datagram must follow to reach its destination.

The specified source route may be either strict (only the listed routers may be visited) or loose (other intermediate routers may also be visited). The network administrator may use both of these Source Route Options to test data throughput over the specified network path.

Time Stamp Option

The Time Stamp Option feature is similar to the Record Route Option, except a source host reserves space in the datagram header for an empty list of router time stamps. Each router is required to record the time and date that it processes the datagram. Network administrators use this option to monitor network performance. In another variation of the Time Stamp Option feature, each router records both a time stamp and its IP address into the datagram's header. This option allows the receiving station to determine the route and performance factors for the datagram as it crosses the internetwork.

IP Packet Encapsulation

The Ethernet Packet Diagram shows that an IP datagram is encapsulated as the data portion of an Ethernet frame.

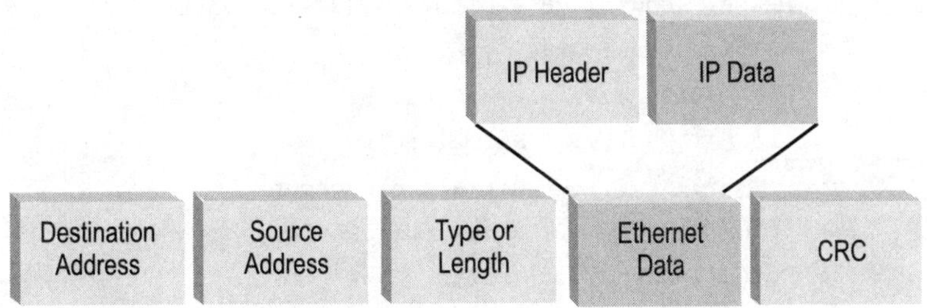

Ethernet Packet

An IP packet encapsulates data sent to it from the Transport Layer. The Data Link Layer protocol (in this example Ethernet, but it could be any LAN or WAN Layer 2 protocol) in turn encapsulates the IP packet as its own data. Physical addresses help the frame find its way across the wire, and when the packet must move to another network, the Data Link Layer frame is stripped away. The next hop device forwards the packet on toward its destination with the source and destination IP addresses and Layer 4 data intact (though possibly fragmented), encapsulated in a new Layer 2 frame or packet.

Activities

The following information is an example of trace data (information that was captured on an Ethernet network). It shows the Ethernet frame encapsulating an IP packet encapsulating a TCP message. Review the information and answer the following questions.

```
Packet 1 captured at 03/24/1998 01:19:35 PM; Packet size is 58(0x3a)bytes
      Relative time: 000:00:05.337
      Delta time: 0.000.000
Ethernet Version II
      Address: 00-60-94-05-11-D9 --->00-60-08-3B-92-06
      Ethernet II Protocol Type: IP
Internet Protocol
      Version(MSB 4 bits): 4
      Header length(LSB 4 bits): 5 (32-bit word)
      Service type: 0x00
            000. .... = 0 - Routine
            ...0 .... = Normal delay
            .... 0... = Normal throughput
            .... .0.. = Normal reliability
      Total length: 44 (Octets)
      Fragment ID: 8706
      Flags summary: 0x40
            0... .... = Reserved
            .1.. .... = Do not fragment
            ..0. .... = Last fragment
            Fragment offset(LSB 13 bits): 0 (0x00)
      Time to live: 32 seconds/hops
      IP protocol type: TCP (0x06)
      Checksum: 0xF1D7
      IP address 205.169.85.162 ->205.169.85.253
      No option
Transmission Control Protocol
      Port 1078 ---> World Wide Web HTTP
      Sequence Number: 4029396
      Acknowledgement Number: 0
      Header Length(MSB 4 bits): 6 (32-bit word)
      Reserved(LSB 4 bits): 0
```

```
    Code: 0x02
          RES: 00.. .... = Reserved
          URG: ..0. .... = Urgent Pointer is Invalid
          ACK: ...0 .... = Acknowledgement Field is Invalid
          PSH: .... 0... = No push Requested
          RST: .... .0.. = No reset Connection
          SYN: .... ..1. = Synchronize Sequence Number
          FIN: .... ...0 = More Data From Sender
    Window: 8192
    Checksum: 0xB09C
    Urgent Pointer: 0x0000
    TCP Option: 020405B4

Packet: 1
0000: 00 60 08 3b 92 06 00 60 94 05 11 d9 08 00 45 00 | .`.;...`...Ù..E.
0010: 00 2c 22 02 40 00 20 06 f1 d7 cd a9 55 a2 cd a9 | .,".@. .ñ×Í©U.Í©
0020: 55 fd 04 36 00 50 00 3d 7b d4 00 00 00 00 60 02 | Uý.6.P.={Ô....`.
0030: 20 00 b0 9c 00 00 02 04 05 b4                   |  .........
```

1. What are the Ethernet and IP addresses of the sender and receiver?

____

____

____

____

2. What is the fragment number of the IP packet?

____

3. Is the information inside of the packet fragmented?

____

4. What does the TTL field indicate?

____

____

Extended Activity

Using the following packet, divide the hexadecimal data into a frame, packet, and message. Draw one line between the Ethernet and IP header, and a second line between the IP and TCP header.

```
Packet 2 captured at 03/24/1998 01:19:35 PM; Packet size is 60(0x3c)bytes
      Relative time: 000:00:05.337
      Delta time: 0.000.410
Ethernet Version II
      Address: 00-60-08-3B-92-06 --->00-60-94-05-11-D9
      Ethernet II Protocol Type: IP
Internet Protocol
      Version(MSB 4 bits): 4
      Header length(LSB 4 bits): 5 (32-bit word)
      Service type: 0x00
            000. .... = 0 - Routine
            ...0 .... = Normal delay
            .... 0... = Normal throughput
            .... .0.. = Normal reliability
      Total length: 44 (Octets)
      Fragment ID: 25170
      Flags summary: 0x40
            0... .... = Reserved
            .1.. .... = Do not fragment
            ..0. .... = Last fragment
            Fragment offset(LSB 13 bits): 0 (0x00)
      Time to live: 128 seconds/hops
      IP protocol type: TCP (0x06)
      Checksum: 0x5187
      IP address 205.169.85.253 ->205.169.85.162
      No option
Transmission Control Protocol
      Port World Wide Web HTTP ---> 1078
      Sequence Number: 163166782
      Acknowledgement Number: 4029397
      Header Length(MSB 4 bits): 6 (32-bit word)
      Reserved(LSB 4 bits): 0
      Code: 0x12
```

```
        RES: 00.. .... = Reserved
        URG: ..0. .... = Urgent Pointer is Invalid
        ACK: ...1 .... = Acknowledgement Field is Valid
        PSH: .... 0... = No push Requested
        RST: .... .0.. = No reset Connection
        SYN: .... ..1. = Synchronize Sequence Number
        FIN: .... ...0 = More Data From Sender
    Window: 8760
    Checksum: 0xEA5B
    Urgent Pointer: 0x0000
    TCP Option: 020405B4

Packet: 2
0000: 00 60 94 05 11 d9 00 60 08 3b 92 06 08 00 45 00 | .`...Ù.`.;....E.
0010: 00 2c 62 52 40 00 80 06 51 87 cd a9 55 fd cd a9 | .,bR@...Q‡Í©UýÍ©
0020: 55 a2 00 50 04 36 09 b9 ba 3e 00 3d 7b d5 60 12 | U..P.6...>.={Õ`.
0030: 22 38 ea 5b 00 00 02 04 05 b4 05 b4             | "8ê[........
```

Lesson 2—Address Resolution

If two hosts on a given network wish to communicate, they must know more than each other's IP address. They must also know each other's physical address so they can use Data Link Layer protocols to transmit datagrams on the local media. This lesson covers ARP, the protocol used to obtain a physical address when an IP address is known. We will use Ethernet LANs in this lesson because Ethernet is the most common type of LAN technology.

Objectives

At the end of this lesson you will be able to:

- Explain the operation of ARP
- Explain the operation of RARP

Key Point

ARP resolves IP addresses to Medium Access Control (MAC) addresses.

ARP

Ethernet designers allocated 48 bits for the Ethernet address. Each Ethernet network interface card (NIC) and interface comes with an address built in from the factory. Vendors who manufacture Ethernet equipment have to register with the Institute of Electrical and Electronics Engineers (IEEE) to ensure that the numbers they assign do not conflict with those of other manufacturers.

Unfortunately, there is no built-in connection or relationship between Ethernet addresses and IP addresses. Instead, IP hosts and routers resolve known IP addresses to MAC addresses using ARP.

ARP's Operation

The ARP Diagram illustrates the basic setup for two hosts communicating:

- Host A desires to communicate with Host B, but does not know Host B's Ethernet address. Host A does know Host B's host name, and thus initiates communication by attempting to contact Host B by its name.
- Host A uses DNS to learn Host B's IP address.

- Host A learns that both devices are attached to the same physical network, because their IP addresses have the same Network field.

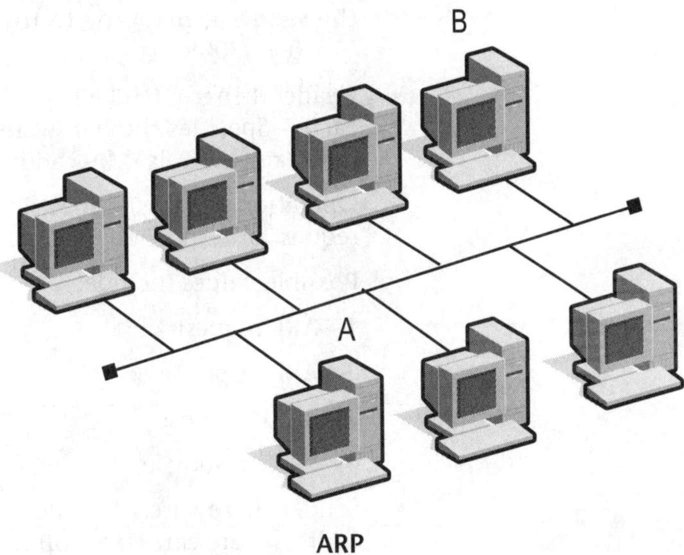

ARP

ARP Request

Though it knows Host B's IP address, Host A does not know Host B's physical address. To learn Host B's physical address, Host A broadcasts an ARP request packet that contains the destination IP address. An ARP request packet takes the form shown on the ARP Packet Format Diagram.

<table>
<tr><td colspan="2">Hardware Type</td><td colspan="2">Protocol Type</td></tr>
<tr><td>HLEN</td><td>PLEN</td><td colspan="2">Operation</td></tr>
<tr><td colspan="4">Sender H/W Address</td></tr>
<tr><td colspan="2">Sender H/W Address</td><td colspan="2">Sender IP Address</td></tr>
<tr><td colspan="2">Sender IP Address</td><td colspan="2">Target H/W Address</td></tr>
<tr><td colspan="4">Target H/W Address</td></tr>
<tr><td colspan="4">Target IP Address</td></tr>
</table>

ARP Packet Format

The entry descriptions are as follows:

- Hardware type (16 bits)—Specifies the hardware interface for which the requester requires a response (for example, 1 for Ethernet).
- Protocol type (16 bits)—Specifies the Network Layer protocol the sender is mapping to the hardware address (for example, IP = 0 x 0800).
- Header Length (HLEN) and Protocol Length (PLEN) (8 bits each)—Specifies the hardware and protocol address lengths in bytes, respectively. MAC addresses are 6, and IP addresses are 4.
- Operation (16 bits)—Specifies whether this is an ARP or RARP request or response.

  Possible values include:

  1—ARP request

  2—ARP response

  3—RARP request

  4—RARP response
- Sender hardware/IP—Sender hardware or IP address. The addresses are carried as follows:

  Packet bytes 8–11—The first 4 hardware address octets

  Packet bytes 12–13—The remaining 2 hardware address octets

  Packet bytes 14–15—The first 2 logical address octets

  Packet bytes 16–17—The remaining 2 logical address octets
- Target hardware/IP—Target hardware address (RARP) or IP address (ARP). The addresses are carried as follows:

  Packet bytes 18–19—The first 2 hardware address octets

  Packet bytes 20–23—The remaining 4 hardware address octets

  Packet bytes 24–27—The 4 logical address octets

Host A asks that the host with the specified IP address respond with its Ethernet address. The sender hardware address is Host A's physical address; the target hardware address is set to all 0s (the receiver's ignore this portion of the packet). The sender IP address is Host A's IP address, and the target IP address is Host B's IP address.

All hosts on the network will receive the request, including those connected by bridges or switches, as illustrated on the ARP Request Diagram. Recall that a broadcast frame is forwarded by all Layer 2 and lower devices (bridges, switches, hubs, and repeaters), but is not forwarded by routers (routers block broadcast frames by default).

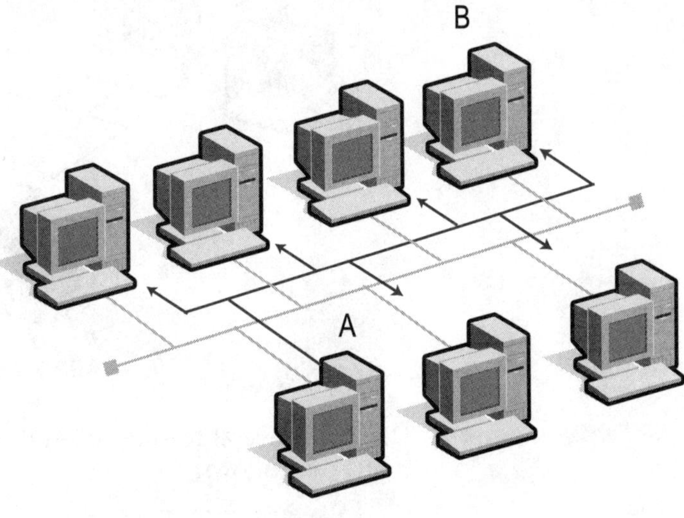

ARP Request

ARP Response

Though all hosts receive the ARP request, only Host B responds. Host B recognizes its IP address and responds to Host A's ARP request by sending an ARP reply containing its own Ethernet address. The ARP Response Diagram illustrates this. Host A now has the Ethernet address it needs to send packets to Host B over the local physical network.

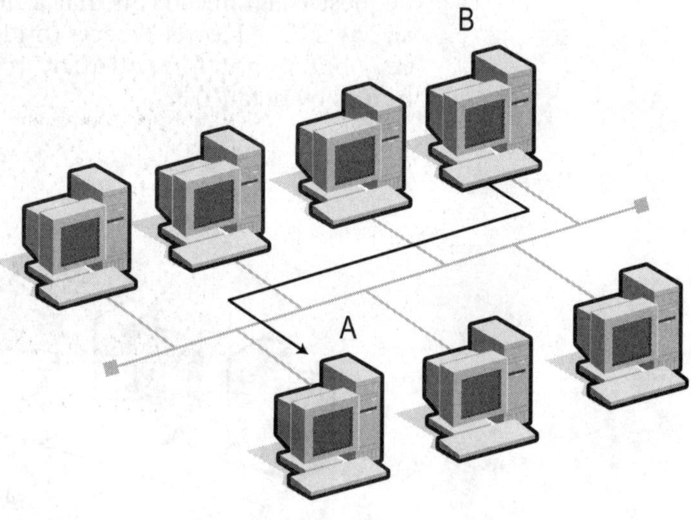

ARP Response

ARP Features

There are several features of ARP that allow it to operate very efficiently, as follows:

- To keep the number of ARP broadcasts to a minimum, hosts that use ARP maintain a cache of discovered Internet-to-Ethernet mappings so they do not have to use ARP every time they want to transmit a packet. To keep the cache from growing too large, an entry is removed if it is not used within a certain period of time. Before transmitting a packet, the host always looks in its cache for a mapping before sending an ARP request.

The ARP Cache Screen Diagram illustrates an ARP cache contents on a Microsoft Windows host.

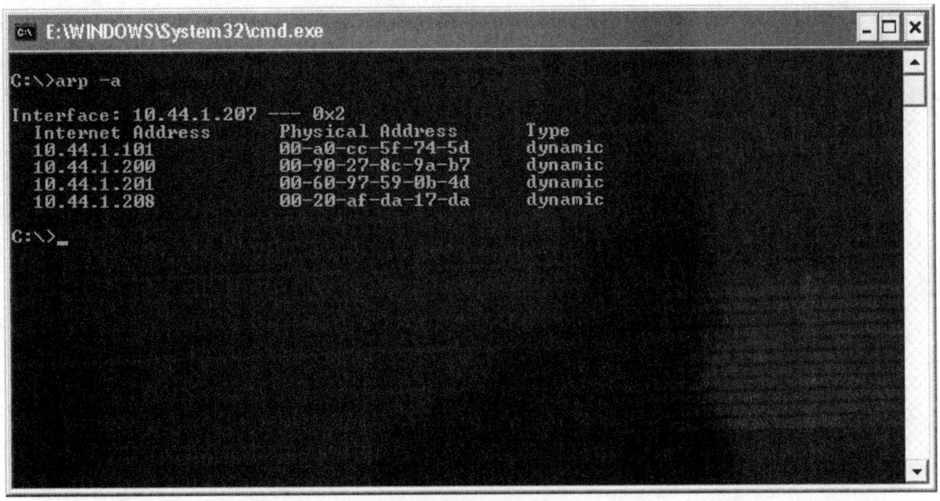

```
E:\WINDOWS\System32\cmd.exe

C:\>arp -a

Interface: 10.44.1.207 --- 0x2
  Internet Address      Physical Address      Type
  10.44.1.101           00-a0-cc-5f-74-5d     dynamic
  10.44.1.200           00-90-27-8c-9a-b7     dynamic
  10.44.1.201           00-60-97-59-0b-4d     dynamic
  10.44.1.208           00-20-af-da-17-da     dynamic

C:\>_
```

ARP Cache Screen

Windows NT maintains an ARP cache entry for a maximum of 10 minutes, by default. If the entry goes unused for more than 2 minutes, it is deleted. Other devices use other time limits. For example, the Cisco routers hold entries for 4 hours, by default.

- Additional network traffic is avoided by having the initiator of an ARP request include its Internet-to-Ethernet mapping in the packet so the recipient can add this mapping to its cache. The recipient need not send an ARP in the opposite direction.
- We can add static ARP entries to avoid the need to broadcast for frequently used host addresses. The implementation varies by operating system (OS) and the entries may be deleted on system restart.

Proxy ARP

An ARP variation is a Proxy ARP, sometimes known as a promiscuous ARP. For example, when host 10.1.50.10/24 needs to send a packet to host 10.2.50.17/24, but does not have the default gateway information necessary to forward the packet to its gateway router, it may issue an ARP request. The local router, configured to answer Proxy ARP requests, will respond to this request for the host 10.2.50.17/24 physical address, and send its physical address instead. The sending host 10.1.50.10/24 believes it now has the receiver's MAC address in its ARP cache, and forwards the packet on to the local router; the local router then forwards the packet to the next hop router, etc. The sending host sends all subsequent packets addressed to host 10.2.50.17/24 to the local router.

Frame Encapsulation

The ARP in an Ethernet Frame Diagram illustrates how an Ethernet frame encapsulates an ARP packet as it travels on the physical network from one computer to another.

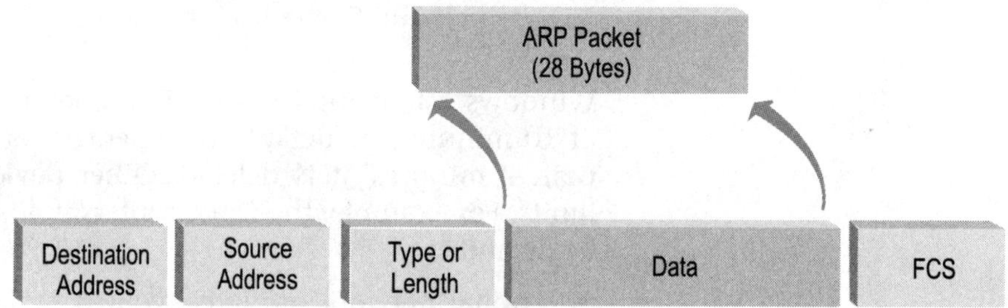

ARP in an Ethernet Frame

Note: ARP is not an IP protocol in the sense that ARP datagrams do not have IP headers. ARP does not use the services of IP, because ARP messages do not leave the logical network and are never routed.

ARP requests are sent as broadcast frames. An Ethernet address of all 1s is used (FFFFFFFFFFFF) as the broadcast address. By convention, every computer on the network is required to listen to packets with this as a destination address.

However, only hosts running the TCP/IP protocol suite respond to ARP requests. When a computer sees an ARP request with its IP address as the target, it must respond. The frame's Ethernet Type field identifies the ARP/RARP packet type carried in the data field, as follows:

- ARP Request/Reply 0x0806
- RARP Request/Reply 0x8035

RARP

The network manager usually configures a computer's IP address when they initially install the communications software. The computer stores its IP address(es) in a configuration file on the disk on which the OS is installed.

However, some devices require an IP address, yet have no disk installed on which to store them. How do these diskless workstations obtain an IP address? Reverse ARP enables a diskless host to broadcast a logical address request to an address mapping server on the local network; the diskless host uniquely identifies itself by sending its Ethernet address. The server searches its cache for the physical to logical address mapping, and responds to the request with the host's IP address. The requesting host may receive responses from one or more servers located on the network, and usually accepts the first response, rejecting all others. After the host learns its IP address, it can communicate across the Internet. Like ARP, a RARP message is encapsulated in the data portion of an Ethernet frame.

Note: Bootstrap Protocol (BOOTP) and Dynamic Host Configuration Protocol (DHCP) are largely supplanting RARP. RARP can only provide a host IP address, where BOOTP and DHCP can provide additional host configuration information.

Operation

The following example shows how a diskless host determines its IP address using RARP.

RARP Request

In the RARP Request Diagram, Host A broadcasts a RARP request packet inside a broadcast Ethernet frame, including its Ethernet address in the packet's Target Hardware Address field. All hosts on the network receive the broadcast frame, but only the RARP server(s) respond.

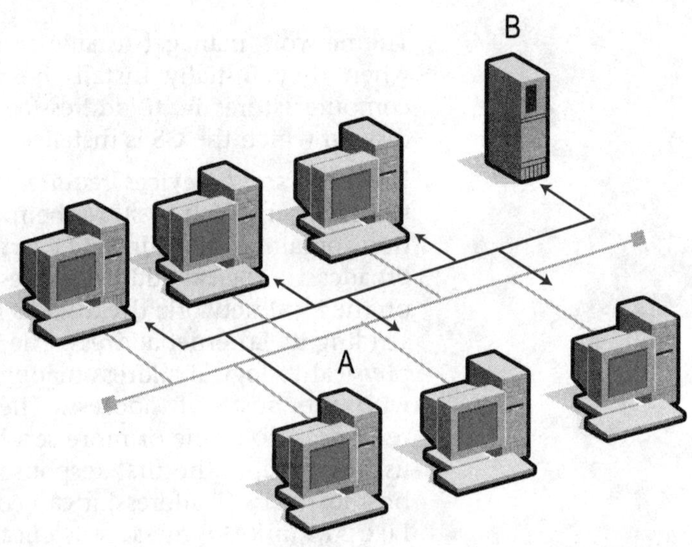

RARP Request

RARP Response

On the RARP Response Diagram, Server B processes the request and sends a reply containing the requesting Host A's IP address in the sender's Internet Address field. For RARP to succeed, the network must contain at least one RARP server. Routers will not forward the broadcast frame to a server located on another network.

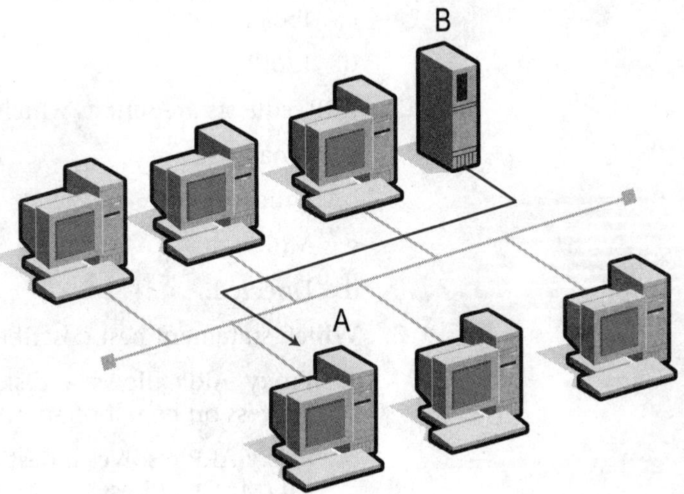

RARP Response

Activities

1. Which IP protocol allows a diskless workstation to contact a server and obtain an IP address?
   a. ARP
   b. IARP
   c. Proxy ARP
   d. RARP
2. ARP requests are sent as which type of Ethernet frame?
   a. Broadcast
   b. Unicast
   c. Multicast
   d. Directed
3. Which statement best describes Proxy ARP?
   a. Proxy ARP allows a diskless workstation to obtain an address on behalf of another, diskless workstation.
   b. Proxy ARP resolves a destination's IP address to its physical (MAC) address.
   c. Proxy ARP allows a router to answer an ARP request on behalf of a local host.
   d. Proxy ARP allows a router to answer an ARP request on behalf of a remote host.
4. Which network segment hosts respond to an ARP request?
   a. All hosts respond
   b. Only the target host responds
   c. The router responds on behalf of all segment hosts
   d. The ARP server responds on behalf of the segment hosts
5. Which ARP feature allows the local host to maintain a mapping of recently discovered IP-to-MAC addresses?
   a. The ARP table
   b. The ARP map
   c. The ARP file
   d. The ARP cache

Extended Activities

This activity has you observe and manipulate your Windows PC's ARP cache. Though created with Windows in mind, with some modifications these procedures will work on other OSs that support TCP/IP communications. See your OS documentation.

1. On your Windows PC, bring up a command or MS-DOS prompt.
2. At the command line, type **arp**. This lists the ARP command switches.
3. Type **arp -a**. This displays your ARP cache's current contents.
4. If you show no ARP cache entries, then locate the IP address of an operational host on your local network, and type at your command prompt **ping <*remotehostIP*>**. Go back and look at your ARP cache; you will now see an entry for the remote host.
5. Delete a single entry from the cache, first recording the IP address: ________________. Type at the command prompt **arp -d <*hostIPaddress*>**.
6. At the command prompt, type **arp -a**. The deleted entry is removed from your ARP cache.
7. Type at the command prompt **ping <*hostIPaddress*>**, where <*hostIPaddress*> is the address you recorded in Step 5.
8. Type at the command prompt **arp -a**. The address is again in your ARP cache.

Lesson 3—UDP

UDP is one of the two major Transport Layer protocols that reside on top of IP. The other protocol residing on top of IP (TCP) will be discussed in a later lesson. UDP provides a transaction-oriented, best-effort delivery service for applications that do not require a reliable data stream service.

Objectives

At the end of this lesson you will be able to:

- Discuss UDP services
- Describe port-number-based demultiplexing
- Describe UDP frame encapsulation
- Describe UDP header fields

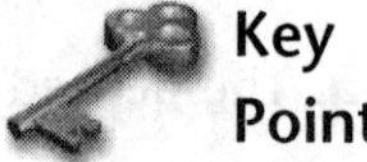

Key Point

UDP is a connectionless counterpart to TCP.

UDP Service

IP is UDP's service provider. The major UDP Application Layer protocol clients are:

- Network File System (NFS)
- DNS
- Trivial File Transfer Protocol (TFTP)
- SNMP

Because UDP uses IP's services, it provides the same connectionless delivery service and lack of reliability as IP. However, UDP does implement flow control to manage the information exchange rate between hosts. UDP does not send or receive acknowledgements to guarantee the successful transmission of data. Neither does UDP provide a method to sequence packets so they can be placed in their proper order by the destination station. Applications requiring reliable and sequenced delivery should use the services of TCP, or should provide reliability on the application itself when using UDP.

Why use UDP? UDP provides a simple transaction service with minimal protocol overhead (unlike TCP). UDP is suitable for carrying protocols that either provide their own error detection and recovery systems or have no need for these services. UDP supports two additional features above those already provided by IP:

- UDP provides the ability to demultiplex data for an application process based on a destination port number. Some common UDP port numbers are:

  Port 53—DNS

  Port 69—TFTP

  Port 123—Network Time Protocol (NTP)

  Port 161—SNMP

- The UDP header includes a checksum that detects errors that occur when data is transmitted from a source host to a destination host.

The UDP and OSI Model Diagram presents the role of UDP relative to the OSI layer protocols.

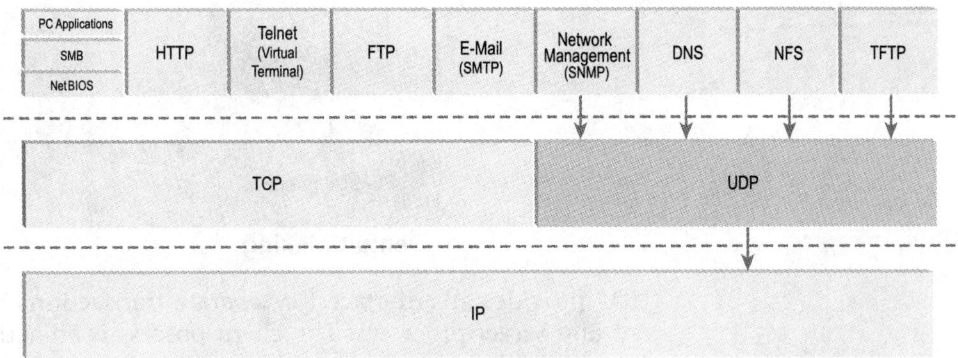

UDP and OSI Model

Demultiplexing Based on Port Number

One of the additional features UDP provides, beyond those that IP provides is the ability to demultiplex data to an application process based on a destination port number. While IP supports the routing function that allows communication between two hosts across an internetwork, UDP creates a mechanism to distinguish among multiple application destinations within a given host. This mechanism allows multiple, simultaneously executing application programs on a given host to send and receive datagrams independently. The Demultiplexing Diagram illustrates this feature of UDP.

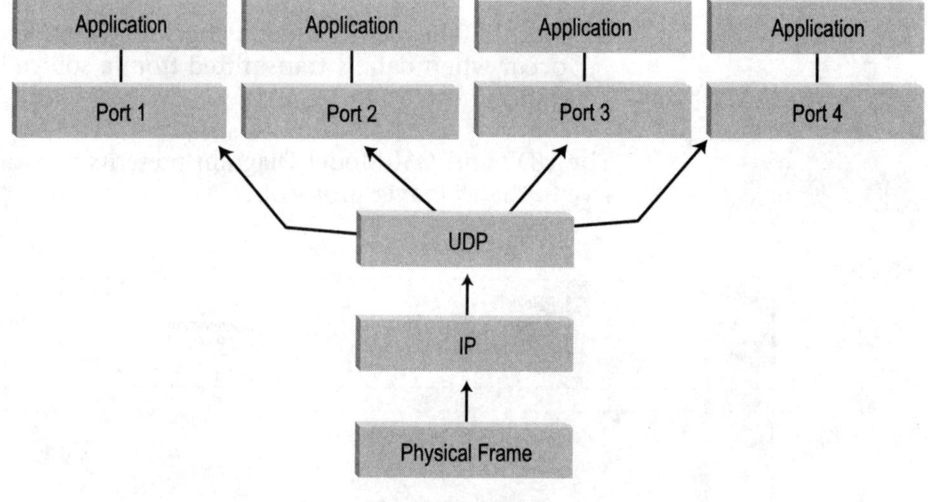

Demultiplexing

UDP provides an interface for separate transactions between client and server processes. The client process is an active UDP client, while the server process runs passively on a server hosting the target application. The passive server application maintains a listening socket on a well-known port number dedicated to the given service. An application creates a socket of its host IP address, the ToS it provides, and the port on which it listens.

The active client requests a service from the remote passive server by sending a packet to the remote server's IP address. The packet carries a UDP segment, part of which specifies the well-known port on which the target application resides. Note that if the server listens on some port other than the well-known port, and the client does not know this alternate port, the transaction will fail.

The passive server listens patiently on this well-known port, waiting for any active client requests. When the server receives a packet sent to its IP address, it reads the packet and decapsulates the IP header, exposing the UDP segment within. It recognizes that the segment specifies one of its available, well-known ports, and passes the data to the associated application. Contained within the UDP segment is the port over which the client wishes the server to answer, and thus, the server targets this client port in its reply. The client can specify any port it wants; this does not have to be a well-known port. The UDP Header Diagram illustrates the UDP Header format.

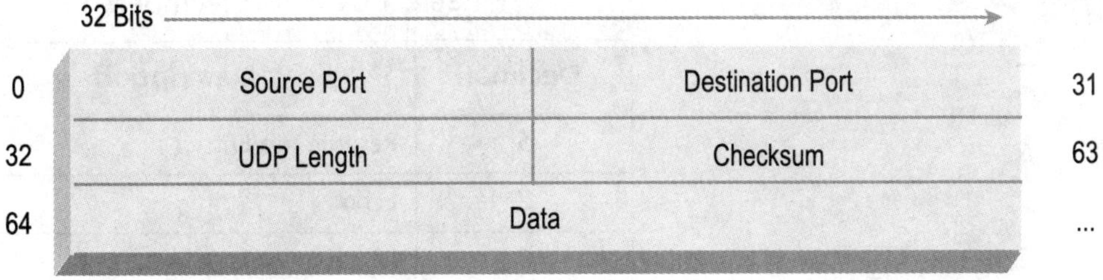

32 Bits

0	Source Port	Destination Port	31
32	UDP Length	Checksum	63
64	Data		...

UDP Header

The fields are as follows:

- Source Port—The 16 bit sending host port number. This is optional, and if unused is set to 0.
- Destination Port—The 16-bit destination host port number. This is the communication's endpoint, responsible for demultiplexing datagrams among the destination computer's processes.
- UDP Message Length—The 16-bit UDP datagram size indicator, expressed in bytes, represents the length of the header and the data combined. The minimum datagram size is 8 bytes (the header alone).
- Checksum—The 16-bit checksum generated from the IP header, the UDP header, and the data, padded with 0s as necessary to fill the field. IP only calculates a header checksum, and thus, this is UDP's only mechanism for verifying data integrity.
- Data—The Application Layer data to which the header is appended.

Network management is a good example of a protocol's use of UDP services. For example, host SNMP agents (the server process) must respond to information requests from network management stations (the requester process). Each SNMP agent waits for management requests on well-known UDP Port 161. If an SNMP manager wants to obtain management information, it sends its request to the destination host's UDP Port 161.

UDP Port Numbers

Examples of UDP port numbers are presented in the Select UDP Port Numbers Table.

Select UDP Port Numbers

Decimal	Description
5	Remote Job Entry
7	Echo
9	Discard
11	Active Users
13	Daytime
15	Who is up or NETSTAT
17	Quote of the Day
19	Character Generator
37	Time
39	Resource Location Protocol
42	Host Name Server
43	Who Is
53	Domain Name Server
67	Bootstrap Protocol Server
68	Bootstrap Protocol Client

Select UDP Port Numbers (Continued)

Decimal	Description
69	Trivial Filter Transfer
79	Finger
111	Sun Microsystems' RPC
123	Network Time Protocol
161	SNMP Message

Frame Encapsulation

A complete UDP message is encapsulated in an IP datagram as it travels across the internetwork. The UDP Frame Encapsulation Diagram illustrates this.

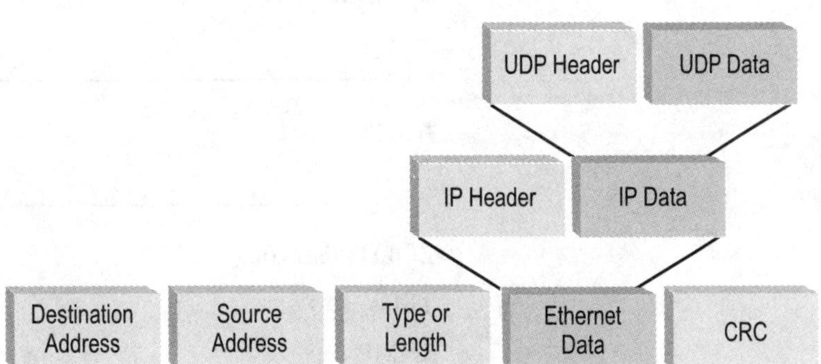

UDP Frame Encapsulation

Activities

1. Match the well-known UDP port numbers with their associated application.

   a. Port 53

   ____

   b. Port 67

   ____

   c. Port 68

   ____

   d. Port 69

   ____

   e. Port 123

   ____

   f. Port 161

   ____

   BOOTP Server

   TFTP

   SNMP

   BOOTP Client

   DNS

   NTP

2. How does UDP support multiple application destinations on the same host?
   a. It supports multiple paths between the source and destination applications.
   b. It carries port numbers in its header, used to logically address a destination application.
   c. It maintains a listening socket for each sending application, which wait for the destination server application server to poll them.
   d. It multiplexes IP packets so they can share the same physical link between the source and destination nodes.
3. Which is a true statement concerning UDP?
   a. UDP is a connection-oriented protocol, used to establish virtual circuits between network applications.
   b. UDP provides error detection and recovery features for reliable communications across an IP network.
   c. UDP clients must listen on well-known ports when awaiting server replies to their service requests.
   d. UDP servers must listen for service requests on well-known ports, or else the transactions may fail.

Extended Activities

1. Draw a diagram illustrating the UDP demultiplexing process.

2. Draw a diagram illustrating an Ethernet frame encapsulation of an IP datagram, in turn encapsulating a UDP message.

Lesson 4—TCP and Connection Establishment

TCP provides applications with a reliable, connection-oriented service, in the form of a virtual point-to-point connection between the client and server applications. TCP causes a connectionless IP end-to-end service to appear as a continuous, uninterrupted data stream carried over a dedicated data channel. This lesson discusses the services and operations TCP uses to create these virtual connections.

Objectives

At the end of this lesson you will be able to:

- Describe fundamental TCP services
- Describe TCP interfaces
- Explain the TCP header fields and format
- Explain fundamental TCP operations
- Describe TCP's use of sequence numbers
- Describe TCP's use of ports and sockets
- List well-known TCP listener ports
- Describe TCP frame encapsulation

Key Point

TCP is a reliable, byte-stream-oriented, virtual circuit protocol.

TCP Features

TCP provides a highly reliable host-to-host communications protocol. The main TCP features include:

- Connection establishment and termination
- Reliable (acknowledged) packet delivery
- Sequenced packet delivery
- Flow control to protect hosts from data overflow

- Lost or duplicated packet error recovery
- Demultiplexing among multiple applications within a given host

The major TCP clients are the following Application Layer protocols:

- Telnet
- FTP
- SMTP

TCP is an IP client, and as such IP provides a vehicle for TCP to send and receive information. The main IP services TCP uses include:

- Addressing, to identify the source and destination stations on different networks
- Ability to route datagrams across different networks
- Ability to fragment and later reassemble datagrams for transmission across small-packet networks
- Ability to demultiplex Transport Layer protocols based on IP-defined protocol numbers
- TTL field to limit the time a datagram remains active on the Internet
- ToS field to indicate the QoS a router should provide

The TCP and OSI Model Diagram illustrates the role of TCP relative to the layout of the OSI reference model.

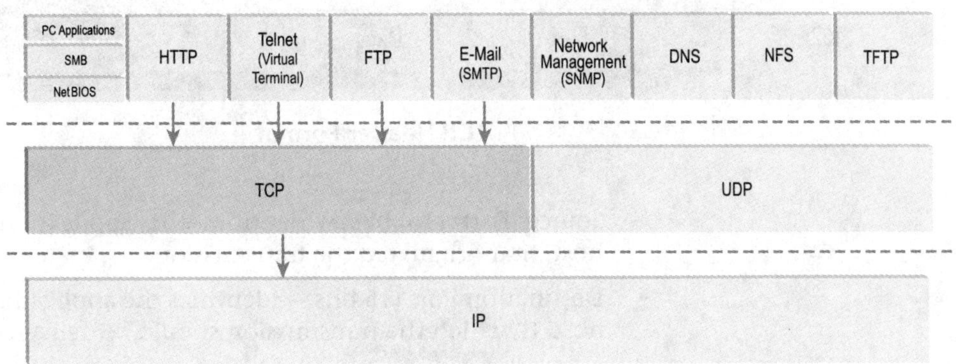

TCP and OSI Model

TCP Interfaces

TCP interfaces with higher layer user-application processes and the lower layer IP Network Layer protocol. A user application transmits data over an IP network by first calling TCP (or UDP), and passing to TCP application data. TCP packages this data into segments, and calls the IP module to transmit each segment to the destination host. The receiving TCP then places the data from a segment into a receiving buffer, reassembles the segments into the application data, and forwards the data to the destination application process.

The TCP Header

The TCP Header Format Diagram presents the format for a TCP header. The header fields are described below.

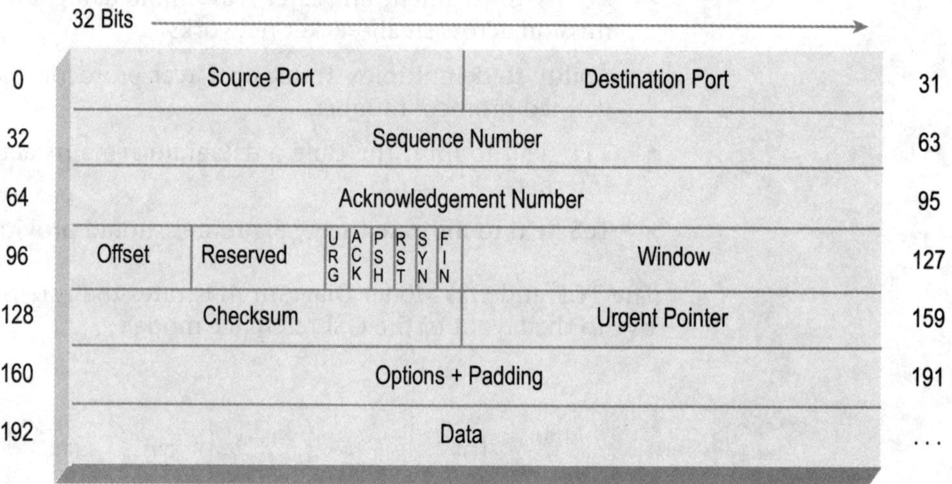

TCP Header Format

- Source Port (16 bits)—Identifies the application, within a host, that originated the transmission.
- Destination Port (16 bits)—Identifies the application, within a host, to which the transmission should be delivered.

- Sequence Number (32 bits)—Identifies the sequence number of the first data byte in the segment (except when the SYN bit is set). When SYN is set, the sequence number is the initial sequence number (ISN) and the first data byte is ISN+1. For example, if SYN is set, the ISN is 100, and the data starts at sequence number 101. SYN is discussed in more detail later in this lesson.
- Acknowledgement Number (32 bits)—Applies only if the ACK control bit is set. The ACK number is the next sequence number the sender of the segment is expecting to receive. For example, if a host receives sequence number 101, it sends a segment back with the acknowledge number set to 102. It expects to receive sequence number 102 next. If a connection is established, this value is always sent.
- Data Offset (4 bits)—Specifies the number of 32-bit words in the TCP header. It indicates where the header ends and the Upper Layer Protocol (ULP) data begins in the segment. This field is needed because the TCP header is of variable length; thus, the position of the ULP data within the segment may vary.
- Reserved—Consists of the 6 bits following the Data Offset field, which are reserved and always zero.
- Control Bits (6 bits)—Accomplishes handshaking and other specific functions. They are from left to right:

  URG—Indicates Urgent Pointer field is significant

  ACK—Indicates Acknowledgement field is significant

  PSH—Push function

  RST—Reset connection

  SYN—Synchronize sequence numbers

  FIN—No more data from sender
- Window (16 bits)—Used for end-end flow control. Indicates the number of bytes, beginning with the one in the Acknowledgement field, that the receiver is willing to accept. The window field is bidirectional, that is, both the sender or receiver can set this value. In this manner, both ends of a connection can control data flowing from the other.
- Checksum (16 bits)—Verifies a segment was transmitted without errors. The devices calculate the checksum from the TCP header and the application data. If the checksum fails when the data is received, an error is detected and the segment is discarded.

- Urgent Pointer (16 bits)—Only significant if the URG control bit is set. This value is a positive offset from the urgent data sequence number, and indicates the beginning of the non-urgent data.
- Options (multiple of 8 bits)—Variable-length field available to indicate TCP options. For example, this field might be used to indicate the maximum segment size the sender is willing to accept.
- Padding—Indicates specific number of 0 bits added to ensure that the header ends on a 32-bit boundary.

Fundamental Operation

The primary purpose of TCP is to provide a reliable, connection-oriented delivery service between processes residing on different hosts. If it is to provide reliable communications over a best-effort network (the Internet, for example), TCP must provide the following services:

- Basic data transfer
- Reliability
- Flow control
- Multiplexing
- Connections

Basic Data Transfer

A segment is the basic TCP transfer unit between communicating hosts. TCP views a data stream as a sequence of bytes, grouped into segments, for transmission. An IP datagram transmits each segment across the internetwork as a single IP data field, unless an intervening small-packet network requires packet fragmentation.

The local TCP determines the number of bytes to include in a particular segment. The many complex issues that affect this decision will be discussed later in this lesson.

Note: After a connection is established, the size of each segment may vary based on network and host conditions. Therefore, all segments do not necessarily contain the same number of bytes.

Though typically TCP waits to fill the segment with data before transmission, applications may at times require immediate data delivery, and cannot wait for the transmit buffer to fill. A Push function forces data delivery even though the transmit buffer is not completely full. On the destination end, the Push function forces the local TCP to immediately deliver the data to the destination application, without waiting for the receive buffer to fill. The TCP header's PSH flag triggers a Push function.

Reliability

TCP must be able to recover from data that is damaged, lost, duplicated, or delivered out of sequence.

TCP assigns a sequence number to each byte transmitted, and requires that the destination TCP return a positive acknowledgement (ACK). If the sender does not receive an ACK within a specified time period, it retransmits the unacknowledged segment(s). The destination station uses the sequence numbers to correctly reorder segments that may have been received out of sequence, and to eliminate duplicate segments.

A checksum included with each segment handles damaged data as it is transferred. The receiving host examines the checksum and discards any damaged segments. Discarded segments are not acknowledged and, therefore, are retransmitted by the source station.

Flow Control

TCP provides a mechanism for the destination station to control the amount of data sent by the source station. A receiving host sets a receive window with each ACK it sends, indicating how many additional bytes it is willing to accept from the source. As the receive buffer fills, the advertised receive window size shrinks. As the receive buffer empties, the receive window's advertised size increases.

Multiplexing

Like UDP, TCP uses ports to identify the destination application, so multiple processes within a single host can use TCP communication services simultaneously.

Combining the host's IP address with a port number creates a TCP socket; sockets are TCP traffic's ultimate destination. A pair of sockets (one for each host) uniquely identifies each connection. Moreover, a socket may be used simultaneously in more than one connection.

Each host independently handles binding ports to processes. For frequently used processes, it may be useful to assign a well-known port number and make that number known to the public. Other devices can then access services assigned to the port through the well-known port addresses. Some processes that benefit from well-known port numbers include:

- Name service
- File transfer services
- Virtual terminal

Connections

TCP's reliability and flow control services require that it initialize and maintain important status information for each data stream; a connection is a combination of this status information. A connection includes socket numbers, sequence numbers, and a great deal of window management information. A pair of sockets uniquely identifies each side of a virtual circuit connection.

When two processes wish to communicate, the TCP on each host must first establish an application connection. The connection initializes the status information for each side of the virtual circuit. After the hosts complete their data exchange, the TCP processes terminate the connection to free up the resources for other users.

During data transfer, the TCP on each host communicate to verify reliable data transfer. If the established connection fails because of network problems, both computers will detect the failure and report it to the appropriate application program.

Sequence Numbers

TCP perceives a data stream as a sequence of bytes grouped into segments for transmission, as illustrated on the Sequence Numbers Diagram.

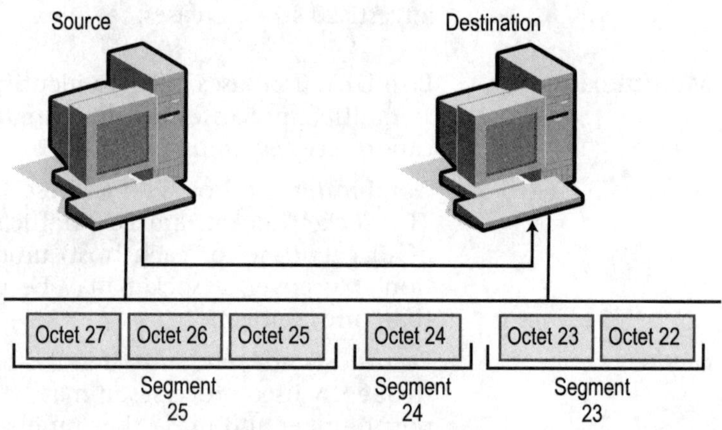

Sequence Numbers

TCP logically assigns each outgoing data byte a unique sequence number. The TCP process assigns a sequence number to the very first byte in the data stream when the connection is established and then increments the sequence numbers for each of the stream's subsequent data bytes.

Sequence numbers range from 0 to 2^{31} (2,147,483,648) and cycle continuously. Though a segment contains multiple data bytes, the TCP header allows for only one sequence number per segment. Therefore, TCP places in the Header Sequence Number field the sequence number of the first byte in the segment. The next segment's sequence number is the first sequence number plus the number of bytes in the first segment. For example, if segment number 1 is assigned sequence number 12,266, and the segment contains 1,500 data bytes, the next segment's sequence number will be 12,266 + 1,500 = 13,766.

Because TCP assigns every byte a sequence number, the communicating hosts could account for each byte in the data stream; however, TCP does not account for each individual byte. Instead, TCP uses a cumulative acknowledgement mechanism to acknowledge a segment's receipt. The TCP receiver sends to the sender an ACK segment, indicating with sequence number X that it has received all transmitted bytes up to, but not including X. If the last segment received has sequence number 13,766, then the receiver will send back an ACK with the sequence number set to 13,767. One advantage of this technique is that a lost acknowledgement does not necessarily force that segment's retransmission. In other words, if the sender does not receive an acknowledgement for one segment, but does receive one for the next, the sender can assume that the receiver received both segments.

Each side of the full-duplex connection sets its own sequence numbers. When a connection is first established, an initial sequence number is defined for each side of the connection. Each end selects its starting sequence numbers at random; thus, for a connection to be established, the two TCPs must synchronize (agree) on each other's initial sequence numbers. If this synchronization did not take place, neither side could keep track of both its send and receive data streams.

Ports

Like UDP, TCP uses a port number as the ultimate destination within a host. When establishing a connection, the local TCP must specify not only the IP address of the target host, but also the application process port number it desires to access.

Servers use well-known port numbers so other devices can open connections to them and start sending commands. The Connecting to a Device—Well-Known Ports Diagram illustrates the concept of connecting by means of ports.

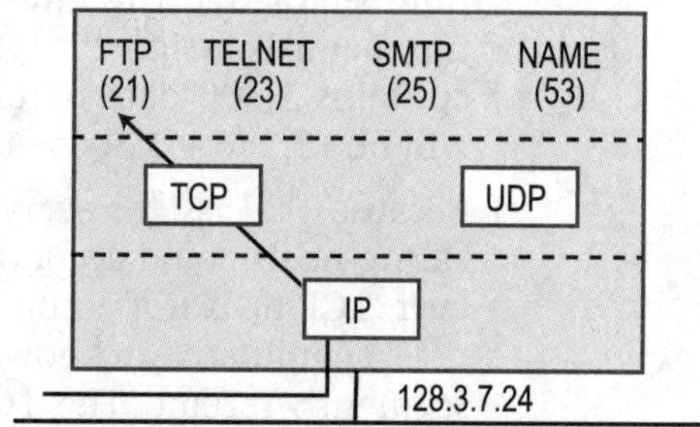

Connecting to a Device—Well-Known Ports

Specific port numbers have been reserved for special server processes that simply wait for client requests. These processes include:

- Name service
- File transfer service
- Remote terminal login
- Mail
- Network management

These ports are often referred to as the well-known ports. Some well-known ports are as follows:

TCP Well-Known Port Numbers

Decimal	Description
1	TCP Multiplexer
5	Remote Job Entry
7	Echo

TCP Well-Known Port Numbers (Continued)

Decimal	Description
9	Discard
11	Active Users
13	Daytime
15	Who is up?
17	Quote of the Day
19	Character Generator
20	FTP (data)
21	FTP (control)
23	Telnet
25	SMTP
37	Time
39	Resource Location Protocol
42	Host Name Server
43	Who Is
53	Domain Name Server
67	Bootstrap Protocol Server
68	Bootstrap Protocol Client
69	Trivial Filter Transfer
75	Any Private Dial-out Server
77	Any Private RJE Service
79	Who is on System
80	HTTP
101	NIC Host Name Server
102	ISO-TSAP
103	X.400 Mail Service
104	X.400 Mail Sending
111	SUN Remote Procedure Call
113	Authentication Service
139	NetBIOS Session Service

Sockets

A TCP socket connection is defined by a set of four numbers:

- IP address at each end (two numbers)
- TCP port number at each end (two numbers)

Every datagram contains these four numbers. IP addresses are placed in the IP header, and port numbers are included in the TCP header. To keep things straight, no two connections can have the same set of numbers; however, each connection can share one number as long as the other ends are unique.

For example, the Connecting to a Device—Identical and Unique Numbers Diagram shows two simultaneous connections between two hosts. Because only two computers are involved, each of the connection's IP addresses are identical. Additionally, both connections are Telnet, thus they each use the server's well-known Telnet Port 23. The client side port numbers are the only difference between the two connections. The TCP Connection of Two Hosts Table summarizes this.

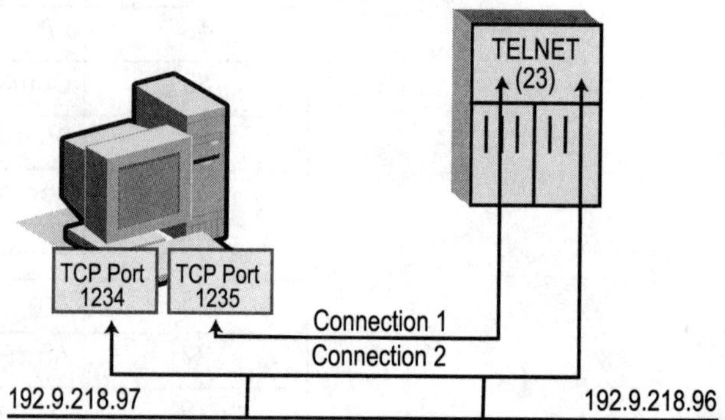

Connecting to a Device—Identical and Unique Numbers

TCP Connection of Two Hosts

Connection	Source IP Address	TCP Port	Destination IP Address	TCP Port
1	192.9.218.97	1234	192.9.218.96	23 Telnet
2	192.9.218.97	1235	192.9.218.96	23 Telnet

The combination of an IP address (defining a host interface) and port number (defining an application on the host) is called a socket. Two sockets (one on each host) uniquely define a TCP connection.

Connection Establishment

When an application program requires a TCP connection from Host A to Host B, one of the hosts must initiate the connection. To open a TCP connection, the initiating application process issues a Call command specifying that the connection request is either active or passive. The Active/Passive Open Diagram illustrates this process.

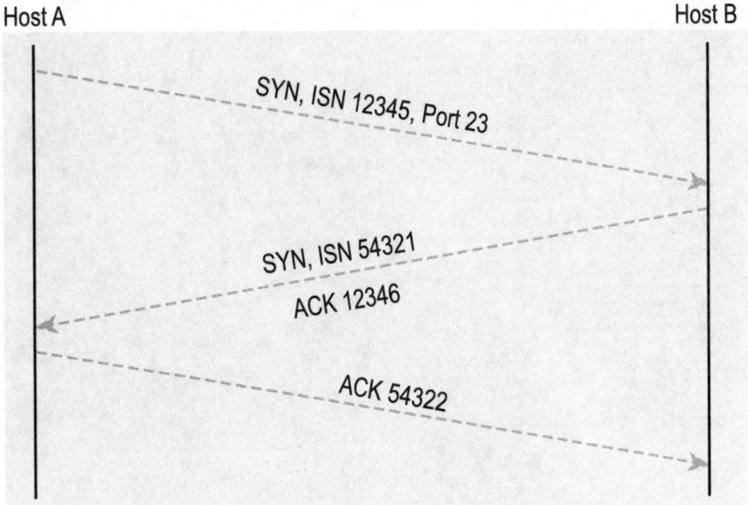

Active/Passive Open

Active Open

As the diagram shows, Host A hosts the application requiring the connection; in this case we want to establish a Telnet session. The Telnet application issues an active Open command request to its local TCP. The local TCP in turn sends a SYN segment to Host B, with the SYN control bit set, and specifying the target hosts well-known port (23) and the ISN. It also sends its listening port and its IP address so Host B knows who and how to answer.

Passive Open

Host B offers the Telnet service Host A's Telnet client wishes to access. Host B, if listening, responds to Host A's active Open with a passive Open command, indicating that it is willing to accept Host A's incoming request. Host B does not request services, but instead indicates that it accepts service requests (Host B is the passive end of the client/server TCP process). Host B's TCP sends a SYN reply segment to Host A, providing its own ISN, and acknowledging Host A's ISN by setting its ACK bit and sending Host A's ISN incremented by 1 (ISN+1).

The connection is established after the successful, synchronized SYN segment exchange between the two TCPs. The transmitted segments synchronize each host's ICNs, and send the basic control information both sides need so they can transfer data over the connection.

Activities

1. Match the well-known TCP port numbers with the associated applications.

   Port

   a. 20

   ____

   b. 21

   ____

   c. 23

   ____

   d. 25

   ____

   e. 53

   ____

   f. 80

   ____

   g. 139

   ____

   Application

   AppliDNS

   HTTP

   SMTP

   NetBIOS session service

   FTP control

   FTP data

   Telnet

The example of trace data (information that was captured on an Ethernet network) is originally shown under the Activities section, Unit 4, Lesson 1. It shows the Ethernet frame encapsulating an IP packet encapsulating a TCP message. Review the information and answer the following questions.

2. Information is being transferred between two Web applications across a TCP/IP network. What is the port number that TCP is using in this example?

    ____

3. What is the sequence number for this TCP message?

    ____

4. What is the socket number for this particular transaction?

    ____

5. What does the syn bit indicate in this trace?

    ____

Extended Activities

Review the information in the example below and answer the following questions.

```
Packet 2 captured at 03/24/1998 01:19:35 PM; Packet size is 60(0x3c)bytes
      Relative time: 000:00:05.337
      Delta time: 0.000.410
Ethernet Version II
      Address: 00-60-08-3B-92-06 --->00-60-94-05-11-D9
      Ethernet II Protocol Type: IP
Internet Protocol
      Version(MSB 4 bits): 4
      Header length(LSB 4 bits): 5 (32-bit word)
      Service type: 0x00
            000. .... = 0 - Routine
            ...0 .... = Normal delay
            .... 0... = Normal throughput
            .... .0.. = Normal reliability
      Total length: 44 (Octets)
      Fragment ID: 25170
      Flags summary: 0x40
            0... .... = Reserved
```

```
            .1.. .... = Do not fragment
            ..0. .... = Last fragment
            Fragment offset(LSB 13 bits): 0 (0x00)
      Time to live: 128 seconds/hops
      IP protocol type: TCP (0x06)
      Checksum: 0x5187
      IP address 205.169.85.253 ->205.169.85.162
      No option
Transmission Control Protocol
      Port World Wide Web HTTP ---> 1078
      Sequence Number: 163166782
      Acknowledgement Number: 4029397
      Header Length(MSB 4 bits): 6 (32-bit word)
      Reserved(LSB 4 bits): 0
      Code: 0x12
            RES: 00.. .... = Reserved
            URG: ..0. .... = Urgent Pointer is Invalid
            ACK: ...1 .... = Acknowledgement Field is Valid
            PSH: .... 0... = No push Requested
            RST: .... .0.. = No reset Connection
            SYN: .... ..1. = Synchronize Sequence Number
            FIN: .... ...0 = More Data From Sender
      Window: 8760
      Checksum: 0xEA5B
      Urgent Pointer: 0x0000
      TCP Option: 020405B4

Packet: 2
0000: 00 60 94 05 11 d9 00 60 08 3b 92 06 08 00 45 00 | .`...Ù.`.;....E.
0010: 00 2c 62 52 40 00 80 06 51 87 cd a9 55 fd cd a9 | .,bR@...Q‡Í©UýÍ©
0020: 55 a2 00 50 04 36 09 b9 ba 3e 00 3d 7b d5 60 12 | U..P.6...>.={Õ`.
0030: 22 38 ea 5b 00 00 02 04 05 b4 05 b4             | "8ê[........
```

1. Packet two in the example above is the response to the packet in the activity. What portion of the trace indicates that the TCP process is now communicating?
2. What is the acknowledgement number?
3. Which client destination port does this message target?

Lesson 5—TCP and Data Transmission

After a connection is established, each side sends and receives data as a stream of bytes. TCP uses a variety of segment delivery mechanisms to ensure efficient and reliable data transmission. This lesson discusses these mechanisms in detail.

Objectives

At the end of this lesson you will be able to:

- Explain how TCP establishes connections
- Describe the TCP three way handshake
- Explain TCP data transmission between ports
- Describe TCP's use of sequence numbers and acknowledgements
- Explain TCP sliding windows
- Explain how TCP terminates connections

Key Point

TCP segments uses several mechanisms to reliably carry data between host ports.

Connection Establishment Functions

TCP connection establishment provides four main functions:

- Through the exchange of connection request and response packets, TCP assures each connecting host process that the opposite process exists
- Provides optional parameter exchange, such as packet size, window size, and QoS
- Allocates transport resources such as buffer space
- Creates an entry in the connection table

Three-Way Handshake

TCP establishes a connection with a "three-way handshake." This ensures that the two ends have synchronized their individual ISNs and can accurately track segments passed back and forth.

The active TCP client process normally initiates the handshake, and in turn the passive server end process responds. Hosts may run both passive and active TCP processes simultaneously, thus the handshake supports multiple simultaneous connections. The Three-Way Handshake Diagram illustrates this connection initiation process.

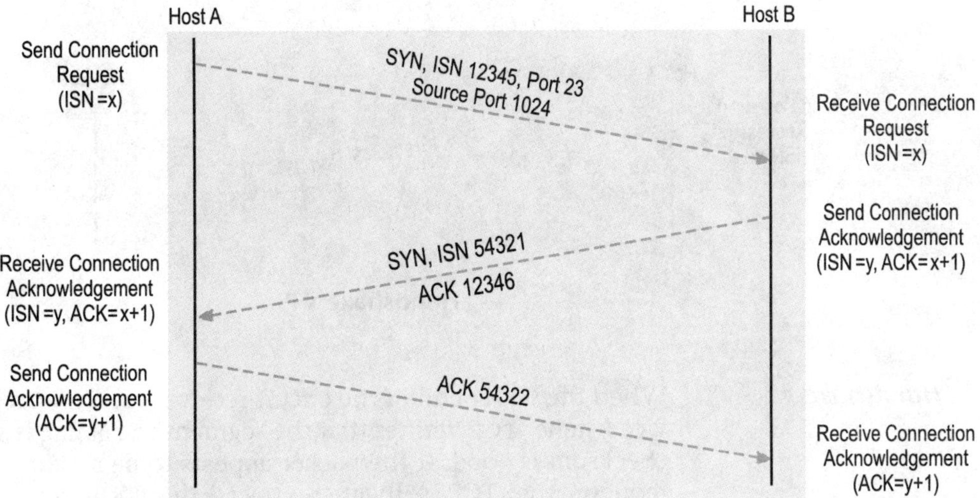

Three-Way Handshake

Handshake #1

When Host A establishes a local socket, its TCP sends an initial SYN packet to Host B's TCP, sets a retransmission timer, and waits until either the timer expires or it receives an ACK packet from the remote socket. A SYN packet consists of an empty TCP segment (a segment with no data, only the header) with the header SYN bit set.

As the Handshake #1 Diagram illustrates, the source station sends a SYN segment requesting a remote server connection. The segment indicates the source station wishes to create a connection, that it will use sequence numbers starting with sequence number 12345, and it wishes to connect to well-known Port 23.

Handshake #1

Handshake #2

When the server end of the circuit receives the SYN packet, its service listener TCP verifies that the segment's SYN flag is set and the checksum is good. If the packet appears to be a valid connection request, the TCP software extracts the local and remote IP addresses and TCP port numbers. It also sets the input buffer pointer to point to the initial SYN packet, allowing the receiver to "hold its place" while it waits for the next segment.

The receiving, passive end TCP records the active side's ISN and returns to the initiator a SYN-ACK packet. It also sets a retransmission timer, and waits until either the timer expires or it receives an ACK packet.

The Handshake #2 Diagram illustrates the server's SYN response to the active Open request, including its ACK that it received the SYN from the initiator.

Note: The ACK field indicates it is now expecting to hear sequence number 12346. This acknowledges the SYN that occupies sequence number space 12345.

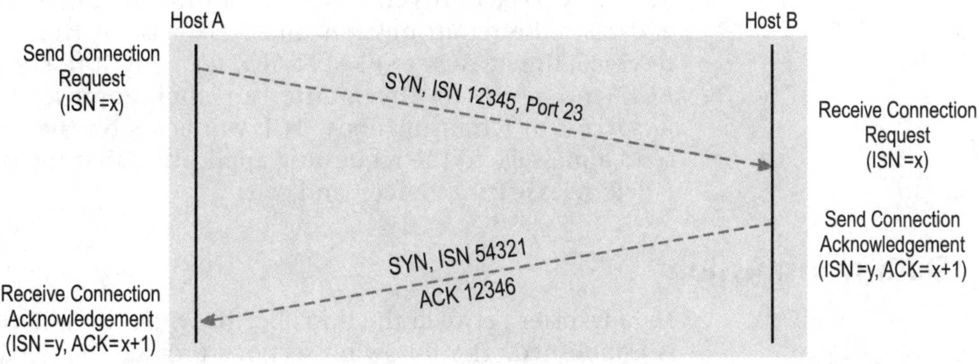

Handshake #2

Handshake #3

When the initiating TCP receives the server's SYN-ACK segment, it returns an ACK packet confirming the SYN-ACK's receipt. When the passive side TCP receives Host A's ACK packet, the end-to-end connection is established. The Handshake #3 Diagram shows the active side sending an empty ACK segment in response to Host B's SYN segment.

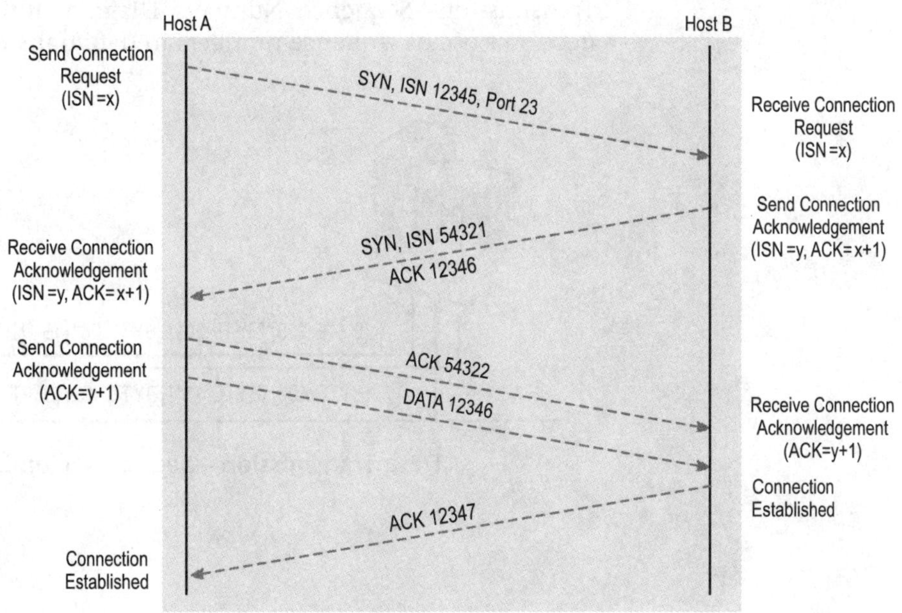

Handshake #3

If Host A's retransmission timer happens to expire before Host B's SYN-ACK packet arrives, it will retransmit the initial SYN packet and reset the retransmission timer. Likewise, if Host B does not receive a timely ACK to its SYN-ACK segment, it resends the SYN-ACK and resets its timer. After an application-set number of unsuccessful retransmissions, TCP will abandon the connection, send a message to the requesting application that the connection failed, release its resources, and exit.

Data Transmission

Data transfer between the hosts begins when the TCP connection is established. The following sections provide the details of how information flows between hosts communicating across TCP virtual circuits.

Sequence Numbers

As we already know, each side of a connection uses its own set of sequence numbers. Each side specifies its first sequence number when the connection is first established (the SYN and SYN-ACK segments). The data flow can be viewed as two independent streams flowing in opposite directions between both ends of the connection. The SYN, SYN-ACK, and FIN packets (used in circuit termination) each consume one sequence number. The Data Transmission—Sequence Numbers Diagram illustrates the connection's use of sequence numbers in data transmission.

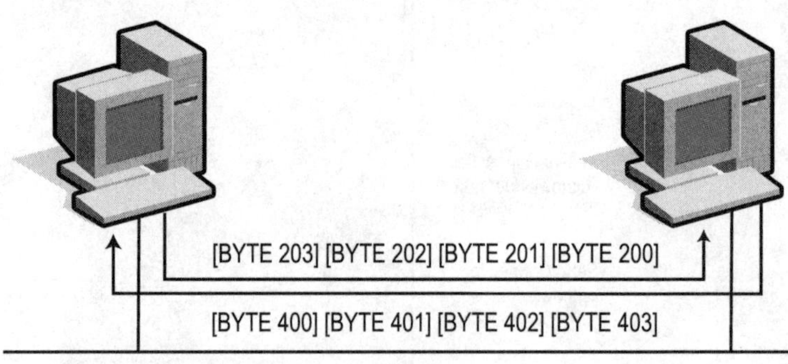

Data Transmission—Sequence Numbers

The source application passes its bytes to the source TCP in order, and the source TCP maintains this byte order as it transmits its segments to the destination TCP process. The destination TCP then delivers the bytes from its receive buffers to the destination application, again maintaining the original byte order. If the receiving TCP receives the segments out of order, it uses the sequence numbers to reorder the bytes before sending them on to the destination application.

Segments

When the source TCP receives data from its client application, it appends the data to the current output buffer queue. If the sending window is open, that is, if the output buffer has room for more segments, TCP sends as much of the new data as fits into the window. TCP has the ability to send and receive more than one segment at a time, and the window size determines how many segments the buffer sends at once. (We will discuss Windows later in this lesson.) TCP sets the segment's sequence number to the sequence number assigned to the first byte of data placed in the segment.

Because TCP is a byte-stream protocol, it is free to divide the source application byte stream into varying size segments. TCP sets each segment's size independent of the application program-supplied data blocks. The Data Transmission—Segments Diagram is an example of this, but is atypical in that the actual segment size may range from 0 to approximately 500 bytes. Notice that each segment's assigned sequence number matches the sequence number allocated to the segment's first data byte.

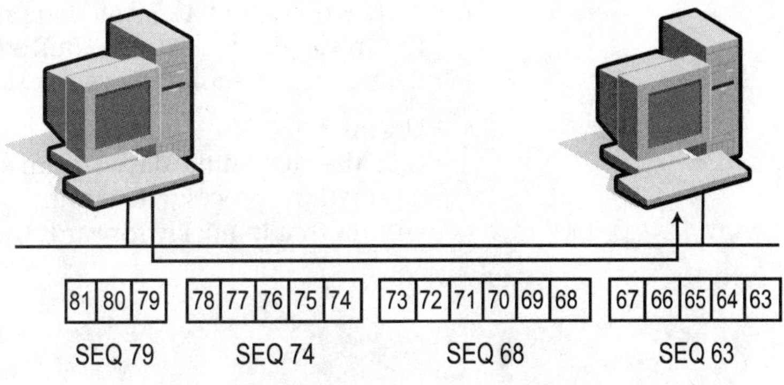

Data Transmission—Segments

Push and Urgent Flags

Recall that a TCP segment's header uses at least 24 bytes of a segment's total size. When segments contain only a few bytes of user data, the segment uses a tremendous amount of communications overhead, wasting network bandwidth. Each transmitted segment must include a fixed amount of header information. Additionally, IP carries a TCP segment across the internetwork, and an IP packet requires its own header information.

A typical TCP over IP packet then must contain 24 bytes of TCP header information, and a minimum of 20 bytes of IP header information. If the packet contains only a few bytes of user data, most of the packet consists of header information. To make data transfer more efficient and minimize network traffic, TCP usually collects enough application data bytes in a buffer to build a reasonably long segment. TCP then transmits the segment across the internetwork.

TCP provides a mechanism to force the delivery of data even though there are not enough bytes to fill the buffer. The mechanism includes use of Push and Urgent flags:

- Push flag—Included as part of the TCP header information, the purpose of the Push flag is to push data through, from the source process to the destination process.

  Normally, TCP decides when enough data has been accumulated to form a segment. However, a source application can require TCP to transmit all outstanding data up to and including that labeled with a Push flag. When the destination TCP notices the Push flag, it does not wait for more data before passing the data up to the destination process.

  This mechanism may be implemented for interactive terminal users who expect an immediate response for each keystroke. If the transmitted data is buffered, the response might be delayed until enough keystrokes fill the output buffer.

- Urgent flag—The Urgent flag informs the destination process that the upcoming data stream contains important data. The destination process determines the appropriate action and ensures that it quickly forwards the data to the receiving process.

ACK and Retransmission

In an established TCP connection, the sending TCP process expects an ACK for each transmitted segment. When the receiving process acknowledges a segment, it acknowledges each byte within the segment. The acknowledgement packet must have the ACK flag set and must contain a valid ACK number. The ACK number is the sequence number for the next data byte the receiving process expects from the source.

The source TCP process must retain all transmitted data until it receives an ACK. If for some reason the sender does not receive an ACK within the time limit specified by the application-set retransmission timer, the transmitting TCP assumes the data is lost or corrupted. The sending TCP retransmits the data, beginning with the first unacknowledged byte. After the application-set number of unacknowledged retransmissions, TCP aborts the connection. On the Data Transmission—ACK and Retransmission Diagram, the numbers 1 through 10 represent a series of segments, each containing 1 byte.

Note: Segments typically contain more than 1 byte.

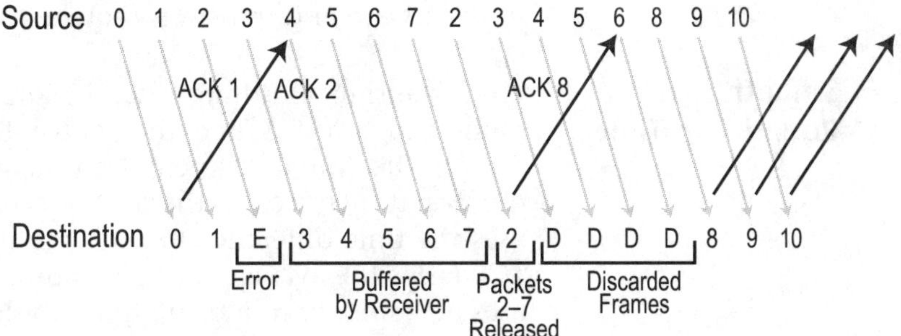

Data Transmission—ACK and Retransmission

During the connection establishment procedure, the source and destination hosts synchronize with an initial transmit sequence number of 0 and a transmit window of 8 bytes. This means that the receiving TCP can hold in its receive buffer 8 data bytes, or in this example, eight 1-byte segments.

In the diagram, segments 0 and 1 are delivered, and the receiving TCP process acknowledges each with the sequence number incremented by one, because this is the next sequence number the host expects to receive. The receiver includes in the ACK packet a window size of 6, stating that the receiver window size remains at 8 bytes; the receiver can hold 6 more bytes of data (6 more segments, in this example).

Segment 2 arrives at the destination host in error (the checksum failed). The source host continues to transmit within its allowed 8-byte window, and the destination host continues to receive these additional segments without error. The receiver buffers the 1-byte segments 3 through 7 with the hope that segment 2 will soon arrive. Because the last ACK the source host received was for segment 1 (ACK 2), and the receive window specified only 8 bytes, the sender must halt transmission at segment 7 until it receives acknowledgement for Segments 2 through 7. Because the senders' segment 2 retransmission timer expired, it begins retransmitting segments 2 through 7.

The destination TCP receives the retransmitted segment 2 without error, and thus can release to the application process the buffered segments 3 through 7, and returns an ACK for segment 7 (ACK 8). Before it sends segment 7, the source host receives the ACK for sequence numbers 2 through 7 (ACK 8 acknowledges receipt of all outstanding sequence numbers). The source station skips forward and transmits sequence number 8.

Smooth Round-Trip Time

The retransmission timer is set dynamically based on the "smooth round-trip time." When the source TCP sends a data packet, it records the initial segment transmission time and its sequence number. It then records the time it receives the segment's ACK, and uses the time difference to calculate the smooth round-trip time. TCP keeps the average round-trip time as a weighted average, and uses new smooth round-trip times to slowly adjust the average.

An internetworking environment presents to the TCP process ever-changing network conditions, such as varying delays and paths across network segments. TCP uses this adaptive round trip time calculation technique to accommodate these changing conditions, adjusting timeouts accordingly. Because the path between two hosts may cross multiple intermediate networks and routers, the source TCP processes can't possibly know in advance how quickly they will receive an ACK segment. Additionally, router performance varies by the amount of traffic they handle, thus the delay each segment experiences at each router varies. Therefore, the round trip time each segment experiences can vary from packet to packet.

Data Reception

The Data Reception Diagram illustrates the data reception concept. A TCP process receives data segments from IP through a mailbox specified in the IP socket block. Using the ACK information contained in the new segment, the local TCP first frees any acknowledged output queue data (segments awaiting transmission to the receiving TCP process). After releasing the acknowledged data, the local TCP inserts any new data from the new packet into its resequencing queue in the appropriate order. If the first segment in the resequencing queue has the next expected sequence number, TCP begins to send the data in the queue to the application.

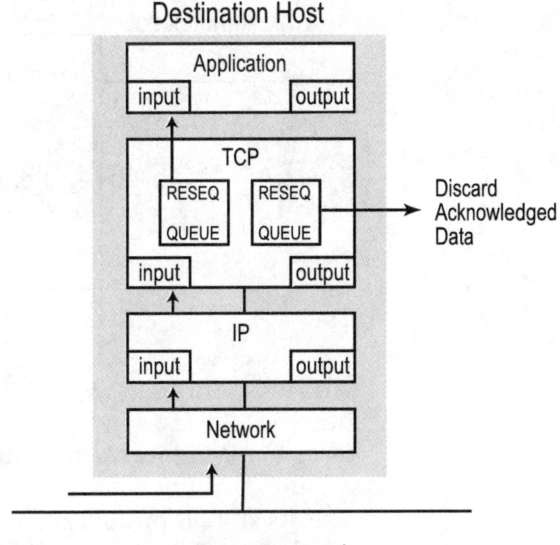

Data Reception

TCP sends the in-sequence data to the client application's mailbox in segments, just as it was received. If the client's mailbox is full, TCP links the inbound segments together and holds them in the resequencing queue, sending the appropriate acknowledgement segments to the source TCP. When the application notifies the local TCP process that its mailbox is no longer full, TCP releases the linked data segments to the application at once.

Window Management

Window management is the TCP process of tracking outstanding TCP segments during information transmission between communicating devices.

Efficient Transmission

A window mechanism provides for efficient data transmission by allowing TCP to send multiple segments before waiting for an ACK. The connection establishment procedure determines the initial window size. The Window Management—Efficient Transmission Diagram illustrates this type of mechanism.

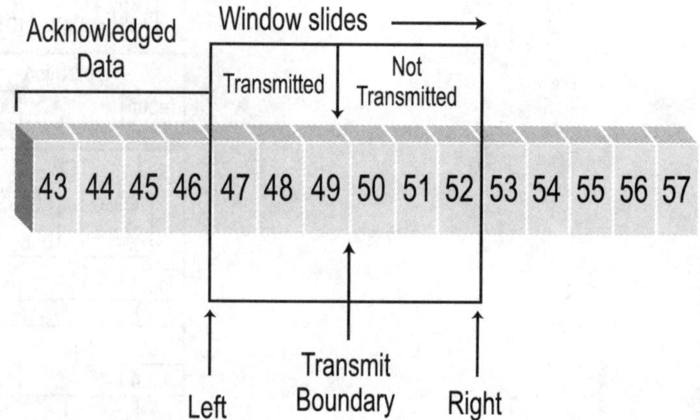

Window Management—Efficient Transmission

The local TCP process manages data flow by placing a transmit window over a sequence of bytes. The source TCP process sequentially groups all bytes bound by the window size into segments, and attempts to transmit the segments without delay. Three pointers define the window:

- The left pointer marks the window's left side. All bytes in the data stream to the left of this pointer have already been sent and acknowledged. Bytes to the right of this pointer are included in the transmission window.

- The right pointer marks the window's right side. All bytes to the right of this pointer are outside the transmission window and cannot yet be sent by TCP. All bytes between this pointer and the left pointer are included in the transmission window. The highest numbered byte within the window boundaries is the last byte that TCP can transmit before it must wait for the next ACK.
- The transmit boundary pointer defines a boundary inside the window. All bytes between this pointer and the left window pointer have already been sent, but the destination has not yet acknowledged their receipt. The source will send the bytes between the transmit boundary pointer and the right window pointer before it stops to wait for an ACK.

The segments' grouping and transmission causes the transmit boundary pointer to move quickly from left to right within the transmit window. When the source TCP process receives an ACK from the destination TCP, the entire window slides to the right 1 byte for each acknowledged byte (to match the window size). Because ACKs are cumulative (they can acknowledge multiple bytes at a time), the window jumps and skips as it moves toward the right.

The window continues to move to the right as the source transmits segments, as long as the source receives timely ACKs and the transmit boundary pointer does not meet the window's right side pointer. If the transmit boundary pointer reaches the right side pointer, the transmitting TCP process must halt segment transmission and wait for an ACK before it can move the window to the right again.

Each TCP connection maintains two windows; one window slides as the data is sent, while the second window slides as the data is received. Because TCP connections are full-duplex, the two connections' windows move simultaneously, one send and receive window on each host.

Flow Control

Flow control describes managing information transferred across a network connection.

Variable-Sized Windows

Variable-sized windows control end-to-end information flow. Each TCP process notifies its remote counterpart of its "receive" window size. The receive window is the range of sequence numbers the source TCP is willing to accept. Normally, the receiving TCP decreases the receive window size as it receives data, and increases the window when it passes data successfully to the client application.

A large window encourages transmissions. In response to an increased receive window advertisement, a sender increases its transmit window size, and sends more unacknowledged bytes. A sender decreases its transmit window size in response to a decreased receive window advertisement. Window size advertisements accompany ACK segments; thus, the source and destination TCPs can change their send and receive window sizes dynamically.

Zero Receive Window

TCP accepts and acknowledges only those segments that fill a window. If TCP cannot accept more data, it closes the receive window by sending an ACK packet with an advertised zero window size. TCP may continue to receive data segments after it has closed the window, but it will not acknowledge them.

A TCP process facing a zero receive window must periodically send probe segments with invalid sequence and ACK numbers and a single byte of invalid data. The receiving TCP responds by sending an ACK immediately, and will include a nonzero window size when it reopens the window. These probes ensure that the source reliably reports the reopened window to the other end of the connection.

Connection Termination

TCP connections are full-duplex, consisting of two independent end-to-end data streams. To terminate a connection, the two TCPs must close both data streams. The Data Streams During a Disconnection Diagram illustrates this concept.

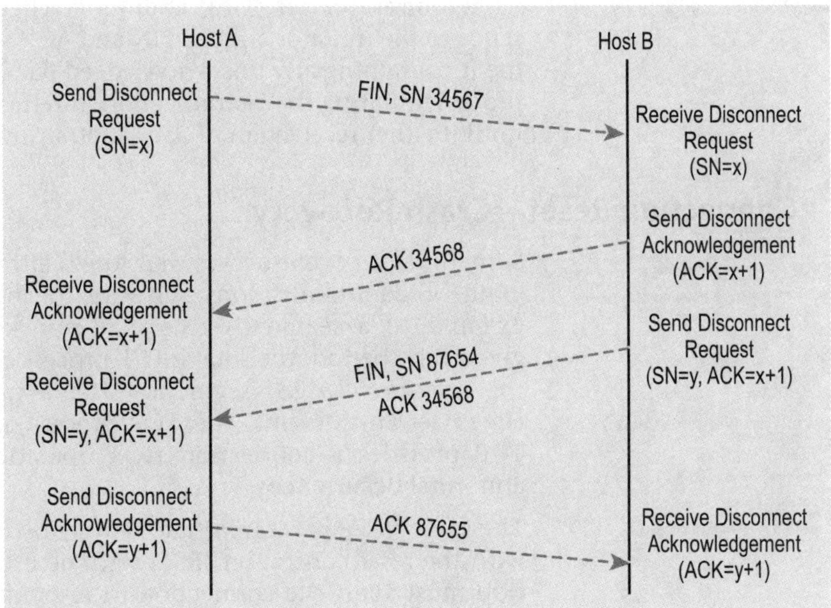

Data Streams During a Disconnection

Side Initiating Disconnection Request

A TCP process that wishes to close a connection transmits a packet containing a set FIN bit to the remote TCP process; this is known as an active close. Because each connection is independent, the initiating TCP process must continue to accept data from the remote process until the remote process responds with an ACK and FIN segment; the remote process' response is called a passive close.

When the initiating TCP process receives the remote process' answering ACK packet, it sends a disconnected message to its client application and waits for a time-out. When the timer expires, the initiating TCP process releases its resources and exits.

Side Responding to Disconnection Request

When a remote TCP process receives a FIN segment from the initiator, it signals its client application with a disconnected message. The remote TCP process continues to accept and transmit data from its client application to the initiating TCP.

After the application sends all remaining client data to the TCP process, the responding TCP process sends a disconnect message to its client application. At this point, the remote TCP process closes its resources for receiving additional client application data. It sends to the initiator either a FIN and ACK segment alone, or a segment containing any unacknowledged data, plus a FIN, to the TCP process initiating the disconnection. It retransmits the FIN segment until it either receives an ACK or a retransmission time out.

Connection Reset—Crash Recovery

Sometimes an event occurs that forces either the application program or communications software to abort a connection. For example, if a segment's receipt is not acknowledged within a given time period, the source TCP process continues to retransmit the unacknowledged segment. After a number of unacknowledged retransmissions, the TCP process aborts the connection. TCP provides a connection reset operation to deal with such abnormal occurrences.

The source TCP process initiates a reset by transmitting a segment with the reset control bit (RST) set. The other side of the connection must abort the connection in response to the RST segment. The receiving side also informs its application process that a reset has occurred, and as a result, both directions immediately stop data transfer and release all resources.

Frame Encapsulations

An IP datagram completely encapsulates a TCP message, including the header and data, as it travels across the network. The Ethernet Frame Diagram provides an example of frame encapsulation.

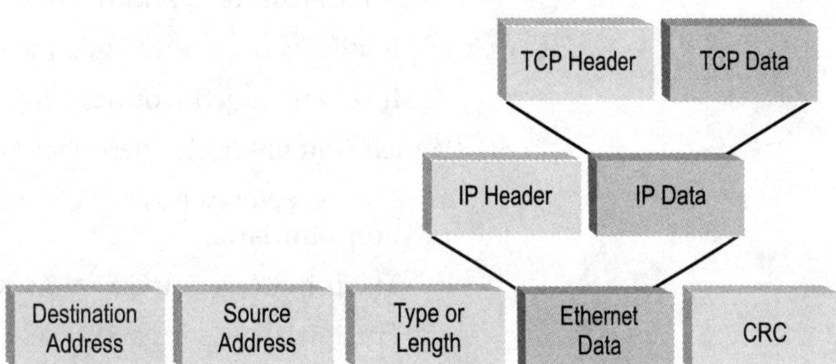

Ethernet Frame

Activities

1. What happens if the retransmission timer set by the sending TCP times out before it receives an acknowledgement.
   a. It abandons the connection.
   b. It retransmits to another destination port.
   c. It adjusts the transmit window size.
   d. It retransmits the outstanding segments.
2. Which statement best describes Handshake #1?
   a. The receiver sends a SYN-ACK segment to the connection's initiator.
   b. The initiator sends a SYN-ACK segment to the receiver.
   c. The initiator sends a SYN segment to the target host's TCP process.
   d. The receiver replies with a SYN segment to the source host TCP process.
3. Which two flags can a sending application set to force the TCP process to send data before filling the transmit buffer? (Choose two.)
   a. FIL
   b. PSH
   c. FIN
   d. URG
4. The destination TCP process has set a 1,000-byte receive buffer window. The source TCP sequence number starts at 23,100.

   The source sends the following segments, in order:

   - Segment 1–200 bytes
   - Segment 2–300 bytes
   - Segment 3–200 bytes
   - Segment 4–300 bytes

As it is sending the segments, it receives the following acknowledgement numbers:

23,300 + Window size 800 bytes (the receive buffer can now hold 1,000–200 bytes)

23,600 + Window size 500 bytes (the receive buffer can now hold 800–300 bytes)

The source continues to send the remaining segments, until it fills the receiver's 1,000-byte buffer. However, the last acknowledgement the source received was 23,600. The retransmission timer for sequence number 23,600 has expired.

What will the source TCP do next?

a. Resend all 4 segments

b. Resend segments 3 and 4

c. Reset the retransmission timer and wait again

d. Continue sending to force the receiver's buffer to enlarge

5. List the four main TCP connection functions.

____

____

____

____

____

____

____

____

Extended Activity

The source TCP is holding in its transmit buffer 6 segments, totaling 2,100 bytes. The receiving TCP has set a receive buffer (window) size of 1,500 bytes. The TCP Buffers Diagram illustrates this concept.

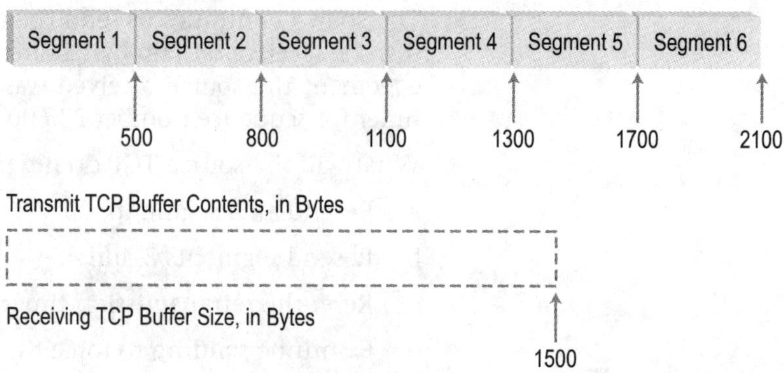

TCP Buffers

The sequence numbers start with 0.

a. Which segments can the receive buffer hold?

____

b. How many receive buffer bytes will these segments use?

____

c. The source TCP sends segment 1 and receives ACK 500. What is the receive window size the receiver sends with ACK 500?

____

d. The source TCP sends segment 2 and receives ACK 800. What receive window size does the receiver send with the ACK segment?

____

e. After receiving ACK 800, what is the next sequence number the source sends?

____

f. The source does not receive ACK 1,100 when expected. Rather than hold transmission waiting for ACK 1,100, the source sends segment 4. What will the source do after sending segment 4?

____

____

____

____

____

____

____

____

Lesson 6—Moving Information Across a TCP/IP Network

The purpose of this lesson is to understand the steps necessary to move information from a computer on one network to a computer on another network. We will review the steps necessary to obtain the proper addresses and establish a virtual circuit between applications, and we will watch the flow of information as it moves across a network.

Objectives

At the end of this lesson you will be able to:

- List the three types of addresses found in most computer networks
- Explain the steps for obtaining the necessary addresses
- Describe the process of moving information between two applications

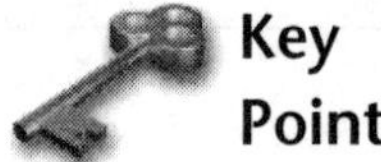

Key Point

Several steps are necessary to move information across a TCP/IP network.

Information Transfer

There are several things that must happen for information to be transferred across a TCP/IP network such as the Internet. In general, the following five steps occur:

1. Obtain logical addresses
2. Obtain physical addresses
3. Establish connection between applications
4. Transfer information
5. Terminate connection

Before going through each of these steps, we will briefly review physical and logical addresses used to move information from application to application.

Primary Functions of Each Layer

The OSI Summary Table provides an overview of the primary functions of each of the OSI model layers. The OSI Summary Table also reviews the unit of information and function of the addresses where appropriate.

OSI Summary

OSI Layer	Layer Function	Unit of Information	Address Type
Application	User Functionality	Program	
Presentation	Character representation Compression Security	Characters and Words	
Session	Establishing, conducting, and ending sessions		
Transport	Getting messages from sending computer process to receiving computer process	Message	Process-to-process between applications
Network	Getting individual packets across a network	Packet	Packet address identifying receiver's network and host location
Data Link	Getting frames containing packets across a link enroute to final destination	Frame	NIC (next node in network)
Physical	Getting bits in the form of signals across physical media	Bit	

Addressing in Computer Networks

There are two classifications of addresses in computer networks: physical and logical. There are two primary types of logical addresses: network and process. Both types of addresses are described in the following sections.

Physical Addresses

A physical address is also referred to as a:

- Hardware address
- Adapter address
- NIC address
- MAC address

A physical address is an address required for information to be ultimately delivered to a given network node. The word "ultimately" is chosen here because information often starts out (at the higher layers) to be simply addressed to some symbolic name, such as the host name in the command Telnet Serverhost. The name serverhost refers to the name of a target host the user is attempting to contact using the Telnet application and protocol. For the user to connect to the above host, a physical address must somehow be derived from the symbolic name and then used in an agreed-upon addressing scheme to reach the target. In this case, an intermediate logical (or software) address (IP address) is first derived from the symbolic name using some sort of a name service process such as DNS.

It is natural to associate a physical address with the Physical Layer, but the physical address is actually processed by the Data Link Layer. Recall that the Physical Layer is just concerned with transmitting bits to, and receiving bits from, the physical medium. This layer does not see bits as organized into meaningful patterns, such as an address.

For the purposes of networking, physical addresses can be categorized into two general types: LAN addresses and WAN addresses. A LAN address is commonly found in an Ethernet or Token Ring environment, and a WAN address is used in High-Level Data Link Control (HDLC) or frame relay addressing.

Logical Addresses

A logical address differs from a physical address in that it is generally implemented as software rather than as a hardware entity. There are two primary types of logical addresses, as follows:

- Network addresses
- Port or process addresses

An example of a logical address is an IP address (network) such as "144.25.54.8." Another example of a logical address is a port number (process address) such as "23."

The most important fact to remember concerning logical addresses is that a logical address will not get the information "into the box." Only the physical address, whether a broadcast address, multicast (group) address, or single destination (unicast) address, can accomplish this.

Obtaining Logical Addresses

There are two logical addresses necessary for moving information across a network. We must know the address of the network, as well as the address of the host within the network. This is the job of IP, and, as previously discussed, an IP address consists of these two parts. We must also know the application within the computer where the information is destined. For example, if we want to retrieve a file from a web server, we must input this information in the browser. The Logical Addresses Screen Diagram illustrates the items found in the "pub" directory at the logical address telnet.westnetinc.com.

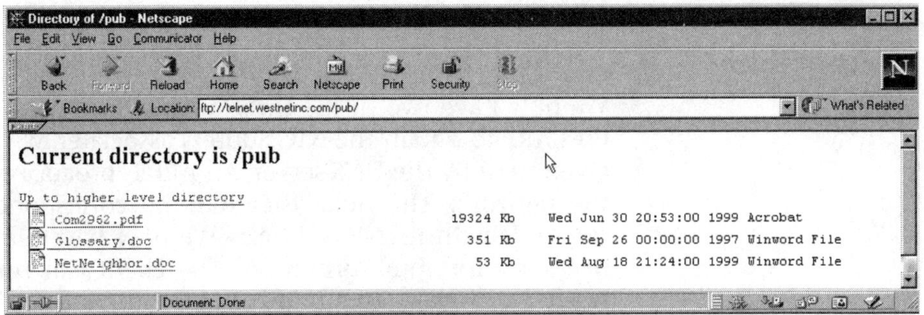

Logical Addresses Screen

At the browser's location or address line, we enter **ftp** to indicate the application we want to invoke, and the address **telnet.westnetinc.com** to represent the host where the application is located. In this case, we have also added the specific directory on the server "pub" where the file is located.

Because ftp is a well-known application, there is a default port number (21) used to access the remote application process. The symbolic address is given, but we still need the numeric address associated with telnet.westnetinc.com; this is where DNS comes in. The requesting client makes a DNS request to a DNS server, which in turn responds with the appropriate IP address, as shown on the DNS Request/Reply Diagram. Each client within a TCP/IP network is preconfigured to connect to a specific DNS server IP address, or to some other type of server that provides name resolution.

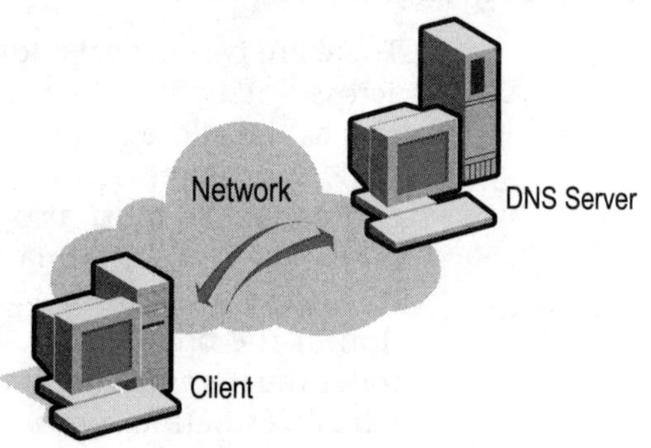

DNS Request/Reply

Obtaining Physical Addresses

We now have two of the three addresses needed. Now the client uses ARP to obtain the NIC address associated with the IP address given to us by the DNS server. An ARP is broadcast to all nodes on the network. The node that has the corresponding IP address responds with its NIC address. We now have all three addresses necessary for communication. The client can now generate the segment, packet, and frame headers to move the information across the physical network.

Establishing a Connection Between Applications

TCP must now establish a connection with the TCP process on the remote computer. Thus, TCP communicates with the TCP peer process on the other end of the network. This virtual circuit is established using socket numbers between communicating applications. After TCP sets up the virtual circuit, information can move between applications. TCP provides reliable information delivery between communication applications. The Connecting to a Device—Well-Known Ports Diagram illustrates how TCP uses port numbers (for example, Port 21), to steer information to the correct process.

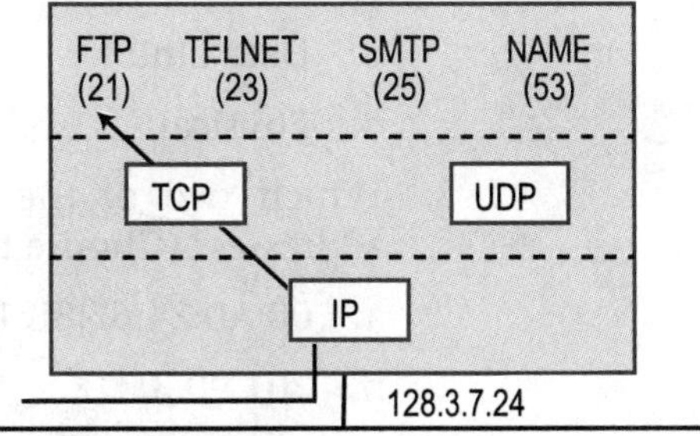

Connecting to a Device—Well-Known Ports

Transferring Information

Information is now transferred across the network. TCP keeps track of application data segmentation and reassembly. TCP relies on IP to get datagrams across the network. IP relies on the underlying LAN or WAN protocol to move the packets across a physical link. If the file server is located on the same physical network, only one frame needs to be built. If the file server is located at a remote site, it will be necessary to build frames at each hop along the way.

Terminating the Connection

After all the information, segment by segment, packet by packet, and frame by frame, has been sent between communicating applications, the communicating hosts terminate the session. The session is terminated after the sending TCP disconnects from the receiving TCP. When terminated, no virtual circuit exists between communicating applications, and no information will travel between TCP ports.

Activities

1. Which three of the following terms refer to a physical address? (Choose three.)
   a. Port address
   b. MAC address
   c. Adapter address
   d. Hardware address
2. At which OSI model layer does the physical address reside?
   a. Transport
   b. Network
   c. Data Link
   d. Physical
3. Which two of the following are examples of LAN logical addresses? (Choose two.)
   a. 00:A0:24:67:8B:1D
   b. 201.90.35.78
   c. Port 23
   d. DLCI 17
4. Which TCP/IP protocol does a network host use to find a physical address, given a logical address?
   a. DNS
   b. RARP
   c. DHCP
   d. ARP
5. TCP establishes which type of circuit between applications?
   a. Virtual
   b. Dynamic
   c. Physical
   d. Connectionless

Extended Activity

1. Download a freeware or shareware packet sniffer, such as that available at **http://www.ufasoft.com**.
   a. Install it on your Windows PC and observe TCP traffic on your local network.
   b. Note the physical and logical addresses recorded for each captured packet.
   c. Also, follow the TCP sequence numbers and windowing information.

Summary

Unit 4 provided an in-depth look at TCP/IP protocols, specifically those used to get application information between source and destination computers. It began by looking at IP protocols. We looked at how IP fragments packets to get large packets across a network.

We learned that to move packets to their destination on a physical network, we must resolve logical IP addresses to physical addresses. ARP performs this function. Additionally, we learned that a router can act as a proxy ARP when the source does not know the destination network gateway address.

UDP is a connectionless protocol that uses IP for getting information between applications using port numbers. The port numbers identify the applications using the TCP/IP network. A client computer, for example, uses UDP to get IP address information from a DNS server. Because UDP is connectionless, it relies on Application Layer protocols to handle error processing and sequencing of information.

TCP is the connection-oriented counterpart to UDP. When two applications need to communicate, TCP first establishes a session between the local and remote applications. It first goes through a handshaking sequence before data can be transmitted between communicating applications. After all the data is sent for a session, TCP is responsible for terminating the session.

Unit 4 Quiz

1. How does a diskless workstation identify itself when requesting an IP address using RARP?
   a. By its subnet mask
   b. By its MAC address
   c. By its IP address
   d. By its network number
2. A host on the local IP network segment has data to send to another host, located on another IP network. The source host needs to resolve the destination host's IP address to a MAC address. Which protocol might the gateway router run in order to answer the local host's ARP request?
   a. RARP
   b. IARP
   c. ARP
   d. Proxy ARP
3. Which best describes IP's use of TTLs?
   a. The TTL designates how long the sending host has been online.
   b. The TTL specifies the time a datagram is allowed to remain on the network.
   c. The TTL designates the number of seconds the packet has been on the network segment.
   d. The TTL counts the number of seconds a datagram has been queued at each router.
4. What happens to a datagram marked as do not fragment if it must be transmitted across a network segment with an MTU smaller than the datagram?
   a. The transmitting network device will adjust the segment's MTU to match the datagram's size.
   b. The sending device will hold the datagram until the destination segment's MTU increases.
   c. The transmitting network device will compress the datagram to fit the segment's MTU.
   d. The transmitting network device will drop the datagram, and notify the source.

5. Which IP packet bits does OSPF use to provide ToS routing?
   a. ToS bits
   b. D-T-R-C bits
   c. TTL bits
   d. OSPF bits
6. Which IP packet frame field ensures that the gateways handling a datagram agree on the datagram's format?
   a. HLEN
   b. ToS
   c. Version
   d. Identification
7. On an IP network, all hosts must be able to handle a packet size of at least how many bytes?
   a. 512
   b. 576
   c. 1,500
   d. 65,536
8. Given the following:
   - A 512-byte destination network segment MTU
   - A 1,500-byte datagram
   - A 20-byte IP header

   How many fragments will the transmitting device have to create to match the datagram to the segment's MTU?
   a. 1
   b. 2
   c. 3
   d. 4
9. Which three of the following applications use UDP services? (Choose three.)
   a. FTP
   b. TFTP
   c. SNMP
   d. DNS

10. Which best describes the UDP demultiplexing process?
    a. UDP enables the destination host to route received packets across multiple IP addresses.
    b. UDP uses link numbers to allow multiple applications to communicate simultaneously on the same host.
    c. UDP uses port numbers to allow multiple applications to communicate simultaneously on the same host.
    d. UDP allows multiple hosts to communicate across a single, virtual circuit.
11. Which three choices are TCP features? (Choose three.)
    a. Best effort packet delivery
    b. Flow control
    c. Packet error recovery
    d. Demultiplexing multiple applications
12. Which statement best describes TCP's use of sequence numbers?
    a. They identify the next expected sequence number.
    b. They identify the next application the source wishes to contact.
    c. They specify the number of SYN bits the host has received during the current session.
    d. They identify the sequence number of the first data byte in the segment.
13. Which best describes TCP's use of the Window Header field?
    a. It is bidirectional, so both ends can control data flow.
    b. It is unidirectional, allowing only the sender to control data flow.
    c. It verifies that the TCP message fits within the segment's MTU.
    d. It allows the sending application to "see" the destination application ports.
14. Which addresses combine to create a TCP socket?
    a. MAC and IP
    b. IP and port
    c. Port and MAC
    d. Port and application

15. The local TCP process sends four segments, each 4 bytes long. The first sequence number is 7,806,002. Which is the acknowledgement number the receiving process returned to indicate it received segment one?
    a. 7,806,003
    b. 7,806,006
    c. 7,8060,010
    d. 7,8090,011
16. Which three parts of the TCP header help the protocol ensure reliable communications between applications? (Choose three.)
    a. ACK control bits
    b. Sequence numbers
    c. Checksum
    d. Urgent pointer
17. Which TCP function forces data delivery before filling the transmit buffer?
    a. Go
    b. Send
    c. Push
    d. Pull
18. Which type of packet does the receiving TCP send to the source indicating its receipt of the source's SYN packet?
    a. SYN-ACK
    b. SYN-2
    c. ACK
    d. RESYN
19. Which types of TCP segments contain window size advertisements?
    a. SYN
    b. ACK
    c. PSH
    d. WIN

20. How does a TCP process handle a failed connection?
    a. It sends FIN segments to poll the destination for status.
    b. It sends a RST segment when the maximum retry count is exceeded.
    c. It sends a RST segment to reset the destination's retransmission timer.
    d. It sends an ACK segment to immediately abort the connection.
21. At which two points in a one-way, multiple hop, end-to-end IP communications session will a frame have to be built? (Choose two.)
    a. At the receiving host's LAN port
    b. At each hop's router outbound port
    c. At the sending host's LAN port
    d. At each hop's router inbound port

Unit 5
TCP/IP Services

As I sit here today, booting my personal computer (PC), logging in to the network, checking my electronic mail (e-mail) and my online courses, I expect everything to work. The PC starts, my network logon succeeds, my e-mail client downloads the latest online sale information, and I can connect to the online course World Wide Web (Web) site and check on my students. Everything works as I desire, and I am able to begin another week.

We rarely think of the underlying network processes that take place millions of times a second. To log on the server, I have to have a network connection, not just physical, but logical. My e-mail client has to find an e-mail server and send my credentials so my Internet service provider's (ISP's) Post Office Protocol (POP) server will release to it my latest e-mail traffic. Finally, my browser has to establish a connection with the online course Web server and download the pages I seek.

In this lesson, we explore some common Transmission Control Protocol/Internet Protocol (TCP/IP) services in depth. We investigate the Domain Name System (DNS), a service that dutifully resolves our Web page Uniform Resource Locators (URLs) to IP addresses.

We explore the Internet Control Message Protocol (ICMP) and how it helps packets find their way from one end of an internetwork to the other. We find that the Internet Group Multicasting Protocol (IGMP) helps multimedia communications work.

Our PCs and servers need IP addresses to communicate, thus we need an avenue for assigning those addresses. Dynamic Host Configuration Protocol (DHCP) and Bootstrap Protocol (BOOTP) provide mechanisms to assign these addresses dynamically, reducing our administrative burden.

Network Address Translation (NAT) allows us to use private IP addresses inside our network, while still accessing public resources. We will learn how NAT makes this happen.

We conclude by discussing IP version 6, the next IP generation, which promises higher quality of service (QoS) capabilities and many more addresses than our currently used version 4.

Lessons

1. DNS
2. ICMP
3. IGMP
4. BOOTP
5. DHCP
6. NAT
7. IPv6

Terms

56-bit Data Encryption Standard (DES) encryption—DES is a popular single-key encryption system that uses a 56-bit key. Triple-DES uses the DES algorithm to encrypt a message three times, using three 56-bit keys. It is considered a hardware solution to encryption because of the time necessary to encrypt and decrypt a message.

address translation table—An address translation table is the internal-to-external IP and/or port address mappings maintained by a NAT device. The table's contents will vary depending on the NAT type used.

anycast—In IPv6, anycast is communication between a single sender and the nearest of several receivers in a group. The term exists in contradistinction to multicast, communication between a single sender and multiple receivers, and unicast, communication between a single sender and a single receiver in a network. Anycasting is designed to let one host initiate the efficient updating of router tables for a group of hosts. IPv6 can determine which gateway host is closest and sends the packets to that host as though it were a unicast communication. In turn, that host can anycast to another host in the group until all routing tables are updated.

BIND—Short for Berkeley Internet Name Domain, a DNS type. BIND is designed for UNIX systems based on BSD, the version of UNIX developed at the University of California's Berkeley campus.

chicken/egg method—The chicken/egg method is a technique used to resolve a first issue dependent on a second, but where the second issue cannot be implemented without the first. Usually, some third issue is used to resolve the first, bypassing the requirement for the second issue.

cut—A DNS cut divides DNS zone responsibilities between the root domain name server and subdomain nameservers, and in turn between subdomains and further subordinate domains. For example, in the domain westnetinc.com, a subdomain contracts.westnetinc.com could exist. When the DNS administrator cuts the westnetinc.com domain, he or she delegates responsibility for the subdomain contracts.westnetinc.com to the subdomain nameserver.

DHCP lease—A DHCP lease is the IP address the DHCP server dynamically issues to DHCP clients. The server maintains the lease for a specific period of time, and as the lease expiration time approaches, the client must renew the lease.

DHCPv6—Short for DHCP version 6, DHCPv6 assigns host IPv6 addresses dynamically. DHCPv6 is specified in Internet Draft form, and adds additional message types and larger Address fields, commensurate with IPv6 addressing, over DHCPv4. DHCPv6 uses UDP Port 546 for the client, and 547 for the server.

DNS zone—The part of the DNS namespace, for which a DNS server has complete information, is organized into units called zones; zones are the main units of replication in DNS. A zone contains one or more RRs for one or more related DNS domains. Each DNS server contains the RRs relating to those portions of the DNS namespace for which it is authoritative (for which it can answer queries sent by a host). When a DNS server is authoritative for a portion of the DNS name space, those systems' administrators are responsible for ensuring that the information about that DNS name space portion is correct. To increase efficiency, a given DNS server can cache the RRs relating to a domain in any part of the domain tree.

flow control—Flow control refers to control of the rate at which hosts or gateways inject packets into a network or internet. Flow control is used to avoid congestion and can be implemented at various protocol levels. Simplistic schemes, like ICMP source quench, instruct the sender to cease transmission until congestion ends. More complex schemes vary the transmission rate continuously.

fully qualified domain name (FQDN)—The FQDN is the full name for an Internet host computer, comprised of the hostname and the domain name. An example of an FQDN is host.westnetinc.com.

IP address translation—IP address translation is a NAT technique used to assign internal IP addresses to external addresses, either statically or dynamically. The NAT needs one public IP for each internal private IP needing a connection.

jumbogram—Using the IPv6, a jumbogram is a packet that contains a payload larger than 65,535 octets.

magic cookie—A magic cookie is a 4-byte field entry in the BOOTREQUEST message set to help the BOOTP server determine the format in which to send vendor-specific information. DHCP also specifies the magic cookie entry.

masquerading—Masquerading is also known as NAPT. Masquerading is a NAT technique that hides all internal devices behind a single public IP address (usually the NAT's outside port IP address). The NAT assigns this address to each internal device connection, and a new TCP or UDP port number taken from the registered port number range. This IP address/registered port number combination identifies a specific internal host on the Internet.

MD5—MD5 is a one-way hash algorithm that takes a message and converts it into a fixed string of digits called a message digest. It is used to create digital signatures.

Packet Internet Groper (Ping)—Ping is a utility used to verify that a computer's IP software is running properly and to verify the connectivity between computers.

registered port—Registered ports are those TCP and UDP ports not controlled by IANA and available for use by ordinary user processes or programs. The registered ports range from 1024–65535. These compare with the well-known ports, which are assigned to specific services.

resolver—The DNS resolver is a DNS system component that performs DNS queries against a DNS server (or servers). The resolver is a part of the DNS client and is usually installed when TCP/IP is installed.

resource record (RR)—An RR is a DNS database record containing information relating to a domain that a DNS client can retrieve and use. For example, the host RR for a specific domain holds the IP address of that domain (host); a DNS client will use this RR to obtain the IP address for the domain.

Resource Reservation Protocol (RSVP)—Sometimes known as Resource Reservation Setup Protocol, RSVP functions to reserve network resources based on an application's QoS requirements. RSVP requests these resources from all devices in a data flow's path and reports to the requesting application that the resources are available for its use.

source quench—Source quench is a congestion control technique in which a congested computer sends a message back to the source causing the congestion, requesting that the source stop transmitting. In a TCP/IP internet, gateways use ICMP source quench to stop or reduce the transmission of IP datagrams.

Tracert—Tracert is a utility that traces the route between two computers and sends information about each router hop along the way.

unauthoritive data—Unauthoritive data is domain namespace information stored on a nameserver on which that server does not maintain authority. The nameserver caches this information for a limited time period and then discards it if it is no longer needed. This caching allows for faster name resolution.

Uniform Resource Locator (URL)—A URL is an Internet address used to locate resources from within a Web browser. It can lead you to an Internet-connected computer anywhere in the world.

zone of authority—A DNS zone of authority is the DNS zone namespace for which a DNS nameserver is responsible. When a DNS domain is created, the new domain's root becomes the domain and its subdomains' zone of authority. A DNS server can maintain responsibility for more than one zone of authority.

Lesson 1—DNS

From a user's point of view, a DNS name, commonly known as a domain name, is a friendly alternative to an IP network address. Although a DNS name technically falls at the Application Layer, it is not a user application per se. This lesson reviews the purpose and function of DNS.

Objectives

At the end of this lesson you will be able to:

- Define a DNS name
- Describe the domain name tree structure
- Represent a domain name
- Describe the functions of a domain name administrator
- Describe how name servers manage domain name information
- Describe how a name is mapped to an IP address

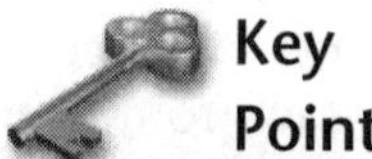

Key Point

DNS resolves user-friendly network names to logical IP addresses.

Overview of DNS

Sit down at your PC, open your browser, and type in a URL, for example, **http://www.westnetinc.com**. Watch the lower left corner (Internet Explorer) and you will see a line that states "Connecting to site 205.169.85.247." This is DNS in action; you type a URL, and your client resolves the user friendly URL to a PC friendly IP address. You could type into your browser the server's IP address, **http://205.169.85.247**, and make the same connection, but imagine how difficult it would be to remember your favorite Web sites if you could only connect by IP address.

Paul Mockapetris invented DNS in 1984. DNS servers, also called name servers, host the name resolution application; the DNS client side is known as a resolver. The term "Domain Name System" refers to the name resolution service vendors provide with their network operating systems (NOSs).

A user sees a domain name as a group of text labels separated by dots (.). The complete entry, host1.westnetinc.com., is called a fully qualified domain name (FQDN). (Notice the last "." following ".com"; this is the root domain designator and is not usually displayed.) The first label is the hostname, and the labels following the first dot constitute the domain. For example, we write the FQDN for host1 located in the westnetinc.com. domain as follows:

host1.westnetinc.com.

When using domain names, the user needs to know whether a given host is in the same domain as his computer. If the host is in the same domain, the user simply types the host name when issuing a command. For example:

http://host1

This individual hostname entry is called the relative name. It represents the hostname relative to the current domain, in this case, westnetinc.com.

On the other hand, if the user's computer and the host are in different domains, the user must include the domain along with the hostname. For example:

http://IBMhost.3Com.com

http://IBMhost.westnetinc.com

The following DNS discussion is for the reader who wants to understand the underlying protocol for this naming system, or who might need to establish a name database for a TCP/IP network that will connect to other TCP/IP networks.

Hierarchical Structure

DNS is a mechanism for naming network resources. It grew from a need to expand the Internet name database, which was centrally managed and maintained. Until DNS, Stanford Research Institute Network Information Center (SRI-NIC) maintained and updated this central database in the form of a hosts table. Network administrators submitted their changes, and the SRI-NIC updated the table. Network administrators then used FTP to download the latest host table and update their local domain name servers. A central database was efficient when there was a small group of users, and database entries seldom changed. However, as TCP/IP became more widely adopted, it became increasingly difficult to keep the central database current.

The Hosts File

Your PC may have its own hosts table, in the form of a hosts file. For example, if you run a Microsoft Windows PC with the TCP/IP protocol suite installed, you will find a file located in the Windows directory named "hosts," with no extension. This text file stores static name resolution entries, to which your PC can refer if it needs to resolve a name to an IP address. Imagine how tedious and time consuming your job would be if you had to update this file every time a new Web site came online!

The file entries are arranged in columns, as follows:

Internet-address   Official-host-name   aliases

The default entry is the local machine's loopback address, used for local diagnostics. The Hosts File Diagram shows a default hosts file from a Windows 2000 workstation, located in the **%systemroot%\system32\drivers\etc** folder. This is the path and folder in which the Windows NT/2000 system files are installed. To identify your systemroot folder, select Start, Run, and type %systemroot%.

```
# Copyright (c) 1993-1999 Microsoft Corp.
#
# This is a sample HOSTS file used by Microsoft TCP/IP for Windows.
#
# This file contains the mappings of IP addresses to host names. Each
# entry should be kept on an individual line. The IP address should
# be placed in the first column followed by the corresponding host name.
# The IP address and the host name should be separated by at least one
# space.
#
# Additionally, comments (such as these) may be inserted on individual
# lines or following the machine name denoted by a '#' symbol.
#
# For example:
#
#      102.54.94.97     rhino.acme.com          # source server
#       38.25.63.10     x.acme.com              # x client host

127.0.0.1       localhost
```

Hosts File

The DNS Hierarchy

As you can imagine, this centralized host table became large and ungainly. Therefore, it was necessary to find a naming system that would allow local name administration and maintenance, while at the same time providing a single, consistent naming scheme.

The DNS protocol extended the Internet name database by devising a system whereby names could be placed into distributed categories that could later be further partitioned. Categories were defined according to domains of authority. This meant that in partitioning the central name database, a scope of authority that included authority for registering, maintaining, and administering names was also defined.

TLDs

The DNS namespace starts at the root level; this is where the domain authority distribution begins, and is designated by a "." (period). Initially, seven top-level domains (TLDs) were defined, located immediately below the root, to reflect current users, as well as new groups adopting TCP/IP networks. These original domain names are:

- gov (government)
- edu (education)
- com (commercial)
- mil (military)
- org (organization)
- net (network service providers)

Each country is assigned a two-letter TLD code; the United States uses .us (though it is often not shown), and other countries have their own codes.

The complete top-level domain country code listing may be found at **http://www.iana.org/cctld/cctld-whois.htm**. Additionally, on November 16, 2000, the Internet Corporation for Assigned Names and Numbers (ICANN) approved seven new TLDs. These are:

- aero (air transport industry)
- biz (businesses)
- coop (cooperatives)

- info (unrestricted)
- museum (museums)
- name (individual name registration)
- pro (professional occupations)

This list is available at **http://www.icann.org/tlds**.

Second-Level Subdomains

Each domain has an administrator who can authorize the formation of a new subdomain. A new subdomain has a specific scope of authority, called zone of authority, usually over the named nodes within a given network system or group of systems. For example, the FQDN host1.westnetinc.com describes host1 located on the westnetinc subdomain, in turn located beneath the .com TLD (we assume the root). Second-level domain administrators register their domain names with ICANN-designated domain name registrars; the ICANN Web site lists the currently authorized registrars. For a fee, these registrars will register your company or private domain name and place the name to address mapping in the global DNS namespace.

Second-level domains can also be categories of top-level domains. For example, the .us TLD is categorized by state, such as Colorado:

.co.us

Some companies subcategorize companies and academic institutions:

.ac.uk

.co.uk

Second level domain administrators may break down their subdomains into smaller subdomains, such as:

support.instructors.westnetinc.com

The entry .support is a subdomain under the .instructor.westnetinc subdomain.

The DNS Hierarchical Structure Diagram shows a partial top-level DNS diagram, and examples of domains partitioned from a TLD.

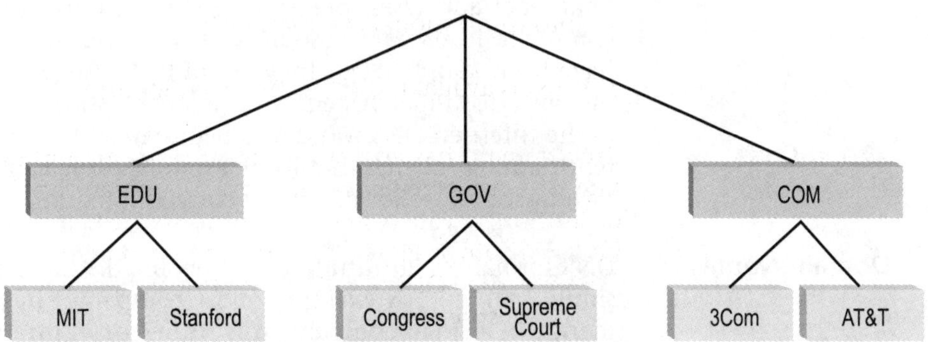

DNS Hierarchical Structure

As illustrated, DNS has a hierarchical structure in which TLDs are defined. These TLDs are centrally administered by ICANN, which authorizes TLD registrars, who in turn maintain the DNS database. Although the final authority and responsibility for DNS names rests with ICANN, each domain has responsibility and authority for names within its jurisdiction, or zone of authority, and can delegate similar authority to subdomains partitioned from it. Domain name information is maintained in databases, managed by applications called name servers, and used for the following purposes:

- Mapping domain names to IP addresses
- Mapping mailboxes to domain names
- Keeping up-to-date information
- Communicating across networks that run different protocols

Consistent Naming Scheme

Computer systems communicate with one another through hardware or network addresses. However, most users find it difficult to remember addresses, preferring instead to give proper names to computer hosts and resources. Various local naming schemes have been adopted, but they are of little use when communicating with dissimilar systems over a large distributed network, such as the Internet. DNS was developed to meet the need for a consistent naming scheme that local administrators can adopt with little adjustment to local naming conventions.

Domain Names

DNS formalizes an intuitive way people distinguish between two similar names. For example, most companies have sales departments. In a small company, it is sufficient in internal documents to say "Refer this to sales." However, to distinguish between two outside firms' sales departments, it would be necessary to say "Send this to the sales departments of company ABC and company XYZ." In this example, the name of each department is Sales. If we were to identify these departments using domain names, the names would appear as follows:

sales.mycompany

sales.ABC

sales.XYZ

Defining Uniqueness

Two computer hosts, both simply known as "host" by the groups connecting to them, might be distinguished by identifying them with the manufacturer, for example, the IBM host or Digital Equipment Corporation (DEC) host. To this intuitive way of distinguishing one host from another, let us introduce a convention of separating each identifier (or label) with a dot notation (.), which would appear as follows:

host.IBM

host.DEC

If a group connects to IBM hosts in two different organizations or locations, they might distinguish these various IBM hosts further, which would appear as follows:

host (referring to a local host, where software supplies the rest of the labels to complete the name)

host.IBM.Atlanta

host.IBM.Denver

host.IBM.Westnetinc

host.IBM.ABC

Using DNS terminology in the example host.IBM, the domain is IBM. However, in the example host.IBM.Westnetinc, the domain is IBM.westnetinc. Given another example, where a domain name is mymail-box.dept.company.state.country, mymailbox's domain consists of all the labels following it, in this example .dept.company.state.country. In another example, consider the FQDN domain sales.mycompany.california.us. The domain for the .mycompany subdomain is california.us.

Viewed as a tree structure, the examples above can be illustrated as shown on the DNS Hierarchical Tree Structure Diagram.

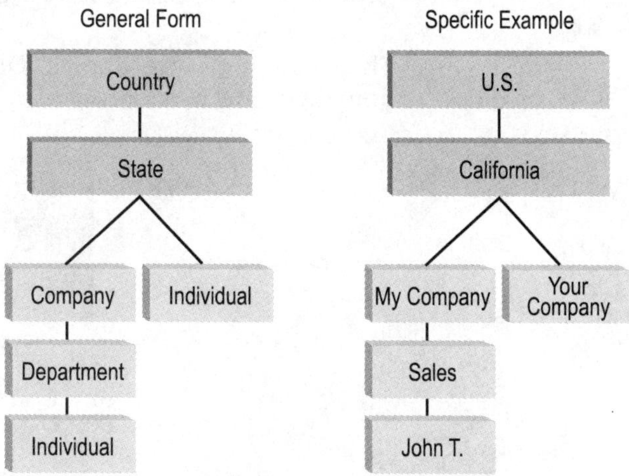

DNS Hierarchical Tree Structure

DNS Tree Structure

DNS defines a nomenclature for referring to hosts and resources. The Hierarchical Structure for Three Top-Level Domains Diagram shows DNS as a tree structure that starts with top-level domains.

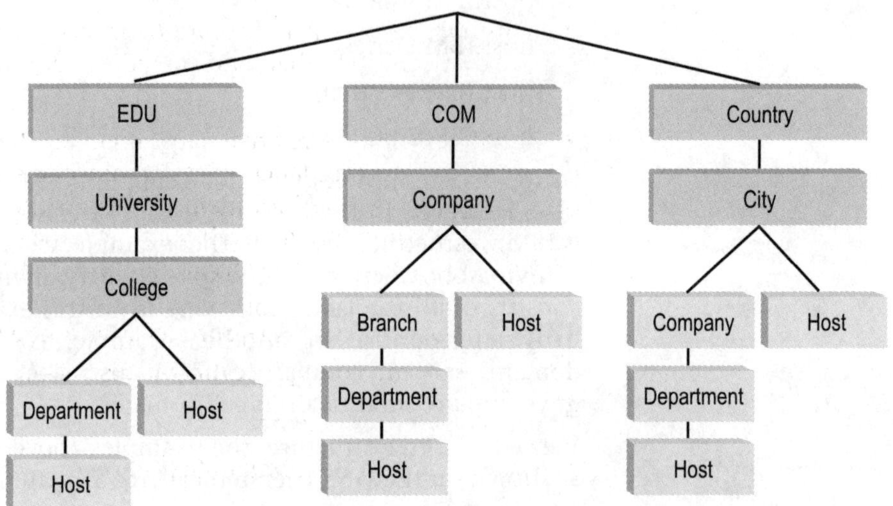

Hierarchical Structure for Three Top-Level Domains

The Domain Name Branch Diagram illustrates an example by domain name.

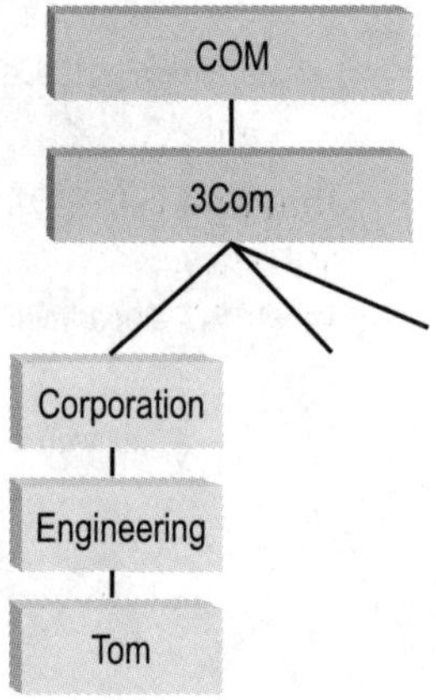

Domain Name Branch

Domain Name Syntax

Domain names are expressed as alphanumeric strings separated by dots. Each part of a domain name is referred to as a label; a label is a character or digit string separated from other labels in the domain name by dots. The maximum length of a label is 64 bytes, and the maximum length of a domain name is 255 bytes.

There are two types of domain names:

- Absolute name—An absolute (complete) domain name ends with a top-level label, and includes a dot after the last label. This is the FQDN.
- Relative name—A relative name includes character strings that represent starting labels of a domain name, usually the minimum ones required for identification within a known system. Relative names are generally entered at the user interface and rely on software at the local domain to complete the names.

The following examples are entered as absolute (FQDN) names:

- This host is in the domain westnetinc.com.

  galaxy.westnetinc.com
- This host is in the domain Stanford.edu.

  jazz.Stanford.edu
- This host has as its domain Sanjo.INS.gov.

  amnesty.Sanjo.INS.gov
- For the host galaxy.westnetinc.com, both of the following names are relative, depending on the resolver's position with the subdomain:

  galaxy

  galaxy.westnetinc

Relative names are used within a subtree or subdomain, where the software can readily resolve the complete name of the host or resource. Domain names are case-insensitive.

Authority Over Domains

The DNS domain authority is distributed. The ICANN authorizes distributed domain registrars to administer the top-level domains, and these registrars authorize qualified organizations to participate as next-level domains in the hierarchy. The ICANN authorized domain registrars give up some of their authority to second-level domain administrators, who administer their domains and can authorize the addition of subdomains. Adding domains and granting authority over names to new subdomains proceeds in a similar manner down the hierarchy.

Although administrators on each level have authority and responsibility for a given subdomain, the ICANN authorized domain registrars, who have top-level authority, remain ultimately and cooperatively responsible for the whole subdomain tree.

Domain Administrators

Domain administrator responsibilities include ensuring the domain satisfies all the parent domain's administration requirements. To find out who has authority over the name space the administrator wishes to join, the administrator should ask the registrar hostmaster to:

- Ensure that the data in the domain is current at all times
- Verify that names are unique within the domain
- Verify that names conform to standard conventions
- Provide access to names and name-related information to users both inside and outside the domain
- Administer the name server, and maintain a current copy of the local domain name database at all times

Zones

Name servers manage the domain database, which contains information about all nodes in the domain system tree. This database's administration is decentralized, and domain administrators cut their domain space subtrees to form zones based on organizational or protocol family requirements. A zone consists of those contiguous domain tree parts for which a domain name server has complete information, and over which it has authority. Zones are domain groupings formed and administered as DNS subtrees.

Each zone consists of at least one domain name, and all nodes within a zone are connected. Within each zone, there is a node that is closer to the root than any other zone node; this node's name often identifies the zone. On the Sample Domain Names in Two-Zone Tree Structure Diagram, Zone X is Education, and Zone Y is Physics.

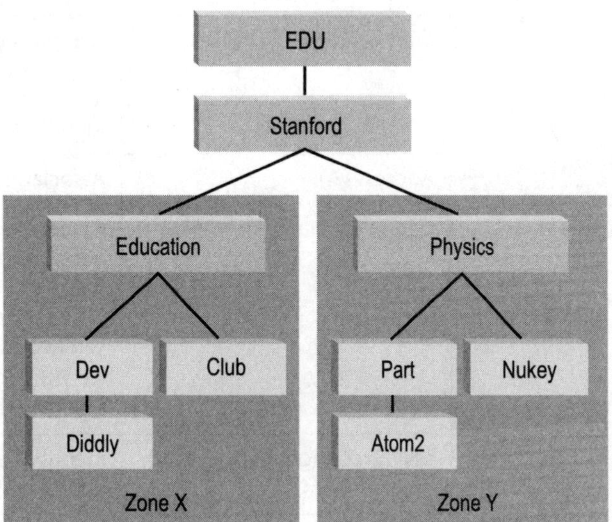

Sample Domain Names in Two-Zone Tree Structure

The first zone is .education.stanford.edu, while the second is .physics.stanford.edu. Each zone is authoritative for all hosts within its tree, and thus is responsible for resolving name inquiries for its particular zone.

The domain name information maintained in each zone is in the form of textual node name entries, called resource records (RRs).

RRs

The host/node name information kept in text format in an RR is described in the RRs Table.

RRs

DNS Record	Function
Name Server (NS)	Identifies DNS servers for a domain.
Start of Authority (SOA)	Identifies the DNS server that is the best information source for a domain. When both primary and secondary DNS servers are used, this record identifies the primary domain DNS server.
Address (A)	Associates a hostname to an IP address.
Canonical Name (CNAME)	Creates an alias for a host. For example, a company's Web server may actually have the hostname marilee.westnetinc.com, but the domain DNS contains a CNAME alias "www," so users can access the server as **http://www.westnetinc.com** rather than as marilee.westnetinc.com.
Mail Exchanger (MX)	Identifies a domain server that provides mail (POP, IMAP, SMTP) services.

RR Format

A DNS RR takes the following basic format:

[name] [ttl] [class] type data

- [name]—This is the alphanumeric entity identifier. After the first of a list of consecutive identically named entities, the Name field may be left out. The Name field can either be a FQDN or relative.
- [ttl] (optional)—The maximum length of time, in seconds, that a resolver should hold the learned domain name in its local cache. If this field is left blank, the TTL value defaults to the minimum value of the SOA record.
- [class]—This is the network type. Three are defined:
  - IN—The Internet
  - CH—ChaosNet, an obsolete network type
  - HS—Hesiod, a database service used on top of the popular BIND DNS implementation.

- type—There are three basic record types:
  - Zone—Identify domains and their name servers
  - Basic—Map names to addresses and route mail
  - Optional—Provide extra information about hosts
- data—The type of data the record supplies. The DNS Record Types Table lists some commonly used record types.

DNS Record Types

	Type	Name	Description
Zone	SOA	Start of Authority	Defines DNS zone of authority
	NS	Name Server	Identifies servers for a zone
Basic	A	Address	Name-to-address translation
	MX	Mail Exchanger	Controls e-mail routing
Optional	CNAME	Canonical Name	Nicknames for a host

Name Servers

Programs called name servers manage zone RRs. Each name server can serve as a repository for more than one zone. In turn, DNS requires that each zone have its information stored in more than one name server.

A name server's main function is to answer queries regarding names, addresses, and name-to-address or address-to-name mappings. Additionally, they maintain a text-based listing of all RRs of the queried type, class, or name.

To provide quick responses to queries, name servers manage the following two domain name information types:

- Local data for the zone(s) that it supports or over which it has authority. Local data can include pointers to other name servers that might provide additional required information.
- Cached data that contains information gathered from responses resolved, or answered, by other name servers.

Authoritative Zone Information

Each zone is a complete database for a particular subtree in the domain space. Every zone has authority over the names in its portion of the database. This means that a zone has responsibility for authoritative information on all nodes of the zone, from the top of the subtree down to the leaf nodes.

Zones have two RRs that are important to zone management and are part of the authoritative information that the zone keeps:

- RR that maintains information identifying and describing which node is at the top of the zone (SOA record)
- RR that lists all name servers in the zone (NS record)

Zones also have RRs that contain nonauthoritative information about name servers in the zone's subzones. These are duplicates of the corresponding RRs of the node at the top of the subzone.

Master Files

Text files, called master files, keep RR information the name servers use. A master file, also called a domain name table, is a sequence of line-oriented entries, entered as RRs.

Two control entries are used when entering an RR:

- Origin—Designate the RR's domain name
- Include—Enter the record in the master file

A name server's master files have RR entries that contain the following information types:

- Authoritative information about all the nodes in the zone(s) that the name server serves. This is the Address (A) record.
- Data that defines the top node of the zone. This is the Start of Authority (SOA) record.
- Data that describes the delegated subzones immediately below it. These are the nameserver (NS) records.
- Data that allows access to name servers for subzones (glue data). This is an A record for a subdomain's name server stored in the parent's zone record.

Glue RRs are A records for a zone's subdomain name servers used when the name servers for a particular subdomain are not located on the subdomain's top node. If a nameserver falls below the subdomain's cut, referrals to the subdomain's nameserver could point to an unresolved name. The following represents a parent domain's referral to an NS record entry and an associated glue record entry for the instruction.westnetinc.com subdomain:

instruction.westnetinc.com IN NS nameserver.instruction.westnetinc.com
nameserver.instruction.westnetinc.com IN A 123.10.17.3

We use DNS glue records when the nameserver to which we delegate authority for a subdomain lives within the subdomain. The Glue RR Diagram illustrates this concept.

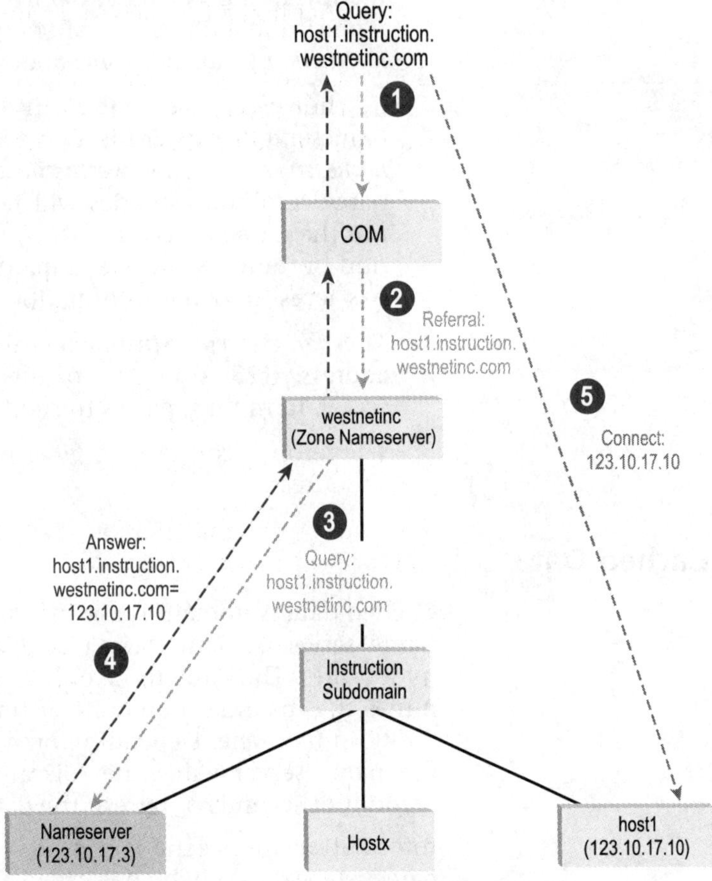

Glue RR

Name resolution works as follows:

1. The *westnetinc.com* domain receives a name resolution request for the host *host1.instruction.westnetinc.com.*
2. The *westnetinc.com* authoritative server refers this request to the nameserver in the *instructor.westnetinc.com* subdomain.
3. The subdomain *instruction.westnetinc.com* references host-name resolution requests to the zone nameserver *nameserver.instruction.westnetinc.com,* located within that sub-domain. These calls try to resolve with the nameserver specified by the hostname *nameserver.instruction.westnetinc.com.* However, the NS record only refers to the nameserver by name, not address, so all name resolution queries to the *instruction.westnetinc.com* subdomain fail.

   If, however, we enter in the *westnetinc.com* domain nameserver's master file a glue RR that resolves the hostname *nameserver.instruction.westnetinc.com* to an IP address, then name resolution queries will target the address 123.10.17.3, not the nameserver's FQDN. A name server uses the information in these RRs to refer a query to another name server that has access to better information regarding the specified query.
4. The *nameserver.westnetinc.com* returns the resolved hostname address, 123.10.17.10, to the *westnetinc.com* authoritative server. It, in turn, passes the address to the requesting resolver.
5. The resolver connects to *host1.instruction.westnetinc.com* by its IP address.

Cached Data

Cached data is domain space information acquired from another name server. A name server also keeps cached information in master files. The Time-to-Live (TTL) information in each RR determines the maximum amount of time the name server will keep an RR in its cache. Depending on a particular RR's requirements, the name server will either discard the RRs after the specified amount of seconds or refresh the data.

Information in a cache is considered unauthoritative data, compared to local data, which is called authoritative data.

Resolvers

A resolver is a program that accesses name servers to resolve queries; a network host that needs to resolve a name to an address is a resolver. When a user program sends out a request to a name server, it sends the request to a program that interfaces with the name server. The resolver is generally located on the same computer as the program that makes the query, whether the request is made from the client directly, or by a referring DNS server.

In some implementations, however, the resolution function is moved from the requesting computer to the name server. This might be done to centralize the cache, or because some requesting computer (such as a PC) does not have the resources to maintain a resolver. A resolver receives a request from a user program, and returns the desired information in a form compatible with the local host's data formats.

A resolver keeps a cache of prior queries and uses this cache to answer new queries, when applicable. A typical resolver has three functions:

- Translation of host name to host address (IP address)
- Translation of host address to host name
- General lookup function that returns all of an RR's content, rather than a processed form

Querying the Name Database

A resolver formulates a query, based on the client's request, and directs the query to name servers that can provide the information. The Querying the Name Database Diagram illustrates this function. The resolver starts with a list of name servers to query.

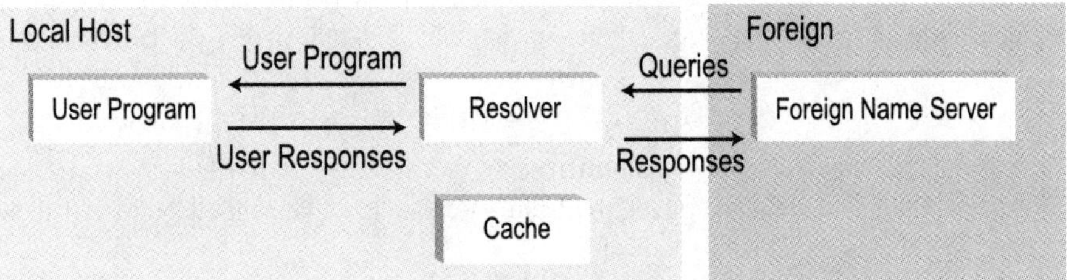

Querying the Name Database

Name servers handle queries iteratively or recursively, as described below:

- Iterative approach—When the requested domain name is not in its database, the name server refers the client to another server and allows the client to pursue the query with that server. A standard query is handled iteratively.
- Recursive approach—The name server takes responsibility for tracking down a response to the client's query. If the domain name requested is not in its database, the name server pursues the query on another server.

Activities

1. Which two mechanisms might a host use to resolve FQDNs to IP addresses? (Choose two.)
   a. LMHosts
   b. Hosts table
   c. WINS
   d. DNS
2. Where does the DNS namespace begin?
   a. The root
   b. Top level domains
   c. Hostnames
   d. Country code domains
3. The maximum DNS domain name length is how many characters?
   a. 64
   b. 128
   c. 200
   d. 255
4. Which two of the following are examples of relative domain names in the westnetinc.com domain? (Choose two.)
   a. telnet.westnetinc.com
   b. telnet
   c. telnet.westnetinc
   d. host1.telnet.westnetinc.com
5. Zones maintain domain name information in which record types?
   a. Zone records
   b. RRs
   c. Domain records
   d. Authority records

6. Which three of the following are typical resolver functions? (Choose three.)
   a. Translation of host name to host address (IP address)
   b. Translation of host address to host name
   c. General lookup function that returns all of an RR's content, rather than a processed form
   d. Name resolution authority for a domain or subdomain

Extended Activities

1. Generate several domain names that you would like to use for your Web site. Research whether the names are already taken. If the names are taken, research who owns them.
2. Log on to the InterNIC network solutions address at **http://www.networksolutions.com/**. Enter a name you would like to register and see whether it is available. If the name is not available, go to the "whois" selection and type the name to see who registered the domain name.

Lesson 2—ICMP

ICMP, documented in Request for Comment (RFC) 792, is a required protocol tightly integrated within IP. ICMP messages are delivered in IP packets and used for out-of-band messages related to network errors and problems.

Objectives

At the end of this lesson you will be able to:

- Discuss the functions of ICMP
- Describe the ICMP header format and data encapsulation
- Describe the various ICMP message types
- Discuss IP multicasting and how it operates
- Discuss how an IP multicast address is mapped into an Ethernet multicast address

Key Point

ICMP is used for packet error reporting.

ICMP and the OSI Model

ICMP is a required companion of IP. This means that all hosts and routers that implement IP must also implement ICMP. The ICMP and OSI Diagram illustrates ICMP's position within the Open Systems Interconnection (OSI) reference model applications.

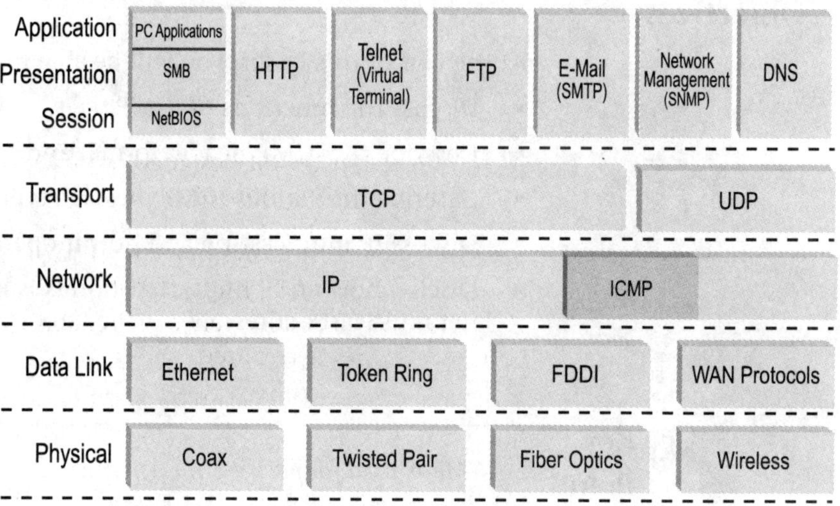

ICMP and OSI

ICMP allows a router or destination host to report an error in datagram processing to the packet's original source. Examples of ICMP messages use include:

- Time exceeded (Type 11, Code 0)—A router must discard a datagram because the TTL counter expires.
- Source quench (Type 4)—A router does not have the buffering capacity to forward a datagram.
- Fragmentation needed and "don't fragment" was set (Type 3, Code 4)—A router must fragment a datagram with the "don't fragment" flag set.

- Parameter problem (Type 12)—A host or router discovers an IP header syntax error.
- Destination network unknown (Type 3, Code 6)—A router does not have a route for the destination network in its routing table.
- Redirect datagram for the network (Type 5, Code 0)—A router asks a source host to use another router that provides a shorter path.

RFCs 792, 950, 1256, 1373, and 1475 list additional ICMP message types.

As we know, IP was not designed to provide a reliable delivery service. The main function of an ICMP message is to provide feedback about various problems that may occur in the communications environment. ICMP was not designed as a quick fix to make IP reliable; higher level protocols that operate as IP clients must implement their own reliability procedures if reliable communication is required.

ICMP messages are encapsulated as the data portion of an IP datagram. As a result, they are routed like any other IP datagram. Because ICMP messages are transmitted in IP datagrams, the ICMP message sender is not guaranteed that the message will be delivered to its ultimate destination.

Because the use of ICMP messages cannot be considered reliable, there is no guarantee they will not be lost or discarded. To avoid complex problems caused by ICMP attempting to track messages about messages, ICMP sends no messages about lost or discarded ICMP messages. Also, ICMP messages are only sent when errors occur in the processing of an unfragmented datagram or in the first fragment of a fragmented datagram.

Encapsulation

ICMP is a member of the TCP/IP protocol architecture's Internet Layer. Despite this position in the TCP/IP stack, ICMP is actually an IP user (client). An IP datagram carries the ICMP header and data, appending to the ICMP message an IP header to carry the message to its destination.

The client constructs an ICMP message and then passes it to the local IP process, as illustrated on the ICMP Encapsulation Diagram. IP appends to the message an IP header and then transmits the resulting datagram over the physical network to the destination host or router.

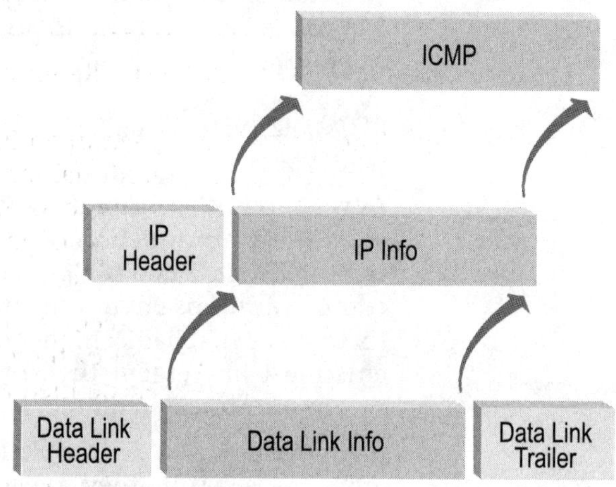

ICMP Encapsulation

The reason that IP was selected to deliver ICMP messages is that the messages may need to traverse several routers and networks to reach their final destination. A simple Data Link Layer protocol encapsulation is not sufficient to deliver a message across a router.

Header Format

Certain ICMP functions provide facilities to test the network. One of the most common debugging tools is the ICMP Echo Request/Reply message, better known as the Packet Internet Groper (Ping) command. The Ping command sends data to a destination address (using the name or address) and, if the destination node is active, the destination node will echo the data back to the sender. The ICMP Echo Request (Ping) Message Format Diagram illustrates this concept. The Echo Reply format will look similar, except it will have a Type field of "0."

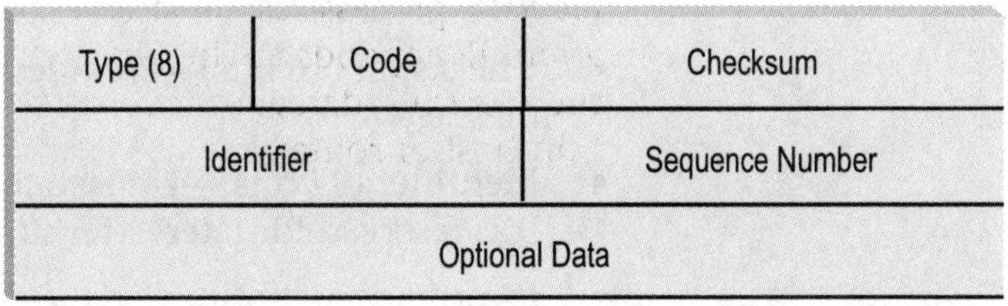

Type (8)	Code	Checksum
Identifier		Sequence Number
Optional Data		

ICMP Echo Request (Ping) Message Format

The Code field is used in an ICMP Destination Unreachable message to provide additional information, such as "5" (source route failed). The Identifier and Sequence Number fields are used by the sender for the purpose of matching replies with requests. The ICMP Echo Request fields are further described below:

- Type (8 bits)—Specifies the meaning of the message and the format of the rest of the packet. Thirteen types of ICMP messages have been defined as presented in the ICMP Header—Type Field Table.

ICMP Header—Type Field

Type Field	Message Type
0	Echo Reply
3	Destination Unreachable
4	Source Quench
5	Redirect
8	Echo Request
11	Time Exceeded
12	Parameter Problem
13	Timestamp Request
14	Timestamp Reply
15	Information Request
16	Information Reply
17	Address Mask Request
18	Address Mask Reply

- Code (8 bits)—Provides additional information about the message type.
- Checksum (16 bits)—Provides a checksum for the entire ICMP message.
- Identifier (32 bits)—Unused for most types of ICMP messages. It is reserved for later extensions and must be 0 when sent.
- Information (optional data)—Includes (for most ICMP message types) the entire IP header and the first 64 bits of the Data field from the datagram that triggered transmission of the ICMP message.

The IP header is included so the source host can match the ICMP message with its own data stream. The first 64 bits of data are included because they contain the Transport Layer header (TCP or User Datagram Protocol [UDP]).

Message Types

The ICMP message types presented in the ICMP Header—Type Field Table are described below.

Destination Unreachable (3)

This message includes a number of contingencies:

- A router will return this message if it does not know how to reach the destination network.
- If the datagram specifies a source route that is unstable, a Destination Unreachable message is returned.

The destination host may send a Destination Unreachable message to the source host if the IP module in the destination host cannot deliver the datagram because the indicated protocol module or process port is not active. A router will return a message and discard the datagram; if the router must fragment the datagram, but the "don't fragment" flag is set, a message is returned and the datagram is discarded.

Time Exceeded (11)

A router will return a Time Exceeded message if it is forced to discard a datagram, because the TTL field has been reduced to zero. A host will also transmit a Time Exceeded message if it cannot complete the reassembly of a fragmented datagram because of missing fragments.

Parameter Problem (12)

A router or host must discard a datagram if the router or host processing the datagram finds a problem with the header parameters and cannot completely process the datagram. The router or host may also use the Parameter Problem message to notify the source host. This Parameter field contains a pointer to the byte in the original header where the error was detected.

Source Quench (4)

This message type provides a basic form of flow control. When datagrams arrive too quickly for a router or host to process, they must be discarded. The computer discarding the datagrams sends an ICMP Source Quench message to request that the original source slow down its rate of sending datagrams. The recipient of a Source Quench message should lower the rate at which it sends datagrams to the specified destination until it no longer receives Source Quench messages. The source host can then gradually increase its transmission rate until it again receives Source Quench messages.

Redirect (5)

Routers send ICMP Redirect messages to hosts on directly connected networks. These messages inform the host that a better route exists for the destination network. ICMP Redirect messages are not sent to other routers. Therefore, Redirect messages are not used to propagate and update routing information among routers.

The ICMP Redirect Message Diagram illustrates the use of an ICMP Redirect message. The source host sends a packet destined for the target network to Router A. Router A examines its routing table, and learns that it must forward the datagram to Router B. Because both Router A and Router B are attached to the same network, the source host should have sent the datagram to Router B. Router A forwards the original datagram to Router B. Router A also sends the source host an ICMP Redirect message advising the host to send future traffic for the target network to Router B.

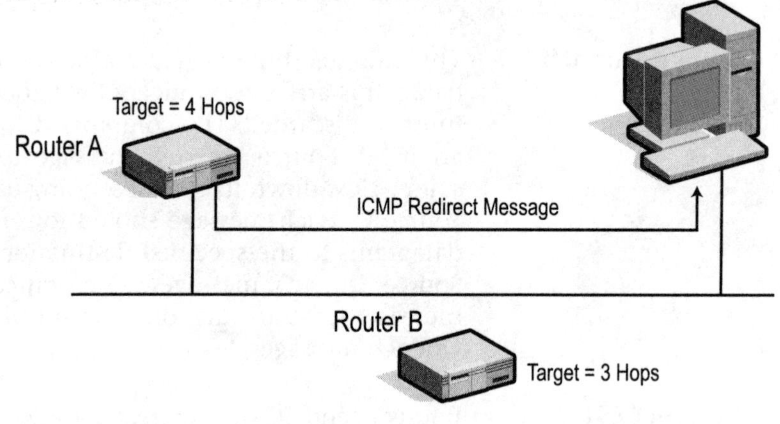

ICMP Redirect Message

Echo Request (8) and Echo Reply (0)

These messages provide a mechanism to determine whether communication is possible between two computers. The recipient of an Echo Request message is required to return the message in an Echo Reply message. Ping uses the Echo Request and Echo Reply ICMP message types to check the reachability between two hosts.

Timestamp Request (13) and Timestamp Reply (14)

These ICMP messages provide a mechanism for sampling the delay characteristics of a network. The sender of a Timestamp Request message includes an identifier in the Parameters field, and places the time that the message was sent in the Information field. The receiver appends a receive timestamp along with a transmit timestamp, and returns the message as a Timestamp Reply message.

Information Request (15) and Information Reply (16)

A host uses an ICMP Information Request message to discover the address of the network to which it is attached. The requesting host sends the message with the network portion of both the source and destination IP Address fields set to 0. Recall that an IP address with a network portion of 0 means "this network." The reply arrives with the address fully specified.

Address Mask Request (17) and Address Mask Reply (18)

A host may use the Address Mask Request message to discover the subnet mask for the network to which it is attached. The host broadcasts the request on the network and waits for a router to respond with an Address Mask Reply message that contains the subnet mask.

Activities

1. Using the Type field values, indicate what you expect given the following situations:
   a. The reply to an ICMP Type 8.

      ____

   b. The ICMP response when a network cannot be located.

      ____

   c. The ICMP type when an IP address does not reply to an echo request after a given amount of time.

      ____

2. Match the ICMP message type to its description.
   a. A router does not have the buffering capacity to forward a datagram __________________.
   b. A host or router discovers an IP header syntax error __________________.
   c. A router asks a source host to use another router that provides a shorter path __________________.
   d. A router wants to sample a network's delay characteristics __________________.
   e. A host wishes to discover the address of the network to which it is attached __________________.

   Descriptions

   Information request (15) and Reply (16)

   Source quench (4)

   Timestamp Request (13) and Reply (14)

   Parameter problem (12)

   Redirect (5)

Extended Activities

1. For each of the following ICMP Message types, describe what situation would occur in a network that would cause the message to occur:

   a. Time exceeded

   ____

   b. Source quench

   ____

   c. Echo Reply

   ____

2. Using the network sniffer you downloaded and installed in Unit 3, Lesson 6, ping some Internet hosts and capture the results. What message types does your PC send, and what types of messages do you receive in reply?

   ____

   ____

   ____

   ____

Lesson 3—IGMP

IGMP is the standard extension to IP that fully supports IP multicasting in a TCP/IP network. IP multicasting (sometimes called multipoint delivery) allows delivery of a single IP multicast datagram to a number of IP hosts identified by a single IP destination address. IP multicasting is critical to many recent applications, such as interactive teleconferencing, online training, and electronic software and information distribution. These applications require simultaneously delivering the same information to multiple recipients. This is in contrast to making several identical copies of the same information and sending a copy to each recipient.

Objectives

At the end of this lesson you will be able to:

- Define IGMP
- Describe how IGMP supports operation of IP multicasting
- Describe the format of an IGMP message

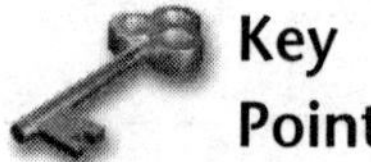

Key Point

IGMP is used to communicate multicast group membership.

IP Multicasting

To participate in multicasting, an IP host must first join a multicast group. A multicast group contains a number of IP hosts that agree to use a unique multicast group ID (that is, a unique Class D IP address). When an IP host becomes a member of the multicast group, it receives all IP multicast datagrams whose destination address is the group's Class D IP address.

IP multicasting works not only when all hosts of a multicast group reside on the same local network, but also when these hosts are on different physical networks. IP multicasting relies on multicasting routers (or gateways) to forward IP multicast datagrams from one network to another in much the same way as IP relies on routers to forward IP datagrams from one network to another.

In order for these multicast routers to work correctly, they need to know which multicast groups are on each network. Moreover, multicast routers need to know which IP hosts belong to these multicast groups; IGMP serves this purpose. IP hosts and multicast routers communicate multicast group membership information by exchanging IGMP messages.

IGMP, like ICMP, is considered an integral part of any IP implementation. An IP datagram carries IGMP data, just like ICMP. The IGMP and OSI Model Diagram illustrates where IGMP fits within the TCP/IP protocol suite.

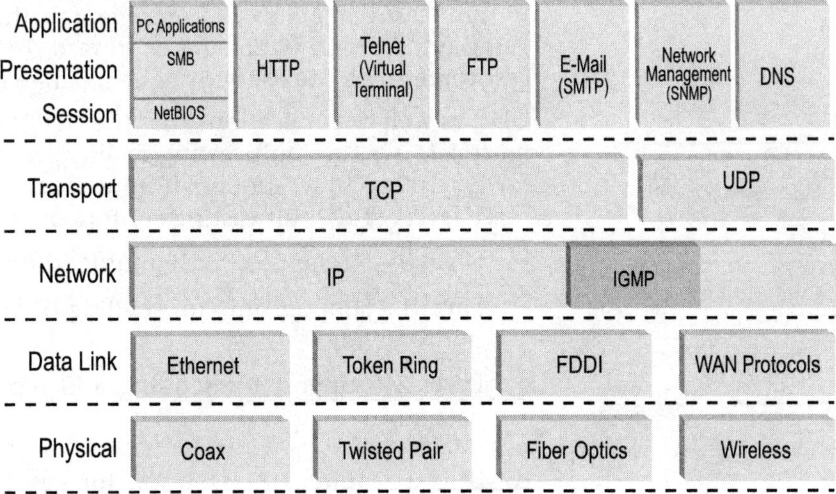

IGMP and OSI Model

Multicast Addressing

Multicast addressing is the transmission and delivery of a single packet to all members of a multicast group (of zero or more hosts) identified by a single multicast address. Unicast addressing (addressing a single host) and broadcast addressing (addressing all hosts) can be considered special multicast addressing cases. In unicast addressing, there is only one member in the multicast group.

In broadcast addressing, all hosts are members of the multicast group. IP multicasting is accomplished by associating a group of IP hosts with a single Class D IP address. An IP datagram whose destination address is a Class D IP address is considered an IP multicast datagram, and will be delivered to all member hosts of the multicast group. Each multicast group has its own unique multicast Class D IP address. Hosts that wish to receive a multicast datagram must first join the multicast group represented by the Class D IP address. Joining an IP multicast group is usually accomplished by a request from application software to join an IP multicast group. This request should be part of the TCP/IP application programming interface (API) (such as the socket interface) that supports IP multicasting.

IP multicasting group membership is dynamic. Hosts can join and leave multicast groups at any time. A host can belong to multiple multicast groups simultaneously. A nonmember host can send a multicast IP datagram to any multicast group. IP multicast routers (or gateways) forward IP multicast datagrams toward their destination, from one network to another. IP multicast routers forward IP multicast datagrams in the same way that Internet routers (or gateways) forward IP datagrams toward their destinations. Multicast routers can coexist with or be separate from IP routers.

UDP, as well as applications that use UDP as their Transport Layer protocol, use the multicasting facility IP provides. The standard for extending IP to support IP multicasting (RFC 1112) specifies three levels of IP multicasting conformance:

- Level 0—No support for IP multicasting
- Level 1—Support only for sending IP multicasting datagrams, not receiving
- Level 2—Support for sending and receiving IP multicasting datagrams

IGMP is a required IP extension for Level 2 conformance. It is used to communicate multicast group memberships between IP hosts and multicast routers.

IP Multicast Addresses and Groups

Every IP multicast group is uniquely identified by a Class D IP address. The Class D IP address is used as the destination address in an IP multicast datagram to specify multicast delivery. The Class D Address Format Diagram illustrates the format of a Class D IP address.

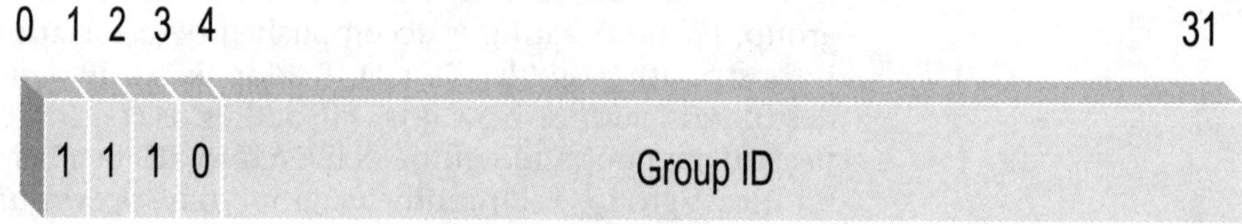

Class D Address Format

Class D IP addresses range from 224.0.0.0 through 239.255.255.255. The first 4 bits in a Class D IP address identify the address, and the remaining 28 bits identify the multicast group ID. There is no further structure to the multicast Group ID field. This is in contrast to IP address Classes A, B, and C, which are further divided into a Network ID field and Host ID field.

Certain Class D IP addresses have been assigned to well-known multicast groups. Examples of these multicast groups are:

- 224.0.0.1—Represents the group "all hosts," that includes all host and multicast routers participating in multicasting on a local network
- 224.0.0.2—Represents the group of all multicast routers on the local network

Note: Membership to these well-known groups varies over time, but the group multicast address is permanent.

Multicast Class D IP addresses outside the well-known group addresses are available as transient multicast groups. They can be used by applications and then discarded when not needed.

Mapping IP Multicast Addresses to Physical Multicast Addresses

In order for IP multicasting to work, it must be supported by a multicasting facility at the network hardware level. Moreover, there must be a way to map an IP multicast address into a physical multicast address.

Fortunately, most network interface hardware supports some form of multicasting. Ethernet network interfaces, for example, support multicasting by setting the lower bit of the high-order byte of an Ethernet destination address to 1 for multicasting and by using 0 for conventional unicasting.

The following are examples of Ethernet unicast, multicast, and broadcast addressing, respectively (in hexadecimal notation, where "x" means any hexadecimal digit):

- Ethernet unicast address 00.xx.xx.xx.xx.xx
- Ethernet multicast address 01.xx.xx.xx.xx.xx
- Ethernet broadcast address FF.FF.FF.FF.FF.FF

IP multicasting maps a Class D IP multicast address into an Ethernet multicast address by placing the low-order 23 bits of the Class D IP address into the low-order 23 bits of the special Ethernet multicast address 01.00.5E.00.00.00. For example, consider the Class D IP multicast address 224.0.0.1. This IP address would map into an Ethernet address of 01:00:5E:00:00:01, as illustrated on the Mapping IP Multicast Addresses into Ethernet Multicast Addresses Diagram.

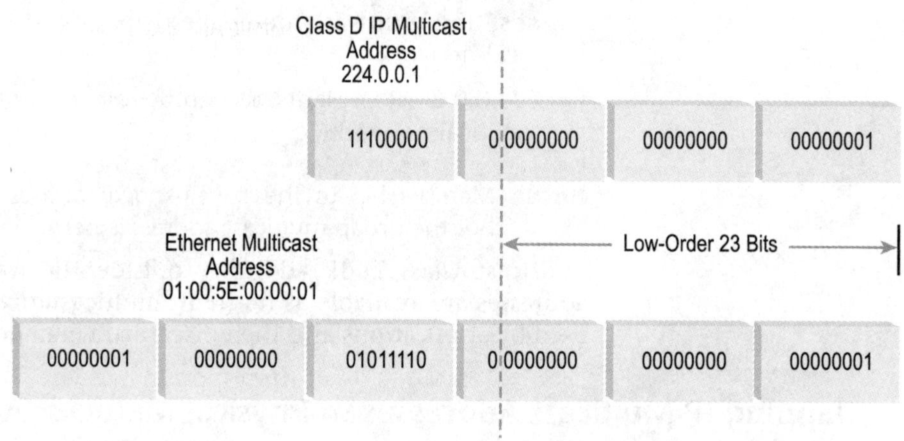

Mapping IP Multicast Addresses into Ethernet Multicast Addresses

Notice that the mapping is not unique. Two Class D IP addresses can map to the same Ethernet multicast address. Although the mapping is not unique, it was selected as an efficient and clean way to support IP multicasting. This mapping also implies that some additional checking should be performed to verify all received IP multicast datagrams.

IGMP Message Format

Multicast hosts and multicast routers use IGMP to communicate multicast group membership information. In turn, multicast routers use a different protocol to communicate routes among themselves. The most widely used multicast router protocol is the Distance Vector Multicast Routing Protocol (DVMRP). DVMRP is similar in many ways to Routing Information Protocol (RIP), which is also communicated among IP routers.

Header Format

The IGMP Message Format Diagram illustrates the format of an IGMP message. Notice that an IGMP message has a fixed length.

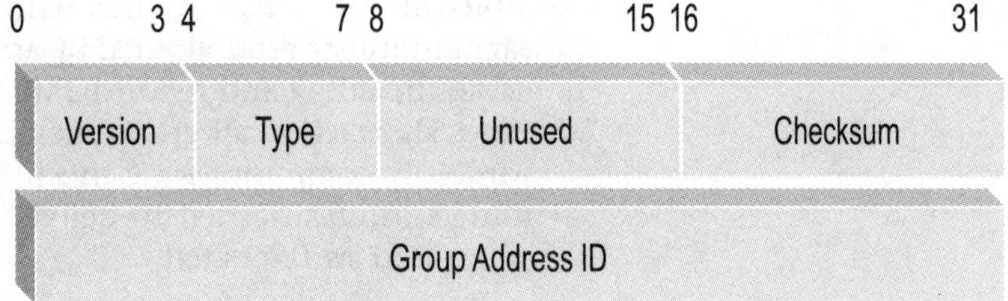

IGMP Message Format

A description of the fields of an IGMP message follows:

- Version—4-bit IGMP version number. The current version is 3.
- Type—4-bit IGMP message type. There are two message types:
  - Type=1—Query message sent by a multicast router to a host.
  - Type=2—Report (or response) message sent by a host to a multicast router.
- Unused—8-bit Unused field that must be set to 0.
- Checksum—16-bit checksum of all eight IGMP message bytes. IGMP performs checksum calculations as do TCP, IP, and ICMP. While the checksum is calculated, the Checksum field is set to 0.
- Group Address ID—Location where a multicast Class D IP address is defined. If this is a query message sent by a multicast router, this field would be set to 0. In a response message sent by a host to its multicast router, this field would contain the Class D IP multicast address of the host.

Operations

When an application joins a multicast group by executing a function in the host TCP/IP API, two major events occur:

1. The host interface is configured to recognize and accept a physical multicast address corresponding to the IP multicast group to which the application requested membership.

2. The host sends an IGMP report informing its immediate multicast router of its multicast group Class D IP address. At regular intervals, multicast routers send query IGMP messages to their physically attached hosts. Each host on the physically attached networks responds with a report IGMP message for each multicast group joined by an application on this host. By using the query and report IGMP messages, a multicast router can keep track of all group memberships on its attached networks. By communicating this information to other multicast routers, routes needed to deliver IP multicast datagrams can be devised and updated.

Encapsulation

Although IGMP is considered an integral part of IP, IGMP messages (like ICMP messages) are encapsulated inside an IP datagram. When encapsulating an IGMP message, the IP header Protocol Number field is set to 2. This allows delivery of the IGMP message to the IGMP module. This encapsulation is illustrated on the IGMP Encapsulation Diagram.

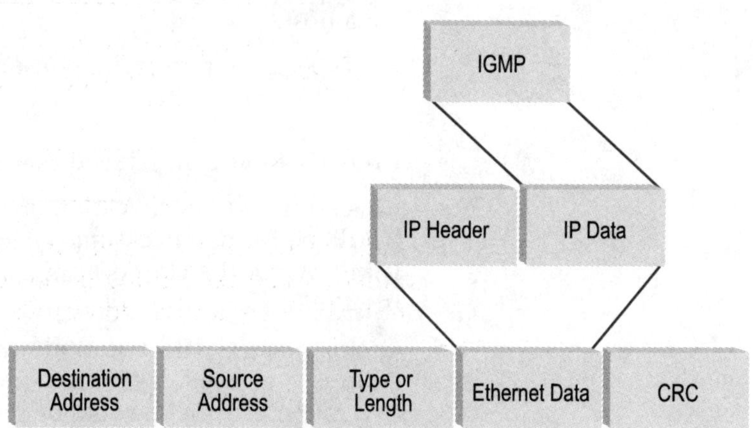

IGMP Encapsulation

Activities

1. Explain why the Class D address range is 224.0.0.0 through 239.255.255.255.

   ____

   ____

   ____

   ____

   ____

   ____

2. What is the binary equivalent of an IP multicast message to "all hosts"?

   ____

   ____

3. What is the binary equivalent of an IP multicast message to multicast routers that are located on a local network?

   ____

   ____

4. Indicate whether the network interface card (NIC), for the Ethernet addresses listed below, could be used for multicast, unicast, or broadcast addressing:

   a. ff.ff.ff.ff.ff.ff

   b. 01.01.01.01.01.01

   c. 00.01.33.44.55.66

Extended Activity

Download and review RFC 1112 from **http://www.ietf.org/rfc**.

Lesson 4—Bootstrap Protocol

Although there are times when we prefer to statically assign IP addresses, such as those we program into our routers, servers, and firewalls, many times network administration is simplified by assigning IP address dynamically. Additionally, if we use devices that cannot store an IP address on our network terminal, such as Windows or UNIX terminals, we would need a method to dynamically assign those addresses, as well.

Though it is not used as frequently as is DHCP, BOOTP provides the basic procedures on which the more capable DHCP is based. This lesson discusses BOOTP, a TCP/IP Application Layer protocol designed to hand out IP addresses on demand, as the groundwork to our upcoming discussion on DHCP.

Objectives

At the end of this lesson you will be able to:

- Define BOOTP
- Describe how BOOTP supports dynamic IP addressing
- Explain a DHCP header format

Key Point

BOOTP provides diskless workstations IP addresses and configuration information.

BOOTP

RFC 951 defines BOOTP as an IP/UDP bootstrap protocol, designed to allow diskless workstations to discover their own IP addresses. Additionally, BOOTP supplies the workstation's BOOTP server host address and a boot file for the workstation to download and execute. RFC 1542 further clarifies the protocol.

BOOTP earned its name from the fact that it is meant to run from within a client workstation's Boot Programmable Read Only Memory (PROM) chip. A BOOTP client broadcasts a request for configuration information (BOOTREQUEST), and a BOOTP server responds (BOOTREPLY).

BOOTP differs from Address Resolution Protocol (ARP) and Reverse Address Resolution Protocol (RARP) in the OSI model layer protocol it addresses. ARP and RARP target Data Link Layer protocols, and only function within their own network segments. BOOTP messages, on the other hand, target the Network Layer, and are carried within IP datagrams. The BOOTP and OSI Diagram illustrate BOOTP's position in the OSI model, and the Bootstrap Protocol Message Header Diagram illustrates a BOOTP message header.

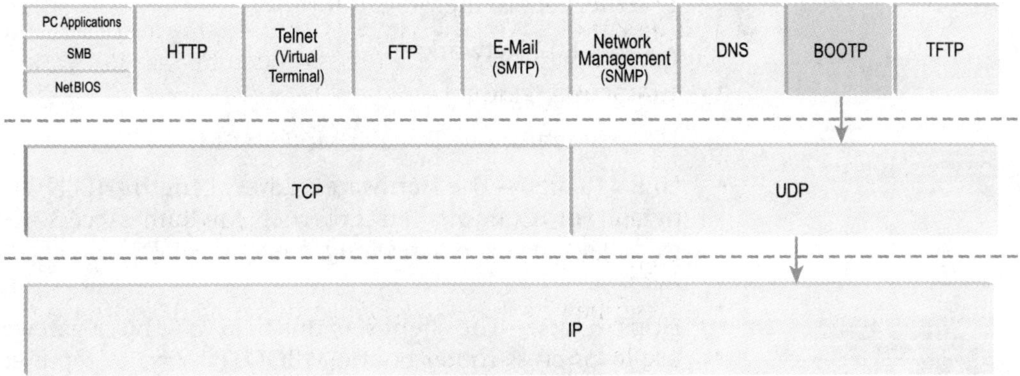

BOOTP and OSI

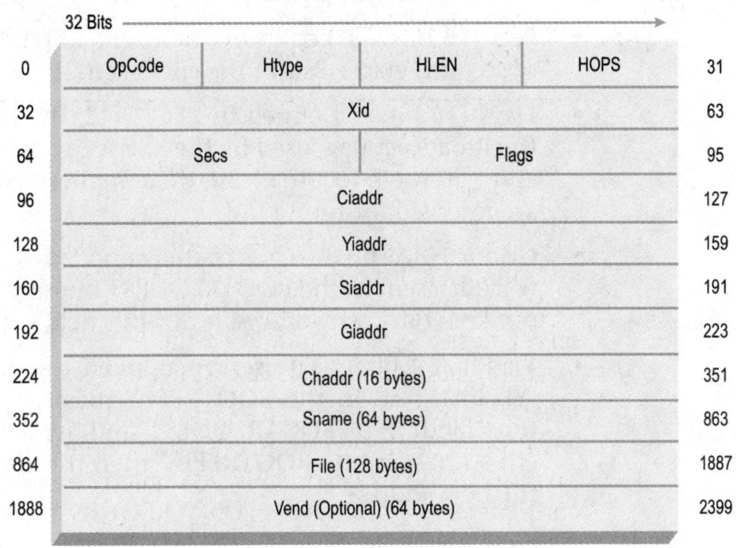

Bootstrap Protocol Message Header

The message fields are as follows:

- OpCode (8 bits)—Carries the message opcode type. There are two BOOTP opcodes:
  - BOOTREQUEST. Send from the workstation to the BOOTP server
  - BOOTREPLY. Send from the server to the workstation
- Htype (8 bits)—Specifies the Hardware Address Type (Htype) field. Some common Htype values are:

  1—Ethernet (10 megabits [Mb])

  6—IEEE 802 Networks

  15—Frame relay

  16—Asynchronous Transfer Mode (ATM)
- HLEN (8 bits)—The Hardware Address Length (HLEN) field, in bytes. For example, an Ethernet Medium Access Control (MAC) address is 6 bytes long, thus the HLEN value for Ethernet is 6.
- Hops (8 bits)—The client sets this field to 0, but a gateway can use it for cross-router booting (BOOTP relay) to represent the number of hops between the BOOTP server and the client.
- Xid (32 bits)—A client-chosen random transaction ID used to match the request with its response.
- Secs (16 bits)—Filled in by the client to represent the number of seconds elapsed since the client sent its first BOOTREQUEST.
- Flags (16 bits)—Defined in RFC 1542, the first bit position is the Broadcast flag, used by the client to tell the BOOTP servers and gateways to broadcast their replies. The remaining bits are reserved for future use.
- Ciaddr (32 bits)—The client supplied Client IP Address (Ciaddr), sent in the BOOTREQUEST message. If the client does not know its own address, it fills this field with 0s (0.0.0.0).
- Yiaddr (32 bits)—The server-supplied Client Your IP Address (Yiaddr), sent in the BOOTREPLY message. If the client sets the Ciaddr in its BOOTREQUEST, and the server sends a different address in the BOOTREPLY, then the client should accept the new address.

- Siaddr (32 bits)—The Server IP Address (Siaddr) sent in the BOOTREPLY message.
- Giaddr (32 bits)—The optional Gateway IP Address (Giaddr) used in cross gateway booting by means of BOOTP relay agents. The client BOOTREQUEST message must set this field to 0.0.0.0. Additionally, the client should ignore this field in BOOTREPLY messages.
- Chaddr (128 bits)—The Client Hardware Address (Chaddr), sent in the BOOTREQUEST message.
- Sname (512 bits)—Optional Server Host Name field, sent in the BOOTREPLY message.
- File (1024 bits)—The boot file name, sent in the BOOTREPLY message.
- Vend (512 bits)—Optional vendor-specific area. The client should always fill the first four octets with a "magic cookie" identifier, even if it does not intend to communicate vendor specific information. This aids the BOOTP server in determining what vendor information it should use in the BOOTREPLY.

BOOTP Operation

BOOTP has a client and a server side. The client workstation boot PROM must contain enough intelligence to:

- Build the BOOTP message
- Maintain a one entry ARP cache so it can answer ARP requests for its own IP address, if known

Client BOOTREQUEST Message

The client builds the BOOTREQUEST message on startup, as follows:

- It sets the OpCode to 1, BOOTREQUEST.
- It sets the Htype to match that of its own MAC address.
- It sets the HLEN to that of its own MAC address length, in bytes.
- It sets the Hops value to 0.
- It sets a random transaction ID (Xid).
- It sets the Seconds field to the number of elapsed seconds since the client sent its first BOOTREQUEST message. The first is set to 0, and incremented on each subsequent attempt. This informs the BOOTP server of how long the client has been trying to obtain its boot information.

- It sets the Broadcast flag if it requests a broadcast reply.
- It sets the BOOTP message Ciaddr to its own IP address, either preconfigured or the last address it was assigned, or to 0.0.0.0 if the address is unknown to the client.
- It sets the Yiaddr, Siaddr, and Giaddr fields to 0.0.0.0.
- It sets its Chaddr field.
- It sets the Sname field to a particular server name, if desired.
- It fills in the File field to match the boot file it desires to use, or to a null value if it only wants client, server, and/or gateway addresses.
- It can fill in the Vendor field with vendor-specific information, if desired. For example, it could fill in its own serial number or hardware type. Though optional, RFC 1542 recommends that the client at least set the "magic cookie" in the first four octets, consisting of either vendor specific information or the hexadecimal equivalent of the dotted decimal value 99.130.83.99. Some operating systems (OSs) or networking packages can be run either alternately or simultaneously on the same machine. In these cases, setting the magic cookie helps the BOOTP server differentiate between multiple BOOTREQUEST messages sent by the same machine.
- It sets the UDP header source port to 68, the BOOTP default client port.
- It sets the UDP header destination port to 67, the BOOTP default server port.
- It builds the IP packet with either the limited broadcast destination address of 255.255.255.255, or the BOOTP server's address, if known.
- Finally, the client calculates the UDP and IP header checksums, and sends the IP packet and message on its way.

The BOOTREQUEST Message Diagram illustrates a sample BOOTREQUEST packet and message.

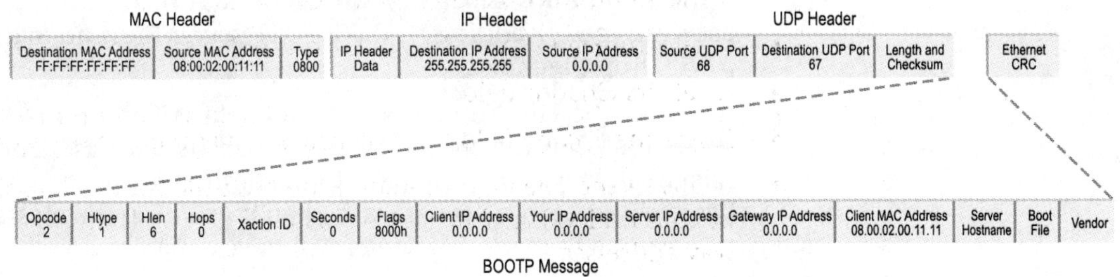

BOOTREQUEST Message

Server BOOTREPLY Message

The BOOTP server responds to the BOOTP request(s) as follows:

- It verifies the packet and message checksums. If the checksums fail, the server discards the message. (Remember, UDP is connectionless, thus the client receives no notification that the message was discarded.)
- It checks that the UDP destination port is BOOTPS, UDP Port 67. If the port is not 67, it drops the message.
- It checks the Server Name field. If the name matches its own, or it is set to null, then it continues message processing. If the client filled in the Sname field with a specific server name, the server can:
  - Drop the message, if not its own.
  - Perform a name lookup for the server in the Sname field, and if it resides on the same segment, drop the message.
  - If the Sname server resides on another segment, forward the message to that address. This requires that the receiving server check the Gateway Address field, and if 0.0.0.0, set the field to match it own address or that of a relay agent that can route the message to its final destination.
- It checks the Ciaddr field. If this field is 0.0.0.0, then the client needs an IP address. If the field is filled, the server should preserve this field's contents in the BOOTREPLY message. The server assigns an address, regardless.

- The server maintains a static database of Chaddr mapped to IP addresses. An administrator must build this database and store it on the BOOTP server.

  If the server finds a match, it fills the Yiaddr field with the client's assigned IP address. If the BOOTP server finds no match, it will drop the message.

- It checks the File Name field. If this field is "non-null," the server looks up the specified filename in its database, and it fills the field with the full path to the desired file. If the server has no file match in its database, then it will drop the message and assume that another server will have a match.
- It checks the Vendor field for recognized data and performs client-specified actions as required. If needed, the server places a response in the Vendor field of the BOOTREPLY message.
- It builds a BOOTREPLY message with the above information. It will include its own address in the Siaddr field.
- It sets the UDP destination port to 68 (BOOTPC), the client port.
- It sends the IP packet to the address specified in the Ciaddr field. If the client knows its own current address, then it can respond to ARPs. If the BOOTREQUEST did not specify the client IP address, but did the Giaddr, then set the UDP destination port to 67 (BOOTPS), and the destination IP address to the relay agent address.

  If neither the client IP address nor the gateway address were specified, then the server uses one of the Chicken/Egg methods to send the reply to the client. The Chicken/Egg method answers the question of how one host sends an IP packet to another host that does not yet have an IP address, as follows:

  1. If the BOOTP server is able to build an ARP cache entry on behalf of the client and place this in its own ARP cache, then it can resolve its own ARP broadcast using the BOOTPREQUEST-supplied Chaddr and the server supplied Yiaddr field contents.
  2. The server can build a BOOTPREPLY IP packet targeted at the receiving interface's IP broadcast address.

  The server may ignore the client IP address entirely, in which case it can handle the BOOTREPLY as if the Ciaddr field is set to 0.0.0.0. Here, it uses one of the Chicken/Egg methods to reply to the client.

- It sets the Broadcast flag appropriately. If the BOOTREQUEST Giaddr field is set to 0.0.0.0, and the BOOTREQUEST also set the Broadcast flag, the BOOTP server will build an IP packet targeting the limited broadcast address, 255.255.255.255, and the Broadcast hardware address (FF:FF:FF:FF:FF:FF). If the BOOTREQUEST reset the Broadcast flag (0), then the server builds a unicast packet targeting the Yiaddr and Chaddr entries.

  The BOOTP Delivery Decision Table summarizes the BOOTREPLY decisions the server makes relative to the BOOTREQUEST supplied information.

BOOTP Delivery Decision

BOOTREQUEST Fields			BOOTREPLY Values		
Ciaddr	Giaddr	Broadcast Flag	UDP Protocol Destination Port	IP Protocol Destination Address	Link Protocol Destination
Non-zero	Don't care	Don't care	68	Ciaddr	ARP
0.0.0.0	Non-zero	Don't care	67	Giaddr	ARP
0.0.0.0	0.0.0.0	0	68	Yiaddr	Chaddr
0.0.0.0	0.0.0.0	1	68	255.255.255.255	Broadcast

- It generates the appropriate checksums and sends the packet on its way.

The BOOTREPLY Message Diagram illustrates a sample BOOTREPLY message and packet.

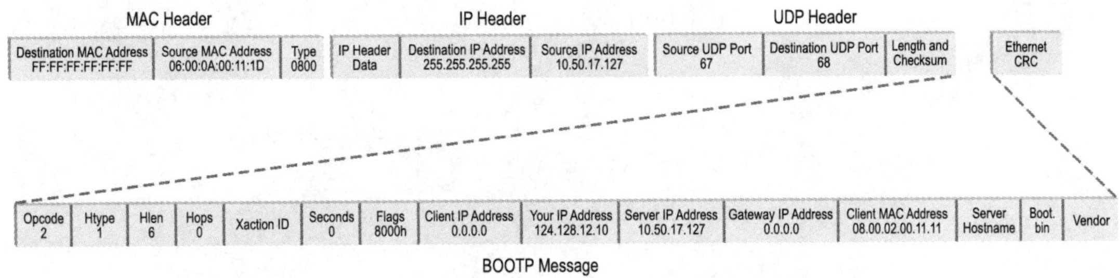

BOOTREPLY Message

Client BOOTREPLY Message Receipt

The client processes the BOOTPREPLY as follows:

- It calculates the IP header and UDP checksums, and discards the packet if the checksum fails.
- It discards the message if:
  - The port address is incorrect. The destination port must be UDP Port 68 (BOOTPC).
  - The BOOTREPLY does not match its own hardware or IP address.
  - The BOOTREPLY does not match its transaction ID.
- It extracts its IP address from the Yiaddr field. It must use this address immediately, even if the client originally supplied a different address in the BOOTREQUEST Ciaddr field.
- It extracts the filename from the Boot File Name field. When it has the IP address, the client can then target this file by means of Trivial File Transfer Protocol (TFTP).
- It extracts the Siaddr and the Giaddr, if present.

Client BOOTREQUEST Retransmission

The client sets a timer so it knows when to retransmit its BOOTREQUEST if it receives no BOOTREPLY. This timer must be carefully set so multiple clients will not flood the network in the case of a server or network component failure.

Random and exponential backoff times can work as a possible retransmission strategy. Client A could retransmit at 4, then 8, then 16, then 32 seconds, and so on. These times could also be randomized so multiple clients won't use the same exponential time simultaneously.

The client updates the Seconds (Secs) field before each retransmission.

The BOOTP Relay Agent

BOOTP provides a mechanism for BOOTP clients to obtain boot information from a server residing on a subnet separate from their own; the BOOTP relay agent performs this task. Although it can operate as a router service, a relay agent performs a function distinct from a router. A router forwards packets from network to network transparently, reading but not altering the packet and its contents. A BOOTP relay agent, on the other hand, accepts BOOTP messages as a final destination, and generates new BOOTP messages as a result. A relay agent can be a router function or a separate device located on the client's subnet.

BOOTP Relay Agent Operations

A BOOTP relay agent, the same as a BOOTP server, listens for BOOTREQUEST messages sent to UDP Port 67 (BOOTPS). A server host listens for IP datagrams sent to the network broadcast, multicast, and its own unicast addresses. A router listens for all the previous addresses, plus addresses sent to remote networks. However, the router only processes local subnet addresses for the BOOTP relay agent, passing remote network addresses to the router function.

An IP host normally discards IP packets sent from the illegal 0.0.0.0 source address. However, hosts supporting BOOTP relay must accept these BOOTREQUEST messages on behalf of the BOOTP server process. Of course, the BOOTP relay host must also accept BOOTREQUEST messages from legal source addresses.

Relay Agent BOOTREQUEST Processing

The BOOTP relay agent processes BOOTREQUEST messages as follows:

- It discards any UDP messages targeting Port 68 (BOOTPC).
- It calculates the IP and UDP header checksums, and discards those messages that fail.
- If the OpCode field does not contain 1 or 2, it discards the message.
- It checks the Hops field. If the hops value exceeds 16, the relay agent must discard the message. If it forwards the message, it increments the Hops field by one.
- It examines the Giaddr field. If set to 0.0.0.0, it fills this field with the interface IP address on which the BOOTREQUEST is received. It maintains the Giaddr field if the BOOTREQUEST message includes a non-zero value.
- It leaves the rest of the fields intact.

- It relays the message, inside an IP packet, to the new destination, which is either the remote BOOTP server or the next hop. These destination IP addresses are administrator configured on the BOOTP relay agent.

  Though some relay agent implementations attempt to load balance BOOTREQUEST messages across multiple BOOTP servers, this concept works well only when a single reply and request occur between the client and the server. In the case of DHCP (discussed next) where multiple exchanges occur, problems arise (requests for the same transaction go to separate servers). Therefore, all related BOOTREQUEST messages must target the same destination server.

- It sets the IP TTL to either the new packet default, or to the original BOOTREQUEST packet's TTL. By setting the TTL to that of the original packet, we can help protect against BOOTREQUEST loops, where a BOOTREQUEST packet circulates infinitely.

- It calculates the IP and UDP header checksums and sends the packet on its way.

The Relay Agent BOOTREQUEST Message Diagram illustrates a sample relayed BOOTREQUEST message.

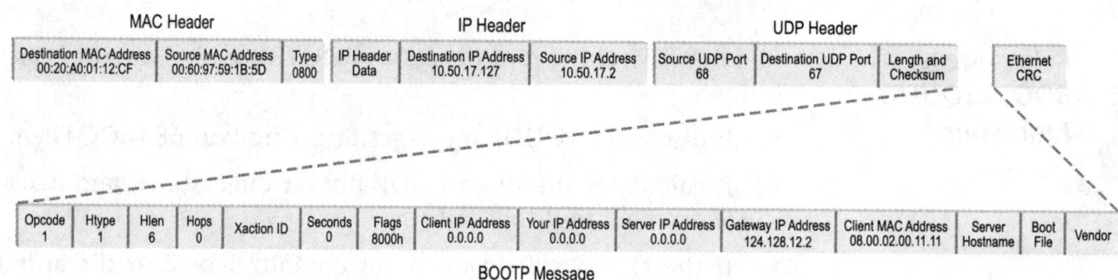

Relay Agent BOOTREQUEST Message

Relay Agent BOOTREPLY Processing

BOOTP relay agents only relay BOOTREPLY messages to BOOTP clients. The BOOTP server sends BOOTREPLY messages directly to the relay agent specified in the BOOTREQUEST Giaddr field.

The relay agent processes BOOTREPLY messages as follows:

- It verifies that it is the destination IP address and discards the packet if it is not.
- It runs the checksums and discards those packets/messages that fail.
- It checks that the destination UDP port is 68 (BOOTPC).
- It checks the Giaddr field to identify the relay agent logical port address from which the BOOTREPLY must be forwarded. If the Giaddr does not specify a directly connected interface's IP address, it discards the message.

  Because the relay agent is administratively configured to point BOOTREQUEST messages to a specified BOOTP server or servers, the relay agent targets the outbound IP packet to that server address. No further examination of the message is necessary, and subsequent relay agents will ignore the packet as it makes its way to the BOOTP server.

  Therefore, the BOOTP server targets the BOOTREPLY at the source BOOTP relay agent IP address. When the target receives the packet, it examines its contents. If the message is a BOOTREPLY (UPD Port 68, OpCode 2), the relay agent processes the message. At this point the message Giaddr field should match the local, logical relay agent interface address from which the BOOTREQUEST originated (the agent set this Giaddr address value in the relayed, original BOOTREQUEST message). If there is no match, the message arrived at this relay agent in error (or a message error occurred).
- It checks the BOOTREPLY message's Yiaddr, Chaddr, HLEN, and Htype fields to obtain the information it needs to forward the message to its destination. These fields must remain intact in the forwarded reply.

- It examines the Broadcast flag. If set to 1, and the client is on a locally connected network, it builds an IP packet targeting the limited IP broadcast address (255.255.255.255). Additionally, it sets the physical address to the broadcast Data Link Layer address.

  If the flag is 0, it builds the IP packet targeted at the unicast IP address specified in the Yiaddr field, and sends the frame to the MAC address specified in the Chaddr field. If the Yiaddr field does not match the address in the Ciaddr field, the Chaddr specified MAC address will find the destination host.
- It sets the UDP port destination address to 68.
- It builds the appropriate IP packets, computes the checksums, and sends the packet on its way.

The Relay Agent BOOTREPLY Message diagram illustrates a relayed BOOTREPLY message.

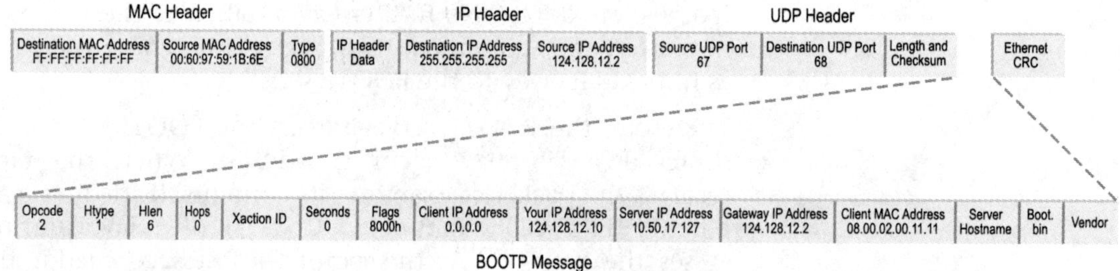

Relay Agent BOOTREPLY Message

Activities

1. Which TCP/IP protocol allows a diskless workstation to discover its IP address, as well as download a boot file?
   a. DHCP
   b. BOOTP
   c. RARP
   d. TFTP
2. Why would you use a BOOTP relay agent on your network?
   a. To load balance BOOTP requests with the server
   b. To multicast BOOTP messages to many hosts
   c. To pass BOOTP messages between subnets
   d. To generate BOOTP messages on the local network
3. Match the BOOTP message field with its description.
   a. The server supplied client IP address _________.
   b. The BOOTP relay agent address _________.
   c. The client's hardware address _________.
   d. The BOOTP server's IP address _________.
   e. The BOOTP server's name _________.
   f. The boot file name _________.
   g. The client supplied IP address _________.
   h. The transaction ID _________.
   i. The message type _________.

   Descriptions

   Chaddr

   Ciaddr

   File

   Giaddr

   OpCode

   Siaddr

   Sname

   OpCode

   Xid

Extended Activities

1. Given the BOOTP Delivery Destination Table, which destination UDP port and IP address will the BOOTP server target in its BOOTREPLY message?

BOOTP Delivery Destination

BOOTREQUEST Fields			BOOTREPLY Values		
ciaddr	giaddr	Broadcast Flag	UDP Protocol Destination Port	IP Protocol Destination Address	Link Protocol Destination
Non-zero	Don't care	Don't care	68	ciaddr	ARP
0.0.0.0	Non-zero	Don't care	67	giaddr	ARP
0.0.0.0	0.0.0.0	0	68	yiaddr	chaddr
0.0.0.0	0.0.0.0	1	68	255.255.255.255	broadcast

a. BOOTREQUEST field information:

Ciaddr = 10.10.120.12
Giaddr = 0.0.0.0
Broadcast flag = 0
BOOTREPLY destination port and address = _____, _________.

b. BOOTREQUEST field information:

Ciaddr = 0.0.0.0
Giaddr = 0.0.0.0
Broadcast flag = 1
BOOTREPLY destination port and address = _____, _________.

c. BOOTREQUEST field information:

Ciaddr = 0.0.0.0
Giaddr = 192.168.12.2
Broadcast flag = 1
BOOTREPLY destination port and address = _____, _________

Lesson 5—DHCP

RFC 1531 originally defined the Dynamic Host Configuration Protocol (DHCP) as an Application Layer TCP/IP protocol used to assign reusable IP addresses and configuration information to hosts. DHCP is an extension to BOOTP, adding functionality to the original BOOTP specification. Various RFCs have refined the original; RFC 2131 is the latest revision.

Objectives

At the end of this lesson, you will be able to:

- Define DHCP
- Identify some more common DHCP option codes
- Explain how DHCP dynamically assigns host addresses
- Describe the use of DHCP relay agents
- Explain how DHCP uses option codes for host configuration

Key Point

DHCP supplies network devices, reusable IP addresses, and configuration information based on a timed lease period.

DHCP

DHCP provides a framework for passing to IP hosts configuration information. Though it is based on BOOTP, DHCP adds capabilities to automatically allocate reusable IP addresses for a finite lease period and pass additional IP configuration information. The DHCP to OSI Diagram shows how DHCP maps to the OSI model.

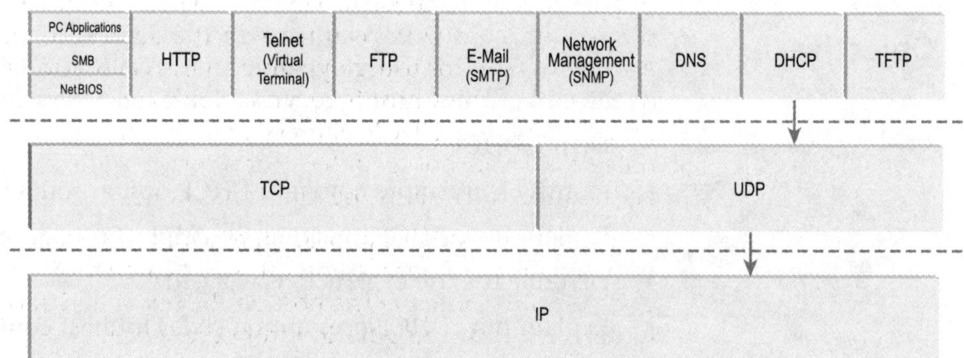

DHCP to OSI

Remember that BOOTP referenced a static, administrator-configured database. Though DHCP does require some initial configuration, it can hand out IP addresses to hosts upon request, without requiring the administrator to manually enter each MAC-to-IP address mapping. Instead, DHCP builds this mapping dynamically and maintains this database as hosts request and release their mapped addresses.

DHCP consists of two components: a protocol for delivering host-specific configuration parameters from a DHCP server, and a mechanism for host network address allocation. DHCP is a client/server application; the host requesting configuration parameters is the client, while the host supplying the configuration parameters is the server.

DHCP Address Allocation Mechanisms

DHCP provides three address allocation mechanisms:

- Automatic allocation—The DHCP server assigns a client a permanent address. The DHCP server cannot reallocate the address after it is assigned.
- Manual allocation—The administrator sets the IP-to-MAC address mapping, and the DHCP server merely passes on this information to the client.

- Dynamic allocation—The DHCP assigns reusable addresses to the DHCP clients.

Dynamic allocation is the most desirable of these three, for a number of reasons. First, dynamic allocation suits instances where hosts only connect to the network for a short time period or when the server has only a small pool of addresses available. Many ISPs use dynamic IP addressing for their clients, both dial-in and directly connected. This way, when the client disconnects or goes offline, the ISP can reassign the address to another host. Another reason for using dynamic address allocation would be in a case where a new host is added to a network when an old host is retired, and the DHCP address pool is limited. The new host obtains the old host's address, or another address; this way, the address pool maintains the same ratio of hosts to addresses.

One might use manual allocation to avoid the error-prone process of manually configuring hosts. Instead, the DHCP administrator can statically configure the host on the server and allow the client to download its configuration from the server.

DHCP Message Format

The DHCP message format is based on the BOOTP message format. The DHCP Message Format Diagram illustrates this.

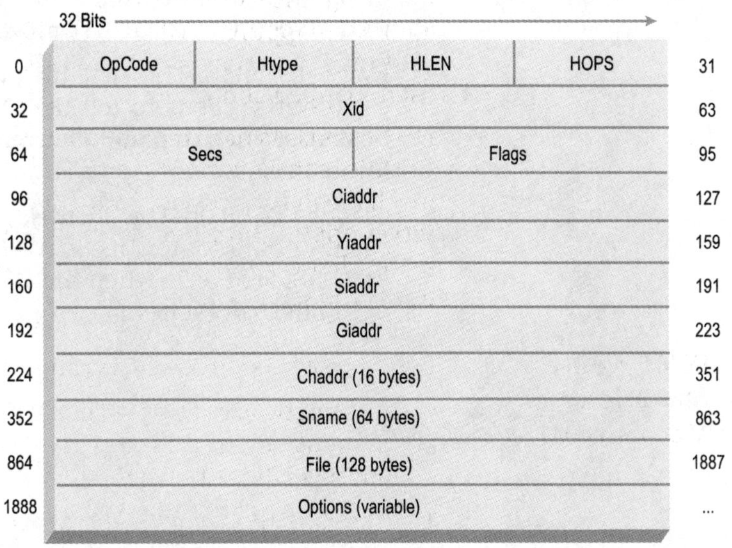

DHCP Message Format

The message fields are as follows:

- OpCode (8 bits)—Carries the message opcode type. There are two BOOTP opcodes:
  - BOOTREQUEST. Send from the client to the DHCP server
  - BOOTREPLY. Send from the server to the client
- Htype (8 bits)—Specifies the hardware address type. Some common Htype values are:

  1—Ethernet (10 Mb)

  6—IEEE 802 Networks

  15—Frame relay

  16—ATM
- HLEN (8 bits)—The hardware address length, in bytes. For example, an Ethernet MAC address is 6 bytes long, thus the HLEN value for Ethernet is 6.
- Hops (8 bits)—The client sets this field to 0, but a relay agent can set it to represent the number of hops between the DHCP server and the client.
- Xid (32 bits)—A client chosen random transaction ID used to match the request with its response.
- Secs (6 bits)—Filled in by the client to represent the number of seconds elapsed since the client sent its first DHCPDISCOVER or DHCPREQUEST message.
- Flags (16 bits)—The first bit position is the Broadcast flag, used by the client to tell the DHCP servers and gateways to broadcast their replies. The remaining bits are reserved for future use.
- Ciaddr (32 bits)—The client-supplied client IP address. If the client does not know its own address, it fills this field with 0s (0.0.0.0). Sent only when the client is in the BOUND, RENEW, or REBINDING states.

- Yiaddr (32 bits)—The server-supplied client your IP address sent in the DHCPOFFER message. If the client sets the Ciaddr in its DHCPDISCOVER, and the server sends a different address in the DHCPOFFER, then the client should accept the new address.
- Siaddr (32 bits)—The address of the next server to use in the bootstrap process, sent in the server's DHCPOFFER and DHCPACK messages.
- Giaddr (32 bits)—The optional gateway address used in cross gateway booting by means of DHCP or BOOTP relay agents. The client DHCPDISCOVER message must set this field to 0.0.0.0. Additionally, the client should ignore this field in DHCPOFFER and DHCPACK messages.
- Chaddr (128 bits)—The Client hardware address, set in the DHCPDISCOVER, DHCPREQUEST, and DHCPNAK messages.
- Sname (512 bits)—Optional server host name, sent in the DHCPOFFER and DHCPACK messages.
- File (1024 bits)—The boot file name, sent in the DHCPOFFER message.
- Options (variable, minimum 312 bytes)—Optional vendor-specific area. The client should always fill the first four octets with a "magic cookie" identifier.

DHCP Operation

Where BOOTP defined only two steps (BOOTREQUEST and BOOTREPLY), DHCP RFC 2131 defines four basic address allocation and configuration steps, and additional optional steps as well. We will concentrate on the four basic steps here: DHCPDISCOVER, DHCPOFFER, DHCPREQUEST, and DHCPACK.

DHCP Services

DHCP provides two services:

- Configuration parameters repository—A DHCP server must provide persistent storage for network client parameters. This is normally in the form of a database, where the client hardware address or hostname references its IP address and other parameters. The DHCP Manager Screen Diagram shows a screen snapshot taken from a Microsoft DHCP server.

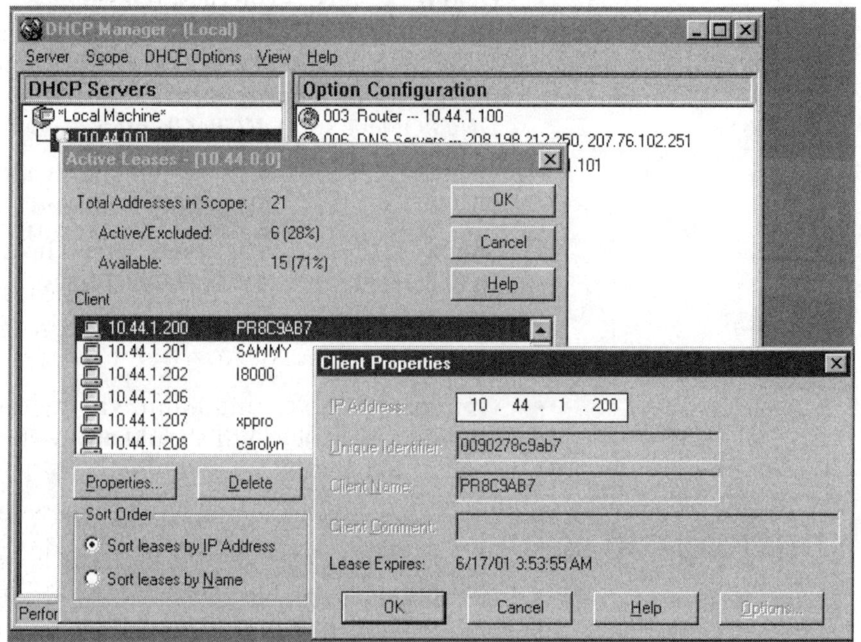

DHCP Manager Screen

The assigned IP address to hostname mappings are shown. You can also see in the background some of the optional parameters passed to the DHCP clients upon their acceptance of the offered lease.

- Dynamic network address allocation—The DHCP server allocates IP addresses to clients, either temporarily or permanently. It does this from the DHCP database, either dynamically or statically.

How DHCP Clients Obtain Configuration Information

As in BOOTP, a DHCP client requests an address, and a server responds. The DHCP Client Initialization Diagram illustrates the DHCP client/server interaction when a client initializes.

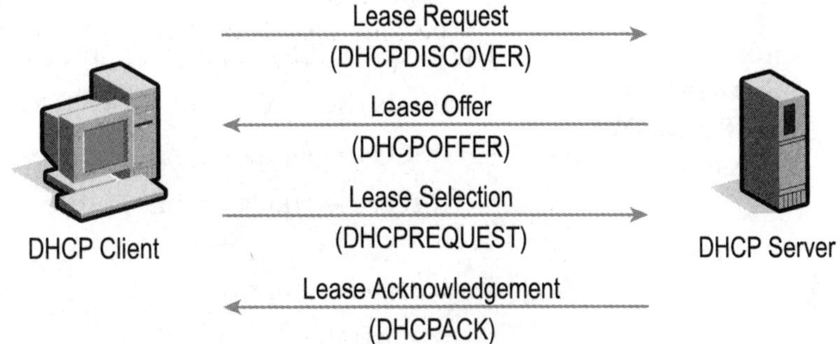

DHCP Client Initialization

When a DHCP client first initializes, it loads a limited version of TCP/IP and enters a number of lease acquisition states in order to obtain an IP address lease from a DHCP server. The process steps are:

1. The client broadcasts a DHCPDISCOVER message to its local subnet. At this point, the client is in the INIT state.
2. A DHCP server responds to the DHCPDISCOVER message with a DHCP offer (DHCPOFFER) message.
3. If no server responds, the client will not initialize TCP/IP. Instead, it continues to resend DHCPDISCOVER messages until it receives a response.
4. When the client receives an offer (or offers), it enters the SELECTING state. It then selects from the received offers a preferred offer, and builds a reply. If more than one server responds to the DHCPREQUEST, the client normally chooses the first offer it receives.
5. The client enters the REQUESTING state by replying to the selected server with a DHCP request (DHCPREQUEST) message.
6. The offering server replies to the DHCPREQUEST with a DHCP acknowledgement (DHCPACK) message.
7. When the client receives the DHCPACK, it configures its TCP/IP properties and joins the network, entering the BOUND state.

In some cases, a DHCP server can return a DHCP negative acknowledgement (DHCPNAK) message in response to the client's DHCPREQUEST message. This occurs if a client requests a duplicate or invalid address. The client initialization process fails in this case, and the client must restart from Step 1.

Client Initialization—DHCPDISCOVER Message

The client builds a DHCPDISCOVER message, as follows:

- It sets the OpCode to 1, BOOTREQUEST.
- It sets the Htype to match that of its own MAC address.
- It sets the HLEN to that of its own MAC address length, in bytes.
- It sets the Hops field to 0.
- It generates a random transaction identifier and places this in the Xid field.
- It sets the Seconds field to the number of elapsed seconds since it sent its first DHCPDISCOVER message. The first is set to 0, and incremented on each subsequent attempt. This informs the DHCP server of how long the client has been trying to obtain its lease information.
- It sets the Broadcast Flags field.
- It sets the Ciaddr field to 0.0.0.0.
- It sets the Yiaddr, Siaddr, and Giaddr fields to 0.0.0.0.
- It places it own MAC address in the Chaddr field.
- It sets the Sname field to a particular server name, if desired.
- It fills in the File field to match the boot file it desires to use, or to a null value if it only wants client, server, and/or gateway addresses.
- It sets the Option field's first four bytes to the RFC 1542 recommended "magic cookie," the hexadecimal equivalent of the dotted decimal value 99.130.83.99. It can follow this magic cookie with a number of optional parameters.

  The client should set the maximum DHCP message size option, using Code 57, to indicate to the server how large a message the client can accept.

It can follow these options with a request for specific configuration parameters by setting the parameter request option, option Code 55, then following this entry with a list of the requested options codes, in preferred order. Though the client can request specific parameters in order, the DHCP server does not have to return them in the requested order. Some examples of client-requested options include:

Code 3—Router. The client requests its subnet's router address.

Code 4—Time server. The client requests an RFC 868 time server address.

Code 6—DNS server. The client requests a DNS server address.

Code 12—Host name. The client requests a hostname (this is not supported in Windows clients).

Code 15—DNS domain name. The client requests a DNS resolver domain name.

The client can request a specific IP address and lease time using the following two option codes:

Code 50—Requested IP address. The client requests a specific IP address.

Code 51—IP address lease time. The client requests a specific address lease time.

The client sends the requested information following the code. A client can only set option Code 50 if it is trying to renew a previously assigned address.

Note: If the client sets parameters in its DHCPDISCOVER message, it must include these in subsequent messages.

- It sets the UDP header source port to 68, the BOOTPC default client port.
- It sets the UDP header destination port to 67, the BOOTPS default server port.
- The DHCP client builds the IP packet with the limited broadcast destination address of 255.255.255.255.
- Finally, the client calculates the UDP and IP header checksums and sends the IP packet and message on its way.

The DHCPDISCOVER Message Diagram illustrates a sample DHCPDISCOVER packet and message.

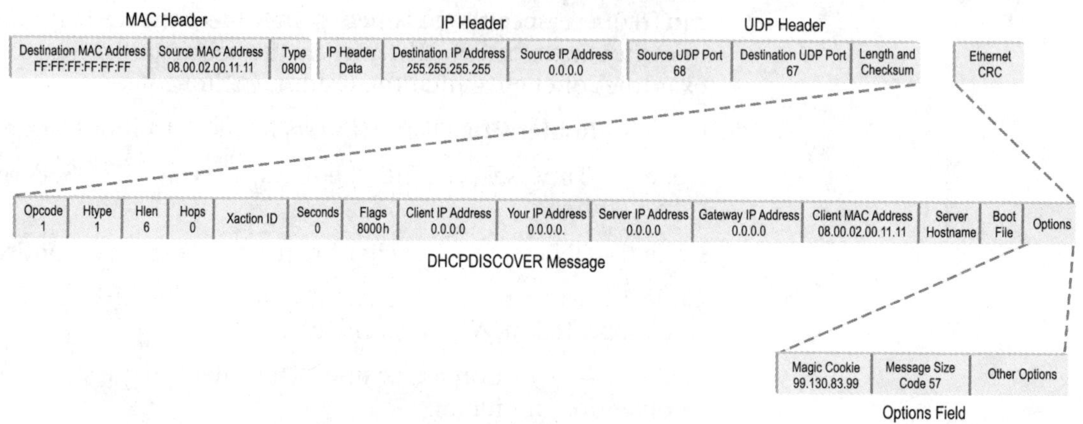

DHCPDISCOVER Message

DHCP Server—DHCPOFFER Message

A DHCP server responds to a DHCPREQUEST with a DHCPOFFER message. The server will respond to any request it receives. The DHCP database is dynamic, not static as in BOOTP; thus the DHCP server can respond to any client requesting an address.

The DHCP server broadcasts its response, because the client does not yet have an IP address. A DHCP server responds to a DHCPREQUEST as follows:

- It verifies the packet and message checksums. If the checksums fail, the server discards the message.
- It checks that the UDP destination port is UDP port 67. If the port is not 67, it drops the message.
- The server chooses from its database a client IP address. It chooses the address as follows:
  1. If the client has an existing, bound address, the server supplies that address. OR,
  2. If the client had a previous, expired, or released address, and that address is available for reuse, the server supplies that address. OR,
  3. If the client has requested a specific address, and the requested address is both available and valid, the server supplies that address. OR,

4. The server allocates to the client a new address from the server's address pool. This address is assigned based on the state of the Giaddr field. If the Giaddr is 0.0.0.0, the address is assigned from the subnet on which the DHCP-DISCOVER message is received. If the message supplied a Giaddr, then the DHCP server assigns an IP address from the subnet on which the Giaddr address resides.

Note: After the server allocates the address, it must not reuse that address until after it receives the client's response to the server's DHCPOFFER message.

- It assigns a lease expiration time, as follows:
  1. If the client did not request a specific lease time, and it has an assigned IP address, the server returns the lease time previously assigned to that address. OR,
  2. If the client did not request a specific lease time, and it has no assigned address, the server assigns the locally configured lease time. OR,
  3. If the client requested a specific lease time, the server may either return the requested lease time, or select another lease time.
- It sets the OpCode to 2, BOOTREPLY.
- It sets the Htype, HLEN, and Hops fields appropriately.
- It includes the original DHCPDISCOVER Xid.
- It leaves the seconds as received.
- It leaves the Ciaddr field as it was received.
- It returns the client's assigned address in the Yiaddr field.
- It supplies its address in the Siaddr field.
- It leaves the Giaddr field as set in the DHCPDISCOVER message.
- It sets the Options Field values as required. It must set a lease time, using option Code 51. It also sends the parameters the client requested, according to the following rules:
  1. If the server has an explicitly configured default for a requested parameter, it includes the parameter's value in the Option field. OR,
  2. If the server recognizes the requested parameter as one defined for that host, it must include that value. OR,
  3. The server will not return the requested parameter.

The server must try to return as many of the requested parameters as it can, and must not return any parameters for which it is not configured.

The DHCP server also supplies the client's subnet mask, using option Code 1.

- It builds a DHCPOFFER message with the above information.
- It sets the UDP destination port to 68 (BOOTPC), the client port.
- It builds the IP packet targeted at the client's limited broadcast address, 255.255.255.255. If the DHCPDISCOVER specified the Giaddr, then it sets the UDP destination port to 67 (BOOTPS), and the destination IP address to the Giaddr. In either case, the server supplies its IP address as the IP packet's source address.
- It generates the appropriate checksums and sends the packet on its way.

The DHCPOFFER Message Diagram illustrates a sample DHCPOFFER message and packet.

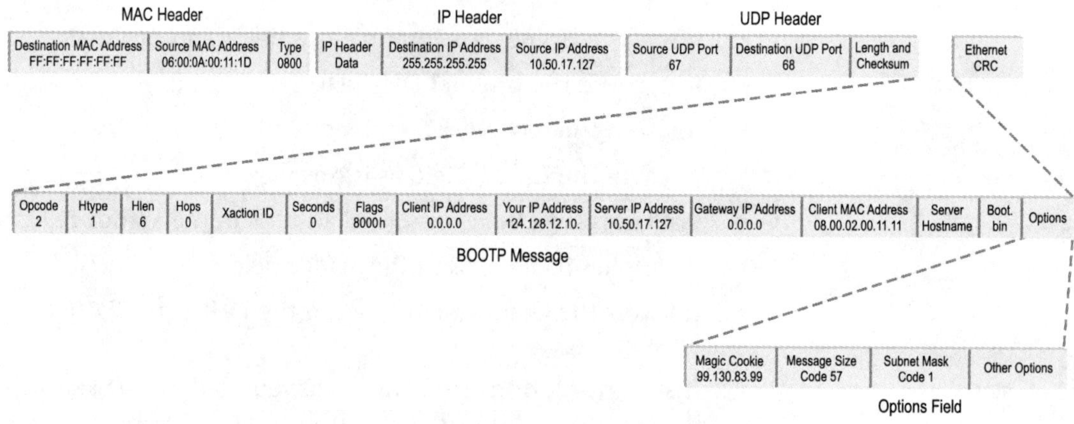

DHCPOFFER Message

DHCP Client—DHCPREQUEST Message

A client responds to the server's DHCPOFFER message with a DHCPREQUEST message. Other reasons a client might send a DHCPREQUEST messages include:

- A client wishes to verify a previously allocated IP address.
- A client wishes to extend its lease.

When a client is responding to an initial DHCPOFFER (called the SELECTING state), it builds the DHCPREQUEST with the following information:

- It inserts the selected server's address in the Siaddr field.
- It leaves the Ciaddr field set to 0.0.0.0.
- It sets the requested IP address option, Code 50, to match the address in the DHCPOFFER Yiaddr field.

The client may receive more than one DHCPOFFER message. In this case, it selects what it thinks is the best offer, and usually it chooses the first DHCPOFFER it receives. In some networks, this can be a problem, as the client cannot discern a valid offer from an invalid one. If, for some reason, a network user has set up an unauthorized DHCP server (known as a rogue server) the client could obtain an invalid or duplicate address and/or invalid configuration parameters.

OS vendors are now making efforts to reduce the threat of rogue DHCP servers. For example, Microsoft Windows 2000 Server maintains in its Active Directory a listing of authorized DHCP servers. Windows 2000 can automatically shut down an unauthorized Windows 2000 DHCP server. Windows 2000 learns of the network's DHCP servers through a DHCPINFORM message, sent by each Windows 2000 DHCP server when it initializes. This is a broadcast message containing Windows 2000 specific options codes that other Windows 2000 servers can interpret.

Any server that sent a DHCPOFFER but does not receive a corresponding DHCPREQUEST is free to reuse the previously reserved, offered address.

The client also reviews the DHCPOFFER's supplied optional parameters. If the client finds all supplied information to its liking, it builds the DHCPREQUEST message, sets the destination UDP port to 67, and broadcasts the message. Because the client does not yet have an assigned IP address, this message is broadcast.

DHCP Server—DHCPACK

The server responds to the client's DHCPREQUEST with a DHCP ACK message. The server returns a lease for the client address, and any additional configuration parameters. For example, a Windows DHCP server can supply many different optional parameters along with the address and lease. These include:

- Code 6—The DNS server address.
- Code 44—A Windows Internet Naming Service (WINS) server IP address.
- Code 46—The Network Basic Input/Output System (NetBIOS) node type.
- Codes 128–254—Vendor specific options limited to a private network.
- The server broadcasts this DHCPACK message to the client.

DHCP Client—DHCPACK Receipt

The client, upon receipt of the DHCPACK, goes into the BOUND state. It binds the offered address to its TCP/IP process and sets any additional optional parameters sent by the offering server. The client should also attempt to verify that the offered address is not already in use. It can do this by issuing an ARP request for the offered address, setting its hardware address as the sender's MAC address and 0.0.0.0 as the sender's IP address. If it receives a reply for the offered address, then the client must decline the offer with a DHCPDECLINE message, sent to the offering server.

DHCP Server—DHCPNAK Message

The server sends a DHCPNAK message to inform a client that it has incorrect configuration information. This can result from:

- The client trying to renew its previous address, and that address is unavailable.
- The client's IP address has become invalid, as the client is now physically located on another subnet.

DHCP Client—DHCPNAK Message

When a client receives a DHCPNAK, it returns to the DHCPDISCOVER phase.

Initializing with an Existing Address

When a client initializes with an existing address, it sends a DHCPREQUEST message. The client enters the INIT-REBOOT state. The client inserts its requested IP address in the Option field, using option Code 50. The client also specifies any other optional parameters it desires. It generates an Xid, and leaves the Siaddr field set to 0.0.0.0. The client broadcasts the DHCPREQUEST, and waits for a DHCPACK message.

If the client receives no reply, or a DHCPNAK, it can still use the address, as long as time remains on the lease.

DHCP Client Lease Renewal

All DHCP clients attempt renewal when 50 percent of the lease time has expired; this is the client RENEW state. They do this with a DHCPREQUEST message sent directly to the server that supplied the lease.

If the server is available, it renews the lease with a DHCPACK message, supplying a new lease time and any updated configuration parameters. The client then updates its configuration with this information.

If the server is unavailable, the client can continue to use the lease. At the 87.5-percent lease time point, the client enters the REBIND state. Here, the client broadcasts a DHCPREQUEST, looking for an answer from any DHCP server. If the client receives a DHCPACK, it renews the lease and other configuration information. If the client receives a DHCPNAK, it must return to the INIT state.

If the client cannot renew its lease, and the lease expires, client TCP/IP communications stops until the client obtains a new address. Any applications running over TCP/IP will experience errors until the client obtains a valid IP address.

DHCP Relay Agents

DHCP relay agents are similar to BOOTP relay agents. As a matter of fact, BOOTP routers which are RFC 1542 compliant can support DHCP, as well. The DHCP Relay Agent Diagram illustrates the use of a DHCP relay agent on a subnet remote from the DHCP server.

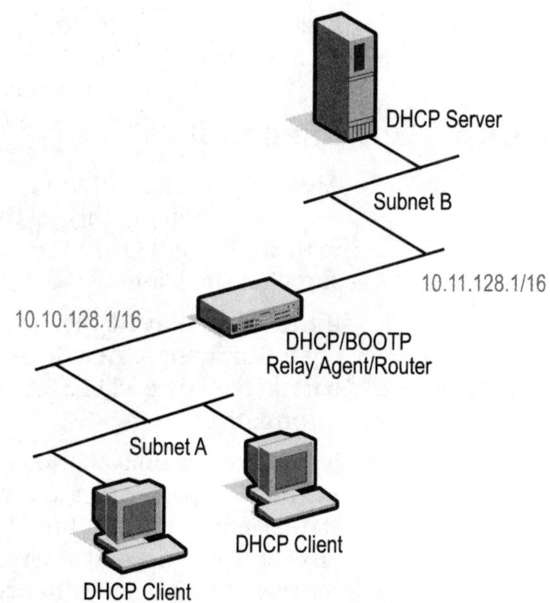

DHCP Relay Agent

A DHCP relay agent works as follows:

1. The relay agent receives a packet containing a DHCPDISCOVER broadcast message. The packet source address is 0.0.0.0, and the destination address is the limited broadcast address 255.255.255.255. The UDP destination port is 67.
2. The relay agent examines the Giaddr field, and if set to 0.0.0.0, fills the field with the relay agent logical interface address on which the request was received. It then forwards the DHCPDISCOVER message to the DHCP server.

3. When the DHCP server receives the packet containing the DHCPDISCOVER message, it examines the Giaddr field; it then determines from which DHCP scope it must assign the client IP address. A DHCP scope is a range of IP addresses an administrator configures on a DHCP server for assignment to requesting hosts. The scope can cover several subnets, thus the server must choose for the client an address on the client's home subnet. Otherwise, the client will not be able to communicate using TCP/IP.
4. The DHCP server sends a DHCPOFFER directly to the relay agent identified in the Giaddr field (the original, forwarding relay agent), containing the client IP address lease offer.
5. The router relays the DHCPOFFER to the client by means of broadcast on the requesting client's subnet.
6. The relay agent forwards the subsequent DHCPREQUEST and DHCPACK messages, as well.

DHCP Client—DHCPRELEASE Message

A client may send a DHCPRELEASE message to a DHCP server when it wishes to release its IP address and cancel its lease.

Activities

1. Which DHCP address allocation method assigns reusable addresses to DHCP clients?
   a. Static
   b. Manual
   c. Automatic
   d. Dynamic
2. What does DHCP provide that BOOTP cannot?
   a. DHCP allows hosts to request configuration information from a server.
   b. DHCP only assigns manually mapped addresses.
   c. DHCP assigns reusable addresses to any requesting host.
   d. DHCP uses relay agents.
3. How many basic operational steps does DHCP define?
   a. 2
   b. 3
   c. 4
   d. 5
4. Match the DHCP lease acquisition state with its description.
   a. The client broadcasts a DHCPDISCOVER message to its local subnet _________.
   b. The client receives a DHCPOFFER message _________.
   c. The client replies to the selected server with a DHCPREQUEST message _________.
   d. The client receives a DHCPACK message _________.

   Descriptions

   BOUND

   INIT

   REQUESTING

   SELECTING

Extended Activities

Note: This activity applies to Windows clients only.

Windows provides a utility, Winipcfg, that displays the local host's IP configuration. With this utility, you may review your IP address, default gateway, subnet mask, and other network information. We will use the Winipcfg utility to review our DHCP settings, and release and renew our DHCP lease.

Note: If your network does not use DHCP, then you will not be able to release and renew your IP address lease.

1. Connect either to your LAN or your ISP's network.
2. Select Start, Run, and type **winipcfg**. Select **OK**.
3. If your PC has both a NIC and a modem, choose whichever device is active using the arrow box at the Window's top. Click the **More Info** >> button.
4. Locate the following information in the resulting window and record it below:
   a. Host name

      ____

   b. Node type

      ____

   c. Adapter address

      ____

   d. IP address

      ____

   e. Subnet mask

      ____

   f. Default gateway

      ____

g. DHCP server address

____

h. Lease obtained date and time

____

i. Lease expires date and time

____

5. Press the **Release** button. This releases your address lease.
6. Locate and record the following information:

a. IP address

____

b. Subnet mask

____

c. Default gateway

____

d. DHCP server address

____

e. Lease obtained date and time

____

f. Lease expires date and time

____

7. Press the **Renew** button.

8. Locate and record the following information:
   a. IP address _________
   b. Subnet mask ________
   c. Default gateway _______
   d. DHCP server address _________
   e. Lease obtained date and time _________
   f. Lease expires date and time _________
9. Which information changed between your previous lease and this new one?

   ____

   ____

10. Press the **Renew** button again. Which information changed this time?

    ____

    ____

11. Select **OK** to close the window.

Lesson 6—NAT

Network Address Translation (NAT) is a means to extend the available IP address ranges. NAT allows a private internetwork to use any range of IP addresses it chooses, only presenting to the public Internet a limited public IP address range. Some NAT implementations also provide a modicum of network security, as the internal network can be effectively hidden from the outside world.

Objectives

At the end of this lesson you will be able to:

- Describe how NAT conserves IP addresses
- Explain how a network can use private addresses and still communicate over the Internet
- Explain NAT security benefits

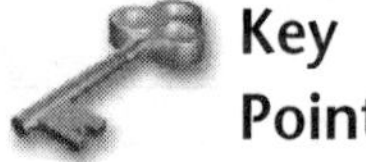

Key Point

NAT helps secure private networks from the public Internet.

NAT

RFC1631, authored in May 1994, describes the Network Address Translator. The author based the original premise on a foreseen need to conserve the quickly depleting globally unique IP address space. CIDR was suggested as a short-term solution, and IPv6 and other competing technologies as long-term solutions. For more on IPv6, see the next lesson in this unit. Address reuse, through the use of NAT, was suggested as a viable, immediate address conservation solution.

What is Address Reuse?

Address reuse takes advantage of the fact that the majority of network traffic remains local; that is, it never leaves the private network. Though this fact is less true now, with the Internet playing such a large part in our day-to-day IP communications, the idea of address reuse is still applicable.

The Stub Domain Diagram illustrates a private enterprise network.

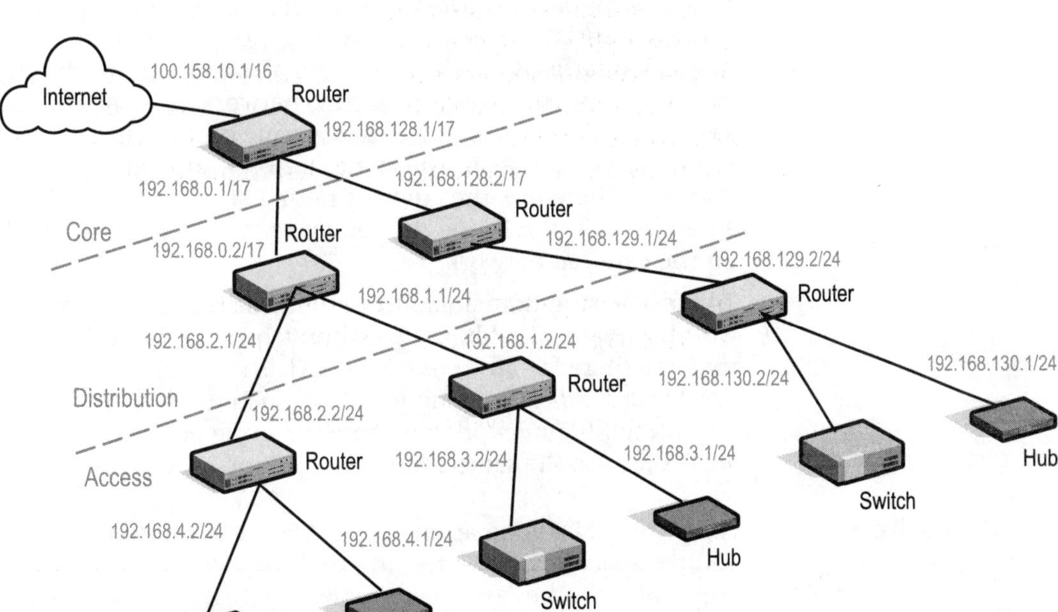

Stub Domain

This network is laid out in the three-layer hierarchy, and most traffic remains within the access and distribution layers. Therefore, the network can use private IP addresses on all hosts and router ports, except for the core layer router port connected to the public Internet. Here, the network is assigned a public Class A address from the ISP's address pool.

The only network traffic needing a public IP address is that leaving the private, stub routing domain. This is where NAT comes in. NAT allows networks to reuse IP addresses, whether public or private, and to do this with minimal impact on day-to-day network operations.

A NAT Overview

A NAT can be a network router or firewall, running network address translator software. It will generally have two physical network interfaces, one on the internal, private network side, and the other on the external, public network side. As we already know, in order for hosts to communicate on the same TCP/IP segment, they must share the same network and subnet IP address portions. Therefore, the administrator assigns the inside NAT port an address on the inside subnet, and the outside port an address on the external network.

The inside, stub domain addresses may be reused anywhere in the world. Private IP address users don't own those address ranges, they are there for all to use. The NAT is installed at the point the private domain needs public access, such as in an Internet gateway router. If a network has more than one public interface, each NAT must use the same address translation table.

NAT Address Spaces

For proper NAT operation, the NAT device must maintain two address spaces: one for the internal, private (local) IP addresses, and one for the external, public (global) IP addresses. Local addresses must not be duplicated, as this will cause the NAT device to lose track of which local device is mapped to which local IP address.

NAT must map private IP addresses to public IP addresses. The NAT device does this in one of two ways:

- Assigns internal devices a unique, global IP address for the extent of the external connection. This is called IP address translation.
- Assigns internal devices the same global IP address and unique TCP or UDP port number. This is called Masquerading or Network Address Port Translation (NAPT).

IP Address Translation

When a NAT uses IP address translation, it assigns global addresses from an address pool. The NAT Address Pool Table is an example of such a pool.

NAT Address Pool

NAT Address Pool: 100.158.0.0—100.158.255.255	
Original Host IP	Translated IP
192.168.2.3	100.158.2.3
192.168.3.4	100.158.3.4
192.168.4.5	100.158.4.5

The NAT device must maintain a table mapping internal addresses to external addresses so it knows which internal device incoming and outgoing packets belong to. NAT devices build these tables in a number of different ways.

Static Address Translation

The above table could represent a simple, static NAT table. The NAT administrator manually configures a set of allowed internal addresses and a NAT netmask of 255.255.0.0. This netmask operates as an inverse mask; thus the first two octets convert to the public address range's first two octets, and the original last two octets remain as they were in the original address.

With this netmask, the NAT first logically ANDs the original address with the inverted netmask:

Original address:

192.168.2.3 11000000.10101000.00000010.00000011

Inverse Netmask:

255.255.0.0 <u>00000000.00000000.11111111.11111111</u>

00000000.00000000.00000010.00000011

Then, the NAT logically ORs the AND function result with the public network and subnet portions. The Binary OR Truth Table illustrates the logical OR function:

Binary OR Truth Table

A	B	Result
0	0	0
0	1	1
1	0	1
1	1	1

The result of this OR function is:

AND result:	00000000.00000000.00000010.00000011
Public network address: 100.158.0.0	01100100.10010110.00000000.00000000
New address: 100.158.2.3	01100100.10010110.00000010.00000011

The assigned public address range is 100.158.0.0/16; thus the NAT maps each internal address's first two octets to the 100.158.0.0/16 network and sets the last two octets as the original host address. Only those devices statically mapped can access the public network.

Dynamic Address Translation

Dynamic address translation is another type of IP address translation. A static NAT administrator must manually map every internal address that needs external network access. For a large number of hosts, this means maintaining a large map, using a large range of public addresses. A solution to this administrative burden, especially where the public address range is limited and cannot match the number of internal hosts needing external access, is a NAT that provides dynamic address translation.

In dynamic NAT, the NAT device hands out IP addresses on demand, from a preconfigured pool. Normally, the pool's internal-to-external address ratio is something more than one-to-one, meaning that there are more internal addresses needing external access than there are available external addresses. This introduces a potential problem with dynamic address translation: the available external address pool can deplete before all external connection requests are satisfied. When no more external addresses are available, the NAT device must refuse additional connection requests, returning to the requesting host a "host unreachable" message, or something equivalent.

Enhanced Network Security

Dynamic address translation provides a security benefit static address translation cannot. Because static address translation maintains a preconfigured internal to external address mapping, someone wishing to hack into a specific internal host can obtain the host's statically mapped IP address and target that address for attack. As long as that host is online, the hacker can repeatedly attempt to break into the host, until they succeed. However, if a host draws its address from a pool, then a hacker with an intercepted address will likely target different hosts, never having enough time to break into one specific host.

When dynamic address translation is used, externally initiated connections are only possible when a device either has a static mapping assigned, or the NAT device has the dynamic mapping active in the NAT table. Outside connections responding to an internally initiated connection request can progress without problems, as the NAT has the internal host-to-external address mapping still stored in its address translation table. However, when an outsider attempts a connection to one of the internal devices, and no mapping exists for that device, then the outside connection will fail. Additionally, if a connection for an internal device is active at the time the external connection is initiated, it is only active for the duration of the original internal-to-external connection, and thus the externally initiated connection will drop when the original connection drops.

The Dynamic Address Translation Diagram illustrates a sample NAT device configuration using dynamic address translation.

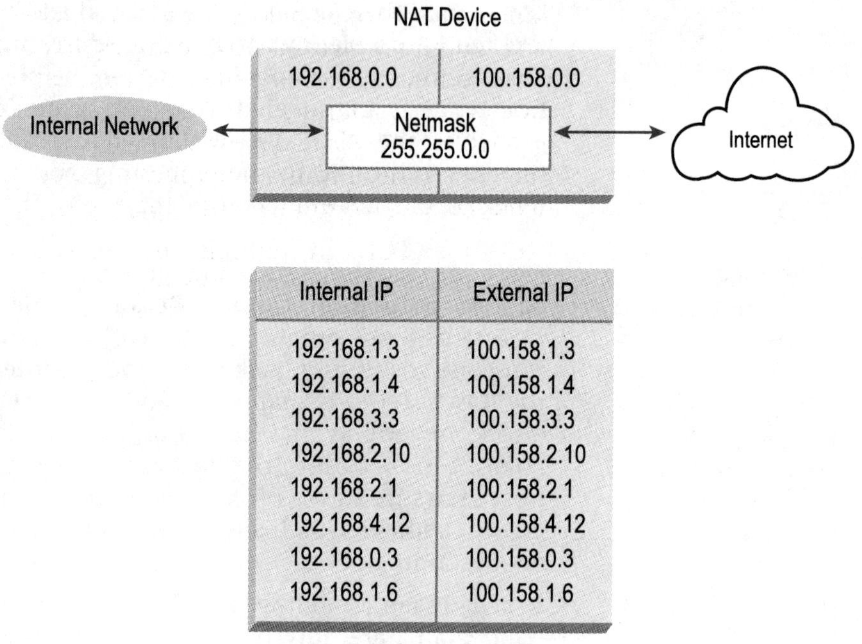

Dynamic Address Translation

The NAT device maintains the address map until the internal device drops the connection and the mapping time out expires. Note that communication is bi-directional, that is, the NAT device not only allows internal-to-external network connections, but also allows devices to respond to internally initiated connections.

Masquerading/NAPT

Masquerading is a NAT technique that hides all internal addresses behind one external address. This is also known as NAPT.

NAPT presents one obvious benefit, and that is that only one public IP address is needed. How can multiple internal hosts use the same address? Instead of the NAT handing each internal host its own external address, NAPT assigns each internal connection a port address associated with a single, shared external IP address. The NAT takes advantage of TCP's ability to multiplex simultaneous connections to the same IP address.

Recall that TCP can multiplex multiple virtual connections; the TCP Multiplexing/Demultiplexing Diagram illustrates this.

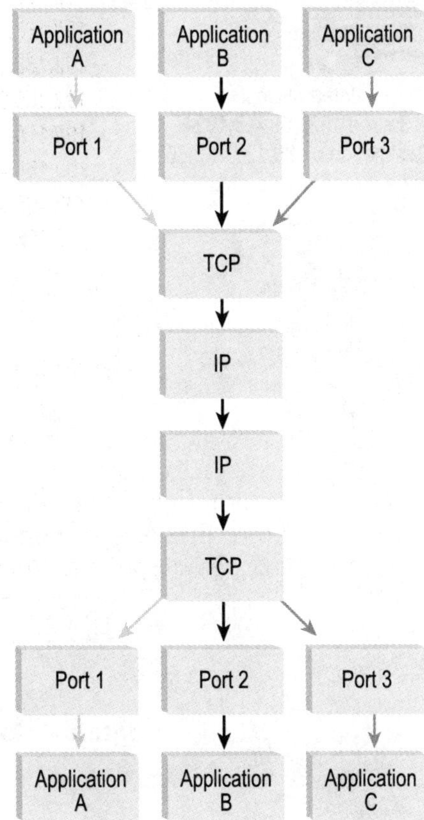

TCP Multiplexing/Demultiplexing

NAPT dynamically assigns each internal connection a TCP port associated with the single external address and maintains a mapping of these internal connections to external ports. For example, suppose that a host with address 192.168.4.3 wanted to connect with the Hypertext Transfer Protocol (HTTP) service on the World Wide Web (Web) server with the address 67.89.127.145. This host initiates a connection to the external network server by means of the NAT device, which is configured as the internal host's default gateway. The internal host specifies its own local address as the source address and its locally assigned TCP port as the source port. It specifies the external Web server as the destination IP address and the server's HTTP service well-known TCP port as the destination port. The Internal Host Connection Diagram illustrates this.

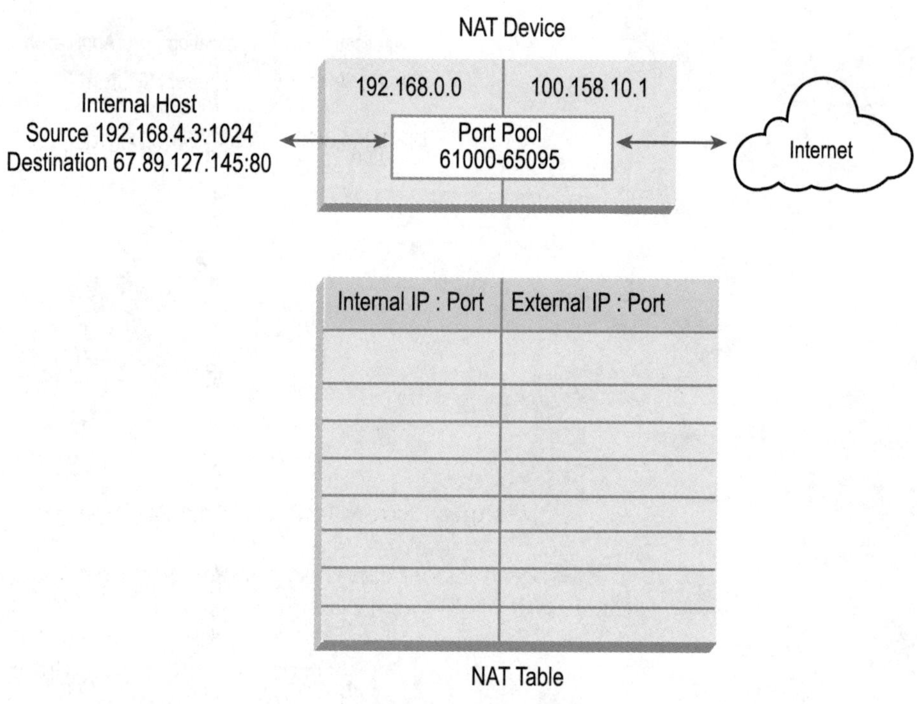

Internal Host Connection

The NAT translates the internal host's IP address to the single, external IP address (in this case, its own external port address), and the source TCP port to one of its available, pooled source ports. It leaves the destination IP and port addresses as the internal host originally specified them. The Assigned External IP and Port Address Diagram illustrates this.

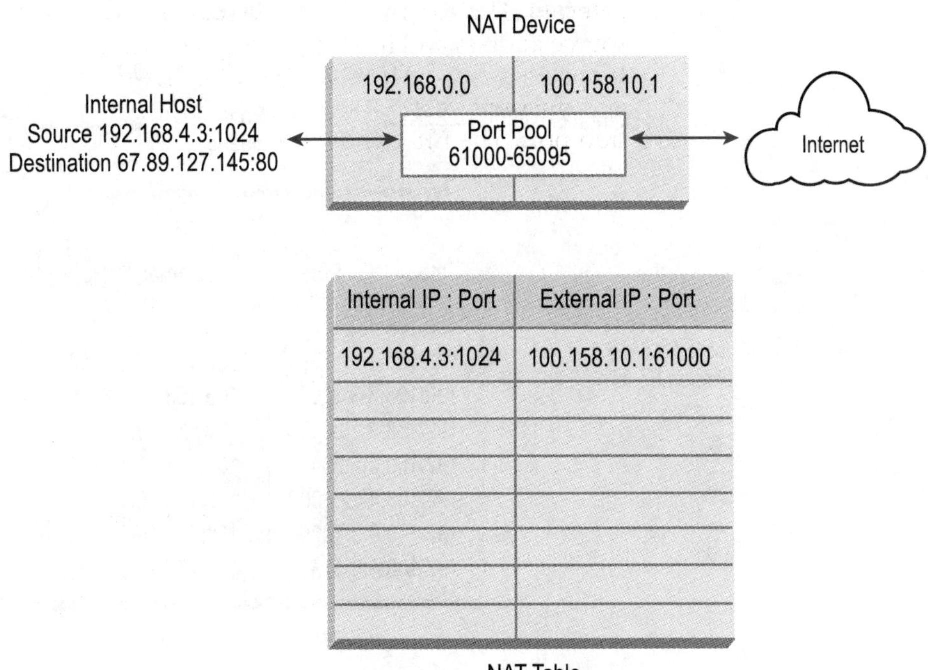

Assigned External IP and Port Address

The internal host can then connect with the external Web server using the NAT-device-assigned shared external address and port. The NAT table reflects this mapping, and the NAT device maintains this mapping for the connection's duration. The Web server can answer the internal host by targeting the NAT assigned public IP address and port, and the NAT will map both connections appropriately.

The NAT can handle additional connections as well, up to the point where either it exhausts its port pool, or its physical resources (central processing unit [CPU], memory, or port throughput). The Multiple NAPT Connections Diagram illustrates a NAPT-capable NAT device with multiple host connections established.

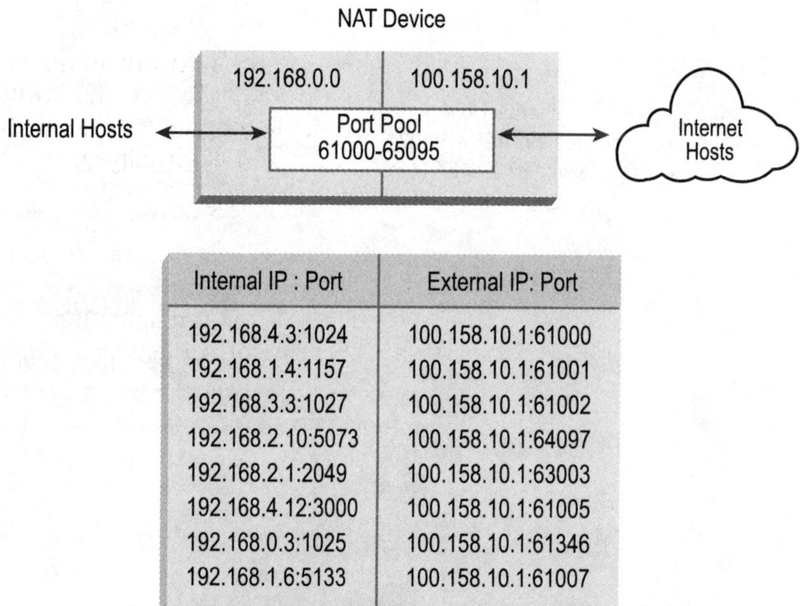

Internal IP : Port	External IP: Port
192.168.4.3:1024	100.158.10.1:61000
192.168.1.4:1157	100.158.10.1:61001
192.168.3.3:1027	100.158.10.1:61002
192.168.2.10:5073	100.158.10.1:64097
192.168.2.1:2049	100.158.10.1:63003
192.168.4.12:3000	100.158.10.1:61005
192.168.0.3:1025	100.158.10.1:61346
192.168.1.6:5133	100.158.10.1:61007

Multiple NAPT Connections

The NAT maps each separate internal host connection to a unique port using the same external IP address, and maintains the mapping for each connection's duration.

NAPT—Even More Security

When using NAPT, incoming externally initiated connections are virtually impossible. When a host has an entry in the NAT table, this entry is only valid for the active TCP connection. This compares with dynamic IP address translation, where as long as the host is connected to the external network, the NAT maintains a mapped entry. Even ICMP replies reporting connection status (*host/port unreachable*) do not automatically get through the NAT to the internal host, but instead must be filtered and relayed by the NAT device's software.

If for some reason the network administrator must allow external connections through the NAT device, they can take additional measures to enable them. For example, they could set up the NAT device so it relays all externally initiated HTTP port connections to a specified internal host. However, because the network has just one externally visible IP address, the NAT device must listen on different ports, one for each service and internal host IP. Because most applications listen on well-known ports that cannot be changed easily (or transparently, to the outside world), this solution is quite inconvenient and often no option at all.

The only solution then is to provide static IP address mappings for whatever internal services we wish to avail to the external network. This means maintaining more than one external IP address on the NAT, but in this manner, the network can provide some externally accessible services while also protecting the internal network's privacy.

Activities

1. How does NAT help secure a private network from outside attacks?
   a. It allows network administrators to assign private IP addresses to public Internet router ports.
   b. It creates a "sandbox" inside which outside applications run before they execute on a local host.
   c. It encloses all inbound traffic in a secure packet directed at only the target host.
   d. It allows networks to use private IP addresses on the internal network, and still access the Internet.
2. Which NAT address mapping technique maps internal IP addresses to a single, external IP address?
   a. Direct Address Port Translation
   b. Unique Address Translation
   c. IP address translation
   d. NAPT
3. How does a NAT netmask work to map internal addresses to external addresses?
   a. It works as a subnet mask, designating the network on which the packets' target host resides.
   b. It works as a wildcard mask, allowing the NAT to filter inbound traffic by the source network address.
   c. It works as a reverse mask, converting the internal host address to a public, outside address.
   d. It works as an inverse mask, converting the internal network address portion to a public address.
4. Which statement best describes NAT masquerading?
   a. It hides all internal addresses behind one external address.
   b. It hides all internal addresses behind one internal address.
   c. It statically assigns all internal addresses to a single external address.
   d. It hides all internal addresses behind a single port number.

5. How does NAPT handle an IP packet's source and destination port and IP addresses?
   a. It leaves the source port and address as is, and changes the destination port and IP address to its own external addresses.
   b. It leaves the source and destination ports as is, and changes the source and destination IP addresses to addresses from its address pool.
   c. It leaves the destination port and address as is, and changes the source port and address to addresses from its address pool.
   d. It changes the source port, but leaves the source address, destination port and address as is.

Extended Activity

You administer a NAPT NAT device, which also serves as your network router. Given the following information, and the NAPT Diagram:

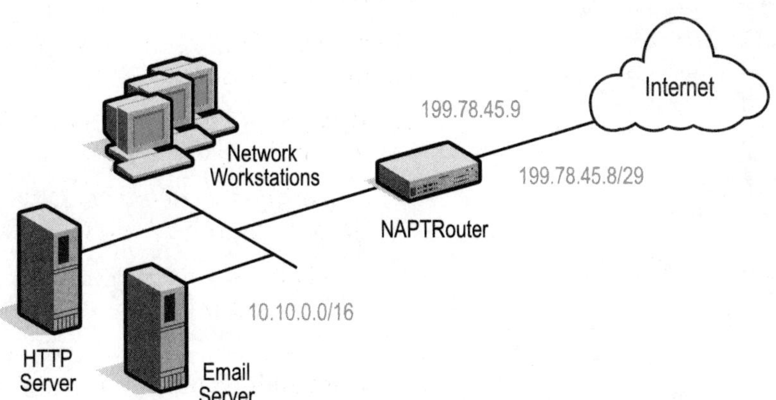

- You own the public IP subnetwork 199.78.45.8/29
- You host internal HTTP and SMTP/POP e-mail servers. Their addresses are as follows:
  - HTTP Server: 10.10.0.250, listens on Port 80
  - SMTP/POP E-Mail Server: 10.10.0.251, listens on Ports 25 (SMTP) and 110 (POP3)

- The NAT device's outside interface IP address is 199.78.45.9/29.
- The NAT maps internal connections to external addresses using the registered TCP and UDP port numbers 1024–65535.

1. Fill out the following table, mapping the HTTP and SMTP/POP e-mail servers and four client connections through the NAT device. The e-mail server only allows internal client connections.

Internal Address	Internal Source Port	External Address	External Source Port
10.10.1.2	1028		
10.10.0.17	4350		
10.10.3.120	1200		
10.10.4.5	1029		
10.10.0.250	80		
10.10.0.251	25		

Lesson 7—IPv6

IP version 6 (IPv6) was designed as an upgrade to IPv4, the current version in use worldwide, and can coexist with the older version. IPv6 was designed to allow the Internet to grow steadily, both in terms of hosts connected and the total amount of data traffic transmitted.

Objectives

At the end of this lesson you will be able to:

- Describe the basic IPv6 features
- Explain the importance of IPv4 compatibility

Key Point

IPv6 expands the IPv4 address field and provides extended QoS support.

IP Next Generation

During the 1980s, when the government was first privatizing the Internet, IPv4 was more than sufficient to handle the total of 213 Internet hosts. By the late 1980s, the host count had increased to over 2,000 and was growing rapidly. By 1996, the number of hosts had risen to over 500,000, and by 1999, the count was over 50,000,000. This rapid growth gave rise to a number of IPv4 problems, the most prevalent being the limited number of IP addresses available.

RFCs to modernize and improve IP were submitted to the Internet Society (ISOC) and Internet Engineering Task Force (IETF) as early as 1995. The IETF appointed a formal group to study the next IP generation, already called IPv6. RFC 1883 specifies IPv6 as the IPv4 replacement and addresses many different protocol issues at once. The following sections describe some of these issues.

Expanded Addresses

IPv6 expands IP addresses from the current 32 bits to 128 bits. The benefits of these larger addresses include:

- Allows continued Internet expansion—Expanding the addresses to 128 bits ensures that the Internet will not exhaust its address supply in the near future. Addresses that are 128 bits allow for 2^{128} individual addresses. This greatly expanded address range ensures that we can assign everything from cellular phones to Personal Digital Assistants (PDA) to wrist-worn communicators their own IP address.
- Improves routing efficiency—Longer IP addresses allow for aggregating addresses by hierarchies of network, access provider, geography, corporation, and other groupings. Such aggregation should increase router lookup speed and reduce router memory requirements, making routing more efficient.
- Accommodates non-IP addressing formats—The long address space provides adequate room for translations of Internetwork Packet Exchange (IPX), network service-access point (NSAP), Ethernet, and other non-IP addresses into IPv6 addresses. This allows existing networks to connect to the Internet with a minimum of address reconfiguration, and reduces setup, debugging, and maintenance loads on network managers.

Multimedia Ready

IPv6 incorporates a variety of functions that make it possible to use the Internet for delivering real-time data requiring guaranteed bandwidth and latency to ensure that packets arrive on a regular basis. Priority and flow label fields enable us to assign priorities to our network data and flows.

Priority Field

The IPv6 header defines a 4-bit Priority field that can indicate 16 different priority levels in much the same way that the IP type of service (ToS) octet does. The Sample Priorities Table lists sample priorities.

Sample Priorities

Priority	Application
0	Normal (nonprioritized) traffic
4	Bulk transfer (FTP)
6	Interactive traffic (Telnet)
7	Control/management traffic (SNMP)

Half of these values are intended for use with non-real-time traffic, such as file transfers, while the other half define eight priority levels reserved for real-time traffic.

Flow Label Field

The IPv6 header also includes a 24-bit flow label that can be used by originating applications to mark a packet stream as belonging to a particular IP flow; thus, routers may classify them without having to look up addresses, application ports, and other information. A flow is simply a sequence of packets sent to a given destination. The actual flow label is a random number chosen from a hexadecimal range of 0x01 to 0xFFFFFF. Packets on the same flow must be sent with the same priority and flow label.

Having flow ID information available within the IP header itself allows routers to reduce the amount of effort, and therefore time, they take to assign a particular QoS to a packet. Note that the flow label does nothing to address the QoS provisioning itself; we must also employ Resource Reservation Protocol (RSVP) and other reservation provisioning protocols.

Multicast Support

IPv6 mandates support for multicast traffic. This function makes it possible to deliver data simultaneously to large numbers of public or private users, without wasting bandwidth broadcasting to the entire network. IPv6 enables us to limit multicast message distribution scopes to a specific region, company, or other criteria, thereby reducing bandwidth usage and providing security.

Bandwidth Reservations

Using the mandated RSVP functionality, users can reserve bandwidth along the route from source to destination. This makes it possible to provide video or other real-time data with a guaranteed QoS.

Packet Prioritizing

Packets are assigned a priority level, ensuring that real-time data flow is not interrupted by lower priority packets.

Jumbograms

IPv6 supports packet sizes of up to four billion bytes. This makes large packet transmission easier, and ensures that IPv6 can make the best use of all the transmission medium's available bandwidth.

Plug and Play Address Discovery

Currently, users or network managers must manually configure each host with an address and other network information. IPv6 alleviates this time consuming chore by including mechanisms to allow hosts to discover their own addresses and automate address changes. By allowing hosts to learn their own addresses from a local router during startup, IPv6 eliminates the need to manually configure addresses or use DHCPv6 on each host. IPv6 also specifies procedures for a host to allocate an address for local site communications and small sites without routers.

Network Information Discovery

DHCPv6 is the dynamic host addressing protocol specified for IPv6. It adds room for larger addresses and additional message types.

Automated Address Changes

Because the router in IPv6 distributes network addresses, changing the address of the network requires updating only the router. In addition, all addresses include lifetimes. Enabling the router to specify a time to switch addresses ensures a smooth, error-free transition to a new address.

Support for Mobile Hosts

IPv6 incorporates algorithms to automatically forward packets from a base address to any other address. This allows users connected to the Internet from any location, even mobile phones, to seamlessly receive their messages.

Dead Neighbor Detection

IPv6 specifies "dead neighbor" and "dead gateway" detection algorithms, ensuring that all implementations of IPv6 are able to efficiently detect problems and reroute packets when necessary.

Increased Efficiency

IPv6 supports several features that increase the overall efficiency of the IP protocol. The following sections describe these features.

Simplified Headers

IPv6 simplifies the packet header from 12 data elements in IPv4 to only 8 elements. This reduces the computation required to process headers, thereby speeding up routing. Fragmentation and other optional control functions are moved into hop-by-hop and end-destination extension headers that follow the standard header. Options in the end-destination extension header are not processed until the final destination, further reducing the computation required to process IPv6 packets as they pass through each router.

Packet Size Optimization

Before sending messages in IPv6, the source determines the maximum packet size supported by all routers along the path to the destination using the Path Maximum Transmission Unit (MTU) Discovery algorithm. The source computer then divides the message into packets that require no fragmentation by routers, reducing the computational load on the routers.

Less Load On Hosts

The multicast function in IPv6 allows hosts and routers to send neighbor discovery messages only to those computers that have registered to receive them, removing the necessity for all other computers to examine and discard irrelevant packets.

Route Aggregation

IPv6 allows multiple addresses per device interface, making route aggregation simple and efficient. For example, if a host is using multiple access providers, it can have separate addresses aggregated under each provider's address space. In IPv4, addresses have little or no connection to routing paths, and therefore routers must maintain enormous tables of routing paths. Address aggregation in IPv6 allows routers to maintain small tables of prefixes that deliver the packets to the correct access provider.

Added Flexibility

IPv6 supports several features that improve the overall flexibility of the IP protocol. The following sections describe these features.

Control Over Options Handling

IPv6 allows applications to specify how to treat unknown options. This provides IPv6 with the flexibility to add new options in the future, without requiring that existing implementations be updated to conform.

Control Over Routing

As opposed to the capability to choose only loose (automatically determined) or strict (user-specified) routing for the entire path in IPv4, IPv6 users can specify loose or strict routing for each hop along the path. IPv6 also provides the flexibility to include additional routing methods in the future.

Anycast Addressing

IPv6 allows a source to specify that it wants to contact any one host from a group by means of a single address.

Configurability of Features

The IPv6 protocol for hosts and routers to discover neighboring computers is called neighbor discovery. IPv6 allows all the features of neighbor discovery, such as retries and time-out parameters, to be locally configured. This provides increased flexibility as well as the capability to optimize neighbor discovery for the needs and constraints of each individual network.

IPv4 Compatibility

Because of the huge installed base of IPv4 hosts and routers, specifications for IPv6 include mechanisms designed to ensure a smooth, gradual transition from IPv4 to IPv6.

IPv4 Address Translation IPv4 addresses are easily translated into IPv6 addresses by adding an IPv6 address prefix of leading 0s.

Dual Protocol Stacks For the foreseeable future, all implementations of IPv6 will also include an IPv4 stack.

IPv6 Tunneled Over IPv4 IPv6 hosts will be able to communicate with each other through IPv4 routers by encapsulating IPv6 packets within IPv4 packets.

Security Infrastructure

IPv6 provides an infrastructure for packet-level encryption and authentication that applications can use to ensure networking security.

Encryption Encryption scrambles data packets to prevent unauthorized people from reading the message. Although 56-bit Data Encryption Standard (DES) encryption is part of the IETF standard, due to conflicts with U.S. export constraints, international users may not have access to this functionality.

Authentication Authentication verifies that the source address was not forged and the packet was not tampered with in route. IPv6 implementations include the Message Digest 5 (MD5) algorithm for message authentication to verify that the message arrives unchanged from the user claiming to have sent the packet.

IPv6 Header Format

The IPv6 Header Format Diagram depicts the new IPv6 header.

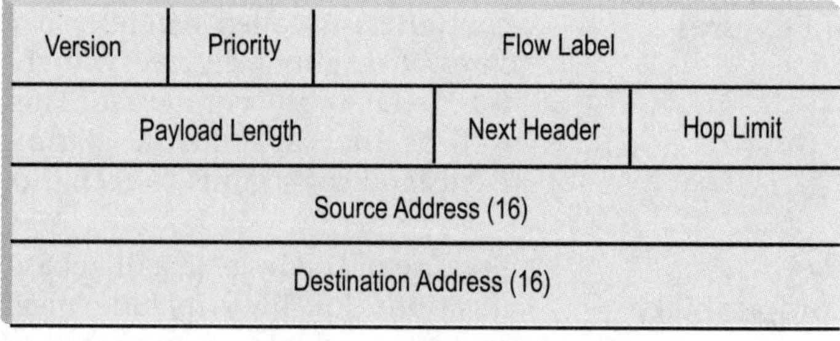

IPv6 Header Format

The fields in the header are described as follows:

- Version field (4 bits)—Indicates version 6.
- Priority field (4 bits)—Is used to enable priorities for various data.
- Flow Label field (24 bits)—Is the former IPv4 ToS field.
- Payload Length field (16 bits)—Is the number of bytes being carried in the packet.
- Next Header field (8 bits)—Identifies the header that immediately follows the IPv6 header. It uses similar values as the Protocol field in the IPv4 header, as shown in the Next Header Field Table.

Next Header Field

Value	Header Type
1	ICMPv4
4	IP in IP (encapsulation)
6	TCP
7	UDP
44	Fragment (replace old fragmentation method)
58	CMPv6
59	None (no next header)

- Hop Limit field (8 bits)—Replaces the TTL field of IPv4 and is decremented at each node (router) that forwards the packet. When it reaches a count of 0, the fragment/packet is discarded.
- Source and Destination Address fields have increased to 16 bytes each.

Dotted decimal notation has been replaced by colon hexadecimal (colon hex) notation. The following examples illustrate colon hexadecimal notation:

1080:0:0:0:8:800:200C:417 unicast address

FF01:0:0:0:0:0:0:43 multicast address

0:0:0:0:0:0:0:1 loopback address

may be represented as:

1080::8:800:200C:417 unicast address

FF01::43 multicast address

::1 loopback address

Transitioning from IPv4 to IPv6 may take place in several different ways. There may be a separate IP stack for each version. Also, version 4 tunneling in a version 6 IP header may occur. Some of these may depend on how individual router manufacturers (for example, 3Com) decide to implement the changes.

Activities

1. How many unique addresses are possible with IPv6?

   ____

2. Why do you think we are running out of IP addresses so quickly?

   ____

   ____

3. Do you think IPv6 offers enough addresses, or will we eventually need more?

   ____

Extended Activity

1. Go to the following Web sites to learn more about IPv6:
   a. **http://www.ietf.org/html.charters/ipngwg-charter.html**
   b. **http://playground.sun.com/pub/ipng/html/ipng-main.html**
   c. **http://www.cis.ohio-state.edu/htbin/rfc/rfc1752.html**
   d. **http://www.ipv6.org/**

Summary

Unit 5 presented details of some key TCP/IP services. First we discussed DNS domain names and the domain name tree structure. We learned that FQDNs represent DNS hosts, and that the DNS uses a hierarchical structure. DNS defines scopes of authority, where specific organizations have responsibility for each portion of the DNS name space.

DNS defines top-level domains based on an organization's industry and country of origin. The second-level is distributed to the individual organizations that maintain their own subdomains; there can be subdomains within these second-level domains, as well. This means that DNS is distributed, not centralized, with responsibility for specific zones spread throughout the tree.

ICMP messages occur at Layer 3 of the OSI model. These messages provide feedback that both users and network devices can use to help resolve network problems. Ping and traceroute are common IP utilities that use ICMP messages.

IGMP messages support multicast applications, such as video or voice conferencing over IP networks. Hosts using IGMP join multicast groups, designated by Class D IP addresses. Hosts can enter and leave multicast groups dynamically. IGMP is an OSI Layer 3 process.

BOOTP is designed to allow diskless workstations to dynamically find their IP addresses and configuration information by broadcasting BOOTPREQUEST messages on the local network. The BOOTP server responds to this address request with a BOOTREPLY message. BOOTP messages travel within UDP segments, which are in turn carried by IP packets. The requesting host broadcasts these messages on the local network because it initially has no IP address and thus cannot communicate by means of directed IP packets. Because routers do not pass broadcast traffic, a relay agent can forward requests and replies across subnet boundaries.

DHCP extends BOOTP to provide additional configuration information. DHCP supports both diskless workstations and standard PCs, simplifying network administration by eliminating the need to manually configure IP addresses and other workstation configuration information. DHCP clients and servers use four basic messages to obtain their configuration information: DHCPDISCOVER, DHCPOFFER, DHCPREQUEST, and DHCPACK. Where BOOTP requires a static address mapping database, DHCP assigns addresses dynamically. Clients must regularly renew their DHCP leases to continue TCP/IP operations. DHCP relay agents can forward DHCP broadcasts across subnets.

NAT allows network administrators to hide their internal network from the public Internet, while at the same time conserving addresses. NAT can be implemented statically, where the administrator manually maps internal addresses to external, public addresses. A network might implement dynamic address translation, where the NAT hands out addresses on demand, from an address pool. Finally, a network might implement masquerading or NAPT, sharing a single external IP address for all internal devices, assigning each outgoing connection a TCP port. NAT helps secure the network by only allowing inbound connections while outbound connections are active, and each consecutive NAT implementation secures the internal network better than the previous. (Dynamic is more secure than static, and NAPT is more secure than either of the others.)

IPv6 is an ongoing project designed to resolve many limitations imposed by the commonly used IPv4. IPv6 provides for more addresses and provides better built-in QoS functions. IPv6 can translate IPv4 addresses and tunnel over existing IPv4 router connections.

Unit 5 Quiz

1. A DNS SOA entry indicates which of the following?
   a. The DNS servers for a domain
   b. An alias name for a specific host
   c. Associates a hostname to an IP address
   d. The domain's primary DNS
2. Which DNS record lists a zone's name servers?
   a. SOA
   b. MX
   c. CNAME
   d. NS
3. Which of the following describes a DNS resolver?
   a. It retrieves ARP information
   b. It stores DNS information
   c. It retrieves IP address information
   d. It retrieves frame information
4. Which are the two control entries found in a master file RR entry?
   a. Origin
   b. Destination
   c. Include
   d. Exclude
5. Which DNS record type specifies name to address translation, such as used in a glue record entry?
   a. A
   b. CNAME
   c. NS
   d. SOA

6. A Ping command uses which ICMP message types?
   a. Echo Request
   b. Source quench
   c. Redirect
   d. Echo Reply
7. Why does ICMP use identifier and sequence numbers?
   a. To provide additional information about the message type
   b. To supply information about the datagram that caused the message
   c. To identify the upper layer protocol that caused the message
   d. To allow the sender to match ICMP reply messages with requests
8. Which IP protocol will a router use to inform neighbor routers of congestion on an interface?
   a. IGMP
   b. ICMP
   c. RARP
   d. IARP
9. Why might we use ICMP testing on an IP network?
   a. To obtain feedback about various problems that might occur on the network
   b. To verify that IP's various reliability mechanisms are properly functioning
   c. To help monitor network traffic
   d. To make IP reliable without the need for higher layer protocols, such as TCP
10. Why might a device send an ICMP source quench message?
    a. The device must discard a datagram because the TTL counter expires.
    b. The device discovers an IP header syntax error.
    c. The device asks a source host to use another router that provides a shorter path.
    d. The device does not have the buffering capacity to forward a datagram.

11. ICMP supports which two TCP/IP utilities? (Choose two.)
    a. Ping
    b. Telnet
    c. ARP
    d. Tracert
12. How would IP multicasting map address 224.0.0.1 to an Ethernet multicast address?
    a. 01:00:24:40:00:01
    b. 01:00:5E:00:00:00
    c. 01:00:5E:00:00:01
    d. 01:00:5E:FF:FF:FF
13. For which three purposes might you use multicasting on an IP network? (Choose three.)
    a. Online training
    b. Teleconferencing
    c. Network management
    d. Software distribution
14. Which two statements concerning multicasting are true? (Choose two.)
    a. IP multicast group membership is dynamic.
    b. A network cannot support both multicast and unicast routers.
    c. UDP uses IP multicast services.
    d. A host can only belong to a single multicast group.
15. When might a BOOTP client discard a BOOTP message? (Choose three.)
    a. If the destination port number is 67
    b. If the BOOTREPLY targets another MAC address
    c. If the BOOTREPLY includes a transaction ID other than its own
    d. If the Yiaddr field contains an address other than its own

16. Which best describes a BOOTP relay agent?
    a. It supplies the client's address and configuration information.
    b. It forwards client BOOTREQUEST messages across subnet boundaries.
    c. It cannot forward BOOTREQUEST messages to other relay agents.
    d. It returns only directed BOOTREPLY messages.
17. In which cases will a BOOTP relay agent discard a BOOTREQUEST message? (Choose three.)
    a. When the packet's source IP address is 0.0.0.0
    b. When the destination port is 68
    c. If the OpCode is not 1 or 2
    d. If the Hops field value exceeds 16
18. Which is the correct DHCP lease message order?
    a. DHCPDISCOVER, DHCPOFFER, DHCPREQUEST, DHCPREPLY
    b. DHCPDISCOVER, DHCPOFFER, DHCPREQUEST, DHCPACK
    c. DHCPREQUEST, DHCPREPLY, DHCPDISCOVER, DHCPOFFER
    d. DHCPREQUEST, DHCPACK, DHCPDISCOVER, DHCPOFFER
19. When can a DHCP server reuse an address offered in a DHCPOFFER message?
    a. After it receives the client's DHCPRELEASE message
    b. After it receives the client's DHCPDISCOVER message
    c. After the server times out waiting for a DHCPREQUEST message
    d. After the client sends a DHCPINFORM message

20. Which DHCP option code is used for specifying vendor specific options?
    a. 6
    b. 44
    c. 46
    d. 128
21. At which point in the lease period does the client first attempt to renew its lease?
    a. 25 percent
    b. 50 percent
    c. 75 percent
    d. 85 percent
22. How might a DHCP client cancel its address lease?
    a. DHCPRELEASE message
    b. DHCPACK message
    c. DHCPNACK message
    d. DHCPCANCEL message
23. NAT IP address translation assigns external addresses to internal devices in which way?
    a. It sends internal address requests to a DHCP server.
    b. It assigns all internal devices the same external IP address.
    c. It converts the internal IP address to a private IP address.
    d. It assigns the internal address to one of a pool of external addresses.
24. What happens when a dynamic NAT device runs out of addresses to assign?
    a. The NAT device refuses new connections.
    b. The NAT device drops the oldest connection.
    c. The NAT device shares addresses between internal devices.
    d. The NAT device uses backup static map entries.

25. Which choice is the best solution for allowing externally initiated connections through a NAPT NAT device?
    a. Use static address mappings for any internal services we wish to make externally available.
    b. Route externally initiated connections to a "honeypot" network, outside the NAT equipped network.
    c. Relay all externally initiated connections to a specific, internal device listening on registered port numbers.
    d. Convert inbound destination port numbers to a range of unregulated port numbers, and insert these new port numbers in the TCP header.
26. Which protocol works with IPv6 QoS mechanisms to provide video and other real-time data with reserved bandwidth across a data flow's path?
    a. RTP
    b. RSVP
    c. TCP
    d. UDP
27. How long is an IPv6 address?
    a. 32 bits
    b. 64 bits
    c. 128 bits
    d. 256 bits

Unit 6
Routing TCP/IP

Routing is the primary reason we choose to deal with the complexities of Transmission Control Protocol/Internet Protocol (TCP/IP); and routing is what makes the protocol suite so desirable in networking. Layer 3 addresses provide us the capability to build within the global Internet individual subnetworks, all able to share information with one another.

Routed protocols are those protocols that carry information from place to place; IP is a routed protocol. Routing protocols allow routers to share path information with one another. This unit is about routing protocols and how they do their jobs.

We will introduce the routing process and illustrate a routed network architecture. We then discuss the different routing types we can configure on a router: static, default, and dynamic. We will learn of the different types of routing protocols we might choose for our internetworks: distance vector, link state, and hybrid. We will discuss Routing Information Protocol (RIP) and Internet Gateway Routing Protocol (IGRP), both distance vector protocols, and learn how shortest path first (SPF) protocols exchange information.

We finish up discussing Exterior Gateway Protocols (EGPs) and advanced routing practices, such as load sharing and least cost and policy routing.

Lessons

1. IP Routing
2. How Routers Share Routing Information
3. RIP
4. IGRP
5. OSPF
6. Advanced Routing

Terms

administrative distance (AD)—A routing table entry's AD represents its source's trustworthiness. A lower number means it is more trustworthy than an entry with a higher number. Cisco routers use ADs that range from 0 (highest trustworthiness) to 255 (lowest, and unusable).

area border routers (ABRs)—An ABR is an OSPF router connected to more than one area. Routing between areas is handled by the ABRs. An ABR maintains a separate link-state database for each area it is connected to, and creates a separate SPF tree from each of those databases.

autonomous system boundary routers (ASBRs)—An ASBR is an OSPF router connected to routers in other autonomous systems. Just as an ABR represents its area to other ABRs, an ASBR represents its AS to other ASBRs. Each ASBR runs OSPF on the interface to its own AS and an inter-AS routing protocol, such as EGP or BGP, on the interface to another AS. These protocols allow ASBRs to exchange routing information that summarizes routes within each AS.

Border Gateway Protocol (BGP)—BGP is an EGP used among BGP routers to exchange reachability information. Each BGP router advertises networks reachable within its AS to other BGP routers in other autonomous systems. BGP remedies many of the limitations of EGP, and provides support for future growth of the Internet.

BGP version 4 (BGP-4)—BGP-4 is documented in RFC 1771 and is the current exterior routing protocol used for the global Internet. BGP-4 is essentially a DVA. BGP runs over TCP Port 179.

class-of-service (CoS) routing—COS routing allows network administrators to specify different routing service categories and associate different performance characteristics with each category. The administrator assigns data packets to different priority queues and specifies the ratio of high-priority packets traversing the network to lower priority packets.

default gateway—A default gateway is a router that provides access to all hosts on remote networks. Typically, the network administrator configures a default gateway for each host on the network.

Exterior Gateway Protocol (EGP)—EGP is the protocol used by a gateway in one AS to advertise IP addresses of networks in the system to a gateway in another AS. All autonomous systems must use EGP to advertise network reachability to the core gateway system.

EGP version 2 (EGP-2)—EGP-2 is an EGP used to exchange network reachability information between routers in different autonomous systems. In each AS, routers share routing information using one or more IGP, for example, RIP or OSPF. The routers that serve as endpoints of a connection between two autonomous systems run an EGP, such as EGP-2.

Gateway-to-Gateway Protocol (GGP)—GGP is a routing protocol that core routers use to exchange routing information between Internet routers. GGP uses an SPF algorithm.

hop count—Hop count is the number of intermediate routers that a packet must traverse to travel from source to destination in a multi-router environment.

interleaf ratio—An interleaf ratio is a value used in CoS routing that specifies the number of high-priority packets to be transmitted for each low-priority packet. For example, if the interleaf ratio is set to five, a router transmits five high-priority packets for each one low-priority packet.

Intermediate System to Intermediate System (IS-IS)—IS-IS is an OSI model link-state, hierarchical routing protocol based on DECnet Phase V routing.

Internet Gateway Routing Protocol (IGRP)—IGRP is a DVA protocol developed by Cisco Systems for use in large, heterogeneous networks. It uses metrics such as bandwidth, delay, MTU, and hop count to compute the best path to a destination network.

least-cost routing—In data networks, least-cost routing describes the methods routers use to determine the lowest cost link between networks. Least cost routing makes these determinations based on cost factors such as bandwidth, delay, and cash costs.

link-state advertisement—Link-state advertisements are sent between routers running LSA routing protocols. These are usually in the form of multicast packets, containing neighbor router information and path costs.

link-state algorithm (LSA)—Also known as Dijkstra algorithm, LSAs allow each router to broadcast or multicast network route cost information concerning its neighbors to every node in the internetwork. LSA routing protocols provide a consistent network view across all routers, and are thus not vulnerable to routing loops.

load splitting—Also known as load balancing, load splitting separates network communications into two or more routes in order to share the load among the separate links. This makes data communications faster and more reliable than does using a single path between networks.

policy routing—Also known as policy-based routing, policy routing allows organizations to implement packet forwarding and routing according to defined policies in a manner that goes beyond traditional routing protocol concerns. By using policy-based routing, organizations can implement policies that selectively cause packets to take different paths, depending on their differentiated, preferential service type.

policy-based routing—Policy-based routing allows network administrators to specify additional routing table and network model information sources. These sources may include information imported from other protocols or information network administrators statically configure. Such policies can be defined on a router-by-router basis and control the advertisement of routing information.

simple password authentication (type 2)—RIPv2 supports simple password authentication by guarding against routers inadvertently joining the routing domain; each router must first be configured with its attached networks' passwords before it can participate in routing. However, simple password authentication is vulnerable to passive attacks; anyone with physical access to the network can learn the password and compromise the security of the routing domain.

shortest path first (SPF) tree—An SPF tree is used by the OSPF protocol to graph a path between OSPF routing nodes.

type-of-service (ToS) routing—ToS routing makes routing decisions based on an IP packet's IP header ToS bit states. This allows the routers to create separate transmission paths for different service types.

variable-length subnet mask (VLSM)—VLSMs are a mechanism for providing subnets of different sizes within a single IP-address block. Routing protocols that support VLSM allow network administrators to subnet a subnet to create more subnets than the default mask will allow.

Lesson 1—IP Routing

The Internet is a large collection of networks and hosts interconnected by routers. Routers are specialized computers that connect two or more packet-switching networks.

Routers function as intermediate packet switches that forward traffic from one network to another. Routers are also called gateways in Internet literature. The Transmission Control Protocol/ Internet Protocol (TCP/IP) protocol suite was designed to provide communication services that allow an individual host to communicate with any other host on any of the networks that make up the Internet or an enterprise internetwork.

Objectives

At the end of this lesson you will be able to:

- Describe the Internet architecture
- Compare direct and indirect routing
- Describe the basic model of operation for the Internet
- Explain static, default, and dynamic routes

Key Point

Routers connect two or more packet-switching networks.

Overview of Internet Architecture

If a host on one network wishes to communicate with a host on another network, the source host must transmit the packet to a router directly connected to its local network. There are many ways a host can learn the identity of the appropriate router; we will learn of some of these throughout this unit. After receiving a datagram, the router forwards the packet through the interconnected system of networks and routers until it eventually reaches a router attached to the same network as the destination host. This final router delivers the packet to the specified host on its local network. The Internet Architecture Overview Diagram illustrates a routed network.

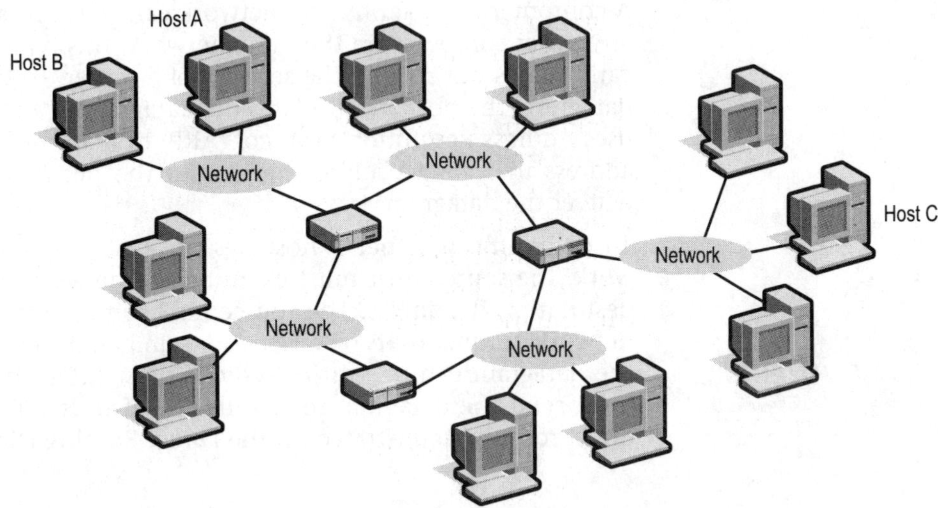

Internet Architecture Overview

Host A can communicate directly with Host B because they are both attached to the same physical network. However, if Host A wishes to communicate with Host C, Host A must transmit the datagram to the nearest exit router, also known as the default gateway, to the outside networks. This gateway router then injects the datagram into the system of routers that connect the internetwork. The datagram is passed from router to router until it eventually reaches the router attached to the same physical network as Host C. This final router uses the services provided by the local network to deliver the datagram to Host C.

A router makes its forwarding decisions based on the information contained in the router's routing table. This information includes the destination network number, rather than the actual physical address of each destination host. Because the routing table is based on network numbers rather than host addresses, the amount of information a router needs to maintain its routing table is directly proportional to the number of networks that make up the internetwork. This reduces the routing table's size, because a router does not have to maintain information about every single host connected to the internetwork.

Direct Routing

A computer on any physical network can transmit a datagram to any other computer on the same network; this type of communication does not require the services of a router. To transmit an IP datagram, the host encapsulates the datagram in a physical frame, uses Address Resolution Protocol (ARP) to map the destination IP address to a media address, and uses the network hardware to deliver the datagram.

To determine whether a host lies on a directly connected network, the source host must examine the network portion of the destination IP address. The source host compares the destination network number to its own network number. If they are the same, the datagram can be sent directly. If they differ, the source host must send the datagram to a router for delivery. The concept of direct routing is illustrated on the Direct Routing Diagram.

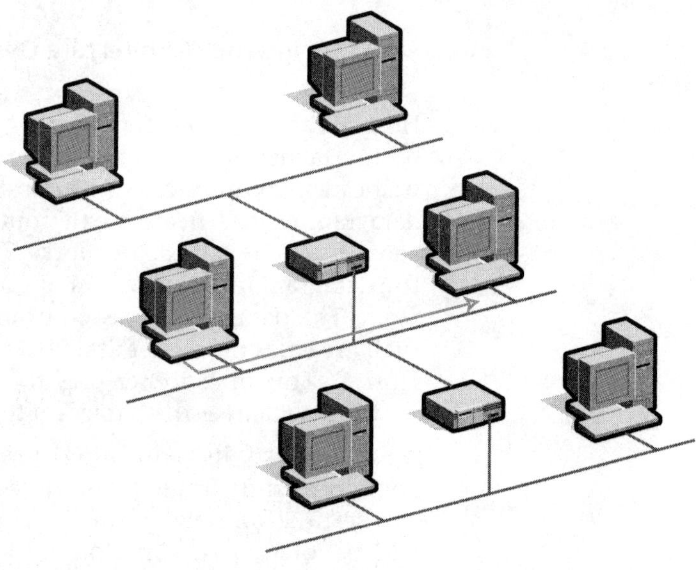

Direct Routing

Indirect Routing

Indirect routing occurs when the destination is not on a directly attached network. Indirect routing requires that the source host send the datagram to a router for delivery. This type of routing is more complex because the source host must identify not only the final destination, but also a router through which the datagram can pass. It is then the router's job to forward the datagram toward its destination network. Indirect routing is illustrated on the Indirect Routing Diagram.

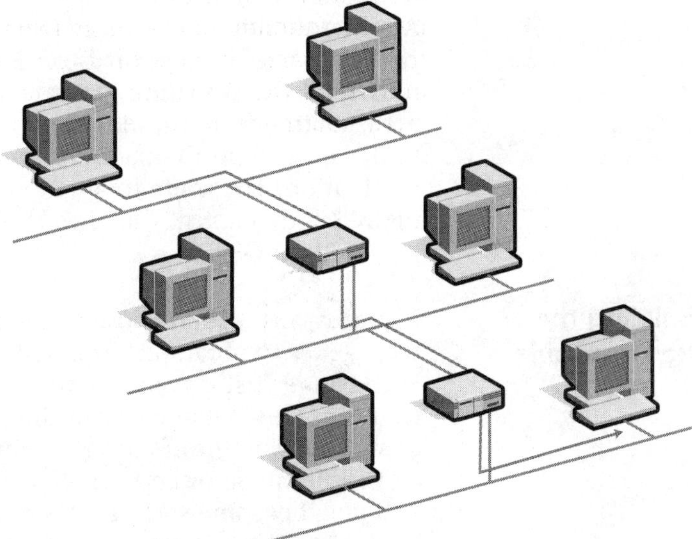

Indirect Routing

There are three different types of indirect routing:

- Static routing—These routes are configured by the network administrator. They have the benefit of reduced router overhead, no bandwidth usage passing updates between routers, and added security. Disadvantages include high administrative overhead updating and maintaining the routing entries and poor scalability on large networks.
- Default routing—These are manually configured routes designed to send any packets without an assigned route to the next hop router by means of a default router port. These can only be used on routers with a single outside interface.

- Dynamic routing—These are routes built by routers sharing routing information. Dynamic routes use routing protocols to pass routing updates between each other. Some dynamic routing protocols are Routing Information Protocol (RIP), Interior Gateway Routing Protocol (IGRP), and Open Shortest Path First (OSPF).

We will discuss these indirect routing types in more detail later in this lesson.

Routing Tables

A router examines its routing table to determine how to forward a packet. If the destination is on a directly attached network, the router can deliver the packet without using the services of another router. If the destination is on a remote network, the router must send the packet to another router closer to the final destination. The route to a remote network can be statically configured or dynamically learned through a routing protocol such as RIP, IGRP, or OSPF.

Building the Routing Table

Typically, most routers use a combination of static and dynamic techniques to obtain information needed for their routing tables. Each router first establishes an initial set of routes. This information is usually obtained by reading a basic routing table from disk at startup. The information for this table is supplied by the network administrator and generally includes the attached networks and possibly some static routes to remote networks. Another way a router might learn initial routing information is by broadcasting to other routers requests for their routing table contents.

After the initial routing table has become memory resident, the router must have the ability to respond to new routes or changes in the network topology. In a small network, the routing table may be managed and updated by the network administrator (static routes). For large networks, such as the ever-growing and evolving Internet, manual updating is too slow and labor intensive, and thus a dynamic method must be used.

The Sample Routing Table Entry Diagram illustrates a sample routing table entry. This is a typical entry for a routing protocol such as RIP, which uses hop count as the routing metric.

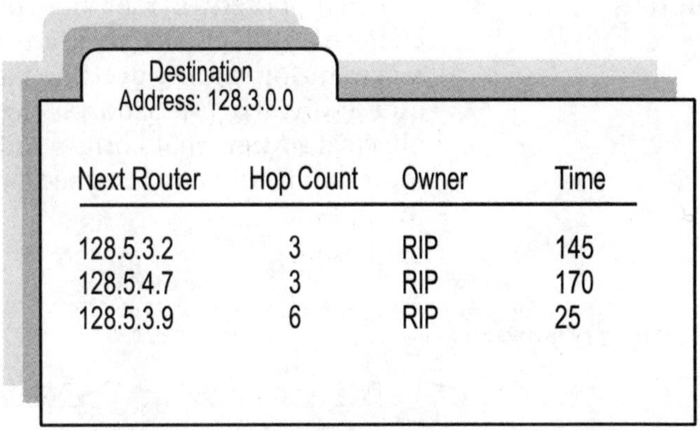

Destination Address: 128.3.0.0

Next Router	Hop Count	Owner	Time
128.5.3.2	3	RIP	145
128.5.4.7	3	RIP	170
128.5.3.9	6	RIP	25

Sample Routing Table Entry

Each entry in the routing table includes the following information that determines how a packet is routed if the router chooses that particular route:

- Destination Address—IP address of the destination network, subnets, or host.
- Next Router—IP address of a remote router to which the local router must send the packet before the packet can be routed to the destination. This is the IP address of the next hop router.
- Hop Count—Number of hops between the router and destination. Each router a packet must pass through is referred to as a hop.
- Owner—Name of the routing protocol that supplied the entry in the routing table.
- Time—Amount of time since the entry was last updated. The timer is reinitialized each time an update for a given network is received. This information "ages out" old routes.

Fundamental IP routers maintain a routing database containing only one route for each possible destination network. Some implementations, however, may contain more than one route to a destination network. The example in the diagram contains three routes to the destination network.

Sample Network Routing Table

The Sample Small Internet Diagram illustrates a small internetwork composed of four networks and three routers. The hosts attached to each network are not shown, because each router makes its forwarding decision based on a network number, not on each individual host address. Again, a router uses ARP to find the physical address that corresponds to the IP address for any host or router on its directly attached networks.

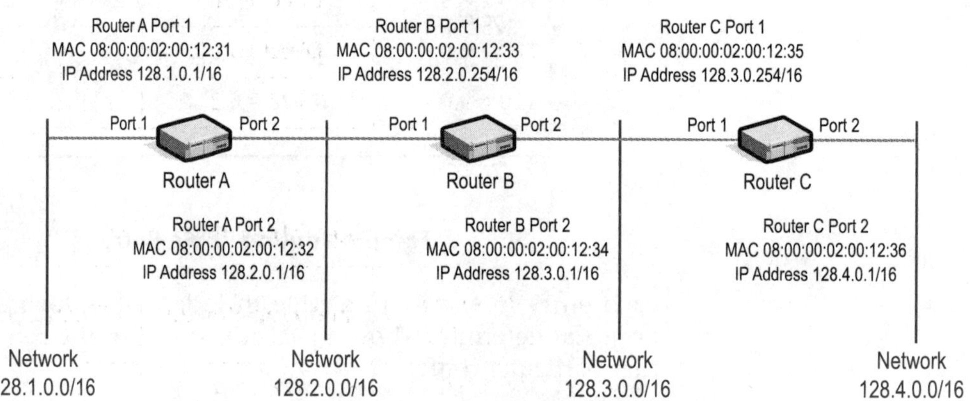

Sample Small Internet

The routing tables for each router shown on the above diagram are presented in the Routing Tables for Routers A, B, and C. The routing tables contain one entry (row) for each route. The columns of the tables include the destination IP network number, IP address of the next hop router, and metric (shown in hops, but metrics can take many forms) used to select the least cost by route if more than one route exists for the destination network.

Routing Table for Router A

Destination Network	Next Hop Router	Metric (Hops)
128.1.0.0	Direct Port 1	0
128.2.0.0	Direct Port 2	0
128.3.0.0	128.2.0.3	1
128.4.0.0	128.2.0.3	2

Routing Table for Router B

Destination Network	Net Hop Router	Metric (Hops)
128.1.0.0	128.2.0.2	1
128.2.0.0	Direct Port 1	0
128.3.0.0	Direct Port 2	0
128.4.0.0	128.3.0.3	1

Routing Table for Router C

Destination Network	Net Hop Router	Metric (Hops)
128.1.0.0	128.3.0.2	2
128.2.0.0	128.3.0.2	1
128.3.0.0	Direct Port 1	0
128.4.0.0	Direct Port 2	0

Model of Operation

The model of operation for transmitting a datagram from one host to another over an internetwork is shown on the Sample Topology of Transmission Over an Internet Diagram. This example involves a source host (Host A), destination host (Host B), three intermediate routers, and four distinct physical networks. The IP and Ethernet addresses for each host and router port are also presented.

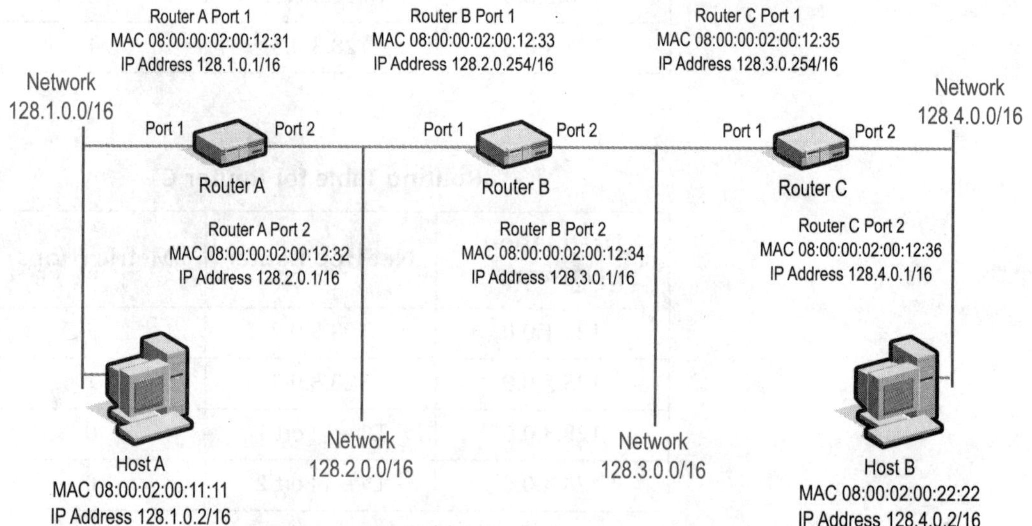

Sample Topology of Transmission Over an Internet

The Internet can be viewed as a large virtual network with the IP datagram taking the place of the network frame. The path a datagram takes is not determined by a central source, but is the result of examining each routing table used in the journey. Each router defines only the next hop in the path and relies on the next hop router to send the IP packet on its way. Intermediate routers pass the datagram up to the IP layer, which routes it back out again onto a different network. Only when the datagram reaches the final destination does the local IP process extract the message and pass it up to the higher protocol layers.

Host A

Host A on Network 128.1.0.0 wishes to make a connection to Host B on Network 128.4.0.0 using the Telnet protocol (illustrated on the next four diagrams). As the packet moves from router to router, the next four diagrams show how the IP header defined by Host A remains constant and does not change. The only addresses that change as the packet moves toward its final destination are the source and destination Ethernet addresses.

Packet on Network 128.1.0.0

Because Host A and Host B are on different networks, Host A must perform indirect routing and use the services of an IP router. Upon initialization, Host A has learned that the IP address of its default gateway is 128.1.0.1. As a result, Host A knows it must use Router A to transmit a packet to any host residing on a different network. If Host A does not have an entry in its ARP cache for device 128.1.0.1, it will issue an ARP request and wait for Router A to respond.

When it has an ARP cache entry for its default router port, Host A transmits an Ethernet frame with a destination Medium Access Control (MAC) address of 080002001231 (Router A), source MAC address of 080002001111 (Host A), and Type field of 0800h (IP). The structure of the packet placed on Network 128.1.0.0 is shown on the Packet on Network 128.1.0.0 Diagram.

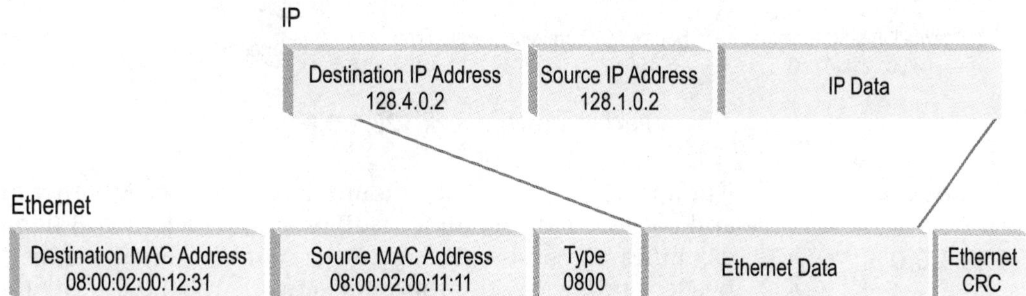

Packet on Network 128.1.0.0

Packet on Network 128.2.0.0

Upon receipt of the packet, Router A removes the Ethernet header and passes the datagram to its IP process. The IP process examines the destination network number contained in the IP header, and locates the route to Network 128.4.0.0 in its routing table (see Routing Table for Router A).

Router A knows that the destination network is two hops away, and that it must forward the datagram to Router B at IP address 128.2.0.254. If Router A does not have the address mapping in its ARP cache, it will make an ARP request and wait for Router B to respond.

Finally, Router A transmits an Ethernet frame on Port 2 with a destination MAC address of 080002001233 (Router B) and a source MAC address of 080002001232 (Port 2 of Router A). The structure of the packet placed on Network 128.2.0.0 is shown on the Packet on Network 128.2.0.0 Diagram.

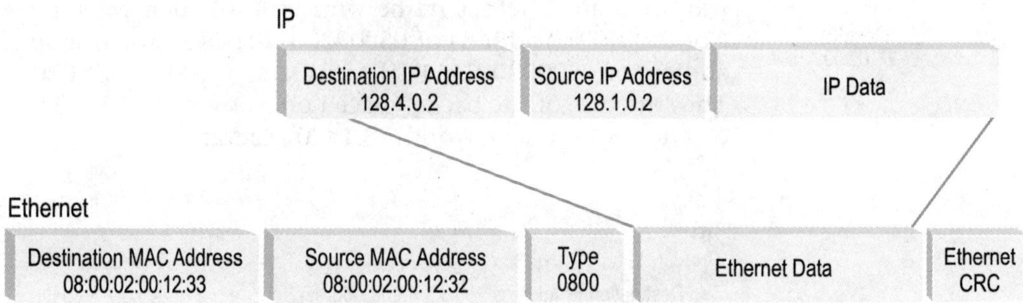

Packet on Network 128.2.0.0

Packet on Network 128.3.0.0

Upon receiving the packet, Router B removes the Ethernet header and passes the datagram to its IP process. The Router B IP process examines the destination network number contained in the IP header and locates the route to Network 128.4.0.0 in its routing table (see Routing Table for Router B). Router B learns that the destination network is one hop away, and that it must forward the datagram to Router C at IP address 128.3.0.254. If Router B does not have the address mapping in its ARP cache, it makes an ARP request, and waits for Router C to respond.

When the mapping is obtained, Router B builds and transmits an Ethernet frame on Port 2 with a destination MAC address of 080002001235 (Router C) and source MAC address of 080002001234 (Router B Port 2). The packet's structure for Network 128.3.0.0 is shown on the Packet on Network 128.3.0.0 Diagram.

Note: Although the MAC addresses change from hop to hop, the destination and source host IP addresses in the IP datagram never change.

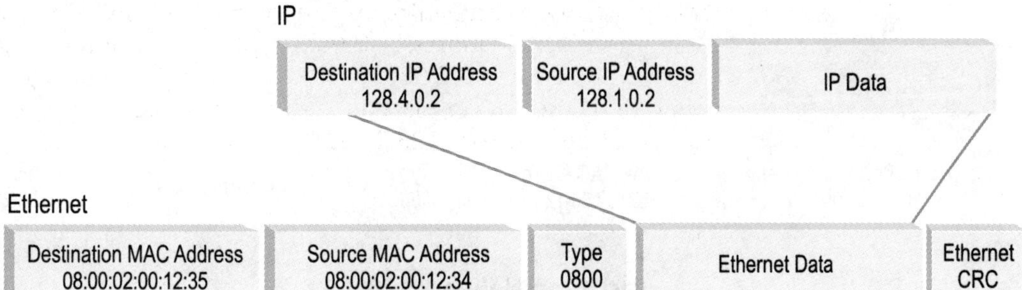

Packet on Network 128.3.0.0

Packet on Network 128.4.0.0

Upon receipt of the packet, Router C removes the Ethernet header and passes the datagram to its IP process. The IP process examines the destination network number in the IP header, and locates the route to network 128.4.0.0 in its routing table (see Routing Table for Router C).

Router C discovers that the destination network is directly connected to its own Port 2, and that it does not need to send the datagram to another router. In other words, Router C can deliver the datagram directly. If Router C does not have the address mapping in its ARP cache, it makes an ARP request and waits for Host B to respond.

When it has the mapping, Router C builds and transmits an Ethernet frame on Port 2 with a destination MAC address of 080002002222 (Host B) and source MAC address of 080002001236 (Port 2 of Router C). The structure of the packet placed on Network 128.4.0.0 is shown on the Packet on Network 128.4.0.0 Diagram.

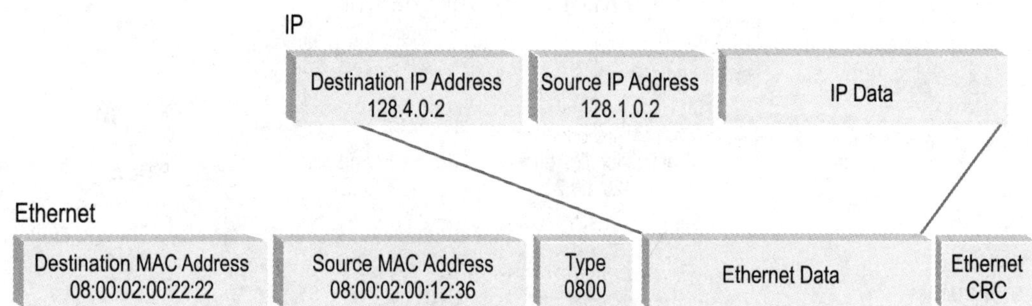

Packet on Network 128.4.0.0

Host B

Host B receives the packet, removes the Ethernet header, and passes the request to the IP module. The IP process determines that the datagram is addressed to the local host, removes the IP header, and passes the datagram to TCP for further processing. TCP examines the port number and passes the datagram to the input queue for the Telnet process.

Static Routing

Routing is the process of a router finding and choosing a path for a packet to its destination. As we learned earlier, there are three types of routing; the first we discuss is static routing.

In static routing, a network administrator must sit down at a router console or Telnet session and enter each destination network and the associated next hop address. Static routes are best used on stub networks, that is, networks with only one entry and exit point. The Sample Small Internet Diagram illustrates a stub network; network 128.1.0.0 has only one entry and exit point into and out of the local network segment. This network is a potential candidate for a static routing table.

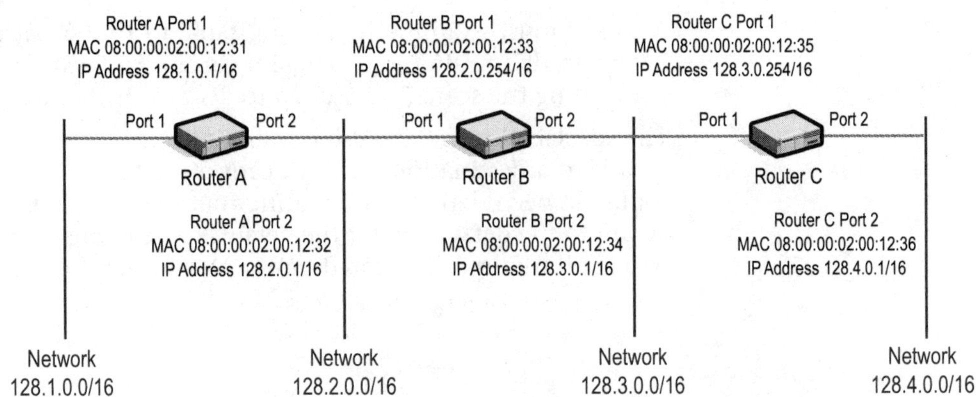

Sample Small Internet

By defining static routes, we can ensure that our packets only take one path to their destination. This could be preferential routing behavior if we only wanted our packets to traverse a particular link between networks. Static routes also protect network topology information, providing added network security. Dynamic routing protocols share network topology information with other routers, exposing information about the internal network we might want to protect. Static routes share no information between routers.

Characteristics of static routing include the following:

- The network administrator keeps a table of networks, and manually updates these tables whenever there is a change within the routing domain.
- Static systems do not operate well in an environment of rapid growth or change. Routing tables cannot be completely responsive in case of failure, because backup routes may need to use the resources of a failed network or device.
- As new networks are added and the physical topology changes, every router in the routing domain must have its tables manually updated. This can require a tremendous amount of time on the part of the network administrator.

Errors in the configuration of static routing tables in large networks may not be easy to find or correct. Static routes require the network administrator to have a good understanding of the network's topology.

Default Routes

A router must examine its routing table to find a path for each datagram. If a route for a datagram cannot be located, the router performing the search is required to discard the packet.

The special address 0.0.0.0/0 is used to describe a default route. If a path to a destination network cannot be located and a default route has been defined, the routing routines will forward the datagram to the default router the default route defines. The concept of default routes is illustrated on the Default Routes Diagram.

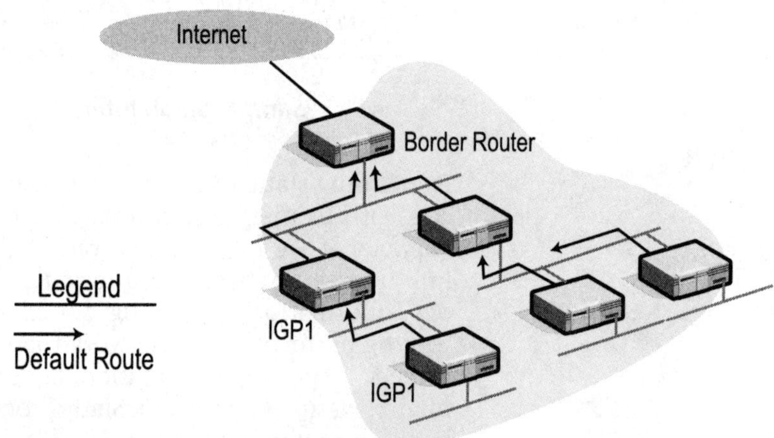

Default Routes

Here, a border router connects the internal subnetworks to the Internet. The internal routers run an Interior Gateway Protocol (IGP), which is a routing protocol used to share routing information within an autonomous system (AS). The border router runs an Exterior Gateway Protocol (EGP), to share routing information with exterior routers. The interior nodes pass routing information between each other and the border router, but are not aware of routes to networks outside of their AS. Instead, when the interior routers need to access a host on an exterior network, they send the packets to the port specified in their default route entries.

Default routes are only suitable for use on stub networks. If we had a router with two external network interfaces and defined default routes for each port, we could experience problems with routing loops and dropped or lost packets. Default routes are generally used to reduce the size of a routing table. As a result, routing is simplified, because it consists of a few tests for local networks and a default for all other destinations. Another advantage of default routes is that the size of the routing table update messages exchanged between routers can be substantially reduced (see Types of Dynamic Routing Protocols in Lesson 2). Some disadvantages of default routes include the possible creation of multiple paths, creation of routing loops, and misconfigurations.

Default routes keep the routing tables small by grouping many routing entries into a single default case, as illustrated on the Default Routes Diagram. The default routes route "up" the tree to the border router, which maintains routes to the other networks on the Internet. The border router implements policy routing and does not propagate these exterior routes to the internal network routers. As a result, the size of the routing table update messages exchanged among internal routers are also greatly reduced. The size of the routing tables maintained at each router can also be reduced.

Dynamic Routing

Dynamic routing protocols share routing information with associated routers. These associated routers can be connected directly, as is the case with RIP, or routers defined within an AS, as in IGRP. We will discuss both of these routing protocols in more detail later in this unit.

Dynamic routing is much less administration intensive than static or default routes, but this comes at a price. Dynamic routing updates use router resources, in the form of increased central processing unit (CPU) and memory usage, when building and sharing routing table updates, and increased network bandwidth usage when routers send and receive updates to and from other routers. Dynamic routing allows routers to choose the best of a number of possible routes between networks based on metrics, such as hop count, bandwidth, delay, and other variables. We can implement load balancing and fault tolerance using dynamic routing.

Dynamic routing presents network management challenges as well, primarily in the form of routing loops. It takes time for routing updates to propagate among all the internetwork routers, thus it is possible for a router or routers to believe they have a good route to a network where, in fact, the link has failed. This routing table update propagation is called convergence, and the faster the protocol can converge, the better. If the routers have not yet converged their routing tables with other routers in the network, a routing loop can occur.

Characteristics of a dynamic routing protocol include the following:

- Dynamic routing protocols respond automatically to changes in the network topology.
- Dynamic routing schemes automatically incorporate these changes by adding or deleting entries from their routing tables.

Administrative Distances

Routers rate routing information source trustworthiness using Administrative Distances (AD). A vendor assigns each routing type and protocol a specific default AD, and routers use these numbers to determine which route to a destination network is most trusted. Cisco Systems set their AD values from 0 to 255, with 0 designating the most trusted route, and 255 disallowing any traffic along that route. The Administrative Distances Table lists some common Cisco router AD values.

Administrative Distances

Route Source	Default AD
Directly connected interface	0
Static route	1
EIGRP	90
IGRP	100
OSPF	110
RIP	120
Unknown	255

A router will always use a directly connected interface over any other route. A router trusts a static route over any dynamically learned route. As the router administrator, you may reset a static route's AD, but on Cisco routers, it will always default to 1.

Activity

1. Fill in the table with the appropriate information. Note that there will always be one port number associated with the sending and receiving applications. There will always be one IP number. However, there may be multiple local area network (LAN) IDs because frames are built when packets are sent across a network. This exercise demonstrates how frames, packets, and port addresses are used together in a TCP/IP network.

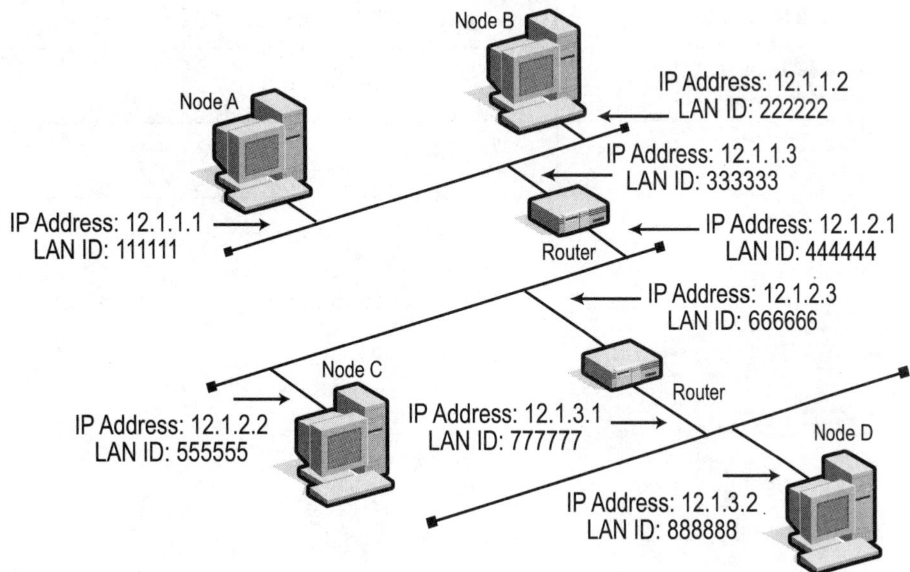

FTP Port = 21 Telnet Port = 23	Direct or Indirect Routing	Source Port	Destination Port	Source IP	Destination IP	Source LAN IDs	Destination LAN IDs
FTP from A to B							
FTP from A to C							
FTP from A to D							
FTP from D to B							
Telnet from D to C							
Telnet from D to A							

Extended Activity

1. Research and summarize the following Requests for Comments (RFCs):

   a. RFC 791

   b. RFC 793

   c. RFC 768

Lesson 2—How Routers Share Routing Information

Routing information between different networks is a complex task. This lesson covers the basic principles of moving (or routing) information between networks.

Objectives

At the end of this lesson you will be able to:

- Define AS
- Define IGP
- Define EGP
- Describe the distance-vector algorithm (DVA) routing protocol
- Describe the link-state algorithm (LSA) routing protocol
- Describe multipath routing
- Explain how a flat network is different from a hierarchical network
- Describe how routing information is distributed differently in flat and hierarchical networks

Key Point

Routers pass routing information to ensure that all routers within an AS share knowledge of the same routes.

Routing Information

During the early history of the Internet, routers that connected the various networks composing the Internet were divided into two groups:

- The first group consisted of a small set of powerful core routers operated and maintained by the Internet Network Operations Center (INOC). These routers made up the core gateway system and maintained reachability information for all networks that made up the Internet and exchanged routing information using the Gateway-to-Gateway Protocol (GGP).
- The second group of routers consisted of a much larger set of less powerful, non-core routers controlled by individual organizations. These routers provided the link between the core system and individual local networks.

The core gateway system was designed to provide reliable and consistent routes for all possible destinations. It operated as the backbone that held the Internet together and made universal communication possible. Local networks attached to the Internet used the core as a transport or "long-haul" system. The Internet Routing—Core and Transport Diagram illustrates these concepts.

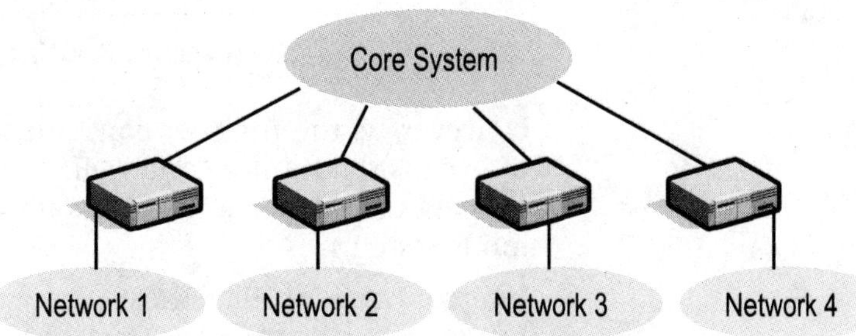

Internet Routing—Core and Transport

Autonomous Systems

As the Internet began to grow, many new routers had to be added to help interconnect the expanding network, as illustrated on the Internet Routing—Growth Diagram. In the past, such growth had taken place in a relatively unstructured and haphazard manner. New routers were simply added to the existing Internet system, with little concern for topological or other issues. The new routers were incorporated using GGP.

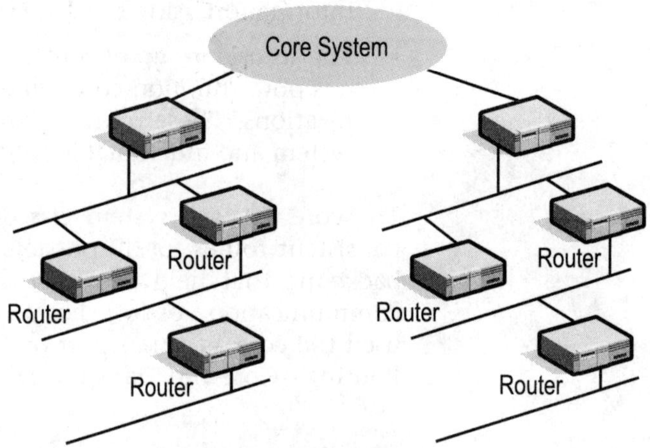

Internet Routing—Growth

However, as the Internet continued to grow, this simple method of expansion did not scale well. As a result, the Internet began to evolve into a collection of separate sections referred to as autonomous systems.

Interconnections like those shown on the Internet Routing—Autonomous Systems Diagram should not be thought of as multiple independent networks, but as a single site having multiple networks under its control. This combination of networks and routers forms an AS.

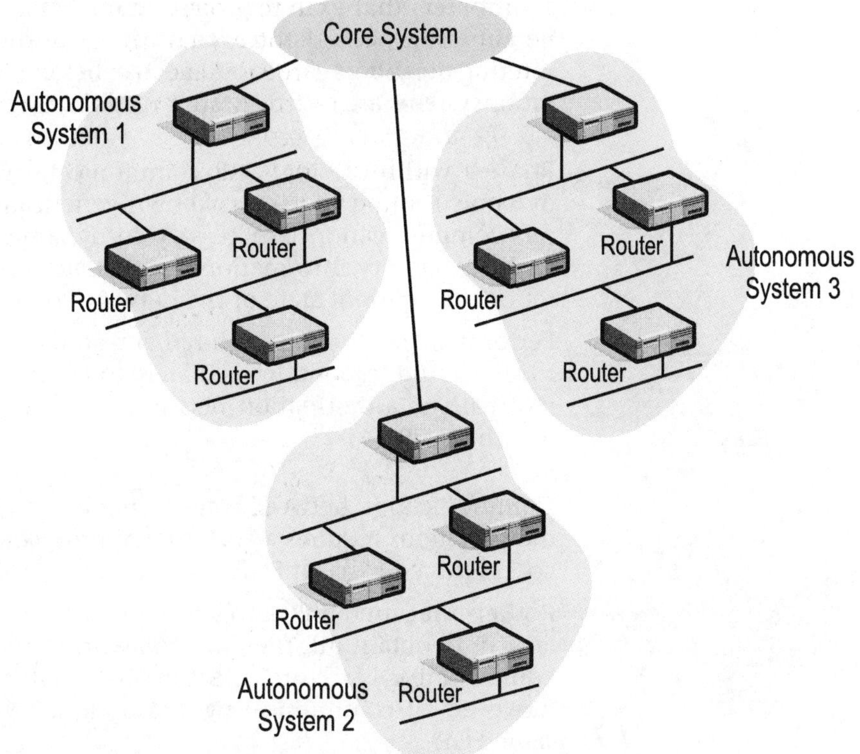

Internet Routing—Autonomous Systems

Networks internal to autonomous systems must be accessible throughout the Internet. To accomplish this, each autonomous system's network administrator assigns one of its routers the responsibility to inform other autonomous systems about the networks contained within its local AS. A separate protocol is exchanged among different autonomous systems. This protocol is referred to as EGP.

To distinguish between multiple autonomous systems, the Internet Network Information Center (InterNIC) assigns each AS a unique identifier; this number is referred to as the AS number. When two routers from different autonomous systems exchange network reachability information, the messages must contain the AS number.

Gateway Protocols

Two routers that exchange routing information are referred to as neighbors or peers. Routers that belong to the same AS are called interior neighbors, and routers that belong to different autonomous systems are called exterior neighbors.

IGPs

Routers within a single AS communicate using one of several dynamic routing protocols, known generically as IGPs. Continuous communication is necessary to dynamically update routing and reachability information within each router so it accurately reflects the current state of the network topology.

Performance is the key requirement of an IGP. The routing algorithm should respond immediately to failures and find the lowest cost path to a destination network. Two examples of an IGP are RIP and OSPF.

EGPs

Communication between routers that belong to different autonomous systems requires an additional protocol. This type of protocol is referred to as an EGP.

Routers that run an EGP to advertise reachability also need to run an IGP to obtain information from within their own AS. Each AS administrator is free to select an IGP that best fits their needs; however, all communicating autonomous systems must use the same EGP.

On the Internet Routing—EGP Diagram, an EGP allows communication between exterior neighbors (peers) in two different autonomous systems.

Note: Exterior neighbors are close to the outer border of their respective autonomous systems.

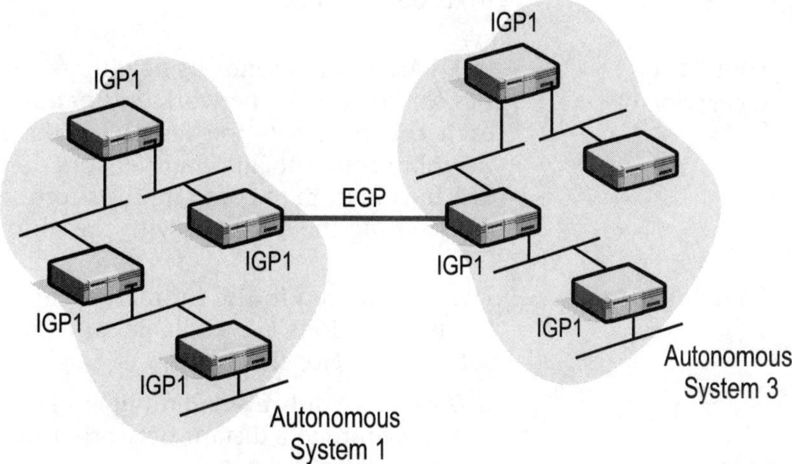

Internet Routing—EGP

There is a greater need for policy routing and control from an EGP than within an IGP. A network administrator would want to avoid remote paths that use backbones that will not accept their packets. They might also want to direct their traffic to backbones that offer an appropriate quality of service (QoS) or lower tariffs. Two of the most popular EGPs are a revision of the first EGP (EGP2) and Border Gateway Protocol (BGP).

Types of Dynamic Routing Protocols

Two types of dynamic routing protocols are used by computer networks to maintain their routing tables and calculate the shortest path to a destination. They are DVAs, also known as Bellman-Ford algorithms, and LSAs, also known as SPF or Dijkstra algorithms. All routing algorithms must use routing metrics stored in routing tables to select the best path to a destination. The shortest path between networks is determined by examining all routes to the destination and selecting the route having the smallest metric, or cost. The metric that selects the least-cost path may be hop count, transmission delay, line capacity, an administratively defined distance, or a composite metric created from two or more individual metrics.

DVAs

DVA is one method of determining routes that a packet can take to its destination.

DVA Basic Operation

In DVAs, a router sends its neighbors a vector of distances or metrics for all possible network destinations (its routing table). Thus, each router knows the length of the shortest path from each neighbor router to all other network destinations. The routers use this information to compute the shortest path to each destination by choosing the neighbor with the shortest available path.

DVA Advantages

DVAs have been in use for many years. As a result, many sample implementations are available, and they are well understood by software developers.

DVAs require only a small number of CPU cycles to determine the shortest route to a distant network. However, this can be misleading because of the potential slow convergence problem that may require multiple updates. These simple calculations may have to be performed many times before routes stabilize and the network enters a state of convergence.

DVA Disadvantages

Depending on the size of the network, the amount of information exchanged between neighbors can be quite large. This is especially true in a routing domain containing many networks and having a complex topology. In DVAs, each router transmits information to its neighbors about its routes to every other destination network. It is impossible for other routers to check this information for accuracy, and as a result, it is difficult for a router to automatically ignore information provided by misbehaving routers. In addition, because the information transmitted by each router is a function of the information that it receives from its immediate neighbors, identifying a misbehaving router supplying inaccurate data is quite difficult.

A change in the routing table of a single router can result in a chain of updates. It can take a considerable amount of time for this information to reach all other routers in the routing domain. As a result of the slow propagation of routing information, DVAs can form routing loops, and be slow to converge. This slow convergence can lead to route instability and increased overhead.

Finally, DVAs do not scale well and experience problems in very large networks because of the potential for slow convergence.

LSAs

LSAs are the second classification of routing protocols used in TCP/IP networks.

LSA Basic Operation

In LSAs, each router must know the entire network topology before computing the shortest path to each destination network. Each router floods update messages to every other router in the routing domain. These messages contain the metric and state of each of the router's attached links. Routes are consistent because every router is using the identical routing algorithm on an identical database. A local router reports any topology changes it detects by broadcasting or multicasting to all other routers in the routing domain. Each node has all the information required to calculate the minimum cost route from itself to any other network in the routing domain.

LSA Advantages

Each router maintains a consistent view of the network, thus eliminating problems of looping and slow adjustment to changes in network conditions. Misbehaving routers are easier to detect when using an LSA, because each router maintains an identical link-state database. Because each router reports on the state of its own links to its neighbors, information from a suspect router may be compared to what a neighbor router is reporting. The link may be considered operational only if each end of the link agrees on the link's state.

LSAs can eliminate problems that occur in very large networks because of their ability to partition an AS into areas. The LSA is calculated on a per-area basis. Inter-area destinations are learned from routers connected to more than one area.

LSA Disadvantages

An excessive amount of memory and communication overhead may be required in large networks, because each router must maintain an up-to-date database containing the entire network topology. LSAs require a larger amount of CPU time per calculation compared to DVAs. However, because new routes are calculated directly, rather than converging toward the solution, the additional CPU requirements are offset by the need to only perform the calculation once.

Multipath Routing

For each destination address (network, subnetwork, or host), some routers may support multiple routes. This means the router can forward packets to the destination through several routes. These routes, either learned or configured, are stored in the routing table.

The ability to route packets through different routes is called multipath routing. Advantages of multipath routing are:

- If the primary route fails, the router can still forward a packet using an alternative route. As a result, the router can immediately respond to network topology changes.
- If there is more than one best-cost route, the network administrator may elect to have the router split the load between the equal-cost routes on a round-robin basis.

When multiple routes exist, the router selects the route with the highest precedence. An example of ordering for route precedence (from highest to lowest precedence) is given below:

1. Static route added without the ability to be replaced by a dynamic route (allows the network administrator to dictate the route despite the existence of a lower cost dynamic route)
2. Route learned using OSPF
3. Route learned using RIP
4. Route learned using an ICMP redirect message
5. Route learned using EGP
6. Static route added with the ability to be replaced by a dynamic route (allows a dynamic route to always take precedence over a static route even if the static cost is lower than the dynamic cost)

If the route with the highest precedence fails, the route with the next highest precedence is used.

Router-Based Network Architectures

The choice of a routing algorithm determines how a network of routers works together and the type of functions each router can perform. There are two types of router-based network architectures in use today:

- Flat—A flat network is like a mesh that connects all routers at the same logical level. The internetwork is not divided into specific areas or specialized functions. In a flat network, there is no distinction between different parts of the network, and all routers play an equal role.
- Hierarchical—A hierarchical network is divided into logical areas and levels. Routers perform different tasks based on their functional position within an area or level.

Flat Router Networks

DVAs, used in routing protocols such as RIP and Inter-Domain Routing Protocol (IDRP), create flat networks.

Flat Networks Are Simple

A flat network is relatively simple, because every router performs the same job in the same way. DVA protocols figure distance based on hop count only, which demands less processing from each router. As a result, DVA-based protocols are common in small router networks.

Flat Networks Are Less Efficient

Unfortunately, this simplicity makes a flat architecture a poor choice for a large network. A protocol such as RIP is inherently inefficient, because it requires every router in a network to frequently exchange a complete routing table with every other router. This approach is acceptable in small groups of routers; however, it quickly becomes a problem as the number of routers increases.

Flat network architectures are also susceptible to routing loops that can cause duplicate update messages to chase themselves through the network. If updates arrive too slowly, a router could receive data packets before it receives routing information indicating where to send the packets. In that case, the router generates additional address-request messages, potentially congesting the network. The presence of loops in a flat network can indicate the network will take a long time to converge.

Hierarchical Networks

In contrast to a flat network, in which all routers are equal, a hierarchical network is typically composed of two levels:

- Routers on Level 1 are generally used for communication within defined areas of the network. Each Level 1 area may consist of several network segments.
- Higher performance routers form a special area called the backbone area. Level 2 backbone routers transmit packets between Level 1 areas, but not directly to end nodes.

LSAs, used in routing protocols such as OSPF and Intermediate System to Intermediate System (IS-IS), create hierarchical networks.

Hierarchical Networks Control Routing Table Updates

The backbone can restrict the dissemination of routing information changes that affect only one Level 1 area. Such messages are not passed along to stations that do not have a "need to know." For example, on the Hierarchical Routed Network Diagram, changes in Area A (Level 1) may only need to be communicated to the backbone routers (Level 2), rather than the entire network.

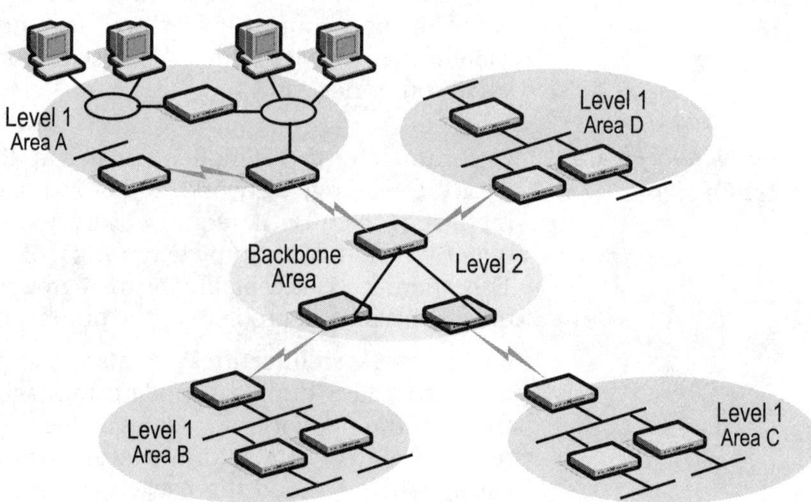

Hierarchical Routed Network

Hierarchical Networks Can Eliminate Routing Loops

The problem of routing loops is solved in hierarchical networks, because path redundancy is provided by the network's backbone area. In hierarchical networks, routing loops are not needed to provide this redundancy and can be avoided altogether.

Simpler Hierarchies Using LSAs

Both the DVA and LSA protocol environments can implement hierarchical architectures. However, LSA routing tables already include topologic data, such as network segment interconnection, necessary to create such architectures. On the other hand, the typical DVA routing table must be manually augmented to create hierarchical architectures in DVA-based protocol environments. Use of an LSA-based protocol makes it simpler to create hierarchical networks, and may save network administrators a considerable amount of time and trouble.

Activities

1. Which of the following protocols do autonomous systems use to exchange routing information between themselves?
   a. IGRP
   b. IGP
   c. EGP
   d. DVA
2. Which of the following is the generic routing protocol type that routers use to communicate within an AS?
   a. IGP
   b. EGP
   c. BGP
   d. IDRP
3. Which two choices are EGP examples? (Choose two.)
   a. OSPF
   b. RIP
   c. EGP2
   d. BGP
4. Which of the following is another name for a DVA?
   a. Dijkstra algorithm
   b. SPF algorithm
   c. Bellman-Ford algorithm
   d. LSA
5. Which three of the following are examples of dynamic routing protocol metrics? (Choose three.)
   a. Hop count
   b. Router capacity
   c. Line capacity
   d. Transmission delay

6. Which routing type allows networks to recover from failed routes?
   a. Multipath routing
   b. Dynamic routing
   c. Static routing
   d. Redundant routing
7. Which type of network architecture allows routers to perform different tasks depending on their functional position within an area?
   a. Flat
   b. Divided
   c. Tiered
   d. Hierarchical

Extended Activity

Given the Gateway Protocols Diagram, fill in each blank with the appropriate gateway protocol type (EGP or IGP). Be prepared to defend your choices.

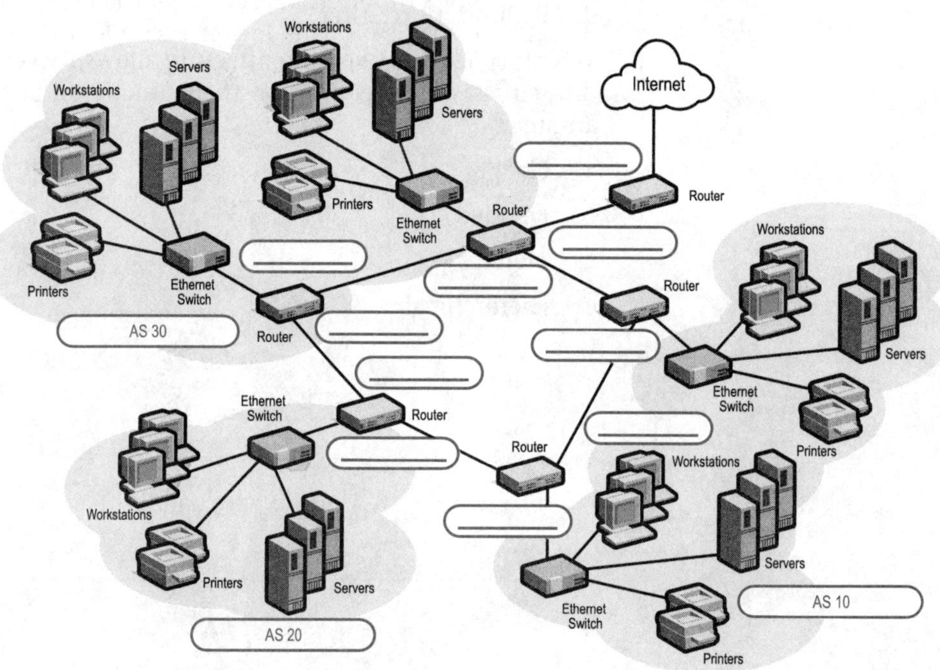

Gateway Protocols

Lesson 3—RIP

As we learned in Lesson 2 of this unit, routers within the same AS are described as being interior in relation to one another. These interior routers use various flavors of IGPs to build routing tables that describe their AS.

Each AS may use a different IGP. Some of the most common IGPs are RIP, IGRP, and OSPF. This lesson presents a detailed description of the way interior routers use RIP to maintain consistent routing information within an AS.

Objectives

At the end of this lesson you will be able to:

- Describe how RIP enables dynamic routing within an AS
- Identify the key advantages and disadvantages of RIP
- Explain the difference between RIP versions 1 (RIPv1) and RIPv2

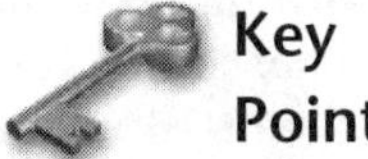

Key Point

RIP was designed to pass routing information inside of small, 15-hop autonomous systems.

Overview of RIP

RIP is a DVA routing protocol used by TCP/IP and Novell Internetwork Packet Exchange/Sequenced Packet Exchange (IPX/SPX) networks. It was originally developed for Berkeley UNIX systems and was named in part for the UNIX daemon program (a daemon is like a DOS Terminate and Stay Resident [TSR]) called routed—pronounced "route d."

RIP, using the simple DVA, was designed for relatively small autonomous systems with a maximum diameter of 15 hops. RIP routes can have a maximum hop count of 15, thus the diameter limitation. RIP considers a network 16 hops away inaccessible. This size limitation is necessary because every RIP router in an AS exchanges entire routing tables with every other router in the same AS. As the number of routers increases, there is an even sharper increase in the number of RIP messages on the network.

RIP Updates

RIP routers send routing updates to adjacent routers every 30 seconds, by default. A RIP router cannot see the network beyond its adjacent routers, and must depend on its neighbors for correct routing information. This is sometimes called routing by rumor, in that a router only knows what other routers tell it.

RIP routers pass routing updates to and from User Datagram Protocol (UDP) Port 520. RIP defines two message types: request messages and response messages. A router sends out a request message to request updates from neighbor routers. The responding router(s) send back response messages. When initialized, RIP routers send out response messages out of every RIP-enabled interface every 30 seconds.

A router stores each new route entry it receives in its routing table, along with the advertising router's address and the hop count. If a router receives a route update with a lower hop count than an existing entry indicates, the router will replace the old route with the new. However, if a router receives an update with a higher hop count than previously recorded and the update came from the same router as had previously advertised the route, the receiving router can put the new route in holddown for an administratively configured time period. Although the RFC 1058 RIP specification does not call for their use, some routers use holddowns to hold route updates to avoid advertising a brief outage across all AS routers, allowing the network to stabilize before passing on the outage information.

If the same router advertises the same route and metric again, the receiving router will lift the holddown and pass on the update. The holddowns section later in this lesson will provide more information.

RIP Stability Features

RIP specifies a number of features designed to make its operation more stable in the face of rapid network topology changes. Remember that DVA routing is susceptible to routing loops caused mainly by slow convergence; DVA stability features help control routing loops when using a DVA routing protocol. These features include a hop-count limit, holddowns, split horizons, and poison reverse updates.

Hop-Count Limit

RIP permits a maximum hop count of 15 and considers any destination network greater than 15 hops away unreachable. RIP's maximum hop count greatly restricts its use in large internetworks; however, it prevents a problem called count-to-infinity from causing endless network routing loops. The count-to-infinity problem is shown in the Count-to-Infinity Problem Diagram.

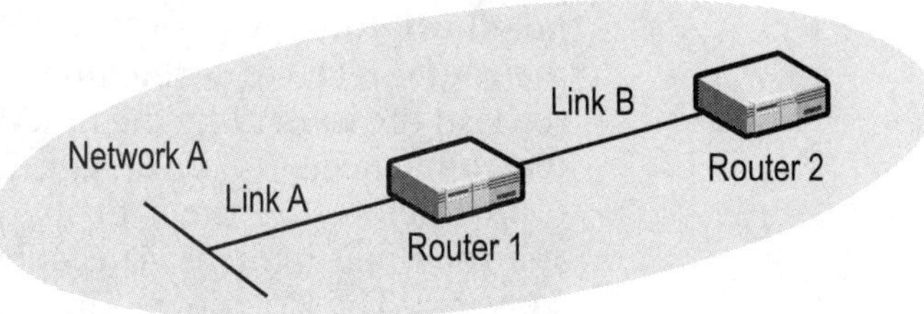

Count-to-Infinity Problem

In the above diagram, consider what will happen if Router 1's (R1's) link (Link A) to Network A fails. R1 examines its information and sees that Router 2 (R2) has a one-hop link to Network A. Because R1 knows it is directly connected to R2, it advertises a two-hop path to Network A and begins routing all traffic to Network A through R2.

This creates a routing loop. When R2 sees that R1 can now get to Network A in two hops, it changes its own routing table entry to show that it has a three-hop path to Network A. This problem, and the routing loop, will continue indefinitely, or until some external limit is imposed; that limit is RIP's maximum hop count. When the hop count exceeds 15, the RIP router marks the route as unreachable. Over time, the route is removed from the table (see RIP Timers later in this lesson).

Holddowns

Holddowns are used to prevent regular update messages from inappropriately reinstating a route that has gone bad. When a route goes down, neighboring routers will detect this. These routers then calculate new routes and send out routing update messages to inform their neighbors of the route change. This activity begins a wave of routing updates that filter through the network.

Holddowns help prevent routes from changing too rapidly by allowing time for the downed route to recover, or for the network to stabilize before changing to the next best route. They are also used to restrict routers from making route changes that might misrepresent downed routes as available. Holddowns tell routers to refrain from propagating any route changes that might affect recently removed routes for some period of time. The holddown period is usually calculated to be just greater than the period of time necessary to update the entire network with a routing change. Holddowns prevent the count-to-infinity problem caused by multiple advertisements for the same network.

When a router receives an update from a neighbor indicating a previously accessible network is now inaccessible, the router's holddown timer will start, and the router propagates the route. If the router receives a new update indicating a better metric than the last, the router lifts the holddown and passes data. However, if the router receives an update with a lower metric (higher hop count) before the timer expires, the router ignores that update and the timer remains. This allows more time for the network to converge. The Holddown Timer Diagram illustrates this concept.

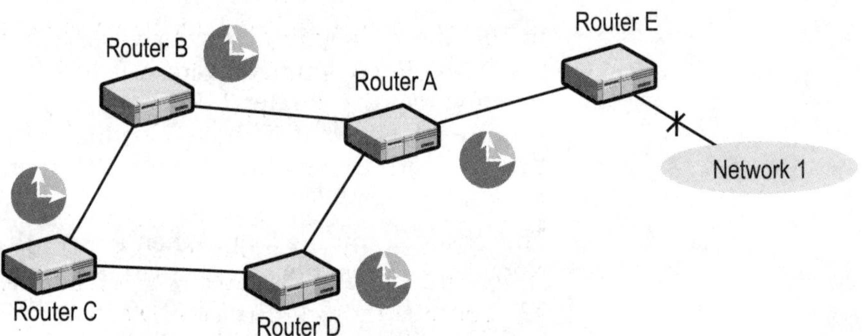

Holddown Timer

Router A receives an update from Router E that its link to Network 1 is down. Router A marks the network as inaccessible and sets a holddown timer. If Router E sends a route update indicating that Network 1 is again accessible, Router A will lift the holddown.

If, during Router A's holddown time period, Router B sends to Router A an updated route to Network 1 with a higher hop count, Router A will ignore this update. If Router A accepted this update immediately, it could end up looping packets destined to Network 1 (which is still inaccessible) through Router B. If, however, Router B sends an update with a lower hop count, Router A will mark Network 1 as accessible and lift its holddown. Eventually, all routers will stabilize and all the timers can be lifted.

Holddowns use triggered updates. Rather than wait for the usual 30-second route update frequency, network changes can trigger an immediate route update. Triggered updates do not instantly arrive at every network device. It is therefore possible that a device that has yet to be informed of a network failure may send a regular update message (indicating a route that has just gone down is still good) to a device that has just been notified of the network failure. In this case, the latter device now contains (and potentially advertises) incorrect routing information.

Routers use a triggered update timer to avoid triggered update storms on a rapidly changing network. When a RIP router sends a triggered update, it sets an update timer for a random time period (between 1 and 5 seconds); this timer stops the router from sending another triggered update for the timer period. This allows the network time to stabilize before the router sends another triggered update.

Triggered updates can reset a holddown timer. These are some instances where a triggered update will reset the holddown timer:

- The holddown timer expires
- Another update indicates the network status has changed (for the better)

Split Horizons

Split horizons derive from the fact that it is never useful to send information about a route back in the direction from which it came. Split horizons are used between adjacent routers. For example, consider the Split Horizons Diagram.

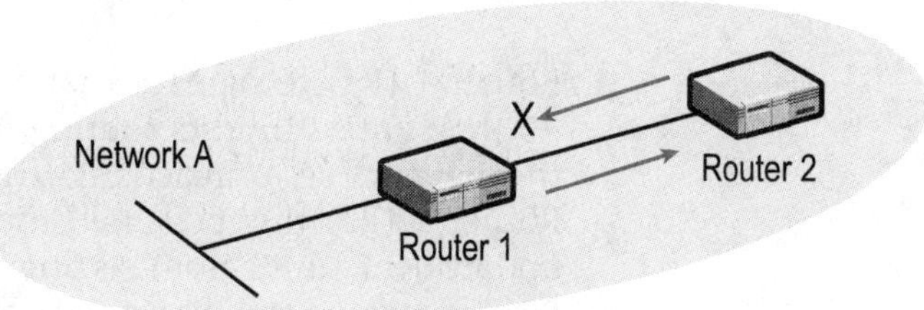

Split Horizons

Router 1 (R1) initially advertises that it has a route to Network A. There is no reason for Router 2 (R2) to include this route in its update back to R1 because R1 is closer to Network A. The split-horizon rule says that R2 should strike this route from any updates it sends to R1.

The split-horizon rule helps prevent two-node routing loops. For example, consider the case where R1's interface to Network A goes down. Without split horizons, R2 continues to inform R1 that it can get to Network A through R1. If R1 does not have sufficient intelligence, it might actually pick up R2's route as an alternative to its failed direct connection, causing a routing loop. Although holddowns should prevent this, split horizon provides extra algorithm stability.

Poison Reverse Updates

Whereas split horizons should prevent routing loops between adjacent routers, poison reverse updates are intended to defeat larger routing loops, as shown on the Poison Reverse Diagram. The idea is that increases in routing metrics generally indicate routing loops. Poison reverse updates are then sent to remove the route and place it in holddown.

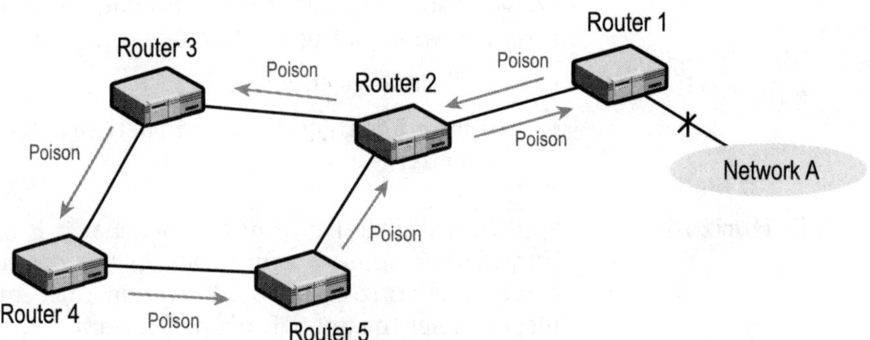

Poison Reverse

Router 1 (R1) recognizes that Network A is no longer accessible. R1 then enters into its routing table a Network A entry reflecting the network as unreachable (hop count 16). R1 then sends to Router 2 (R2) this poisoned route update, preventing any other update sent to R2 from setting an incorrect route to Network A. R2 propagates this poisoned route information throughout the AS, including back to R1. This poison reverse update is not subject to split horizon rules, as the update sent from R2 back to R1 reflects the same metric as the one R1 initially sent.

Poison reverse can speed network convergence when used with holddowns, as route poisoning can trigger route updates. Routers may propagate the poisoned update quicker than the default RIP update period of 30 seconds allows.

RIP Timers

RIP uses three timers to regulate its performance:

- Routing update timer—These set the time interval between regular route update messages. This time period is normally set to 30 seconds, but depending on the router can range from 0 to more than 4 billion seconds.
- Route invalid (expiration) timer—Determines how long the router holds active in its routing table a route for which it has not received an update. This range is also administratively alterable and varies by vendor implementation. It is set as a multiple of the routing update timer.
- Route flush timer—Also known as garbage collection, this is the time period that elapses between the time a route becomes invalid and the time the router removes the route from its route table entirely. Normally, this is configured at some multiple of the update timer, but greater than the invalid timer.

Additionally, if the vendor uses holddowns, a fourth timer is set—the holddown timer. This is set somewhere between the invalid and flush timer settings.

Novell RIP

An important feature of RIP is its ability to route both TCP/IP and IPX/SPX network protocols. Novell RIP operates similar to IP RIP, in that the protocol sends out regular updates and passes the entire routing table.

However, Novell RIP differs from IP RIP in a few ways:

- Novell RIP sends updates by default every 60 seconds.
- Novell RIP adds a new metric called ticks; a tick is 1/18 of a second. The protocol uses ticks as its first metric, and if multiple routes exist to a network, the protocol chooses the one the fewest ticks away. If the routes' tick count ties, then Novell RIP will use the hop-count metric as the tie breaker.
- Novell RIP can load share between tied routes. If the ticks and hop counts between multiple network paths tie, then Novell RIP can load share between the paths. This balances traffic across the routes.

IPX (Novell) network addresses are 10 bytes long, including 4 network address bytes and 6 bytes of host (node) address. RIP communicates the type of network address in use by the "network family" value in the RIP message, as illustrated on the Novell RIP Message Diagram. As we can see on the diagram, each 4-byte Network Address field is sufficient to carry all information required for Novell (IPX) routing.

32 Bits

0 1 2 3 4 5 6 7 8 9 10 11 12 13 14 15 16 17 18 19 20 21 22 23 24 25 26 27 28 29 30 31

Command 1-5	Version = 1	Always Zero
Family of Network 1		Always Zero
Address of Network 1		
Always Zero		
Always Zero		
Distance to Network 1		
Family of Network 2		Always Zero
Address of Network 2		
Always Zero		
Always Zero		
Distance to Network 2		

Novell RIP Message

RIPv2

RIPv1 was created before the development of subnet masks for IP addresses. When subnetting became common, RIPv2 was created to handle this additional routing information.

The four elements added to RIPv1 to create RIPv2 were:

- Route tag
- Subnet mask

- Next hop
- Authentication

It is important to remember that RIPv2 is an extension to RIPv1; it is not a new protocol. The restrictions on AS diameter (maximum 15 hops) and complexity, which applied to RIPv1, also apply to RIPv2. RIPv2 allows the smaller, simpler DVA protocol to be used in environments that require authentication or use of variable-length subnet masks (VLSMs).

The RIPv2 Diagram illustrates a network divided into subnets. Each subnet's address is now part of the extended network address created by the subnet mask in the IP address.

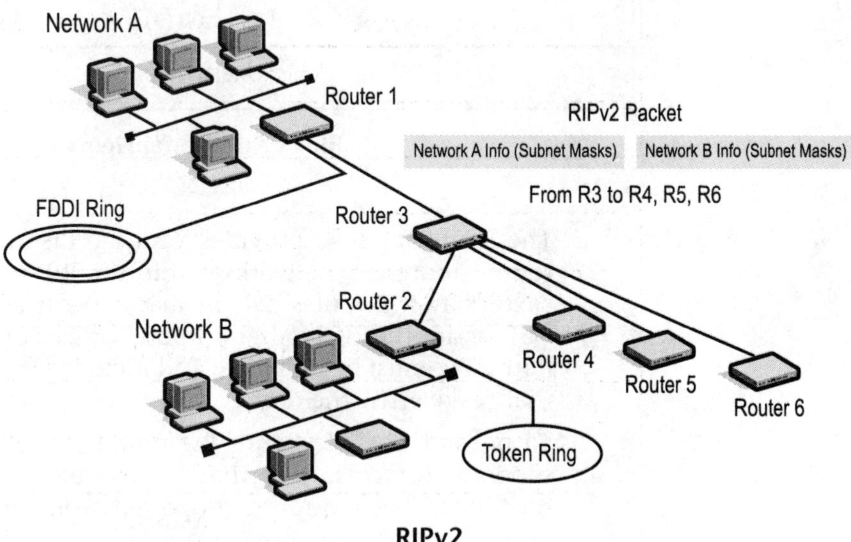

RIPv2

On the diagram, we can see that Router 3 is sending a RIPv2 packet to describe its configuration to Routers 4, 5, and 6. Router 3 is connected to two subnets (Network A and Network B); thus, Router 3's RIPv2 packet must include subnet mask information that will allow the other routers to address packets to those subnets.

RIPv2 carries this extra information by simply adding a few new fields to the existing RIPv1 packet header. The RIPv2 Additional Fields Diagram illustrates the additional fields added to RIPv2.

32 Bits

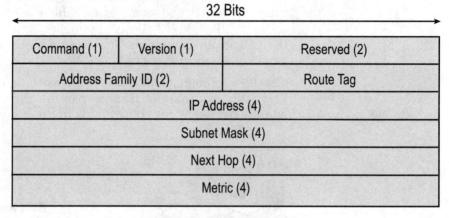

Command (1)	Version (1)	Reserved (2)
Address Family ID (2)		Route Tag
IP Address (4)		
Subnet Mask (4)		
Next Hop (4)		
Metric (4)		

RIPv2 Additional Fields

Route Tag

The Route Tag field provides a way to distinguish "internal" RIP routes (routes for networks within the RIP routing domain) from "external" RIP routes, which may have been imported from an EGP or another IGP. After a Route Tag is assigned to a route, the Route Tag must be preserved and included in future RIPv2 packets that re-advertise the route.

To prevent possible Route Tag number duplication, routers that support protocols other than RIP should be configured to reset the Route Tag for routes imported from different sources. For example, routes imported from EGP or BGP should be able to have their Route Tags set to an arbitrary value, or at least to the number of the AS from which the routes were learned.

Subnet Mask

The Subnet Mask field contains the subnet mask that is applied to the IP address to yield the nonhost portion of the address. If this field is zero, no subnet mask has been included for this entry.

Next Hop

This field indicates the IP address to which packets on the route should be forwarded. In other words, packets addressed to the destination specified in this routing table entry should be forwarded to the next hop address. The purpose of the Next Hop field is to prevent packets from being routed through extra hops in the system. It is particularly useful when RIP is not being run on all routers on a network.

A value of 0.0.0.0 in this field indicates packets should be routed by means of the originator of the RIP advertisement. An address specified as a next hop must be directly reachable on the logical subnet over which the advertisement is made.

Metric

The metric is the same as the "Distance to Network" value in a RIPv1 message. It represents the hop count to a given network.

Authentication

It is not usually important to conceal information in RIP messages; however, it is essential to prevent unauthorized people from inserting bogus routing information into routing tables. RIPv2 allows an administrator to configure each router with a simple password. Routers then use this password to authenticate RIP messages to each other.

The authentication mechanism specified in RIPv2 is less than ideal, because passwords are transmitted unencrypted and can potentially be intercepted. However, it does prevent anyone who cannot directly access the network (someone who cannot capture and analyze the RIP packets to determine the password) from damaging routing tables by inserting bogus information.

Authentication is performed for each RIPv2 message packet. Because there is only one 2-octet field available in the packet header, and any reasonable authentication scheme will require more than 2 octets, the authentication scheme for RIPv2 uses the space of an entire RIP message packet. The RIPv2 Authentication Packet Diagram illustrates this type of RIP message.

32 Bits

Command (1)	Version (1)	Reserved (2)
0 x FFFF		Authentication Type (2)
Authentication (16)		

RIPv2 Authentication Packet

If the Address Family Identifier of the first (and only the first) entry in the message is FFFF, the remainder of the entry contains authentication. This means there can be, at most, 24 routing table entries in the remainder of the message. If authentication is not in use, no entries in the message should have an Address Family Identifier of FFFF.

Currently, RIPv2 only supports simple password authentication (type 2), thus the Authentication Type field is set to 2. The remainder of the 16 bytes contains the plain text password. If the password is under 16 bytes, it must be left justified and padded to the right with nulls (00).

Activities

1. Which two protocol suites use RIP as a routing protocol? (Choose two.)
   a. DECnet
   b. IPX/SPX
   c. NetBEUI
   d. TPC/IP
2. Concerning RIP, what is meant by the term "maximum diameter of 15 hops"?
   a. The router can only have a maximum of 15 ports.
   b. The router may only connect up to 15 separate networks.
   c. Any single network cannot be more than 15 hops away.
   d. Any connected segment can only support 15 hosts.
3. Which three of the following are DVA stability features? (Choose three.)
   a. Shutdowns
   b. Holddowns
   c. Hop-count limits
   d. Split horizons
4. You maintain an autonomous routing network that runs RIPv1 as its routing protocol. You calculate that at the workday's busy hours, routing changes occurring on the nearest router take 45 seconds to propagate to the furthest router. In the past, this slow convergence has resulted in routing loops.

   How might you configure your routers to avoid creating routing loops when route changes occur within the network?
   a. Set maximum hop-count limits on all routers to 50 seconds.
   b. Set poison reverse updates on the nearest router.
   c. Set routing loop limits on the furthest router.
   d. Set 50-second route update holddowns on all routers.

5. Which RIP stability feature sets a route's hop count to 16, preventing further updates from setting an incorrect route to an unreachable network?
   a. Split horizons
   b. Poison reverse
   c. Holddowns
   d. Hop-count limits
6. Match each type of RIP timer to its description below.
   a. The amount of time between when a route becomes invalid and the router removes the route ______________
   b. The amount of time a router holds a route active when it has not received an update message for that route ______________
   c. The timer interval between regular route update messages ______________
   d. The amount of time a router refrains from updating a route which it has recently removed from its routing tables ______________

   Description

   Route invalid timer

   Route flush timer

   Holddown timer

   Routing update timer
7. Novell RIP differs from IP RIP in which way?
   a. It uses a delay metric in addition to hop counts.
   b. It adds a metric called ticks.
   c. It sends hop count updates every 90 seconds, by default.
   d. It does not use hop counts as a metric.
8. In which three of the following ways does RIPv2 differ from RIP? (Choose three.)
   a. RIPv2 adds a Route Tag routing table entry.
   b. RIPv2 sets an AS diameter of 30 hops.
   c. RIPv2 supports variable length subnet masks.
   d. RIPv2 provides update message authentication.

Extended Activity

Divide into teams of two or three people and analyze the following RIP trace. Review the RIP portion and describe what is happening. In your analysis, describe (diagram) the protocol stack showing all protocols at the correct layer of the OSI model.

RIP Trace

```
DLC: ----- DLC Header -----
DLC:
DLC: Frame 37 arrived at 13:34:00.259; frame size is 74 (004A hex) bytes.
DLC: AC: Frame priority 0, Reservation priority 0, Monitor count 1
DLC: FC: LLC frame, PCF attention code: None
DLC: FS: Addr recognized indicators: 11, Frame copied indicators: 11
DLC: Destination = BROADCAST FFFFFFFFFFFF, All Fs Broadcast
DLC: Source     = Station 000083208FEE
DLC:
LLC: ----- LLC Header -----
LLC:
LLC: DSAP = AA, SSAP = AA, Command, Unnumbered frame: UI
LLC:
SNAP: ----- SNAP Header -----
SNAP:
SNAP: Type = 0800 (IP)
SNAP:
IP:  ----- IP Header -----
IP:
IP:  Version = 4, header length = 20 bytes
IP:  Type of service = 00
IP:     000. .... = routine
IP:     ...0 .... = normal delay
IP:     .... 0... = normal throughput
IP:     .... .0.. = normal reliability
IP:  Total length = 52 bytes
IP:  Identification = 43
IP:  Flags = 0X
IP:  .0.. .... = may fragment
IP:  ..0. .... = last fragment
IP:  Fragment offset = 0 bytes
```

```
IP:  Time to live = 128 seconds/hops
IP:  Protocol = 17 (UDP)
IP:  Header checksum = BE8B (correct)
IP:  Source address = [141.1.239.1]
IP:  Destination address = [255.255.255.255]
IP:  No options
IP:
UDP: ----- UDP Header -----
UDP:
UDP: Source port = 520 (Route)
UDP: Destination port = 520
UDP: Length = 32
UDP: No checksum
UDP:
RIP: ----- RIP Header -----
RIP:
RIP: Command = 2 (Response)
RIP: Version = 1
RIP: Unused = 0
RIP:
RIP: Routing data frame 1
RIP:   Address family identifier = 2 (IP)
RIP:   IP Address = [141.2.0.0]
RIP:   Metric   = 1
RIP:

ADDR HEX                          ASCII
0000 18 40 FF FF FF FF FF FF   00 00 83 20 8F EE AA AA .@.........  ....
0010 03  00 00 00 08 00 45 00  00 34 00 2B 00 00 80 11 ......E..4.+....
0020 BE 8B 8D 01 EF 01 FF FF   FF FF 02 08 02 08 00 20 ...............
0030 00 00 02 01 00 00 00 02  00 00 8D 02 00 00 00 00 ................
0040 00 00 00 00 00 00 00 00  00 01             ..........

--------------------- Next  Frame ----------------------

DLC: ----- DLC Header -----
DLC:
DLC: Frame 38 arrived at 13:34:00.260; frame size is 74 (004A hex) bytes.
DLC: AC: Frame priority 0, Reservation priority 0, Monitor count 1
```

```
DLC: FC: LLC frame, PCF attention code: None
DLC: FS: Addr recognized indicators: 11, Frame copied indicators: 11
DLC: Destination = BROADCAST FFFFFFFFFFFF, All Fs Broadcast
DLC: Source   = Station 000083208FEE
DLC:
LLC: ----- LLC Header -----
LLC:
LLC: DSAP = AA, SSAP = AA, Command, Unnumbered frame: UI
LLC:
SNAP: ----- SNAP Header -----
SNAP:
SNAP: Type = 0800 (IP)
SNAP:
IP:  ----- IP Header -----
IP:
IP:  Version = 4, header length = 20 bytes
IP:  Type of service = 00
IP:     000. .... = routine
IP:     ...0 .... = normal delay
IP:     .... 0... = normal throughput
IP:     .... .0.. = normal reliability
IP:  Total length = 52 bytes
IP:  Identification = 44
IP:  Flags = 0X
IP:  .0.. .... = may fragment
IP:  ..0. .... = last fragment
IP:  Fragment offset = 0 bytes
IP:  Time to live = 128 seconds/hops
IP:  Protocol = 17 (UDP)
IP:  Header checksum = BE8A (correct)
IP:  Source address = [141.1.239.1]
IP:  Destination address = [255.255.255.255]
IP:  No options
IP:
UDP: ----- UDP Header -----
UDP:
UDP: Source port = 520 (Route)
UDP: Destination port = 520
UDP: Length = 32
```

```
UDP: No checksum
UDP:
RIP: ----- RIP Header -----
RIP:
RIP: Command = 1 (Request)
RIP: Version = 1
RIP: Unused = 0
RIP:
RIP: Routing data frame 1: Request for entire table
RIP:   Address family identifier = 0
RIP:   Metric    = 16
RIP:

ADDR HEX                              ASCII
0000 18 40 FF FF FF FF FF FF  00 00 83 20 8F EE AA AA .@.......... ....
0010 03 00 00 00 08 00 45 00  00 34 00 2C 00 00 80 11 ......E..4.,....
0020 BE 8A 8D 01 EF 01 FF FF FF FF 02 08 02 08 00 20 ...............
0030 00 00 01 01 00 00 00 00   00 00 00 00 00 00 00 00 ................
0040 00 00 00 00 00 00 00 00   00 10             ..........
```

Lesson 4—IGRP

IGRP is another distance-vector IGP; developed by Cisco Systems to overcome some of RIP's limitations.

This lesson presents a detailed description of the way interior routers use IGRP to maintain consistent routing information within an AS.

Objectives

At the end of this lesson you will be able to:

- Describe how IGRP improves upon RIPv1
- Identify the key advantages and disadvantages of IGRP

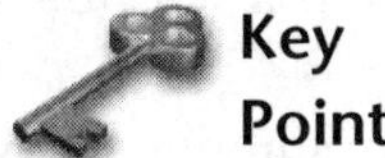

Key Point

IGRP is a Cisco Systems proprietary distance-vector protocol designed to improve upon RIP.

Overview of IGRP

Because IGRP is a Cisco Systems proprietary routing protocol, using IGRP on a network requires that all internetwork routers be Cisco routers. IGRP improves upon IP RIP in a number of ways:

- Maximum hop count—IGRP sets a maximum hop count of 255, with a default of 100. This makes IGRP suitable for large networks.
- IGRP uses different metrics than does IP RIP—IGRP's default metrics are the link's bandwidth and delay, but it can also build a composite metric using the link's reliability, load, and Maximum Transmission Unit (MTU).
- Longer update period—The IGRP default update period is three times (90 seconds) that of IP RIP.

IGRP Updates

Like RIP, IGRP is a classful routing protocol. IGRP does not pass subnet information within the route update packets. IGRP broadcasts its entire routing table to adjacent neighbor routers (with the exception of those suppressed with split horizon rules). IGRP uses split horizons with poison reverse updates, triggered updates, and holddown timers for stability.

IGRP differs from RIP in that it uses AS numbers to designate a routing domain. Route updates are limited to the routers within a specific AS. IGRP classifies route entries in one of three ways:

- Interior routes—An interior route is a path to a subnet defined from a major network directly attached to the router interface. If the directly attached network is not subnetted, IGRP will not advertise interior routes.
- System routes—A system route is a path to a network summarized by a boundary router. In other words, a system route is a route to other networks within the AS, learned from directly connected networks.
- Exterior routes—An exterior route links autonomous systems. The border router chooses a gateway of last resort, similar to a default route, from a list of available exterior routes, to which it will forward packets destined for other autonomous systems. If it knows of no better route to the destination network, it chooses the gateway of last resort.

The Autonomous System Diagram illustrates these three different routes.

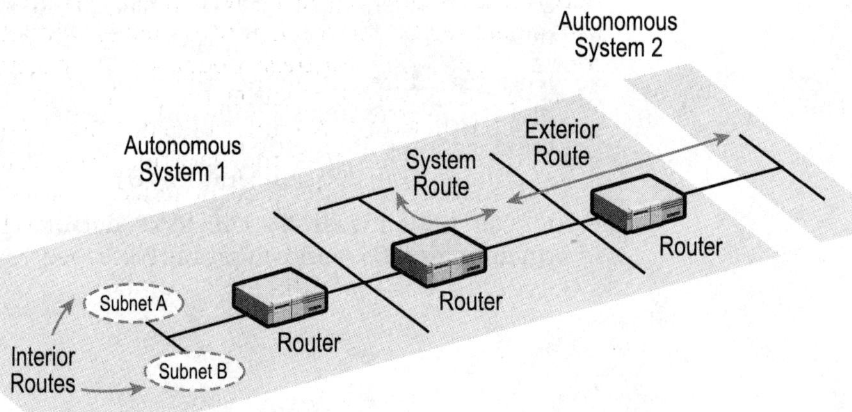

Autonomous System

An IGRP router sends route updates every 90 seconds, by default. These, like RIP updates, contain the entire routing table. The receiving router sets a new route's invalid timer to 270 seconds, three times the update timer, and sets the flush timer to seven times the update timer (630 seconds). When a router receives a new update, it resets the timers.

The router marks the route as unreachable if the invalid timer expires before the router receives an update. This invalid route is held in the route table and advertised as unreachable until the flush timer expires. The router then deletes the route from its route table.

IGRP Stability Features

IGRP's use of a 90-second update timer means updates use less network resources than do RIP updates. This can also mean that IGRP updates can propagate slower than can RIP updates. IGRP uses the following stability features to aid in faster route convergence.

Holddowns

When a router learns of a route with a poorer metric than it previously recorded, the router will accept the update and put the route in holddown. The router advertises this route change but will not update its route table with any new advertisements concerning that route, except for those received from the original route entry source.

As with RIP, IRGP uses holddowns to prevent regular route updates from reinstating a bad route. When a router learns of a change in a route's status, for instance, if the router connecting a network goes down, the routers directly attached to the failed router will recalculate their routing tables and advertise the new routes. It takes time for these updates to propagate, thus a distant router could advertise to other routers an available route to the unavailable network. An intermediate router could learn from one adjacent router that the network is unavailable, and then learn from another router that the failed network is available, but with a different metric than before. Without holddowns, the intermediate router could reinstate the failed route, advertising false information about the route's status.

Split Horizons

Split horizons apply only to adjacent routers. As with RIP, IGRP split horizons prevent a router from advertising to an adjacent router an alternative to a route the adjacent router knows has failed, creating a routing loop. Without split horizons, routers could continue routing packets to an unavailable network, using valuable network and router resources in the process.

Poison Reverse Updates

IGRP routers use poison reverse updates to mark a network as unreachable. The router that first learns of the route failure sets the route's metric to infinity (unreachable) and forwards this update to adjacent routers. These adjacent routers receive the update and place the route in holddown. They return a poison reverse update to the source, indicating that they received the original route poisoning message.

Flash Updates

IGRP uses flash updates to send an update sooner than the regular update timer setting would dictate. These flash updates work with poison reverse to quickly remove a route and place it in holddown.

IGRP Timers

Like RIP, IGRP defines several timers to regulate its performance:

- Routing update timer—This sets the time interval between regular route update messages. This time period defaults to 90 seconds.
- Route invalid (expiration) timer—Determines how long the router holds active in its routing table a route for which it has not received an update. This range is also administratively alterable, and varies by vendor implementation. It is set as a multiple of the routing update timer; the default is three times the update timer (270 seconds).
- Holddown timers—The holddown timer specifies the hold-down period. It is set somewhere between the invalid and flush timer settings, and the IGRP default is the update timer times three, plus 10 seconds (280 seconds).
- Route flush timer—This is the time period that elapses between the time a route becomes invalid and the time the router removes the route from its route table entirely. Normally, this is configured as some multiple of the update timer, but greater than the invalid timer. The IGRP default is seven times the update timer (630 seconds).

IGRP Metrics

As mentioned earlier, IGRP can create a composite metric of several individual metrics. For each path within an AS, IGRP records the bandwidth, accumulated delay, MTU, reliability, and load. It then uses variables to weigh each metric, giving bandwidth the most importance. On a network with only one medium, such as an all 100-megabits-per-second (Mbps) Ethernet network, the IGRP metric reduces to hop count alone. On a mixed media network, the route with the lowest composite metric becomes the most desirable path.

Activities

1. In which instance could you use IGRP as a routing protocol?
   a. 3Com routers in the same AS as Cisco routers
   b. Bay Networks routers in the same AS as 3Com routers
   c. Cisco routers in the same AS as Bay Networks routers
   d. Cisco routers in the same AS as other Cisco routers
2. Which two of the following are default IGRP metrics? (Choose two.)
   a. Hop count = 255
   b. Update period = 90 seconds
   c. Hop count = 100
   d. Update period = 30 seconds
3. A classful routing protocol passes which three types of information in its routing table update messages? (Choose three.)
   a. Metrics
   b. Network numbers
   c. Subnet information
   d. AS numbers
4. Which three choices are IGRP stability features? (Choose three.)
   a. Holddowns
   b. Redundant loops
   c. Split horizons
   d. Poison reverse updates
5. Which metric does IGRP use on a network with only one medium, such as one running 16-Mbps Token Ring exclusively?
   a. Delay
   b. Bandwidth
   c. MTU
   d. Hop count

Extended Activities

This activity has you configure and verify IGRP on a Cisco router. To perform this activity, you will need access to a Cisco router or a router simulator. You can gain free access to Cisco routers at **http://www.r1r2.com**.

1. Access your router or router simulator.
2. Log in to the router, and go into privileged mode by typing **enable** at the router> prompt.
3. At the router# prompt, type **config t**. This takes you into global configuration mode.
4. At the router(config)# prompt, type **router igrp 10**. This turns on IGRP routing, and sets the AS to 10.
5. At the router(config-router)# prompt, type network **10.10.4.0**. This is a network number you will advertise.

Note: The advertised network is normally a directly connected network. In this case, we are merely demonstrating the IGRP configuration process, and thus will advertise a fictitious network.

6. At the router(config-router)# prompt, type **ctrl-z**. This takes you back to privileged mode.
7. At the router# prompt, type **show ip protocol**. This shows your routing protocol information. What type of information is available here?
8. At the router# prompt, type **exit**. This will log you out of the router.

Lesson 5—OSPF

Open Shortest Path First is one of the most popular IGPs used in IP networks today. The "Open" in OSPF means this protocol is based on open standards; it is not proprietary.

Objectives

At the end of this lesson you will be able to:

- Describe the problems RIP can cause in large networks
- Explain how OSPF solves RIP's large network problems
- Describe SPF tree, Hello protocol, neighbors, and adjacencies
- Explain how routing areas work
- Describe the roles of the area border router (ABR), backbone area, AS border router (ASBR), and designated router (DR)

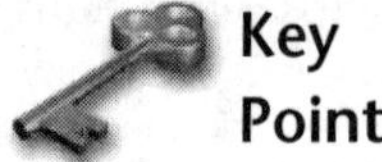

Key Point

OSPF is an IGP that can calculate "best path" in a number of different ways.

Review of Link-State Routing

OSPF uses an LSA. This algorithm provides a mechanism that maintains the status of all links to a given router and provides that information to all other routers in the domain.

Each router maintains an identical link-state database that describes the topology of its domain. When a router's link state changes, it immediately floods link-state advertisements from all ports. A link-state advertisement is a broadcast packet link-state protocols use to share information about neighbors and paths. Each router that receives a link-state advertisement adds the new information to its own link-state database, then forwards the link-state advertisement to its neighbors. In this way, all routers in the domain receive link-state advertisements and maintain identical link-state databases.

With itself as the root, each router uses this common link-state database to build its own SPF tree, which describes the cost to reach each destination network. This cost metric factors in the number of hops to each destination, as well as additional considerations such as line speed, line delay, QoS, and cash costs. The resulting SPF tree is used as the basis for creating the routing table.

The flexible and detail-rich OSPF was designed to overcome several key limitations of the RIP.

RIP Limitations

RIP was the first standard TCP/IP protocol to ensure interoperability between routers manufactured by different vendors. Unfortunately, the rapid growth in networking has pushed RIP beyond its capabilities.

RIP, a DVA protocol, has several limitations that can cause problems in large networks:

- RIP's update mechanism consists of frequent broadcasts of each router's entire routing table. In a large AS, these routing tables can become quite large, and broadcasts can consume a considerable amount of network bandwidth.
- Because of this update mechanism, RIP supports a maximum of 15 hops between destinations. A destination that requires more than 15 consecutive hops is simply classified as unreachable. This restricts the maximum size of an AS to 16 consecutive connected networks.
- RIP only considers hop count when determining the best path; RIP cannot consider a network link's speed, reliability, or delay. This means RIP sometimes fails to select the most efficient and economical path, because it bypasses faster lines with larger hop counts in favor of slower lines with lower hop counts.
- The RIP specification provides for a maximum route advertisement packet size of 512 bytes. This packet size allows for only 25 destination-hop pairs to be exchanged in a single packet. This means that 12 back-to-back RIP packets are required to broadcast a routing table containing 300 entries.
- Slow convergence is another serious DVA protocol problem. When a routing link changes in a large AS, it may take several minutes for the new routing information to propagate through the AS. During this time, routing inconsistencies can result in the formation of routing loops. Routing loops can cause update packets to circulate continuously in the AS until either the Time-to-Live (TTL) field reaches zero or the routing loop is corrected.

OSPF Solution

OSPF solves RIP's main problems, while providing many new features.

- OSPF supports configurable metrics, allowing an administrator to assign each path a cost metric based on a combination of factors, such as cash cost, reliability, delay, and hop count. For example, a fast T1 line could be assigned a cost metric of 10, while a slower 56-kilobits-per-second (Kbps) line would get a cost metric of 100. OSPF will always select the path with the lowest cost metric, regardless of hop count. Of course, an administrator can include hop count with other factors when determining the cost of a route.
- SPF technology converges quickly and is resistant to routing loops.
- Orderly update procedures reduce network traffic. Routers exchange information about changes only, and do not exchange entire routing tables. All updates are acknowledged to ensure reliability.
- All routing exchanges are authenticated. This allows only "trusted" routers to participate in routing within an AS, and prevents both accidental and malicious routing table corruption inside an OSPF-based system.
- OSPF uses multicasts, rather than broadcasts, to exchange routing updates. Only those routers and hosts participating in the OSPF protocol are included in these exchanges.
- Equal-cost multipath routing allows a router to perform load balancing over multiple routes with equal costs.
- Subnet masks can be attached to routes, thereby allowing the use of variable-length subnet masks. This feature extends the IP subnet addressing model and allows network managers to make efficient use of the IP address space.
- OSPF supports area routing. This allows the network manager to limit network-wide traffic by partitioning the AS into subdomains. Area routing provides another level of information hiding, reduces network traffic, and protects routing within an area from outside interference. Routing areas are explained in detail later in this lesson.

- OSPF supports type-of-service (ToS) routing. OSPF allows a sending host to use the IP packet header ToS field to request from an OSPF router one of several classes of service (CoSs). ToS routing is explained in detail later in this lesson.
- OSPF supports the transfer of external routing information through an AS, through external route tagging.

Routing Areas

Within an AS, OSPF allows for grouping collections of contiguous networks and hosts. One of these groups, along with the routers having interfaces connected to networks in the group, is called an area. Area routing provides three major advantages:

- Routing areas greatly reduce the amount of routing information traffic in the entire AS. Routers that belong to the same area only flood link-state advertisements within that area.
- Routers within the same area maintain identical link-state databases that describe the topology of just that area. Therefore, link-state databases are smaller, and each router in an area computes its SPF tree just for that area.
- Areas allow the development of a routing information hierarchy. Each area is protected from external routing information, and each area's information is hidden from routers outside that area. This "information hiding" is important for security, because it prohibits one area from identifying the physical topology of another area.

Area Routing Components

OSPF routing can take place at three general levels. From lowest to highest, these are:

- Routing within areas
- Routing between areas, by means of ABR and the backbone area
- Routing between autonomous systems, by means of ASBRs

ABR

An ABR is an OSPF router connected to more than one area, as shown on the ABR Diagram. ABRs handle routing between areas. An ABR maintains a separate link-state database for each area to which it is connected and creates a separate SPF tree from each of those databases.

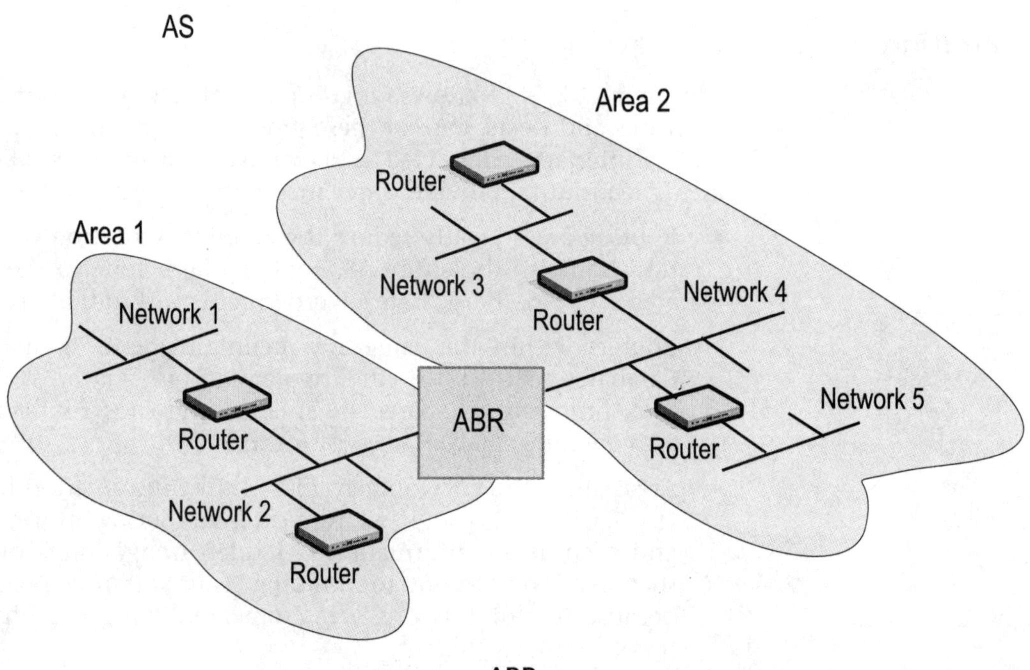

ABR

An ABR speaks for its area. It summarizes information learned from its area, then floods that information to other areas with a summary links advertisement (SLA). Each SLA includes the cost, ToS, and subnet mask for each route within the area. This tells other ABRs how to route traffic, without disclosing details about the topology of an area.

An ABR must always be reachable through intra-area routing. As long as an ABR can be reached, the networks that it summarizes can be reached. The cost to reach the summarized networks is equal to their link-state advertisement cost, plus the intra-area cost to reach the ABR.

Backbone Area

Areas are connected to each other by means of a special area called the backbone area, which is assigned an area ID of 0. As shown on the Backbone Area Diagram, the backbone area consists of those networks not contained in any area, routers attached to those networks, and all ABRs.

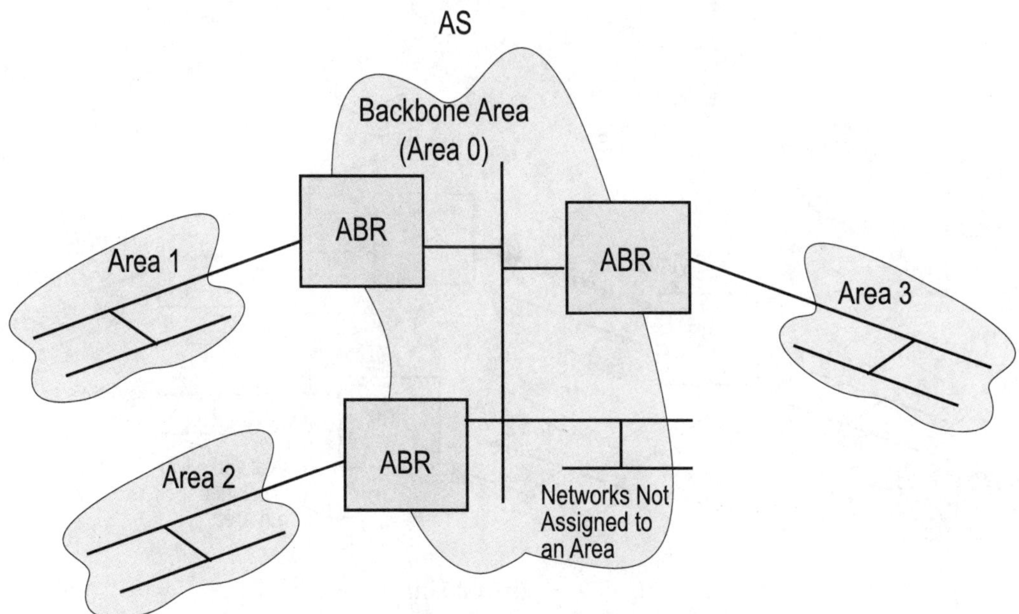

Backbone Area

The main function of the backbone area is to distribute routing information between areas. The backbone area executes the same OSPF procedures and algorithms as any other area to maintain its own link-state database and SPF tree. The backbone topology is invisible to its attached areas, and the areas' topologies are invisible to the backbone.

An ABR executes two copies of the OSPF protocol. The first copy operates on the interface connected to its local area, and accepts flooded link-state advertisements from other routers that belong to that area. A second copy executes over the interface that connects to the backbone. This backbone copy sends and receives SLAs over the backbone; thus, all areas can learn about backbone reachability without directly participating in the backbone's routing advertisements.

Virtual Links

When an ABR and its area are not contiguous to the backbone, that is, there is a break in the link between ABRs or ABRs must connect over a nonbackbone area, a virtual link can connect the ABR to the backbone. The discontiguous ABR forms one end of the virtual link; an ABR attached to the backbone forms the other. Both of these ABRs must belong to at least one common non-backbone area, as shown on the Virtual Link Diagram.

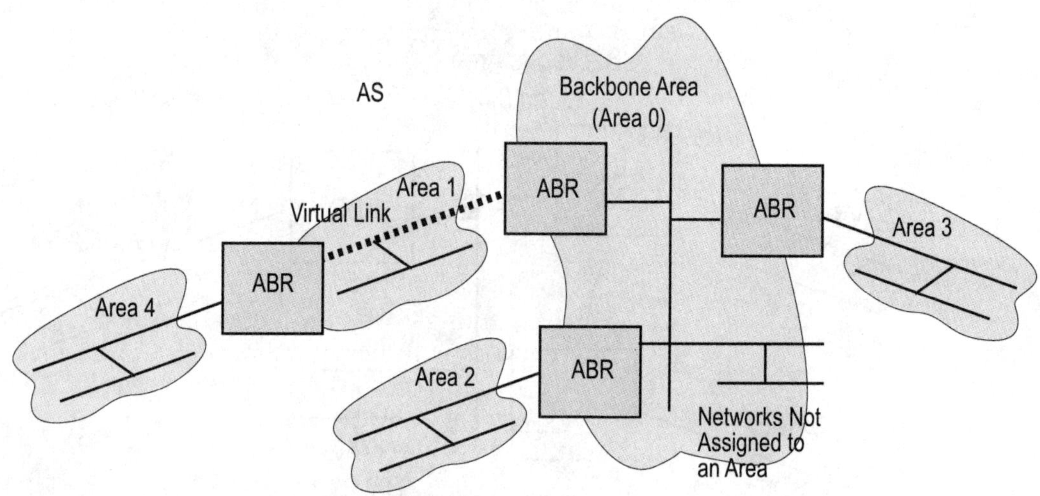

Virtual Link

The virtual link forms a tunnel over any available physical link, and thus is not associated with any one particular physical link. This forms an optimized path for routing packets between discontiguous ABRs.

When interarea routing information is flooded among backbone-area members, the backbone ABR connected to Area 1 forwards the information over the virtual link to Area 4. Likewise, when conditions change in Area 4, its ABR sends an SLA across the virtual link to the backbone.

ASBR

An ASBR is connected to routers in other autonomous systems. Just as an ABR represents its area to other ABRs, an ASBR represents its AS to other ASBRs.

Each ASBR runs OSPF on the interface to its own AS. On the interface to another AS, the ASBR runs an inter-AS routing protocol such as the EGP or BGP. These protocols allow ASBRs to exchange routing information that summarizes routes within each AS.

As an ASBR learns about a destination outside its AS (or a manually configured route, such as a default route), it shares the information with its AS by flooding an external links advertisement throughout the AS. External links advertisements are the only type of link-state advertisements flooded into every area of an entire AS.

Stub Areas

When all traffic into and out of an area flows through a single router, only that router needs to maintain routing information about other autonomous systems. Hosts in that area only need to know to send all outgoing traffic to that router. In that case, the administrator can designate the single entry/exit router as the default route for that area, and block the flow of external links advertisements into that area. This reduces the size of the "stub" area's link-state database.

Neighbors and Adjacencies

As we have seen thus far, OSPF's hierarchical approach avoids clogging the network with heavy traffic that results when every router exchanges information with every other router in its AS. In an AS that uses OSPF, a router only exchanges information with a few of its immediate neighbors. This special relationship between neighbors is called an adjacency, and it is a vital OSPF concept.

Neighboring routers are those that share a common network, or are directly connected through a serial link. An adjacency is a two-way communication between selected neighboring routers for the purpose of exchanging routing information. When a pair of routers forms an adjacency, they synchronize their link-state databases. Because every router will become adjacent to at least one other, all routers in an area will eventually contain identical link-state databases.

DR and BDR

Although a router may have many neighbors, not every pair of neighboring routers becomes adjacent. On multiaccess networks such as Ethernet, routers form adjacencies only with the designated router (DR) (and backup designated router [BDR]). Point-to-point networks do not select a DR. Establishing a DR reduces routing information traffic within individual networks, just as ABRs reduce traffic within autonomous systems.

The network administrator selects the network's most dependable router as its DR; the second-most dependable router becomes the BDR, which immediately takes the place of the DR in the event of its failure. If the administrator does not select a DR, the router with the highest configured Router Priority value becomes DR (second-highest value becomes BDR).

Forming Adjacencies

The process of forming adjacencies occurs in three phases, as described below.

Phase 1: Finding Neighbor Routers

First, a router must find its neighbors and maintain bidirectional relationships between each of them and itself. To locate its neighbors, a router sends a Hello message out all ports, targeted at IP multicast address 224.0.0.5. All OSPF routers belong to this multicast group. Each Hello packet contains:

- The router's Router Priority value, used to determine the DR and BDR if the administrator has not specified them
- Interval (in seconds) between new Hello packets from the router
- Time (in seconds) within which the router expects to receive a Hello packet from a neighbor before determining the neighbor is down
- List of routers from which Hello packets have been recently received
- Router's current choice for DR (if the administrator has not specified it)

The router's neighbors respond to the first router by sending their own Hello packets. When the first router sees itself listed in the "recently received" list of a neighbor's Hello packet, it knows that that neighbor has received its Hello packet.

After routers establish bidirectional relationships, a network's routers elect a DR and BDR based on the highest Router Priority value (if the administrator has not specified a DR and BDR). The BDR "shadows" the DR, and only takes over the DR's function if the DR fails. Remember that a DR and BDR are only necessary on a multiaccess network.

Phase 2: Synchronizing Link-State Databases

After a router has identified all of its neighbors, it begins the process of forming at least one adjacency by synchronizing link-state databases with a neighbor. On a multiaccess network, all routers become adjacent to the DR and BDR.

A pair of routers attempting to become adjacent exchange summaries of their link-state databases. Each summary is called a Database Description packet, and it contains a list of abbreviated link-state advertisements.

Based on the Database Description packet received from its neighbor, each router builds a list of requests for complete link-state advertisements, required to update its own link-state database. A router builds this list by checking its link-state database for a copy of each link-state advertisement received in the summary. If a router does not have a link-state advertisement, or determines its neighbor has a more recent version of a link-state advertisement, it adds that link-state advertisement to its request list.

The pair of routers exchange their request lists in Link-State Request packets. Each router responds with Link-State Update packets containing the requested link-state advertisements.

When both neighbors have received all requested link-state advertisements, their link-state databases are synchronized and they become fully adjacent. Each adjacent router uses its link-state database to create its SPF tree, with itself at the root, and then uses the tree to generate its routing table.

Phase 3: Maintaining Database Synchronization

Each router floods link-state advertisements to notify all routers of changes to its link state. When a link-state advertisement is flooded, it is passed from one router to its adjacent router until it has updated every router in the routing domain. Each router determines whether to pass on a link-state advertisement. For example, a router will not forward a link-state advertisement that it originally created, or a link-state advertisement that is too old.

Each link-state advertisement's age is recorded in a field in its packet header. This age value is periodically incremented while the link-state advertisement resides in a router's link-state database. If a link-state advertisement's age reaches a certain limit, it is flushed from the link-state database.

A router will also replace a link-state advertisement with a more recent version received from adjacent neighbors. Routers detect new link-state advertisements by a 32-bit link-state sequence number, which is also part of the packet header. Each time a router generates a new link-state advertisement, it uses the next available sequence number.

The link-state advertisement flooding process is reliable because an adjacent router that receives or forwards a link-state advertisement must send an acknowledgment message to the router that originates the link-state advertisement. The source router retransmits a link-state advertisement until it is acknowledged.

Link State Advertisement Types

OSPF defines multiple packet types. Each packet type carries within it an LSA message payload. Several packet types (Database Description, Link State Update, Link State Acknowledgement) define an LSA Message payload. This LSA Message carries within it a header containing information concerning the message's age, the router type from which the packet originated, and other information. The Link State Advertisement Header Diagram illustrates this header's format.

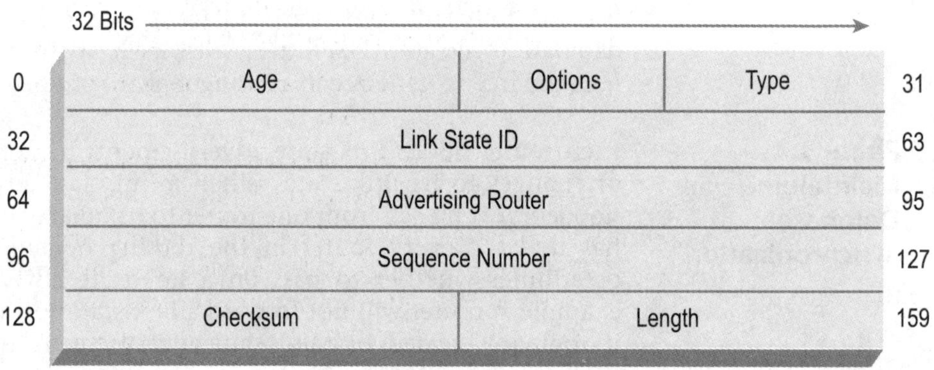

Link State Advertisement Header

For example, when an OSPF router builds an adjacency, it sends an OSPF Database Description packet containing LSAs as the message field content. The LSA Header specifies the following:

- Age—This is the time in seconds since the LSA was originated.
- Options—Specifies the OSPF domain's optional capabilities.

- Type—OSPF defines several router types (area routers, ABRs, and ASBRs). To identify the router type originating an LSA Message, OSPF includes a Type field in the LSA Message header. Some router type examples are:
  - Type1 (Router LSA)—Every OSPF router produces this LSA. It lists a router's link state to the area, along with the outgoing link cost. OSPF floods these LSAs only within the originating area.
  - Type 2 (Network LSA)—DRs initiate Network LSAs. These LSAs advertise a multi-access network and all routers attached to it. As with Router LSAs, OSPF floods these LSAs only within the originating area.
  - Type 3 (Network Summary LSA)—These LSAs advertise networks external to an area, including default routes. OSPF floods these LSAs only into a single area.
  - Type 4 (ASBR Summary LSA)—ASBR Summary LSAs advertise ASBRs external to an area. As with Network Summary LSAs, OSPF floods these LSAs only into a single area.
  - Type 5 (AS External LSA)—ASBRs originate AS External LSAs. These LSAs advertise destinations external to the OSPF AS, including default routes to external destinations. OSPF floods these into all the OSPF domain's nonstub areas.
- Link state ID—Identifies the portion of the OSPF domain described by the LSA.
- Advertising router—The advertising router is the router ID of the router originating the LSA.
- Sequence number—The originating router increments the sequence number each time it sends out an LSA. This helps other routers identify the most recent instance of the LSA.
- Checksum—Used to verify the LSA's validity.
- Length—Specifies the LSA's length, in octets.

ToS Routing

The IP header contains a 4-bit ToS field, used by a source host to request a particular type of routing service. Each bit represents one service factor, as shown in the ToS Field Table.

ToS Field

Bit Position	Delay	Throughput	Reliability	Cost
Set to 1	Low delay	High throughput	High reliability	Low cost
Cleared to 0	Normal delay	Normal throughput	Normal reliability	Normal cost

By setting or clearing different combinations of bits in the ToS field, a host can select up to 16 different types of routing service. Each ToS, from ToS 0 to ToS 15, is the decimal equivalent of its 4-bit field value, as shown in the ToS Values Table.

ToS Values

ToS Value	ToS Field	ToS Requested
ToS 0	0000	Default: all factors normal
ToS 1	0001	Low cost
ToS 2	0010	High reliability
ToS 3	0011	High reliability, low cost
ToS 4	0100	High throughput
ToS 5	0101	High throughput, low cost
ToS 6	0110	High throughput, high reliability
ToS 7	0111	High throughput, high reliability, low cost
ToS 8	1000	Low delay
ToS 9	1001	Low delay, low cost
ToS 10	1010	Low delay, high reliability

ToS Values (Continued)

ToS Value	ToS Field	ToS Requested
ToS 11	1011	Low delay, high reliability, low cost
ToS 12	1100	Low delay, high throughput
ToS 13	1101	Low delay, high throughput, low cost
ToS 14	1110	Low delay, high throughput, high reliability
ToS 15	1111	Low delay, high throughput, high reliability, low cost

An OSPF router can use a packet's ToS field to choose its best route. To do this, it first creates a separate SPF tree and routing table for each ToS. For example, assume a router can reach the same destination by means of two paths: a satellite link and 56-Kbps telephone line. The satellite offers high throughput, but with a high delay. To direct high-throughput applications (such as file transfers) over the satellite link, the administrator sets the ToS 4 metric lower on the satellite link than on the 56-Kbps line. On the other hand, the slower 56-Kbps line offers low delay. Thus, to guide low-delay applications (such as interactive processes) over the telephone line, the administrator sets the ToS 8 metric lower on the telephone line than the satellite link.

Therefore, an OSPF router uses its ToS 4 routing table to direct ToS 4 traffic (to the satellite), and it uses its ToS 8 table to direct ToS 8 traffic (to the telephone line). If a preferred link goes down, a router can still route traffic over a less-desirable link, using the ToS 0 (default: normal service) routing table. Routers use the ToS 0 table for any ToS request not specified in its routing table.

Creating a separate SPF tree and routing table for each ToS can be expensive in terms of router memory and CPU cycles. Therefore, OSPF allows an administrator to configure OSPF routers to calculate and use only a single ToS 0 routing table. A router that uses a single table informs its peers by clearing the "ToS-capable" bit in the header of its Router Links Advertisement packets (0 = not ToS-capable). The multiple-table routers will attempt to bypass single-table routers when forwarding nonzero ToS traffic. However, if a route cannot be found that uses a non-zero ToS value, the traffic is forwarded along the ToS 0 route.

Activities

1. The broadcast packets used by link-state protocols to share routing information about neighbor routers are called what?
    a. PDU
    b. LSA
    c. DVA
    d. SPF
2. What does each link-state router build to describe the cost to reach each destination network?
    a. LSA tree
    b. DNS tree
    c. STP tree
    d. SPF tree
3. In what three ways does OSPF control network routing table update traffic? (Choose three.)
    a. It provides for partitioning networks into subdomains, called area routes.
    b. It supports multicast, rather than broadcast route update messages.
    c. It passes only route table changes, rather than entire tables.
    d. It defines an AS diameter of 15 hops.
4. Which two of the following result from using OSPF routing areas? (Choose two.)
    a. Greatly reduced routing information traffic within the entire AS
    b. Routers maintain unique link-state databases that describe only directly connected networks
    c. The development of a routing information hierarchy
    d. Larger link-state databases describing the entire AS

5. Which statement best describes an OSPF virtual link?
   a. It designates the network's backbone area.
   b. It designates a physical connection between ABRs.
   c. It connects ABRs over a nonbackbone area.
   d. It is associated with a specific physical link.
6. OSPF routers send which type of packet to locate their neighbors?
   a. Discover
   b. Hello
   c. Locate
   d. LSA

Extended Activities

This activity will have you configure and verify IGRP on a Cisco router. To perform this activity, you will need access to a Cisco router or router simulator.

1. Access your router or router simulator. You can gain free access to Cisco routers at the **http://www.r1r2.com**.
2. Log in to the router, and go into privileged mode by typing **enable** at the router> prompt.
3. At the router# prompt, type **config t**. This takes you into global configuration mode.
4. At the router(config)# prompt, type **router ospf 1**. This turns on OSPF routing, and sets the OSPF process ID to 1. The process ID is not an AS number, as in IGRP; OSPF allows multiple OSPF processes to run on the same router.
5. At the router(config-router)# prompt, type **network 10.10.4.0 0.0.0.255 area 0**. This sets the interface address on which OSPF runs, and defines the area.

Note: OSPF has us specify a *wildcard* mask along with the network number. The OSPF process uses this mask to identify router interfaces that belong in the specified area. In our example, all interfaces within the network 10.10.4.0 will belong to area 0.

6. At the router(config-router)# prompt, type **ctrl-z**. This takes you back to privileged mode.
7. At the router# prompt, type **show ip protocol**. This shows your routing protocol information. What type of information is available here? How does it differ from the IGRP information you recorded in Lesson 4?
8. At the router# prompt, type **exit**. This will log you out of the router.

Lesson 6—Advanced Routing

Not only must autonomous systems share routing information internally, but they also must share information externally. The routing protocols that make this route information sharing between autonomous systems possible are called EGPs.

This lesson discusses the relationship between IGPs and EGPs. It also discusses some advanced routing features some of the previously discussed protocols can support.

Objectives

At the end of this lesson you will be able to:

- Explain the difference between an IGP and an EGP
- Describe key advanced routing functions: least-cost routing, load splitting, CoS, ToS/QoS routing, and policy-based routing

Exterior Gateway Protocols allow routers to share routing information between autonomous systems.

IGP and EGP

We have studied the two major algorithms used for routing protocols: distance-vector and link-state. However, we need to keep in mind that there is yet another way we can classify protocols: EGP and IGP. Routing protocols are either used within an AS or between autonomous systems; both distance-vector and link-state protocols are used within an AS.

An Internet service provider (ISP) is an example of an AS; routers within an ISP's network use IGPs to share route information. When the ISP must share routing information with other ISPs, it uses an EGP between these autonomous systems.

The term "gateway" is an older term for "router"; now "router" is the preferred terminology. This means you may see IGPs also referred to as interior routing protocols, although "gateway" is still more commonly used.

The main difference between IGPs and EGPs is that the former is used to communicate routing information within the confines of an AS. The administrator within the AS sets routing policies and other important parameters, such as path cost and ToS where applicable. On the other hand, an EGP is a protocol used to pass network reachability information between autonomous systems using a standard protocol that all communicating autonomous systems understand, such as BGP-4. The term "reachability" simply means communicating to a given AS (for example, AS "1"), information about another network that is located inside another AS (for example, AS "2").

The AS Routing Diagram illustrates gateway protocol communications between and within autonomous systems. Some important terms included on the diagram are as follows:

- End system—A host at the "end of the branch." It can receive packets from a router but can only forward them to other end systems on the same local network.
- Intermediate system—Any router that can receive packets from a neighboring router, then forward the packets to at least one other host (router or end system). Intermediate systems (routers) that belong to the same AS are called interior neighbors, and they exchange routing information using one of several IGPs. Each AS may choose the IGP that best fits its needs.
- Border system—An intermediate system specially designated by the administrator to forward packets from its own AS to other autonomous systems. Border systems are called exterior neighbors, and they exchange routing information using a standard EGP. All communicating autonomous systems must use the same EGP.

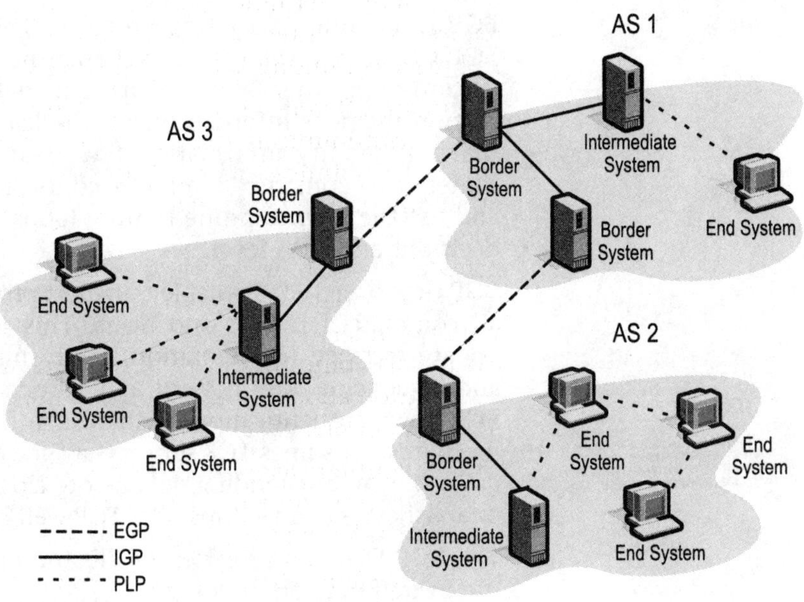

AS Routing

EGP

Before one AS can use another as a transport medium (for IP packet routing), routers that are exterior neighbors of each other (border systems) must be able to find out which networks can be reached through the other. EGPs allow for this information to be exchanged between border systems.

Although EGP is a generic term applied to all EGPs, there was once an EGP in use that was actually called "EGP." EGP did not have all the capabilities needed in larger, more complex networks. The BGP is an improved way to exchange network reachability information between autonomous systems. BGP operates as a DVA, and therefore remains true to the associated "hop-by-hop" (or the hop count as the distance between networks) model. BGP uses the TCP protocol to exchange information over a reliable connection. BGP, currently at version 4, is the most commonly used EGP. Another popular EGP is the International Standards Organization's (ISO's) Inter-Domain Routing Protocol (IDRP).

BGP-4

BGP is an inter-AS routing protocol. The primary function of a BGP-speaking system is to exchange network reachability information with other BGP systems. This network reachability information includes information on the list of autonomous systems that reachability information traverses. Using this information, routers can construct a map of connected autonomous systems and use the map to prune routing loops and enforce some policy decisions at the AS level.

BGP runs over TCP, a reliable transport protocol present in virtually all commercial routers and hosts. This means that TCP handles update message fragmentation, retransmission, acknowledgment, and sequencing. Any TCP authentication scheme may be used with BGP's own authentication mechanisms. The BGP error notification mechanism assumes TCP supports a "graceful" connection closure, delivering all outstanding data before closing the connection. BGP establishes its connections over TCP well-known Port 179.

The BGP Diagram provides an illustration of where BGP fits into the overall network topology.

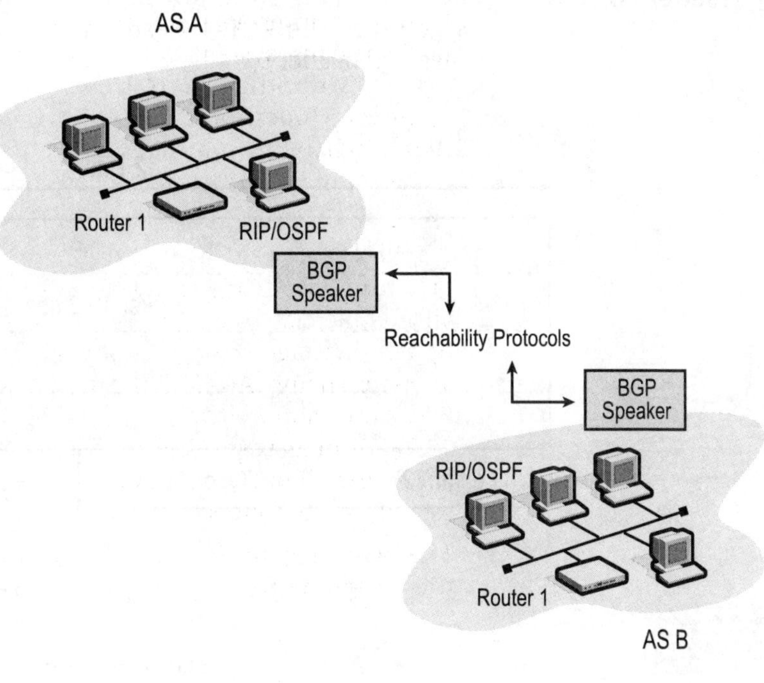

BGP

BGP in Practice

The BGP Diagram shows two autonomous systems. Each AS, "A" and "B," have a BGP speaker at the edge of their networks.

When the two BGP-speaking routers establish a TCP connection, they exchange messages to Open and confirm the connection parameters, and then they exchange their entire BGP routing tables. Each router sends Updates as its routing table changes; BGP does not require periodic refreshes of the entire BGP routing table. Therefore, a BGP speaker must retain the current version of the entire BGP routing table of all its peers for the duration of the connection. BGP sends KeepAlive messages periodically to test the connection. Notification messages are sent in response to errors or special conditions. If a connection encounters an error condition, a Notification message is sent and the connection is closed.

Hosts executing the BGP need not be routers. A nonrouting host, such as a gateway (protocol converter), could exchange routing information with routers by means of an EGP or an IGP. The nonrouting host could then use BGP to exchange routing information with a border router in another AS.

BGP-4 Message Header Format

Each BGP message has a fixed-size header. There may or may not be a data portion following the header, depending on the message type. The BGP-4 Header Diagram shows the layout of the message header.

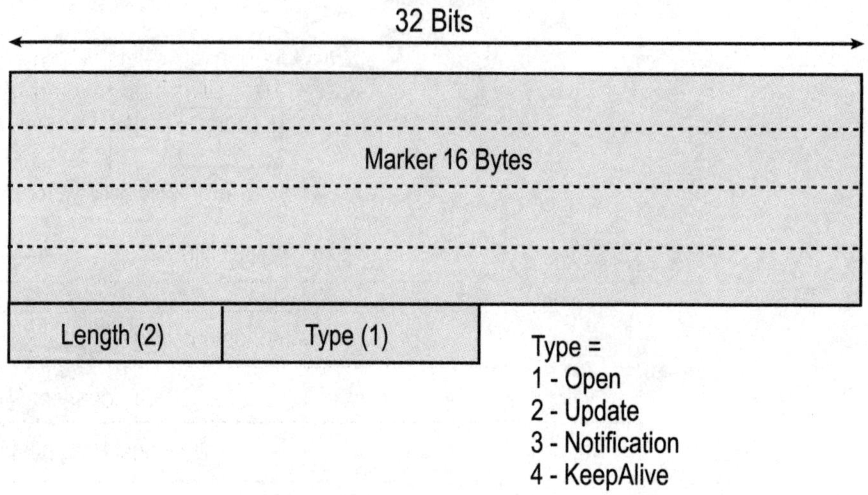

BGP-4 Header

The message header fields are as follows:

- Marker—The Marker can be used to detect loss of synchronization between a pair of BGP peers, and authenticate incoming BGP messages. This 16-byte field contains a value that the receiver of the message can predict. If the Type of the message is Open, or if the Open message carries no authentication information (as an Optional Parameter), the Marker must be all 1s. Otherwise, the value of the Marker can be predicted by some computation specified as part of the authentication mechanism (specified as part of the authentication information) used.
- Length—This field is a 2-byte number that indicates the total length of the message, including the header, in bytes. No padding of extra data after the message is allowed; thus, the Length field must have the smallest value required given the rest of the message.
- Type—The Type field is a 1-byte number code that indicates the type of the message. The following Type codes are defined:

- OPEN—Open a BGP connection with an adjacent speaker
- UPDATE—Update reachability information
- NOTIFICATION—Notify of an adjacency outage
- KEEPALIVE—Test the connection to see whether the speakers are still active

BGP-4 Open Packet Format

BGP speakers exchange Open packets when they want to make a connection to share and propagate reachability information. The BGP-4 Open Packet Diagram illustrates the various field values present.

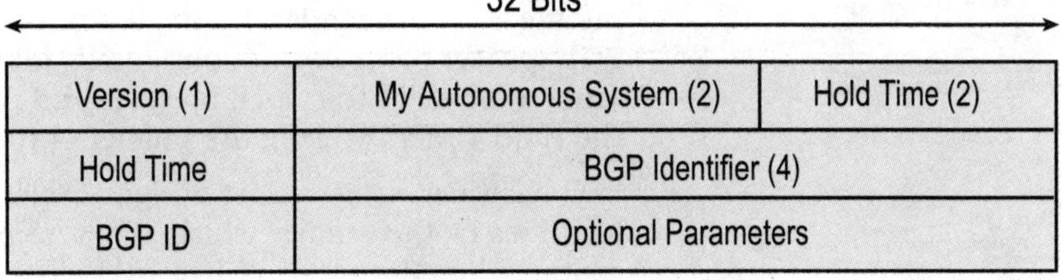

32 Bits

Version (1)	My Autonomous System (2)	Hold Time (2)
Hold Time	BGP Identifier (4)	
BGP ID	Optional Parameters	

BGP-4 Open Packet

After a TCP connection is established, the first message sent by each side is an Open message. If the Open message is acceptable, a KeepAlive message confirming the Open message is sent back. After the Open message is confirmed, Update, KeepAlive, and Notification messages may be exchanged. The message fields are as follows:

- Version—This 1-byte number indicates the protocol version number of the message. The current BGP version number is 4.
- My Autonomous System—This 2-byte number indicates the AS number of the sender.
- Hold Time—This 2-byte number indicates the number of seconds the sender proposes for the value of the Hold Timer. The Hold Timer is the maximum number of seconds that may elapse between receipt of successive KeepAlive and/or Update messages by the sender. Upon receipt of an Open message, a BGP speaker compares its configured Hold Time and the Hold Time received in the Open message and then sets the value of the Hold Timer by using the smaller of those values.
- BGP Identifier—This 4-octet unsigned integer indicates the BGP Identifier of the sender, which is the same as the sender's IP address. The value of the BGP Identifier is determined on startup.
- Optional Parameters—This field may contain a list of optional parameters, each one encoded as a <Parameter Type, Parameter Length, Parameter Value> triplet. An example of an optional parameter would be an authentication code used to authenticate BGP peers.

Advanced Routing Functions

Advanced router functionality depends primarily on which routing protocols (and algorithms) are supported, and how particular vendors implement these protocols. Extra processing may be necessary to calculate a packet's best available path to a destination.

As discussed previously, the best path is the one with the least number of hops, adequate bandwidth, or fastest transmission, depending on the routing algorithm in use. Correctly configured routers should be able to split up packets for efficient line use and route different protocols over various communication links. Although these functions have different names in different protocol environments, generally they include the following:

- Least-cost routing
- Load splitting

- CoS routing
- ToS routing
- Policy-based routing

Least-Cost Routing

Least-cost routing allows network administrators to configure the router so that it will always compute the minimum-cost path for a packet. Cost factors used in this calculation may include, for example, bandwidth and line delay, as well as cash costs. Packets may be assigned to least-cost paths based on their type or destination.

Load Splitting

Routers use load splitting, also known as load balancing, to effectively use redundant paths through the network. Load splitting allows routers to send all packets from a single network transaction over several paths simultaneously. Thus, if there is more than one best-cost route, the network administrator may choose to have the router split the load between the equal-cost routes.

Load splitting can result in much faster transmission of high-priority messages and helps to maximize overall network efficiency. However, load splitting is dependent on the network protocol. For example, IPX does not implement load splitting in the same way as IP.

CoS Routing

CoS routing allows network administrators to specify different routing service categories and associate with each category different performance characteristics. The network administrator assigns packets to different priority queues, and configures an interleaf ratio that specifies the number of high-priority packets to be transmitted for each low-priority packet. An interleaf ratio represents the number of one particular packet type sent for the number of another type.

For example, if the interleaf ratio is set to five, five high-priority packets are transmitted for each one low-priority packet. Typically, packets from interactive processes (voice or video) would be assigned to the high-priority queue, while packets from background or batch processes (data) would be assigned to the low-priority queue. CoS routing allows network managers to customize routing service to the business requirements of the organization. For example, connections between global and regional headquarters might be assigned to classes that ensure the fastest possible transmission speeds.

ToS/QoS Routing

This type of routing allows the network administrator to specify up to 16 ToSs (using the IP packet header ToS field) and establish a separate transmission path for each one. Service types typically include factors such as line speed, error correction, and line delay. For example, this type of routing can transmit large files over a long-delay, high-capacity satellite link, while interactive or bursty traffic is sent over short-delay leased lines. ToS routing is the term used by the OSPF protocol. The IS-IS protocol refers to this type of routing as QoS routing.

Policy-Based Routing

Policy-based routing allows network administrators to specify additional sources of information for the routing table and network model. These sources may include information imported from other protocols or information network administrators statically configure. Such policies can be defined on a router-by-router basis and control the advertisement of routing information. They define who can talk to whom, who can listen to whom, and what types of information are transmitted and received.

Policy-based routing is often part of network security procedures. For example, a network administrator might specify that network information imported from other protocols can be included in the routing table and network model, and subsequently shared with outside routers as part of update messages. However, routers with custom security settings and other private configuration information would only share that information with other routers that share the same security settings.

Activities

1. A router that can receive packets from a neighboring router and forward them to at least one other router is called what?
   a. End system
   b. AS
   c. Border system
   d. Intermediate system
2. A router that an administrator designates to forward packets between autonomous systems is call what?
   a. End system
   b. AS
   c. Border system
   d. Intermediate system
3. BGP, though an EGP, operates as which type of routing protocol?
   a. LSA
   b. DVA
   c. IGP
   d. SPF
4. Which advanced routing function allows for redundant paths between networks?
   a. Load splitting
   b. Least cost routing
   c. CoS routing
   d. QoS routing
5. Which three of the following cost factors might least cost routing use to calculate a minimum-cost path for a packet? (Choose three.)
   a. Bandwidth
   b. Delay
   c. Router load
   d. Cash costs

Extended Activity

Advanced routing techniques, such as CoS, ToS/QoS, and policy routing, support such converged communications as Voice over IP (VoIP) and Unified Messaging. Research these advanced routing functions and summarize how they support convergent technologies.

Some URLs to visit include:

- **http://www.cisco.com/networkers**
- **http://www.cisco.com/warp/public/784/packet/technology.html**
- **http://www.protocols.com**
- **http://www.telephonyworld.com/**

Summary

In this unit, we introduced the key point of using TCP/IP in a network; its ability to carry information across separate network segments. We learned that the Internet is a collection of smaller networks connected together with routers. These routers must know paths to other networks so hosts can communicate with other hosts in those other networks. Routers maintain routing tables that contain information about a network, such as its network number and associated costs. Routing tables point packets to specific remote router interfaces, called next hop routers, where the packets are then routed to the next hop, and so forth, until they reach their destination. Routers use one of three routing types to build routing tables: static routing, default routing, and dynamic routing.

Networks are grouped together as autonomous systems; IGPs share route information between routers within an AS. EGPs carry routing information between autonomous systems. We learned of two dynamic routing protocol types: those using DVA, and those using LSA. RIP and IGRP are examples of DVA protocols, and OSPF is an LSA protocol. DVA protocols create a flat network, while LSA protocols create a hierarchical network.

RIP is a commonly used DVA protocol. It uses a simple hop count as its metric, with a maximum value of 15. RIP supports both TCP/IP and IPX/SPX networks. RIP, as are other DVA protocols, is susceptible to routing loops, and thus provides a number of mechanisms to control these loops and stabilize the network. These mechanisms are maximum hop counts, poison reverse, split horizon, and holddowns. Holddowns work with triggered updates to speed router convergence. RIP provides a number of configurable timers to help us adjust our network to suit our application. RIPv2 adds four elements to RIP: Route Tags, subnet masks, next hop, and authentication, and supports variable-length subnet masks.

IGRP is a Cisco Systems proprietary DVA protocol designed to overcome some of RIPs limitations. IGRP uses hop counts as one potential metric, but combines this with a number of other metrics to create a composite metric. The IGRP maximum hop count is 255, and the IGRP default metrics are bandwidth and delay. IGRP is still susceptible to routing loops, and thus uses the same stabilizing mechanisms as does RIP. IGRP timers default to different values than do RIP timers. IGRP also requires the use of AS numbers in its routing tables.

OSPF is an LSA protocol and is an open protocol. As an LSA protocol, it learns much more information about its AS topology than do RIP and IGRP. OSPF solves many of RIP's problems handling large networks. OSPF supports multiple, configurable metrics, where RIP only supports hop count. OSPF converges rapidly and is resistant to routing loops. OSPF routers only pass route updates when topology changes occur, and each router authenticates routing exchanges to protect routing tables from corruption. OSPF multicasts updates to cut down on network traffic, can load balance across equal cost links, pass subnetting information, and supports ToS routing. OSPF supports area routing to control routing update traffic, maintain area topology information, and develop an area hierarchy. OSPF identifies neighboring routers and establishes adjacencies between them.

For autonomous systems to communicate routing information with each other, EGP can be used. One of the more common BGPs is BGP-4. An ISP is an example of an AS that would need to exchange routing information with other autonomous systems by means of BGP-4. BGP-4 establishes connections between autonomous systems using TCP, and the communicating autonomous system's send KeepAlive messages to maintain the connection. Advanced routing function support varies by the routing protocol used. Least-cost routing makes routing decisions based on path costs. Load-splitting balances the load between redundant network paths. CoS routing queues and interleaves packets based on an administrator-assigned CoS. ToS/QoS routing uses the IP header ToS field to establish a separate path for each service type. Policy-based routing uses external sources to establish policies that routers use to determine the best method to handle specific traffic.

Unit 6 Quiz

1. A router makes its packet forwarding decisions based on what information?
   a. The router's MAC address table
   b. The router's routing table
   c. The router's host table
   d. The router's NAT table
2. What type of network communication does not require a router's services?
   a. Indirect routing
   b. Point-to-point routing
   c. Default routing
   d. Direct routing
3. Which three choices are indirect routing types? (Choose three.)
   a. Static
   b. Default
   c. Stub
   d. Dynamic
4. In order to automatically build a routing table, which type of indirect routing must a router use?
   a. Static
   b. Default
   c. Stub
   d. Dynamic
5. RIP uses which metric to make path decisions?
   a. Cost
   b. Bandwidth
   c. Tick count
   d. Hop count

6. On which network type is a static route best used?
   a. Enterprise
   b. Dynamic
   c. Stub
   d. IPX
7. In which two ways might using static routes provide additional network security over other routing options? (Choose two.)
   a. They require the network administrator to know the password for each route.
   b. They can limit packet traffic to only a single, dedicated route.
   c. They share no routing information with other routers.
   d. They can restrict routing table updates to a single, dedicated link.
8. Which router protocol type shares routing information within an AS?
   a. IGP
   b. EGP
   c. BGP
   d. AS-RIP
9. Which routing type allows network administrators to implement route load balancing and fault tolerance?
   a. Static
   b. Dynamic
   c. Redundant
   d. Default
10. Which three of the following are IGP protocol examples? (Choose three.)
   a. IGRP
   b. RIP
   c. OSPF
   d. IDRP

11. DVAs operate in which manner?

    a. Each router must know the entire network topology before computing the best path to a destination network.

    b. They send routing messages containing the attached links' states and metrics.

    c. They limit routing update traffic by multicasting updates to specific routers.

    d. They advertise their routing tables to directly connected neighbor routers.

12. Which two dynamic routing protocols create flat network topologies? (Choose two.)

    a. RIP

    b. IGRP

    c. LSA

    d. IGRP

13. By default, how frequently do RIP routers send out response messages to neighbor routers?

    a. Every 60 seconds

    b. Only upon initialization

    c. Every 30 seconds

    d. Only when topology changes occur

14. Which would cause a router to update a route entry still in the holddown period set by a previously received update?

    a. A triggered update with a lower hop count than previously received

    b. A triggered update received from the same router that sent the previous update

    c. A triggered update received with a new holddown timer setting

    d. A triggered update with a loop count lower than that previously received

15. How does RIPv2 authentication protect routing table information?
    a. It encrypts routing table entries.
    b. It sends encrypted passwords between routers.
    c. It password protects routing table updates between routers.
    d. It limits routing table entries within the update message to a maximum of 12.
16. Which two of the following are the IGRP default metrics? (Choose two.)
    a. Hop count
    b. Reliability
    c. Bandwidth
    d. Delay
17. An IGRP interior route is which of the following?
    a. A path to a network summarized by a boundary router
    b. A link between autonomous systems
    c. A route to other networks within the AS
    d. A path to a directly attached, subnetted route
18. What type of routing table update message does IGRP send to quickly remove a route and place it in holddown?
    a. Flash updates
    b. Poison reverse updates
    c. Split horizons
    d. Holddown updates
19. Which statement best describes split horizons?
    a. It is a router load balancing technique that splits network traffic across multiple network links.
    b. It ensures that routers don't advertise route information to failed links.
    c. It prevents regular update messages from reinstating a failed route.
    d. It prevents a router from advertising a route out to the interface on which the route was learned.

20. Considering the default Cisco router default ADs, which of the following routes will a router consider more trustworthy than the others?
    a. RIP
    b. Static route
    c. EIGRP
    d. OSPF
21. In an LSA SPF tree, which three of the following are metrics the router uses to describe the cost to reach each destination network? (Choose three.)
    a. Line speed
    b. Line distance
    c. Line delay
    d. Hop counts
22. Which statement best describes an OSPF ABR?
    a. It maintains a link-state database for only a single area's topology.
    b. It maintains a link-state database for each area to which it is connected.
    c. It floods SLAs to only its assigned area, dropping all other SLAs.
    d. It connects to routers located in other autonomous systems.
23. An OSPF ASBR runs which two routing protocols? (Choose two.)
    a. OSPF on interfaces on its own AS
    b. OSPF on interfaces on other autonomous systems
    c. EGP on interfaces on other autonomous systems
    d. EGP on interfaces on its own AS
24. To reduce routing information traffic between adjacent networks, OSPF networks elect which two devices? (Choose two.)
    a. Designated router
    b. ABR
    c. ASBR
    d. Backup designated router

25. What message type does BGP send to test a connection's state?
    a. KeepAlive
    b. Notification
    c. Hello
    d. Update
26. Which statement correctly describes CoS routing?
    a. It determines the route a packet takes based on the path's cost.
    b. It makes routing decisions based on the packet's ToS bits.
    c. It looks up route information from an administrator-configured database.
    d. It makes routing decisions based on the packet's service category.
27. QoS routing uses which IP header field to make route decisions?
    a. QoS
    b. ToS
    c. Options
    d. Fragmentation

Unit 7
How TCP/IP Applications Work

This unit covers operation of the most common application protocols. We will see how the protocols are used to transfer information between client and server. We begin with the Hypertext Transfer Protocol (HTTP) and the mechanism for transferring information between World Wide Web (Web) clients and Web servers. We then look at the operation of Telnet, File Transfer Protocol (FTP), Simple Mail Transfer Protocol (SMTP), and Simple Network Management Protocol (SNMP). We complete the unit with an introduction to the ITU-T H.323 packet multimedia recommendations, which are designed to carry voice, video, and data across TCP/IP packet-based networks.

HTTP, Telnet, FTP, and SMTP use Transmission Control Protocol (TCP) and Internet Protocol (IP) as the transport and network protocols for sending information. The last application, SNMP, uses the User Datagram Protocol (UDP) and IP. H.323 uses additional protocols that run on top of UDP and IP, and includes standards for encoding analog voice and call signaling into packet data.

Lessons

1. Web Browser and Web Server Step-by-Step
2. Telnet
3. FTP
4. SMTP
5. Network Management
6. H.323 Standard for Packet Multimedia

Terms

Abstract Syntax Notation 1 (ASN.1)—ASN.1 is a LAN "grammar" with rules and symbols used to describe and define protocols and programming languages. ASN.1 is the OSI standard language for describing data types.

Acknowledgement (ACK)—The TCP header field that indicates the Acknowledgement field is significant.

Acknowledgement (ACK) Number—The ACK number applies only if the ACK control bit is set. The ACK number is the next sequence number a sender of a segment is expecting to receive. If a connection is established, this value is always sent.

Asynchronous Transfer Mode (ATM)—ATM is a connection-oriented cell relay technology based on small (53-byte) cells. An ATM network consists of ATM switches that form multiple virtual circuits to carry groups of cells from source to destination. ATM can provide high-speed transport services for audio, data, and video.

basic encoding rules (BERs)—BERs are the data unit encoding rules used in the ASN.1 LAN encoding grammar.

Broadband-ISDN (B-ISDN)—B-ISDN is a set of ITU-T services requiring transmission channels that support data rates in excess of the primary rate, DS1. Three underlying technologies are critical to B-ISDN: SS7, ATM, and SONET.

Data Offset—The data offset specifies the number of 32-bit words in the TCP header. It indicates where the data begins in a segment. This field is necessary because the Options field is of variable length, as is the header.

default gateway—A default gateway is a router that provides access to all hosts on remote networks. Typically, the network administrator configures a default gateway for each host on the network.

Finish (FIN)—FIN is the TCP header field (ACK number 50) that indicates no more data should be sent from the sender.

Fragment Offset—Fragment offset is the IP header field that specifies the offset in the original datagram of the data being carried in the fragment, measured in units of 8 bytes, starting at 0.

G.711—G.711 is one of a series of ITU-T voice digitizing algorithms. G.711 transfers digitized audio at 48, 56, and 64 Kbps.

G.722—G.722 is one of a series of ITU-T voice digitizing algorithms. G.722 transfers digitized audio at 32 Kbps.

G.723—G.723 is one of a series of ITU-T voice digitizing algorithms. G.723 transfers digitized audio at 5.3 or 6.3 Kbps.

G.728—G.728 is one of a series of ITU-T voice digitizing algorithms. G.728 transfers digitized audio at 16 Kbps.

G.729—G.729 is one of a series of ITU-T voice digitizing algorithms. G.729 transfers digitized audio at 8 Kbps.

gatekeeper—A network device or process that controls data flow on a transmission channel or allocates transmission bandwidth among multiple competing signals is referred to as a gatekeeper.

H.225—H.225 is the ITU-T recommended standard that describes how audio, video, data, and control information on a packet-based network can be managed to provide conversational services in H.323 equipment.

H.245—H.245 is line transmission of nontelephone signals. It includes receiving and transmitting capabilities as well as mode preference from the receiving end, logical channel signalling, and control and indication. Acknowledged signalling procedures are specified to ensure reliable audiovisual and data communication.

H.261—H.261 describes a video stream for transport using RTP with any of the underlying protocols that carry RTP.

H.263—H.263 specifies the payload format for encapsulating an H.263 bitstream in the RTP.

H.310—H.310 is the ITU-T recommendation for videoconferencing in an ATM environment.

H.320—H.320 is the most common ITU-T family of videoconferencing standards. H.320 standards allow videoconferencing systems to communicate over ISDN-BRI connections.

H.321—H.321 is the adaptation of the H.320 videoconferencing standards to an ATM environment.

H.322—H.322 is the ITU-T recommended adaptation of H.320 to a guaranteed QoS LAN environment.

H.323—H.323 is an umbrella recommendation from ITU that sets standards for multimedia communications over LANs that do not provide a guaranteed QoS, such as over IP networks.

H.324—H.324 is the ITU-T recommended standard for videoconferencing by means of modems over POTS lines. H.324 uses H.263 for video compression, G.723 for audio encoding, and H.245/H.225 for control and multiplexing.

IEEE 802.1p—IEEE 802.1p is the IEEE extension to 802.1D that allows Layer 2 bridges and switches to filter and prioritize LAN traffic. 802.1p modifies the 802.1Q 3-bit priority identification tag to represent one of eight topology-independent priority values.

IEEE 802.1Q—IEEE 8021Q is the IEEE specification for implementing VLANs in Layer 2 LAN switches, emphasizing but not limited to Ethernet. 802.1Q modifies the 802.10 Clear Header 2-byte field to indicate a frame's VLAN membership.

Integrated Services Digital Network (ISDN)—ISDN is a digital multiplexing technology that can transmit voice, data, and other forms of communication simultaneously over a single local loop. ISDN-BRI provides two bearer channels (B channels) of 64 Kbps each, plus one control channel (D channel) of 16 Kbps. ISDN-PRI offers 23 B channels of 64 Kbps each, plus one D channel of 64 Kbps.

International Telecommunications Union Telecommunications Standardization Sector (ITU-T)—ITU-T is an intergovernmental organization that develops and adopts international telecommunications standards and treaties. ITU was founded in 1865 and became a United Nations agency in 1947.

management information base (MIB)-2—MIB-2, also known as MIB-II, is the RFC 1213 specified MIB format for TCP/IP networks. MIB-2 includes such information as system uptime, interface counters, and IP layer address tables.

Multipoint Control Unit (MCU)—MCUs are hosts that coordinate multipoint conferences of three or more terminals that use the H.323 packet multimedia standards. All H.323 terminals participating in a conference must establish a connection with the MCU.

Optical Carrier (OC)-3—OC-3 is the SONET optical signal standard that corresponds to a data rate of 155.52 Mbps. SONET is an optical transmission standard that defines a numbered signal hierarchy. The optical signal standards are designated OC-1, OC-2, and so on. The basic building block is the OC-1 51.84-Mbps signal, chosen to accommodate a T3 signal.

public-switched telephone network (PSTN)—PSTN is the worldwide voice telephone network accessible to anyone with a telephone.

Real-Time Transport Control Protocol (RTCP)—RTCP, a counterpart of RTP, is an OSI model Presentation Layer protocol that provides control services and feedback on the quality of the data transmission.

Real-Time Transport Protocol (RTP)—RTP is an OSI model Presentation Layer protocol that provides end-to-end delivery of real-time audio and video by prioritizing this traffic ahead of connectionless data transfers.

sequence number—This is the sequence number of the first data byte in a segment (except when synchronize [SYN] is present). When SYN is present, the sequence number is the ISN, and the first data byte is ISN+1.

switched circuit network (SCN)—SCN is another term for the PSTN.

Synchronize (SYN)—SYN is the TCP header field used to synchronize sequence numbers.

Uniform Resource Identifier (URI) —A URI is the generic term for all types of names and addresses that refer to objects on the Web. A URL is one kind of URI.

Version—This 4-bit field in a datagram contains the version of IP used to create the datagram. The Version field is used to ensure that the sender, receiver, and intervening gateways agree on the format of the datagram.

window—A window is the number of bytes, beginning with the one in the ACK field, that can be accepted by the sender of this segment.

X.500—The ITU-T X.500 standard designates a distributed, global Directory that permits applications, such as e-mail, to access information either stored centrally or distributed across numerous servers. A Directory contains information about objects; these objects may be files or network entities, such as the user accounts and resources listed in Novell's NetWare Directory Services or Microsoft's Windows 2000 Active Directory.

Lesson 1—Web Browser and Web Server Step-by-Step

The purpose of this lesson is to detail, step-by-step, the flow of information from the Web browser to the Web server and back. We begin with a client request for a Web page and show several transactions between Web browsers and Web servers. The trace information was taken using a Network Associates NetXRay product. The steps involved include:

1. Name resolution
2. TCP connection establishment
3. HTTP request
4. HTTP response

Objectives

At the end of this lesson you will be able to:

- Describe the functionality of all layers of the Web client communications software
- Describe the functionality of all layers of the Web server communications software

Key Point

Web communication requires a TCP connection.

Server Waits for a Client Request

When a Web server is not processing a request from a client, it is in a "wait state," waiting for a client request. The request can be from any client on the network that knows the address of the Web server. The Web Server Waiting for a Connection Diagram illustrates this concept.

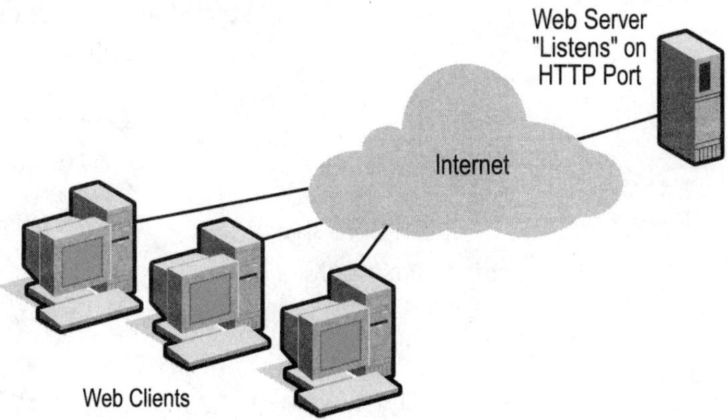

Web Server Waiting for a Connection

Client Resolves Server IP Address

The first step on most client requests is address resolution. Address resolution can be performed at the IP layer (Domain Name System [DNS]) or at the Link Layer (Address Resolution Protocol [ARP]). This may or may not happen depending on the stored client information. If the client has recently made a request to the same server, address resolution may not take place. The DNS Request/Response Diagram illustrates the information flow, protocol stacks, and devices involved in a DNS request.

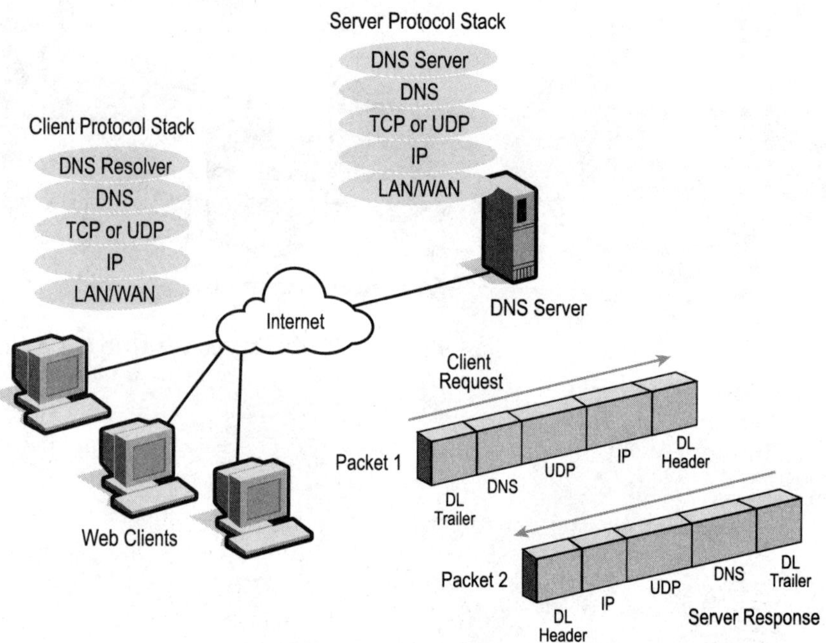

DNS Request/Response

The details of the information transferred from client to server and from server to client are shown below in trace format. A trace is the information captured from the network. In the case of the following traces, the network is 10-megabits-per-second (Mbps) Ethernet. The information gathered is displayed in packets by the trace program (Network Associate's NetXRay) that is capturing the information. The frame, packet, message, and application information is shown.

The first two captures show the client server pairs for the DNS lookup. The first packet consists of the DNS lookup. The DNS server is located at IP address 205.169.85.240. This server is normally located at the Internet service provider (ISP), and the request is sent to the gateway (router) of the corporate network, and then to the ISP. However, in this example, the Domain Name Server is on the local network, thus the lookup goes there first. The destination Web site that is trying to be reached is **http://www.westnetinc.com**.

```
Packet 1 captured at 02/25/1999 06:49:52 PM; Packet size is 78(0x4e)bytes
      Relative time: 000:00:09.822
      Delta time: 0.000.000
Ethernet Version II
      Address: 00-60-97-DB-88-A1 --->00-60-97-9D-32-06
      Ethernet II Protocol Type: IP
Internet Protocol
      Version(MSB 4 bits): 4
      Header length(LSB 4 bits): 5 (32-bit word)
      Service type: 0x00
            000. .... = 0 - Routine
            ...0 .... = Normal delay
            .... 0... = Normal throughput
            .... .0.. = Normal reliability
      Total length: 64 (Octets)
      Fragment ID: 43591
      Flags summary: 0x00
            0... .... = Reserved
            .0.. .... = May be fragmented
            ..0. .... = Last fragment
            Fragment offset(LSB 13 bits): 0 (0x00)
      Time to live: 32 seconds/hops
      IP protocol type: UDP (0x11)
      Checksum: 0xA9DE
      IP address 205.169.85.68 ->205.169.85.240
      No option
User Datagram Protocol
      Port 1506 ---> Domain Name Server
      Total length: 44 (Octets)
      Checksum: 0x5056
```

```
Domain Name Service
      HEADER SECTION:
      Identifier: 1
      Flags:
            0... .... = Request packet
            .000 0... = OP Code is 0x00 - Query
            .... .0.. = Non-Authoritative Answer
            .... ..0. = No Truncation Packet
            .... ...1 = Recursion Desired
            0... .... = Recursion Not Available
            .000 .... = Reserved Bits
            .... 0000 = Response Code is 0 - No Error
      Section Entries:
            Question   Section: 1 Entrie(s)
            Answer     Section: 0 Entrie(s)
            Authority  Section: 0 Entrie(s)
            Additional Section: 0 Entrie(s)
      QUESTION SECTION[1]:
            Domain Name: www.westnetinc.com
            Query  Type: 1 = A - a host address
            Query Class: 1 = IN - the ARPA internet
```

The hexadecimal equivalent of the above information is shown below. The Data Link Layer header consisting of the destination address (first 6 bytes), the source address (next 6 bytes), and the protocol type are listed first, starting at hexadecimal address 0000h and ending at 000Dh. Notice the preamble, start of frame delimiter, and error detection information is not shown.

The arrow marks the end of the frame header (Ethernet) and the start of the packet header (IP).

```
Hexadecimal Detail
Packet: 1
                                                ↓
0000: 00 60 97 9d 32 06 00 60 97 db 88 a1 08 00 45 00 | .`..2..`.Û....E.
0010: 00 40 aa 47 00 00 20 11 a9 de cd a9 55 44 cd a9 | .@ªG.. .©Þí©UDí©
0020: 55 f0 05 e2 00 35 00 2c 50 56 00 01 01 00 00 01 | Uð...5.,PV......
0030: 00 00 00 00 00 00 03 77 77 77 0a 77 65 73 74 6e | .......www.westn
0040: 65 74 69 6e 63 03 63 6f 6d 00 00 01 00 01       | etinc.com.....
```

The packet is shown next, beginning with the hexadecimal byte 45 at address 000Eh. As noted in the previous detail, this indicates that this is IPv4, and the IP packet is five 32-bit words long, ending with the hexadecimal number f0. F0 is the last number in the destination address, decimal 240 (205.169.85.240 is the address of the DNS server).

Following the packet is the UDP message, beginning at address 0022h. The UDP message begins with the source port number, two hexadecimal bytes, 05 and E2. These are equivalent to decimal 1506, the port number associated with the UDP request. The next two bytes are the destination port, 00 35, equivalent to decimal 53. This relates to Port 53, the well-known port of DNS. For more information on port numbers, refer to Request for Comment (RFC) 1700 at an RFC repository such as the one at **http://www.rfc-editor.org/rfc.html**.

The second packet is the response from the DNS server. The DNS server responds with the 32-bit IP address (205.169.85.253) of the requested web site (**http://www.westnetinc.com**). The client can now send a request to the Web server because it has the 32-bit IP address.

```
Packet 2 captured at 02/25/1999 06:49:52 PM; Packet size is 94(0x5e)bytes
      Relative time: 000:00:09.823
      Delta time: 0.000.637
Ethernet Version II
      Address: 00-60-97-9D-32-06 --->00-60-97-DB-88-A1
      Ethernet II Protocol Type: IP
Internet Protocol
      Version(MSB 4 bits): 4
      Header length(LSB 4 bits): 5 (32-bit word)
      Service type: 0x00
            000. .... = 0 - Routine
            ...0 .... = Normal delay
            .... 0... = Normal throughput
            .... .0.. = Normal reliability
      Total length: 80 (Octets)
      Fragment ID: 60365
      Flags summary: 0x00
            0... .... = Reserved
            .0.. .... = May be fragmented
            ..0. .... = Last fragment
```

```
        Fragment offset(LSB 13 bits): 0 (0x00)
    Time to live: 128 seconds/hops
    IP protocol type: UDP (0x11)
    Checksum: 0x0848
    IP address 205.169.85.240 ->205.169.85.68
    No option
User Datagram Protocol
    Port Domain Name Server ---> 1506
    Total length: 60 (Octets)
    Checksum: 0xD9EA
Domain Name Service
    HEADER SECTION:
    Identifier: 1
    Flags:
        1... .... = Response packet
        .000 0... = OP Code is 0x00 - Query
        .... .1.. = Authoritative Answer
        .... ..0. = No Truncation Packet
        .... ...1 = Recursion Desired
        1... .... = Recursion Available
        .000 .... = Reserved Bits
        .... 0000 = Response Code is 0 - No Error
    Section Entries:
        Question   Section: 1 Entrie(s)
        Answer     Section: 1 Entrie(s)
        Authority  Section: 0 Entrie(s)
        Additional Section: 0 Entrie(s)
    QUESTION SECTION[1]:
        Domain Name: www.westnetinc.com
        Query  Type: 1 = A - a host address
        Query Class: 1 = IN - the ARPA internet
    ANSWER SECTION[1]:
        Domain Name (w/Pointer): www.westnetinc.com
        RR  Type: 1 = A - a host address
        RR Class: 1 = IN - the ARPA internet
        RR Time To Live: 3600 second(s)
        RR Data  Length: 4 Octet(s)
        An ARPA internet address: 205.169.85.253
Hexadecimal Detail
```

```
Packet: 2
0000: 00 60 97 db 88 a1 00 60 97 9d 32 06 08 00 45 00 | .`.Û...`..2...E.
0010: 00 50 eb cd 00 00 80 11 08 48 cd a9 55 f0 cd a9 | .Pëí.....Hí©Uðí©
0020: 55 44 00 35 05 e2 00 3c d9 ea 00 01 85 80 00 01 | UD.5...<Ùê......
0030: 00 01 00 00 00 00 03 77 77 77 0a 77 65 73 74 6e | .......www.westn
0040: 65 74 69 6e 63 03 63 6f 6d 00 00 01 00 01 c0 0c | etinc.com.....À.
0050: 00 01 00 01 00 00 0e 10 00 04 cd a9 55 fd       | ..........í©Uý
```

Client TCP Sends a Connection Request to Web Server TCP Process

HTTP is a relatively simple protocol that defines methods as a part of the HTTP header used to pass messages between the client and the server. These seven basic methods, as defined in RFC 2068 are:

- DELETE—A request that the receiving station delete the resource specified if it exists on the listed Uniform Resource Identifier (URI). The receiving station is not required to grant a DELETE request.
- GET—A request for transfer of a resource, such as a Web page, from the server to the client.
- HEAD—A request for transfer of header information without transfer of the entire resource. This method is most frequently used for testing purposes and verifying modification and update information. Search engines also use HEAD to display TITLE and META information.
- OPTIONS—A request by the client for additional information relating to the communications options available. The purpose of this method is to allow the client to obtain additional information regarding options and requirements without initiating any actions on the part of the server.
- POST—A request that the receiving station make the enclosed resource a subordinate of the listed URI. Specific uses for POST are annotation of existing resources, posting a message to a bulletin board, newsgroup, mailing list, and so on, providing a block of data to a data-handling process, and appending to a database.
- PUT—A request that the enclosed resource be stored under the specified URI. If the PUT request references a resource that already resides under the URI, the receiving station should (but is not required to) treat it as though it were an update to the previously existing resource.

- TRACE—A request to the receiving station to return a copy of the sender's request message, exactly as it was received (loopback). A TRACE request is used for testing; it allows the sending station to see how a message was received.

Before the actual HTTP GET request for the document on the Web server takes place, a connection must be established between the client TCP process and the Web server TCP process. The client HTTP request for a document follows after a TCP session has been successfully negotiated. The Client Request Diagram illustrates the protocol stacks on the client and server, and the direction of the information transfer.

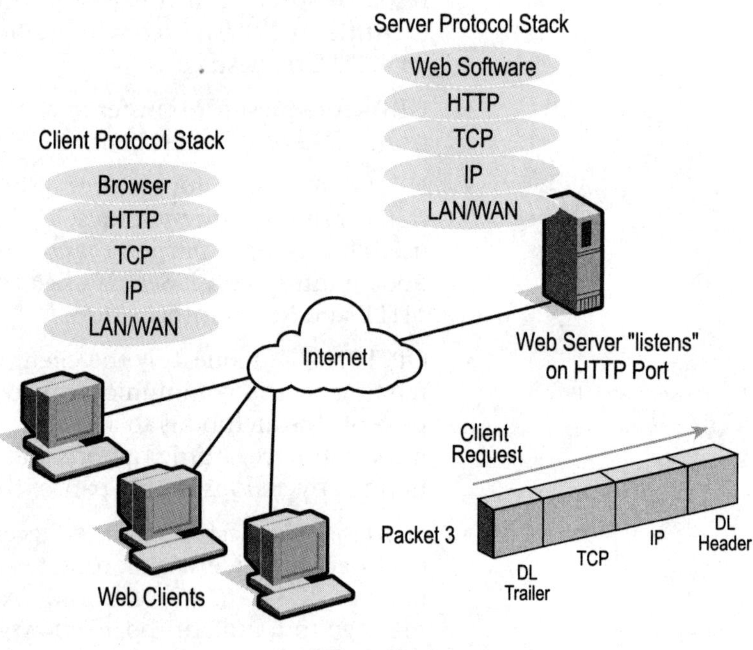

Client Request

The details of the transfer of information from the client, directly to the server, are shown next. This is the frame and frame contents that are sent across the physical link to the Web server. Inside the frame are the packet and the message. In this message, the client TCP process is requesting a session to be established with the remote (Web server) TCP process. In the next two packets (3 and 4), the client TCP process establishes sequencing and synchronization parameters with its peer TCP process. The connection is targeted to the destination port of the Web server (HTTP) process, which is Port 80. Notice the Sequence Number of 32592973 and the fact that the SYN (Synchronize Sequence Number) bit is set. If the server TCP process accepts the connection, it increments this number by one, and puts the result in the Acknowledgement Number field. The server also includes its starting sequence number in the Sequence Number field (this is illustrated in Packet 4).

```
Packet 3 captured at 02/25/1999 06:49:52 PM; Packet size is 58(0x3a)bytes
      Relative time: 000:00:09.832
      Delta time: 0.000.173
Ethernet Version II
      Address: 00-60-97-DB-88-A1 --->00-60-94-2E-6B-7A
      Ethernet II Protocol Type: IP
Internet Protocol
      Version(MSB 4 bits): 4
      Header length(LSB 4 bits): 5 (32-bit word)
      Service type: 0x00
            000. .... = 0 - Routine
            ...0 .... = Normal delay
            .... 0... = Normal throughput
            .... .0.. = Normal reliability
      Total length: 44 (Octets)
      Fragment ID: 43847
      Flags summary: 0x40
            0... .... = Reserved
            .1.. .... = Do not fragment
            ..0. .... = Last fragment
            Fragment offset(LSB 13 bits): 0 (0x00)
      Time to live: 32 seconds/hops
      IP protocol type: TCP (0x06)
      Checksum: 0x68F0
```

```
        IP address 205.169.85.68 ->205.169.85.253
        No option
Transmission Control Protocol
        Port 1507 ---> World Wide Web HTTP
        Sequence Number: 32592973
        Acknowledgement Number: 0
        Header Length(MSB 4 bits): 6 (32-bit word)
        Reserved(LSB 4 bits): 0
        Code: 0x02
                RES: 00.. .... = Reserved
                URG: ..0. .... = Urgent Pointer is Invalid
                ACK: ...0 .... = Acknowledgement Field is Invalid
                PSH: .... 0... = No push Requested
                RST: .... .0.. = No reset Connection
                SYN: .... ..1. = Synchronize Sequence Number
                FIN: .... ...0 = More Data From Sender
        Window: 8192
        Checksum: 0xD520
        Urgent Pointer: 0x0000
        TCP Option: 020405B4

Hexadecimal Detail
Packet: 3
0000: 00 60 94 2e 6b 7a 00 60 97 db 88 a1 08 00 45 00 | .`..kz.`.Û....E.
0010: 00 2c ab 47 40 00 20 06 68 f0 cd a9 55 44 cd a9 | .,.G@. .hðÍ©UDÍ©
0020: 55 fd 05 e3 00 50 01 f1 54 4d 00 00 00 00 60 02 | Uý.ã.P.ñTM....`.
0030: 20 00 d5 20 00 00 02 04 05 b4                   |  .Õ ......
```

The Server TCP Process Responds to the Client TCP Process

The server TCP process responds to the client TCP process by sending a message back to the client. The Server TCP Response Diagram shows the direction of information flow, the client and server protocol stacks, and the format of the frame going across the network.

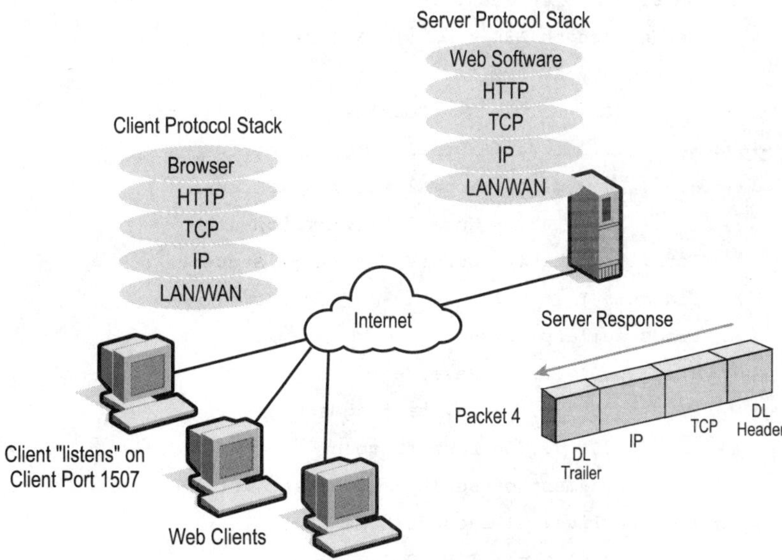

Server TCP Response

Details of the transfer of the Ethernet/IP/TCP information are shown next. This is the frame that is sent across the physical link from the Web server. Inside the frame are the packet and the message. In this message, the server TCP process is responding to the previous request of the client TCP process. Notice the Sequence Number from the previous packet (3), has been incremented by one (32592974), and placed into the Acknowledgement Number field. The server has placed its own starting sequence number (4033327865) into the Sequence Number field. The client TCP process acknowledges the server's connection request in the same manner, by incrementing the sequence number by one and putting the result in the Acknowledgement Number field. The client's acknowledgement appears in Packet 5.

```
Packet 4 captured at 02/25/1999 06:49:52 PM; Packet size is 60(0x3c)bytes
      Relative time: 000:00:09.832
      Delta time: 0.000.506
Ethernet Version II
      Address: 00-60-94-2E-6B-7A --->00-60-97-DB-88-A1
      Ethernet II Protocol Type: IP
Internet Protocol
      Version(MSB 4 bits): 4
      Header length(LSB 4 bits): 5 (32-bit word)
      Service type: 0x00
            000. .... = 0 - Routine
            ...0 .... = Normal delay
            .... 0... = Normal throughput
            .... .0.. = Normal reliability
      Total length: 44 (Octets)
      Fragment ID: 10213
      Flags summary: 0x00
            0... .... = Reserved
            .0.. .... = May be fragmented
            ..0. .... = Last fragment
            Fragment offset(LSB 13 bits): 0 (0x00)
      Time to live: 64 seconds/hops
      IP protocol type: TCP (0x06)
      Checksum: 0x0C53
      IP address 205.169.85.253 ->205.169.85.68
      No option
Transmission Control Protocol
      Port World Wide Web HTTP ---> 1507
      Sequence Number: 4033327865
      Acknowledgement Number: 32592974
      Header Length(MSB 4 bits): 6 (32-bit word)
      Reserved(LSB 4 bits): 0
      Code: 0x12
            RES: 00.. .... = Reserved
            URG: ..0. .... = Urgent Pointer is Invalid
            ACK: ...1 .... = Acknowledgement Field is Valid
            PSH: .... 0... = No push Requested
            RST: .... .0.. = No reset Connection
            SYN: .... ..1. = Synchronize Sequence Number
```

```
        FIN: .... ...0 = More Data From Sender
    Window: 32736
    Checksum: 0xD1CD
    Urgent Pointer: 0x0000
    TCP Option: 020405B4

Hexadecimal Detail
Packet: 4
0000: 00 60 97 db 88 a1 00 60 94 2e 6b 7a 08 00 45 00 | .`.Û...`..kz..E.
0010: 00 2c 27 e5 00 00 40 06 0c 53 cd a9 55 fd cd a9 | .,'å..@..SÍ©UýÍ©
0020: 55 44 00 50 05 e3 f0 67 b2 f9 01 f1 54 4e 60 12 | UD.P.ãðg.ù.ñTN`.
0030: 7f e0 d1 cd 00 00 02 04 05 b4 7e 7e             | .à.Í......~~
```

There are several things to note in the message that is returned from the Web server. First of all, notice that only TCP responds; there is nothing inside of the TCP message regarding Web information. This is because TCP has to establish a connection first. Ethernet and IP are connectionless; no connection is established between peer network interface card (NIC) driver processes or peer IP processes. However, TCP is connection-oriented, and the two communicating TCP processes must establish synchronization before higher layer communication can take place. For more details on TCP connection establishment, synchronization, sequencing, and so on, refer to RFC 793.

Client Acknowledges the Server TCP Connection Request

In the last packet, the server sent its own connection request. Packet 5 is the acknowledgment to that request. At the end of this exchange, there is a logical connection between the Web client and the Web server applications.

```
Packet 5 captured at 02/25/1999 06:49:52 PM; Packet size is 54(0x36)bytes
      Relative time: 000:00:09.833
      Delta time: 0.000.216
Ethernet Version II
      Address: 00-60-97-DB-88-A1 --->00-60-94-2E-6B-7A
      Ethernet II Protocol Type: IP
Internet Protocol
      Version(MSB 4 bits): 4
      Header length(LSB 4 bits): 5 (32-bit word)
      Service type: 0x00
            000. .... = 0 - Routine
            ...0 .... = Normal delay
            .... 0... = Normal throughput
            .... .0.. = Normal reliability
      Total length: 40 (Octets)
      Fragment ID: 44359
      Flags summary: 0x40
            0... .... = Reserved
            .1.. .... = Do not fragment
            ..0. .... = Last fragment
            Fragment offset(LSB 13 bits): 0 (0x00)
      Time to live: 32 seconds/hops
      IP protocol type: TCP (0x06)
      Checksum: 0x66F4
      IP address 205.169.85.68 ->205.169.85.253
      No option
Transmission Control Protocol
      Port 1507 ---> World Wide Web HTTP
      Sequence Number: 32592974
      Acknowledgement Number: 4033327866
      Header Length(MSB 4 bits): 5 (32-bit word)
      Reserved(LSB 4 bits): 0
```

```
    Code: 0x10
          RES: 00.. .... = Reserved
          URG: ..0. .... = Urgent Pointer is Invalid
          ACK: ...1 .... = Acknowledgement Field is Valid
          PSH: .... 0... = No push Requested
          RST: .... .0.. = No reset Connection
          SYN: .... ..0. = No synchronize Sequence Number
          FIN: .... ...0 = More Data From Sender
    Window: 8760
    Checksum: 0x4733
    Urgent Pointer: 0x0000

Hexadecimal Detail
Packet: 5
0000: 00 60 94 2e 6b 7a 00 60 97 db 88 a1 08 00 45 00 | .`..kz.`.Û....E.
0010: 00 28 ad 47 40 00 20 06 66 f4 cd a9 55 44 cd a9 | .(.G@. .fôÍ©UDÍ©
0020: 55 fd 05 e3 00 50 01 f1 54 4e f0 67 b2 fa 50 10 | Uý.ã.P.ñTNðg..P.
0030: 22 38 47 33 00 00                               | "8G3..
```

Client Sends HTTP Request to Web Server

The next message is from the client to the server. The TCP connection has been established and the client now makes a request to Port 80, the HTTP port. This is the request that is processed by the Web server application (in this case, Apache), and the Web page is returned in the ensuing packets. The HTTP GET request does not specify an HTML document, thus the Web server returns the default document. The default document name is often called INDEX.HTML.

```
Packet 6 captured at 02/25/1999 06:49:52 PM; Packet size is 382(0x17e)bytes
    Relative time: 000:00:09.836
    Delta time: 0.002.972
Ethernet Version II
    Address: 00-60-97-DB-88-A1 --->00-60-94-2E-6B-7A
    Ethernet II Protocol Type: IP
Internet Protocol
    Version(MSB 4 bits): 4
    Header length(LSB 4 bits): 5 (32-bit word)
    Service type: 0x00
          000. .... = 0 - Routine
          ...0 .... = Normal delay
```

```
        .... 0... = Normal throughput
        .... .0.. = Normal reliability
    Total length: 368 (Octets)
    Fragment ID: 44615
    Flags summary: 0x40
        0... .... = Reserved
        .1.. .... = Do not fragment
        ..0. .... = Last fragment
        Fragment offset(LSB 13 bits): 0 (0x00)
    Time to live: 32 seconds/hops
    IP protocol type: TCP (0x06)
    Checksum: 0x64AC
    IP address 205.169.85.68 ->205.169.85.253
    No option
Transmission Control Protocol
    Port 1507 ---> World Wide Web HTTP
    Sequence Number: 32592974
    Acknowledgement Number: 4033327866
    Header Length(MSB 4 bits): 5 (32-bit word)
    Reserved(LSB 4 bits): 0
    Code: 0x18
        RES: 00.. .... = Reserved
        URG: ..0. .... = Urgent Pointer is Invalid
        ACK: ...1 .... = Acknowledgement Field is Valid
        PSH: .... 1... = Push Requested
        RST: .... .0.. = No reset Connection
        SYN: .... ..0. = No synchronize Sequence Number
        FIN: .... ...0 = More Data From Sender
    Window: 8760
    Checksum: 0x86C2
    Urgent Pointer: 0x0000
HyperText Transfer Protocol
    GET / HTTP/1.1
    Accept: image/gif, image/x-xbitmap, image/jpeg, image/pjpeg, application/vnd.ms-
excel, application/msword, application/vnd.ms-powerpoint, */*
    Accept-Language: en-us
    Accept-Encoding: gzip, deflate
    User-Agent: Mozilla/4.0 (compatible; MSIE 4.01; Windows 95)
    Host: www.westnetinc.com
```

```
    Connection: Keep-Alive
    <\r><\n><\r><\n> End of TEST HTTP header
```

```
Hexadecimal Detail
Packet: 6
0000: 00 60 94 2e 6b 7a 00 60 97 db 88 a1 08 00 45 00 | .`..kz.`.Û....E.
0010: 01 70 ae 47 40 00 20 06 64 ac cd a9 55 44 cd a9 | .p.G@. .d.Í©UDÍ©
0020: 55 fd 05 e3 00 50 01 f1 54 4e f0 67 b2 fa 50 18 | Uý.ã.P.ñTNðg..P.
0030: 22 38 86 c2 00 00 47 45 54 20 2f 20 48 54 54 50 | "8.Â..GET / HTTP
0040: 2f 31 2e 31 0d 0a 41 63 63 65 70 74 3a 20 69 6d | /1.1..Accept: im
0050: 61 67 65 2f 67 69 66 2c 20 69 6d 61 67 65 2f 78 | age/gif, image/x
0060: 2d 78 62 69 74 6d 61 70 2c 20 69 6d 61 67 65 2f | -xbitmap, image/
0070: 6a 70 65 67 2c 20 69 6d 61 67 65 2f 70 6a 70 65 | jpeg, image/pjpe
0080: 67 2c 20 61 70 70 6c 69 63 61 74 69 6f 6e 2f 76 | g, application/v
0090: 6e 64 2e 6d 73 2d 65 78 63 65 6c 2c 20 61 70 70 | nd.ms-excel, app
00a0: 6c 69 63 61 74 69 6f 6e 2f 6d 73 77 6f 72 64 2c | lication/msword,
00b0: 20 61 70 70 6c 69 63 61 74 69 6f 6e 2f 76 6e 64 |  application/vnd
00c0: 2e 6d 73 2d 70 6f 77 65 72 70 6f 69 6e 74 2c 20 | .ms-powerpoint,
00d0: 2a 2f 2a 0d 0a 41 63 63 65 70 74 2d 4c 61 6e 67 | */*..Accept-Lang
00e0: 75 61 67 65 3a 20 65 6e 2d 75 73 0d 0a 41 63 63 | uage: en-us..Acc
00f0: 65 70 74 2d 45 6e 63 6f 64 69 6e 67 3a 20 67 7a | ept-Encoding: gz
0100: 69 70 2c 20 64 65 66 6c 61 74 65 0d 0a 55 73 65 | ip, deflate..Use
0110: 72 2d 41 67 65 6e 74 3a 20 4d 6f 7a 69 6c 6c 61 | r-Agent: Mozilla
0120: 2f 34 2e 30 20 28 63 6f 6d 70 61 74 69 62 6c 65 | /4.0 (compatible
0130: 3b 20 4d 53 49 45 20 34 2e 30 31 3b 20 57 69 6e | ; MSIE 4.01; Win
0140: 64 6f 77 73 20 39 35 29 0d 0a 48 6f 73 74 3a 20 | dows 95)..Host:
0150: 77 77 77 2e 77 65 73 74 6e 65 74 69 6e 63 2e 63 | www.westnetinc.c
0160: 6f 6d 0d 0a 43 6f 6e 6e 65 63 74 69 6f 6e 3a 20 | om..Connection:
0170: 4b 65 65 70 2d 41 6c 69 76 65 0d 0a 0d 0a       | Keep-Alive....
```

The Server Processes the Web Page Request

The server now responds with the information requested, the Web page. The server knows to respond with the Web page based on the IP address and the port number of the client request. The IP address of 205.169.85.253 is the address of the Web server (**http://www.westnetinc.com**). Port number 80 is the well-known port number for HTTP. The combination of the two triggers the Web server to respond with the initial web page (INDEX.HTML). The Web Page Response Diagram shows the response, the protocol stacks, and the direction of the information flow from server to client.

The Web page is returned to the client that made the request. The Web page is contained within the message, within the packet, and within the frame. This is detailed in the following trace information.

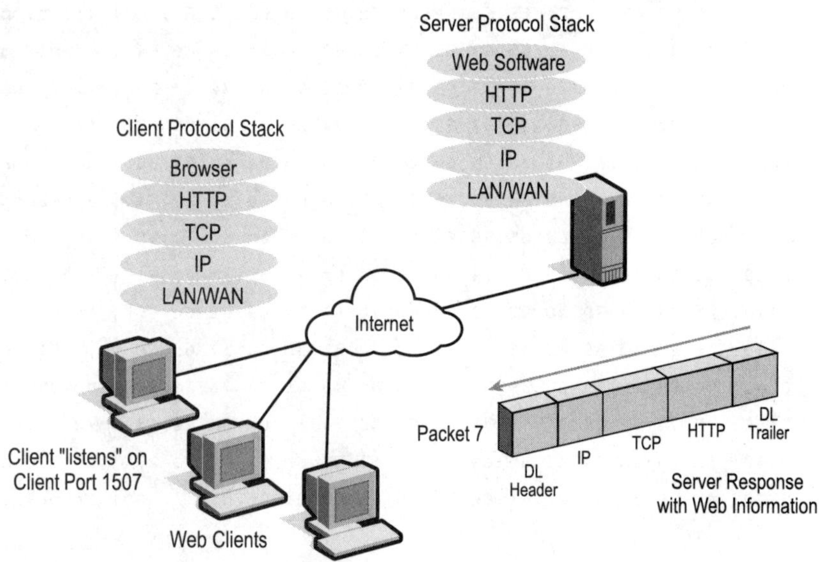

Web Page Response

```
Packet 7 captured at 02/25/1999 06:49:52 PM; Packet size is 1514(0x5ea)bytes
      Relative time: 000:00:09.841
      Delta time: 0.005.587
Ethernet Version II
      Address: 00-60-94-2E-6B-7A --->00-60-97-DB-88-A1
      Ethernet II Protocol Type: IP
Internet Protocol
      Version(MSB 4 bits): 4
      Header length(LSB 4 bits): 5 (32-bit word)
      Service type: 0x00
            000. .... = 0 - Routine
            ...0 .... = Normal delay
            .... 0... = Normal throughput
            .... .0.. = Normal reliability
      Total length: 1500 (Octets)
      Fragment ID: 10214
      Flags summary: 0x40
            0... .... = Reserved
            .1.. .... = Do not fragment
            ..0. .... = Last fragment
            Fragment offset(LSB 13 bits): 0 (0x00)
      Time to live: 64 seconds/hops
      IP protocol type: TCP (0x06)
      Checksum: 0xC6A1
      IP address 205.169.85.253 ->205.169.85.68
      No option
Transmission Control Protocol
      Port World Wide Web HTTP ---> 1507
      Sequence Number: 4033327866
      Acknowledgement Number: 32593302
      Header Length(MSB 4 bits): 5 (32-bit word)
      Reserved(LSB 4 bits): 0
      Code: 0x18
            RES: 00.. .... = Reserved
            URG: ..0. .... = Urgent Pointer is Invalid
            ACK: ...1 .... = Acknowledgement Field is Valid
            PSH: .... 1... = Push Requested
            RST: .... .0.. = No reset Connection
            SYN: .... ..0. = No synchronize Sequence Number
```

```
            FIN: .... ...0 = More Data From Sender
        Window: 32736
        Checksum: 0xE0B3
        Urgent Pointer: 0x0000
HyperText Transfer Protocol
        HTTP/1.1 200 OK
        Date: Fri, 26 Feb 1999 02:36:14 GMT
        Server: Apache/1.3.3 (Unix)  (Red Hat/Linux)
        Last-Modified: Thu, 25 Feb 1999 20:12:49 GMT
        ETag: "af008-278e-36d5aec1"
        Accept-Ranges: bytes
        Content-Length: 10126
        Keep-Alive: timeout=15, max=100
        Connection: Keep-Alive
        Content-Type: text/html
        <\r><\n><\r><\n> End of TEST HTTP header
Data:
0000: 3c 68 74 6d 6c 3e 0d 0a 3c 68 65 61 64 3e 0d 0a | <html>..<head>..
0010: 3c 74 69 74 6c 65 3e 57 65 73 74 4e 65 74 20 4c | <title>WestNet L
0020: 65 61 72 6e 69 6e 67 20 54 65 63 68 6e 6f 6c 6f | earning Technolo
0030: 67 69 65 73 3c 2f 74 69 74 6c 65 3e 0d 0a 3c 6d | gies</title>..<m
0040: 65 74 61 20 68 74 74 70 2d 65 71 75 69 76 3d 22 | eta http-equiv="
0050: 43 6f 6e 74 65 6e 74 2d 54 79 70 65 22 20 63 6f | Content-Type" co
0060: 6e 74 65 6e 74 3d 22 74 65 78 74 2f 68 74 6d 6c | ntent="text/html
0070: 3b 20 63 68 61 72 73 65 74 3d 69 73 6f 2d 38 38 | ; charset=iso-88
0080: 35 39 2d 31 22 3e 0d 0a 3c 6d 65 74 61 20 6e 61 | 59-1">..<meta na
```

```
Hexadecimal Detail

Packet: 7

0000: 00 60 97 db 88 a1 00 60 94 2e 6b 7a 08 00 45 00 | .`.Û...`..kz..E.
0010: 05 dc 27 e6 40 00 40 06 c6 a1 cd a9 55 fd cd a9 | .Ü'æ@.@...Í©UýÍ©
0020: 55 44 00 50 05 e3 f0 67 b2 fa 01 f1 55 96 50 18 | UD.P.ãðg...ñU.P.
0030: 7f e0 e0 b3 00 00 48 54 54 50 2f 31 2e 31 20 32 | .àà³..HTTP/1.1 2
0040: 30 30 20 4f 4b 0d 0a 44 61 74 65 3a 20 46 72 69 | 00 OK..Date: Fri
0050: 2c 20 32 36 20 46 65 62 20 31 39 39 39 20 30 32 | , 26 Feb 1999 02
0060: 3a 33 36 3a 31 34 20 47 4d 54 0d 0a 53 65 72 76 | :36:14 GMT..Serv
0070: 65 72 3a 20 41 70 61 63 68 65 2f 31 2e 33 2e 33 | er: Apache/1.3.3
0080: 20 28 55 6e 69 78 29 20 20 28 52 65 64 20 48 61 |  (Unix)  (Red Ha
0090: 74 2f 4c 69 6e 75 78 29 0d 0a 4c 61 73 74 2d 4d | t/Linux)..Last-M
00a0: 6f 64 69 66 69 65 64 3a 20 54 68 75 2c 20 32 35 | odified: Thu, 25
00b0: 20 46 65 62 20 31 39 39 39 20 32 30 3a 31 32 3a |  Feb 1999 20:12:
00c0: 34 39 20 47 4d 54 0d 0a 45 54 61 67 3a 20 22 61 | 49 GMT..ETag: "a
00d0: 66 30 30 38 2d 32 37 38 65 2d 33 36 64 35 61 65 | f008-278e-36d5ae
00e0: 63 31 22 0d 0a 41 63 63 65 70 74 2d 52 61 6e 67 | c1"..Accept-Rang
00f0: 65 73 3a 20 62 79 74 65 73 0d 0a 43 6f 6e 74 65 | es: bytes..Conte
0100: 6e 74 2d 4c 65 6e 67 74 68 3a 20 31 30 31 32 36 | nt-Length: 10126
0110: 0d 0a 4b 65 65 70 2d 41 6c 69 76 65 3a 20 74 69 | ..Keep-Alive: ti
0120: 6d 65 6f 75 74 3d 31 35 2c 20 6d 61 78 3d 31 30 | meout=15, max=10
0130: 30 0d 0a 43 6f 6e 6e 65 63 74 69 6f 6e 3a 20 4b | 0..Connection: K
0140: 65 65 70 2d 41 6c 69 76 65 0d 0a 43 6f 6e 74 65 | eep-Alive..Conte
0150: 6e 74 2d 54 79 70 65 3a 20 74 65 78 74 2f 68 74 | nt-Type: text/ht
0160: 6d 6c 0d 0a 0d 0a 3c 68 74 6d 6c 3e 0d 0a 3c 68 | ml....<html>..<h
0170: 65 61 64 3e 0d 0a 3c 74 69 74 6c 65 3e 57 65 73 | ead>..<title>Wes
0180: 74 4e 65 74 20 4c 65 61 72 6e 69 6e 67 20 54 65 | tNet Learning Te
0190: 63 68 6e 6f 6c 6f 67 69 65 73 3c 2f 74 69 74 6c | chnologies</titl
01a0: 65 3e 0d 0a 3c 6d 65 74 61 20 68 74 74 70 2d 65 | e>..<meta http-e
01b0: 71 75 69 76 3d 22 43 6f 6e 74 65 6e 74 2d 54 79 | quiv="Content-Ty
01c0: 70 65 22 20 63 6f 6e 74 65 6e 74 3d 22 74 65 78 | pe" content="tex
01d0: 74 2f 68 74 6d 6c 3b 20 63 68 61 72 73 65 74 3d | t/html; charset=
01e0: 69 73 6f 2d 38 38 35 39 2d 31 22 3e 0d 0a 3c 6d | iso-8859-1">..<m
```

The majority of this message is the application (HTTP) data that contains the information needed to build the Web page. The client Web browser (for example, Netscape) would take this information and display it on the screen. The Web Response Summary Diagram illustrates the overall process. Notice that more information must be retrieved from the Web site in order to build the screen, including buttons, pictures, animations, and so on. These are shown in the full trace.

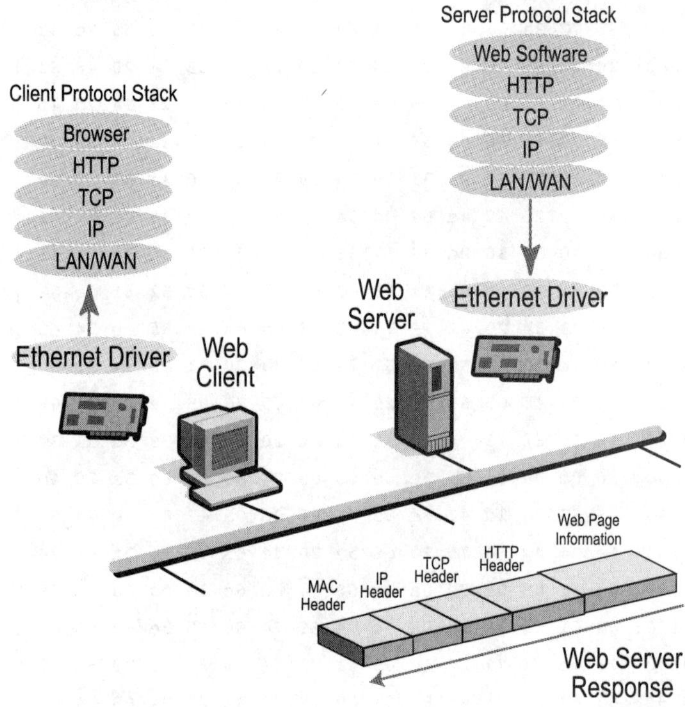

Web Response Summary

Activity

For the following trace, indicate in the hexadecimal information the frame header, packet header, and TCP header. Indicate which of the bytes (code) is used to indicate TCP connection synchronization. Draw the binary equivalent of this byte, and circle the SYN bit.

```
Packet 3 captured at 04/15/1998 01:37:58 PM; Packet size is 58(0x3a)bytes
      Relative time: 000:00:19.969
      Delta time: 0.005.203
Ethernet Version II
      Address: 00-A0-24-BF-6F-B3 --->00-60-08-3B-92-06
      Ethernet II Protocol Type: IP
Internet Protocol
      Version(MSB 4 bits): 4
      Header length(LSB 4 bits): 5 (32-bit word)
      Service type: 0x00
            000. .... = 0 - Routine
            ...0 .... = Normal delay
            .... 0... = Normal throughput
            .... .0.. = Normal reliability
      Total length: 44 (Bytes)
      Fragment ID: 3855
      Flags summary: 0x40
            0... .... = Reserved
            .1.. .... = Do not fragment
            ..0. .... = Last fragment
            Fragment offset(LSB 13 bits): 0 (0x00)
      Time to live: 32 seconds/hops
      IP protocol type: TCP (0x06)
      Checksum: 0x04A4
      IP address 205.169.85.201 ->205.169.85.253
      No option
Transmission Control Protocol
      Port 1143 ---> World Wide Web HTTP
      Sequence Number: 7718008
      Acknowledgment Number: 0
      Header Length(MSB 4 bits): 6 (32-bit word)
      Reserved(LSB 4 bits): 0
```

```
      Code: 0x02
            RES: 00.. .... = Reserved
            URG: ..0. .... = Urgent Pointer is Invalid
            ACK: ...0 .... = Acknowledgment Field is Invalid
            PSH: .... 0... = No push Requested
            RST: .... .0.. = No reset Connection
            SYN: .... ..1. = Synchronize Sequence Number
            FIN: .... ...0 = More Data From Sender
      Window: 8192
      Checksum: 0x6758
      Urgent Pointer: 0x0000
      TCP Option: 020405B4

Hexadecimal Detail
Packet: 3
0000: 00 60 08 3b 92 06 00 a0 24 bf 6f b3 08 00 45 00 | .`.;....$.o³..E.
0010: 00 2c 0f 0f 40 00 20 06 04 a4 cd a9 55 c9 cd a9 | .,..@. ...Í©U.Í©
0020: 55 fd 04 77 00 50 00 75 c4 78 00 00 00 00 60 02 | Uý.w.P.u.x....`.
0030: 20 00 67 58 00 00 02 04 05 b4       |  .gX......
Packet 3 captured at 04/15/1998 01:37:58 PM; Packet size is 58(0x3a)bytes
      Relative time: 000:00:19.969
      Delta time: 0.005.203
Ethernet Version II
      Address: 00-A0-24-BF-6F-B3 --->00-60-08-3B-92-06
      Ethernet II Protocol Type: IP
Internet Protocol
      Version(MSB 4 bits): 4
      Header length(LSB 4 bits): 5 (32-bit word)
      Service type: 0x00
            000. .... = 0 - Routine
            ...0 .... = Normal delay
            .... 0... = Normal throughput
            .... .0.. = Normal reliability
      Total length: 44 (Bytes)
      Fragment ID: 3855
      Flags summary: 0x40
            0... .... = Reserved
            .1.. .... = Do not fragment
            ..0. .... = Last fragment
```

```
            Fragment offset(LSB 13 bits): 0 (0x00)
      Time to live: 32 seconds/hops
      IP protocol type: TCP (0x06)
      Checksum: 0x04A4
      IP address 205.169.85.201 ->205.169.85.253
      No option
Transmission Control Protocol
      Port 1143 ---> World Wide Web HTTP
      Sequence Number: 7718008
      Acknowledgment Number: 0
      Header Length(MSB 4 bits): 6 (32-bit word)
      Reserved(LSB 4 bits): 0
      Code: 0x02
            RES: 00.. .... = Reserved
            URG: ..0. .... = Urgent Pointer is Invalid
            ACK: ...0 .... = Acknowledgment Field is Invalid
            PSH: .... 0... = No push Requested
            RST: .... .0.. = No reset Connection
            SYN: .... ..1. = Synchronize Sequence Number
            FIN: .... ...0 = More Data From Sender
      Window: 8192
      Checksum: 0x6758
      Urgent Pointer: 0x0000
      TCP Option: 020405B4

Hexadecimal Detail
Packet: 3
0000: 00 60 08 3b 92 06 00 a0 24 bf 6f b3 08 00 45 00 | .`.;....$.o³..E.
0010: 00 2c 0f 0f 40 00 20 06 04 a4 cd a9 55 c9 cd a9 | .,..@. ...Í©U.Í©
0020: 55 fd 04 77 00 50 00 75 c4 78 00 00 00 00 60 02 | Uý.w.P.u.x....`.
0030: 20 00 67 58 00 00 02 04 05 b4       |  .gX......
```

Extended Activities

1. Using a Web browser, access a Web page such as **http://www.westnetinc.com**. List the messages that appear while the Web pages are being accessed. What do each of these mean, such as "looking up host" or "contacting host"?

____

____

____

____

____

____

2. Try to access a Web site with an invalid Web name. What are your results? What does this tell you?

____

____

____

____

____

____

Lesson 2—Telnet

Telnet is a network application program that uses the reliable service of TCP to provide remote terminal access. Remote terminal access allows a user to log in and communicate with a process on another host, as if the user were directly connected to the remote host. The goal of providing users with remote terminal capability was one of the major reasons for the creation and development of large data networks.

Objectives

At the end of this lesson you will be able to:

- Describe the advantages of remote terminal access over direct wiring
- Describe the need for Virtual Terminal Protocol (VTP) on larger networks
- Describe the concept of a Network Virtual Terminal (NVT)
- Describe Telnet NVT and its options
- Describe the fundamentals of Telnet data transfer
- Describe Telnet single command option negotiation
- Describe negotiations
- Describe Telnet options

Key Point

Telenet provides remote terminal access.

Remote Terminal Access

Remote terminal access is especially useful in an organization where users must have access to many different hosts on a network. The Direct (Terminal-to-Host) Wiring Diagram illustrates some of the problems created by "spaghetti" wiring, when direct terminal-to-host connections are used to access multiple hosts from a single location. The spaghetti becomes more entangled when access to a new host is required. This happens because a new terminal must be added to each desktop, and multiple cables may have to be pulled the entire length of the building.

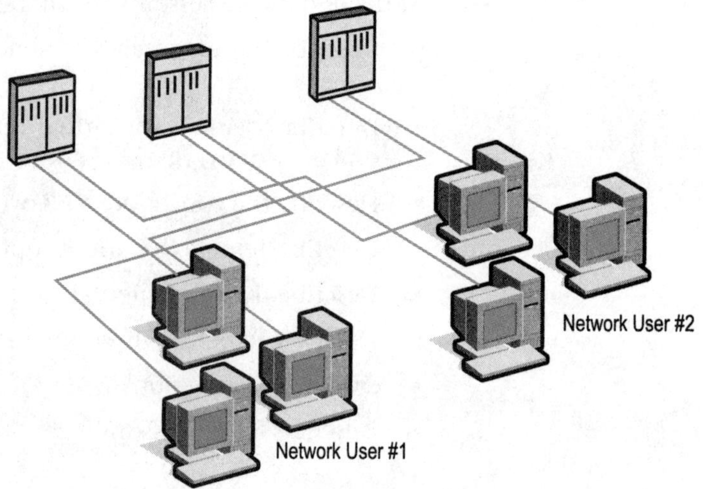

Direct (Terminal-to-Host) Wiring

Instead of having a separate terminal directly connected to each host, a remote terminal access process allows a user to access all hosts on the network from a single terminal. The user first establishes a TCP connection from his terminal to the desired remote host. After the connection is established and the logon procedure is completed, the user begins sending keystrokes to the remote host and reading the screen output generated by the remote host. The Remote Terminal Access Diagram illustrates a sample network topology with remote terminal access.

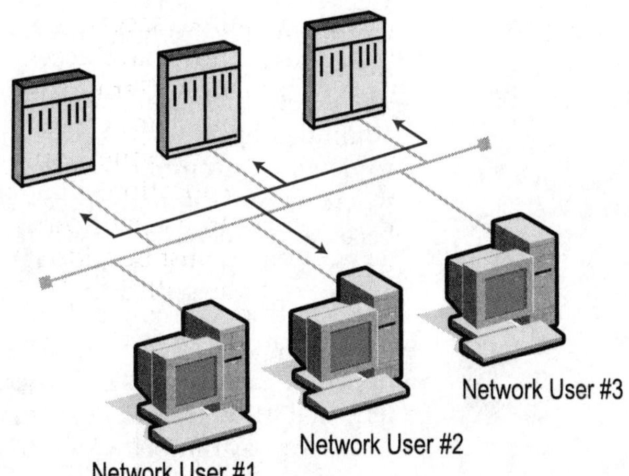

Remote Terminal Access

Remote terminal access has several advantages over direct terminal-to-host connections, as follows:

- Reduces the number of physical terminals and connections required to access remote hosts
- Provides access to geographically separate sites
- Makes it easier to move users to another workspace and support their network access requirements
- Makes it easier to add a new host to the network and make it immediately available to many users in the organization
- Increases user productivity because users can simultaneously connect to multiple remote hosts and switch back and forth between them

VTP

Remote terminal access attempts to provide the same type of service (ToS) available from direct terminal-to-host connections. Unfortunately, remote hosts generally support only a limited number of terminal types. Each terminal type has a well-defined set of terminal characteristics that must be strictly followed for communication to take place. This limitation can make it difficult to develop a remote terminal access protocol on large networks where many different types of terminals are used. This occurs because characteristics of a terminal requesting host access may not be known or supported by the remote host.

The solution to this problem is to use VTP. VTP is used as a common language to transfer data and control information across a network. VTP uses a data structure, referred to as NVT, as a generic terminal interface. All hosts map their local device characteristics, so as to appear to be talking to NVT over the network.

The sending host translates its own device characteristics to NVT for transmission on the network. The receiving process translates the received NVT data stream to its own local terminal characteristics. This translation procedure is illustrated on the VTP Diagram.

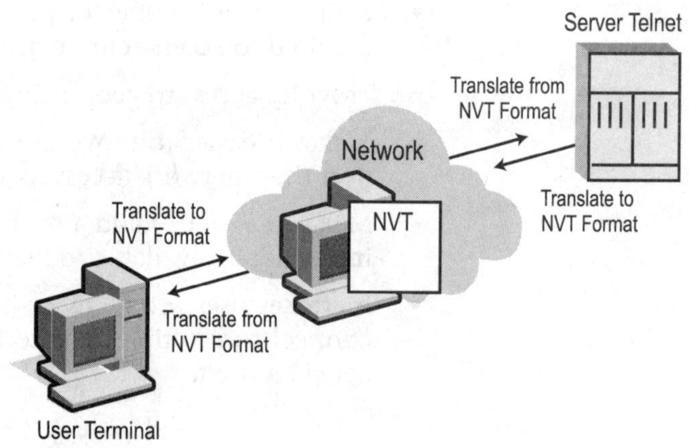

VTP

Telnet Overview

Telnet is a network application program that uses the reliable service of TCP to provide remote terminal access. The Telnet protocol (RFC 854) defines an NVT. The Telnet and OSI Diagram illustrates the relationship of Telnet to other protocols in the TCP/IP suite.

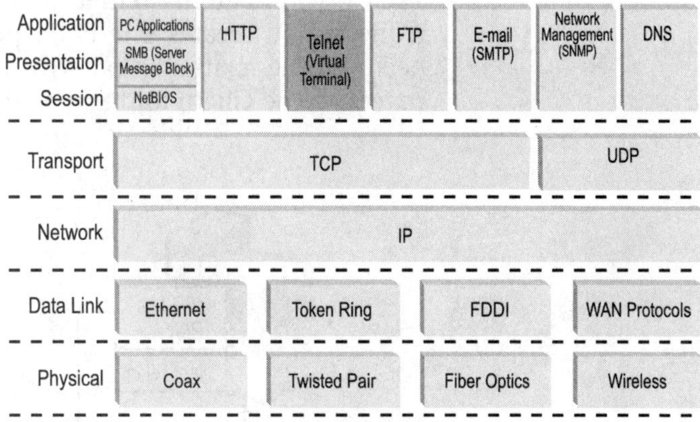

Telnet and OSI

The following describe several Telnet characteristics:

- Telnet uses the underlying reliability provided by TCP. No additional data validation procedures are included in the Telnet specification.
- All communication between the local and remote Telnet process occurs on a single, two-way data stream with encoded commands interspersed with data.
- There is support for both 7-bit (American Standard Code for Information Interchange [ASCII]) data encoded in 8-bit bytes, and full 8-bit binary encodings.

Client Telnet and Server Telnet

Telnet, like all other TCP/IP applications, conforms to the client/server paradigm. The client Telnet process resides at the user's terminal, personal computer (PC), or host. The client is responsible for establishing a TCP connection over the network with the server. The server is responsible for providing the desired service of remote terminal access.

The server Telnet process resides on the host that provides the requested service to the client. The Server Telnet process listens on TCP well-known Port 23 for incoming connection requests. The server must be able to support multiple concurrent connections to various clients.

Typically, a parent Telnet process waits for new connection requests and creates one child process (CP) for each active connection. The relationship between client and server Telnet is illustrated on the Client and Server Telnet Diagram.

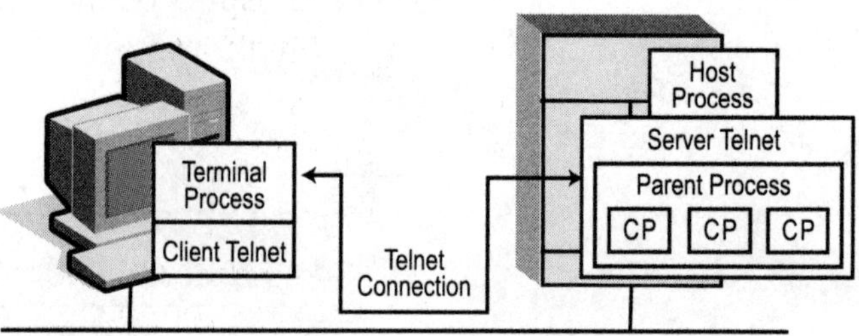

Client and Server Telnet

Telnet NVT

When a Telnet session is first established, each end of the connection is assumed to use the NVT interface. The designers of Telnet elected to define an extremely basic virtual terminal. The Telnet NVT was designed to provide remote terminal access that can be used by the simplest user terminals.

The Telnet Model Diagram illustrates the concept of a Telnet connection originating and terminating at NVT. On the diagram, the client Telnet performs a translation between the local terminal process and NVT. The server Telnet performs the same type of translation between NVT and the host process.

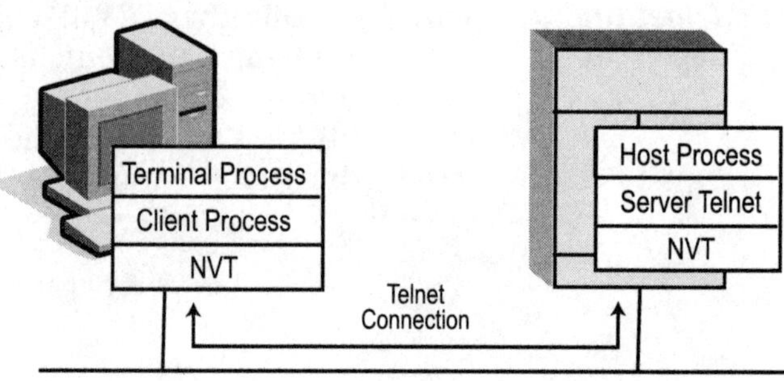

Telnet Model

Negotiated Options

Some users may have more complex terminals that have the ability to use a more sophisticated ToS than provided by the basic Telnet NVT. For this reason, RFCs that define the Telnet protocol include the concept of negotiated options. This feature allows a host to request services over and above those available from the basic NVT.

Either end of a Telnet session can offer to use an option or initiate a request that some option take effect. The other end of the connection can either accept or reject the offer or request. If the option is accepted, it will take effect immediately. If the option is rejected, the associated aspect of the connection remains as specified for NVT. If no options are selected, the default NVT will be used.

The various options are not actually defined in the original Telnet specification (RFC 854). The specific options are documented in subsequent RFCs. Options may be selected with the "Do, Don't, Will, Won't" option negotiation procedure. This procedure allows both ends of a Telnet connection to agree to use different or more complex features for their Telnet connection. The "Do, Don't, Will, Won't" process will be detailed later in this lesson.

Default NVT

The Telnet NVT is a bidirectional character device consisting of a keyboard (to produce outgoing data sent over the Telnet connection) and a printer (to display incoming data). The outgoing data can also be echoed to the local NVT printer. Before options are negotiated, the NVT appears as a simple terminal with the following characteristics:

- NVT operates as a scroll-mode asynchronous terminal with an unlimited line length and number of lines.
- The keyboard can generate all 128 ASCII codes.
- Data is transmitted as a 7-bit ASCII value in an 8-bit field.
- Telnet control commands are embedded in the data stream and encoded using byte values outside the range defined by ASCII codes.
- When inspecting the data stream, the receiving Telnet program is only required to check for the inclusion of embedded control commands indicated by the presence of the Interpret as Command (IAC) character. This character (255) must precede any other command bytes.

- In most cases, input from the NVT keyboard is buffered at the local host until a complete line of data is ready for transmission, or until some locally defined explicit signal to transmit the data occurs. The signal to transmit can be generated by a process executing on the local host. The signal can also be generated by a human user pressing the ENTER key.

Telnet Data Transfer

A Telnet connection is built upon the reliable transport services provided by TCP. A TCP connection allows data to be transmitted in both directions simultaneously (full-duplex). However, by default, Telnet data is actually sent in one direction at a time (half-duplex).

In the client-to-server direction, the new line character (carriage return or line feed) signifies the end of user input. The server can begin transmitting data. In the server-to-client direction, the Telnet Go Ahead (GA) command indicates that the client can begin transmitting data. The Telnet Transmission Turnaround (Default Half-Duplex Operation) Diagram illustrates the default half-duplex operation of the Telnet transfer protocol.

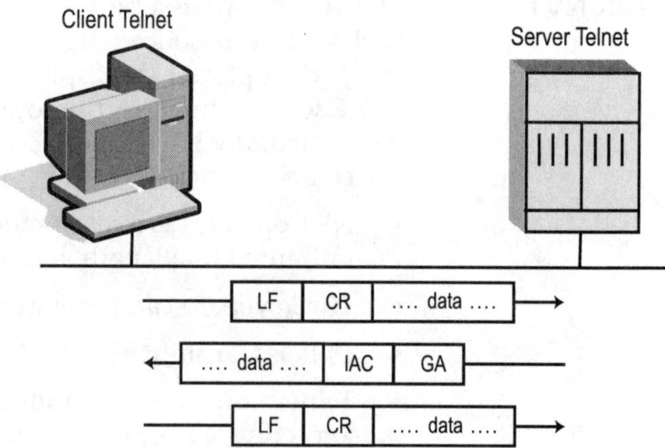

Telnet Transmission Turnaround (Default Half-Duplex Operation)

Despite the fact that data transmission is half-duplex, control signals can be sent in both directions regardless of the data transmission direction, because of the full-duplex nature of the TCP connection.

Transmission of Control Functions

All Telnet commands are embedded in the data stream and encoded using a minimum 2-byte command sequence. When inspecting the data stream, the receiving Telnet program is only required to check for the inclusion of embedded control commands, indicated by the presence of an Interpret as Command (IAC) character. An IAC character is a TELNET escape character. The 2-byte command sequence consists of an IAC character (255), followed by the code for the command. If an ASCII value of 255 is included as part of the data stream, it must be preceded by an IAC character to prevent it from being interpreted as IAC.

Several Telnet control commands are described below:

- Interrupt Process (IP)—Allows a user to signal the remote end of a Telnet connection to interrupt or abort the operation of a process. This function is often invoked when a user believes a remote process is in an infinite loop. The command can also be used when an unwanted process has been mistakenly executed. The IP command is represented by ASCII code 244, and illustrated on the Transmission of the Interrupt Process Command Diagram.

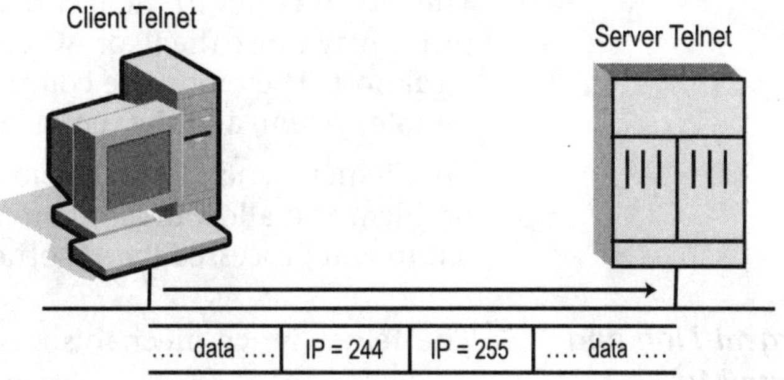

Transmission of the Interrupt Process Command

- Abort Output (AO)—Allows a user to run a remote process to completion without sending the output to the user's terminal. Typically, this command deletes any output already produced but not actually displayed on the user's terminal. The AO command is represented by ASCII code 245.

- Are You There (AYT)—Provides a user with a printable indication that a remote process is still executing. This command can be invoked by a user when the remote process appears to be "silent" for a long period of time. The remote process may be silent due to the performance of a lengthy calculation or unexpectedly high system demands. The AYT command is represented by ASCII code 246.
- Erase Character (EC)—Provides a user with the ability to erase the last character entered. This command is typically used to edit user keystrokes when typing errors are made. The EC command is represented by ASCII code 247.
- Erase Line (EL)—Provides a user with the ability to erase the last line of input entered. This command is typically used to edit user input when typing errors are made. The EL command is represented by ASCII code 248.

Out-of-Band Signaling (Telnet Synch)

The IP and AO commands are examples of control commands that allow a terminal user to halt a process that is out of control. The ability to stop a "runaway" process becomes more difficult when the terminal is connected to the remote system through a network.

The difficulty lies in the fact that the network flow control mechanisms may cause the IP or AO command to be buffered in the user's local host. Therefore, the command is not sent immediately to the remote system, and the remote process continues to execute.

The Telnet Synch mechanism was developed to overcome this problem and allow urgent commands to be immediately transmitted to and processed by the other end of the Telnet connection.

Urgent Flag and Data Mark Command

The Telnet Synch mechanism is composed of two parts:

- Setting the Urgent flag in the TCP header
- Sending the Telnet Data Mark (DM) command

A TCP packet with a set Urgent flag is not subject to the network flow control provided by the Telnet connection. The packet will not remain buffered in the local host by flow control, but will be sent immediately to the remote host. Upon receipt, the remote Telnet will begin reading its input looking for the expected DM command. As the remote Telnet reads the data stream, it will execute any interesting Telnet commands encountered. An interesting command is defined as an IP, AO, or AYT (not EC or EL) command. All user data from the Urgent flag to the DM command is discarded.

The DM command functions as the synchronization point in the data stream. It indicates that any special commands have already occurred, and the receiving process can return to normal handling of the data stream. The DM command is represented by ASCII code 242.

In the out-of-band signaling mode, the Urgent flag alerts the remote Telnet process. The embedded interesting commands are acted upon by the next higher level process. The DM instructs the remote process to return to normal handling of the data stream. The Telnet Synch Diagram illustrates the operation of this type of Telnet mechanism.

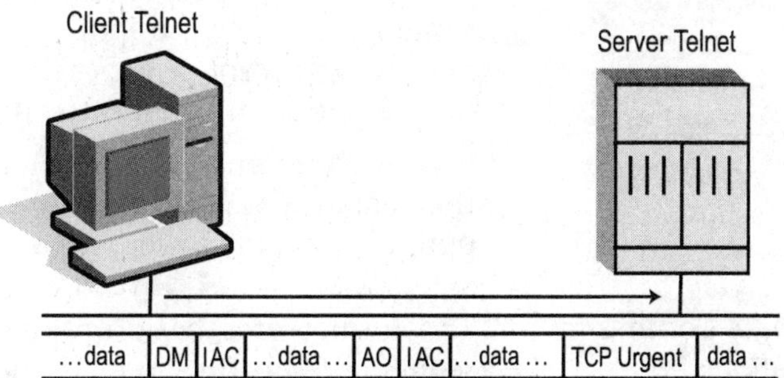

Telnet Synch

Options Negotiations

Up to this point, we have discussed a relatively simple scroll-mode NVT. Through use of the Telnet option specifications defined in RFC 855, additional features may be added to the basic NVT originally defined in RFC 854. These additional features can be used to create a more sophisticated NVT that is specialized to the particular needs of the current session, and takes advantage of more complex terminal-host interaction.

RFC 855 defines a method to assign option codes, and describes a standard for documentation of options. It does not define the actual options available. Individual Telnet options are defined separately in subsequent RFCs.

There are two possible types of options negotiations:

- Negotiations completed in a single command—This type of negotiation can be viewed as a request to enable or disable a flag. For example, options of this type are Binary Transmission (RFC 856), Echo (RFC 857), and Suppress Go Ahead (RFC 858).

- When agreed upon, negotiations that require additional information to be passed between negotiating processes—The exchange of this additional information is known as subnegotiations. The additional data can be of any length and format specified by the option's subnegotiation protocol defined in the option's RFC. An example of an option that uses subnegotiations is a request to use a particular terminal type (RFC 1091).

Options negotiations are most likely exchanged immediately after the Telnet/TCP connection is established. Each host attempts to obtain the best possible service from the other end of the connection as early as possible in the session.

Either side of the Telnet connection can request that an option be supported, offer to support an option, or do both. The other side may either accept or reject the request or offer. If both sides agree on the option, it is put into effect immediately.

Because both ends of a connection must be prepared to support the default NVT, a host can always refuse a request to enable some option, but must never refuse a request to disable an option.

Single Command Options Negotiation Format

The format of a basic options negotiation consists of a 3-byte sequence. The first byte is the traditional IAC command field, which alerts the remote process that a Telnet command follows in the data stream. The second byte specifies the Request Code field. The third byte is the Option Code field, which identifies the specific option being negotiated.

The format of a basic options request is illustrated on the Telnet Single Command Options Negotiation Diagram.

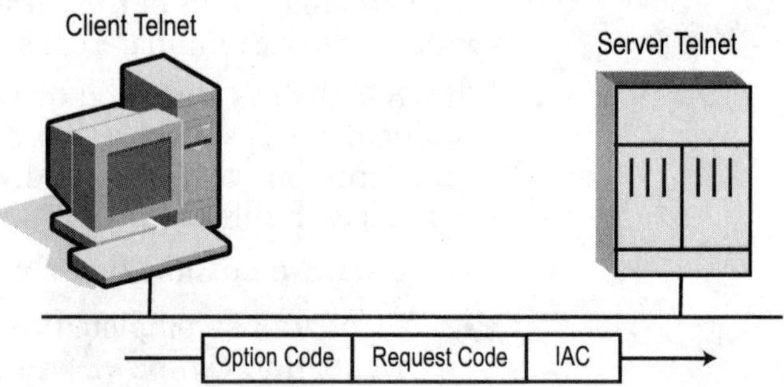

Telnet Single Command Options Negotiation

The request code must be one of the following four codes:

- Will (251)—Indicates the desire to begin performing some specified option ("I would like to do local echoing of characters").
- Won't (252)—Indicates that the Telnet process will not perform the option ("I can't locally echo").
- Do (253)—Indicates that the sending Telnet desires the other party to perform some specified option ("Please perform local echoing").
- Don't (254)—Indicates that the other side should not perform the option ("You shouldn't locally echo").

Through the use of options' negotiations, one side is free to ask for options of which the other side is completely unaware. This occurs because the other side can simply cancel the request by responding with a Won't or Don't message.

Subnegotiations

When a remote host initially agrees to an option that requires subnegotiations, the local Telnet can safely assume that the other end of the connection will be able to understand the subnegotiation protocol. Formats for subnegotiations are predefined in the RFCs that document each option.

Subnegotiations are transmitted by use of the SB (250) and SE (240) command bytes. The SB command is placed at the beginning of the data to be transmitted, and the SE command is placed at the end. As a result, the data can be of any length and format required by the particular option subnegotiation protocol. The format for transmitting subnegotiated options is illustrated on the Telnet Subnegotiations Diagram.

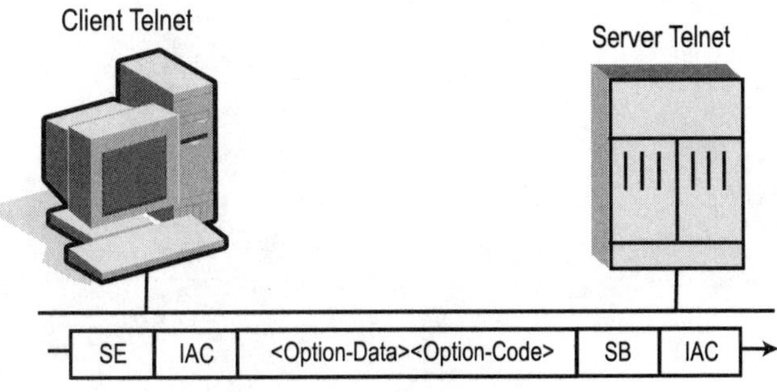

Telnet Subnegotiations

For example, RFC 1091 documents the terminal type option that requires the use of subnegotiations. This option provides a mechanism to request or change the terminal type. It defines the Option Code value to be 24, and the Option Data to be any NVT ASCII string meaningful to both ends of the negotiations. The latest Assigned Numbers RFC specifies a list of terminal type names (with correct spellings). Some terminal type names from Assigned Numbers are DEC-VT100 and IBM-3278-4.

Extended Options List

RFC 861 defines the Option Code value of 255 as the Extended Options List (EXOPL) code. The value 255 is now reserved to allow an additional 256 Telnet option codes.

Telnet Options

The defined Telnet options can be roughly divided into three major groups:

- Options that modify the default NVT, such as RFC 857, which controls echoing of data received or sent
- Options that modify Telnet transfer procedures, such as RFC 858, which eliminate the GA command and makes transmission full-duplex
- Options that allow information that is not part of the user data or transfer protocol to be defined and transmitted over the Telnet connection, such as RFC 859, which allow status information to be sent over the link

The Select Assigned Telnet Options Table lists many of the popular Telnet options.

Select Assigned Telnet Options

RFC	Description	Option ID
856	Telnet Binary Transmission	0
857	Telnet Echo Option	1
858	Telnet Suppress Go Ahead Option	3
859	Telnet Status Option	5
860	Telnet Timing Mark Option	6
861	Telnet Extended Options List	34
885	Telnet End of Record Option	25
927	TACACS User Identification	26
933	Output Marking Telnet Option	27
947	Telnet Terminal Location Number	28
1041	Telnet 3270 Regime Option	29
1053	Telnet X.3 PAD Option	30
1073	Telnet Window Size Option	31
1079	Telnet Terminal Speed Option	32
1080	Flow Control Option	33
1091	Telnet Terminal Type Option	24
1096	Subliminal-Message Option	257

Activities

1. Which best describes Telnet's use of subnegotiations?
   a. They occur prior to the negotiation process.
   b. They occur within a single command.
   c. They define basic NVT characteristics.
   d. They can vary in length and format.
2. Which Telnet single command option code tells the requestor that the remote cannot perform the option?
   a. Will (251)
   b. Won't (252)
   c. Do (253)
   d. Don't (254)
3. How does the Telnet NVT support complex terminals?
   a. It transmits data as 7-bit ASCII.
   b. It embeds controls in the data stream.
   c. It echoes characters to the local printer.
   d. It supports a 3-byte negotiation sequence.
4. How does VTP support remote terminal access?
   a. It eases development of multiple terminal access protocols.
   b. It changes the host characteristics to match the remote's.
   c. It reduces the number of each terminal's characteristics.
   d. It provides generic terminal interfaces for data and control transfer.
5. Which best describes using a remote terminal versus direct access to a number of different hosts?
   a. Remote terminal access requires a number of physical connections between hosts.
   b. Remote terminal access provides single terminal access to a number of remote hosts.
   c. Direct access can connect to multiple remote hosts over a single connection.
   d. Remote terminal access can only access local devices.

6. Which best describes the Telnet single commands options Do (253) code?
   a. It indicates the desire to begin performing some option.
   b. It indicates that the Telnet option process will not perform the option.
   c. It indicates that the sending Telnet desires the other party perform some specified option.
   d. It indicates that the other side should not perform the option.

Extended Activities

1. A host is about to telnet to a Telnet server that it has never accessed before. List the necessary steps, including locating the proper addresses.

   ____

   ____

   ____

   ____

   ____

   ____

   ____

2. Using the Web, download and familiarize yourself with the following RFC:

   RFC 854 "Telnet Protocol Specification," J. B. Postel and J. K. Reynolds

Lesson 3—FTP

FTP is used to transfer information from a client on a TCP/IP network to a server on a TCP/IP network, and vice versa. This lesson details operation of FTP and the underlying layers FTP uses.

Objectives

At the end of this lesson you will be able to:

- Describe the objectives of FTP
- Describe the data types that FTP defines
- Describe the file structures that FTP defines
- Describe the transmission modes that FTP supports
- Describe the file transfer procedure from the user's perspective
- Describe the file transfer in terms of control connections

Key Point

FTP uses a control and transfer connection and provides reliable and efficient data transfer.

Overview of FTP

FTP is another TCP/IP application that comes standard with the TCP/IP protocols. The FTP and OSI Diagram shows how FTP relates to the Open Systems Interconnection (OSI) model.

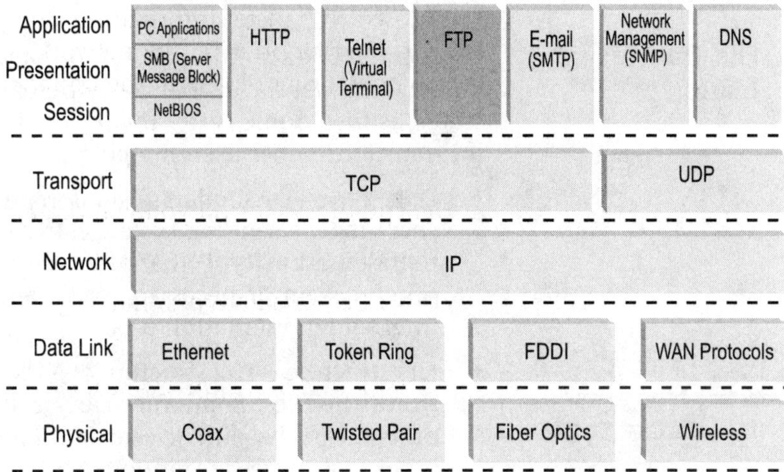

FTP and OSI

The discussion in this lesson is based on RFC 959, which contains FTP specifications for file transfer using TCP. FTP has the following objectives:

- File sharing
- Remote access to files
- File storage technology that is transparent to the user
- Reliable and efficient transfer of data

FTP allows users to log on, provide a user name and optional password, list directories, and send or receive files. Although users can transfer files interactively, FTP can also be used for program-to-program data transfer. Data can be in the form of text files, encoded data, or programs.

A user process can request that a file be transferred from a host to a user computer. It can also initiate third-party transfers between two remote hosts.

To effect a data transfer, FTP uses two TCP connections:

- Control commands
- Data transfer

FTP uses Telnet protocols for its command channel, making use of Telnet access control procedures for user identification.

File Transfer Issues

Users transfer data either by sending the data to another user or making the data available for other users to copy. The data is stored as files. Some issues involved when making a file available for transfer to other users are presented below:

- Data type—Dissimilar systems represent data differently. To share data, a sending system translates the data to a standard representation type that the other system can receive. The other system, if necessary, can then translate the data to its internal representation type.
- File structure—The structure of a file depends on the host that stores the files. Some files can be stored as sequential bytes, others can be line (record)-oriented, and others can be indexed as pages for random access.
- Transmission mode—Data can be transmitted as a stream of bytes, compressed, or it can be formatted to include markers used when data needs to be re-sent after an error occurs.

The sections that follow discuss data types, file structures, and transmission modes in more detail.

Data Type

FTP defines a limited number of data types that systems must make available. A user process can specify a data type using the Type command. The data types are:

- Text Files—Text must be represented in either of the following data types. Common text file extensions are .TXT (plain text) and .ASC (ASCII text):
  - ASCII—Default data type required for all FTP implementations. Data is prepared for transmission by converting it from the local data type to an 8-bit ASCII representation, following the Telnet NVT specification.
  - Extended Binary Coded Decimal Interchange Code (EBCDIC)—Data type used by IBM hosts to store their data. It is more efficient to keep the data in this form when transferring it from one IBM host to another. EBCDIC data is represented in 8-bit EBCDIC characters.

- Non-Text Data—Non-text data can be transmitted in one of the following data types:
  - Image (binary)—Used between similar systems for exchange of executable programs or encoded data. An Image transfer is executed by maintaining the sequence of bits in the source at the destination, with no bits skipped or modified. Common image file extensions include .BMP (bitmap), .GIF (graphics interchange format), and .JPG (Joint Photography Experts Group).
  - Local—Uses the Logical Byte Size value when the byte size of data sent needs to be preserved. For example, when a 36-bit computer sends data to a 32-bit computer, the Logical Byte Size parameter enables the receiving computer to store the data in a format meaningful to the 32-bit computer and yet retrievable in the original 36-bit format.

    Other binary file extensions include .EXE (program executable files), .SEA (Macintosh self-extracting archive), SIT (Stuffit compressed files), .TAR (TAR archive format), and .ZIP (PKZIP compressed files).
- Format Control—When ASCII and EBCDIC data types are transmitted, FTP specifies an optional parameter to indicate the vertical format of the file. These vertical file control formats are as follows:
  - Non-print—Used when no vertical file format is specified (default format).
  - Telnet format controls—Used for carriage return, line feed, new line, form feed, and end of line. The printer process interprets these controls appropriately.
  - Carriage control—Used for moving paper one or two lines up, moving paper to top of next page, and overprinting.

File Structure

The structure of a file affects both the transfer mode of the file and the interpretation and storage of the file. A user can specify the file structure for transmission using the Structure command. The three file structures defined by FTP are as follows:

- File Structure—There is no internal structure, and a file is considered to be a continuous sequence of data bytes. This is the default if the Structure command has not been used.
- Record Structure—A file is made up of sequential records. It must be accepted for text files (ASCII or EBCDIC data) by all FTP implementations.

- Page Structure—A file is made up of independent indexed pages available for random access. Each page is sent with a page header that includes the HLEN, Page Index, Data Length, Page Type, and Options fields.

Transmission Mode

Commands to transfer data between hosts include the Mode command, which specifies how data bits are to be transmitted. FTP uses three transmission modes for data transfer:

- Stream
- Block
- Compressed

For the block and compressed mode of data, FTP defines a procedure that allows a sender to insert a special marker code in the data, referred to as a restart marker. FTP uses this marker to mark the block in a file from which to re-send, in case there is a system failure. The three transmission modes are described below:

- Stream Mode—The default stream mode, which transmits data as a stream of bytes, is an available transmission mode regardless of data representation type. For some systems, the stream mode might move data faster, because it transmits the data with little or no processing. Thus, it can be an efficient mode for transferring data between two identical systems.
- Block Mode—The block mode transmits a file as a series of data blocks preceded by a header. The header provides information regarding the total length of the data block (in bytes), and includes descriptor code defining the following:
  - Last block in the file (end of file [EOF])
  - Last block in the record (end of record [EOR])
  - Restart marker (discussed later in this lesson)
  - Suspect data (data suspected to contain errors) for certain types of data (for example, seismic or weather data sent despite local errors such as magnetic tape read errors)
- Compressed Mode—The compressed mode sends three kinds of information:
  - Regular data sent in a byte string
  - Compressed data of replicated strings (such as consecutive bytes of blank spaces or consecutive string of 0 bytes)
  - Control information

  The compressed mode is rarely used or supported.

Sample File Transfer

The Sample File Transfer Diagram illustrates an example of a file transfer. The user process initiates the connection. When the control connection is made, the user process provides a user name. The server process validates the name, and then asks for a password. When the user provides the password, the user is logged on. The user may now request that a file on the server be retrieved. The server process finds the file, opens a data connection, sends the file, and then closes the connection when the transfer is made successfully. The control connection remains open until terminated by the user process.

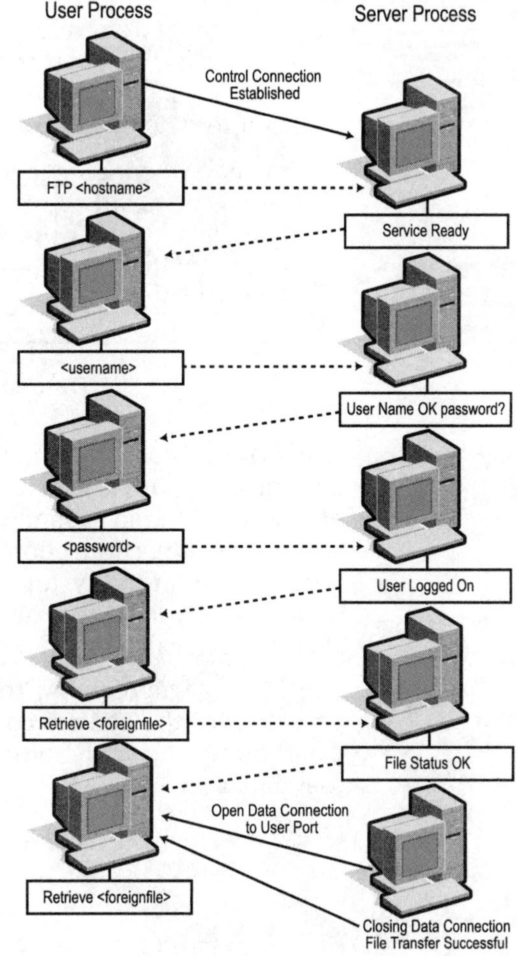

Sample File Transfer

User and Server Processes

The following sections discuss file transfer from a slightly different perspective, focusing on FTP processes involved in the transfer of data.

In FTP, both the user and server processes have a control connection and data port. The control connection ports remain active and open throughout the FTP session. The data ports and data connection are created each time a file is transferred and are terminated thereafter. The server control and data ports are TCP well-known port numbers 21 and 20, respectively. The Data and Control Ports Diagram illustrates these two concepts.

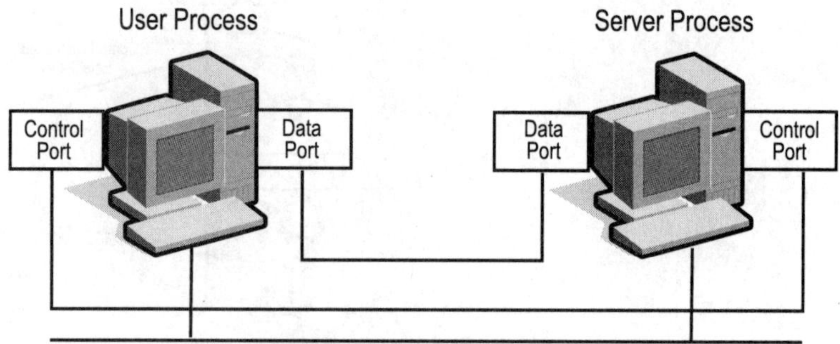

Data and Control Ports

DTP

The server protocol interpreter "listens" for a connection from the user protocol interpreter and establishes a control connection. The server is then responsible for initiating, maintaining, and closing the data connection. The user data transfer process (DTP) assumes responsibility for closing the connection only when it sends data in a transfer mode that requires the connection be closed to indicate EOF.

The DTP Diagram shows the transfer request made by the user process over the control connection. The server then initiates a data connection and transmits (transfers) the data back to the user data port.

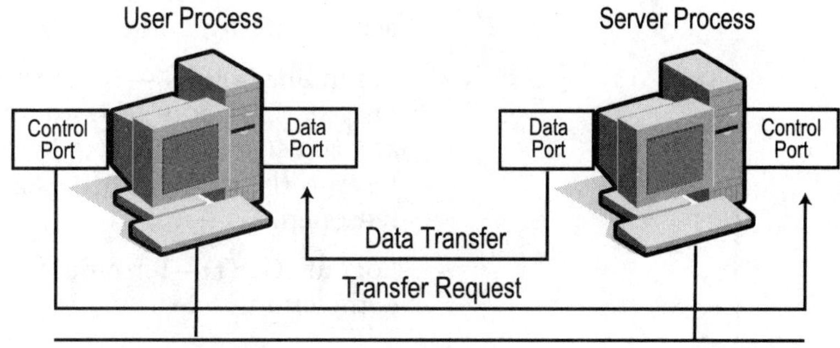

DTP

FTP Command Structure

FTP follows specifications of the Telnet NVT ASCII protocol for all communications over the control connection. Therefore, all FTP commands are Telnet strings terminated by the Telnet end of line code.

FTP commands fall into three areas:

- Access control commands
- Transfer parameter commands
- Service commands

Commands begin with a command code followed by an argument field. Command codes are four or less alphabetic characters and are not case sensitive. The three command types are as follows:

- Access Control Commands—Access controls define user access privileges to a system and files within the system. Access controls are necessary to prevent unauthorized or accidental use of files. The server-FTP process invokes access control commands as follows:
  - UserName (USER)—Identifies a user.
  - Password (PASS)—Identifies a user's password.
  - Account (ACCT)—Identifies a user's account.
  - Change Working Directory (CWD)—Allows a user to work with a different directory for file storage or retrieval without altering login or account information.
  - Change to Parent Directory (CPUD)—Special case of CWD: indicates change to parent of current working directory.

  - Structure Mount (SMNT)—Allows a user to mount a different file system data structure without altering login or account information.
  - Reinitialize (REIN)—Terminates a user, flushing all input/output (I/O) and account information, except to allow any transfer in process to be completed. All parameters are reset to the default settings and the control connection is left open.
  - Logout (QUIT)—Terminates a user and closes the control connection.

- Transfer Parameter Commands—Commands that contain data transfer parameters can be given in any order, but they must precede an FTP service request. All data transfer parameters have default values.

  The following commands are only required if the default parameters are to be changed:

  - Data Port (PORT)—Specifies a data port to be used in the data connection.
  - Passive (PASV)—Requests that the server DTP "listens" on a nondefault data port and waits for a connection.
  - Representation Type (TYPE)—Specifies the representation type (ASCII, EBCDIC, Image, or Local).
  - File Structure (STRU)—Specifies the file structure (file, record, or page).
  - Transfer Mode (MODE)—Specifies the transmission mode (stream, block, or compressed).

- Service Commands—Service commands are used to define the file transfer or file system function requested by a user. The argument supplied with the command is normally a path name. FTP does not specify a standard path name convention. Each user must follow the file naming conventions of the file systems involved in the transfer.

  The following service commands define file transfer or file system functions:

  - Retrieve (RETR)—Causes the server DTP to transfer a copy of a file to the other end of the data connection.

- Store (STOR)—Causes the server DTP to accept the data transferred by means of the data connection, and store the data as a file at the server site.
- Append (APPE)—Causes the server DTP to accept the data transferred through the data connection and store the data as a file at the server site. If the file already exists at the server site, the data is appended to that file.
- Allocate (ALLO)—May be required by some servers to reserve sufficient storage to accommodate a new file to be transferred.
- Restart (REST)—Resumes a file transfer at the specified checkpoint.
- Rename to (RNTO)—Specifies a new path name of a file.
- Abort (ABOR)—Instructs the server to abort the previous FTP service command and any associated transfer of data.
- Delete (DELE)—Deletes the file specified in the path name to be deleted at the server site.
- Remove Directory (RMD)—Causes a specified directory to be removed.
- Make Directory (MKD)—Creates a specified directory.
- Print Working Directory (PWD)—Causes the name of a current working directory to be printed as a reply.
- List (LIST)—Causes a list (of files or text) to be sent from the server to a user's passive DTP.
- Name List (NLST)—Causes a directory listing to be sent from the server to a user site.
- System (SYST)—Learns the type of operating system (OS) at the server.
- Status (STAT)—Causes a status response (current status of the operation in progress) to be sent over the control connection as a response.
- Help (HELP)—Causes the server to send helpful information regarding its implementation over the control connection to the user.
- No operation (NOOP)—Causes no action, but the server sends an OKAY reply.

Sample FTP Implementation

The following is a sample of FTP implementation on a DOS system.

Start FTP

Command Line TCP has three ways of starting FTP from the DOS prompt:

- To start FTP and connect to a host simultaneously, use the following command:

  ftp <hostname>

- To start FTP first and then connect to a host, use the following sequence of commands:

  ftp open <hostname>|<IP_address>

- To start FTP as well as load and unload files that minimize memory use, use the following sequence of commands:

  ftp <hostname>|<IP_address>

  open <hostname>|<IP_address>

Transfer Files

To transfer files from a PC to a host, use the Put command:

put <local_filename> [<remote_filename>]

To transfer files from a host to a PC, use the Get command:

get <remote_filename> [<local_filename>]

Close Connection

To close the FTP connection, use the Close command at the FTP prompt. If you want to terminate the connection as well as close it, use the Quit command at the FTP prompt.

Activities

1. Download the protocol trace file PROTOCOLTRACES.PDF from the following FTP site:

   telnet.westnetinc.com/pub

2. List the protocol layers shown on the TCP NetBIOS and TFTP traces.

   ____

   ____

   ____

   ____

Extended Activity

1. Download file DV_ALL.HLP from the following FTP site:

   telnet.westnetinc.com (This is a very large file [16 Mbytes]).

   After the file has been downloaded, perform the following tasks using Microsoft Windows:

   a. Go to the directory where the file was downloaded.

   b. Double click on the file.

   c. After the application has started, click on the Search button.

   d. Search on the term "telnet" to find additional information about Telnet.

Lesson 4—SMTP

The Simple Mail Transfer Protocol (SMTP) is the protocol used to move electronic mail (e-mail) across a TCP/IP network, whether the network is on the other side of the world or across a room. SMTP runs on top of TCP/IP and uses well-known port number 25. SMTP is referred to as "simple" because of the English-like commands used in the protocol header.

Objectives

At the end of this lesson you will be able to:

- Describe the relationship of SMTP to other protocols in the TCP/IP suite
- Describe basic SMTP commands

SMTP uses simple commands for transferring mail.

SMTP Commands

The SMTP Commands Table presents some of the more common commands used by SMTP.

SMTP Commands

SMTP Command	Command Syntax	Command Function
Hello	HELO <sending host>	Identification of sending SMTP program
Quit	QUIT	End current SMTP session
From	MAIL FROM: <sender IP address>	Sender's IP address
Recipient	RCTP to: <receiver IP address>	IP address of host to receive information
Data	DATA	Begin SMTP message

SMTP Commands (Continued)

SMTP Command	Command Syntax	Command Function
Verify	VRFY <data>	Verify username
Expand	EXPN <data>	Expand mailing list
Help	HELP <data>	Request online help

As with other protocols that use TCP/IP, a TCP connection must be established before SMTP information can be transferred. After the connection is established, the sending host identifies itself, and the "from" and "to" addresses are sent between sender and receiver. The message is transferred beginning with the Data command and ending with a period. The Quit command is used to end the session. Other commands can be used as well, but these are the most common.

Overview of SMTP

SMTP is an Application Layer protocol that uses the lower layers to reliably transport messages between hosts. SMTP is not concerned with the content of e-mail messages. Its main goal is to efficiently and reliably transfer messages between computers. The SMTP and OSI Diagram illustrates the relationship of SMTP to other protocols in the TCP/IP suite.

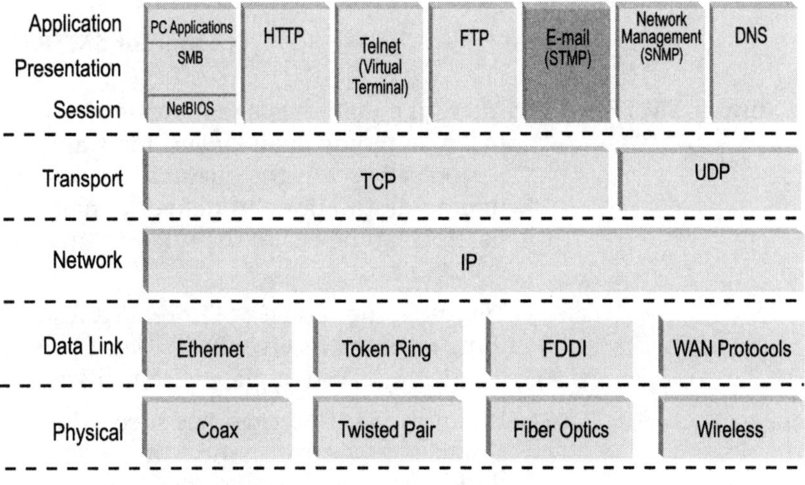

SMTP and OSI

SMTP Mail Process

The SMTP mail process is composed of two parts:

- Sender SMTP—Concerned with transmission of outgoing e-mail messages
- Receiver SMTP—Involved with reception of incoming e-mail messages from the internet

SMTP is only concerned with the delivery of e-mail from one computer to another. It does not specify how a user edits and presents e-mail to the e-mail system for delivery. SMTP is not concerned with how a user receives notification and retrieves incoming e-mail. SMTP does not specify how e-mail is to be stored or how often messages should be sent. SMTP simply defines the conversation that takes place between the sender SMTP and receiver SMTP. The Model for SMTP Use Diagram illustrates the relationship between sender SMTP and receiver SMTP.

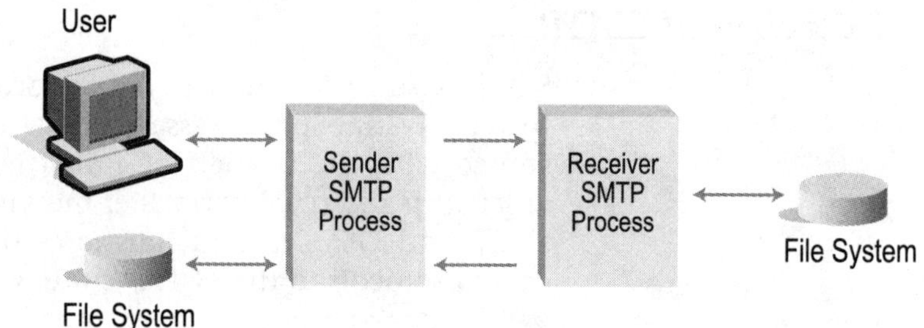

Model for SMTP Use

Sender SMTP

After an e-mail message is created by the user process, it is placed in an outgoing mail queue for transmission. The sender SMTP periodically scans the queue and opens TCP connections with the remote destinations to deliver e-mail. The other end of the connection can be either the final destination or an intermediate forwarding host.

Typically, the sender SMTP retains responsibility for all error handling until the receiver SMTP data transfer is complete. As a result, errors may cause duplicate transmissions, but not lost messages.

When the SMTP sender has successfully completed delivery to an e-mail message destination, it deletes the corresponding destination from the message's destination list. When all destinations have been reached, the e-mail message is deleted from the queue.

Receiver SMTP

The main function of the receiver SMTP is to accept incoming e-mail messages on local TCP Port 25. After an e-mail message is received, SMTP either places the message in the user mailbox or copies it to the outgoing mail queue to be forwarded to another host. The receiver SMTP's error responsibility is limited to abandoning TCP connections that fail or are inactive for long periods of time.

Mail Addresses

The following sections describe components of names used in e-mail applications.

Two-Part Names

The source and destination of Internet e-mail are identified by using a two-part name structure. A typical e-mail address consists of a character string that has the following format:

<user>@<domain-name>

The domain name identifies a specific host that has the ability to send and receive e-mail. The user identifies a particular mailbox on a computer identified by the domain name.

SMTP Mail Transfer

SMTP e-mail messages are transmitted over a TCP connection between a sender SMTP and a receiver SMTP. Mail transfer over the TCP connection consists of three distinct phases:

- The connection establishment phase creates the TCP connection for reliable data transfer.
- The data transfer phase involves transfer of an e-mail message to one or more mailboxes on the remote host.
- The connection closure phase terminates the TCP connection.

Connection Establishment

The connection establishment phase initializes the TCP connection using the traditional three-way handshake. It also includes some basic exchanges to ensure that the sender SMTP and receiver SMTP are willing to accept each other for e-mail transfer.

The Connection Establishment Exchange Diagram illustrates the exchanges involved in the connection establishment phase. After the TCP connection is established, the receiver SMTP identifies itself with a 220 positive connection ACK. The sender SMTP identifies itself to the receiver SMTP with the Hello command. The receiver SMTP accepts the sender's identification by responding with the standard 250 success response.

```
S: <TCP Connection Request>
R: <TCP Connection Confirm>
R: 220 Beta.CSO.westnetinc.com Service Ready
S: HELO Alpha.CSO.westnetinc.com
R: 250 Beta.CSO.westnetinc.com
```

Connection Establishment Exchange

Data Transfer

The data transfer phase may be used to transmit one or more e-mail messages. Each transfer is implemented through the use of three SMTP commands:

- From—identifies the source of the following message
- Recipient—identifies recipients of the message (beep)
- Data—includes the message header and body

The following provides greater detail for the transfer commands:

- From Command—The From command identifies the originator of a message. The From Command Diagram shows that the message is from JimF at host Alpha.CSO.westnetinc.com.

```
S: MAIL FROM:<JimF@Alpha.CSO.westnetinc.com>
R: 250 OK
```

From Command

- Recipient Command—The sender SMTP process issues a separate Recipient command to identify the mailbox for each recipient of the e-mail. The receiver SMTP process responds with a separate reply for each desired destination.

The Recipient Command Diagram illustrates the Recipient commands for the sample e-mail message. In the example, MaryC will not receive the message and (unfortunately for her) will continue to come to work for the remainder of the week.

```
S: RCPT TO:<AdrianB@Beta.CSO.westnetinc.com>
R: 250 OK
S: RCPT TO:<MaryC@Beta.CSO.westnetinc.com>
R: 550 No such user here
S: RCPT TO:<CherylB@Beta.CSO.westnetinc.com>
R: 250 OK
```

Recipient Command

If MaryC's mailbox was not on Beta.CSO.westnetinc.com, but the host Beta knew of her forwarding address on host Sigma, the receiver SMTP would have responded with the message *251 User not local; will forward to <MaryC@Sigma.CSO.westnetinc.com>*. In this case, MaryC would receive the message and take off the rest of the week.

- Data Command—After all Recipient commands have been transmitted and acknowledged, the sender SMTP issues a Data command. The receiver SMTP responds to the Data command with the response *354 Start Mail Input.* This part of the mail transfer process is illustrated on the Data Command Diagram.

```
S: DATA
R: 354 Start mail input; end with
<CR><LF>.<CR><LF>
```

Data Command

The text of the e-mail message is now entered into the transaction process. E-mail messages transported by SMTP use the format specified in RFC 822. The RFC 822 format is a recommendation for the message header that precedes the body of the e-mail message containing the text. The most commonly used RFC 822 keywords are Date, From, Subject, and To.

Note: SMTP does not differentiate between To: and CC: recipients. Both are originally identified with a separate Recipient command.

The body of the e-mail message may use as many lines as required and is terminated by the five-character sequence: *<CR><LF>.<CR><LF>*. The complete SMTP e-mail message, including the RFC 822 header and body, is illustrated on the SMTP Message: RFC 822 Header Format and Body Diagram.

```
S: Date: 28 May 91 11:41:56 PDT
S: From: JimF@Alpha.CSO.westnetinc.com
S: Subject: Vacation Time
S: To:
AdrianB@Beta.CSO.westnetinc.com,MaryC@Beta.CSO.w
estnetinc.com
S: CC: CherylB@Beta.CSO.westnetinc.com
S:
S: Dear Staff:
S:
S: Take the rest of the week off!
S:
S: Jim
S: <CR><LF>.<CR><LF>
```

SMTP Message: RFC 822 Header Format and Body

Connection Closure

After the sender SMTP has completed sending all e-mail messages for a particular destination, the sender SMTP issues a Quit command to terminate the TCP connection. The Connection Closure Exchange Diagram illustrates the steps involved in the connection closure exchange.

```
S: QUIT
R: 250 Beta.CSO.westnetinc.com Service Closing
Transmission Channel
R: <TCP Close Request>
S: <TCP Close Confirm>
```

Connection Closure Exchange

Very rarely, if ever, do users use e-mail in this fashion for sending and receiving information. Today, almost all e-mail is sent using an e-mail application program that sits on top of SMTP and hides the details from the user. This lesson, however, demonstrates the underlying protocol and operation of SMTP.

Activities

1. Which of the following services does SMTP use?
   a. UDP
   b. TCP
   c. RTP
   d. POP
2. Which of the following statements concerning SMTP is correct?
   a. SMTP notifies users when mail is received.
   b. SMTP defines the message format.
   c. SMTP retrieves mail for the client application.
   d. SMTP delivers mail from one computer to another.
3. The SMTP receiver accepts incoming e-mail on which well-known port?
   a. TCP Port 23
   b. TCP Port 25
   c. UDP Port 23
   d. UDP Port 25
4. Which three of the following are the three SMTP mail transfer phases? (Choose three.)
   a. Connection closure
   b. Data transfer
   c. Mail delivery
   d. Connection establishment
5. How does the receiver SMTP respond to the sender SMTP issued Data command?
   a. 354 send mail input
   b. 354 start mail input
   c. 250 OK
   d. 220 positive acknowledgement

6. Which command does the sender SMTP issue to terminate the TCP connection?
   a. QUIT
   b. EXIT
   c. 250 OK
   d. END

Extended Activity

Describe the steps necessary to send an e-mail message from one person to another by means of an e-mail server.

____

____

____

____

____

____

Lesson 5—Network Management

This lesson demonstrates the underlying architecture and operation of the SNMP. SNMP is a simple protocol by which management information for a network element can be inspected or altered by a management station.

Objectives

At the end of this lesson you will be able to:

- Describe the manager/agent model
- Describe the basic operation of SNMP
- Explain the role of the management information base (MIB)
- Explain the basic issues of SNMP encoding

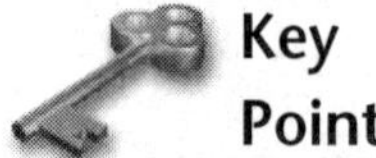

Key Point

PDUs are used to send and receive SNMP data. SNMP models all management functions as the alteration or inspection of variables.

SNMP and OSI Model

The SNMP and OSI Diagram illustrates how SNMP compares to the OSI model. SNMP uses UDP to send and receive information between the source and destination hosts.

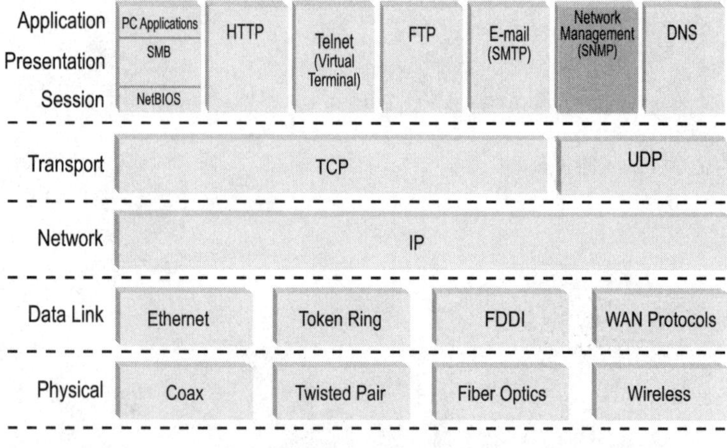

SNMP and OSI

Basic Operation

The SNMP strategy allows monitoring the status of a network by having a network management station poll for appropriate information. A limited number of unsolicited messages (traps) from the network elements guide the timing and focus of the polling. Limiting the number of unsolicited messages is consistent with the goal of simplicity and minimizing the amount of traffic generated by the network management function.

SNMP Architecture

Network management, by means of SNMP, consists of several elements that work together, including the managed elements and manager, and means by which they communicate. The SNMP Architecture Diagram illustrates these elements. The functions of the elements are briefly described below and further explained throughout the rest of this lesson.

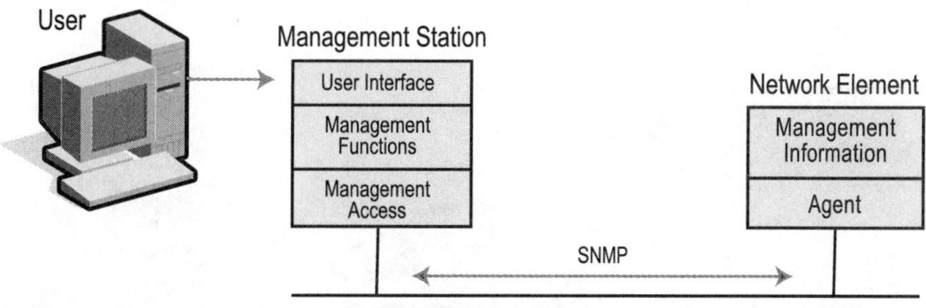

SNMP Architecture

A management station executes management applications that monitor and control network elements. A management station reports its findings to the human administrator.

Network elements (devices) such as hosts, bridges, routers, bridges/routers, hubs, terminal servers, and other "intelligent" network devices have management agents (software installed). It is by means of these management agents that a management station manages network elements using SNMP. The agents are responsible for performing network management functions requested by a network management station.

SNMP is a simple request/response protocol that exchanges management information between a network management station and management agents residing in the network elements. The protocol does not define objects that can be managed. SNMP may be used with any network management variable that can be inspected or altered.

SNMP applications are implemented in network elements through the use of management agents. Management agents reside in the network elements and have access to MIB data. They are also responsible for acting as a server to perform network management functions requested by a network manager.

Management agents are simple elements, and, for the most part, are passive. They perform operations only under the direction of a remote managing process. Only when certain well-defined error conditions occur does a management agent take any action on its own initiative. These events are called traps, and SNMP's use of traps is limited.

Management agents only manage a specific set of resources on a given network element. This simple scope makes an agent relatively simple and inexpensive to implement. The SNMP Agents Diagram illustrates the concept of management agents.

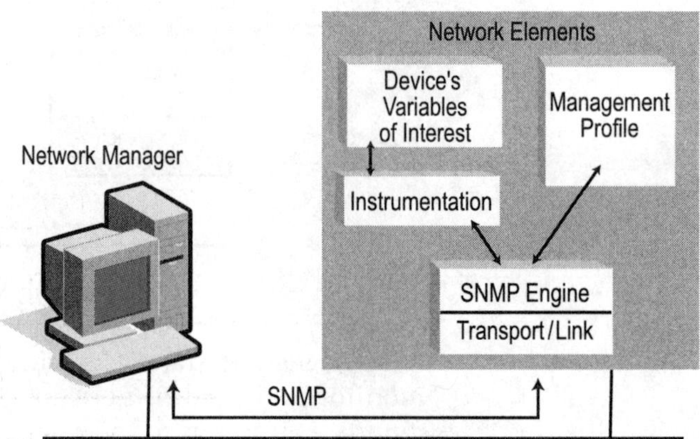

SNMP Agents

A typical implementation of a management agent includes the following four components:

- Transport protocol—Provides for the transmission (sending and receiving) of datagrams between devices on a network.
- SNMP engine—Implements SNMP and is responsible for the peer-to-peer message exchange between manager and management agent, and the encoding/decoding of requests and responses into a platform-independent form.

- Instrumentation—Provides a management protocol access to a management agent's variables of interest. This is usually achieved by an internal communications mechanism in which data structures for the device can be accessed and manipulated at the request of the management protocol.
- Management profile—A set of rules that define access to the variables of interest. Each object in the profile has an SNMP access mode: read-only, read-write, or not-accessible. This is also known as an SNMP MIB view.

SNMP Proxy Agents

A powerful aspect of SNMP architecture is the use of proxy agents. They serve as translators between SNMP and proprietary management systems. SNMP proxy agents receive SNMP directives from a managing process, translate the directives into proprietary operations, collect information, and respond to the managing process with standardized SNMP messages and traps.

Proxy agents extend the scope of SNMP management control to products and management systems that do not implement SNMP MIB or object definitions. The SNMP Proxy Agents Diagram illustrates the role of these agents.

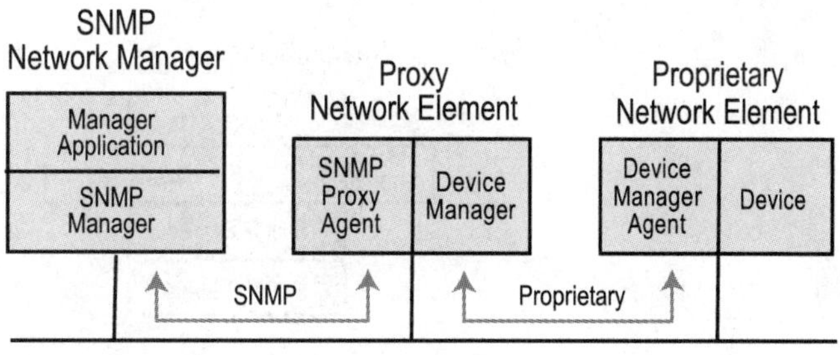

SNMP Proxy Agents

There are several reasons for the development of SNMP proxy agents, as follows:

- The managed system is limited in memory or processing resources, and therefore cannot support the required agent.
- The management access protocol for the managed system is not supported by a manager.
- The managed system has special security constraints.
- The underlying transport protocol cannot provide a path between a manager and agent.

SNMP Management Station

An SNMP manager application controls a group of management agents. These manager applications (also called managers) have the ability to direct individual management agents to deliver management information or change the operation of their particular elements. Managers are more complex than management agents. Managers can take information from a set of management agents, correlate the information, and then issue a set of directives that coordinate the activity of the set of management agents. The SNMP Management Station Diagram illustrates the role of a management station.

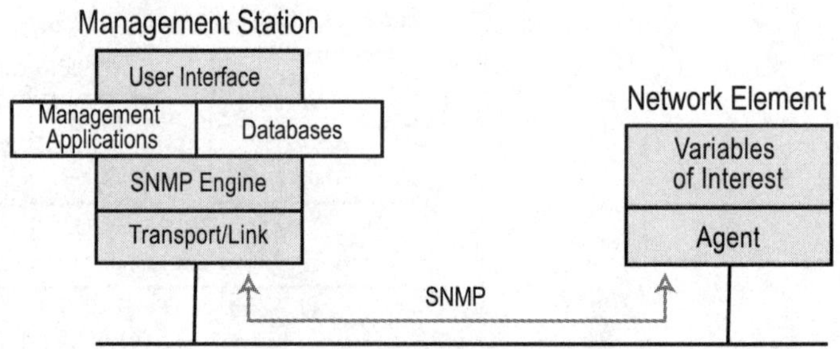

SNMP Management Station

A network manager implementation typically includes five components:

- User interface—Enables a human operator to enter management commands and receive responses. The management agent responses may be either solicited or unsolicited.
- Management applications—Assist in the analysis of network management information obtained from management agent processes.

- Databases—Contain all configuration, performance, and audit data. A distinction between MIB and other databases should be noted. MIB is the management information contained in all managed systems composing a network. The other databases are physical storage for specific instances (values) of MIB objects and other types of data collected and used for management functions as follows:
  - MIB database
  - Network element database
  - Management application databases:
    - Map database
    - Event log
    - Monitor logs
- SNMP engine—The process that implements SNMP, exchanges SNMP messages, and allows a managing system to remotely access management information in the network elements.
- Transport/Link—Provides access to the underlying data communications paths. SNMP uses UDP for transport.

This type of structure follows the primary SNMP goal of simplicity:

- Only a single manager has to have complex functions, while management agents can remain simple and relatively inexpensive to implement.
- Placing additional resources in development of management applications provides a foundation for long-term development of increasingly sophisticated management applications that can do more and more tasks without human intervention. Meanwhile, management agents can remain simple and easy to implement.
- Management applications can be isolated from particular details of network management communication protocol. This allows the applications to be moved to another type of architecture, such as OSI, in the future. Hopefully, this transition can be made without major modifications to the applications.

MIB

MIB is an integrated collection of information about all objects under the control of a particular management agent or manager. MIB is organized in a very simple table that makes it easy to implement on almost any system.

Management Objects

Management objects are representations of actual resources being managed in the SNMP environment. Currently, there are several hundred objects that have been defined and registered as standard members of the Internet MIBs.

MIB Object Definitions

Definitions for various MIB objects are presented below:

- Object Name—Objects are named through the use of object identifiers and object descriptors. An object identifier is an administratively assigned numeric name that specifies an object type. The object identifier is a sequence of integers that denotes the path of travel through the MIB name tree to the data element. (The organization of the name tree is discussed later in this lesson.) The object descriptor is a text string that is a synonym for the object identifier. It is used for human convenience.
- Object Syntax—The syntax of an object type defines the data structure corresponding to that object type. A well-defined subset of the Abstract Syntax Notation One (ASN.1) language is used for this purpose. ASN.1 is an International Organization for Standardization (ISO) standard that defines the syntax and encoding rules that specify protocol packet formats.
- Object Encoding—The encoding of an object type on the media is implied by the object type's syntax and the basic encoding rules (BERs) of ASN.1.
- MIB Object Groups—MIB has collected managed objects into related groups to further facilitate and simplify management functions. Not all groups of defined variables are mandatory for all Internet components. What is mandatory, however, is that all variables of a group are supported if any element of the group is supported.

  It was originally expected that additional MIB groups and variables would be assigned as management needs grew and evolved on the Internet. This vision became reality with the introduction of the new groups contained in MIB-2.

Names of some of the various SNMP MIB-II object groups are presented below. The number following each group indicates the group's branch in the MIB subtree.

Systems Group (1)

Implementation of the Systems Group is mandatory for all devices. A description of each system in the environment, including computer type, serial number, OS, available resources, and other attributes, is mandatory.

Interface Group (2)

Implementation of the Interface Group is required for all systems. Each system interface to a communication facility is a member of this group. Some of the attributes include the total number of interfaces and an interfaces table. This table includes the interface type, transmission speed, Maximum Transmission Unit (MTU) size, physical address, interface state, and various statistical counters.

Address Translation Group (3)

Implementation of the Address Translation Group is mandatory for all systems. This group monitors services supplied by the Address Resolution Protocol (ARP). It contains a single indexed table composed of mappings of IP addresses to physical addresses.

IP Group (4)

Implementation of the IP Group is required on each system. It defines configuration parameters for each IP computer. Select objects include the number of IP datagrams received without error, number of IP datagrams discarded, and number of fragments received. This group also includes two tables. The IP address table contains a device's IP addressing information. The IP routing table contains an entry for each route presently known to the device.

ICMP Group (5)

Implementation of the Internet Control Message Protocol (ICMP) Group is mandatory for all systems. This group defines configuration parameters for an ICMP computer. The ICMP Group contains ICMP input and output statistics for each type of ICMP message.

TCP Group (6)

Implementation of the TCP Group is mandatory for all systems that implement TCP. Select objects include the maximum number of connections supported, current number of established connections, and a table containing connection-specific information (connection state, local address, local port, remote address, and remote port).

UDP Group (7) Implementation of the UDP Group is mandatory for all systems that implement UDP. Select objects include the total number of transmitted and received UDP datagrams and error counters.

MIB Name Tree and Internet Subtrees

Management information is structured through use of a name tree. All variables in MIB are identified using the name tree. To facilitate the eventual transition to OSI, the SNMP name tree has been registered with ISO as an internationally recognized part of the ISO service registry.

The Name Tree Diagram presents the concept used to identify MIB variables. The root of the tree is unlabeled. It has three successors: Consultative Committee for International Telephony and Telegraphy (CCITT) (0), ISO (1), and Joint ISO/CCITT (2). The ISO node has another subtree for international organizations (3). One subnode of the tree has been given to the U.S. Department of Defense (DOD) Internet (6). All subtrees under this subnode are managed by the DOD Internet. Currently, there are four such subtrees: Directory (1), Management (2), Experimental (3), and Private (4). The following sections describe the structure of name trees.

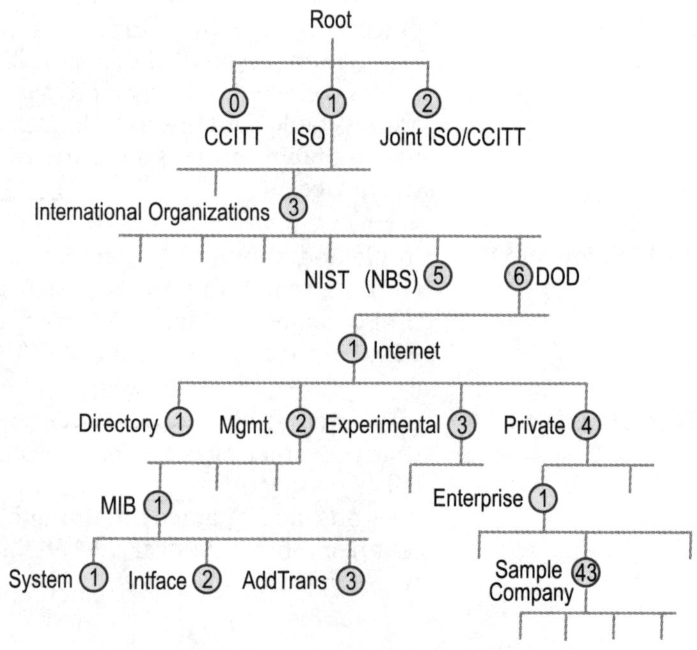

Name Tree

Directory

The Directory (1) subtree is reserved for use with a future memo that discusses how the OSI Directory Service can be used in the Internet. The directory subtree will eventually incorporate the OSI X.500 Directory Service.

Management

The Management (2) subtree identifies objects defined in Internet Architecture Board (IAB)-approved documents. As RFC-defined new versions of MIB are approved, the Assigned Numbers authority for identifying objects defined by the memo assigns the RFCs an object identifier. For example, all MIB variables start with the object identifier:

```
{mgmt 1} or 1.3.6.1.2.1 (ISO.International
Organizations.DOD.Internet.Management.MIB)
```

The Management subtree contains the MIB (1) subtree. Each of the managed object groups is defined as a subtree to MIB.

The path from the root through the tree to the object identifies the object. Each type of object is viewed as a logical table reached by branching through the sequence of integers, as illustrated on the Management Subtree Diagram.

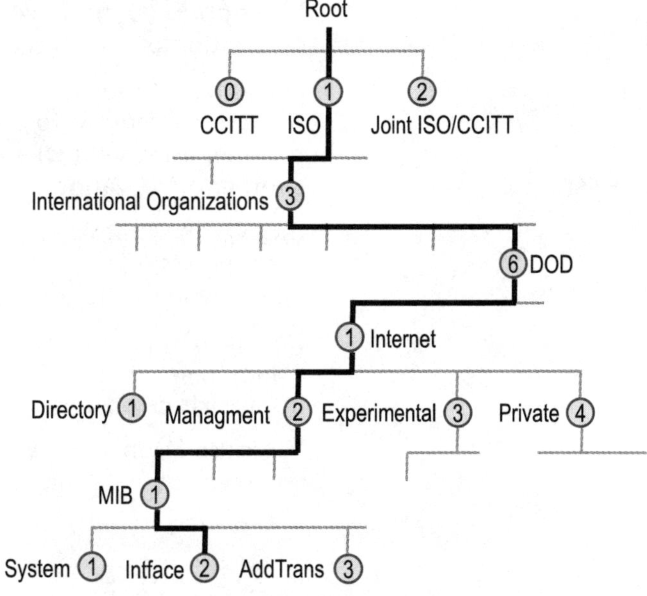

Management Subtree

For example, an object in the Interface (Intface) Group can be reached with 1.3.6.1.2.1.2. All objects within this group are ordered by the lexicographical value (as in dictionary ordering) of the remainder of their addresses.

Managed Objects

The following section provides examples of common MIB objects used with the SNMP protocol:

- Format of Definitions—The Structure of Management Information and Concise MIB Definition RFCs specify a format to be used by other documents when defining managed objects. The definition of a managed object in a MIB consists of eight possible fields:
  - Syntax (Required)—The Syntax field is the abstract syntax notation for the object type. This defines the data type that models the object.
  - Access (Required)—The Access field defines the minimal level of access required for the object type. The field must be read-only, read-write, write-only, or not-accessible.
  - Status (Required)—The Status field is either mandatory, optional, obsolete, or deprecated.
  - Description (Optional)—The Description field is a textual description of the object type.
  - Reference (Optional)—The Reference field contains a textual cross-reference to an object defined in another MIB module. It is useful when interpreting a MIB produced by another organization.
  - Index—The Index field is present only if the object type corresponds to a row in a table. It defines how SNMP can unambiguously access a logical row.
  - Defval (Optional)—The Defval field defines a default value that can be assigned to an object when a new instance is created by a management agent.
  - Value Notation—The Value Notation field is the name of an object, which is an object identifier.

The following are examples of formats used when defining managed objects:

Example #1

if Mtu OBJECT-TYPE

SYNTAX: INTEGER

ACCESS: read-only

STATUS: mandatory

DESCRIPTION: "The size of the largest IP datagram which can be sent /received on the interface, specified in bytes."

::= { ifEntry 4 }

Example #2

sysUpTime OBJECT-TYPE

SYNTAX: TimeTicks

ACCESS: read-only

STATUS: mandatory

DESCRIPTION: "The time (in hundredths of a second) since the network management portion of the system was last reinitialized."

::= { system 3 }

Experimental

The Experimental (3) subtree identifies objects used in Internet experiments. For example, an experimenter might receive number 23, and would have the object identifier available:

```
{experimental 23} or 1.3.6.1.3.23
```

Private

The Private (4) subtree identifies vendor-specific objects. The Enterprise (1) subtree permits parties providing networking subsystems to register models of their products. Upon receiving a subtree, an enterprise can define new MIB objects in the subtree.

Example—Sample Company has been assigned node number 43 in the Enterprises subtree. Sample Company might choose to register its bridge/router under the name:

1.3.6.1.4.1.43.2

Sample Company's proprietary bridge/router object identifiers would be assigned this prefix.

Operations and PDUs

SNMP uses a minimum set of operations and protocol data units (PDUs). This set provides management capability across a diverse set of networks and systems. To facilitate transition to OSI, object definitions and PDUs are encoded using OSI ASN.1. Only the ASN.1 types of integer, byte string, object identifier, null, sequence, and sequence of are used. The more complex encodings of full ASN.1 are not used.

SNMP uses a connectionless transport service such as UDP to convey PDUs between managers and management agents. UDP reflects the transaction-based nature of most management interactions. Managers can issue multiple directives to a management agent and match each response, even when they arrive out of sequence. A simple timer can detect unanswered directives and re-send them.

PDU Types

The following sections demonstrate different types of PDUs used by SNMP:

- GetRequest PDU—This PDU requests the management agent to return attribute values for a list of managed objects. The management station issues one request at a time to the management agent specifying a list containing the name of each object in which it is interested. In response, the management agent sends a reply indicating the success or failure of the request. If the request is successful, the resulting message contains the values of any objects requested.
- GetNextRequest PDU—This PDU traverses a table of objects. Because object attributes are stored in lexicographical (that is, dictionary) order, the result of the previous GetNextRequest PDU can be used as an argument in a subsequent GetNextRequest. In this way, a manager can traverse a variable length table until it has extracted all the information for the same type of object.
- GetResponse PDU—This PDU is used by an SNMP agent to return the requested attribute values to the managing process. GetResponse PDUs are also used by an agent to report error conditions. An error response can be generated by an agent when it receives an invalid object name or nonexistent object.

- SetRequest PDU—This PDU type is used by a management station to request that a management agent set attribute values of select objects. The management station sends both a list of object names and values to the management agent. The management agent attempts to alter the MIB objects to the specified values, but may fail for three reasons:
  - The MIB objects cannot be changed. For example, the object was defined to be read-only.
  - The value specified is illegal.
  - The management station was only given read-only access to a read-write object.
- Trap PDU—A trap is issued by a management agent on its own. The trap reports certain conditions and status changes to the managing process. SNMP supports a limited number of traps from network elements as follows:
  - Cold Start Reinitialization—The management agent configuration or protocol entity implementation may be altered.
  - Warm Start Reinitialization—Neither the management agent configuration nor protocol entity implementation is altered.
  - Link Down Change—Provides the status of attached communication facilities.
  - Link Up Change—Provides the status of attached communication facilities.
  - Authentication Failure—System detects an attempt to access resources by unauthorized parties.

Actions Supported by SNMP Protocols

The following sections list actions supported by the management agent and network management station.

Agent Actions

Receive GetRequest; Read Variable; Return GetResponse

Receive GetNextRequest; Read Variable; Return GetResponse

Receive SetRequest; Set Variable; Return GetResponse

Detect Event; Send Trap Message

Network Management Station Actions

Send GetRequest; Wait for and process response

Send GetNextRequest; Wait for and process response

Send SetRequest; Wait for and process response

Listen for Trap Messages; Modify Behavior as required

SNMP Encoding

SNMP uses the ASN.1 encoding scheme so a wide variety of computers can understand the contents of SNMP data.

ASN.1

One of the major goals of SNMP is to allow transfer of management information from one computer's internal representation to another computer's internal representation using a computer-independent abstract syntax. The SNMP Encoding: ASN.1 Diagram illustrates the role of this abstract syntax.

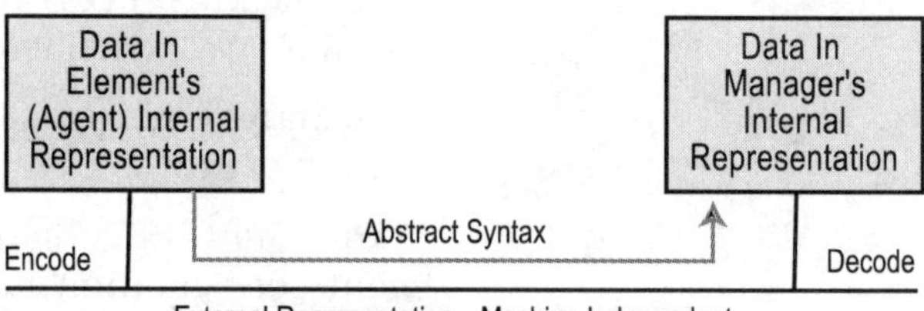

SNMP Encoding: ASN.1

ASN.1 defines management data in a computer-independent, widely understood, and widely accepted format. Characteristics of ASN.1 include:

- Allows complicated data types to be defined in printed notation.
- Allows values for these data types to be specified.
- Defines encoding rules for values of ASN.1 types. These rules completely specify the representation of a value's encoded form on the wire. They allow a receiving station to identify transferred information as containing a specific value of a specific ASN.1 type.

The syntax of a managed object defines the abstract data structure that corresponds to the object type. A well-defined subset of ASN.1 is used for this purpose. Only the ASN.1 types of integer, byte string, object identifier, object descriptor, null, sequence, and sequence of are used. The more complex encodings of full ASN.1 are not used.

Encoding SNMP management information using ASN.1 results in a variable-length SNMP message.

Protocol Layering

The SNMP Encoding: Protocol Layering Diagram illustrates frame encapsulation and protocol layering of a typical SNMP message.

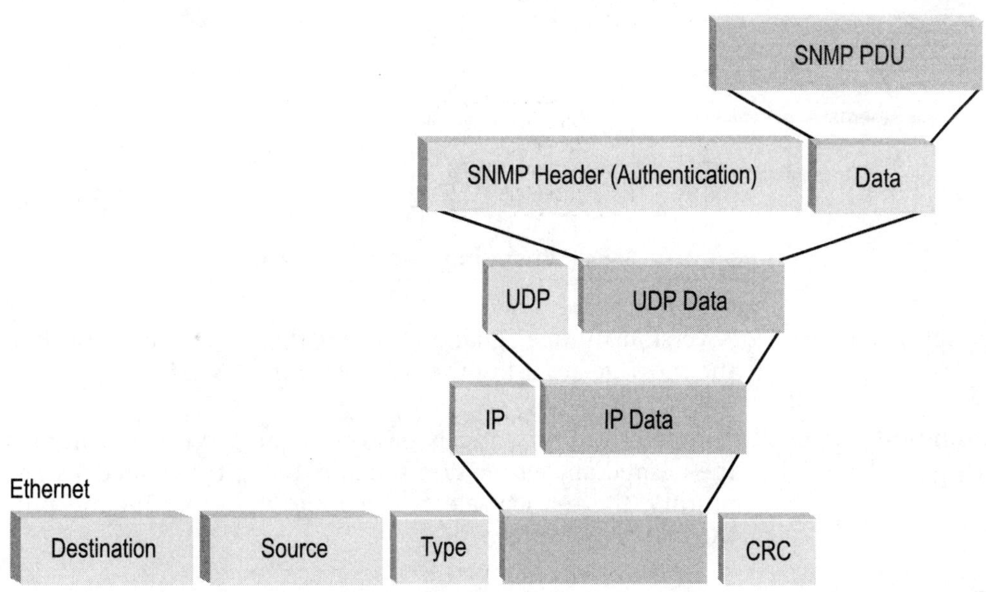

SNMP Encoding: Protocol Layering

Message Format

A typical SNMP message consists of three parts, as illustrated on the SNMP Encoding: Message Format Diagram.

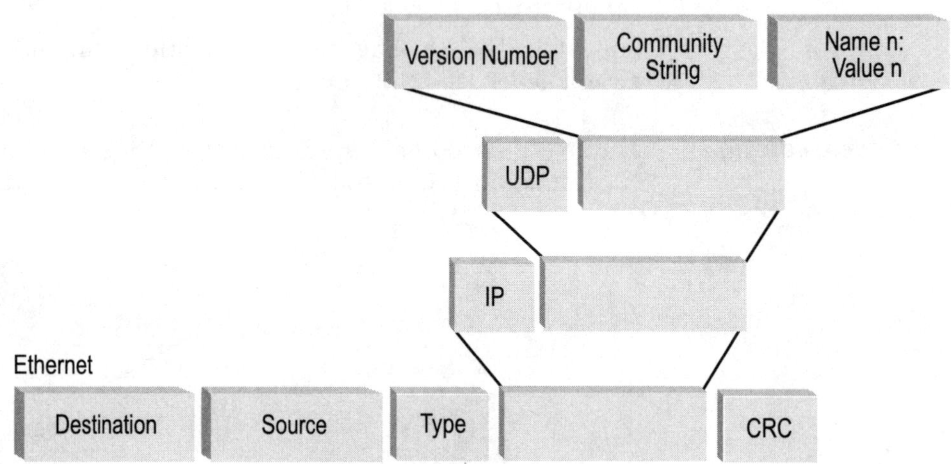

SNMP Encoding: Message Format

Version Number

A version number guarantees that the source and destination of the message are using the same version of SNMP.

Community String

The community string is passed to the service that implements the desired authentication scheme. Using the named SNMP community, the service selects the appropriate profile and processes the PDU accordingly.

PDU

There are five SNMP PDUs as follows:

- GetRequest
- GetNextRequest
- GetResponse
- SetRequest
- Trap

The PDU portion of an SNMP message is illustrated on the PDU Portion of the SNMP Message Diagram.

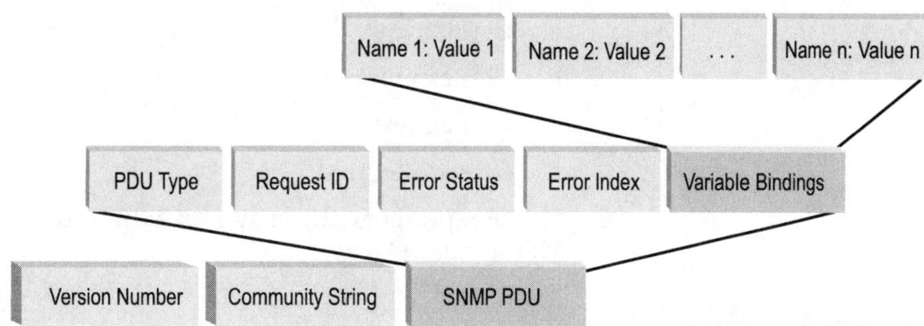

PDU Portion of the SNMP Message

The PDU fields are as follows:

- Protocol Data Unit Type—The PDU type indicates the type of PDU encapsulated in the SNMP message:
  - 0—GetRequest
  - 1—GetNextRequest
  - 2—GetResponse
  - 3—SetRequest
  - 4—Trap
- Request ID—Distinguishes among outstanding requests. By using a Request ID value, an SNMP application entity can correlate incoming responses with outstanding requests.
- Error Status—A nonzero value that indicates an exception occurred while processing a request.
- Error Index—Provides additional error information by indicating which variable in a list caused the exception.
- Variable Bindings—The pairing of the name of a variable (object identifier) to the variable's value. This field is simply a list of variables and their corresponding values.

Activities

1. Which SNMP PDU type requests that the management agent return attribute values for a list of managed objects?
   a. GetListNow
   b. GetResponse
   c. GetRequest
   d. ForwardRequest
2. SNMP represents object syntax with a subset of which ISO standard?
   a. ASN.1
   b. AS1.N
   c. ASCII
   d. ANS.1
3. Which choice best describes an SMTP proxy agent?
   a. Proxy agents perform network management functions requested by the network manager.
   b. Proxy agents direct individual management agents to deliver management information.
   c. Proxy agents define the managed resources in the SNMP environment.
   d. Proxy agents translate between SNMP and proprietary management systems.
4. Which three of the following are typical management agent components? (Choose three.)
   a. Proxy agents
   b. Transport protocol
   c. SNMP engine
   d. Management profile
5. Which three of the following are typical network manager components? (Choose three.)
   a. SNMP engine
   b. Transport/link
   c. MIB database
   d. Management profile

6. Given the Name Tree Diagram, answer the following problem:

   A server vendor is preparing to market their newest server line. They own a private MIB node number of 63, and will assign this particular server identifier number 176. Which is the correct server object identifier syntax?

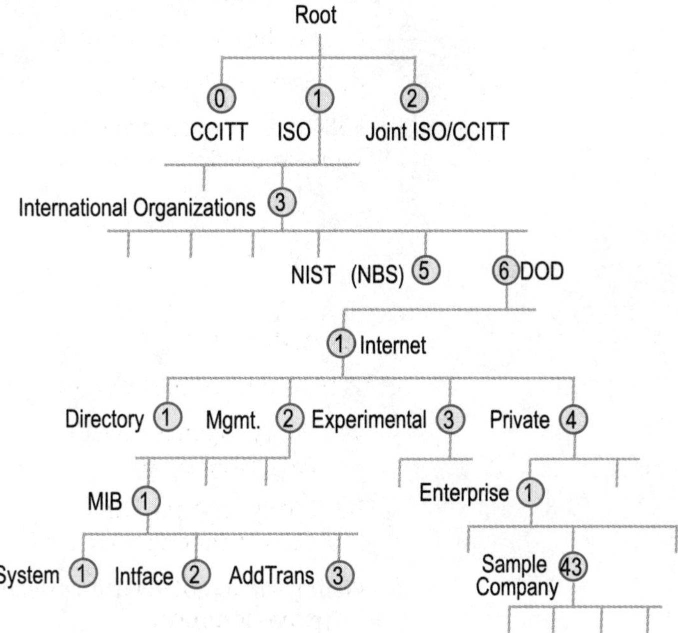

Name Tree

   a. 1.2.6.1.4.1.63.176
   b. 1.3.6.1.4.1.63.176
   c. 1.3.6.1.4.1.176.63
   d. 1.3.6.1.3.1.63.176

Extended Activities

1. Draw a diagram showing a frame and how SNMP information would be encapsulated in this frame.

2. Using the Web, locate at least 10 different MIBs and list the purpose of each.

Lesson 6—H.323 Standard for Packet Multimedia

H.323 is a standard that specifies the components, protocols, and procedures that provide multimedia communication services (real-time audio, video, and data communications) over packet networks, including IP-based networks. H.323 is part of a family of International Telecommunication Union-Telecommunications Standardization Sector (ITU-T) recommendations, called H.32x, that provides multimedia communication services over a variety of networks.

Objectives

At the end of this lesson you will be able to:

- Describe the different versions of the H.323 standard
- List the H.32x family of recommendations
- Name the components used in an H.323 network
- Name the protocols and associated layers in the H.323 protocol stack

Key Point

H.323 provides for multimedia transmission over packet-based networks.

Overview of the H.323 Standard

The H.323 standard specifies the components, protocols, and procedures for transmitting real-time audio, video, and data communications over packet-based networks. Packet-based networks include IP-based (including the Internet) or Novell Internetwork Packet Exchange (IPX)-based local area networks (LANs), enterprise networks (ENs), metropolitan area networks (MANs), and wide area networks (WANs).

H.323 can be applied in a variety of ways, depending on the type of traffic to be transmitted:

- Audio only (IP telephony)
- Audio and video (videotelephony)
- Audio and data
- Audio, video, and data
- Multipoint-multimedia communications (audio or video conferencing)

Because H.323 provides myriad services, it can be applied in a wide variety of areas, including consumer, business, and entertainment applications.

Version 1: Videophone

Version 1 of the H.323 standard was accepted in October 1996. It defined visual telephone systems and equipment for LANs that provide a nonguaranteed quality of service (QoS). As this suggests, Version 1 was heavily weighted toward multimedia communications in a LAN environment. Version 1 of the H.323 standard does not provide guaranteed QoS.

Version 2: Packet-Based Multimedia

The emergence of voice-over-IP (VoIP) applications, also called IP telephony, was not guided by any standard. The absence of a standard resulted in incompatible IP telephony products, and necessitated a revision of H.323.

VoIP introduced new requirements, such as providing communication between a PC-based telephone and a telephone on the switched circuit network (SCN) of the public telephone system. Version 2 of H.323 accommodated these additional requirements and was accepted in January 1998.

Version 3: Under Development

New features are currently being added to the H.323 standard, which will evolve to Version 3 shortly. The features being added include fax-over-packet networks, gatekeeper-to-gatekeeper communications, and fast-connection mechanisms.

Other Standards of the H.32x Family

The H.323 standard is part of the H.32x family of recommendations specified by ITU–T. The other recommendations of the family specify multimedia communication services over different networks:

- H.324—SCNs such as the public telephone system
- H.320—Integrated Services Digital Network (ISDN)
- H.321 and H.310—Broadband Integrated Services Digital Network (B–ISDN)
- H.322—LANs that provide guaranteed QoS

One of the primary goals in the development of the H.323 standard was interoperability with other multimedia services networks. This interoperability is achieved through the use of a gateway, which is a node that performs any translation necessary for traffic to pass between two dissimilar networks.

Components of an H.323 Network

The H.323 standard specifies four kinds of components. When networked together, these components provide the point-to-point and point-to-multipoint multimedia communication services:

- Terminals (client end stations)
- Multipoint control units (MCUs)
- Gateways
- Gatekeepers

Not all of these components are required in every H.323 network. Furthermore, gatekeepers, gateways, and MCUs are logically separate functions of an H.323 network, but can be implemented within a single physical device.

Terminals

Used for real-time bidirectional multimedia communications, an H.323 terminal can either be a PC or a stand-alone device running an H.323 protocol stack and the desired multimedia applications. A terminal must support audio communications, and can optionally support video or data communications. Because the basic service provided by an H.323 terminal is audio communication, such a terminal plays a key role in IP telephony services.

The primary goal of H.323 is to interwork with other multimedia terminals. Therefore, H.323 terminals are compatible with terminals that comply with the other members of the H.32x family of standards, listed above.

MCUs

MCUs coordinate multipoint conferences of three or more H.323 terminals. All terminals participating in a conference must establish a connection with the MCU. The MCU manages conference resources, negotiates between terminals to choose the audio or video coder/decoder (codec) to use, and may handle the media stream. If multipoint conferencing is not used in an H.323 network, an MCU is not required.

Gateways

All LAN-based telephony systems need to connect to the public-switched telephone network (PSTN). Gateways convert the format of a voice signal between packet-switched and circuit-switched transmission. In general, an H.323 gateway provides connectivity between an H.323 network and a non-H.323 network. A gateway is not required, however, for communication between two terminals on an H.323 network.

For example, a gateway provides communication between an H.323 terminal and the PSTN. This connectivity of dissimilar networks is achieved by translating protocols for call setup and release, converting media formats between different networks, and transferring information between the networks connected by the gateway.

The gateway converts packetized voice (sound that has been digitized and placed into an Ethernet frame) to a format that can be accepted by the PSTN. Because the digitization format for voice on the packet network is often different than on the PSTN, a gateway can also convert each format to the other; thus, these devices are often called transcoding gateways. Gateways also pass telephone signaling information, including dial tone.

Gateways support four types of connections:

- Analog (standard telephone)
- T1 or E1
- ISDN, generally Primary Rate Interface (PRI)
- Asynchronous Transfer Mode (ATM), at speeds of Optical Carrier (OC)-3c and higher

Gatekeepers

A gatekeeper can be considered the brain of the H.323 network. It is the focal point for all calls within the H.323 network. Although it is not a required component, a gatekeeper provides important services such as addressing, authorization and authentication of terminals and gateways, accounting, billing, and charging. Gatekeepers may also provide call control and voice switching services.

The gatekeeper's most important function is to limit the number of real-time network connections so they do not exceed the available bandwidth. Real-time applications register themselves with the gatekeeper before attempting to bring up a session. The gatekeeper may refuse a request to bring up a session, or grant the request at a diminished data rate. This function is most important for video connections, which can consume vast amounts of bandwidth for a high-quality connection.

A gatekeeper is not required; however, if one is available, terminals must use its services. All terminals, gateways, and MCUs managed by a single gatekeeper are referred to as an H.323 zone. A zone may be independent of network topology and composed of multiple network segments connected using routers or other devices. The H.323 Zones Diagram illustrates the zone concept.

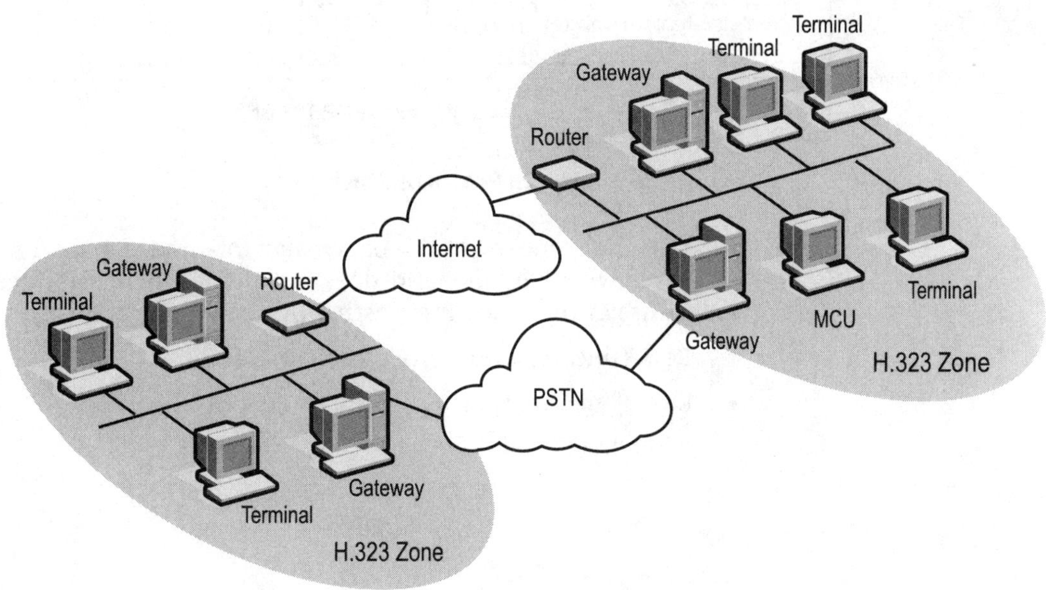

H.323 Zones

H.323 Protocols

The H.323 series of recommendations defines a family of protocols, shown shaded on the H.323 Protocol Stack Diagram:

- Audio codecs—Recommendations G.711, G.722, G.723, G.728, G.729
- Video codecs—H.261, H.263
- Registration, admission, and status (RAS)—H.225
- Control signaling—H.245
- Document conferencing and multipoint communications transport—T.120 series

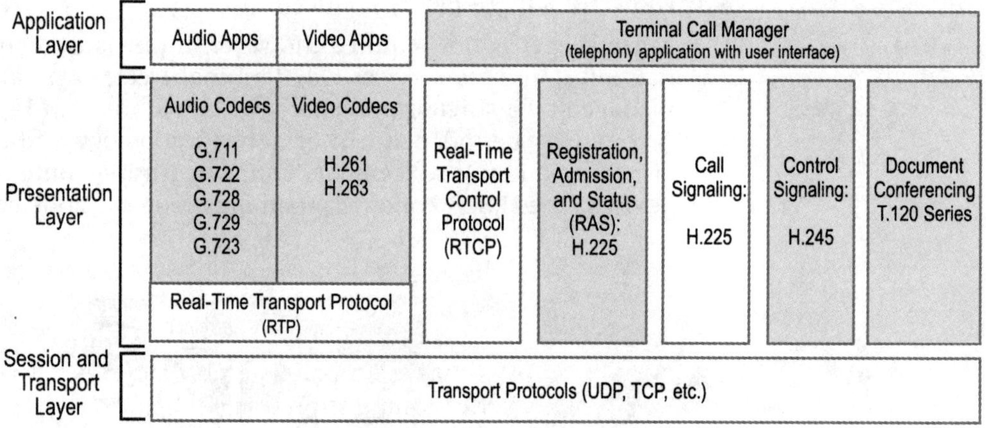

H.323 Protocol Stack

H.323 is independent of the packet network and transport protocols over which it runs and does not define them. However, it makes use of the following existing protocols:

- Real-Time Transport Protocol (RTP)—H.245
- Real-Time Transport Control Protocol (RTCP)

Audio Codecs

An audio codec encodes the audio signal from the microphone of a sending H.323 terminal and decodes the received audio code sent to the speaker of a receiving H.323 terminal.

Each audio codec is described in a separate ITU-T recommendation, as shown in the list below. Because audio is the minimum service provided by the H.323 standard, all terminals are required to support at least the G.711 audio codec. In addition to this codec, terminals may support additional codecs from the following list:

- G.711—Audio coding at 64 kilobits per second (Kbps) (required)
- G.722—64, 56, and 48 Kbps
- G.723—5.3 and 6.3 Kbps
- G.728—16 Kbps
- G.729—8 Kbps

Video Codecs

A video codec encodes video from the camera of a transmitting H.323 terminal and decodes the received video code sent to the video display of the receiving H.323 terminal. Because video support is optional under H.323, video codecs are optional as well. However, any H.323 terminal that provides video communications must support video encoding and decoding as specified in the ITU-T H.261 recommendation: compressed video transmission at 64 Kbps, at a resolution of 176 x 44 pixels.

H.323 terminals may optionally support the H.263 video codec, which offers better compression than H.261.

RTP

RTP is not defined in the H.323 specification; it is an existing protocol that H.323 simply uses. RTP provides end-to-end delivery of real-time audio and video by prioritizing this traffic ahead of connectionless data transfers. Whereas H.323 is used to transport data over IP-based networks, RTP is typically used to transport data by means of the UDP. RTP can also be used with other transport protocols. However, the faster, but less reliable, UDP is used because speed is more important than accuracy in audio/video transmission. In other words, a video or audio signal is still understandable if a few packets are lost, but will be garbled if too many packets are late.

RTP, together with UDP, provides transport protocol functionality. RTP provides payload-type identification, sequence numbering, timestamping, and delivery monitoring. UDP provides multiplexing and checksum services.

RTCP

RTCP is the counterpart of RTP that provides control services. The primary function of RTCP is to provide feedback on the quality of the data distribution. Other RTCP functions include carrying a transport-level identifier for an RTP source, called a "canonical name," which is used by receivers to synchronize audio and video.

RAS: H.225

RAS is the protocol that synchronizes communication between endpoints (terminals and gateways) and gatekeepers. The RAS protocol (H.225) is used to perform registration, admission control, bandwidth changes, status, and disengage procedures between endpoints and gatekeepers. A RAS channel is used to exchange RAS messages. This signaling channel is opened between an endpoint and a gatekeeper prior to the establishment of any other channels.

Call Signaling: H.225

The Call Signaling protocol (H.225) is used to establish a connection between two H.323 endpoints. This is achieved by exchanging H.225 protocol messages on the call-signaling channel. The call-signaling channel is opened between two H.323 endpoints or between an endpoint and the gatekeeper.

Control Signaling: H.245

The Control Signaling protocol (H.245) is used to exchange end-to-end control messages governing the operation of the H.323 endpoint. These control messages carry information such as:

- Capabilities exchange
- Opening and closing of logical channels used to carry media streams
- Flow-control messages
- General commands and indications

Document Conferencing: T.120 Series

The T.120 series of recommendations defines the rules for viewing, editing, and transferring files as part of a multimedia conference. This multilayered system of protocols allows dispersed users to share and annotate computer documents in real time.

Network Infrastructure Requirements

In addition to the hardware and software components necessary to create an H.323 packet telephony network, a robust packet network is required to support IP telephony and other real-time applications. At a minimum, switched 10-Mbps Ethernet to the desktop is required. The switches themselves must be nonblocking and support multiple internal queues to enable traffic prioritization.

Telephony traffic traversing an intranet will go through a Layer 3 switch, which must support multiple queues and QoS features such as IEEE 802.1p or 802.1Q. Switches and routers must also support the Resource Reservation Protocol (RSVP), which guarantees QoS by prioritizing traffic and reserving the network bandwidth necessary for each telephony connection.

In addition, each user's desktop must include one of two types of systems that either mimic or replace their existing telephone sets. Many users have an Ethernet telephone, a network device that plugs into an Ethernet RJ-45 wall jack. Other users, such as call center agents who use a telephone extensively in conjunction with a PC, use headsets that plug into their PCs.

Activities

1. Which three of the following are H.323 gatekeeper functions? (Choose three.)
   a. Admissions control
   b. Call signaling
   c. Bandwidth management
   d. Conference control
2. Which two codecs support audio coding at 64 Kbps? (Choose two.)
   a. G.711
   b. G.722
   c. G.726
   d. G.728
3. Which H.323 recommendation protocol handles RAS?
   a. H.225
   b. H.245
   c. H.261
   d. H.263
4. Which multimedia protocol specifies a multipoint conferencing transport?
   a. T.120
   b. H.261
   c. H.263
   d. T.038
5. Describe each of the following H.323 recommendation specified components.
   a. MCU

      ____

      ____

   b. Terminal

      ____

      ____

c. Gateway

d. Gatekeeper

6. Describe how the four components of an H.323 network are used.

7. Describe the process an audio codec goes through at the sending and receiving stations.

Extended Activities

1. Based on the H.323 protocol stack, draw an Ethernet frame carrying video information.

2. Using the Web, research additional information on the following topics:

   a. H.323 terminals

   b. H.323 MCUs

   c. H.323 gateways

   d. H.323 gatekeepers

   e. RTP

Summary

This unit provided a detailed look at how TCP/IP application information is transferred between two computers. Previous units helped us to understand why applications are used and details of the underlying protocols. This unit built upon the previous three units, and looked at details of information going "across the wire" between two computers attached to a TCP/IP network.

Lesson 1 looked at how information is transferred between a PC attached to an Ethernet network accessing information from a Web server. We first saw how a client uses DNS to resolve a URL to an IP address. Once the client learns the server's address, its TCP process establishes a connection with a TCP process on a server. After the connection is established, information flows between communicating ports using services of IP and the underlying LAN protocol.

Lesson 2 reviewed operation of Telnet and how a client Telnet process communicates with a Telnet server. Options are first negotiated between client and server, and then data transfer takes place. Several RFCs specify Telnet options that can be used between Telnet clients and servers.

Lesson 3 covered details of moving files between client servers using FTP. FTP is a very common TCP/IP application used to move all types of files across the Internet. It provides an efficient mechanism for sharing files and giving clients access to files transparently.

Lesson 4 covered details of the e-mail protocol SMTP and how SMTP is used to transmit and receive messages. SMTP uses the connection-oriented TCP to move e-mail from client to server. SMTP defines the conversation that takes place between a client and server, rather than how e-mail is stored or retrieved.

Lesson 5 covered details of SNMP and how information is sent between SNMP agents and management software. There are several different modes of network management covered by the SNMP specification, including passive management, active management, and exception management.

Finally, Lesson 6 introduced us to the H.32x family of ITU-T packet multimedia standards. We learned that H.323 specifies four components: terminals, MCUs, gateways, and gatekeepers. H.323 uses the services of other protocols such as voice and video codecs (H.225) and H.245 to handle call signaling, control, and management, and RTP and RSVP. H.323 networks require specific qualities of service, and thus require the QoS services of protocols such as 802.1Q and 802.1p.

Unit 7 Quiz

1. Before data can be sent between applications using TCP, which of the following must occur?
   a. IP connection must be established.
   b. TCP connection must be is established.
   c. TCP messages must be divided into segments.
   d. IP packets must be divided into frames.
2. IP packet addresses most likely come from which of the following?
   a. User entering a URL
   b. ARP
   c. Router in a network
   d. Web server
3. The concept of a virtual terminal allows for which of the following?
   a. High-speed data transfer
   b. Connectivity to multiple host computers
   c. Multiple users of the same terminal
   d. Multitasking host computers
4. An FTP control port is used by an FTP server to perform which of the following?
   a. Interpret requests from a client
   b. Control the amount of data in a packet
   c. Control the speed at which data is sent across a LAN
   d. Send data to and from a client
5. Which of the following is the reason some TCP/IP applications are referred to as simple?
   a. They are easy to understand.
   b. They are easy to replicate.
   c. They use easy-to-read commands.
   d. They use easy-to-process data.

6. A Web browser client sends a Web page request message to an HTTP server. In which order will the server decapsulate the request message?
   a. Application Layer, Transport Layer, Network Interface Layer, Internet Layer
   b. Transport Layer, Application Layer, Internet Layer, Network Interface Layer
   c. Network Interface Layer, Internet Layer, Application Layer, Transport Layer
   d. Network Interface Layer, Internet Layer, Transport Layer, Application Layer
7. How does a TCP application acknowledge the last message's receipt?
   a. In its response message, it increments the TCP port number by one.
   b. It increments the received sequence number by one and sends it in the response message's Acknowledgement Number field.
   c. It increments the response sequence number by one and sends it in the response message's Acknowledgement Number field.
   d. It clears the response message's acknowledgement and synchronization bits.
8. If an HTTP client does not specify a document name in its HTTP request message, what will the HTTP server return in response?
   a. An empty page
   b. An error message
   c. Default document
   d. An HTTP NACK
9. Which combined information triggers a TCP or UDP application to respond to an information request?
   a. The MAC and IP addresses
   b. The IP address and port number
   c. The MAC address and port number
   d. The filename and port number

10. Which three of the following are advantages of remote terminal access (Telnet) over direct terminal-to-host access? (Choose three.)
    a. Reduction in the number of remote hosts
    b. Increased user productivity
    c. Access to multiple, separate sites from the same terminal
    d. Reduction in the number of physical terminals
11. Which protocol reduces the number of client terminal protocols the remote host must support?
    a. HTTP
    b. TCP
    c. UDP
    d. VTP
12. What is the Telnet character device responsible for displaying incoming data?
    a. Printer
    b. Display
    c. LPD
    d. Monitor
13. The Telnet default NVT provides which fundamental characteristics? (Choose three.)
    a. It embeds control commands in the data stream.
    b. The keyboard generates 128 ASCII codes.
    c. It transmits data as a 7-bit ASCII value in an 8-bit field.
    d. Color-coded characters representing different data types.
14. When do a Telnet terminal and remote host negotiate options?
    a. Prior to establishing the TCP connection
    b. Prior to establishing the UDP connection
    c. After establishing the TCP connection
    d. After data transmission begins

15. Which three of the following are FTP objectives? (Choose three.)
    a. File sharing
    b. Transparent file storage technology
    c. Remote terminal access
    d. Reliable data transfer
16. Which application protocols does FTP use on its command channel?
    a. HTTP
    b. TFTP
    c. Uuencode
    d. Telnet
17. Which text file type is the FTP default?
    a. ASCII
    b. EBCDIC
    c. Binary
    d. Local
18. Which three modes does FTP use to transfer data? (Choose three.)
    a. Stream
    b. Flow
    c. Block
    d. Compressed
19. Which are the FTP server control and data well-known ports? (Choose two.)
    a. TCP Port 20
    b. TCP Port 21
    c. TCP Port 22
    d. TCP Port 23

20. Which is the FTP command used to place files on an FTP server?
    a. Send
    b. Put
    c. Get
    d. Transfer
21. Which SMTP command identifies the sending host?
    a. IAM
    b. FROM
    c. HELO
    d. IDSEND
22. Which SMTP command does the sender process use to identify separate recipient mailboxes?
    a. HELO
    b. RCPT
    c. MBOX
    d. TO
23. Which SMTP command designates that the message's text follows?
    a. DATA
    b. START
    c. TEXT
    d. HELO
24. An SNMP management agent's implementation includes which components? (Choose three.)
    a. SNMP engine
    b. instrumentation
    c. transport protocol
    d. user interface
25. Which are SNMP MIB view access modes? (Choose three.)
    a. Write-only
    b. Read-only
    c. Read-write
    d. Not-accessible

26. Which portion of the SNMP architecture is responsible for implementing SNMP and exchanging messages between the management station and the managed elements?
    a. The MIB database
    b. The network transport protocol
    c. The user interface
    d. The SNMP engine
27. SNMP structures MIB management information in which of the following trees?
    a. A MIB tree
    b. An SNMP tree
    c. A name tree
    d. A directory tree
28. Which services does RTP provide to add reliability to packet voice networks? (Choose three.)
    a. Delivery monitoring
    b. Sequence numbering
    c. Packet priorities
    d. Time-stamping
29. You wish to implement VoIP services on your existing data network. Part of your plan is to allow telecommuters to call network users from their home PSTN telephones. Which H.323 device must you install in your existing data network to allow for these remote connections?
    a. A PSTN telephone switch
    b. An MCU
    c. H.323 terminals in each telecommuter's home office
    d. A PSTN gateway
30. Which of the following are H.323 audio codecs? (Choose two.)
    a. G.711
    b. G.728
    c. H.245
    d. H.320

31. Which protocols assist H.323 in controlling and monitoring connections? (Choose two.)
    a. H.225
    b. H.245
    c. H.310
    d. H.321
32. Which QoS protocols must a network support to provide robust VoIP services? (Choose two.)
    a. 802.1p
    b. 802.11b
    c. RSVP
    d. 802.3

Unit 8
Troubleshooting a TCP/IP Network

This unit covers a general approach for troubleshooting a Transmission Control Protocol/Internet Protocol (TCP/IP) network. A logical approach should be taken when identifying a problem and coming up with a solution. The network troubleshooter follows a methodical series of steps to resolve issues and is careful to document both findings and results.

This unit also covers specific tools that can be used to troubleshoot a network, including Address Resolution Protocol (ARP), Ipconfig, Nbtstat, Netstat, packet Internet groper (Ping), and Tracert. These tools are used in the isolation and testing of problems found in a TCP/IP network.

Lessons

1. Troubleshooting Principles
2. Winipcfg
3. Ping
4. Tracert
5. Nbtstat and Netstat
6. ARP
7. A Troubleshooting Problem

Terms

Address Resolution Protocol (ARP)—ARP is a TCP/IP protocol used to convert an IP address into a physical address, such as an Ethernet address. A host wishing to obtain a physical address broadcasts an ARP request onto the TCP/IP network. The host on the network that has the IP address in the request then replies with its physical hardware address.

fat ping—A fat ping is a ping issued with the -l option, specifying a large packet size. This can be used to test for intermittent network component or link failures between end nodes. A useful packet size is 512 bytes, although sizes up to the network segment's MTU can also be used. This term also refers to a TCP/IP denial of service attack, where the sender floods the receiver's network with oversized packets.

Ipconfig—Ipconfig is one of the configuration tools, such as the Windows Winipcfg, used to display addressing information on a host computer.

Nbtstat—Nbtstat is a utility that can be used to display statistics and current TCP/IP connections using NetBIOS over a TCP/IP connection.

Netstat—Netstat shows the current status of all connections on a computer. The Netstat utility shows remote connected computer IP addresses and port numbers and the corresponding computer name; the local computer IP address, port, and name; and the protocol the connection uses.

Packet Internet Groper (Ping)—Ping is used to verify that a computer's IP software is running properly and to verify the connectivity between computers.

Reverse ARP (RARP)—RARP can be used by a host to discover its IP address. In this case, the host broadcasts its physical address and a RARP server replies with the host's IP address.

Tracert—Tracert is a utility that traces the route between two computers and sends information about each router hop along the way.

Lesson 1—Troubleshooting Principles

It is good to have a systematic approach to determine whether a problem is attributable to an operator or a system and, given a problem scenario, to select the appropriate next step based on this approach. This lesson reviews steps that can be used in troubleshooting a TCP/IP network.

Objectives

At the end of this lesson you will be able to:

- Explain the importance of a troubleshooting methodology

Key Point

Effective troubleshooting requires a systematic and logical approach.

Troubleshooting Steps

Troubleshooting a network is as much art as it is skill. Following a systematic approach is important, as is documenting the steps taken and the findings. Although this approach may seem laborious, it helps to do it right the first time. The steps for troubleshooting a network include:

1. Identify the exact issue
2. Recreate the problem
3. Isolate the cause
4. Formulate and implement a correction
5. Test the solution
6. Document the problem and solution and provide feedback

Identify the Exact Issue

The most important step in troubleshooting is to identify the exact issue. Knowing the normal operating conditions of a network is important in identifying an issue. It helps to sort out symptoms from probable causes. To identify an issue, ask the following questions:

- When the problem occurred, what took place?
- When the problem occurred, was something new being done or something routine?
- Has anything changed recently that might have had an impact?
- Can the problem be recreated easily?

Recreate the Problem

If possible, recreate the problem that occurred. For example, if Internet connectivity is lost, try it again and note what occurs. Messages displayed by a browser can give some indication as to what might have happened. In some cases, it may not be possible to recreate the problem, but it is helpful to recreate the steps taken when the problem occurred.

At this point, a list of likely problems can be generated and slowly narrowed as more information is gathered. To do this, we will need some of the tools mentioned in the upcoming lessons.

Isolate the Cause

The next step in the troubleshooting process is to isolate the cause of the problem. Is the problem related to physical connectivity, computer hardware, computer software, operator error, or some other identifiable source? By this time, we should have a good idea which computer is causing the problem, or which area of the network is suspicious. We continue to isolate the problem until we discover its cause. It is also important at this phase to review the information gathered thus far, to see whether there are other possible causes of the problem.

Formulate and Implement a Correction

Now it is necessary to implement a correction to the problem. There may be several solutions to the problem, and tradeoffs may exist. Tradeoffs often occur between different solutions and the economic differences between solutions. After a solution is determined, the corrective action can be taken.

Test the Solution

After a solution is implemented, we should test our resolution to see whether it solved the problem. We should also test "around" the solution to ensure that no other part of the system has been impacted by the corrective action. We do not want to fix one thing and break two more!

Document the Problem and Solution and Provide Feedback

The final step in the troubleshooting process is to document the findings and solution. A solution may be as elaborate as redesigning a network, or as simple as restarting a server or plugging in a loose cable. When documented, it is also good to obtain feedback from the impacted user or group to close the loop and complete the troubleshooting process.

Tools Used for Troubleshooting a TCP/IP Network

There are a number of tools used to assist with troubleshooting TCP/IP networks. These can be used in a number of the troubleshooting steps, including identifying the exact issue and testing the solution. These tools, covered in the next series of lessons, include:

- Ipconfig—Ipconfig is one of the configuration tools, such as the Windows Winipcfg, used to display addressing information on a host computer
- Ping—Ping is used to verify that a computer's IP software is running properly and to verify the connectivity between computers
- Tracert—Tracert is a utility that traces the route between two computers and sends information about each router hop along the way
- Nbtstat—Nbstat is a utility that can be used to display statistics and current TCP/IP connections using Network Basic Input/Output System (NetBIOS) over a TCP/IP connection
- Netstat—Netstat shows the current state of all connections on a computer
- ARP—ARP is used to show the ARP cache of a computer

Activities

1. Why is it necessary to follow a systematic approach when troubleshooting a network?

2. Is it necessary to document everything you find when you troubleshoot a problem? Why?

3. Why is it important to recreate a problem?

4. After a correction is formulated, why is it necessary to test the solution?

5. If the testing process determines that the solution does not fix the problem, what should you do next?

6. After the solution is implemented and the issue is resolved, is documentation still necessary? Why?

Extended Activity

Your customer reports that all network users can no longer connect to the company's intranet Web site. Yesterday, everyone could access the site. The company DNS services were moved to a new server.

Explain how you would use each of the troubleshooting steps mentioned in this lesson to identify and isolate the problem and implement and document a solution. Which troubleshooting tools will you use?

Lesson 2—Winipcfg

Winipcfg is a Microsoft Windows tool used to display important information about a computer's addressing and connectivity parameters. Winipcfg is frequently used as a starting point for problem isolation. Winipcfg is a Windows 95/98/Me utility; the Windows NT and Windows 2000 equivalent is ipconfig.

Objectives

At the end of this lesson you will be able to:

- Use Winipcfg to verify the local computer's TCP/IP configuration
- Use Winipcfg to update the local computer's TCP/IP configuration

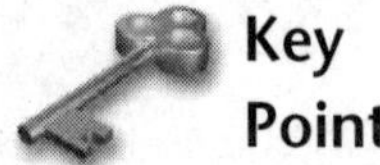

Key Point

Winipcfg displays a computer's addressing information.

TCP/IP Applications and Tools

The Winipcfg command displays current TCP/IP network configuration values. These values include the host name, Domain Name System (DNS) server name, and other pertinent information. To initiate the Winipcfg command, click on the Start button in the lower left corner of your Windows 95/98 screen. Scroll up to Run and release the mouse. The Run menu screen will appear, as shown on the Run Menu Screen Diagram.

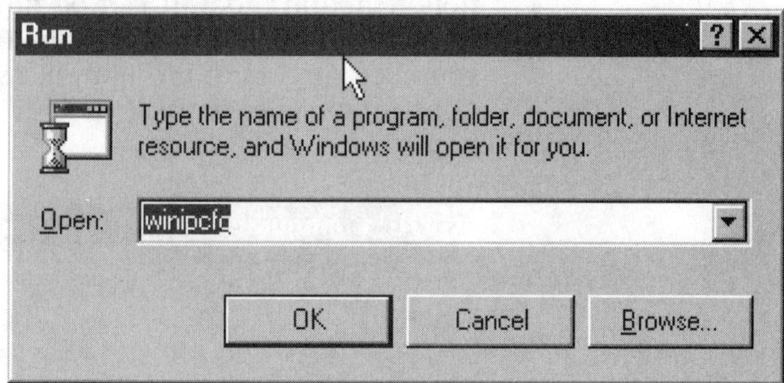

Run Menu Screen

Type **winipcfg** in the open window and press ENTER. The following screen will appear, as shown on the IP Configuration Screen Diagram.

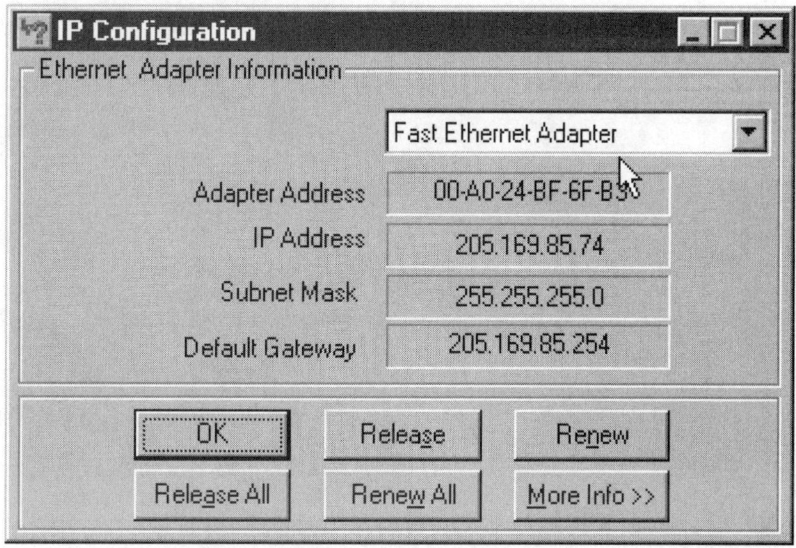

IP Configuration Screen

The IP Configuration screen can be very helpful as a resource and troubleshooting tool. It can be run from a DOS prompt or the Windows 95/98 Run menu. More information is available when you click the More Info button, as shown on the Expanded IP Configuration Screen Diagram.

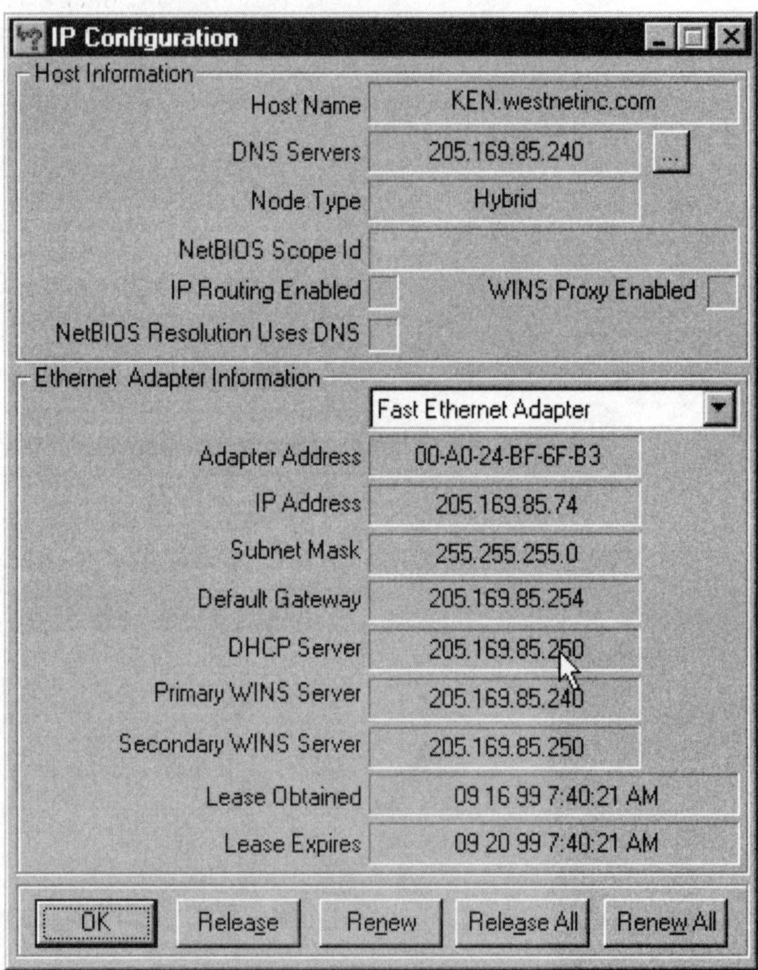

Expanded IP Configuration Screen

This screen tells us a lot about the computer. It tells us the host name, KEN. It also gives us quite a bit of addressing information, including the address of the first DNS server that will be used for name resolution. It also tells us the Fast Ethernet network interface card (NIC) address referred to on this screen as the adapter address. It includes the IP address and subnet mask associated with this IP address. And finally, it includes the address of the router (default gateway) used for connectivity to the Internet.

Additional information is available as well. Clicking the button next to the DNS Servers entry will cause it to cycle through additional DNS server addresses, if so configured. Clicking the down arrow next to the Fast Ethernet Adapter entry selects additional adapters and shows their configuration information.

The buttons along the Windows' bottom control the local computer's Dynamic Host Configuration Protocol (DHCP) information. The Release button releases the currently selected adapter's address lease and related information. The Renew button updates the current adapter's lease information. The Release All button releases configuration information for all adapters, and the Renew All button renews all adapter information.

Activities

Refer to the IP screen shot used earlier in this lesson to answer the following questions:

1. What is the class of IP address in this network?

   ____

2. How many subnets are used in this network?

   ____

3. What part of the IP number is associated with KEN, and what part of the IP number is the network portion?

   ____

4. What is the speed of the portion of the network where this device is connected?

   ____

Extended Activities

1. Perform the Winipcfg or Ipconfig command on a Windows-based computer and list your findings.

   ____

   ____

   ____

   ____

2. Using the Web, find other tools that can be used to find out information about computers. What are similar tools that are used in a Macintosh or UNIX workstation?

   ____

   ____

   ____

   ____

Lesson 3—Ping

The quickest and easiest way to evaluate whether a computer is up and running and attached to a TCP/IP network is to use the Ping command. This command tells a lot about the condition of the network and the device of concern. This lesson reviews the Ping command and how it is used in troubleshooting network problems.

Objectives

At the end of this lesson you will be able to:

- Use the Ping utility to verify TCP/IP operation
- Display the various Ping utility options
- Gather additional information using the Ping utility

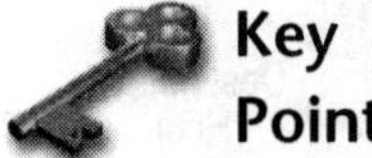

Key Point

Ping is used to verify whether an IP process is running on another host.

Ping Operation

Ping is a program that tests to see whether another host on a TCP/IP network is reachable. Ping sends an IP packet to another computer on the network and expects a reply. Ping is actually an Internet Control Message Protocol (ICMP) "echo message," meaning a packet is sent to another computer, and it is expected the information will be echoed back to the sender with the exact data that was transmitted, as illustrated on the Ping Diagram. Round-trip times are reported when Ping is used to give the troubleshooter some indication as to how long it took to move information between sender and receiver. Ping uses ICMP echo request (ICMP Message Type 8) and reply (ICMP Message Type 0) messages.

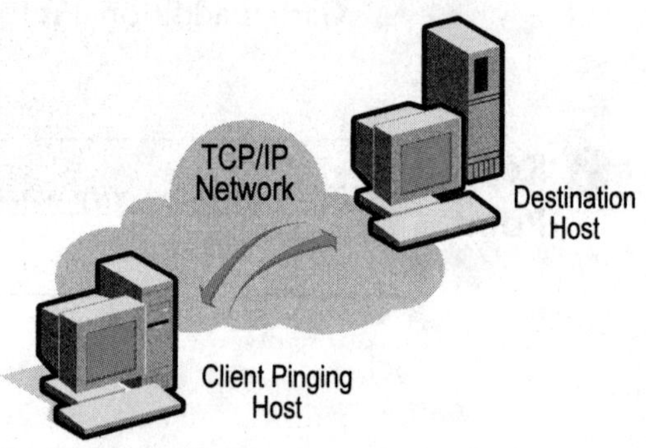

Ping

Simply typing **ping** from a command line will give you the list of options available with the PING command. These are shown on the Ping Command Screen Diagram.

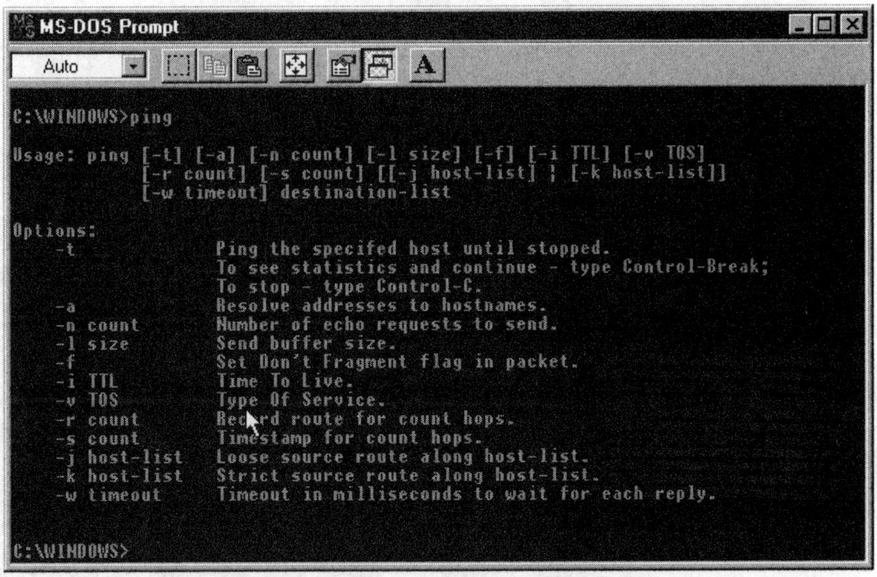

MS-DOS Prompt

Auto

```
C:\WINDOWS>ping

Usage: ping [-t] [-a] [-n count] [-l size] [-f] [-i TTL] [-v TOS]
            [-r count] [-s count] [[-j host-list] | [-k host-list]]
            [-w timeout] destination-list

Options:
    -t             Ping the specifed host until stopped.
                   To see statistics and continue - type Control-Break;
                   To stop - type Control-C.
    -a             Resolve addresses to hostnames.
    -n count       Number of echo requests to send.
    -l size        Send buffer size.
    -f             Set Don't Fragment flag in packet.
    -i TTL         Time To Live.
    -v TOS         Type Of Service.
    -r count       Record route for count hops.
    -s count       Timestamp for count hops.
    -j host-list   Loose source route along host-list.
    -k host-list   Strict source route along host-list.
    -w timeout     Timeout in milliseconds to wait for each reply.

C:\WINDOWS>
```

Ping Command Screen

The options can be used to receive different types of information depending on the problem. For example, by running ping with the "-t" option, a ping operation will continue until we interrupt it by issuing the Ctrl+C key combination. Another option used is the "-l" option; this option allows us to specify the packet buffer size. By setting this to a large value, such as 512 bytes, we can issue what is known as a "Fat Ping." This "Fat Ping" exercises the various network components between the end devices, testing for intermittent component or link failures.

The quickest and easiest way to use the Ping command is to simply type **ping** and the hostname. For example, typing **ping www.cudenver.edu** might give the results shown on the Ping Command www.cudenver.edu Screen Diagram.

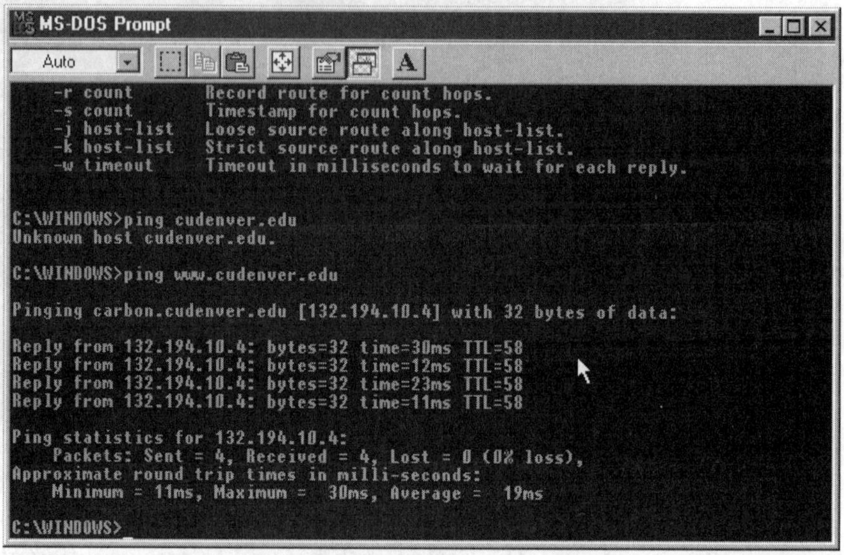

```
MS-DOS Prompt
Auto
    -r count       Record route for count hops.
    -s count       Timestamp for count hops.
    -j host-list   Loose source route along host-list.
    -k host-list   Strict source route along host-list.
    -w timeout     Timeout in milliseconds to wait for each reply.


C:\WINDOWS>ping cudenver.edu
Unknown host cudenver.edu.

C:\WINDOWS>ping www.cudenver.edu

Pinging carbon.cudenver.edu [132.194.10.4] with 32 bytes of data:

Reply from 132.194.10.4: bytes=32 time=30ms TTL=58
Reply from 132.194.10.4: bytes=32 time=12ms TTL=58
Reply from 132.194.10.4: bytes=32 time=23ms TTL=58
Reply from 132.194.10.4: bytes=32 time=11ms TTL=58

Ping statistics for 132.194.10.4:
    Packets: Sent = 4, Received = 4, Lost = 0 (0% loss),
Approximate round trip times in milli-seconds:
    Minimum = 11ms, Maximum =  30ms, Average =  19ms

C:\WINDOWS>_
```

Ping Command www.cudenver.edu Screen

There are several things that can be noted from the results of this Ping. First, the host computer's (World Wide Web [Web] server at the University of Colorado-Denver) IP process is up and running. We know this because a reply is returned from the requested IP process. We also know the IP address of this host (132.194.10.4). We could just as easily have used the IP address itself if we had known it ahead of time.

This particular Ping program (shipped with Windows 98) also provides some statistics, such as the number of packets sent and packets lost, round-trip delay, and other statistics associated with Ping. If we want a better sample, we could request that 10 packets be sent using the -n option. This is shown in the Ping command -n Option Screen Diagram.

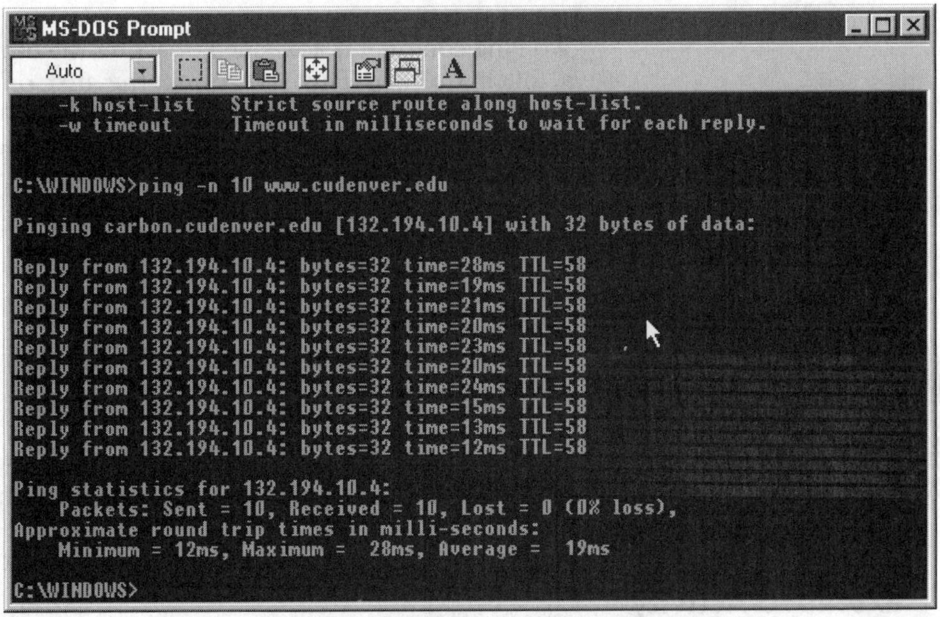

MS-DOS Prompt

```
    -k host-list    Strict source route along host-list.
    -w timeout      Timeout in milliseconds to wait for each reply.


C:\WINDOWS>ping -n 10 www.cudenver.edu

Pinging carbon.cudenver.edu [132.194.10.4] with 32 bytes of data:

Reply from 132.194.10.4: bytes=32 time=28ms TTL=58
Reply from 132.194.10.4: bytes=32 time=19ms TTL=58
Reply from 132.194.10.4: bytes=32 time=21ms TTL=58
Reply from 132.194.10.4: bytes=32 time=20ms TTL=58
Reply from 132.194.10.4: bytes=32 time=23ms TTL=58
Reply from 132.194.10.4: bytes=32 time=20ms TTL=58
Reply from 132.194.10.4: bytes=32 time=24ms TTL=58
Reply from 132.194.10.4: bytes=32 time=15ms TTL=58
Reply from 132.194.10.4: bytes=32 time=13ms TTL=58
Reply from 132.194.10.4: bytes=32 time=12ms TTL=58

Ping statistics for 132.194.10.4:
    Packets: Sent = 10, Received = 10, Lost = 0 (0% loss),
Approximate round trip times in milli-seconds:
    Minimum = 12ms, Maximum =  28ms, Average =  19ms

C:\WINDOWS>
```

Ping Command -n Option Screen

The ICMP Echo Request (Ping) Message Format Diagram presents this type of message. The Echo Reply format would look similar, except it would have a Type field of "0."

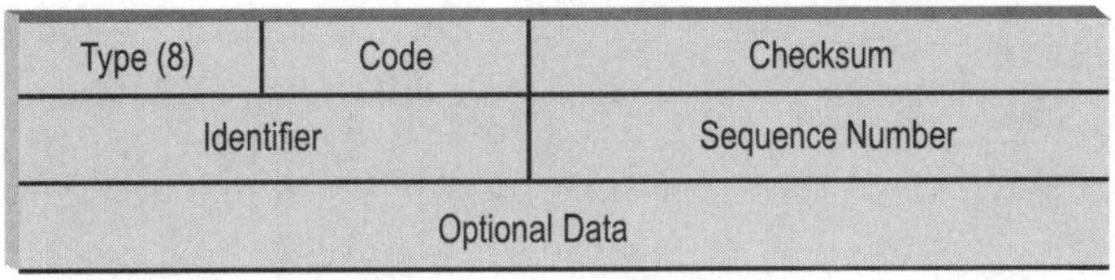

Type (8)	Code	Checksum
Identifier		Sequence Number
Optional Data		

ICMP Echo Request (Ping) Message Format

The Code field would be used in an ICMP Destination Unreachable message to provide additional information, such as "5," Source Route Failed. The Identifier and Sequence Number fields are used by a sender for the purpose of matching replies with requests.

Activities

1. Issue a Ping to a computer on another network. Notice that if two Ping commands are issued one after the other, the second is much quicker. This is because the first one most likely requires an ARP that takes a bit longer. The second uses the information in the ARP cache and takes much less time. Sample sites to ping are:
   a. westnetinc.com (Arvada, CO)
   b. csn.org (Boulder, CO)
   c. dartmouth.edu (Hanover, NH)
   d. cudenver.edu (Denver, CO)
   e. concorde.inria.fr (France)
   f. munnari.oz.au (Melbourne, Australia)
2. Send a Ping to a computer on your network with different size packets.

Extended Activity

Go through each of the Ping options to see how each can be used when troubleshooting a network.

Lesson 4—Tracert

Tracert is another TCP/IP tool often used in troubleshooting a network. Tracert lets us see the route that IP datagrams follow from one host to another. It tells us each router that the packet goes through from source to destination across a TCP/IP network.

Objectives

At the end of this lesson you will be able to:

- Use the Tracert program to check the number of hops between a source and destination node
- Gather additional information about a route using the Tracert options

Key Point

Tracert tells us the route a packet takes from source to destination.

How Tracert Works

Tracert measures a packet's round trip time by sending ICMP echo messages to a destination host. The sender sends packets in sets of three.

Each time a sender sends a packet set to a destination, the sending host increments the packet's Time-to-Live (TTL) field by one. For example, the sending host sets the first three packets' TTL field to 1. The first router "kills" the packets by decrementing their TTLs to 0 and sending back to the sender an ICMP response Message Type 11, indicating the packets' TTL has been exceeded.

The sender sets the next set's TTL to 2. The first router decrements each packet's TTL by one and forwards them on to the next hop router. The second router kills the packets (sets the TTLs to 0), and sends a response saying the TTLs have been exceeded. This procedure continues until the sending host contacts the final router, or the maximum hop count is reached. This allows the Tracert program to track which routers a packet goes through from source to destination.

The Tracert Example Diagram demonstrates the fact that the first tracert packet is sent to the first router and then returned. The second tracert packet is sent to the second router (because now the TTL field has been set to two), and then returned.

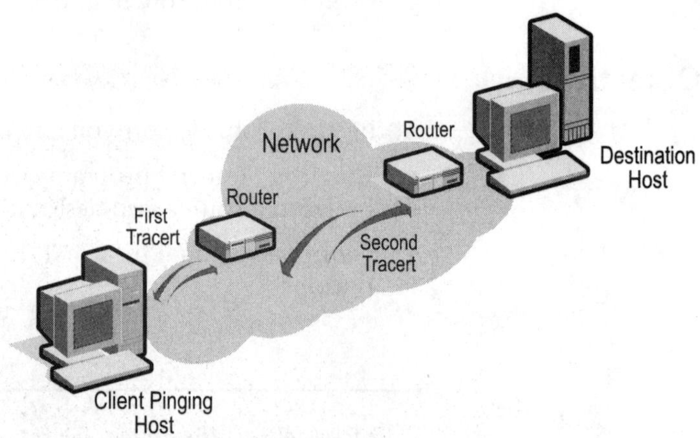

Tracert Example

If we type **tracert** from the command line of a personal computer (PC) operating system (OS) such as Windows 95, we get the options for the Tracert command, as shown on the Tracert Command Options Screen.

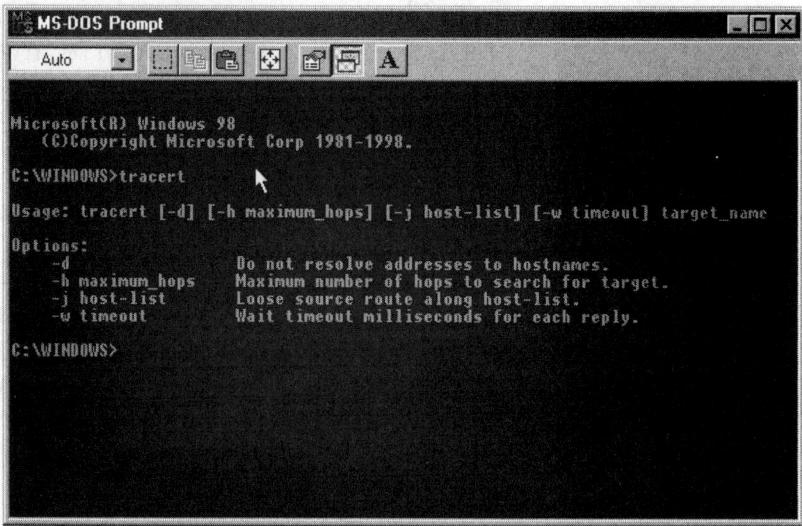

Tracert Command Options Screen

If we simply type **tracert** with a host name, the program logs each hop along the way toward the final destination. For example, if we type **tracert www.cudenver.edu**, we will get the following results, as shown on the Tracert Command www.cudenver.edu Screen Diagram.

```
MS-DOS Prompt
Auto

Usage: tracert [-d] [-h maximum_hops] [-j host-list] [-w timeout] target_name

Options:
    -d                  Do not resolve addresses to hostnames.
    -h maximum_hops     Maximum number of hops to search for target.
    -j host-list        Loose source route along host-list.
    -w timeout          Wait timeout milliseconds for each reply.

C:\WINDOWS>tracert www.cudenver.edu

Tracing route to carbon.cudenver.edu [132.194.10.4]
over a maximum of 30 hops:

  1     2 ms     2 ms     2 ms  gateway.westnetinc.com [205.169.85.254]
  2     8 ms     7 ms     9 ms  den-edge-14.inet.qwest.net [205.169.243.9]
  3     8 ms     8 ms     8 ms  cnb7505.sni.net [205.169.234.254]
  4    10 ms    10 ms     9 ms  cuatm.inet.qwest.net [205.169.250.50]
  5    23 ms    25 ms    24 ms  denatm.inet.qwest.net [204.131.62.30]
  6    22 ms    37 ms    12 ms  chief100.cudenver.edu [132.194.100.1]
  7    43 ms    21 ms    22 ms  carbon.cudenver.edu [132.194.10.4]

Trace complete.

C:\WINDOWS>_
```

Tracert Command www.cudenver.edu Screen

This screen first shows the value of the TTL field in the IP datagram, beginning with 1, then 2, and so forth. It then shows the time it takes to get to a specific router. Every packet is sent three times to each router. In the example above, the first packet sent took 2 milliseconds (ms) to get from the client to the first router in the network. In general, the time increases with each hop because it is farther and farther toward the final destination. However, because of congestion and other variables, times do not always increase with the number of hops. The sixth router in the example above has a time of 12 ms, shorter than the previous packet's, using a TTL of 5. The last part of each line is the router IP address and name, if available.

The roundtrip times are calculated by the Tracert program on the sending computer. They are the total roundtrip times from the Tracert program to the router. If we are interested in the link time between routers, we have to subtract the time for TTL n from the value printed for TTL n + 1.

For example, if we wish to measure the roundtrip time between router 1 and 2, we would subtract the roundtrip time between the sending host and router 1 (n) from the roundtrip time from the sending host and router 2 (n + 1). The time from router 1 to router 2 is 9 ms – 2 ms = 7 ms. This calculation does not always work, however, as network conditions can varying widely over a matter of milliseconds.

Activities

1. Trace the route to the following sites and record your results.
   a. mcdata.com (Broomfield, CO)

   ____

   ____

   b. csn.org (Boulder, CO)

   ____

   ____

   c. dartmouth.edu (Hanover, NH)

   ____

   ____

   d. regis.edu (Denver, CO)

   ____

   ____

   e. concorde.inria.fr (France)

   ____

   ____

   f. munnari.oz.au (Melbourne, Australia)

   ____

   ____

Extended Activity

1. Use the various Tracert options with each example above and record your findings.
2. Look for other programs that provide a visual output for the Tracert program. Begin with the following URL:

   http://www.visualroute.com/

Lesson 5—Nbtstat and Netstat

The tools covered in this lesson provide information about the connectivity of a computer on a TCP/IP network. Nbtstat is a utility that can be used to display statistics and current TCP/IP connections using NetBIOS over a TCP/IP connection. Netstat shows the current status of all connections on a computer.

Objectives

At the end of this lesson you will be able to:

- Use the Nbtstat command to gather NetBIOS over TCP/IP network information
- Use the Netstat command to gather active TCP connection information

Netstat shows the current status of a computer's connections.

Nbtstat

The Nbtstat command is used to display protocol statistics for a given computer on a TCP/IP network. It displays these statistics using NetBIOS, the PC local area network (LAN) protocol. If we type **nbtstat** from a DOS command line, we get the following results, as shown on the Nbtstat Screen Diagram.

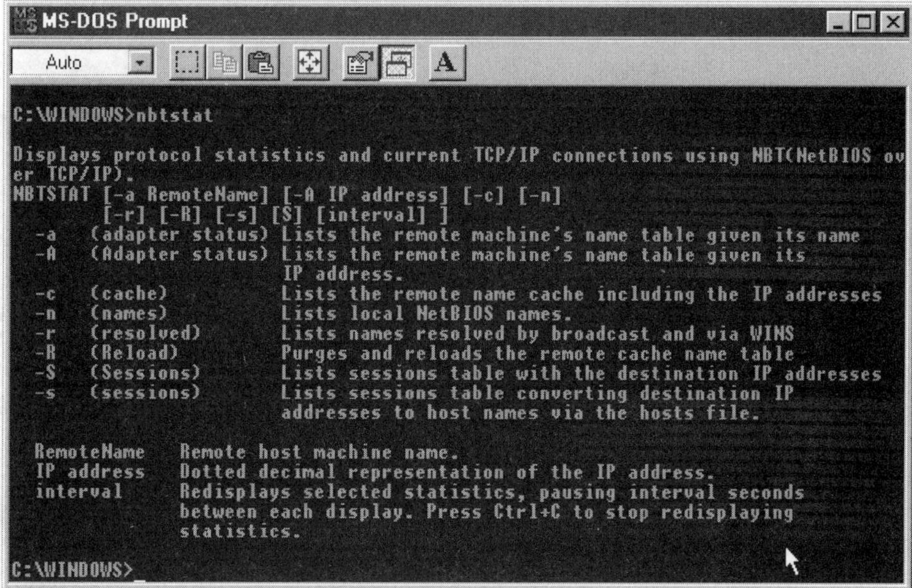

MS-DOS Prompt
Auto
C:\WINDOWS>nbtstat
Displays protocol statistics and current TCP/IP connections using NBT(NetBIOS ov
er TCP/IP).
NBTSTAT [-a RemoteName] [-A IP address] [-c] [-n]
[-r] [-R] [-s] [S] [interval]]
-a (adapter status) Lists the remote machine's name table given its name
-A (Adapter status) Lists the remote machine's name table given its
IP address.
-c (cache) Lists the remote name cache including the IP addresses
-n (names) Lists local NetBIOS names.
-r (resolved) Lists names resolved by broadcast and via WINS
-R (Reload) Purges and reloads the remote cache name table
-S (Sessions) Lists sessions table with the destination IP addresses
-s (sessions) Lists sessions table converting destination IP
addresses to host names via the hosts file.
RemoteName Remote host machine name.
IP address Dotted decimal representation of the IP address.
interval Redisplays selected statistics, pausing interval seconds
between each display. Press Ctrl+C to stop redisplaying
statistics.
C:\WINDOWS>_

Nbtstat Screen

This screen displays all of the options that can be used with the Nbtstat command. We can view the status for all communications parameters of a given device, including the status of the NIC, all current active sessions, and so forth. For example, if we type **nbtstat -s** (lowercase s), we get the following results, as shown on the Nbtstat -s Screen Diagram.

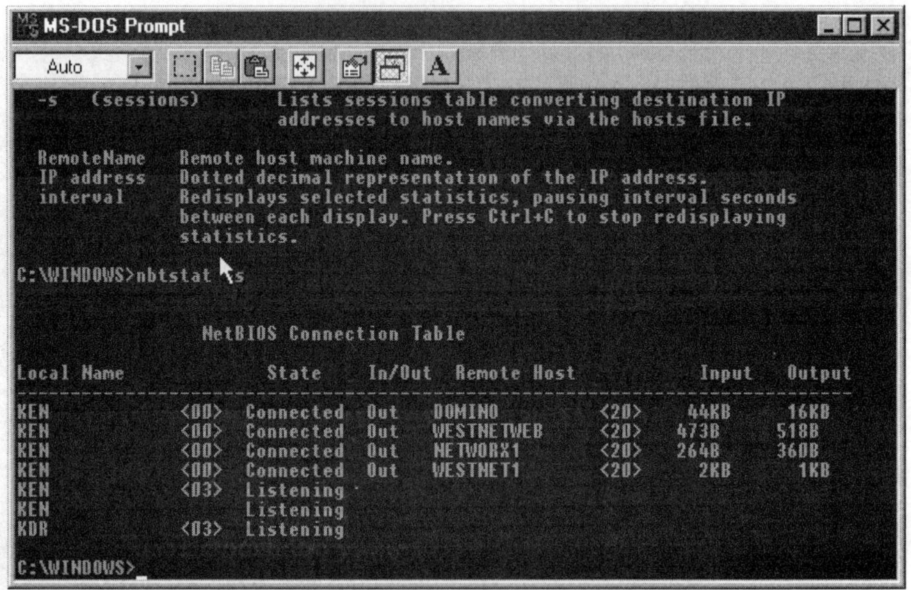
MS-DOS Prompt
Auto
A
-s (sessions) Lists sessions table converting destination IP addresses to host names via the hosts file.
RemoteName Remote host machine name.
IP address Dotted decimal representation of the IP address.
interval Redisplays selected statistics, pausing interval seconds between each display. Press Ctrl+C to stop redisplaying statistics.
C:\WINDOWS>nbtstat -s
NetBIOS Connection Table
Local Name State In/Out Remote Host Input Output
KEN <00> Connected Out DOMINO <20> 44KB 16KB
KEN <00> Connected Out WESTNETWEB <20> 473B 518B
KEN <00> Connected Out NETWORX1 <20> 264B 360B
KEN <00> Connected Out WESTNET1 <20> 2KB 1KB
KEN <03> Listening
KEN Listening
KDR <03> Listening
C:\WINDOWS>_

Nbtstat -s Screen

This screen shows that the current computer (NetBIOS name KEN) is connected to four servers. These servers are Domino (a mail server), Westnetweb (a Web server) (this is the internal name for the **http://www.westnetinc.com** Web server), and Networx1 and WestNet1 (two internal servers). If we want to see the IP addresses associated with each of these computers, we can type the same command, but this time with a capital "S." The result is shown on the Nbtstat -S Screen Diagram.

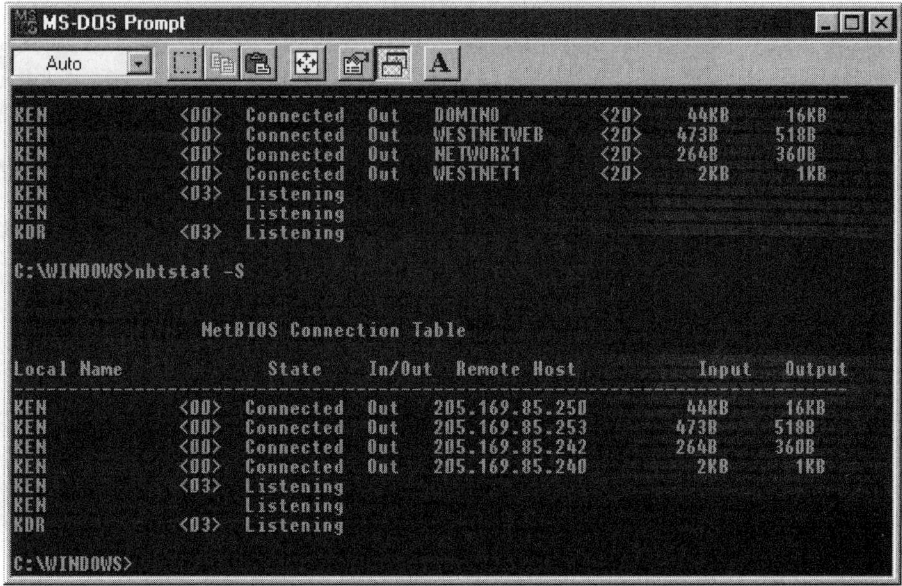

Nbtstat -S Screen

This screen reveals the IP address for each server mentioned above. If, for example, we were having connectivity problems to one of the servers, we might use the Ping or Tracert command to isolate a problem.

Netstat

The Netstat command is another command used in troubleshooting a TCP/IP network. This command is used to display the active sessions for a given computer. If we type **netstat** at the command line, we get the following results, as shown on the Netstat Command Screen Diagram.

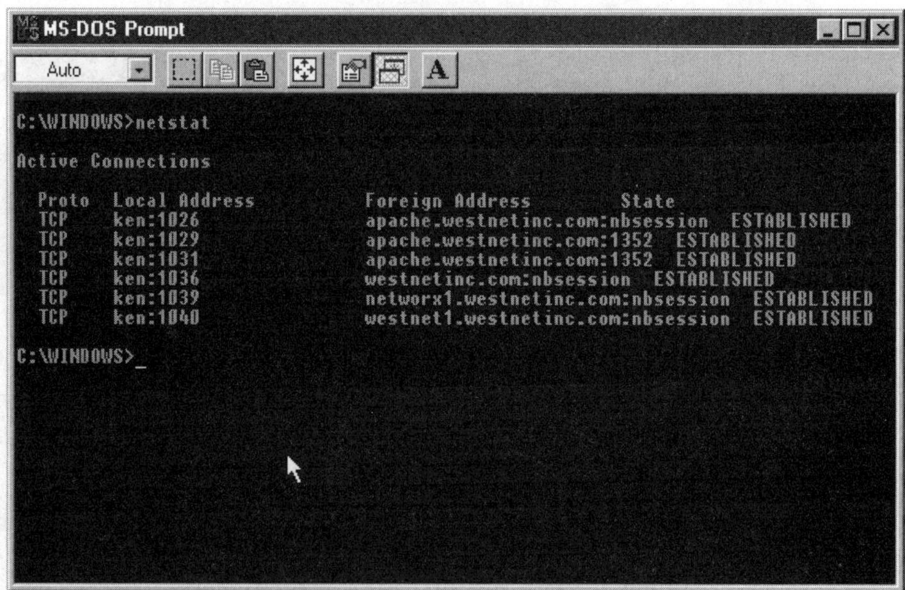

Netstat Command Screen

This screen reveals the active connections for this particular computer. It shows the protocol being used, in this case TCP. It also shows the port numbers that are active for each session. For example, there are current active sessions with the Web server (Apache server software running on a Linux box). Local port numbers 1026, 1029, and 1031 are being used, and the server is using port number 1352. HTTP sessions often open multiple TCP connections, and this is the case here.

Activity

1. Review each option that can be used with the Nbtstat command, and list how they might be used to troubleshoot a network.

Extended Activities

1. Issue the Nbtstat and Netstat commands and record your findings.

2. Use the Web to find additional information about the Nbtstat and Netstat commands.

Lesson 6—ARP

ARP is used to provide a mapping between IP addresses and Data Link Layer addresses, such as those found in LANs (for example, Ethernet).

Objectives

At the end of this lesson you will be able to:

- Use the ARP command to resolve IP addresses to Medium access Control (MAC) addresses
- Use the ARP command options to gather additional ARP information

Key Point

ARP is used to map IP addresses to Data Link Layer addresses.

ARP Operation

The ARP command is used to view the ARP cache on a local computer. We may also use ARP to return the NIC address of a computer with a known IP address. Typing "ARP" at the command line provides options that can be used with the ARP command. The ARP Command Screen Diagram illustrates what is displayed when we invoke the ARP program.

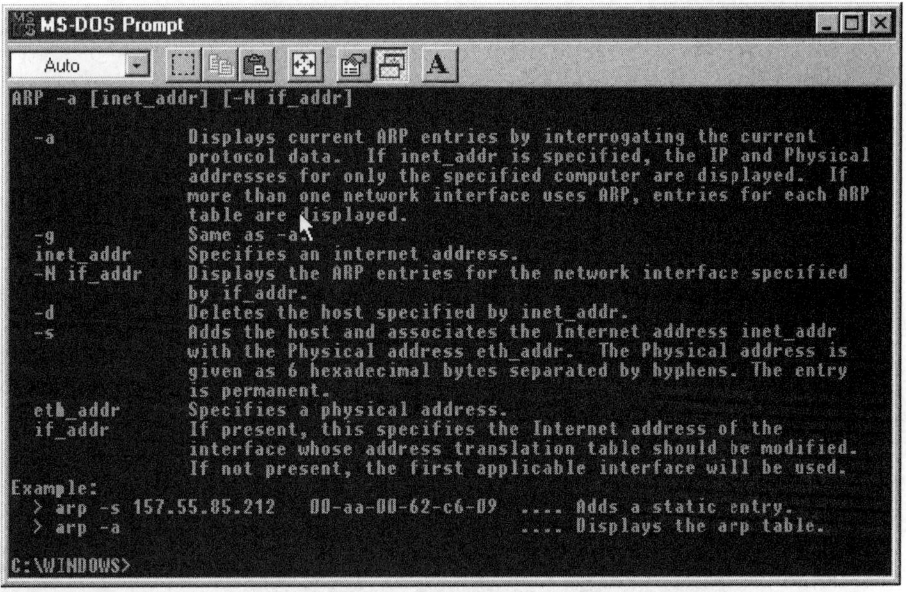

MS-DOS Prompt
Auto
ARP -a [inet_addr] [-N if_addr]
-a Displays current ARP entries by interrogating the current protocol data. If inet_addr is specified, the IP and Physical addresses for only the specified computer are displayed. If more than one network interface uses ARP, entries for each ARP table are displayed.
-g Same as -a.
inet_addr Specifies an internet address.
-N if_addr Displays the ARP entries for the network interface specified by if_addr.
-d Deletes the host specified by inet_addr.
-s Adds the host and associates the Internet address inet_addr with the Physical address eth_addr. The Physical address is given as 6 hexadecimal bytes separated by hyphens. The entry is permanent.
eth_addr Specifies a physical address.
if_addr If present, this specifies the Internet address of the interface whose address translation table should be modified. If not present, the first applicable interface will be used.
Example:
> arp -s 157.55.85.212 00-aa-00-62-c6-09 .... Adds a static entry.
> arp -a .... Displays the arp table.
C:\WINDOWS>

ARP Command Screen

With the ARP command, we can display the current status of the ARP cache of a computer and manipulate it's contents. If we want to display the contents of our ARP cache, we can type **ARP -a** and the following results will appear, as shown on the ARP - a Command Screen Diagram.

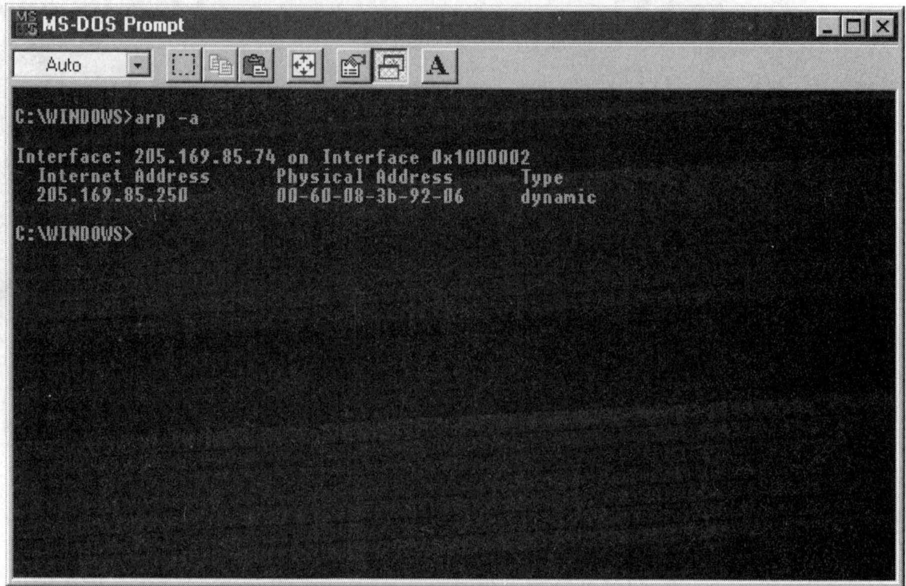

ARP -a Command Screen

This screen indicates there is one entry in the ARP cache, the IP address of a computer on the network. We can use the Nbtstat command to determine which computer this IP address is indicating, or we can Ping the IP address. From the previous lesson, we learned this particular address is the address of a Domino mail server.

We can change the contents of the ARP cache by sending information to another computer. To do this artificially, we might use the Ping command. For example, if we Ping the www.cudenver.edu host and then display the ARP cache, we will get the following results as shown on the Ping www.cudenver.edu Display ARP Cache Screen Diagram.

```
MS-DOS Prompt
  205.169.85.250          00-60-08-3b-92-06     dynamic

C:\WINDOWS>ping www.cudenver.edu

Pinging carbon.cudenver.edu [132.194.10.4] with 32 bytes of data:

Reply from 132.194.10.4: bytes=32 time=43ms TTL=58
Reply from 132.194.10.4: bytes=32 time=22ms TTL=58
Reply from 132.194.10.4: bytes=32 time=16ms TTL=58
Reply from 132.194.10.4: bytes=32 time=21ms TTL=58

Ping statistics for 132.194.10.4:
    Packets: Sent = 4, Received = 4, Lost = 0 (0% loss),
Approximate round trip times in milli-seconds:
    Minimum = 16ms, Maximum =  43ms, Average =  25ms

C:\WINDOWS>arp -a

Interface: 205.169.85.74 on Interface 0x1000002
  Internet Address      Physical Address      Type
  205.169.85.240        00-60-97-9d-32-06     dynamic
  205.169.85.250        00-60-08-3b-92-06     dynamic
  205.169.85.254        00-c0-7b-6e-12-35     dynamic

C:\WINDOWS>
```

Ping www.cudenver.edu Display ARP Cache Screen

The last entry in the ARP cache shows the IP and NIC addresses of the destination computer. In this case, it is the router of the internal network that provides connectivity to the Internet. ARP only caches addresses on the local network segment; if a destination host is on another subnet, then ARP cannot obtain the destination host MAC address. Because we Pinged an external Web server (**http://www.cudenver.edu**), we had to go to the router first (205.169.85.254). The router was then responsible for getting the Hypertext Transfer Protocol (HTTP) request from the internal network to the Internet, where it was sent on to the final destination.

Activity

Review each ARP parameter and list the functions it serves.

____

____

____

____

____

____

Extended Activity

1. Describe how ARP might be used in troubleshooting a network. Given the following scenarios, what tools would you use to isolate the problem?
   a. A user complains that he no longer has connectivity to the Internet. The symptom is that when he starts Netscape, he gets a "server not found" message.

      ____

      ____

   b. A user complains that he cannot access his mail server.

      ____

      ____

Lesson 7—A Troubleshooting Problem

In this lesson, we use the various tools we have studied in Unit 8 to troubleshoot an Internet access problem experienced by several network users attempting to connect to a company Web site.

Objectives

At the end of this lesson you will be able to:

- Identify the steps required to troubleshoot IP connectivity problems
- Use IP troubleshooting tools to locate and isolate the problem
- Choose the correct course of action to resolve the problem

The Problem

Users on your network complain that they intermittently receive browser messages stating the company's Internet site is unreachable. Outside user's have no such problem. You are to isolate and correct the problem.

Identify the Exact Issue

You first need to find as much information as possible about the problem. You ask the following questions:

- When the problem occurred, what took place?

  The answer from the users is that their browser window shows an "HTTP 404 Not Found" message after they enter the site URL, **http://www.bigdotcom.com**. They can refresh the page, and sometimes the home page loads and the error goes away; other times it does not.

- When the problem occurred, was something new being done or something routine?

  The answer predominantly is that users were only performing routine network tasks. The problem is widespread across all internal network users.

- Has anything changed recently that might have had an impact?

  You look in the network maintenance logs and talk to your coworkers. The only recent network change is a new router installed to replace a failed router on your Internet connection. Because the Web server is located offsite, you note this as a possible cause.

- Can the problem be recreated easily?

  Yes, you are able to recreate the problem from any browser. You use only one vendor's browser.

Recreate the Problem

You find that when attempting to access the company Web site from the internal corporate network, any user workstation browser displays the same "HTTP 404 Not Found" message. You verify, by contacting external customers and professional acquaintances, that external users experience no problems connecting to the site.

Potential explanations are as follows:

- The new router is misconfigured
- The new router is faulty
- The internal client TCP/IP settings are incorrect
- The internal browsers are misconfigured
- An internal network component is faulty (switch, bridge, or hub)
- There is a problem at your Internet service provider (ISP)
- There is a problem at the Web site hosting firm

This is a fairly long list of potential problems, thus you must now eliminate each of these potential problems, gradually narrowing the list down to the one problem source.

Note: It is not uncommon for the solution to include more than one option on the potential problem list. Often, a problem's root is a combination of individual issues. The only way to know if eliminating an individual problem corrects the failure is to test thoroughly after the repair.

Isolate the Cause

This is where we spend most of our time. Because we have potential causes located both on the local network and at remote locations, we will have to systematically test each point on the network and work outward, eliminating each potential cause along the way. Although we could have just as easily chosen to work from the outside in, general troubleshooting techniques work from the inside out, eliminating those areas for which we are responsible. This also provides reinforcing documentation in the case that you run into resistance from the external network support personnel. With good troubleshooting documentation, you stand a better chance of obtaining their cooperation in resolving the problem.

The IP Troubleshooting Diagram illustrates the various points on the network where we will test.

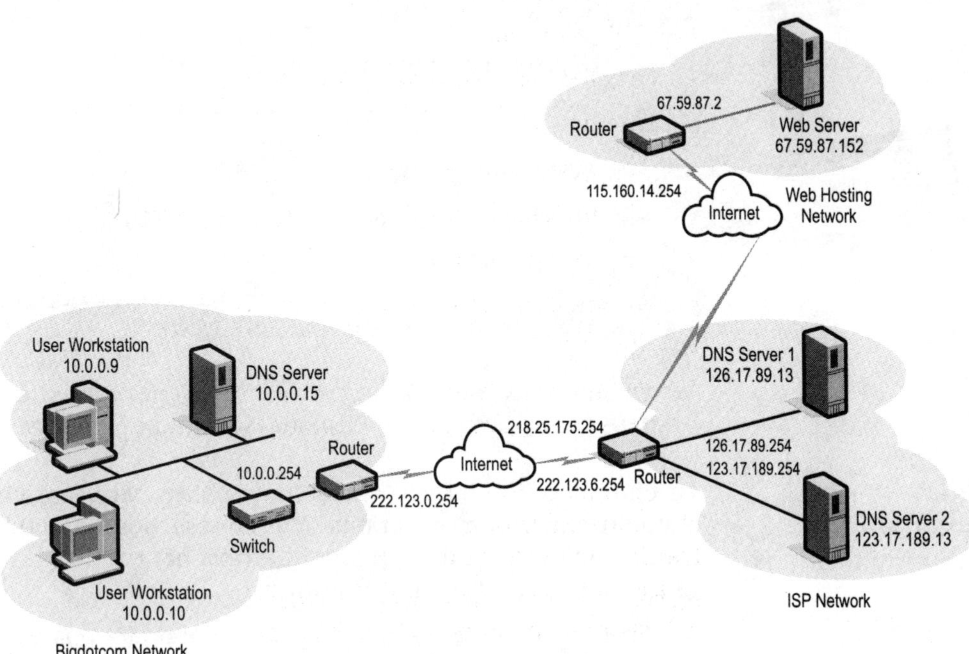

IP Troubleshooting

The various network devices are assigned the following IP addresses:

- The Bigdotcom network uses the following addresses:
  - 10.0.0.0/8 IP address range
  - The router's internal address is 10.0.0.254/8
- The local DNS Server address is 10.0.0.15/8
  - The router's external address is 222.123.0.254/24
- The ISP router uses the following addresses:
  - External to Bigdotcom, 222.123.6.254/24
  - External to the Web hosting firm, 218.25.175.254/24
  - Internal to DNS Server 1, 126.17.89.254/24
  - Internal to DNS Server 2, 123.17.189.254/24
- The ISP provides two DNS servers
  - DNS Server 1 with address 126.17.89.13/24
  - DNS Server 2 with address 123.17.189.13/24
- The Web hosting firm's router addresses are:
  - External to Internet, 115.160.14.254/16
  - Internal 67.59.87.2/8
- The Web server address is 67.59.87.152/8

We will test in phases, starting with the local network, then moving on to test communications with our ISP and the Web hosting firm.

Phase 1—Internal Communications

To eliminate any internal network problems, we first choose to test internal communications. We choose host 10.0.0.9 as our internal test host and verify that this host has the same symptoms as the others. We then begin testing.

1. First, we successfully ping the local loopback address, 127.0.0.1, to test that TCP/IP is working on the test host.
2. Next, we successfully ping the test host's address, 10.0.0.9. This verifies that TCP/IP works to the NIC port.

3. We choose to ping another network host, host 10.0.0.10. This successfully verifies communications on the network.
4. We successfully ping the local DNS server, 10.0.0.15. This verifies communications with the local DNS server.
5. We then successfully ping host 10.0.0.10 by its fully qualified domain name (FQDN), host10.bigdotcom.com. This verifies that our local DNS resolves our local host names correctly. The DNS server resolves the name host10.bigdotcom.com to the correct IP address, 10.0.0.10. We can also choose to ping other hosts by name to ensure that the DNS resolves these names correctly.
6. Next, we successfully ping the local router's internal port address, 10.0.0.254. This verifies that we can communicate with the router.
7. We successfully ping the router's external address, 222.123.0.254. This verifies that the router can route and switch packets to the outside network.

Note: This step may fail if the router uses access control lists (ACL) or packet filters to block Internet Control Message Protocol (ICMP) replies. Many networks use filters to protect the internal network from denial of service attacks. If this is the case, then you will have to modify the filters or ACLs, or try some other testing method, like Telneting to the external router port.

8. We can, if we wish, examine the test host's ARP cache contents for the IP-to-MAC address mappings for all our contacted hosts. We should at least see entries for those devices we have pinged in the last 2 minutes. Remember that a router does not pass ARP broadcasts, thus instead of an entry for the router's external port MAC address, we will see the internal port MAC address.

Phase 2—ISP Communications

We are now satisfied that our internal network is functioning and can now move on to the external networks. We next choose to test communications with our ISP. This will likely mean coordinating efforts with the ISP support staff; they may also block ICMP replies. Your documentation of your troubleshooting efforts to this point will be helpful here.

1. First, we successfully ping the ISP's external router port address, 222.123.6.254. This verifies communications across the Internet from our network to the ISP router.
2. We then successfully ping the ISP's router internal ports, 123.17.189.254 and 126.17.89.254. This verifies the ISP router routes and switches packets correctly.
3. We ping DNS Server 1, 126.17.89.13, by name and address. The ping by address succeeds, but the ping by name fails intermittently. We note this in our troubleshooting logs.
4. We ping DNS Server 2, 123.17.189.13, by name and address. Both succeed.
5. We successfully ping the ISP router's external interface to the Web hosting firm's network, address 218.25.175.254. This verifies that the router can switch and route packets to our Web server host's network.

As a result of these testing efforts, we note that pings by name to the ISP's DNS Server 1 fail intermittently. However, rather than prematurely jump on this as our potential solution, we choose to continue our testing to verify all is well with the Web host's network.

Phase 3—Web Host Firm Communications

We finish our testing with the Web hosting firm's network. As with the ISP's network, this will likely require us to coordinate our efforts with the Web host's network support group.

1. First, we successfully ping the Web hosting firm's router external address, 115.160.14.254. This verifies that we can contact the Web hosting firm's network.
2. Next, we successfully ping the inside router port, 67.59.87.2. This verifies that the hosting firm's router can route and switch packets.

3. We successfully ping the Web server by address, 67.59.87.152, several times. This verifies that we can communicate with the Web server.
4. We ping the Web server by name, **http://www.bigdotcom.com**, and find that this fails intermittently. We first see the ping succeed to address 67.59.87.152, then later see it fail and present a message stating "Bad IP address www.bigdotcom.com."

Tallying the Results

As a result of our testing, we observe the following symptoms:

- Pings by name to DNS Server 1 intermittently fail.
- Pings by name to the Web server intermittently fail.

We conclude that we have an intermittent name resolution problem, as indicated by the above symptoms. Pings by address always succeed, and the only failures occur when TCP/IP must resolve a hostname to an address. Additionally, these failures occur only on external hosts, thus the internal DNS is likely functioning properly.

Isolating the Cause

We know now that we have a name resolution problem. We know that external network users do not have this problem, thus we determine that they use a different DNS than we use. We do not use the internal DNS to resolve external names, we depend on the ISP's DNS to resolve external FQDNs.

Because our ISP provides two DNS servers, the next step is to verify that the clients use the correct DNS server to resolve names. We look at the client TCP/IP configuration using the Winipcfg utility, and find that the client's are configured to use DNS servers 10.0.0.15, 126.17.89.13, and 123.17.189.13. These addresses match those of the three DNSs we use to resolve names internally and externally, and thus determine that the clients are configured correctly.

The next step then is to isolate the servers. Because our clients download their TCP/IP configurations from a local DHCP server, including their DNS server information, we decide to manually configure our local test host, excluding one of the external DNS servers from the list. Because DNS Server 1 failed, we remove its entry from the test host's DNS configuration first, as shown on the Test Host DNS Configuration Screen Diagram.

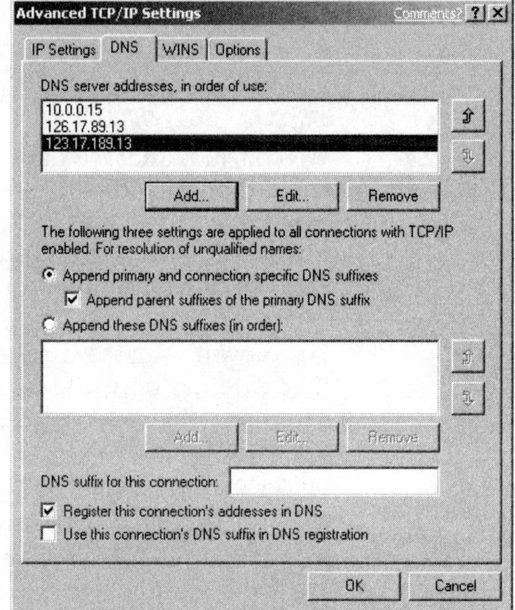

Test Host DNS Configuration Screen

We attempt a ping by name to DNS Server 1, and find that it succeeds each time. We then attempt to ping **http://www.bigdotcom.com** by name, and again find it succeeds each time.

We then reconfigure our local test host to use only the local DNS and DNS Server 1, removing the address for DNS Server 2. This time, both pings fail by name, but still succeed by address.

Formulate and Implement the Solution

We have now isolated the problem to DNS Server 1. We contact our ISP and suggest that there might be a malfunction on DNS Server 1. They troubleshoot, and find that indeed, DNS Server 1 is failing to resolve names to IP addresses and that there is a problem with the DNS server software. They suggest we reconfigure our clients to use an alternate DNS server, DNS Server 3, using IP address 126.17.89.14, leaving the DNS Server 2 entries intact.

Because we use DHCP to download client TCP/IP configuration information, including IP addresses, the subnet mask, the default gateway address, and DNS server information, we can easily set up our DHCP scopes to download the new DNS server information. We set the DHCP server with the new information and select the Renew button on our test host.

We then ping by name both of the ISP DNS servers and the Web server; all three pings succeed. We use the test host's browser to contact our Web site, and find that the site comes up each time.

We know that the remaining internal clients will renew their leases in a maximum of three days, and thus decide to allow each client to download the new DNS information on the next lease renewal cycle. We will have the Help desk tell all who call and complain to run Winipcfg and select the Renew button to manually update the DNS server information.

Test the Solution

To verify that the solution works across the board, we contact each user who has opened a helpdesk ticket on this problem and have them renew their DHCP leases. We then have them contact the Web server, and verify that communications succeeds.

Document the Problem and Solution and Obtain Feedback

We complete the appropriate troubleshooting logs and Help desk tickets and provide written procedures to the Help desk personnel so they can walk users through the lease renewal process. We write an e-mail to the Chief Technology Officer (CTO) describing our problem isolation and troubleshooting efforts, and copy the e-mail to our ISP's tech support manager. We then follow-up with each affected user to ensure that the problem is resolved and does not reoccur. Finally, we e-mail a Quality Assurance questionnaire to all users who logged a Help desk call, asking for their feedback on the problem resolution process.

Tools Used in Resolving this Problem

We used the following tools in resolving this problem:

- Ping—We used ping extensively, both internally and on the two external networks. We pinged not just by IP address, but also by name. This helped us isolate the problem to a name resolution issue, rather than a network communications issue.
- ARP—We used ARP to verify that the local ARP cache was gathering address mappings correctly. Although ineffective in troubleshooting this problem, we nonetheless determined that ARP was working correctly and thus was not an issue here.
- Winipcfg—We used Winipcfg to verify the local client TCP/IP configuration. We also later used it to renew the DHCP client leases, causing them to download the new DNS information. If we ran Windows NT or Windows 2000 clients, we would have used the Ipconfig utility.

We could have used tracert, nbtstat, and netstat as part of the testing phase, if we wished. Though these utilities played no part in troubleshooting and isolating the problem, nonetheless we could have used them to verify that all else was well with the network after we implemented the fix.

Activities

1. How would we verify that TCP/IP is working on the local host?
    a. Ping the default gateway
    b. Ping the subnet mask
    c. Ping the wire address
    d. Ping the local loopback address
2. How can we verify that name resolution is working correctly?
    a. Ping the local loopback address on the DNS server
    b. Ping one or more network hosts by both name and address
    c. Ping the DNS server by IP address to verify it is operational
    d. Ping the local host by name and IP
3. Which ping tests would indicate that TCP/IP is working correctly on a network segment? (Choose three)
    a. Ping the local IP address
    b. Ping other local segment hosts by IP address
    c. Ping the local network segment router port
    d. Ping the local loopback address
4. Which TCP/IP client/server service would allow an administrator to quickly reconfigure host configuration information?
    a. DNS
    b. DHCP
    c. Ipconfig
    d. RARP
5. When troubleshooting a problem crossing network responsibilities, why is it best to start with the local network and work out? (Choose three.)
    a. It allows us to eliminate and resolve any internal problems first.
    b. It provides information we can use to support our case, if the problem proves to be external to our network.
    c. It eliminates the need for cooperation from outside sources, if troubleshooting moves outside the local network.
    d. It breaks up the troubleshooting effort to specific areas of responsibility.

Extended Activity

Note: Your instructor has the solution to the following problem. Once you complete the activity, discuss your conclusions with your class.

Background Information

You are a network administrator, responsible for a multisubnet, routed network. The Routed Network Diagram illustrates your company's network.

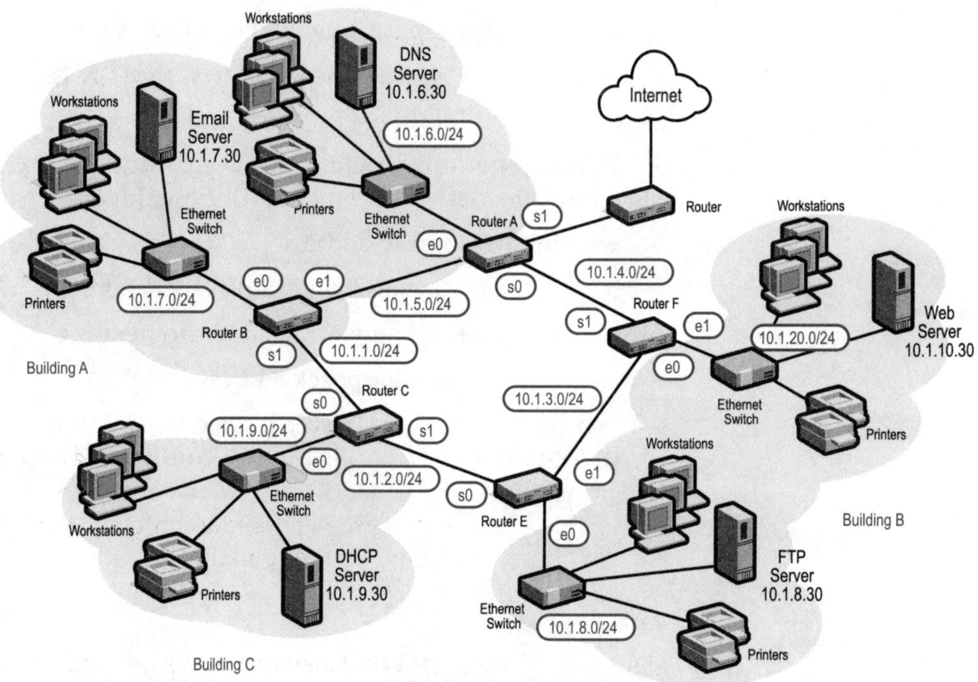

Routed Network

The internal network addresses are shown. The router port IP addresses are as follows, where *x.y.z* is the directly connected network address (for example, on subnet 10.1.1.0, *x.y.z* = 10.1.1):

- Interfaces labeled as e0 are addressed as *x.y.z*.253
- Interfaces labeled as e1 are addressed as *x.y.z*.254
- Interfaces labeled as s0 are addressed as *x.y.z*.253
- Interfaces labeled as s1 are addressed as *x.y.z*.254

You maintain the following network services:

- A DNS server on network 10.1.6.0
- A POP3/SMTP e-mail server on network 10.1.7.0
- An FTP server on network 10.1.8.0
- A DHCP server on network 10.1.9.0
- A Web server on network 10.1.10.0
- Each router operates as a DHCP relay agent
- Router A is a NAPT NAT device

Additional network information is as follows:

- The backbone links are 100BaseTX Ethernet
- The following subnets create workgroup segments, isolating workgroup traffic to those subnets:

  10.1.6.0

  10.1.7.0

  10.1.8.0

  10.1.9.0

  10.1.10.0
- Each workgroup has dedicated printers
- The routers use RIP
- The network e-mail server handles internal e-mail, and forwards and retrieves Internet e-mail

The Problem

Help desk tickets state that network users are unable to send and receive e-mail, yet they are able to access all other services. You must isolate the problem's cause.

Identify the Exact Issue

You interview the complaining users and find the following:

- When they open their e-mail clients, the client application prompts them to logon to the e-mail server. You note that this is not standard behavior (you configured the e-mail clients to store the user passwords and logon to the e-mail server automatically)
- Some users complain that Internet access is slow.

- Users on the 10.1.7.0 subnet complain that they cannot access the Internet, but that communications within the workgroup seems fine. They also complain of communications problems with other workgroups. They suffer the e-mail problem, as well.

You interview your peers and look in the network maintenance logs. You discover the following:

- Last weekend, all routers were upgraded to the latest operating system version. All were tested and deemed operational.
- Because the router upgrade required more router memory than the previous operating system version, one of the Building A routers was replaced, but no one remembers which one. The maintenance logs don't specify.

Recreate the Problem

You attempt to recreate the problem. Here are your findings:

- You open an e-mail client on each workgroup subnet. All fail as indicated (both when accessing the e-mail server by name and IP), except on subnet 10.1.7.0. On subnet 10.1.7.0, e-mail works fine as long as you access the e-mail server by IP address. You can send and receive e-mail, but only with users within the subnet. Access by name fails.

Isolate the Cause

You begin to gather your own information:

- While still on subnet 10.1.7.0, you attempt to access other network services. All attempts fail.
- You attempt to renew a 10.1.7.0 DHCP client address, and the renewal attempt fails. You remember that your DHCP lease duration is six days.
- Lease renewal works from all other workgroups.
- All other subnets can access the Web and FTP servers by name.

What additional steps will you take and what tools will you use to isolate the problem? Make a list of potential problem areas and how you would eliminate or confirm them as the cause.

What do you think is the failed component or components? How would you repair the problem?

Summary

This unit covered troubleshooting a TCP/IP network. It began by covering some basic steps used in the analysis and troubleshooting of a network. Lesson 1 looked at the six general steps used to troubleshoot a network, including identification, re-creation, and isolation of the problem, as well as correction, testing, and documentation of the results of the findings.

The remaining lessons looked at software tools commonly found with implementations of TCP/IP software. These include tools that show the configuration of computers, such as Winipcfg, Netstat, and Nbtstat. It also included tools that help understand the connectivity of a network, such as Ping and Tracert. Other tools, such as ARP, can be used for finding addressing information.

Unit 8 Quiz

1. Which of the following commands shows the addresses loaded in a PC?
   a. Ping
   b. Winipcfg
   c. Tracert
   d. Nbtstat
2. Which of the following commands shows the path between source and destination in a TCP/IP network?
   a. Ping
   b. Winipcfg
   c. Tracert
   d. Nbtstat
3. Which of the following echoes information back from an IP process?
   a. Ping
   b. Winipcfg
   c. Netstat
   d. Nbtstat
4. How many times is a Ping issued per router when performing a Tracert to a destination computer?
   a. 1
   b. 2
   c. 3
   d. 4
5. Which utility is used to display current TCP/IP connections using NetBIOS over a TCP/IP connection?
   a. Ping
   b. Winipcfg
   c. Tracert
   d. Nbtstat

6. Which of the following helps to determine local addressing information?
   a. Ping
   b. Winipcfg
   c. Tracert
   d. ARP
7. Which of the following troubleshooting tools tells how many hops to the destination computer?
   a. Ping
   b. Winipcfg
   c. Tracert
   d. Nbtstat
8. When troubleshooting a network, we begin by performing which of the following?
   a. Isolating the problem
   b. Documenting the results
   c. Testing the problem
   d. Issuing a Ping command
9. Tracert uses which of the following commands and IP fields to carry out its operation?
   a. Ping and header
   b. Nbtstat and trailer
   c. Ping and TTL
   d. Ping and type
10. Which is the most important of the network troubleshooting steps?
    a. Recreate the problem
    b. Isolate the cause
    c. Test the solution
    d. Identify the exact issue

11. Which are TCP/IP network troubleshooting tools? (Choose three.)
    a. Netstat
    b. Ping
    c. Tracert
    d. TFTP
12. Which two TCP/IP tools will allow you to display a workstation's network configuration values? (Choose two.)
    a. Netstat
    b. Nbtstat
    c. Winipcfg
    d. Ipconfig
13. Winipcfg displays which three of the following pieces of client configuration information? (Choose three.)
    a. Adapter address
    b. Listening ports
    c. IP address
    d. Lease expiration
14. Which TCP/IP troubleshooting tool is the fastest and easiest method to evaluate whether a host is available across a TCP/IP network?
    a. Winipcfg
    b. Telnet
    c. Nbtstat
    d. Ping

15. You are troubleshooting a communication error on a TCP/IP network. Your users complain that whenever they try to connect to your new Internet Web site, **http://www.newserver.com**, the connection fails.

    You attempt a connection to the site from your workstation, and that too fails. However, you try to connect to the Web server by IP address, and it succeeds. You suspect that your ISP entered the Web server in their DNS incorrectly.

    The server is configured as follows:

    IP address–125.38.79.124

    FQDN–www.newserver.com

    Which command can you issue to verify that name resolution is the problem's source?

    a. Ipconfig 125.38.79.124
    b. Ping 125.38.79.124
    c. Ping www.newserver.com
    d. Ipconfig/all

16. Which key combination will terminate a continuous ping issued with the ping -t option?

    a. Ctrl+S
    b. Ctrl+C
    c. Ctrl+Esc
    d. Ctrl+T

17. To determine the path your IP packets take to reach a remote office router, you issue the Tracert command from a local network host, targeted at the remote office routers outside interface. Previous tracert replies showed the router 9 hops away, so you set the Tracert command's maximum hops option to 10.

    You ping the remote router interface, 191.67.17.2, and it succeeds. You issue the command Tracert -h 10 191.67.17.2, but the tracert result does not list the router interface's IP address. Which might be a reason why this occurred?

    a. You did not include the subnet mask in the Tracert command.

    b. DNS is not correctly resolving the name tracert to an IP address.

    c. Your ISP has added routers between your local and remote network.

    d. You should have issued the Tracert command by name, not by IP address.

18. Which command uses NetBIOS to display protocol statistics on a local host?

    a. Netstat

    b. Netbeui

    c. Winipcfg

    d. Nbtstat

19. You are running an active browser session with your employer's Human Resources intranet Web server. You issue the Netstat command from your local workstation's command prompt. The resulting screen shows several connections to the Web server, each using a separate TCP port.

    Why does your client workstation have multiple active port connections open to the same Web server?

    a. The Netstat command opens new port connections to test communications with active applications.

    b. The Web server is listening for HTTP traffic on multiple well-known ports.

    c. HTTP sessions often open multiple connections between the client and the server.

    d. You are using NAPT NAT on your local router port.

20. Your customer called and stated that they have installed a new border router in their subnetted network. This router supports CIDR, and they are excited that they can now advertise a single network route to the Internet, instead of the six they had advertised before.

    They own the Class C address range 220.68.0.0/18, and use the following class C network addresses on their internal network segments:

    220.68.7.0

    220.68.11.0

    220.68.17.0

    220.68.21.0

    220.68.23.0

    220.68.24.0

    They state that some of the networks can no longer connect to Internet services. You Telnet into their border router and look at the routing table entries. You see that their router administrator configured their router to advertise the following internal network:

    220.68.0.0/21

    Which of the following might be the problem's cause?

    a. The router is not passing route information to the ISP router.

    b. They do not own all the addresses specified in the advertised network.

    c. The CIDR prefix is incorrect for this range of addresses.

    d. The internal routers must also support CIDR.

21. Which ARP command option shows the contents of the local ARP cache?

    a. ARP -a

    b. ARP -c

    c. ARP - N

    d. ARP -s

22. Which command can we use in conjunction with the ARP command to determine the hostname of a cached NetBIOS-over-IP address?
    a. ARP -host <IPaddress>
    b. Whois <IPaddress>
    c. Netstat -A <IPaddress>
    d. Nbtstat -A <IPaddress>
23. Which two of the following might cause a ping across network boundaries to fail? (Choose two.)
    a. Pinging by name instead of IP address
    b. Access Control Lists on the router ports
    c. ICMP filters on the router ports
    d. Pinging a host on an indirectly connected network

Course Quiz

1. Which of the following best describes an e-mail message's communication flow through the TCP/IP model layers?

   a. The Internetwork Layer breaks the message into pieces, the Network Access Layer forwards the datagram to its final destination, and the Transport Layer places the packets into frames.

   b. The Network Access Layer passes the data stream to the Transport Layer, which breaks the data into pieces. The Transport Layer passes the pieces to the Internetwork Layer, which build frames to carry the datagrams to the next node on the physical network.

   c. The Transport Layer breaks the data stream into pieces, which it passes to the Network Access Layer. The Network Access Layer adds the source and destination IP addresses, and forwards the packets to the Internetwork Layer. The Internetwork Layer builds frames and converts them to bits for transport across the physical network.

   d. The Transport Layer breaks the data stream into pieces, which it passes to the Internetwork Layer. The Internetwork Layer adds the source and destination IP addresses and forwards the packets to the Network Access Layer. The Network Access Layer builds frames, and converts them to bits for transport across the physical network.

2. Which two of the following are Class C addresses? (Choose two.)
   a. 10.1.23.46
   b. 192.17.89.253
   c. 192.168.40.15
   d. 172.16.45.134
3. ICANN recommends organizations use private IP addresses under which condition?
   a. The network hosts require access to other enterprises or the Internet.
   b. The organization anticipates future Internet access requirements.
   c. A corporate merger is pending between organizations using private IP addresses.
   d. The network uses gateways, routers, or firewalls to act on the network host's behalf.
4. Bridges and Layer 2 switches filter traffic in which way?
   a. By building routing tables and making forwarding decisions based on packet addresses
   b. By building physical address to port mappings and making forwarding decisions based on these mappings
   c. By looking at the source MAC address and forwarding frames only to the same segment on which the source resides
   d. By looking at the destination IP address and forwarding all unknown packets to all ports
5. Which network device can isolate broadcast traffic to the local network segment?
   a. Router
   b. Hub
   c. Bridge
   d. Switch

6. RMON differs from SNMP in which way?
   a. RMON presents to the monitoring station a collection of separate entities.
   b. SNMP uses SNMP probes, where RMON uses no probes.
   c. RMON agents gather information about a segment and its devices.
   d. SNMP allows the management station to see the network as a whole.
7. Which protocol allows clients to locate and download IP addressing and configuration information on an automatically renewable (lease) basis?
   a. BOOTP
   b. DHCP
   c. TFTP
   d. SNMP
8. Which statement best describes IMAP?
   a. IMAP uses POP3 for client/server e-mail communications.
   b. IMAP allows users to search e-mail messages for keywords directly on the e-mail client.
   c. IMAP depends on SMTP for client and server communications.
   d. IMAP is a protocol for transferring e-mail messages between servers.
9. In which two ways does an SNMP agent respond to the management station? (Choose two.)
   a. By actively polling the management station for permission to send updates
   b. By responding to the management station's requests for updated data
   c. By trapping information that exceeds a set threshold and forwarding the data to the management station
   d. By trapping information from the management station and forward the information to the managed devices

10. What is the binary equivalent of the subnet mask 255.248.0.0?

    a. 11111111.11111000.00000000.00000000

    b. 11111111.11110000.00000000.00000000

    c. 11111000.11111111.00000000.00000000

    d. 11111111.11111100.00000000.00000000

11. Which two of the following are reasons why an organization would choose to subnet their network? (Choose two.)

    a. To control collisions across multiple sites

    b. To build a more scalable network

    c. To support a single site from one address range

    d. To conserve network addresses

12. In a Class B network, if you borrowed 9 bits, how many usable subnets would you create?

    a. 62

    b. 126

    c. 254

    d. 510

13. Your customer owns a full Class C address, 220.14.56.0. They currently operate a flat network using the default Class C subnet mask, 255.255.255.0, and use a single router to connect to the Internet.

    To better control broadcast traffic, they wish to segment their network. They operate four workgroups, currently connected with Ethernet hubs. You evaluate their current network and find the following:

    - The administrative workgroup operates 15 workstations and primarily access a single combined file and e-mail server.
    - The technical support workgroup operates 23 workstations and accesses 2 file servers and a single database server.
    - The warehouse workgroup operates 3 workstations and accesses a single database server.

- The executive workgroup operates 4 workstations and accesses a single e-mail server.
- They plan 10 percent growth in the next five years.

To better control traffic, you decide to use routers to segment the network by workgroups, placing the workgroup's primary servers on each workgroup segment. Your next job is to determine the appropriate subnet mask to assign each new subnet.

How many usable subnets will you create, and what is the resulting subnet mask?

a. 30 subnets, 255.255.255.248

b. 14 subnets, 255.255.255.240

c. 8 subnets, 255.255.255.224

d. 6 subnets, 255.255.255.224

14. Using the subnet mask 255.255.255.192, which sets of host addresses will be able to communicate on the same network segment?

    a. 210.68.165.13, 210.68.166.48

    b. 210.68.165.30, 210.68.165.67

    c. 210.68.165.65, 210.68.165.120

    d. 210.68.165.131, 210.68.165.201

15. Given the IP address 67.89.124.189 and the subnet mask 255.224.0.0, which is the subnetted octet, and how frequently will it increment?

    a. The second octet, by 32

    b. The second octet, by 64

    c. The third octet, by 32

    d. The third octet, by 64

16. Your employer has merged with several competitors, each with its own Class C network. The network addresses are as follows:

    201.36.35.0/24

    201.36.72.0/24

    201.36.78.0/24

    201.36.79.0/24

    201.36.80.0/24

    201.36.141.0/24

    You need to integrate these networks and present them to the network border router routing tables with as few entries as possible. You will do this using CIDR.

    Which of the following best represents the border router's routing table entries for these networks, after you apply CIDR techniques?

    a. 201.36.35.0/24
       201.36.78.0/26
       201.36 141.0/24

    b. 201.36.32.0/26
       201.36.72.0/26
       201.36.141.0/26

    c. 201.36.35.0/24
       201.36.64.0/26
       201.36.128.0/25

    d. 201.36.35.0/24
       201.36.64.0/26
       201.36.141.0/24

17. What happens first when an IP host needs to resolve an IP address to a MAC address?

    a. The sending host looks in its ARP cache for the necessary mapping.

    b. The sending host immediately sends an ARP broadcast.

    c. The receiving host activates its ARP cache in preparation to receive packets.

    d. The sending host flushes its ARP cache of all old entries.

18. IP provides which three of the following services to TCP? (Choose three.)
    a. Datagram routing
    b. Error recovery
    c. TTL
    d. ToS
19. Which portion of the TCP header specifies the next sequence number the receiver expects from the connection source?
    a. Data offset
    b. Acknowledgement number
    c. ISN
    d. Control bits
20. How does the TCP receiver control the data flowing from the source?
    a. It discards any packets too large to fit in the MTU window.
    b. It sets the receive window size with each ACK segment it returns.
    c. It sets the acknowledgement window size with each WIN segment it returns.
    d. It sets the window size once in the SYN packet when the connection is initiated.
21. How does a sending TCP process handle a zero receive window size?
    a. It sets its transmit window to zero and halts transmission.
    b. It waits for periodic probe segments sent by the receiving TCP process.
    c. It sends periodic probe segments and waits for an ACK with a nonzero window size.
    d. It changes its receive window size to zero, flushes its buffers, and terminates the connection.

22. If a DHCP client fails to renew its lease at the 50-percent point, what happens next?
    a. It must immediately cease using the lease.
    b. It enters the REBIND state at 75-percent lease time.
    c. It broadcasts a DHCPREQUEST message.
    d. It tries to renew again at 87.5-percent lease time.
23. Which best describes a DHCP scope?
    a. A list of DHCP servers from which the client can choose to obtain its configuration
    b. A list of clients the server is allowed to answer
    c. A range of addresses from which the server chooses a client address assignment
    d. A range of addresses from which a server can choose a client address assignment, limited to a single subnet
24. How does dynamic address translation enhance network security?
    a. It assigns each host the same address, making each internal connection easily traceable.
    b. It only maps internal hosts to external addresses for the duration of the connection.
    c. It blocks external attacks while the internal host is online.
    d. It disconnects any externally initiated connections while the internal host is online.
25. In order to communicate with a host on a remote network, the source IP device must forward its packets to which of the following?
    a. The remote host's default gateway
    b. The remote host's nearest exit router
    c. The source host's default gateway
    d. The source host's nearest internal router

26. Which two of the following are advantages gained from using static routes? (Choose two.)
    a. Reduced network overhead
    b. Added network security
    c. Increased scalability
    d. Reduced administrative overhead
27. Which statement is true concerning IP routing?
    a. The Data Link Layer PDU changes at each hop.
    b. The IP Layer PDU changes at each hop.
    c. The Transport Layer PDU changes at each hop.
    d. The Application data changes at each hop.
28. Which two statements are true concerning DVA routing protocols? (Choose two.)
    a. They must know the entire network topology before computing the best path to a destination network.
    b. Each node maintains enough information to compute the least cost route to any other network in the routing domain.
    c. Slow convergence can cause such problems as routing loops and lost packets.
    d. They usually require fewer router resources to compute the best path to a destination network than do other routing protocols.
29. How does RIP resolve the count-to-infinity problem?
    a. Hop-count limits
    b. Split horizons
    c. LSAs
    d. Holddowns

30. A RIP router, Router 1, in a two-router network informs its neighbor, Router 2, of a new route to a directly connected network, Network A. Router 2 updates its routing table accordingly.

    Almost immediately, Router 1's link to Network A fails; Router 1 informs Router 2 of this change. Router 2 updates its routing table with this information, and then in its regular update message tells Router 1 that it has a new route to Network A, with a hop count of 1. This route is through Router 2 back to Router 1. Router 1's link to Network A is still failed.

    This is an example of which RIP routing problem?

    a. Split horizons

    b. Count-to-infinity

    c. Route poisoning

    d. Holddowns

31. In what two ways does OSPF improve upon the limitations of DVA protocols, such as RIP and IGRP? (Choose three.)

    a. It eliminates hop counts as a metric.

    b. SPF technology resists routing loops.

    c. Routers exchange routing table updates only.

    d. All routing table exchanges are authenticated.

32. A client DNS resolver wishes to resolve a Web server FQDN to an IP address. It sends its first message to its designated DNS server, requesting name to IP address resolution. This message contains the following information:

    The LAN protocol Data Link Layer header and trailer

    The IP header

    The UDP header

    The DNS resolver request

    Why did the resolver send the DNS request in the first packet, rather than send an initial empty SYN packet?

    a. UDP does not use SYN and ACK packets.

    b. UDP provides more room for data in the SYN packet than does TCP.

    c. UDP includes the SYN packet in the application data portion of the packet.

    d. UDP combines SYN and ACK packets.

33. An H.323 MCU provides which service on a converged network?
    a. Name resolution
    b. Voice-to-data conversion
    c. Authorization and authentication
    d. Terminal conferencing
34. You wish to measure the round-trip time your IP packets experience between your local router, RouterA, and a directly connected router, RouterB. You issue a Tracert command to measure the round trip time between the routers. The routers are configured as follows:

    Local router:

    - Router name—RouterA
    - Internal network port IP address—10.0.12.1
    - External network port IP address—10.0.14.1

    Remote router:

    - Router name—RouterB
    - Directly connected port IP address—10.0.14.2

    Next hop port IP address—171.68.123.250

The tracert command results are as follows:

Tracing route to routerb.bigdotcom.com [10.0.14.2] over a maximum of 30 hops

1 2ms 2ms 2ms routera.bigdotcom.com [10.0.12.1]

2 5ms 7ms 6ms routerb.bigdotcom.com [10.0.14.2]

Trace complete

The Tracert command results are as follows:

You calculate the round-trip time based on each hop's third ICMP packet set. Based on your calculations, which of the following choices represents the round-trip time your packets experience traveling between RouterA and RouterB?

a. 2 ms

b. 4 ms

c. 6 ms

d. 7 ms

35. You are troubleshooting a name resolution problem on your local network. You run two internal DNS servers, and they resolve all local hostnames. Where would you look to verify that your Windows clients are configured to use the correct DNS servers?

    a. The local ARP cache

    b. The nbtstat window

    c. The winipcfg window

    d. The DNS server hosts file

GLOSSARY

100BaseFX—100BaseFX is a 100BaseT variant that runs over fiber optic cabling. 100BaseFX is generally used for high-speed LAN backbones.

100BaseT—100BaseT is based on 802.3 Ethernet and uses twisted pair cabling, as does 10BaseT Ethernet. However, 100BaseT runs 10 times faster than 10Base2 and 10Base5, at 100 Mbps.

10Base2—10Base2 is one of several physical cabling standards for 802.3 Ethernet networks. 10Base2 uses thin RG-58A/U coaxial cabling for connecting nodes on a bus topology, as does 10Base5. 10Base2 is also known as Thinnet.

10Base5—Also known as Thicknet, 10Base5 was the original Ethernet cabling standard. It is called Thicknet because it used a coaxial cable approximately 0.5 inches thick.

10BaseT—10BaseT is one of several physical cabling standards for 802.3 Ethernet LANs. 10BaseT networks use twisted pair cabling for connecting nodes in a star topology.

56-bit Data Encryption Standard (DES) encryption—DES is a popular single-key encryption system that uses a 56-bit key. Triple-DES uses the DES algorithm to encrypt a message three times, using three 56-bit keys. It is considered a hardware solution to encryption because of the time necessary to encrypt and decrypt a message.

Abstract Syntax Notation 1 (ASN.1)—ASN.1 is a LAN "grammar" with rules and symbols used to describe and define protocols and programming languages. ASN.1 is the OSI standard language for describing data types.

Acknowledgement (ACK)—TCP header field that indicates the Acknowledgement field is significant.

Acknowledgement (ACK) Number—The ACK number applies only if the ACK control bit is set. The ACK number is the next sequence number a sender of a segment is expecting to receive. If a connection is established, this value is always sent.

address mask—An address mask is a bit mask used to select bits from an IP address for subnet addressing. The mask is 32 bits long and selects the network portion of the IP address and one or more bits of the local portion.

Address Resolution Protocol (ARP)—ARP is a TCP/IP protocol used to convert an IP address into a physical address, such as an Ethernet address. A host wishing to obtain a physical address broadcasts an ARP request onto the TCP/IP network. The host on the network that has the IP address in the request then replies with its physical hardware address.

address translation table—An address translation table is the internal-to-external IP and/or port address mappings maintained by a NAT device. The table's contents will vary depending on the NAT type used.

administrative distance (AD)—A routing table entry's AD represents its source's trustworthiness. A lower number means it is more trustworthy than an entry with a higher number. Cisco routers use ADs that range from 0 (highest trustworthiness) to 255 (lowest, and unusable).

Advanced Research Projects Agency Network (ARPANET)—ARPANET is a long-haul network funded by the ARPA (later DARPA) and built by Bolt, Beranek, and Newman, Inc. From 1969 through 1990, ARPANET served as the basis for early networking research, as well as a central backbone during development of the Internet.

American Standard Code for Information Interchange (ASCII)—ASCII is one of the most widely used codes for representing text in computers. ASCII codes represent letters, numerals, punctuation, and keyboard characters as numbers. For example, when the character "A" is pressed on the keyboard, the ASCII binary representation of that character is 100 0001 (hexadecimal 41). The basic ASCII character set uses 7 bits to represent the 128 text and keyboard elements.

AND function—The AND function is a Boolean operator that only returns a true (1) value when both operands are true. Otherwise, the result is false (0).

anycast—In IPv6, anycast is communication between a single sender and the nearest of several receivers in a group. The term exists in contradistinction to multicast, communication between a single sender and multiple receivers, and unicast, communication between a single sender and a single receiver in a network. Anycasting is designed to let one host initiate the efficient updating of router tables for a group of hosts. IPv6 can determine which gateway host is closest and sends the packets to that host as though it were a unicast communication. In turn, that host can anycast to another host in the group until all routing tables are updated.

AppleTalk—AppleTalk is Apple's proprietary protocol suite for Macintosh networks. It provides a multilayer, peer-to-peer architecture that uses built-in OS services. AppleTalk corresponds to the OSI seven-layer model.

area border routers (ABRs)—An ABR is an OSPF router connected to more than one area. Routing between areas is handled by the ABRs. An ABR maintains a separate link-state database for each area it is connected to, and creates a separate SPF tree from each of those databases.

Asynchronous Transfer Mode (ATM)—ATM is a connection-oriented cell relay technology based on small (53-byte) cells. An ATM network consists of ATM switches that form multiple virtual circuits to carry groups of cells from source to destination. ATM can provide high-speed transport services for audio, data, and video.

attribute—When related to HTML, an attribute is used to distinguish elements of the same type by their details. An example of an HTML attribute is the SIZE attribute, which specifies an element's height. Another HTML attribute is HREF, which specifies a referenced file's URL.

autonomous system boundary routers (ASBRs)—An ASBR is an OSPF router connected to routers in other autonomous systems. Just as an ABR represents its area to other ABRs, an ASBR represents its AS to other ASBRs. Each ASBR runs OSPF on the interface to its own AS and an inter-AS routing protocol, such as EGP or BGP, on the interface to another AS. These protocols allow ASBRs to exchange routing information that summarizes routes within each AS.

base10—See decimal.

base2—See binary.

Base64—Base64 is a standard algorithm for encoding and decoding non-ASCII data for attachment to an e-mail message; it is the foundation for MIME. Base64 uses a 65-character subset of ASCII to represent non-ASCII data in e-mail attachments.

basic encoding rules (BERs)—BERs are the data unit encoding rules used in the ASN.1 LAN encoding grammar.

BGP version 4 (BGP-4)—BGP-4 is documented in RFC 1771 and is the current exterior routing protocol used for the global Internet. BGP-4 is essentially a DVA. BGP runs over TCP Port 179.

binary—The binary number system is one that uses just two unique digits, 1 and 0. Computers and other networking devices are based on the binary numbering system. All operations that are possible in the decimal system (addition, subtraction, multiplication, division) are equally possible in the binary system. For network devices, because of their electrical nature (on versus off), the binary system is more natural than the decimal system.

BIND—Short for Berkeley Internet Name Domain, a DNS type. BIND is designed for UNIX systems based on BSD, the version of UNIX developed at the University of California's Berkeley campus

Bootstrap Protocol (BOOTP)—BOOTP is an Internet protocol for enabling a diskless workstation to boot and determine its configuration information, such as its IP address, from information available on a BOOTP server.

Border Gateway Protocol (BGP)—BGP is an EGP used among BGP routers to exchange reachability information. Each BGP router advertises networks reachable within its AS to other BGP routers in other autonomous systems. BGP remedies many of the limitations of EGP, and provides support for future growth of the Internet.

bridge—A bridge is a hardware device that connects LANs. It can be used to connect LANs of the same type, such as two Token Ring segments, or LANs with different types of media such as Ethernet and Token Ring. A bridge operates at the Data Link Layer of the OSI reference model.

bridge router (Brouter)—A Brouter is an internetworking device that combines the functions of both a bridge and a router. See router.

Broadband-ISDN (B-ISDN)—B-ISDN is a set of ITU-T services requiring transmission channels that support data rates in excess of the primary rate, DS1. Three underlying technologies are critical to B-ISDN: SS7, ATM, and SONET.

broadcast—The term broadcast is used in several different ways in communications and networking. With respect to LANs, the term refers to information (that is, frames) sent to all devices on the physical segment. For example, a bus topology, in which a common cable is used to connect devices, is considered a broadcast technology. Another common use of the term broadcast relates to frames. Broadcast frames contain a special destination address that instructs all devices on the network to receive the frame.

cc:Mail—cc:Mail is a Lotus Development Corporation proprietary mail system. cc:Mail does not provide Internet mail access, and thus must use an e-mail gateway to send and receive SMTP mail.

checksum—A checksum is a simple error detection strategy that computes a running total based on a packet's transmitted byte values and then applies a simple operation to compute the checksum value. The receiver compares the checksums computed by the sender and the receiver, and, if they match, assumes error-free transmission.

chicken/egg method—The chicken/egg method is a technique used to resolve a first issue dependent on a second, but where the second issue cannot be implemented without the first. Usually, some third issue is used to resolve the first, bypassing the requirement for the second issue.

classful protocol—A classful protocol is a routing protocol that does not send along subnet mask information along with routing updates. A classful routing protocol cannot differentiate between a default network's network address and the all 0s subnet, making that subnet unusable.

Classless Interdomain Routing (CIDR)CIDR replaces the older network addressing system based on classes A, B, and C. With CIDR, a single IP address can be used to designate many unique IP addresses. A CIDR IP address looks like a normal IP address except that it ends with a slash followed by a number, called the IP prefix. The IP prefix specifies how many addresses are covered by the CIDR address, with lower prefix values covering more addresses. For example, an IP prefix of /16, can be used to address 256 former Class C addresses.

classless protocol—A classless protocol is a routing protocol that passes subnet mask information with its routing updates. This makes subnetting more efficient and is the basis for CIDR.

class-of-service (CoS) routing—COS routing allows network administrators to specify different routing service categories and associate different performance characteristics with each category. The administrator assigns data packets to different priority queues and specifies the ratio of high-priority packets traversing the network to lower priority packets.

collision—A collision occurs in an Ethernet network when two frames are put onto the physical medium at the same time and overlap fully or partially. When a collision occurs, the data on the physical segment is no longer valid.

convergence—Convergence is the speed and ability of a group of internetworking devices running a specific routing protocol to agree on the topology of an internetwork after a change in that topology.

country code top level domain (ccTLD)—Each country in the world is assigned an Internet country code, a two-character code designating the country in which a domain resides. This country code is appended to the end of the FQDN.

cut—A DNS cut divides DNS zone responsibilities between the root domain name server and subdomain nameservers, and in turn between subdomains and further subordinate domains. For example, in the domain westnetinc.com, a subdomain contracts.westnetinc.com could exist. When the DNS administrator cuts the westnetinc.com domain, he or she delegates responsibility for the subdomain contracts.westnetinc.com to the subdomain nameserver.

daemon—A daemon is a UNIX process that runs in the background and performs an operation at a specified time or in response to a certain event. A Microsoft Windows equivalent to a daemon is a service or system agent.

Data Offset—The data offset specifies the number of 32-bit words in the TCP header. It indicates where the data begins in a segment. This field is necessary because the Options field is of variable length, as is the header.

datagram—A datagram is a unit of information processed by the Network Layer of the OSI reference model. The packet header contains the logical (network) address of the destination node. Intermediate nodes forward a packet until it reaches its destination. A packet can contain an entire message generated by higher OSI layers or a segment of a much larger message.

decimal—Decimal refers to numbers in base 10 (the numbers we use in everyday life), represented by the digits 0–9. Decimal numbers are more natural for us to work with, thus most network devices perform binary-to-decimal and decimal-to-binary conversion for us.

DECnet—DECnet is a proprietary network architecture created by DEC (now Compaq). The most recent DECnet model, DECnet Phase V, specifies seven layers that correspond to the OSI reference model. The DECnet architecture specifies 20-byte addresses and allows for the creation of separate routing and administration domains.

default gateway—A default gateway is a router that provides access to all hosts on remote networks. Typically, the network administrator configures a default gateway for each host on the network.

DHCP lease—A DHCP lease is the IP address the DHCP server dynamically issues to DHCP clients. The server maintains the lease for a specific period of time, and as the lease expiration time approaches, the client must renew the lease.

DHCPv6—Short for DHCP version 6, DHCPv6 assigns host IPv6 addresses dynamically. DHCPv6 is specified in Internet Draft form, and adds additional message types and larger Address fields, commensurate with IPv6 addressing, over DHCPv4. DHCPv6 uses UDP Port 546 for the client, and 547 for the server.

digital signature—A digital signature is a digital code that can be embedded into a document to prove its authenticity. Digital signatures are an application of public-key encryption technology; the sender of a document uses a private encryption key to encrypt a text string or the digest of the message. Document recipients use the sender's public-encryption key to decrypt the signature and authenticate the sender.

disk operating system (DOS)—DOS is the low-level software that resides on many PCs and controls the operation of a computer and its peripheral devices. MS-DOS is the operating system that preceded Microsoft Windows and still exists as an extension of the Windows OS.

DNS zone—The part of the DNS namespace for which a DNS server has complete information is organized into units called zones; zones are the main units of replication in DNS. A zone contains one or more RRs for one or more related DNS domains. Each DNS server contains the RRs relating to those portions of the DNS namespace for which it is authoritative (for which it can answer queries sent by a host). When a DNS server is authoritative for a portion of the DNS name space, those systems' administrators are responsible for ensuring that the information about that DNS name space portion is correct. To increase efficiency, a given DNS server can cache the RRs relating to a domain in any part of the domain tree.

Domain Name System or Service (DNS)—In a TCP/IP network, a user can communicate with another user by specifying a name, such as johnd@engr.company.com. TCP and IP require Internet addresses for messages, thus one must be translated to the other. This is the job of the DNS; given a name, it returns an Internet address.

dotted decimal notation—Dotted decimal notation is the syntactic representation for a 32-bit integer that consists of four 8-bit numbers with periods (dots) separating them. Many TCP/IP application programs accept dotted decimal notation in place of destination computer names (205.169.85.200).

Dynamic Host Configuration Protocol (DHCP)—DHCP is used on a TCP/IP network to allow hosts to obtain configuration information from a DHCP server. DHCP provides for address leases, which release an address after a set lease period. DHCP can pass to a DHCP client computer such information as its DNS server and default gateway addresses and subnet mask.

EGP version 2 (EGP-2)—EGP-2 is an EGP used to exchange network reachability information between routers in different autonomous systems. In each AS, routers share routing information using one or more IGP, for example, RIP or OSPF. The routers that serve as endpoints of a connection between two autonomous systems run an EGP, such as EGP-2.

Ethernet—Ethernet technology, originally developed in the 1970s by Xerox Corporation in conjunction with Intel and DEC, is now the primary medium for LANs. The original Ethernet has 10-Mbps throughput and uses the CSMA/CD method to access the physical media. Fast Ethernet (100-Mbps Ethernet) and Gigabit Ethernet (1,000-Mbps Ethernet) are also used.

expansion card—An expansion card is a printed circuit board that can be inserted into a PC to add capabilities. Expansion card examples are NICs, video cards, and modems.

Exterior Gateway Protocol (EGP)—EGP is the protocol used by a gateway in one AS to advertise IP addresses of networks in the system to a gateway in another AS. All autonomous systems must use EGP to advertise network reachability to the core gateway system.

extranet—An extranet is an external intranet offering select Internet users controlled access to an internal network segment. External users can view and update data stored on the internal network without actually traversing the network.

fat ping—A fat ping is a ping issued with the -l option, specifying a large packet size. This can be used to test for intermittent network component or link failures between end nodes. A useful packet size is 512 bytes, although sizes up to the network segment's MTU can also be used. This term also refers to a TCP/IP denial of service attack, where the sender floods the receiver's network with oversized packets.

Fiber Distributed Data Interface (FDDI)—FDDI is a LAN standard specifying a 100-Mbps token-passing network using fiber optic cable.

File Transfer Protocol (FTP)—FTP is a TCP/IP Application Layer protocol used to transfer files between two computers.

Finish (FIN)—FIN is the TCP header field (ACK number 50) that indicates no more data should be sent from the sender.

flow control—Flow control refers to control of the rate at which hosts or gateways inject packets into a network or internet. Flow control is used to avoid congestion and can be implemented at various protocol levels. Simplistic schemes like ICMP source quench instruct the sender to cease transmission until congestion ends. More complex schemes vary the transmission rate continuously.

Fragment Offset—Fragment offset is the IP header field that specifies the offset in the original datagram of the data being carried in the fragment, measured in units of 8 bytes, starting at 0.

fragmentation—Fragmentation is the IP process of dividing a datagram into smaller pieces that will better suit the transporting network's MTU.

fully qualified domain name (FQDN)—The FQDN is the complete Internet system name. The FQDN includes the hostname and the domain name. An example of a FQDN is ken.westnetinc.com.

G.711—G.711 is one of a series of ITU-T voice digitizing algorithms. G.711 transfers digitized audio at 48, 56, and 64 Kbps.

G.722—G.722 is one of a series of ITU-T voice digitizing algorithms. G.722 transfers digitized audio at 32 Kbps.

G.723—G.723 is one of a series of ITU-T voice digitizing algorithms. G.723 transfers digitized audio at 5.3 or 6.3 Kbps.

G.728—G.728 is one of a series of ITU-T voice digitizing algorithms. G.728 transfers digitized audio at 16 Kbps.

G.729—G.729 is one of a series of ITU-T voice digitizing algorithms. G.729 transfers digitized audio at 8 Kbps.

gatekeeper—A network device or process that controls data flow on a transmission channel or allocates transmission bandwidth among multiple competing signals is referred to as a gatekeeper.

Gateway-to-Gateway Protocol (GGP)—GGP is a routing protocol that core routers use to exchange routing information between Internet routers. GGP uses an SPF algorithm.

graphical user interface (GUI)—A GUI provides easy access to computer programs and often hides details of a program from the user.

graphics interchange format (GIF)—GIF is one of two graphic image formats used in HTML. (JPEG is the other type.) GIF files, the more popular format for small or simple images, are limited to 256 colors, have a lower resolution than JPEG files, offer lossless compression, and can be made transparent for a popular type of borderless effect.

H.225—H.225 is the ITU-T recommended standard that describes how audio, video, data, and control information on a packet-based network can be managed to provide conversational services in H.323 equipment.

H.245—H.245 is line transmission of nontelephone signals. It includes receiving and transmitting capabilities as well as mode preference from the receiving end, logical channel signalling, and control and indication. Acknowledged signalling procedures are specified to ensure reliable audiovisual and data communication.

H.261—H.261 describes a video stream for transport using RTP with any of the underlying protocols that carry RTP.

H.263—H.263 specifies the payload format for encapsulating an H.263 bitstream in the RTP.

H.310—H.310 is the ITU-T recommendation for videoconferencing in an ATM environment.

H.320—H.320 is the most common ITU-T family of videoconferencing standards. H.320 standards allow videoconferencing systems to communicate over ISDN-BRI connections.

H.321—H.321 is the adaptation of the H.320 videoconferencing standards to an ATM environment.

H.322—H.322 is the ITU-T recommended adaptation of H.320 to a guaranteed QoS LAN environment.

H.323—H.323 is an umbrella recommendation from ITU that sets standards for multimedia communications over LANs that do not provide a guaranteed QoS, such as over IP networks.

H.324—H.324 is the ITU-T recommended standard for videoconferencing by means of modems over POTS lines. H.324 uses H.263 for video compression, G.723 for audio encoding, and H.245/H.225 for control and multiplexing.

hop count—Hop count is the number of intermediate routers that a packet must traverse to travel from source to destination in a multi-router environment.

hub—Also referred to as a wiring concentrator, a simple hub is a repeater with multiple ports. A signal coming into one port is repeated out the other ports.

Hypertext Markup Language (HTML)—HTML is the authoring language used to create documents for use on the Web.

Hypertext Transfer Protocol (HTTP)—HTTP is the Application Layer protocol used to request and transmit documents by means of the Web.

IEEE 802.1p—IEEE 802.1p is the IEEE extension to 802.1D that allows Layer 2 bridges and switches to filter and prioritize LAN traffic. 802.1p modifies the 802.1Q 3-bit priority identification tag to represent one of eight topology-independent priority values.

IEEE 802.1Q—IEEE 8021Q is the IEEE specification for implementing VLANs in Layer 2 LAN switches, emphasizing but not limited to Ethernet. 802.1Q modifies the 802.10 Clear Header 2-byte field to indicate a frame's VLAN membership.

Institute of Electrical and Electronic Engineers (IEEE)—IEEE is a professional organization composed of engineers, scientists, and students. Founded in 1884, IEEE publishes computer and electronics standards, including the 802 series that defines shared-media networks such as Ethernet and Token Ring.

Integrated Services Digital Network (ISDN)—ISDN is a digital multiplexing technology that can transmit voice, data, and other forms of communication simultaneously over a single local loop. ISDN-BRI provides two bearer channels (B channels) of 64 Kbps each, plus one control channel (D channel) of 16 Kbps. ISDN-PRI offers 23 B channels of 64 Kbps each, plus one D channel of 64 Kbps.

interleaf ratio—An interleaf ratio is a value used in CoS routing that specifies the number of high-priority packets to be transmitted for each low-priority packet. For example, if the interleaf ratio is set to five, a router transmits five high-priority packets for each one low-priority packet.

Intermediate System to Intermediate System (IS-IS)—IS-IS is an OSI model link-state, hierarchical routing protocol based on DECnet Phase V routing.

International Telecommunications Union Telecommunications Standardization Sector (ITU-T)—ITU-T is an intergovernmental organization that develops and adopts international telecommunications standards and treaties. ITU was founded in 1865 and became a United Nations agency in 1947.

Internet—The Internet is the worldwide internetwork of various research, defense, and commercial networks, all tied together for sharing information with one another and public and private users of all sizes and concerns. The Internet consists of millions of interconnected hosts.

Internet Control Message Protocol (ICMP)—ICMP is an integral part of IP that handles error and control messages. Gateways and hosts use ICMP to report problems about datagrams back to the original source that sent the datagram. ICMP also includes an echo request/reply used to test whether a destination is reachable and responding.

Internet Corporation of Assigned Names and Numbers (ICANN)—ICANN is a private, nonprofit organization responsible for overseeing the domain name registration process, assigning IP addresses, assigning protocol parameters, and managing the DNS root servers. Learn more about ICANN at **http://www.icann.org**.

Internet Engineering Task Force (IETF)—IETF is a large, open, international community of network designers, operators, vendors, and researchers concerned with the evolution of the Internet architecture and smooth operation of the Internet.

Internet Gateway Routing Protocol (IGRP)—IGRP is a DVA protocol developed by Cisco Systems for use in large, heterogeneous networks. It uses metric such as bandwidth, delay, MTU, and hop count to compute the best path to a destination network.

Internet Group Management Protocol (IGMP)—IGMP is the Internet standard by which hosts can communicate their multicast group membership status to multicast routers. IGMP is used to keep up-to-date information on which host is in which multicast group.

Internet Message Access Protocol (IMAP)—IMAP is a protocol used for retrieving e-mail messages from a mail server. IMAP4 is a version of IMAP similar to POP3, but it supports additional features such as allowing keyword searches in e-mail messages while the messages remain on the mail server.

Internet Packet Exchange/Sequenced Packet Exchange (IPX/SPX)—IPX is NetWare's proprietary Network Layer protocol. SPX is the connection-oriented transport protocol concerned with connection-oriented services such as sequencing packets and guaranteeing their delivery, which provides reliability for IPX communications.

Internet Protocol (IP)—IP is the TCP/IP standard protocol that defines the IP datagram as the unit of information passed across an internet. IP provides the basis for connectionless, best-effort packet delivery service, and includes ICMP. The entire protocol suite is often referred to as TCP/IP because TCP and IP are the two most fundamental protocols.

internetwork—Internetwork is a term used to describe a set of connected networks communicating across routers using routable protocols such as TCP/IP or IPX/SPX. The Internet is a very large internetwork; smaller internetworks are corporate networks spanning several floors, buildings, or sites.

intranet—An intranet is a local Internet. An intranet is generally only accessible by corporate network users, but it runs all the same protocols and services as does an Internet site.

IP address translation—IP address translation is a NAT technique used to assign internal IP addresses to external addresses, either statically or dynamically. The NAT needs one public IP for each internal private IP needing a connection.

IP Version 6—IPv6, also known as IP next generation, is a new version of the IP currently being reviewed in the IETF standards committees. IPv6 adds features over the current IPv4, including longer addresses (128 bits) and better QoS support.

Ipconfig—Ipconfig is one of the configuration tools, such as the Windows Winipcfg, used to display addressing information on a host computer.

Joint Photographic Experts Group (JPEG)—JPEG is an open standard that defines a method of compressing still images. See JPEG File Interchange Format.

JPEG File Interchange Format (JFIF)—JFIF is a public domain graphic compression format that conforms to the JPEG standard for image compression. It is one of two popular graphic image formats used in HTML pages (GIF is the other). JPEG/JFIF files offer higher resolution, with up to 16.7 million colors, and are generally used in continuous-tone images such as photographs. However, JPEG/JFIF compression is lossy (some image information is lost), even at the highest quality setting.

jumbogram—Using the IPv6, a jumbogram is a packet that contains a payload larger than 65,535 octets.

least significant bit (LSB)—In a binary number, the LSB is the bit position with the lowest place value (2^0).

least-cost routing—In data networks, least-cost routing describes the methods routers use to determine the lowest cost link between networks. Least cost routing makes these determinations based on cost factors such as bandwidth, delay, and cash costs.

link-state advertisement—Link-state advertisements are sent between routers running LSA routing protocols. These are usually in the form of multicast packets, containing neighbor router information and path costs.

link-state algorithm (LSA)—Also known as Dijkstra algorithm, LSAs allow each router to broadcast or multicast network route cost information concerning its neighbors to every node in the internetwork. LSA routing protocols provide a consistent network view across all routers, and are thus not vulnerable to routing loops.

load splitting—Also known as load balancing, load splitting separates network communications into two or more routes in order to share the load among the separate links. The makes data communications faster and more reliable than does using a single path between networks.

loopback—The TCP/IP loopback function allows a network administrator to test IP software without concern for the hardware or drivers. The loopback address 127.0.0.1 is the designated software loopback interface for the machine.

magic cookie—A magic cookie is a 4-byte field entry in the BOOTREQUEST message set to help the BOOTP server determine the format in which to send vendor-specific information. DHCP also specifies the magic cookie entry.

mailbox—When referring to IP sockets, this is a software-specified storage area where the local IP process forwards inbound segments to the TCP process. TCP, in turn, forwards the data to the destination application.

management information base (MIB)-2—MIB-2, also known as MIB-II, is the RFC 1213 specified MIB format for TCP/IP networks. MIB-2 includes such information as system uptime, interface counters, and IP layer address tables.

masquerading—Masquerading is also known as NAPT. Masquerading is a NAT technique that hides all internal devices behind a single public IP address (usually the NAT's outside port IP address). The NAT assigns each internal device connection this address and a new TCP or UDP port number taken from the registered port number range. This IP address/registered port number combination identifies a specific internal host on the Internet.

Maximum Transmission Unit (MTU)—MTU is the maximum amount of information that can be carried by a datagram or frame. For example, the MTU of Ethernet is 1,500 bytes of information.

MD5—MD5 is a one-way hash algorithm that takes a message and converts it into a fixed string of digits called a message digest. It is used to create digital signatures.

Medium Access Control (MAC)—MAC is one of the media-specific IEEE 802 standards (802.3, 802.4, and 802.5) that defines the protocol and frame formats for Ethernet, Token Bus, and Token Ring. It is the lower sublayer of the Data Link Layer of the OSI model used to transmit frames between NICs.

most significant bit (MSB)—In a binary number, the MSB is the bit position with the highest place value. In an 8-bit number, the MSB in the bit position with the place value of 2^7.

Motion Picture Experts Group (MPEG)—A standard for com- pressing video to fewer bits for storage and transmission.

multicast—Multicast is a technique that allows copies of a single packet to be passed to a select subset of all possible destinations. Some hardware (such as Ethernet) supports multicast by allowing a network interface to belong to one or more multicast groups. IP supports an internet multicast facility.

Multipoint Control Unit (MCU)—MCUs are hosts that coordinate multipoint conferences of three or more terminals that use the H.323 packet multimedia standards. All H.323 terminals participating in a conference must establish a connection with the MCU.

Multipurpose Internet Mail Extension (MIME)—MIME is an extension of SMTP that supports the exchange of a wide variety of document files by means of an e-mail system.

Nbtstat—Nbtstat is a utility that can be used to display statistics and current TCP/IP connections using NetBIOS over a TCP/IP connection.

Netstat—Netstat shows the current status of all connections on a computer. The Netstat utility shows remote connected computer IP addresses and port numbers and the corresponding computer name; the local computer IP address, port, and name; and the protocol the connection uses.

Network Address Translation (NAT)—NAT is an Internet standard that enables a LAN to use one set of IP addresses for internal traffic and a second set of addresses for external traffic. A network device, such as a router or a firewall, located where the LAN meets the external network, translates the internal addresses to external addresses, and external to internal. NAT serves two main purposes: it provides a type of firewall by hiding internal IP addresses and enables a company to use more internal IP addresses than ICANN has assigned them. Since these addresses are used internally only, there is no possibility of conflict with IP addresses used by other companies and organizations.

Network Basic Input/Output System (NetBIOS)—IBM and Sytek developed NetBIOS to link a NOS to specific hardware, augmenting DOS to provide LAN functions to the operating system. NetBIOS uses SMBs as the message format for sharing Windows files, directories, and devices.

network interface card (NIC)—A NIC is an expansion board inserted into a computer to enable the computer to be connected to a network.

network mask—The network mask is the number of mask bits in an IP address class used to determine the network on which a host resides. The mask octets set to all 1s determines the network, while the mask octets set to all 0s determines the host.

Network News Transfer Protocol (NNTP)—NNTP is the TCP/IP protocol used to distribute news article collections, or news feeds, over the Internet.

Open Systems Interconnection (OSI)—OSI began as a reference model, that is, an abstract model for data communications. However, now the OSI model has been implemented and is used in some data communications applications. The seven-layer OSI model falls logically into two parts. Layers 1 through 4, the "lower" layers, are concerned with the communication of raw data. Layers 5 through 7, the "higher" layers, are concerned with the networking of applications.

Optical Carrier (OC)-3—OC-3 is the SONET optical signal standard that corresponds to a data rate of 155.52 Mbps. SONET is an optical transmission standard that defines a numbered signal hierarchy. The optical signal standards are designated OC-1, OC-2, and so on. The basic building block is the OC-1 51.84-Mbps signal, chosen to accommodate a T3 signal.

OR function—The OR function is a Boolean operator that returns a true (1) when the operands are both true, or when either is true and the other is false (0). The only time the OR function results in a false condition is when both operands are false.

Packet Internet Groper (Ping)—Ping is used to verify that a computer's IP software is running properly and to verify the connectivity between computers.

PC card—Previously known as a PCMCIA card, a PC card is a small rectangular expansion card for portable devices, such as laptop and palm computers. PC cards can be NICs, modems, and hard drives, to name a few.

policy routing—Also known as policy-based routing, policy routing allows organizations to implement packet forwarding and routing according to defined policies in a manner that goes beyond traditional routing protocol concerns. By using policy-based routing, organizations can implement policies that selectively cause packets to take different paths, depending on their differentiated, preferential service type.

policy-based routing—Policy-based routing allows network administrators to specify additional routing table and network model information sources. These sources may include information imported from other protocols or information network administrators statically configure. Such policies can be defined on a router-by-router basis and control the advertisement of routing information.

Post Office Protocol (POP)—POP is used to transfer information from a mail server to a user's computer so the information can be read by a mail program at the user's desk. POP3 is the latest iteration of the protocol.

protocol data unit (PDU)—A PDU is a datagram created by a particular layer of an open system reference model. A PDU is used to provide peer-to-peer communications between local and remote processes.

Proxy ARP—Proxy ARP is a variation of the ARP protocol, where an intermediate device, such as a router, sends an ARP response to the requesting host on behalf of the end node.

public-key encryption—Public-key encryption is a cryptographic system that uses two mathematically related keys; one key is used to encrypt a message and the other is used to decrypt it. People who need to receive encrypted messages distribute their public keys but keep their private keys secret.

public-switched telephone network (PSTN)—PSTN is the world-wide voice telephone network accessible to anyone with a telephone.

Real-Time Transport Control Protocol (RTCP)—RTCP, a counterpart of RTP, is an OSI model Presentation Layer protocol that provides control services and feedback on the quality of the data transmission.

Real-Time Transport Protocol (RTP)—RTP is an OSI model Presentation Layer protocol that provides end-to-end delivery of real-time audio and video by prioritizing this traffic ahead of connectionless data transfers.

registered port—The registered ports are those TCP and UDP ports not controlled by IANA and available for use by ordinary user processes or programs. The registered ports range from 1024–65535. These compare with the well-known ports, which are assigned to specific services.

Remote Monitoring (RMON)—The Remote Monitoring protocol gathers network information at a central workstation. RMON defines additional SNMP MIBs that provide more detailed information about network usage and status.

repeater—A repeater connects one cable segment of a LAN to other segments, including connecting differing media. For example, a repeater connects thin Ethernet cables to thick Ethernet cables. It regenerates electrical signals from one segment of cable onto all other segments. Because a repeater reproduces exactly what it receives, bit by bit, it also reproduces errors.

Request for Comment (RFC)—RFCs are the working documents of the Internet research and development community. A document in this series may be on essentially any topic related to computer communication and may be anything from a meeting report to the specification of a standard.

resolver—The DNS resolver is a DNS system component that performs DNS queries against a DNS server (or servers). The resolver is a part of the DNS client and is usually installed when TCP/IP is installed.

resource records (RRs)—An RR is a DNS database record containing information relating to a domain that a DNS client can retrieve and use. For example, the host RR for a specific domain holds the IP address of that domain (host); a DNS client will use this RR to obtain the IP address for the domain.

Resource Reservation Protocol (RSVP)—Sometimes known as Resource Reservation Setup Protocol, RSVP functions to reserve network resources based on an application's QoS requirements. RSVP requests these resources from all devices in a data flow's path and reports to the requesting application that the resources are available for its use.

Reverse Address Resolution Protocol (RARP)—RARP is the protocol a diskless computer uses at startup to find its IP address. The computer broadcasts a request that contains its physical hardware address, and a server responds by sending the computer its IP address. RARP takes its name and message format from the IP ARP.

RMON probe—A RMON probe is a firmware or hardware device installed in a network component, or attached to a network segment, designed to monitor the network and its devices. The probe sends information it has gathered to the network monitoring station.

RMON2—RMON2 improves upon RMON by providing traffic data at the Network Layer in addition to the Physical Layer. This allows administrators to analyze traffic by protocol.

routed protocol—A routed protocol is one that is routed across an internetwork. Routed protocols contain source and destination network and host addresses, in the form of logical addresses, to enable network devices to move data from its source host and network to the destination network and host.

router—A router is a Layer 3 device with several ports that can each connect to a network or another router. The router examines the logical network address of each packet, then uses its internal routing table to forward the packet to the routing port associated with the best path to the packet's destination. If the packet is addressed to a network that is not connected to the router, the router forwards the packet to another router that is closer to the final destination. Each router, in turn, evaluates each packet and then either delivers the packet or forwards it to another router.

routing protocol—A routing protocol is a protocol that implements the movement of Layer 3 protocol traffic across an internetwork. Routing protocols gather network path information from neighboring network devices and use this information to determine the best path over which to forward traffic towards its destination.

Secure/MIME (S/MIME)—S/MIME is a MIME version that supports message encryption using public-key encryption technology. This ensures that e-mail is sent and received in a manner that is secure from interception or tampering.

Sendmail—Sendmail is a UNIX application that handles electronic mail. Sendmail supports back-end message routing and handling for SMTP-based e-mail systems.

sequence number—This is the sequence number of the first data byte in a segment (except when synchronize [SYN] is present). When SYN is present, the sequence number is the ISN, and the first data byte is ISN+1.

shell—A shell is another term for a user interface. OSs sometimes provide an alternative shell to make program interaction easier. For example, the shell may provide a menu-driven system that translates user menu choices to OS commands.

shortest path first (SPF) tree—An SPF tree is used by the OSPF protocol to graph a path between OSPF routing nodes.

Simple Network Management Protocol (SNMP)—SNMP is a TCP/IP Application Layer protocol used to send and receive information about the status of network resources on a TCP/IP network.

simple password authentication (type 2)—RIPv2 supports simple password authentication by guarding against routers inadvertently joining the routing domain; each router must first be configured with its attached networks' passwords before it can participate in routing. However, simple password authentication is vulnerable to passive attacks; anyone with physical access to the network can learn the password and compromise the security of the routing domain.

socket—A socket is a software object that connects an application to a network protocol. In UNIX, for example, a program can send and receive TCP/IP messages by opening a socket and reading and writing data to and from the socket. A TCP process creates a socket from the host's IP address combined with a port number, and each TCP connection includes two sockets, one for each connected host.

source quench—Source quench is a congestion control technique in which a congested computer sends a message back to the source causing the congestion, requesting that the source stop transmitting. In a TCP/IP internet, gateways use ICMP source quench to stop or reduce the transmission of IP datagrams.

store-and-forward—In a messaging system, a store-and-forward application accepts messages on their way to their final destination and stores them until the destination host requests them. When the destination host requests the messages, the store-and-forward system forwards them on to the requesting host. POP3 is a store-and-forward application protocol.

subnet address— Subnet address is an extension of the IP addressing scheme that allows a site to use a single IP network address for multiple physical networks. Gateways and hosts using subnet addressing interpret the local portion of the address by dividing it into a physical network portion and host portion.

subnetwork—A subnetwork is a smaller network created by borrowing host bits (subnetting), from a larger Class A, B, or C network.

supernet—A supernet is an aggregate of smaller, classful networks presented to a border router as a single, routing table entry. Supernetting is the basis for CIDR.

switch—A switch is a device that operates at the Data Link Layer of the OSI reference model. It can connect LANs or segments of the same media access type and dedicates its entire bandwidth to each frame it switches.

switched circuit network (SCN)—SCN is another term for the PSTN.

Synchronize (SYN)—SYN is the TCP header field used to synchronize sequence numbers.

Systems Network Architecture (SNA)—SNA is IBM's architecture for computer networking, which was designed for transaction processing in mission-critical applications. SNA networks usually involve a large number of terminals communicating with a mainframe.

tag—A tag is an HTML command inserted in a document that specifies how a Web browser should format the document or a portion of the document.

Telnet—Telnet is a TCP/IP Application Layer protocol that provides a remote login capability to another computer on a network.

terminal emulation—A terminal emulation program allows a local computer to connect to a remote computer and appear to be logged on to the remote computer locally. Terminal emulation programs are often used to access mainframe computers.

Time to Live (TTL)—TTL is a technique used in best-effort delivery systems to avoid packet loops. Each IP datagram is assigned an integer TTL when it is created. IP gateways decrement the TTL field when they process a datagram and discard it if the TTL value reaches zero.

Token Ring—Token Ring is a network architecture that uses a ring topology and a token passing strategy to control network access. The IEEE 802.5 standard defines the token ring architecture and how it operates at the OSI model Physical and Data Link Layers.

top level domain (TLD)—TLDs are the groupings of lower level domain types. A TCP/IP network can be segmented into a hierarchy of domains or groupings; the Internet is an example of this segmentation type. For example, the .com TLD groups commercial domains, while the .edu TLD groups educational institutions.

Tracert—Tracert is a utility that traces the route between two computers and sends information about each router hop along the way.

Transmission Control Protocol (TCP)—TCP is the TCP/IP Transport Layer protocol that provides reliable, full-duplex, stream service. TCP allows a process on one computer to send data to a process on another computer. TCP software implementations normally reside in the OS and use IP to transmit information across the underlying internet.

Trivial File Transfer Protocol (TFTP)—TFTP is a simple file transfer protocol designed for use on top of connectionless UDP. TFTP requires an acknowledgement for each packet before it sends another.

type-of-service (ToS) routing—ToS routing makes routing decisions based on an IP packet's IP header ToS bit states. This allows the routers to create separate transmission paths for different service types.

unauthoritive data—Unauthoritive data is domain namespace information stored on a nameserver about which that server does not maintain authority. The nameserver caches this information for a limited time period and then discards it if it is no longer needed. This caching allows for faster name resolution.

unicast—A unicast is a transmission sent to a single network address. This is in contrast to a broadcast, which is sent to all network addresses simultaneously, and a multicast, which is sent to several addresses at once.

Uniform Resource Identifier (URI) —A URI is the generic term for all types of names and addresses that refer to objects on the Web. A URL is one kind of URI.

Uniform Resource Locator (URL)—A URL is an Internet address used to locate resources from within a Web browser. It can lead you to an Internet-connected computer anywhere in the world.

UNIX to UNIX Copy Program (UUCP)—UUCP is an Application Layer protocol used for transferring files between UNIX systems.

USB adapter—A USB adapter is a PC expansion device that conforms to the USB standard. USB devices support data transfer rates of up to 12 Mbps and up 127 devices on the same bus. USB device examples include NICs, modems, scanners, and CD-ROM drives.

Usenet—Usenet is a global news distribution service that relies on the Internet for much of its news traffic. News servers agree to share and distribute newsfeeds, which are collections of related news articles. Users post news messages in newsfeeds using a news reader client.

User Datagram Protocol (UDP)—UDP is the TCP/IP protocol that allows an application program on one computer to send a datagram to an application program on another computer. UDP uses IP to deliver datagrams. The difference between UDP datagrams and IP datagrams is that UDP includes a protocol port number, allowing the sender to distinguish among multiple destinations (application programs) on the remote computer. UDP also includes a checksum for the data being sent.

Uuencode—Uuencode is a set of algorithms for converting e-mail attachments into a series of 7-bit ASCII characters for transmission over the Internet. Uuencode originally stood for UNIX-to-UNIX encode, but is now considered a universal protocol used to transfer file attachments between different operating system platforms. Nearly all e-mail applications support uuencoding.

variable-length subnet mask (VLSM)—VLSMs are a mechanism for providing subnets of different sizes within a single IP-address block. Routing protocols that support VLSM allow network administrators to subnet a subnet to create more subnets than the default mask will allow.

Version—This 4-bit field in a datagram contains the version of IP used to create the datagram. The Version field is used to ensure that the sender, receiver, and intervening gateways agree on the format of the datagram.

Waveform Audio File (WAV)—WAV is one of several formats for storing sound in files developed jointly by Microsoft and IBM. Support for WAV files is built-in to Windows 95 making it the de facto standard for sound on PCs. WAV sound files end with a .WAV extension and can be played by nearly all Windows applications that support sound.

window—A window is the number of bytes, beginning with the one in the ACK field, that can be accepted by the sender of this segment.

Windows Internet Naming Service (WINS)—WINS is a Microsoft client/server application that resolves network computer host names to IP addresses. WINS works in conjunction with DHCP, where the WINS server maintains a dynamic database of host-name-to-address mappings. Because DHCP clients may not maintain the same address over time, WINS works well for this application. Standard DNS supports only hosts with statically assigned IP addresses.

Windows service—A Windows service is the equivalent of a UNIX daemon. Windows services provide specific functions, such as enabling file sharing or automatic virus protection, and can start automatically on system startup, manually as directed by the user, or when scheduled to run at a particular time of the day.

WINS node type—A WINS node type designates the type of NetBIOS name resolution the client uses; WINS support several different node types. For example, a client might broadcast for name resolution (B-node) or first broadcast then directly request name resolution (M-node).

X.500—The ITU-T X.500 standard designates a distributed, global Directory that permits applications such as e-mail to access information either stored centrally or distributed across numerous servers. A Directory contains information about objects; these objects may be files or network entities, such as the user accounts and resources listed in Novell's NetWare Directory Services or Microsoft's Windows 2000 Active Directory.

zone of authority—A DNS zone of authority is the DNS zone namespace for which a DNS nameserver is responsible. When a DNS domain is created, the new domain's root becomes the domain and its subdomains' zone of authority. A DNS server can maintain responsibility for more than one zone of authority.

INDEX

Numerics

A

B

C

D

E

F

T

U

V

W

X

Z